The
Disorganized
Personality

The Disorganized Personality

Third Edition

George W. Kisker
Professor of Psychology
University of Cincinnati

McGraw-Hill Book Company

New York • St. Louis • San Francisco • Auckland • Bogotá • Düsseldorf
Johannesburg • London • Madrid • Mexico • Montreal • New Delhi • Panama
Paris • São Paulo • Singapore • Sydney • Tokyo • Toronto

The Disorganized Personality

1234567890 DODO 783210987

Library of Congress Cataloging in Publication Data

Kisker, George W
The disorganized personality.

Bibliography: p.
Includes index.
1. Psychology, Pathological. I. Title.
RC454.K57 1977 616.8'9 76-48732
ISBN 0-07-034878-2

This book was set in Melior by Black Dot, Inc.
The editors were Richard R. Wright, Helen Greenberg, and Susan Gamer;
the designer was J. Paul Kirouac, A Good Thing, Inc.;
the production supervisor was Charles Hess.
The drawings were done by Danmark & Michaels, Inc.
R. R. Donnelley & Sons Company was printer and binder.

See Figure Credits on pages 459–460. Copyrights included on this page by reference.

Cover: Detail from *John the Baptist*, by Peter Breughel the Elder.
Photo by Erich Lessing/Magnum.

Contents

List of Case Studies

Preface

Every new edition of a textbook involves both a promise and an obligation. The promise is that the new book will offer significant changes and improvements over earlier editions. The obligation is for the author to make certain that the promise has been fulfilled. This objective was the primary consideration in the planning and development of the third edition of *The Disorganized Personality.* The most substantial changes and improvements will be found in three areas: new and updated content, the reorganization of material, and improved readability.

The content of this edition was selected to reflect recent developments, new techniques, and changes in emphasis and orientation in the field of abnormal paychology. More than 80 percent of the text material is completely new. Although the overall biological emphasis has been retained, much of the technical detail related to the nervous system, hormones, and nutrition has been eliminated or simplified. Similarly, psychodynamic interpretations have been balanced by a greater emphasis on behavioral, cognitive, and sociocultural factors. Also, the detailed medical material on psychophysiological disorders and the descriptions of relatively rare forms of mental retardation will not be found in this edition. Other changes in content have to do with psychodiagnosis, where projective techniques have lost much of their attraction, and with physical methods of treatment which have little or no place in current psychiatric therapy.

Those who have used the second edition of *The Disorganized Personality* will find that the material on comparative admission rates to public mental hospitals is no longer presented. The reason is that the increasing availability and use of mental health services in the local community make admissions to public mental hospitals an uncertain index of the true prevalence of mental disturbance.

Although weeding out of irrelevant material is required of every new edition, it is also expected that new content will be presented. Current models of abnormality, community mental health programs, crisis intervention, genetics of mental disorder, concepts of depression, biofeedback, behavior modification, and trends in group therapy are some of the topics introduced or more fully developed in the present edition.

The reorganization of this edition has involved the addition of three chapters, and the elimination of the final chapter, on experimental psychopathology. Despite these changes, the book is considerably shorter than the second edition. This change, made possible by the curtailment of detailed technical material in all chapters, is designed to increase students' interest and to make the book more flexible for the instructor.

Perhaps the most significant change in the third edition is the greatly improved readability of the book. *The Disorganized Personality* is directed to both the psychology major and to the increasingly large number of nonpsychology majors who have relatively little background in psychology and who probably will not pursue the subject. For this reason, the vocabulary and technical concepts have been simplified, chapter objectives have been added, and summaries have been shortened. Suggested readings for students have been carefully selected for their general interest and ready availability.

During the preparation of this edition I was helped immeasurably by Patricia E. Christie, who served with great competence as my research and editiorial assistant; Helen Greenberg, the skillful and efficient McGraw-Hill editor, whose sound advice and sympathetic assistance guided the project to completion; Professor Norman Garmezy of the University of Minnesota, who read the early drafts of the revision and made numerous valuable suggestions; and the many helpful staff members of the medical library of the University of Cincinnati. The book is dedicated with a most special acknowledgment to Florence Ray Kisker for her ever-needed and always present support and encouragement during the long and sometimes difficult months of the revision.

George W. Kisker

The Disorganized Personality

1
Abnormal Psychology in a Changing World

Objectives

To indicate the general nature of abnormal psychology

To emphasize the importance and prevalence of abnormal behavior in our society

To explain what is meant by *theoretical models* and why they are important in thinking about abnormality

To discuss descriptive models of abnormality and to show why they have limited usefulness

To describe the more helpful biological, psychological, and sociocultural types of explanatory models of abnormality

To discuss the roles of the psychologist, psychiatrist, and other professionals and paraprofessionals who work with psychologically disturbed people

To indicate why the study of abnormal psychology is important to education, business, law, religion, and other areas of everyday life

D.A. Pleads Guilty to Beating Women in Bondage Survey

Wellsville, N.Y., Sept. 20—The Allegany County District Attorney pleaded guilty to five counts of an indictment charging him with tying up women and whipping them after saying he was conducting an official survey on bondage.

The 30-year-old official admitted writing letters on official letterheads to women asking them to participate in a bondage survey. Seven women, including two girls under 18, accepted the invitation. The D.A. was arrested after one of the teenaged girls complained to her parents.

Police Seek Phantom Foot Kisser

New Haven, Conn., Feb. 15—A mysterious attacker with the penchant for kissing the feet of coeds has been haunting the stacks of the Sterling Memorial Library at Yale University. On at least four occasions coeds studying in isolated sections of the library have been accosted. The young man approached his victims, dropped to his knees and began kissing their feet. One coed commented, "I've had some pretty weird passes made at me, but nothing like this!"

The district attorney who tied up women and beat them and the young man who kissed the feet of coeds in the library at Yale University were psychologically disturbed. People who behave in such peculiar ways are assumed to have personality problems. We say they are emotionally unstable or mentally disturbed. Whatever the behavior is called, it is subject matter of *abnormal psychology*.

The study of abnormal psychology helps us to understand some of the strange and seemingly incomprehensible actions and thoughts of ourselves and others. Such understanding is one of the ways by which people are able to protect themselves from many minor emotional upsets and personality disturbances. More important, when these minor upsets are avoided, the chances of developing more serious personality problems are decreased.

A knowledge of abnormal psychology is of value to us in ways other than self-understanding. It is one of the most important avenues to the understanding of others, particularly of behavior which is odd, strange, unusual, different, and apparently inexplicable. Anyone who takes the trouble to keep up with news events is faced with the daily reminder that abnormal behavior is the concern of everyone.

The statistics on the extent and cost of psychological disturbances in our country indicate why mental health is considered one of the most important public health problems of our time. While it is true that the middle of the present century has been marked by the beginning of a new revolution in the care and treatment of many of the

---

**Mental Health in Our Society:
Some Startling Statistics**

More than 25 million people in the United States have some form of psychological disorder.

Over 40 percent of the nation's hospital beds are occupied by patients with psychological disturbances.

Between 10 and 15 percent of all students in elementary schools, high schools, colleges, and universities are disturbed enough to need professional help.

There are about 8 million alcoholics in our country.

More than 50,000 men, women, and children will commit suicide this year.

About 2.5 million men, women, and children in the United States are receiving some form of treatment for mental health problems.

The cost of personality disturbance in the United States is about $25 billion per year for treatment services, operation of mental hospitals, and loss of productivity. (National Institute of Mental Health, 1975)

---

more serious mental conditions, the rapidly changing social and physical world in which we live has been responsible for a sharp increase in personal tensions and anxieties which are leaving less obvious, but no less real, scars on modern humanity.

The Illusion of Normality

Most people like to think of themselves as being normal. They are convinced that they act normally and do things in a normal way. They even believe they are more normal than their friends and neighbors. Yet in spite of the widespread insistence on being considered normal, it is not clear that normality is such a desirable state.

A distinguished expert on mental health once said, "To be normal seems shockingly repellent to me. I see neither hope nor comfort in sinking to that low level." Another assures us that "Only a fool would continue to wish to be normal after he discovered what it would be like." And the head of one of America's most famous private mental hospitals commented that all the normal people in any city could be housed in its city hall.

Ronald D. Laing, the Scottish psychiatrist, said in the introduction to his book *The Politics of Experience* (1967), "We are all murderers and prostitutes—no matter to what culture, society, class, nation we belong, no matter how normal, moral, or mature, we take ourselves to be." In a more recent book (1971) he continued, "We are bemused and crazed creatures, strangers to our true selves, to one another, and to the spiritual and material world—mad."

How is it possible to reconcile the popular desire to be normal with the opinion of these established authorities who scoff at the very notion of normality? The answer, in part, is to be found in the confusion and lack of clarity associated with the words *normal* and *abnormal*. Such words have a wide range of meaning and imply different things to different people. It is extremely difficult to define abnormality in a generally meaningful way. On the surface, it would appear to be a simple matter. Anything not normal must therefore be abnormal. The difficulty is in trying to decide what is normal.

The word *normal* comes from the Latin *norma*, which means a carpenter's square. A *norm* therefore became a rule, pattern, or standard, and it was in this sense that the word was introduced into the English language. The word *abnormal*, with its prefix *ab* ("away from"), means a variation from the normal. Human behavior and experiences which are strange, unusual, or merely different are often considered abnormal. In any case, the words *normal* and *abnormal* are abstract concepts that do not correspond to anything in the physical world. They can, and have been, defined in many different ways.

Models of Abnormality

How do we decide whether or not a person is normal? Think about some of the people you know. You can probably rank them from the most normal to the least normal. How do you do it? Upon what do you base your judgment? Ordinarily we arrive at our decision by means of *theoretical models* or tentative ways of viewing a problem. Models are developed by making a series of assumptions which may or may not lead to an eventual theory. Models are useful even though they are incomplete and may have recognized flaws. The usefulness of the model is in its convenience and flexibility. Since models are not necessarily incompatible, it is quite possible for different models to be equally valid. Such is not the case with theories, which are generally more complete and complex. If one theory proves to be correct, other theories must be rejected.

Abnormal psychology makes use of two general types of models. *Descriptive models* tell us which types of behavior are considered to be abnormal; *explanatory models* are based upon the assumed processes underlying abnormal behavior. They attempt to tell us *why* the behavior is abnormal.

Models That Describe

Descriptive models of abnormality tell us something about behavior but do not touch on what causes the behavior. Such models are based upon the personal judgments and biases of the observer, social customs, and statistical measures and criteria. Among some of the more common descriptive models are the views that abnormality is a moral defect, an impairment, an imperfection, social deviancy, or statistical variance.

Abnormality as moral defect The moral model of abnormal behavior is based on value judgments made by people who observe behavior. Behavior is "good" or "bad" to the extent that it is irritating, irresponsible, disgusting, frightening, or troublesome. Friends, relatives, hospital ward personnel, and other nonprofessionals frequently use this model of abnormality without realizing it. It is not unusual for alcoholics and sexual deviates to be considered morally defective. In all cases of the moral model, the appropriateness of the individual's behavior is more important than the underlying causes (Siegler & Osmond, 1974).

The moral model is expressed by one writer who said: "There is no such thing as mental illness; there are only responsible and irresponsible people" (Glasser, 1965). Another proponent of the moral model believes that a mentally disordered person has the right to be hanged for a murder he or she committed, rather than to be considered "ill" (Szasz, 1963).

Abnormality as impairment The impairment model of abnormality views the disturbed person as an individual who has a limited capacity to function effectively but who is nevertheless expected to do what he or she can within the limits of the condition. Our public mental hospitals became a depository for impaired people. Those who did not respond to treatment and were considered to be too impaired to leave the hospital became the bulk of the hospital population. These patients found themselves doing the cleaning, dishwashing, laundering, coal shoveling, and general maintenance jobs.

The impairment model of mental illness has been closely related to the degradation and dehumanization of patients in public psychiatric hospitals. When the first mental hospitals were built early in the nineteenth century, the number of patients was small, and it was possible to deal with them on an individual basis. Enlightened superintendents exerted direct and beneficial influence on the patients.

However, as mental hospitals increased in size, it became increasingly difficult to give patients the personal care and attention they demanded and deserved. It was the beginning of the inevitable deterioration of patient care and of the growing numbers of impaired persons who were to make the institution their home for the rest of their lives.

At one public mental hospital a head nurse received a call asking the nurses to select and supervise a group of patients who

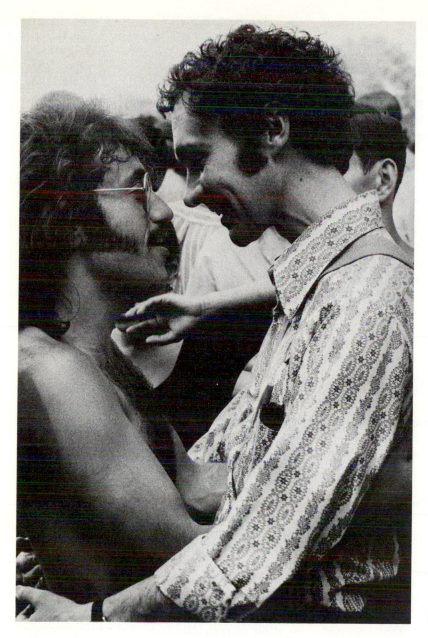

Figure 1.1 These two young men are obviously delighted with one another. Not many years ago, such a public display of homosexual affection would have been impossible. Today, as a result of more permissive attitudes and the efforts of gay liberation groups, many men and women feel free to express their feelings openly.

were to dig a grave for a patient who had died. The nurse was justifiably outraged at this blatant misuse of nurses. But grave-digging as an activity for patients is even more outrageous. "In a general hospital . . . what would one say if a nurse came around to whistle up a group of patients to dig a grave for a patient who died? This is so inconceivable that it sounds like a sick joke" (Siegler & Osmond, 1974, p. 40). But the incident points out the major difference between impairment and illness. What is considered acceptable for an impaired person would be an outrage for someone who is ill.

Abnormality as imperfection This model of abnormality is based on the idea that perfection is the ideal form of behavior. Since perfection is a value judgment, the ideal person may be seen differently by different people. Some may find their ideal in a religious figure, a humanitarian, a business executive, a political leader, or even a popular hero. A rare few manage to reach degrees of perfection far beyond anything attained by the masses of people. These few become idealized, and serve as models of behavior to which others aspire. The great philosophers, members of nobility, and creative geniuses also have been regarded from time to time as models of normality.

A major weakness in the model is that seemingly ideal personalities, when examined closely, reveal a full share of human frailties and shortcomings. A more fundamental flaw in the normative model is that it is based ultimately on the idea of "what ought to be." Such a concept has no place in scientific investigation. Science is not concerned with what ought to be or what should be. It is concerned with the world as it exists.

Abnormality as social deviancy This definition of abnormality is based on the assumption that normality is the standard approved by the greatest number of people. If enough people adopt a hairstyle, article of clothing, type of dance, manner of speech, or way of behaving, it is assumed to be normal.

There are many examples of the cultural determination of normality and abnormality. Homosexuality is frowned upon and considered abnormal by some people in our society. But at other times and in other places, such behavior has been considered quite acceptable and normal. The severe view of this type of behavior in the Old Testament is indicated by the admonition: "If a man also lieth down with a man as he lieth with a woman, both of them have committed an abomination. They shall verily be put to death. Their blood shall be upon them." However, in ancient Greece, sexual love among members of the same sex was looked upon favorably, and even encouraged. Plato said: "They [homosexuals] act in this way because they have a strong soul, manly courage, and a virile character" (Jowett, 1953). Today, in our culture, homosexual behavior is neither an abomination nor a sign of strong character. It is looked upon as an expression of a personality problem. Here, then, are three sets of attitudes toward the same behavior. Each attitude is a function of the culture in which the behavior occurs.

During the mid-1970s a controversy erupted as a result of the announcement by the American Psychiatric Association that homosexuality was no longer to be considered a mental disorder, and would be dropped from the next edition of *The Diagnostic and Statistical Manual*. Many psychologists and psychiatrists who viewed homosexuality as being determined by psychosocial influences applauded the decision; most of those who held to the medical view of homosexuality as being the expression of endocrine imbalance or other physical disturbance objected to the proposed change.

Changes in attitude toward what is acceptable and "normal" are also seen in the relaxation of restrictions on "obscene" language in literature. When the movie version of Tennessee Williams's play *A Streetcar Named Desire* was made, the producers were required to eliminate the last three words from the line "I would like to kiss you softly and sweetly *on the mouth.*" And Norman Mailer had to invent the word "fug" to give the flavor of profanity to his war novel *The Naked and the Dead.* But by the 1970s, all barriers to erotic realism in acceptable literature had been demolished.

Abnormality as statistical variance The statistical conception of normality implies that the "average" is normal. There is an average weight, height, hat size, shoe size, and clothing size. The more closely the average is approached, the more normal the person is considered to be. A man would not be normal if he wore a size 10 hat, or a size 14 shoe.

The statistical model is best illustrated by the normal distribution curve. This curve is derived by plotting cases along a base line, with the number of cases indicated on the vertical axis. The bell-shaped appearance of the curve is due to the fact that most cases fall in the middle of the distribution, with fewer and fewer cases trailing off at the lower and upper ends. According to the statistical

model, cases falling around the middle of the distribution most closely approximate the distribution of normal cases. As cases fall farther and farther toward the ends of the distribution, the degree of abnormality increases.

Unfortunately, this approach does not lend itself conveniently to the analysis of personality disturbance. While the statistical model is a precise means of portraying traits and representing biological measurements, it cannot reflect the subtle complexities of maladaptive behavior. The difficulty is not in the nature of the model, but in the fact that not all maladjusted people are high or low on a given dimension of personality. With the increased sophistication of statistical methods, we have come to a better knowledge of *who* is abnormal. However, statistical methods tell us very little about *why* people become abnormal.

Models That Explain

While descriptive models may be convenient for certain purposes, most of us are

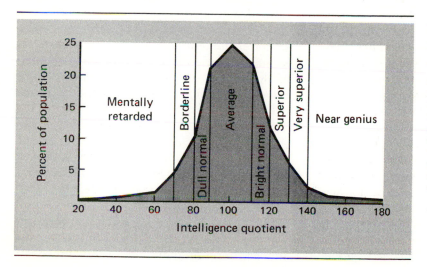

Figure 1.2 The statistical view of abnormality is an example of a theoretical model that describes but does not explain. The curve indicating the distribution of intelligence shows that the mentally retarded and the near-genius group represent two extremes of intellectual ability. These people can therefore be considered abnormal in a statistical sense. But there is no explanation as to why some people are retarded while others are geniuses.

more concerned with underlying processes than with the way in which abnormal behavior differs from normal behavior. Explanatory models can aid in learning *why* deviation in behavior occurs. The principal explanatory models are biological, psychological, and sociological.

Abnormality as a biological problem
Some of the oldest and most firmly established explanations of abnormal behavior have their origins in biology and medicine. Before the present century, biological and medical explanations of disturbed behavior remained unchallenged. Except for a few isolated voices anticipating the psychological and social sciences, the biological model of abnormality was generally accepted and the only question was the nature of the physical changes responsible for the abnormal behavior.

Abnormality as illness   The view that abnormal behavior, especially behavior seen in those conditions usually referred to as mental disorder, is an illness or disease has a long history reaching back to the time of Hippocrates and ancient Greek medicine. Today this view is often called the *medical model* and is under severe attack by some workers outside and within the medical profession. Nevertheless, the medical model has maintained a firm hold on the thinking of many psychiatrists, psychologists, and other professionals. For a number of centuries—and until less than a hundred years ago—most of the interest in mental disorder was limited to patients in mental hospitals and asylums. Few people questioned the accepted view that the inmates were mentally ill as a result of some type of disease.

The medical model of mental disorder has lost much of its appeal for a number of reasons. Many psychologists and psychia-

trists believe that there is insufficient evidence to support the explanation of most mental disturbances on the basis of biology. Others are concerned that continued adherence to the illness model tends to deprive nonmedical health professionals of the right to diagnose and treat such conditions. Another criticism of the medical model is based on the argument that people are considered mentally ill only because of the way in which society defines what is psychologically healthy and psychologically "sick." The situation is quite different in some parts of the medical field, where a diseased kidney is a diseased kidney regardless of what other people say or think. But behavior standards are established in an arbitrary manner by social definition, and variations in behavior can be judged only in terms of this definition. Such reasoning, which has much to say for it, is difficult for many people to accept because it runs counter to what appears to be the "commonsense" view that abnormal behavior is somehow an indication of an illness.

However, the apparent failure to demonstrate a disease process does not rule out the importance of biological factors in the causation of mental disorder. In fact, while the illness view of abnormal behavior has been under systematic attack, there has been an increasing interest in the biological aspects of the more serious mental disorders. This interest is reflected in the growing numbers of biologically oriented investigations reported in the professional journals, in the many new books dealing with the biology of mental disorder, and in the increased emphasis on the biological approach in departments of psychology and psychiatry in our colleges and universities.

Abnormality as an inherited condition.
The genetic view of abnormality is based on the assumption that there is an inherited

factor involved in pathological behavior. It is certainly the case that some patterns of abnormal behavior appear to run in families in a way which is highly suggestive of biological inheritance. Many people are convinced that a genetic basis will eventually be found for at least some types of abnormal behavior. Other specialists in the field of abnormal psychology are equally convinced that heredity is not involved in deviant behavior, and that the apparent transmission of behavior patterns from parents to children is a matter of social learning.

However, while the genetic basis of many forms of abnormal behavior has not been established for most of the less serious personality disturbances, there is clear evidence of genetic influences in some types of mental deficiency (see Chapter 15), and an increasing likelihood of genetic involvement in some of the more severe depressive disorders and in *schizophrenia*, one of the most serious of all mental disturbances (see Chapter 12). There is also recent evidence pointing to the possibility that the genetic background may play a part in the development of alcoholism (see Chapter 7).

Abnormality as constitutional deficit. The word *constitution* has a special meaning in psychology and medicine. It refers to the basic biological unit as determined not only by heredity but by all the early factors which operate to shape a person's fundamental physical nature. These factors include everything that happens to the organism from the moment the female ovum is fertilized by the male sperm cell until birth has taken place. During the weeks immediately following fertilization, the developing organism is called the *embryo*. Later it is known as the *fetus*. During the embryonic and fetal stages, the genetic code determines the organism's growth sequence, but a wide range of other factors also influence it. The chemistry of the mother's body fluids, physical strains and pressures exerted by the uterus, and the birth experience itself are some of the early shaping influences.

While some psychologists include events of the early hours and days following birth as constitutional influences, the experiences of the infant are usually considered to be learned behaviors susceptible to modification later in life. The conventional view is that constitutional factors are strongly resistant to such later change. For example, as a result of adverse developmental conditions while he or she was in the uterus of the mother, a person might have an inherent instability of the nervous or endocrine system. This biological characteristic would be part of his or her constitutional makeup. As a result, the person might show disturbed resistance to physical and psychosocial stress, or atypical learning responses. In either case, the risk of maladaptive behavior later in life would be increased.

Abnormality as biochemical imbalance. The most exciting and promising of the biological models of abnormality involves the possibility that some forms of abnormal behavior may be due to disturbances of the body chemistry. For many years biochemists interested in mental disorder have been convinced that biochemical imbalance is somehow related to disturbances of thinking and emotion. Many approaches were used in the attempt to obtain evidence to support this view, but most efforts failed.

Today there is growing evidence that the biochemists may be right in their belief that chemical factors are involved in certain types of abnormal behavior. Rapid advances in the biochemistry of behavior have grown out of interest in LSD (lysergic acid diethylamide) and other hallucination-inducing drugs, and in the wide use of drugs to control disturbed thinking and emotions.

One example of biochemical imbalance related to abnormal behavior is in connection with certain types of severe depression and elation. There is growing evidence that chemicals involved in the transmission of the nerve impulse also play a role in extreme swings in mood. The problem of biochemistry and behavior disturbance will be discussed in greater detail in Chapter 3.

It is of considerable interest that the mental disturbances for which there is the most evidence of biochemical involvement are the same conditions in which genetic factors are suspected. It is not surprising that this should be the case, since the biochemical model is not inconsistent with the genetic model.

It is entirely possible that a genetic defect may result in subsequent biochemical error. While much of the clinical and experimental evidence for biological influences in abnormal behavior is tentative and suggestive rather than well established, such influences undoubtedly exist. However, it would be just as inappropriate to view abnormal behavior as always due to an underlying physical defect as it would be to completely deny the influence of biological factors. The highly complex nature of human behavior grows out of the continuous interplay of biological, psychological, and sociological influences.

Abnormality as a psychological problem
The explanations of abnormal behavior offered by scientific psychology are of much more recent origin than are biological explanations. Earlier explanations of a nonbiological nature were based upon superstition, philosophy, and religious beliefs. While there were many explanations of this kind over the centuries, psychological explana-

Figure 1.3 Sigmund Freud (1856–1939), an Austrian physician, developed the theory and treatment method known as psychoanalysis. Although his original ideas have been modified over the years by many of his followers, the fundamental principle is that maladaptive behavior is a result of a conflict, at the unconscious level, between instinctual drives (id) and the demands of society (superego). The self (ego) is caught in the middle of this struggle.

tions with some degree of scientific justification did not appear until the late 1800s. At that time, two completely different psychological developments, which were to dominate the theory and treatment of abnormal behavior during our century, began to take shape. One was the view that mental disorder is a symptom, or sign, of conflicts taking place at the unconscious levels of the personality. This view was advanced by the Viennese physician Sigmund Freud, whose theories and treatment techniques came to be known as *psychoanalysis*. The other view was that most behavior is learned, and that abnormal, or maladaptive, behavior is learned in the very same way that normal, or adaptive, behavior is learned. According to this view, the principles of learning can explain the appearance of abnormal behavior and can be used to modify maladaptive behavior in desired directions.

Abnormality as inner conflict. This view was developed at the beginning of the present century, when psychiatrists began to study and treat the personality disturbances of people who were not in hospitals or other institutions. When it became clear that personality disturbances can also develop in individuals who appear to be physically healthy, the traditional view that abnormality is due to some type of underlying disease process had to be reexamined. The new approach provided by Freud and his colleagues sought to explain abnormal behavior and mental disorder in terms of psychological processes taking place at the hidden levels of the personality. The concept of unconscious mental activity was used to describe these processes, which ordinarily are beyond the range of our awareness. This view emphasizes unconscious motivation, hidden conflict, and the struggle to rid ourselves of the conflict. When this inner drama is unsuccessful, the symptoms of personality disturbance appear. The form these symptoms take is determined by a combination of inborn, developmental, and learned influences. This *psychodynamic* view of abnormal behavior will be discussed in greater detail in Chapter 4.

Abnormality as learned behavior. While the psychodynamic view was the dominant psychological model of abnormality during the first half of this century, the second half has been increasingly influenced by the view that abnormal behavior is maladaptive behavior that has been learned in the same way that normal adaptive behavior is learned. The behavior model of mental disorder holds that most behavior, normal and abnormal, is shaped by our previous experience. Whether such behavior is adaptive or maladaptive is determined by what has been learned.

The learning approach to abnormal behavior grew out of the principles of normal learning. These began to evolve late in the nineteenth century and early in the present century as a result of the conditioning experiments of I. P. Pavlov in Russia and the animal-learning experiments of E. L. Thorndike in the United States. The Russian work demonstrated that behavior disturbances can be induced in animals by means of conditioned learning. This technique, which came to be known as *classical* conditioning, will be discussed in Chapter 4.

Thorndike's work took a different direction. He and his students were interested in the effects of reward and punishment on the learning process. It was found that both conditions could be used successfully to reinforce learning. At the time, few psychologists sensed the implications of this finding for the understanding and treatment of mental disorder. Abnormal psychology was dominated by the biological view that mental disturbances are diseases and by the psychological theories of psychoanalysis. It was not until the middle of our century that these two divergent but influential models of abnormality began to be seriously challenged. Largely as a result of the work of the Harvard psychologist B. F. Skinner, the principles of reward and punishment were ready to be applied to the understanding and treatment of behavior disorders. In contrast to the

Figure 1.4 Ivan P. Pavlov (1849–1936), a Russian physiologist, was a pioneer in establishing the foundations of learning theory. The learning technique developed in his laboratory is now known as classical conditioning, to distinguish it from operant conditioning, which began with E. L. Thorndike and was brought to its present high level of development by B. F. Skinner and his followers.

classical conditioning techniques developed by Pavlov, the basic methods used by Skinner and the behaviorists are called *operant*, or *instrumental*, conditioning. The principles of the behavioral approach will be discussed in detail in Chapter 4, and the ways in which learning techniques are being used to modify maladaptive behavior will be presented in Chapter 17.

Abnormality as a sociocultural problem

Some of the recent attempts to establish explanatory models of abnormal behavior have come from the social scientists. The social approach to abnormality takes several forms. One approach, which is an extension of the learning model, holds that mental disorder grows out of disturbances of the normal process of socialization during childhood. Such factors as parental rejection or overprotection, excessive rivalries and jealousies, and difficulties in communication are later developed into socially maladaptive, or abnormal, behavior.

Another sociocultural explanatory model emphasizes the importance of social disorganization in the causation of abnormal behavior patterns. Emotionally disturbed family members and family relationships, migration, poverty, racism, and other sources of group tension tend to cause psychological problems and personality disturbances in some of the people exposed to the social turmoil.

A third sociocultural model looks upon abnormal behavior as being culturally defined. According to this view, each culture determines the forms of behavior that are considered "abnormal." The shamans, or priests, hold exalted positions in some cultural groups. By our standards, many of these people would be considered severely disturbed. Yet the behavior we would look upon as being maladaptive is adaptive in a different cultural framework.

The most extreme sociocultural view of abnormality is that mental illness is a myth and in fact does not exist at all. Exception is taken to the fact that people are labeled as being mentally ill because it is believed that such labeling is unjustified and potentially damaging. The position is taken that the person who is called abnormal is really no different from those not so called, but that this person has—for economic or other non-psychological reasons—been singled out by society because of his or her behavior. The "radical psychology movement" holds that many people are considered mentally ill simply because they hold unconventional and unpopular social and political views.

The most widely quoted advocate of the view that mental disorder is a myth is the psychiatrist Thomas Szasz. He has stated on numerous occasions that "there is no such

Figure 1.5 Thomas S. Szasz (1920–   ), one of the leading proponents of the idea that mental illness is a myth. This psychiatrist believes that those conditions traditionally called mental illness are merely forms of behavior society has arbitrarily defined as being abnormal.

thing as mental illness." This startling view proposed by a psychiatrist has had a peculiar fascination for many lay people and for some professionals in the field of mental health.

The major sociocultural models will be discussed in Chapter 5. These models of abnormality, like the biological and psychological models already mentioned, should be regarded merely as convenient ways of thinking about certain types of disturbed behavior. Most human behavior, normal and abnormal, involves biological, psychological, and social components. The relative weight of each of these components varies from person to person, and from one situation to another.

The Mental Health Team

An effective understanding of the field of abnormal psychology must include a clear idea of how this branch of psychology fits into the broader field of general psychology and how it is related to other professions concerned with the problems of mental health. Psychology is the science of behavior and experience, and it is made up of a wide range of specialties.

Abnormal psychology is that phase of psychology which studies deviations in behavior and experience. The field is oriented toward the description of personality disturbances, the development of theories to explain the observed conditions, and the use of experimental techniques in the attempt to validate models, hypotheses, and theories. As such, abnormal psychology is not in itself an applied field. It is primarily concerned with providing the raw material for the professional and paraprofessional workers who are concerned with the everyday problems of mental health.

Mental Health Professionals

The traditional mental health team is made up of the clinical psychologist, psychiatrist, psychiatric social worker, psychiatric nurse, and psychiatric aide. Each of these skilled professionals plays an important and specialized role in preventing, identifying, and treating personality disturbances and behavior disorders. While the work of the mental health team was at one time limited largely to the mental hospital, much of its work has shifted from the institution to the community.

The clinical psychologist is a nonmedical professional whose principal strengths are knowledge of normal behavior development and skills in behavior assessment and intervention. The clinical psychologist is quite capable of making psychological diagnostic evaluations and engaging in nonmedical treatment. Moreover, the research training of clinical psychologists makes it possible for them to play a key role in clinical and experimental investigations of abnormal behavior.

The psychiatrist is the medical member of the mental health team. As a physician, the psychiatrist is qualified by training and authorized by law to make medical diagnoses and to prescribe and carry out physical treatments. Ordinarily the psychiatrist has neither a research background nor training in the principles of normal behavior. Many clinical psychologists and psychiatrists regard themselves as rivals and competitors since their professional work inevitably overlaps. However, psychologists and psychiatrists have quite different skills and have unique contributions to make to the mental health field. Potential areas of cooperation far outnumber those of conflict. For example, clinical psychologists and psychiatrists have been working together in program development and evaluation, staff training, and the establishment and operation of community outreach services.

Paraprofessionals in Mental Health

One of the results of the emphasis on innovation in the mental health field has been the rapid advance in the use of nonprofessional, or *paraprofessional*, personnel to assist and supplement the traditional mental health team. The paraprofessional has not completed the formal training in any of the professional disciplines, but he or she helps provide mental health activities and services to individual patients, clients, their families, and community members through face-to-face contacts. Clerical and administrative activities, even though they be in a mental health setting, are not considered paraprofessional work.

The paraprofessional in mental health serves two major functions: (1) to enrich the lives of disturbed people and to augment community services by volunteering special skills and talents and (2) to increase the effectiveness of the professional members of the mental health team by relieving them of a certain amount of routine and time-consuming work, thus freeing them for the diagnostic and treatment procedures which are beyond the training of paraprofessionals.

The job titles of paraprofessionals in nearly two hundred projects sponsored by the National Institute of Mental Health (Table 1.1) give some idea of the variety of ways in which nonprofessionals contribute to the mental health effort.

Mental health paraprofessionals are drawn from every age group, beginning with high school dropouts and other teenagers. One project found that youthful workers were especially effective in teaching home management and personal adjustment skills needed by elderly mental patients after leav-

Table 1.1 Paraprofessional workers in the mental health field. The wide variety of job titles indicates the many new areas in which nonprofessional people are contributing to the care and treatment of people with psychological problems

Staff Category	Number	Percent
Tutor teacher-aides	2,267	21.7
Recreation and groupwork aides	2,092	20.0
Nursing and ward personnel	1,758	16.9
Other staff categories	1,122	10.8
Home visitors–enablers	1,020	9.8
Case aides	666	6.4
Physical, occupational, vocational rehabilitation aides	355	3.4
Neighborhood community organizers	293	2.8
Special skill instructors	279	2.7
Community mental health aides	268	2.6
Reach-out aides	185	1.8
Foster parents	60	0.6
Homemakers	52	0.5
Total staff	10,417	100.0

(Sobey, 1970, p. 76)

ing the hospital environment and returning to normal life. Other mental health projects were staffed by black youths in a public school in Rochester, New York, and by Mexican youths who worked in mental hospitals in Utah and Wyoming. In addition to providing practical help in such areas as tutoring and assisting in group activities, it was hoped that the work experience would interest the young volunteers in mental health careers (Sobey, 1970).

At the other end of the age range, some mental health projects have made good use of elderly paraprofessionals. A great many men and women over 65 are eager to fill their time with meaningful volunteer work, since the social security system offers little incentive for gainful employment. These elderly people serve as case aides, home visitors, rehabilitation aides, tutors, and recreation

aides. Groups of senior citizens have proved to be unexpected sources of highly motivated and well-educated volunteers. Moreover, the retired person frequently is able to contribute a degree of patience, warmth, and interest that younger adults cannot manage because of their own involvement in the stressful tasks of making a living and raising a family (Sobey, 1970).

It has also been found that the poor, "indigenous" paraprofessionals are often more successful in working with their deprived, undereducated, and socially disadvantaged neighbors than are middle-class or professional volunteers (Sobey, 1970). The psychological principle that people learn more readily from their peer group (that is, people of similar culture, education, social class, and economic situation) than from other groups is being substantiated in a number of mental health projects.

Abnormal Psychology and Everyday Life

The study of abnormal psychology touches upon most of the problems of community life. Whenever human relationships are involved, there is the possibility that one or more of the group members may be psychologically disturbed. For this reason the principles of abnormal psychology are relevant to education, business and industry, law and law enforcement, politics, and religion.

The Educational Establishment
A knowledge of abnormal psychology is of the greatest importance to all teachers. It is the classroom teacher who must detect the early signs of personality disorder and take the responsibility for pointing out the danger

signals to the school administration. Where psychological or psychiatric services are not available, the teacher should have some idea of how to handle the problem and when and where to make a referral.

Every teacher sooner or later is confronted with personality problems among the pupils. Mental retardation, hostile and aggressive behavior, sexual acting out, vandalism and destructiveness, seclusiveness and withdrawal, and similar symptoms are frequent.

A study of nursery school youngsters found that 30 percent of the children received mental health services during their later school careers. More than half received service during the first four grades. This unusually high incidence of maladjustment might be explained in part by the fact that youngsters with behavior problems at home tend to be placed in nursery schools in an attempt to correct the difficulty. But the most significant finding was that observations made in nursery schools tended to be more sensitive in predicting maladjustment than observations made by teachers in the early grades of school. Another important finding was that more maladjusted children who received mental health service in nursery school showed improvement at the high school level than did those who did not receive such help (Westmen, Ferguson, & Wolman, 1971).

Teachers at the junior and senior high school levels also need to be knowledgeable about personality difficulties. Because of the nature of adolescence and the transition from the dependency of childhood to the relative independence of adult life, many personality difficulties first occur during the adolescent years. Difficult problems of social adjustment, conflict with parents, and relations with members of the opposite sex are rich sources of stress leading to emotional disorders of many kinds.

Teachers at the college level are frequently faced with the need to identify and understand the various forms of personality disturbance. The disturbances seen on the campus are roughly comparable to emotional problems observed in outpatient psychiatric clinics in the community.

Many colleges and universities offer psychological and psychiatric services in the form of psychological clinics, counseling centers, and other mental hygiene services. Such facilities are widely used by students. At the Massachusetts Institute of Technology, 23.4 percent of the class of 1965 was seen in the psychiatric service at least once during the four years (Snyder & Kahne, 1971).

Unfortunately, students are not the only victims of disturbed behavior. Teachers and administrators also break down under stress. This is most destructive when teachers in the primary and elementary grades are involved. In such cases the damage to schoolchildren can be very great indeed. A first-grade boy, caught whispering by the teacher, was made to sit the rest of the morning in a wastepaper basket, with his arms and legs dangling over the hard metal rim. Another teacher encouraged her pupils to chant, "Jimmy is a baby! Jimmy is a baby!" when a youngster broke his crayon. Other teachers gratify deviant and often unrecognized needs through cruel actions and excessive demands upon students.

The problem of mental health in the educational establishment is one of continuing concern, since more than 25 percent of the population of the United States is involved as student, teacher, or administrator. While the educational experience carries with it the danger of the development of disturbed behavior, it represents our first opportunity for detecting, treating, and preventing personality problems and behavior disorders.

The World of Work

Work plays a deep and powerful role in the lives of most people. It is not only a means of economic survival and of maintaining self-esteem but also a source of constant and shifting stress. For this reason the world of work is important in terms of mental health and mental disturbance.

A knowledge of the role of inner conflict is helpful in dealing with many problems related to the selection and upgrading of employees and the handling of problem employees, executive evaluation and development, employee grievances, and similar matters. While the diagnosis and treatment of personality disturbances must be left to trained professionals, a knowledge of abnormal psychology enables people in business to be more sensitive to human problems within their organizations.

Mental disturbance is industry's most costly health problem. Every business and industry has problem employees. White-collar and blue-collar workers—laborers, skilled workers, and executives—all may be vulnerable to emotional disturbances and personality problems.

Business and industry are based on a complex series of human relationships which is subject to intrapersonal, as well as interpersonal, disorganization. A knowledge of abnormal psychology makes it possible to avoid some of the difficulties and to minimize the damaging effects of others. Among the more common types of emotional disturbance in the work situation are the frustration of not being recognized for the job one does, conflicts of personality among employees, marital or financial difficulties which reach into the job situation, and damaging attitudes such as overaggressiveness or pronounced passivity.

As an example of a company's interest in improving the mental health of employees,

Mental Health in Business and Industry

Accidents, low productivity, and high personnel turnover are concrete industrial problems significantly related to mental health and mental illness.

Emotional problems are responsible for approximately 20 to 30 percent of employee absenteeism.

Personal factors cause 80 to 90 percent of industrial accidents.

It is estimated that from 15 to 30 percent of the work force are seriously handicapped by emotional problems. This may be only a guess, but evidence shows that about a quarter of any large work force is in serious need of help for some kind of psychological and social trouble.

At least 65 and possibly as much as 80 percent of the people who are fired by industry are dropped from their jobs because of personal rather than technical factors.

Although exact dimensions are unknown, there are considerable data which suggest that drug abuse and addiction is emerging as a serious and major problem in many work settings.

At least a $15 billion loss to the economy occurs annually as a result of alcohol abuse. Of this total, lost work time in industry, government, and the military accounts for $10 billion. Health and welfare services provided to alcoholics and their families cost $2 billion. An estimated $3 billion to $3.5 billion may be attributed to property damage, medical expenses, increased insurance costs, and wage losses. (Adapted from Weiner, Akabas, & Sommer, 1973, p. 11)

the Xerox Corporation made funds available to the local family service organization so that the agency could provide a full-time mental health staff member at the company's headquarters. Xerox employees also are encouraged to see a mental health counselor at the central office or a branch office of the family service organization (Mills, 1972).

The labor unions are also becoming interested in the mental health of their members. One of the first studies of the relationship between labor unions and mental health delivery systems was made in the garment industry in New York City. The study concentrated on those workers who, because of emotional problems, were having difficulty functioning on the job.

During the four-year project, 442 people received mental health services. Of these, 350 were union members; the others were husbands, wives, and immediate relatives. The striking feature was that a very large number of the referrals proved to be very disturbed. Of the workers seen in the mental health clinic, 41 percent were diagnosed as being seriously disturbed mentally (Weiner, Akabas, & Sommer, 1973).

The Political Scene

There has been increasing interest in the application of abnormal psychology and psychiatry to the problems of political life and to government agencies and organizations. The matter of psychologically disturbed political figures has attracted the attention of the press, the public, and mental health professionals. The implications of the mental and emotional imbalance of men and women in high places in government as well as in other areas of influence have been recognized by the Group for the Advancement of Psychiatry, which issued a report on the problem (GAP, 1973).

The political implications of mental health became apparent during Senator Barry Goldwater's campaign for the Presidency when a group of psychiatrists, who had never examined or treated the Senator, had no hesitancy in labeling him as having been mentally disturbed in spite of the fact that this type of "distance diagnosis" is both unwise and unprofessional. In 1972, Thomas Eagleton was dropped as the Democratic

Figure 1.6 Senator Thomas Eagleton of Missouri appeared to be destined for a brilliant political career when he was chosen by George McGovern to be the Democratic Vice-Presidential candidate at the 1972 nominating convention. Then, it was revealed that Eagleton has been the victim of periods of depression so severe that electroshock treatment was required. The revelation of the psychological disability resulted in his being replaced as McGovern's running mate.

Vice-Presidential candidate when it was revealed that he had received electroshock therapy for his depression; and there were widespread rumors of Richard M. Nixon's emotional instability following the Watergate scandal. More recently one of the most powerful congressmen in Washington became publicly involved with a striptease dancer as a result of his alcoholic excesses.

Abnormal Psychology and the Law

There has been noticeably increased recognition of the fact that psychiatry and other mental health specialties can make a contribution to the legal field. Increasing numbers of medicolegal cases are being referred to hospitals and clinics for examination and expert opinion. Moreover, courts have been increasingly ready to seek psychiatric treatment for certain classes of offenders.

Lawyers need a knowledge of abnormal psychology to help them understand some of the deviant motives of clients and witnesses in the courtroom. Another problem is the

Figure 1.7 (*a*) The face of an assassin. Sirhan B. Sirhan stares at the body of Robert F. Kennedy moments after fatally shooting him. Although the motivation for the slaying remains obscure, the reproduction of the page from his diary (*b*) reflects the disturbed nature of his thinking.

validity of testimony by psychiatrists, psychologists, and other professionals in the field of mental health. Expert testimony often presents difficulties in the courtroom because of the restrictions placed upon the witness. Psychiatric testimony is probably the most precarious and uncertain of all expert testimony.

During the trial of Sirhan Sirhan for the assassination of Robert Kennedy, the nature and quality of psychiatric testimony came in for sharp and deserved criticism. The man on trial was described by two psychiatrists and six clinical psychologists as being the victim of assorted emotional damage during childhood, fantasies of persecution, and psychological problems. One psychiatrist claimed that Sirhan murdered Kennedy while in a hypnotic "trance." A clinical psychologist described Sirhan in words taken without acknowledgement from a recently published book.

The legal world is still burdened to some extent by the archaic concept of determining "insanity" by the test of whether a person knows right from wrong. The assumption is that if this distinction can be made, the person is "sane"; if the distinction cannot be made, he or she is "insane." Nothing could be more incorrect. Serious forms of personality disorganization are found in some men and women who would have little trouble in making such a distinction, while the distinction cannot be made by many antisocial people who have never shown any symptoms of personality disturbance (see Chapter 8).

Abnormal Psychology and Religion

There has been a growing interest in the relationship between religion and psychopa-

Figure 1.8 Religious counseling has been used as a form of psychological therapy throughout the ages. Today, informal counseling by the clergy can be aided by techniques used in the field of abnormal psychology.

thology, particularly in connection with the treatment process. With the possible exception of magic, religion is the oldest form of psychological treatment. Throughout the centuries, religious advisers have performed therapeutic roles. They give emotional support to men and women who are discouraged, depressed, frightened, and guilt-laden.

For the most part, religious counseling

has, in the past, been done on an intuitive basis. More recently, the priest, the rabbi, and the minister have reached into the field of abnormal psychology for techniques to improve their religious counseling. The clergy and mental health professionals are in agreement that there are a number of areas in which pastoral counselors need to be better informed in order to perform their functions more effectively. These areas include the stresses of divorce and broken homes, premarital problems, the plight of the aged, the troubles of alcoholics and their families, and the problem of suicide.

The organized interest of the clergy in the clinical problems of mental health was expressed when the Council for Clinical Training of Theological Students was established. The purpose of this organization was to provide internships in psychiatric hospitals for pastors in training. Since that time, a number of mental health programs have been undertaken by the clergy as well as by church groups and religious organizations.

One example of the cooperation between psychiatry and religion is the Menninger Foundation program at Topeka, Kansas. This organization extends psychiatric training facilities to members of the clergy, teaching them viewpoints and skills helpful in carrying out their pastoral work. The Foundation also looks to the clergy for help in dealing with patients in mental hospitals, in marriage counseling situations, and in the many phases of outpatient care and inpatient aftercare. Each year the Foundation holds a series of conferences which include psychiatrists, psychologists, and theologians of all faiths.

The Chapter in Review

Abnormal psychology is a specialized field of psychology dealing with personality disturbances and behavior disorders. While such conditions are widely recognized, it is not easy to define the terms *normality* and *abnormality* since they are merely abstractions. Nevertheless, a number of attempts have been made to explain the meaning of abnormality.

1 Mental Health in Our Society
   The problem of mental disorder is one of major concern. Statistics on abnormal behavior indicate that at least one of every ten men, women, and children is psychologically disturbed enough to require treatment.

2 Models of Abnormality
   Theoretical models are tentative ways of looking at a problem. Different models represent different points of view and are not necessarily incompati-

ble. The two principal types of models are those that describe behavior and those that attempt to explain it.

a Models That Describe
Among the descriptive models are those positing abnormality as a moral defect, an impairment, or an imperfection. Other descriptive models are the views that abnormality represents social deviancy or statistical variance.

b Models That Explain
The explanatory models can be classified as biological, psychological, and sociocultural. The biological approaches emphasize abnormality as illness, constitutional deficit, or biochemical imbalance. The psychological approaches deal with the effects of inner conflict or the learning of maladaptive behavior. The sociocultural models look upon abnormality as a form of disturbed socialization, as a product of social disorganization, or as culturally defined behavior. An extreme social view is that mental illness does not really exist since society is sick and not the individual.

3 The Mental Health Team
The mental health team which deals with serious individual psychological problems is made up of the clinical psychologist, psychiatrist, and psychiatric social worker. In hospitals, the psychiatric nurse and psychiatric aide also form a part of the team. In recent years the nonprofessional assistant, or paraprofessional, has offered valuable support in the mental health field.

4 Abnormal Psychology and Everyday Life
The facts and principles of abnormal psychology have far-reaching applications to many of the problems of everyday life. Some of the applications are in the areas of education, business and industry, politics, law and law enforcement, and religious counseling.

Recommended Readings

Nature of Normality and Abnormality

Offer, D., & Sabshin, M. *Normality: Theoretical and clinical concepts of mental health* (Rev. ed.) New York: Basic Books, 1974.

Siegler, M., & Osmund, H. *Models of madness, models of medicine*. New York: Macmillan, 1974.

The Mental Health Team

Sobey, F. *The non-professional revolution in mental health*. New York: Columbia University Press, 1970.

Applications to Everyday Life

Kellem, S. G., et al. *Mental health and going to school.* Chicago: University of Chicago Press, 1975.

Weiner, H. J., et al. *Mental health care in the world of work.* New York: Association Press, 1973.

2

Abnormal Psychology in Historical Perspective

Objectives

To discuss the reasons for the decline of the public mental hospital program in the United States

To show the various ways in which community involvement in mental health is being accomplished

To describe some of the mental health problems of minority groups and to indicate what is being done about them

To trace the historical influences that led to the development of the field of abnormal psychology

To indicate some of the prescientific attitudes toward people who showed abnormal behavior

To show how the mental hygiene movement began and influenced the care and treatment of mentally disturbed people

The story of abnormal psychology as a science has a relatively brief history. You will recall that psychology did not exist as an independent discipline until about one hundred years ago. However, the preoccupation with problems of a psychological nature reaches back for many centuries. These problems—which involved the nature of motivation, emotion, learning, thinking, and similar behavior—were dealt with by philosophers, theologians, and physicians. Similarly, disturbances of behavior were observed, thought about, and discussed from at least the beginning of recorded history. For convenience we will study the history of abnormal psychology by dividing it into three parts: the prescientific period, modern origins in the nineteenth and early twentieth centuries, and the situation today.

Prescientific Origins of Abnormal Psychology

The early history of every present-day science shares an accumulation of human experience and knowledge that preceded the emergence of the special approach we call *scientific*. The beginnings of this prescientific period are lost in the mists of time, long before there was a recorded history. In the case of abnormal behavior, it is not unlikely that the roots of such behavior are to be found in the prehuman stages of animal development. Primitive human beings most probably had their full share of personality disturbances and behavior disorders.

Belief in Animism
The earliest attitudes toward personality disturbances grew out of the primitive concept of *animism*, or the belief that the world is controlled by spirits, gods, and other kinds of supernatural beings. Primitive people believed that the winds blew, streams flowed, stones rolled, and trees grew because of spirits residing within the objects. All behavior which was not understood was explained in the same way.

Even a primitive form of head surgery was undertaken as a result of the belief in animism. In the late nineteenth century, a large number of ancient skulls with small holes cut through the bone were discovered in Peru. While in some cases the skulls have fracture lines suggesting the holes had been cut for therapeutic purposes, in most instances the skulls are intact. It is not unlikely that the purpose of the holes was to allow demons, devils, spirits, and other supernatural beings to escape from the head of the patient.

The influence of Greek thought in medicine, particularly in connection with mental disorder, began during the Homeric period, approximately three thousand years ago. The belief was that people became mentally disturbed because angry gods took their minds away. People were treated by prayer, charms, and sacrifice in order to appease the gods who had taken possession of them. It was believed that if those who were possessed participated in the mysteries of Hecate at Aegina, or in the rites of the Corybantes, the god responsible for the disorder might be persuaded to leave the body of the sufferer.

Rise of Naturalism
A most important change in the tradition of animism, spirit possession, and temple medicine came about with Hippocrates (460–367 B.C.). This physician and his followers developed a revolutionary point of view in

medicine. This new and daring approach was *naturalism*, which held that disorders of any kind, mental or physical, are the result of natural causes. Hippocrates had the courage and vision to challenge the beliefs that had been accepted almost without question since people first started to think about the problem. He denied the influence of spirits, gods, and demons as a cause of disease. In his treatise *The Sacred Disease,* Hippocrates wrote, "If you cut open the head, you will find the brain humid, full of sweat, and smelling badly. And in this way you may see that it is not a god which injures the body, but disease."

In ancient Rome, the early period was marked by animism, a concept later replaced by the belief in divine intervention. The Greek gods were adopted by the Romans and given Latin names. Here and there, however, the naturalistic views of Hippocrates and his followers were taken over and elaborated by a few Roman physicians.

The most influential figure of the Roman period was Galen (ca. A.D. 130–200), a Greek physician who accepted and extended the naturalistic ideas of Hippocrates and carried out important work in the area of animal dissection. His most outstanding original contributions were made in connection with the anatomy of the nervous system. Galen also developed a treatment program that was substantially medical, physical, and psychological.

Retreat into Superstition

The decline of medicine began with the death of Galen in A.D. 200. Roman physicians reverted to popular superstition and, later, to demonology and sorcery. The general trend of medicine was one of rapid and almost incredible deterioration. The natural-istic approach of Hippocrates and Galen came to be discarded almost completely in the Christian world.

The ideas of Plato and Aristotle, with emphasis on a mind divorced from the body, and the Judeo-Christian concept of demons and devils struggling for possession of the body led to a preoccupation with magic, sorcery, satanism, and finally witchcraft. The medical treatment of the mentally disturbed was abandoned because such conditions were no longer looked upon as natural disorders, but rather as signs that the victims were possessed by devils or demons.

It is not surprising that the first mental institutions were developed in the non-Christian countries where physicians continued to be influenced by the ideas of Hippocrates. In Baghdad, a large building called the House of Grace was used to detain the mentally ill until they recovered. Magistrates visited the institution from time to time and released those who seemed to be well. Similar institutions were common among the Moors, and as a result of their influence the first mental hospital in Europe was opened in Spain in the early part of the fifteenth century.

The most famous of all historic institutions for mental patients, Bethlehem Royal Hospital in London, was established in 1547 after Henry VIII had seized various church properties. The institution had been founded 300 years earlier as a priory and received a few "lunatics" as early as 1400. After the institution became a mental hospital, the name was corrupted to "Bedlam." Applications for admission were so numerous that most patients were released before they were cured. Some of the inmates were permitted to roam the countryside begging for alms. These demented beggars were identified by foxtails hanging from their hats, and frequently they carried long sticks with many-colored ribbons. Shakespeare referred to this practice in *King Lear* (Act II, Scene III) when he wrote:

The country gives me proof and precedent
Of Bedlam beggars, who, with roaring voices,
Strike in their numb'd and mortified bare arms
Pins, wooden pricks, nails, sprigs of rosemary;
And with this horrible object, from low farms,
Pour pelting villages, sheep-cotes, and mills,
Sometimes with lunatic bans, sometimes with
    prayers,
Enforce their charity.

The true nature of mental disorder was obscured at the time by ignorance and superstition. Since evil spirits were believed to be responsible for mental disturbance, certain saints were thought to have special power in the exorcism of these spirits. Afflicted people by the thousands were taken to religious shrines where it was believed they might be cured. At St. Nun's pool in England, the mentally ill were plunged backward into the water and dragged back and forth until their emotional excitement ceased. The "valley of lunatics" in Kerry, Ireland, had two famous wells. The mentally ill were brought to drink the waters, which were thought to have supernatural powers in curing madness.

Visits to sacred shrines were the mildest form of treatment during the Middle Ages. More frequently the mentally disturbed were burned, starved, flogged, immersed in painfully hot water, and otherwise tortured in an effort to rid them of the evil spirits that had taken possession of them.

At many institutions, the patients were exhibited to visitors on Sundays and holidays. A fee was charged, and people visited the patients' cells just as one might today visit the zoo. The practice continued for several hundred years. As late as the eighteenth century, as many as ninety thousand

Figure 2.1 Tom o'Bedlam, a name given to mentally disturbed people released from Bethlehem Hospital (Bedlam), was a familiar figure in the English countryside several centuries ago. These people wandered along the roads begging for food and shelter. This woodcut shows the sad plight of released persons. The bat, moon, and toad symbolize the powers of darkness aligned against these unfortunate people.

visitors paid admission each year to see the mental patients at Bethlehem Hospital in London. At the same time, patients were displayed in cages on the continent of Europe. Only a hundred years ago, the public paid admission to stare at inmates at the Hospital of St. Andre in Lima, Peru.

During the fifteenth century, the belief in demon possession reached its most virulent form. Two Dominican monks in Germany became the leaders of a movement for the extermination of witches. With the publication of their infamous book *Malleus Maleficarum* (*The Hammer of Evil*), a campaign to rid the world of witches got under way in earnest. This treatise confirmed the existence of witches, described the signs by which they could be detected, and pre-

Figure 2.2 Albrecht Durer's grotesque and frightening figure with wings, tail, and pendulous breasts is an example of the demons believed to be responsible for mental disorder during the Middle Ages.

The Hammer of Evil:
An Excerpt from *Malleus Maleficarum*

QUESTION XI

That Witches who are Midwives in Various Ways Kill the Child Conceived in the Womb, and Procure an Abortion; or if they do not this Offer New-Born Children to Devils.

Here is set forth the truth concerning four horrible crimes which devils commit against infants, both in the mother's womb and afterwards. And since the devils do these things through the medium of women, and not men, this form of homicide is associated rather with women than with men.

Certain witches, against the instinct of human nature, and indeed against the nature of all beasts, with the possible exception of wolves, are in the habit of devouring and eating infant children. And concerning this, the Inquisitor of Como, who has been mentioned before, has told us the following: that he was summoned by the inhabitants of the County of Barby to hold an inquisition, because a certain man had missed his child from the cradle, and finding a congress of women in the night-time, swore that he saw them kill his child and drink its blood and devour it.

We must add that in all these matters witch midwives cause yet greater injuries, as penitent witches have often told to us and to others, saying: No one does more harm to the Catholic Faith than midwives. For when they do not kill children, then, as if for some other purpose, they take them out of the room and, raising them up in the air, offer them to devils.

scribed the legal form for examining and sentencing them. The result was two hundred years of witch-hunting and the torture and violent death of hundreds of thousands of mentally ill men, women, and children.

The laws against witchcraft were not repealed until the eighteenth century. As late as 1768, the eminent Protestant clergyman John Wesley declared, "The giving up of witchcraft is in effect the giving up of the Bible." And in America, where thirty-two witches had been put to death over the years, an official trial for witchcraft took place in New England in 1793.

The Return to Reason

The great changes generated by the Renaissance, in the form of the reappearance of scientific method, emphasis on individual dignity, and the political belief in liberty and human rights, were reflected in the latter part of the eighteenth century in an emerging concern for the mentally ill. By the late 1700s, the return to the naturalistic approach of Hippocrates was well under way. Emphasis was placed once again on anatomy and physiology, and the physical treatment of mental disorders was stressed by physicians.

In France, the writings of Montaigne at the end of the sixteenth century and of Voltaire in the middle of the eighteenth century were important milestones in returning to a naturalistic, nontheological interpretation of mental disorder.

It remained for a French physician, Philippe Pinel (1745–1826), to apply a new social and political philosophy to the problems of mental illness. Pinel was chosen to head the Bicêtre Hospital for the Insane in Paris. The hospital was recognized as a disgrace to the nation, with patients chained to posts, walls, and beds. On Sundays and holidays, the attendants charged a fee for allowing sightseers to visit the cells and to tease and taunt the patients.

One of Pinel's first actions was to demand the removal of the chains from some of the patients. After considerable difficulty, permission was obtained to undertake this daring plan. Most of the officials considered Pinel to be as mad as his patients for even contemplating it. However, within a few days the chains were removed. The results were sensational. Even the most excited and maniacal patients became easier to handle.

Figure 2.3 Philippe Pinel (1745–1826), a French physician, has been called the father of modern psychiatry. He was one of the first to remove the chains from asylum inmates and to treat them as human beings rather than as dangerous animals. His humane and progressive attitudes influenced the care and treatment of mentally disturbed people throughout the civilized world.

Patients who had been chained for twenty or more years, and who had been considered extremely dangerous, strolled about the hospital in camisoles or restraining jackets. They showed no inclination to harm anyone. Noise and excitement decreased, and the discipline of the hospital improved remarkably. J. E. D. Esquirol (1772–1840), a pupil of Pinel and later his assistant, was one of the first clinicians, if not the first, to give lectures in psychiatry. He described the state of mental patients early in the nineteenth century:

I have seen them naked, or covered with rags, and protected only by straw from the cold damp pavement upon which they were lying. I have seen them coarsely fed, deprived of fresh air, or water to quench their thirst, and of most of the necessary things for life. I have seen them delivered and abandoned to the brutal supervision of veritable jailers. I have seen them in squalid, stinking little hovels, without air or light, chained in caves where wild beasts would not have been confined. These unfortunate beings, like the criminals of the state, are cast into dungeons, or into dark cells into which the eye of humanity never penetrates. There they remain to waste away in their own filth under the weight of chains which lacerate their bodies. Their faces are pale and emaciated; they await only the moment which will end their misery and conceal our disgrace. They are exhibited to the public gaze by greedy keepers, who make them appear as wild beasts. They are huddled together in a disorderly manner with no known means of maintaining order among them, except terror. Whips, chains and dungeons are the only means of persuasion employed by keepers who are as barbarous as they are ignorant. (Esquirol, 1838)

The conditions described by Esquirol were typical of those found throughout Europe and the United States. In many parts of the world, the plight of the mental patient was far worse. It was not unusual to confine a mentally disordered man or woman in a hole dug in the floor with a grid fitted over the top. The patient sat or crouched in the hole, received food, excreted wastes, and finally, sometimes after many years of such confine-

Figure 2.4 This inmate of an early French asylum is restrained in a camisole, or straitjacket. The sleeves, which are tied together in front, have no openings for the hands. This type of restraint was used in most mental hospitals in the United States until the introduction of tranquilizing drugs in the early 1950s.

Figure 2.5 The early asylums for mentally disturbed people were often nothing more than damp dungeons with thick stone walls and barred windows. Inmates were sometimes herded together in wild and noisy confusion growing out of the mixture of delusions, hallucinations, and bizarre behavior.

Figure 2.6   Restraining chairs were used in the late 1700s and early 1800s as a method for keeping unruly inmates of insane asylums under control. Such people were restrained for many hours at a time. They were fed while strapped in the chair, and a bucket underneath served as a toilet.

Figure 2.8   Many mechanical devices were used in asylums from the late 1700s until the early 1900s. One such device was this rotating cagelike chair. The inmate was restrained in the chair, which could be rotated rapidly until the person became dizzy. The device was designed as a form of treatment but soon became a method of control and punishment.

Figure 2.7   The Aubanel bed was a crib used to restrain, and frequently to punish, inmates who were difficult to control. Such cribs were used in asylums in the United States up to the early 1900s.

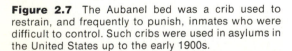

ment, died in misery in these cramped and filthy quarters.

Modern Origins of Abnormal Psychology

Abnormal psychology and psychiatry began in the United States in 1783, when Benjamin Rush (1745–1813) became a member of the medical staff of the Pennsylvania Hospital. There were twenty-four patients who had been admitted as "lunatics." Little was known about the cause of such conditions and less about how to cure them. As a result, the patients were confined to damp and poorly ventilated cells which were cold in the winter, hot in the summer, and foul smelling.

Rush took the matter to the people of Philadelphia through newspaper articles, speeches, and personal influence. Finally, after thirteen years, a separate ward for mental patients was established in 1796. Rush continued to push for enlightened treatment

Figure 2.9 This lithograph depicts a ward scene in a mental hospital in the late 1800s. There is little difference between the behavior of these women and that of the men a century earlier in the dungeon shown in Figure 2.5. While improvements had been made in physical facilities, there had been very little progress in understanding and treating the inmates.

of these patients, insisting that they be given interesting work as well as recreation and amusement. Later he advocated separate wards for men and women and isolation buildings for noisy and disturbed patients.

The Mental Hygiene Movement

In the United States, the objectives of all humane efforts in behalf of mental patients came to be embodied in the *mental hygiene movement*. Historically this movement began with the efforts of Dorothea Lynde Dix (1802–1887), a Massachusetts schoolteacher who became interested in the plight of mentally disturbed men and women confined in jails, prisons, and almshouses. Miss Dix began a forty-year crusade to improve the condition of the mentally ill. Directing her efforts primarily toward the need for special hospitals for mental patients, she pointed out the widely prevalent brutality toward mentally disturbed people and the neglect of those in almshouses and jails. She emphasized statistics which tended to show that most of the mentally ill could be cured if sent to hospitals during the early stages of their disorders. Meeting a degree of success, she was encouraged to carry her investigation to other parts of the United States and eventually to England and Scotland. Her work was an important factor in awakening public consciousness to the needs of the mentally disturbed.

By 1878, the concept of mental hygiene was in more or less general use and was accepted as referring to the prevention of personality disturbances and the promotion of mental health. The mental hygiene movement gained momentum in 1880 with the organization of the National Association for the Protection of the Insane and the Prevention of Insanity. While this organization ex-

Figure 2.10   This inmate of an asylum in the United States was kept restrained in irons and chains for a period of twelve years. His terrible experience was not unique. Thousands of disturbed men and women throughout the country were subjected to this kind of inhuman treatment.

isted for only a few years, it was the first important organized effort to prevent mental disability and promote mental health.

Early in the present century the mental hygiene movement in the United States gained unexpected public support when Clifford W. Beers published his autobiography, *A Mind That Found Itself.* After graduating

Dorothea Dix Visits the Sudbury Poorfarm: An excerpt from a report submitted to the Legislature of the State of Massachusetts in January, 1843

Sudbury. First week in September last I directed my way to the poorfarm there. Approaching, as I supposed, that place, all uncertainty vanished as to which, of several dwellings in view, the course should be directed. The terrible screams and imprecations, impure language and amazing blasphemies, of a maniac, now, as often heretofore, indicated the place sought after. I know not how to proceed. The English language affords no combinations fit for describing the condition of the unhappy wretch there confined. In a stall, built under a woodshed on the road, was a naked man, defiled with filth, furiously tossing through the bars and about the cage portions of straw (the only furnishing of his prison) already trampled to chaff. The mass of filth within diffused wide abroad the most noisome stench. I have never witnessed paroxysms of madness so appalling: it seemed as if the ancient doctrine of the possession of demons was here illustrated. I hastened to the house overwhelmed with horror. The mistress informed me that ten days since he had been brought from Worcester Hospital, where the town did not choose any longer to meet the expenses of maintaining him; that he had been "dreadful noisy and dangerous to go near" ever since. It was hard work to give him food at any rate; for what was not immediately dashed at those who carried it was cast down upon the festering mass within. "He's a dreadful care; worse than all the people and work on the farm beside." "Have you any other insane persons?" "Yes: this man's sister has been crazy here for several years. She does nothing but take on about him; and maybe she'll grow as bad as he." I went into the adjoining room to see this unhappy creature. In a low chair, wearing an air of deepest despondence, sat a female no longer young; her hair fell uncombed upon her shoulders; her whole air revealed woe, unmitigated woe. She regarded me coldly and uneasily. I spoke a few words of sympathy and kindness. She fixed her gaze for a few moments steadily upon me, then grasping my hand, and bursting into a passionate flood of tears, repeatedly kissed it, exclaiming in a voice broken by sobs: "Oh, my poor brother, my poor brother. Hark, hear him, hear him!" then, relapsing into apathetic calmness, she neither spoke nor moved; but the tears again flowed fast as I went away. I avoided passing the maniac's cage; but there, with strange curiosity and eager exclamations, were gathered, at a safe distance, the children of the establishment, little boys and girls, receiving their early lessons in hardness of heart and vice; but the demoralizing influences were not confined to children.

---

from Yale in 1897, Beers started on a business career. However, he experienced an emotional disturbance that prompted him to attempt suicide. For the next several years he was in three different mental hospitals. While in these hospitals, he was the victim of a variety of brutalities, and he observed his fellow patients being subjected to indifference, lack of consideration, humiliation, and inhuman restraints.

Beers wrote to many officials, including the Governor of Connecticut and the President of the United States, demanding an investigation of conditions in mental hospitals. Since he was himself a patient, his letters were disregarded. Nevertheless, he continued to make detailed notes on his observations, and five years after leaving the hospital, in 1908, he published his explosive autobiography.

The book exposed existing evils and suggested ways in which these unfortunate conditions could be corrected. The volume was an immediate success and was read widely and quoted extensively. Soon after publication of the book, the Connecticut Society for Mental Hygiene was founded, and Beers was made executive secretary.

A national mental health committee was established a little later on, and the movement spread throughout the country. In 1975, there were more than a thousand local mental health associations in the United States. In other parts of the world, the mental hygiene movement is being carried on by the World Federation for Mental Health and the World Health Organization.

Abnormal Psychology Today

While the historical foundations of abnormal psychology remain unchanged, the situation at any given time reflects current research interests, shifts in theoretical emphasis, and the overall impact of social and technological change. Apart from the ever-present preoccupation with the possible causes of abnormal behavior, and methods for treating it, the major concerns today are directed toward community involvement in mental health problems.

Crisis in Custodial Care

The custodial public mental hospital has come in for sharp criticism in recent years. A large number of critical studies and a series of popular novels such as Ken Kesey's *One Flew over the Cuckoo's Nest* have alerted the public and mental health professionals to the apparent failure of the custodial mental hospital to provide personalized care or effective rehabilitation. As long ago as 1963, President John F. Kennedy spoke out against the "cold mercy of custodial isolation" and urged that mental patients no longer be placed in institutions to "wither away."

As indicated in the earlier part of this chapter, the public mental hospital was the principal source of mental health service during the 1800s and the first half of the present century. These public hospitals were large, isolated, overcrowded, and understaffed. Those who entered these gloomy institutions frequently remained for many

years, and it was not unusual for inmates to live out their lives in the locked wards.

With all the advances in our attitudes toward the mental patient and all our upgrading of psychiatric hospitals, there continue to be reports of abuses and injustice. A patient who had been confined to the Matteawan (New York) State Hospital for the criminally insane for more than fourteen years was awarded $300,000 in damages by a New York judge who described practices at the hospital as "incredible." In his legal opinion, the judge said, "He (the plaintiff) was struck, kicked and beaten by attendants. After a beating he was stripped and placed in a small dark room without toilet facilities, without water, and without a bed or mattress. He was kept in the room for about eight days on bread and water, and with a full meal once every three days." The damages were awarded for the brutality and for the lack of meaningful psychiatric care.

Was this merely an isolated case of the abuse of a mental patient? Unfortunately not. The state legislature of New Jersey investigated charges that female patients at the state's largest mental hospital had been abused sexually by hospital employees. Girls were smuggled out of the wards by attendants for acts of prostitution. The attendants received $10 each time a girl was smuggled out, and the girl received a bar of candy or a coin. The activity came to light when the parents of a teenage girl complained to the hospital authorities that she was pregnant.

Perhaps the most dramatic and shocking revelation of brutal and inhuman treatment of mental patients is seen in the documentary film *Titicut Follies*, filmed at the Bridgeport Hospital for the Criminal Insane in Connecticut. A Boston judge of the Superior Court described the film as "a nightmare of ghoulish obscenities." He then declared that the film "exceeded the public's right to know" about conditions in mental institu-

(a)

(b)

Figure 2.11 (a, b) Scenes such as these from the film *One Flew Over the Cuckoo's Nest* have played an important part in sensitizing the public to the continuing problems of mental hospitals in the United States.

tions such as Bridgewater. Nevertheless, the film was eventually released throughout the United States and Canada.

An investigative committee reporting on conditions in public institutions for the mentally retarded in Massachusetts listed the following findings of neglect and mistreatment:

> We found not only the children nude, filthy and bruised, but also sitting, sleeping, and eating with moist and dried feces covering them and their surroundings.
>
> We found children heavily medicated and lying on filthy sheetless beds, uncovered and with flies crawling up and down, and in and out of their noses and mouths.
>
> We found children playing in, and eating, garbage.
>
> We found cockroaches and other bugs infesting exposed foods and greasy dishes, and having the run of the building.
>
> We found unlocked medical cabinets, and observed unsupervised and poor dispensing of medicines.
>
> We found poor plumbing, locked bathroom doors, exposed electrical cords, poor ventilation, poor lighting, broken windows and screening, knobless and broken doors, drainless floors, broken and inadequate furnishings.
>
> We found hopeless, apathetic, and frustrated patients and employees with no supervision, no evident instruction in procedures, and no schedule or program to follow; their plea to us was that there was continual lack of cooperation from the nursing office. (Blatt, 1970, p. 86)

It is an unfortunate fact that the conventional mental hospital environment literally teaches patients to remain sick. Endless hours and days of boredom, inactivity, and lack of stimulation are combined with little treatment, or none at all, and a complete lack of meaningful human contact. Even the best-intentioned hospital finds itself overwhelmed by the large numbers of patients and the relatively few staff members. The use of volunteers from the community helps ease the situation to a slight degree, but the basic and depressing aura of the institution cannot be erased from the minds of the patients. The result is a gradual giving in to the psychologically damaging influence of institutional life.

The degrading and dehumanizing character of the mental hospital is seen in the lack of privacy, lack of a place for personal belongings, lining up for meals at appointed times, absence of free communication by mail and phone, restricted visiting procedures, lack of beds for naps, ward odors, and similar frustrations. While many hospitals try to offset these negative aspects of hospital life by providing programs of resocialization and remotivation, most institutions eventually become victims of their own lethargy.

Conditions in some mental hospitals are scandalous. Patients are herded together during the day and crowded together at night. There is little or no privacy. Food is tasteless and sanitary conditions are highly objectionable. The attitudes of custodial staff members are impersonal and unsympathetic. Physical abuse is not uncommon.

But it should be kept in mind that public mental hospitals, like other social institutions such as schools, correctional facilities, general hospitals, and so on, fall on a continuum from the worst to the best. What is important is the marked shift that has taken place in recent years. Until World War II, most public mental hospitals clustered very close to the worst end of the scale. Today, most hospitals of this type are closer to good than to poor. This is not to say that improvements are not needed, because they are. But the wholesale condemnation of the public mental hospital is not justified.

In spite of the general notion that people with mental disorders are isolated, outcast, and discriminated against by society, anyone

Figure 2.12 In spite of many advances in the care and treatment of people with mental disorders, conditions in some hospitals remain shockingly inadequate. The idyllic scene depicted by the photomural on the wall stands in sharp contrast to the depressing reality of everyday life in this hospital ward.

who has observed the problem at first hand over a number of years cannot fail to be impressed by the truly enormous gains that have been made since World War II. The worst ward in any hospital today would have been the average ward not many years ago. Locked doors have been opened, patients have a degree of freedom that would have been unthought of thirty years ago, crowding has been eased, the once pervasive smell of urine has been eliminated, and, with few exceptions, patients are reasonably neat and clean.

Mental Health in the Community

As a result of the growing recognition that the conventional psychiatric hospital cannot solve all the problems of mental disorder, there has been a rapidly accelerating movement toward community mental health programs. Most American communities cannot provide comprehensive mental health services. It was to help provide these services that the national Community Mental Health Centers Program was established.

Early in the 1960s the federal government proposed the establishment of a number of community mental health centers throughout the country. Each center would serve a segment of the population to be known as a "catchment area," and would offer five basic services to every resident. These services were to be twenty-four-hour emergency care, short-term hospitalization, partial hospitalization, outpatient care, and programs of consultation and education.

Community Mental Health Centers

The goal of the Community Mental Health Centers Program is to improve the organization and delivery of mental health services, with the objective of making the most effective mental health care available to all the people of the nation. It seeks to reduce suffering and costly disability and to deploy resources so that greater progress can be made toward preventing personality disturbances.

The diversity of the areas served by these centers is remarkable. They range from the very poorest counties in Appalachia to the affluent urban-suburban fringes of our major cities. While the general objectives of the community mental health centers are similar, the forms and functions of the center are determined by local resources and needs.

The community mental health movement has not been without its problems and disappointments. Many of the newly opened half-way houses, day clinics, workshops, and similar facilities designed to care for the people released from mental hospitals are in dilapidated buildings with a depressing atmosphere and minimal medical and other professional assistance. Segregation within

---

The Northeast Kingdom: A Rural Success

The Northeast Kingdom is a comprehensive mental health center serving three counties in Northeastern Vermont near the Canadian border. The catchment area covers about 2,500 square miles. Much of the country is so remote that it has been said about one of the counties that there are more black bears than people.

In this unlikely setting, the mental health center offers the full range of services recommended by the government. However, the center has been able to extend its services in a number of directions. For example, there is a foster home for the placement of troubled children and unmanageable adolescents. And there is a summer program for younger children who have been identified as having personality problems and behavior disorders. Professional counseling is available to problem children and their parents and teachers.

Special classes and a sheltered workshop were established to help mentally retarded and educationally disadvantged children and adults. The center also operates a drug and alcohol rehabilitation program. These various services and facilities involve not only professional and paraprofessional staff members but more than a hundred citizen participants who have volunteered to assist in the work of the mental health center. (National Institute of Mental Health, 1975)

---

the isolated public mental hospital has too often been replaced by relegation to the slum areas of our cities.

Some of the most disappointing aspects of the community mental health movement have grown out of unrealistic expectations, group pressures, conflicts resulting from overlapping services, and the many administrative difficulties which plague any new large-scale undertaking. Negative reactions in some communities have also grown out of their having been forced to assume responsibility for a "medical problem" that is actually a complex and poorly understood illness.

While the bright hopes at the beginning of the Community Mental Health Centers Program have been realized only incompletely, the changes that have taken place in the care and treatment of emotionally disturbed people have been unequalled by anything that has happened since the hospitals replaced dungeons in the late eighteenth century.

Crisis Intervention

One of the most striking developments in connection with the community mental health approach has been the concept of crisis intervention. As early as World War II, it was found that immediate treatment of psychiatric casualties, with an early return to combat, was the best guarantee against psychological deterioration. The longer treatment was delayed and the farther from the zone of combat the soldier was removed, the less were his chances of making a full and rapid recovery (Menninger, 1948). This finding was later confirmed by psychiatrists during the wars in Korea and Vietnam (Glass, 1954; Hausman & Rioch, 1967).

The first crisis intervention centers, established in the late 1950s, were in connection with medical departments of general hospitals. The purpose was to provide first aid for

The Lincoln Experiment: An Urban Failure

The community mental health program of Lincoln Hospital was developed to serve the South Bronx, a large slum area in New York City that previously was without psychiatric services. The program employed nearly three hundred professionals and indigenous nonprofessionals who were residents of the ghetto neighborhoods served by the center. Initial enthusiasm resulted in a success so remarkable that in 1968 the program won an achievement award from the American Psychiatric Association for "its innovative efforts in making mental health services available when and where they are needed . . . demonstrating how to reach the unreachables."

Only one year later, this model program was torn apart by a crisis which destroyed its effectiveness and threatened its existence. The trouble began as a struggle for power between professional and nonprofessional staff members. Soon the problem became one of open hostility between racial and ethnic minorities, the members of which made up 95 percent of the Lincoln Hospital staff. Eventually the disunity spread to other hospital departments, the medical school and university, community groups, and municipal, state, and national agencies and organizations.

Rivalry and jealousy erupted into threats and violence. Picketing and mass resignations brought the program to a standstill. In the utter deterioration that took place, the people who were to be served by the project were neglected and ignored. Eventually services and facilities again became available. But the program was never able to escape the shadow of the earlier events.

emotional problems on a walk-in basis. Appointments were not necessary and there were no restrictions on who could take advantage of the service. Within a few years crisis centers were opened throughout the country.

Today a variety of crisis programs give immediate support to people experiencing emotional disturbances (Lieb et al., 1973). The support may be the mere answering of troublesome questions, or it may involve psychological counseling or psychiatric treatment. In large cities these clinics are sometimes in storefronts in disadvantaged neighborhoods.

Another type of crisis intervention program is the "hot line" telephone center where paraprofessional workers are available to take calls at any hour of the day or night. The first crisis telephone service was started at Children's Hospital in Los Angeles. It was recognized that most young people, and many adults, are reluctant—through fear or reticence—to appear in person at community clinics and other mental health facilities. The purpose of the hot line was to provide information and to give emergency counseling when needed. The success of the experiment was so immediate and pronounced that similar telephone emergency services appeared in most large cities and university communities.

Much of the work of the telephone crisis center involves giving information about the availability of services and facilities in the community. A mother called seeking help for a problem child. A young man asked to be referred to a psychiatrist in private practice. Another caller wanted to know how to locate a clinic for her mentally retarded brother.

Other callers are more interested in immediate help for themselves. They are often experiencing an emotional crisis at the time they call the hot line number. One of the most frequent calls of this type is made by a person who is depressed and may be having suicidal thoughts. Calls are also received as a result of frightening reactions to drugs.

Mental Health and Minority Groups

It is in the nature of our society that the benefits of recent advances in mental health care are unevenly distributed. Since each

"I Need Help, or I'll Die!"
Crisis Intervention in an LSD Emergency

Tom, a young college student, contacted a crisis intervention center by telephone, saying he knew he "was going to die; I can't control it . . . I must!" He denied the receptionist's repeated requests for more information and kept repeating, "I need help, or I'll die!" Attempts to elicit information about where he was and how he was going to die were answered by desperate sounds of sobbing and saying, "I don't know . . . I don't know." After the second telephone call he was connected directly to a therapist. While attempting to extract more information, the therapist discerned that Tim was confused and disoriented and suspected the use of drugs. When questioned about the use of drugs, Tom stated that a week ago he had taken LSD but had not taken any drugs since. He added that he had "a bad trip; I feel the same way now . . . I'm so depressed . . . life isn't worth living. I've tried three times to jump out of the window of the dorm, but I can't do it . . . but I know I will!" When asked where he was, he said he was in a telephone booth (approximately two blocks from the center). The therapist very specifically told him how to reach the center and emphasized that she would be waiting for him.

Tom arrived ten minutes later and, because of the urgency of the situation, bypassed the usual admission procedure and was seen immediately by the therapist. He exhibited a high state of anxiety and was almost incoherent. The therapist managed to secure information as to age, residence, friends, family, and so on. When Tom explained about his trip on LSD a week ago and that he was feeling "the same way now," he was reassured that it was possible he was "reliving" the previous experience. A medical consultation was arranged, and he received medication. His roommate, Jake, was contacted and came immediately. In approximately thirty minutes Tom was calmer, although still confused, and he did not reiterate his previous wish to die. He still found it difficult to believe that he could be reexperiencing his previous trip. The therapist thought that he could go home with his roommate, since Jake was aware of the situation and felt able to cope with Tom's feelings and behavior. Jake was given medication to sustain Tom and the twenty-four-hour emergency telephone number, and an appointment was made for Tom to return for therapy. (Aguilera & Messick, 1974, pp. 80–82)

Figure 2.13 Every large city has street gangs such as this one in the Spanish Harlem section of New York City. The young people in these gangs are often members of the minority groups which have been served least effectively by community mental health programs. Although efforts to correct this situation are being made in some cities, much remains to be done.

community mental health center was designed to deliver services to catchment areas involving very large segments of the population, the program has favored the white middle-class group. "While exceptions and changing trends are discernible, it is nonetheless a fact that race and class have decisively determined the character of the mental health movement" (Kramer, 1973).

The objection has been that the mental health movement has been unresponsive to the needs of various minority groups, including the lower socioeconomic classes, older people, blacks, women, residents of rural areas, and such ethnic minorities as Puerto Ricans, Mexicans, Indians, and Orientals. Treatment has been a long and costly undertaking, waiting lists have been long, and admission procedures have been complicated. The mental health delivery system was not geared to offer low-cost services when and where they were most needed.

Racial and other minorities In 1970, the Center for Minority Group Mental Health was established within the National Institute of Mental Health. The Center was the result of two years of negotiations between the Black Psychiatrists of America and NIMH officials. The black professionals had severely criticized federal agencies for failing to include more blacks in decision making and the formulation of policies affecting members of minority groups (Ochberg & Brown, 1973).

Some psychiatrists believe that racism should be regarded as a mental disorder. While this radical view is not accepted by most mental health professionals, there is general agreement that racial minorities, along with other minorities, are at a definite disadvantage when it comes to sharing mental health services and facilities.

Another example of the effort to meet the mental health needs of a minority group are the programs directed toward American Indians. In one such project in Montana a number of Northern Cheyenne Indians have been trained to serve as mental health "helpers" or intermediaries between outside professionals and the Indians on the reservation, where rates of alcoholism and suicide are abnormally high.

In another Indian project, Navajo medicine men have trained apprentices in important native ceremonials and have themselves received instruction in conventional medical techniques. It has become quite clear that tribal "medicine" cannot be dismissed or neglected. The ceremonial procedures are deeply rooted in the culture of the Indians and play an important role in maintaining the emotional stability of the individual and the group.

Medicine men are combinations of physicians, teachers, psychiatrists, artists, and priests. Among a people with a group orientation to living, where decisions are made by consensus without centralized authority, medicine men are the cultural leaders—the carriers of tribal knowledge, pharmacology, and symbolism. Without them, traditions would vanish. Although many Navajos live in two very different worlds, even the most acculturated members gain sustenance from the ceremonies. (Segal, 1973, p. 151)

Women as a minority Women cannot be considered a minority in terms of numbers, but their limited rights and privileges and their restricted opportunities place them in a minority position. This minority role carries over to the field of mental health, where the fact of being a woman often results in less than adequate consideration and service (Chesler, 1972).

An example of the bias against women in mental health has been seen in connection with victims of rape. As if this experience were not stressful and degrading enough, police, hospital, and court procedures have added to the emotional shock by callous questioning, crude physical examinations, and the public recital of previous sexual activities. The anticipation of such traumatic experiences has deterred a very large number of women from reporting the crime or seeking medical help.

Fortunately there are increasing signs that some of these emotionally damaging procedures can be bypassed or eliminated through legislation. Privately sponsored "rape crisis centers," where a rape victim can receive sympathetic help and advice, are appearing in our larger cities; the more enlightened police departments and hospital emergency services are providing women interviewers and counselors; and a few states are moving to eliminate the need for a rape victim to reveal her sexual history in court.

The rural minority Rural Americans also make up a minority group. They are defined by the Bureau of the Census as those who live in the open country or in communities of less than 2,500 people. While rural Americans constitute only about 25 percent of the total population, they live in rural counties that occupy about 90 percent of the land area of the United States.

The rural population has been at a disadvantage in terms of availability of mental health services and facilities. Most of the professional and paraprofessional workers in mental health are concentrated in the large urban areas. This situation has made it difficult even for the financially able rural resident to receive mental health services. For the low-income rural population, mental health help has been virtually nonexistent. More than two-thirds of the rural counties in the United States are still not within the catchment areas of community mental health centers (Segal, 1973).

The Chapter in Review

The history of abnormal psychology can be divided into three phases: the prescientific period, from primitive times until the end of the eighteenth century; the period of modern origins, from the beginning of the nineteenth century until the 1950s; and the present period, covering the immediate past and reaching into the future.

1 The Prescientific Period

The prescientific period was characterized by the concept of animism among primitive people; a belief in the power of gods and goddesses; and the development of naturalism by Hippocrates and his followers in Greece and Rome. Then, for more than a thousand years, the Judeo-Christian world was plunged into a period of superstition marked by a belief in devils, demons, and witches. It was not until the late 1700s that reason and humanity appeared once again. The revolution in the care and treatment of disturbed individuals began with the work of the French physician Philippe Pinel.

2 Modern Origins of Abnormal Psychology

The modern period in abnormal psychology began in the United States with the development of the public mental hospital program early in the 1800s. Another important factor was the increased attention given to the plight of mental hospital inmates by Dorothea Dix and other concerned people who were responsible for the mental hygiene movement. The history of abnormal psychology is also related to the early interest in classifying abnormal behavior, in seeking to discover physical causes and treatments, and in the attempts to develop psychological explanations for mental disorders.

3 Abnormal Psychology Today

Abnormal psychology today is marked by a shift in emphasis from the custodial mental hospital to mental health services in the community. These services are offered through a national network of community mental health centers as well as through a variety of more specialized facilities. Considerable emphasis is being placed on making services available where and when they are needed in the local community.

4 Mental Health and Minority Groups
An important aspect of abnormal psychology today involves the mental health needs of minority groups. Ethnic minorities, women, children, and the elderly as well as residents of rural areas are receiving increasing attention through innovative programs and facilities.

Recommended Readings

Early History of Abnormal Psychology

Howells, J. G. (Ed.) *World history of psychiatry*. New York: Brunner/Mazel, 1975.

Neiman, J. S. *Suggestion of the devil*: *Insanity in the Middle Ages and the twentieth century*. Garden City, N.Y.: Anchor Books, 1975. (Paperback.)

Skultans, V. (Ed.) *Madness and morals*: *Ideas on insanity in the nineteenth century*. London: Routledge, 1975.

Custodial Care

Glenn, M. *Voices from the asylum*. New York: Harper & Row, 1974. (Paperback.)

Community Mental Health

Gottesfeld, H. *The critical issues of community mental health*. San Francisco: Holden-Day, 1970.

Renner, K. E. *What's wrong with the mental health movement*. Chicago: Nelson-Hall, 1975.

Crisis Intervention

McGee, R. K. *Crisis intervention in the community*. College Park, Md.: University Park Press, 1974.

Specter, G. A., & Claiborne, W. L. *Crisis intervention*. New York: Behavioral Publications, 1973.

Mental Health Problems of Minority Groups

Chesler, P. *Women and madness*. Garden City, N.Y.: Doubleday, 1972.

Giordano, J. *Ethnicity and mental health*. New York: Institute of Human Relations, 1973.

Segal, J. (Ed.) *The mental health of rural America*. Rockville, Md.: National Institute of Mental Health, 1973.

Weiner, H. J., et al. *Mental health care in the world of work*. New York: Association Press, 1973.

Willie, C. V., et al. (Eds.) *Racism and mental health.* Pittsburgh: University of Pittsburgh Press, 1973.

General Interest

Fadiman, J., & Kewman, D. (Eds.) *Exploring madness: Experience, theory and research.* Monterey, Calif.: Brooks/Cole, 1973.

Snyder, S. H. *Madness and the brain.* New York: McGraw-Hill, 1974. (Paperback.)

Szasz, T. (Ed.) *The age of madness.* Garden City, N.Y.: Anchor/Doubleday, 1973. (Paperback.)

3
Biological Models of Abnormal Behavior

Objectives

To show that some forms of psychological disorder have their origins in organic disturbances and that other disorders may be indirectly influenced by physical conditions

To present evidence that genetic influences apparently operate in some types of abnormal behavior

To indicate that constitutional factors may play a role in the development of psychological disturbance

To discuss the possible relationship of nutritional and hormonal disturbances to abnormal behavior

To show how chemicals involved in the transmission of the nerve impulse are suspected of being related to some forms of mental disorder

To describe various types of brain damage and show how brain damage can result in disturbed behavior

To demonstrate the potential role of stress in the development of maladaptive behavior.

Biological models of abnormal behavior grew out of the observation that many physical conditions contribute to, and are frequently causes of, personality disturbance and behavior disorder. The origins of this type of model can be traced to the naturalistic medicine of ancient Greece, when Hippocrates declared that body fluids, or "humors," were responsible for mental disorder. Since that time, except when superstition and demonology have been prevalent, there has been a persistent belief that the physical condition of the body plays an important part in personality disorganization.

Today, the search for physical causes of maladaptive behavior occupies the attention of many investigators. It is recognized that not all personality disturbances and behavior disorders develop as a result of biological influences. But it is also believed that some conditions are determined in a significant way by physical factors. Most of the emphasis is on genetic influences; nongenetic, or constitutional, conditions prior to birth or at the time of birth; defects, or errors, in the biochemistry of the body; and brain damage. There is also a very considerable interest in the impact on behavior of the physical changes accompanying stress. The biological model holds that any one of these conditions or influences, or any combination of them, can result in psychological disturbances.

Genetic Model

An understanding of the role of heredity in personality disorganization must start with the realization that psychological characteristics in themselves are not inherited. What is inherited is encoded information which, under given conditions, is able to determine or to influence psychological characteristics. Mental disorders are not passed on from generation to generation. What is transmitted is a potential for physical variations which make it difficult, if not impossible, for those affected to meet the demands of their environment. This is what Henry Maudsley meant many years ago when he said, in his book *The Pathology of Mind*, "A person does not inherit insanity, but a predisposition or tendency" (1879).

Long before the genetic discoveries of the Austrian monk Gregor Mendel in 1860, there was a general conviction that mental disorder was in some way passed on from one generation to another. While it is known today that few conditions are based simply upon hereditary mechanisms, there remains a reasonable likelihood that some personality disturbances develop only because the soil has been prepared by a highly complex hereditary pattern.

Early studies of the inheritance of mental disorder were concerned with the idea that there is a common underlying inherited weakness, or *neuropathic constitution*, that expresses itself in a variety of abnormal conditions (Tuke, 1892). However, this concept was eventually abandoned because of its vagueness. Attention was then directed to the possible inheritance of more specific kinds of abnormal behavior. Attempts were made to isolate genetic characteristics and to demonstrate the operation of hereditary factors in the families of people with mental disorder. But the complexity of the problem of human inheritance and the limited understanding of underlying genetic mechanisms at the time combined to prevent any substantial increase in the knowledge of the inheritance of personality disorder.

Recent advances in behavioral genetics have increased the interest in, and knowledge of, the influence of inherited factors in certain types of maladaptive behavior. The evidence for such influence comes from three principal sources: family-risk studies, twin studies, and studies of adopted children.

Family-risk studies involve the investigation of abnormal behavior in the relatives of a disturbed person. For example, if a son is alcoholic, what are the chances that the father, mother, sisters, brothers, or other relatives will also be alcoholic? The higher the incidence of the disorder in close relatives, the more likely it is that a genetic influence is present. Such evidence is only suggestive of genetic involvement, since the higher incidence of disorder among relatives could also be explained by social factors.

Since family-risk studies are inconclusive in themselves, other types of genetic evidence have been sought. Some of the most persuasive findings have grown out of the study of fraternal (dizygotic) twins as compared with identical (monozygotic) twins. The genetic makeup of fraternal twins is no different from that of nontwin brothers and sisters, while the genetic makeup of identical twins is the same.

If one of a pair of twins shows abnormal behavior, it would be expected that if the behavior is influenced by heredity, an identical twin would also show it in a very high number of cases. Fraternal twins, however, would be expected to show the abnormal behavior only about as often as would nontwin brothers and sisters. This pattern of incidence in twins has been found for such serious mental disorders as schizophrenia and the manic-depressive conditions (see Chapters 12 and 13).

A third type of genetic evidence comes from the study of adopted children. In this approach, children who have been separated very early in life from a disturbed parent are compared with children who have remained with such a parent. If a genetic influence is present, it would be expected that the adopted child would be likely to show disturbed behavior beyond normal expectancy, even in the completely new environment. As in the case of twin studies, the investigation of adoptees gives strong support to the assumption of a genetic factor in some types of abnormal behavior.

When the children of schizophrenic mothers are adopted and reared away from the family, the children develop schizophrenia to about the same extent as those reared at home with a schizophrenic parent (Heston, 1966). Another study found that children separated from alcoholic parents during the first six weeks of life, and having no later contact with the parents, are more likely to develop alcohol problems as they grow older than are children of nonalcoholic parents (Goodwin et al., 1973a).

In spite of the mounting evidence of genetic influence in certain types of abnormal behavior, there has been a persistent reluctance on the part of some psychologists and psychiatrists to accept the findings. Their criticisms and objections, however, have not been able to obscure the growing likelihood that genetic components are involved in at least some personality disturbances and behavior disorders.

Constitutional Model

In addition to genetic influences in personality disturbances and behavior disorders, there are additional factors that become operative during the development of the fetus, at the time of birth, and during the period immediately following birth. These factors are not learned in the conventional sense even though they are determined in part by the environment. They are a relatively unalterable part of the individual and are highly resistant to change or modification.

Our everyday observation tells us that people differ in body type. Moreover, it is not difficult to group people according to their physical characteristics. The assumption, however, that specific psychological traits and personality disturbances are associated with identifiable body types has not been supported by recent investigations. Nevertheless, since basic physical characteristics are genetically determined, and since there is a strong possibility that genetic factors are also involved in certain types of abnormal behavior, a possible relationship between biotypes and mental disorder cannot be completely discounted.

Biotypes and Abnormal Behavior

A person's body formation is determined by a combination of genetic and early developmental factors. Once the pattern has been established, it remains relatively constant throughout life. Even though the person may lose or gain weight, the underlying physique is unchanged. People are tall or short, broad or narrow, and large boned or small boned. This relatively constant body structure is called the *biotype*.

The belief that biotypes are intimately related to psychological characteristics has a long history. In ancient Greece, Theophrastus suggested that people were similar in their natures to the animals they resembled. The person who looked like a bulldog was said to have the tenacious characteristics of that breed. Since that time there have been many attempts to establish a relationship between physical structure and abnormal behavior.

Earlier in this century, evidence was presented in support of a relationship of this kind (Kretschmer, 1925; Sheldon, 1940). However most psychologists and psychiatrists remained skeptical and unconvinced that biotypes and mental disorders were related in a significant way.

Biorhythms and Abnormal Behavior

Another area of interest involving constitutional factors related to abnormal behavior is that of *biorhythms.* While the rhythmic nature of such body functions as heart rate, sleep, respiration, brain waves, and menstrual activity has been widely recognized, a large number of other bodily functions follow cycles, show rhythms, and exhibit periodicity. It has been suggested that these biorhythms, which have been called the *biological clock*, may be involved in some forms of abnormal behavior (Luce, 1971).

Tension, temper, and depression are frequently observed during the premenstrual period. There is little doubt that these personality changes are related to physiological events in the body. This being the case, it is not unreasonable to suppose that other biological rhythms might also be related to changes in behavior and experience.

One investigation demonstrated a daily rhythm in the level of serotonin, a chemical involved in the transmission of the nerve impulse, in extremely withdrawn children (Yuwiler et al., 1971); another concerned itself with the daily rhythms of chemicals in individuals with emotional depression (Riederer et al., 1974). Still another studied the biorhythm of the activity level of overactive people who were mentally retarded (Wade, et al., 1973); and one investigation demonstrated a daily rhythm in the susceptibility to convulsive seizures (Schreiber & Schlesinger, 1971).

While strong evidence for a relationship

The Strange Behavior of Two Brothers: Biorhythm or Coincidence?

Harry M. was a teaching assistant in the psychology department of a large midwestern university. He was a quiet and well-mannered young man who joined other young colleagues each day for lunch in the Student Union. Conversation was usually animated and often argumentative. But Harry had little to say on most occasions. Then one noon he began to talk about a variety of matters, but his talkativeness went unnoticed in the extremely talkative group. However, after a day or two, Harry began to interrupt others who were talking and soon dominated the conversation. Within a few days, it was difficult for anyone else to say anything because Harry had taken over completely. Not only was he talking constantly, but his stories were becoming increasingly improbable. He frequently jumped up from the table to dash across the dining room to greet a student or acquaintance. He became more and more talkative and expansive in his classes, and insisted that his introductory class meet on Saturday morning even though the regular meeting days were Monday, Wednesday, and Friday. The students did not object to the extra class because they sensed the instructor's excitement, and they were eager to see what would happen. When they met on Saturday, Harry soon had two projectors going full blast showing films on both side walls of the classroom while he was shouting at the top of his voice to be heard over the uproar of the films and the hilarity of the students who were caught up in the pandemonium. Before the unusual class was half over, the head of the psychology department and the dean became aware of the problem and hurried to the scene. When Harry saw them he dashed out of the classroom, raced across the campus, and barricaded himself in his room. When the college officials finally managed to batter down the door, they were bombarded with empty beer cans. Soon Harry was strapped in an ambulance on the way to a nearby mental hospital. The only relative listed in Harry's personnel file was a brother living in a distant city. When a telephone call was put through to him, it was discovered that he was a psychiatrist on the staff of a well-known private mental hospital. The only difficulty was that the psychiatrist brother had also been admitted as a patient on that very day. He had developed such a degree of excitement that he could no longer be controlled. It was only later that college officials discovered that Harry and his brother were identical twins.

between biorhythms and abnormal behavior is lacking, the episodes of the mental disorder known as manic-depressive psychosis (See Chapter 13) frequently appear with an impressive degree of regularity. Clinicians have been impressed for many years with the rhythmic nature of this mental disturbance. Such clinical observations suggest the possibility that the symptoms might be based upon some as yet obscure type of internal biological timing mechanism. It is also possible that environmental relationships with time might account for the rhythmic occurrence of symptoms.

Biochemical Model

The biochemistry of personality disturbance has been a matter of research interest for the greater part of the present century. This interest was intensified in the 1950s by the development of a wide range of *psychoactive* drugs.

While the gap between brain chemistry and emotional life is still too great to correlate behavior with specific chemical changes in most cases, modern science is moving in this direction, and with steadily increasing acceleration. Research into brain biochemistry may lead to the solution of some of the more elusive problems associated with personality disorganization.

Neurohumors and Abnormal Behavior

Neurohumors are chemicals involved in the transmission of the nerve impulse. These chemicals are stored in various areas of the body; when they are released, they facilitate or inhibit the activity of the nervous system. Once they have served their purpose, they are broken down chemically and destroyed.

The importance of the neurohumors in the transmission of nerve impulses was first shown in 1921. It was then demonstrated that, following the stimulation of the vagus nerve of a frog's heart, a chemical appeared which, when transferred to a second isolated heart, produced an effect similar to that of vagus stimulation (Loewi, 1921). The substance responsible for this stimulation was later identified as *acetylcholine*.

It was not until the middle of this century that serious study was directed to the possible role this chemical plays in abnormal behavior. While acetylcholine is not normally present in the cerebrospinal fluid, it is found in the majority of people with convulsions, particularly in those who have frequent seizures. It is also possible to induce convulsive seizures in a person by injecting acetylcholine into the veins. Similarly, there have been reports linking acetylcholine with other types of mental disorder.

Most of the current interest in the neurohumors involves chemicals in the *catecholamine* and *indoleamine* groups. The principal catecholamines are *norepinephrine* (*noradrenalin*) and *dopamine*; an important indoleamine is *serotonin*. These chemicals are intimately involved in the regulation of nervous system activity; they have been implicated in emotional depression and elation as well as the disturbed behavior of schizophrenics.

Catecholamine hypothesis The rapid advance in our knowledge of the chemical action of the neurohumors has resulted in the catecholamine hypothesis, which states that the level of catecholamines is an important factor in the development of some forms of abnormal behavior.

The hypothesis is based on the finding that certain drugs which deplete or inactivate dopamine and norepinephrine in the central nervous system cause sedation in animals or depression in human beings or both, and that drugs which increase the level of dopamine and norepinephrine tend to produce stimulation in animals and elation in human beings (Schildkraut, 1965).

Some findings that tend to question the catecholamine hypothesis include the fact that some chemicals which are thought to exert their effects through their action on amines are stimulants but not antidepressants. Cocaine and amphetamine are drugs of this type. It is also the case that some antidepressant drugs are effective in one type of depression but not in other types. And at least one drug (lithium) can be used in the treatment of both depression and elation (Sack & Goodwin, 1974).

Indoleamine hypothesis The most important substance of the indoleamine group of chemicals is serotonin. The indoleamine hypothesis is based on the observation that drugs which inactivate or deplete serotonin lead to depression. These findings led to the hypothesis that depression is associated with a relative deficiency of serotonin, whereas elevation of mood is associated with an excess of serotonin at critical sites in the brain (Ban, 1975).

The evidence in favor of the indoleamine hypothesis is that a variety of drugs with a depressant action tend to lower the level of serotonin or to block its action in the nervous system (Ban, 1974). However, one drug (para-chlorophenylalanine), which produces an 80 to 90 percent reduction of serotonin, does not induce depression (Mendels & Frazer, 1974). This latter finding is the principal argument against the indoleamine hypothesis.

It is of considerable interest that several naturally occurring substances that cause abnormal behavior are very closely related chemically to serotonin. One of these is the ergot alkaloid *lysergic acid diethylamide*, or LSD. The psychologically disturbing effects of this drug are now well known. Another substance related to serotonin is bufotenine, which is found in the narcotic mushroom *Amanita muscaria*. This mushroom produces marked psychological disturbances when eaten and has been used for many years by Siberian tribes of the Kamchatka Peninsula. It is also used in the United States and abroad among students, other young people, and some adults.

Nutrition and Abnormal Behavior

Although the importance of nutrition in physical and mental health has been recognized for many centuries, the precise role of nutritional deficiencies in behavior disorders and personality disturbances has been relatively neglected. But it is known that the tissue of the brain, spinal cord, and peripheral nerves depends in a very critical way upon a variety of nutritional elements.

It is probable that nutritional deficiencies are the direct cause of psychological disorders in some cases. On the other hand, personality disturbances from other causes tend to interfere with food intake and in this way produce secondary deficiencies which reinforce the damaging cycle.

Malnutrition There is good reason to believe that inadequate nourishment of the brain during infancy and early childhood has lasting effects on both the physical and psychological development of the individual. When it is realized that there are more than 300 million malnourished children under 5 years of age in the world and that about 60 percent of preschool children lack sufficient protein food, the implications for physical and mental health are very grave indeed.

Animal experimentation also indicates that diet and nutrition are critically important in the early stages of growth and development. There is consistent and clear brain damage in many species as a result of early protein deficiency. The human brain is also susceptible to protein deficiency, especially during the growth spurt in the last few weeks of pregnancy and the first six months following birth.

Studies of the effects of malnutrition on the mental health and mental growth of children have found that the degree of malnutrition is positively related to the level of intellectual deterioration. The malnourished child is usually apathetic and shows little interest in the surroundings. Reactions tend to be slow, and crying is monotonous and plaintive (Mönckeberg, 1972). A higher incidence of psychiatric disorders among malnourished children also has been found (Sharma, 1973).

However, a major study of the impact of famine on human development—based on the Dutch "hunger winter" of 1944–1945 during World War II—found that exposure to famine did not appear to interfere with the mental competence of the infants who survived to adulthood. Since the nutritional deprivation was more severe than in even the harshest and most deprived environmental conditions of today, the finding is of considerable interest.

The Dutch study concerned *prenatal* nutritional deprivation on the part of the mother and did not involve *postnatal* food deprivation of the infant. It is possible that brain damage did in fact occur but that there was an excessive death rate of children with damaged brains; or that postnatal learning contributes such an important part to adult mental function that the brain cell damage was compensated for by later learning; or that there is a reserve of brain cells large enough to offset any later loss in function (Stein et al., 1975).

The Dutch study did not deal with the effects of nutritional deprivation on infants and children who are malnourished during their developmental years. Here the evidence is more clear-cut.

Mineral deficiency Among lower animals, diet has a pronounced influence on behavior. Chickens lacking a proper diet become irritable, and young rats brought up on a magnesium-deficient diet show excitability. They may become apprehensive and fearful and may finally develop convulsions. The common saying "feeling your oats" reflects the fact that horses fed too heavily on oats become extremely high-spirited.

While manganese deficiency does not result in obvious malformations, it is not unusual for offspring to show a disturbance of gait and balance when the maternal diet was lacking in manganese during pregnancy. In the case of zinc deficiency during pregnancy, fetuses are usually malformed and stunted in growth, with almost all body systems affected (Winick, 1970).

Vitamin deficiency Our present knowledge of vitamin functions and vitamin deficiencies suggests that there is no causal relationship between vitamin lack and specific clinical conditions. However, because of the initimate and diffuse functions of the vitamins in the biochemistry of the body, any significant lack of these substances might be expected to be reflected in a variety of psychological symptoms.

The major impact of the vitamins on the personality is through *avitaminosis*, or vitamin deficiency. Such deficiencies are brought about in a number of ways. A faulty or improperly balanced diet may furnish the body with inadequate amounts of a vitamin, or there may be an incomplete absorption of the vitamins from the alimentary canal. It is possible also that the vitamin storage may be defective, the cells may be unable to use the vitamins made available to them, or vitamins may be used up at an excessive rate due to stress.

Of the various vitamins, those in the B group have the most immediate implications for abnormal behavior. *Thiamine*, or vitamin B_1, was the first of this group to be identified. A deficiency in thiamine results in neurological changes and in a variety of circulatory symptoms. The deficiency also brings about a neurotic-like reaction characterized by lack of appetite, sleep disturbances, irritability, and increased feelings of fatigue. Those affected are likely to have many vague physical complaints. Psychologically, they are forgetful, find it difficult to think in an orderly way, and are unable to concentrate. Occasionally, there are ideas of persecution. In more serious forms of thiamine deficiency, there is severe depression with loss of memory, confusion, distorted thinking, and perceptual disorders.

In a study of the effects of thiamine deficiency on behavior, ten normal men were subjected over a span of seven months to a prolonged period of partial restriction of thiamine, a shorter period of acute thiamine deprivation, and a recovery period of thiamine supplementation. Psychological testing during the study showed pronounced personality changes. The men became depressed and showed signs of hypochondria (i.e., physical complaints and preoccupation with body functions). These symptoms disappeared as soon as the thiamine level was brought back to normal (Brozik & Gentzkow, 1971).

Vitamin B_{12} deficiency is known to produce central nervous system damage and has been implicated in a variety of neurological and psychiatric disorders in the elderly. In a study of chronically hospitalized geriatric patients in a psychiatric outpatient clinic, vitamin B_{12} deficiency was found in 15 percent of the cases (Whanger & Wang, 1970).

While vitamin deficiency appears to play a part in some cases of mental disturbance, its actual role is complicated by the fact that related conditions such as malnutrition, physical illness, alcoholism, or drug abuse may also be involved.

Hormones and Abnormal Behavior

The human organism is made up of a complex network of body systems, including the skeleton, muscles, nerves, blood vessels, glands, and other specialized parts of the body. Of these body systems, the nervous and glandular systems are most closely related to the onset and course of personality disorganization.

The glandular system consists of (1) duct glands and (2) ductless, or *endocrine*, glands. The duct glands are those whose product is secreted to the external or internal surface of the body by means of a duct or canal. Tear glands and sweat glands are examples of duct glands. For the most part, glands of this type are relatively unimportant in psychopathology. The endocrine glands, however, frequently play a critical role in the development and form of personality disturbance. These glands produce chemical substances called *hormones* and secrete them directly into the bloodstream.

These substances have a powerful regulatory effect on various functions of the body.

There is considerable evidence that the hormones are involved in abnormal behavior. For example, a substantial number of depressed individuals have been shown to release excessive amounts of the adrenal cortex hormone *cortisol*. The pattern of secretion returns to normal limits after clinical recovery (Sachar et al., 1973).

The problem of the relationship between the hormones and personality disorder is a most complicated one. The endocrine system is intimately tied in with the nervous system through the hypothalamus, an important brain center located close to the pituitary gland. The nerve cells which connect the nervous system with the endocrine system form the bridge which makes possible an intimate and powerful relationship that plays a part in normal and abnormal behavior.

The relation of hormones to abnormal behavior is indicated by the finding that when the level of the hormone *progesterone* drops suddenly during pregnancy, there is an increase in crying, depression, and episodes of mental disorder. Similarly, when progesterone drops during the second half of the menstrual cycle—to a level of virtually no detectable hormone on the first day of menstruation—mental depression often follows. This hormonal change has also been related to suicide attempts, crimes of violence, mental hospital admissions, and assaultive behavior among hospitalized psychiatric patients (Hamburg, Moos and Yalom, 1968).

Other Biochemical Factors

Research in biochemistry has also centered on blood chemistry, water metabolism, urinary constituents, analysis of the cerebrospinal fluid, the relation of brain enzymes and coenzymes to personality disorganization, and similar problems.

The relationship of brain enzymes, or chemical regulators, to personality disorganization is in an early stage of investigation. There is evidence, however, that future knowledge of certain mental disturbances will be increased as a result of advances in our understanding of the action of the enzyme systems in the body.

Biochemical studies of people with mental disorders are difficult to evaluate and interpret because of a number of factors which can confuse the findings. Some of these factors are the ordinary hazards of all clini-

cal and experimental investigations. Some of the more general sources of error are the accuracy of the diagnosis, the adequacy of control groups, and the bias of the investigator. In addition, biochemical findings can be complicated by the effect of institutionalization on diet and the greater risk of infection, the influence of treatment with various drugs, and the emotional stress related to the hospital experience.

Brain-Damage Model

Some of the most striking personality disturbances grow out of physical damage to the brain in the form of infection, toxic condi-

---

**"The First Time I Died"—
Some Psychological Effects of Brain Injury**

Lisa was an attractive and well-dressed woman in her late twenties who sat quietly in the ward of a psychiatric hospital. She smiled pleasantly whenever anyone passed or looked in her direction. One might have thought she was a visitor rather than a patient. But she had been at the hospital for nearly six years, and during that entire time she had never once initiated a conversation or even asked a question. Lisa was able to speak and readily answered questions put to her. However, if the question concerned her life before coming to the hospital, she always answered by saying, "I forgot all about that the first time I died."

Lisa was quite convinced that she had died, but she was unable to say how or when her death had occurred. It did not seem strange or inconsistent to her that she was eating and sleeping and living in the ward of the hospital, or that she was able to talk about her own death.

Few people at the hospital knew the story behind Lisa's condition. Her father and mother were intellectuals who had been forced to flee from an Eastern European country when Lisa was a child. Since both parents were highly educated, cultured, and talent-

ed, the daughter grew up surrounded by books, paintings, and music. She excelled in school, became fluent in four languages, and continued on to the university where she received her Ph.D. degree in biochemistry. Upon graduating, she took a position with a large laboratory and later married.

One afternoon Lisa and a friend were driving in the country. There was an accident—no one knows how or why, since there were no witnesses. The car overturned, and her companion was killed. Lisa was unconscious when she was found pinned in the wreckage. She had a severe head injury and was taken to a hospital, where surgeons worked for six hours in an attempt to repair the damage to her brain.

When Lisa finally recovered consciousness some days later, it was soon apparent that she had suffered severe psychological deficit. She had no memory of the accident or the events that had preceded it. She responded to her name, and she recognized her husband and members of her family when they visited her, but she had no memory of them when they were not present. She lost her ability to use the foreign languages she had learned, and she apparently forgot the technical information and skills she had acquired as a scientist. While Lisa's loss of memory is typical of most brain injury cases, her delusion of having already died was probably related to experiences of a more private nature.

tions, injuries, and similar organic disturbances. Each of these conditions is a stressful situation in the body. The nervous system is affected, and its functioning is impaired. The result may be a personality disturbance. The severity of the symptoms depends on the location, extent, and persistence of the damage.

Brain Injury

Personality disorganization sometimes occurs as a result of injuries to the head and brain. In most cases, such injuries show neurological changes as the primary symptoms, but it is not unusual for psychological symptoms to be present as well. It is a commonplace observation that injuries of this type result in personality change. Such everyday expressions as "She fell on her head" and "He must have fallen out of the cradle when he was a baby" are evidence of the popular acceptance of the role of head injury in personality disturbance.

The earliest account of head injury appears in the Edwin Smith papyrus of the seventeenth century B.C. This document refers to three classes of head injuries, including superficial lacerations in which the bone of the skull is uninjured, injuries in which the bone is perforated and the victim unable to turn his or her head, and injuries in which both the bone and the brain tissue are wounded. Treatment consisted merely in sewing the skin of the scalp and dressing the wound with lint, honey, and grease. A fifteenth-century physician who wrote about personality changes in persons who had suffered head injury observed peculiarities in sexual habits and eating.

The symptom picture varies in different forms of cerebral trauma, depending upon the extent and location of the damage. However, the initial and most frequent symptoms include fluctuating impairments of consciousness, ranging from mild confusional states to deep stupor. Another early symptom of brain damage is a defective memory. Such defects range from brief lapses to a complete loss of memory. In more serious cases of head injury, the victim may experience illusions, visual and auditory perceptual disturbances, and disordered thinking. In addition, irrelevant and incoherent speech is often part of the symptom picture.

Infection

Infectious disease has been recognized as a source of personality disturbance for many years. Sometimes the psychological effects result from the direct action on the nervous system by the microorganism of a disease, and sometimes the effects are a result of secondary factors in the form of elevated body temperature, disordered water balance, deficient oxygen consumption, or other homeostatic disturbances. In either case, there is always the possibility of organic changes which may interfere with the function of the nervous system, resulting in psychological symptoms of various kinds.

Clinical reports of mental changes during the fever and toxic phases of infectious disease have been a part of the medical literature for many centuries. It was not until the early 1800s, however, that medical knowledge was sufficiently advanced and concern with mental disturbances sufficiently strong to draw serious attention to the problem.

The clearest example of the role of infection in personality disturbance is in connection with syphilis of the brain. It was established beyond question early in the present century that the microorganism of syphilis is responsible for the wide range of psychological symptoms that had been observed for several centuries in certain cases of mental disorder. Infections such as malarial fever, influenza, pneumonia, smallpox, scarlet fever, and typhoid fever can also result in temporary, or sometimes permanent, changes in the personality. These conditions, and the changes associated with them, will be discussed in Chapter 14.

Intoxication

The effect of intoxicating beverages and other toxic substances on the behavior of human beings and animals has been observed for many centuries. Naturalists have observed that woodpecking birds become intoxicated from drinking fermented sap, that the behavior of ants becomes disorganized when they eat the exudations of certain beetles, and that European thrushes occasionally develop a craving for certain berries which eventually cause paralysis and death. It has also been observed that sheep and goats in the pastures of certain parts of Africa become intoxicated and aggressive from eating the beans of the coffee plant. Cattle, sheep, and horses contract serious nervous disorders from feeding on the loco weed found in the Western plains of the United States. The taste for this plant develops into an addiction which sometimes leads to death. In the Eastern states, cattle acquire the "trembles" from eating the white snakeroot plant.

For human beings, the principal intoxicant is alcohol. While this substance affects nearly every tissue of the human body, it has a particularly toxic effect upon the tissues of the central nervous system. Alcohol is essentially a physiological depressant, although some of the effects appear to be psychologically stimulating. Characteristically, the more delicate shades of feeling are blunted, the cares of life are minimized, and the tongue is loosened. Typical behavior patterns, determined in part by the fundamental personality type, are released in the form of expressions of affection, maudlin self-pity or sympathy, or hostility and aggression. Finally, the alcoholic shows increasing signs of physical and psychological disorganization. The usual sequence is confusion and disorientation, incoordinate speech and movements, and finally sleep and unconsciousness.

Other intoxicating beverages also can result in abnormal behavior. When the Dutch artist Vincent van Gogh cut off his ear and presented it to a prostitute on Christmas Day, he may have been trying to rid himself of auditory hallucinations brought on by a toxic condition due to heavy drinking of absinthe (Lubin, 1972).

Less widespread than alcoholism, but no less important to abnormal psychology, are the toxic conditions brought on by addiction to drugs. The psychological distortions of reality produced by drugs have been observed for many centuries. The modern clinical psychologist and psychiatrist are familiar with the special effects of the sedatives and hypnotics, the opiates, cocaine, marihuana, and, most recently, the tranquilizers, antidepressants, and hallucinogens.

Each drug, or group of drugs, produces a more or less unique effect on the human organism, depending upon the particular pharmacodynamic action of the drug. Excessive use of sedatives and hypnotics may result in prolonged states of delirium. The opiates induce distortions in visual perception, cocaine results in disturbed body sensations, and marihuana interferes with the perception of time. The hallucinogens produce complicated psychological states bearing a strong resemblance to the more serious mental disorders. Prolonged drug intoxication can result in chronic brain damage.

Much less frequent than alcoholism and

Figure 3.1 A young man spaced out on drugs. The expression on his face reflects the pleasant experience of escaping from the sordid surroundings. Not all drug experiences are so pleasant.

drug addiction are cases in which metal poisons produce personality disturbances. The toxic effects of lead on the nervous system have been recognized for centuries. By the nineteenth century, the effects of lead on the nervous system were fully recognized.

Within recent years there has been a renewed interest in lead poisoning and its effects on central nervous system activity. This interest has been brought about by the increasing number of young children who have become the victims of the disorder by licking and chewing on toys, windowsills, woodwork, and plaster walls coated with lead-based paint. The symptoms include irritation, lethargy, abdominal pain, vomiting, disturbances of balance, and convulsions.

It is not only young paint-eaters who are in danger of lead poisoning. In some cities the lead intake of inhabitants approaches—or

The Day a Town Went Mad

It was late summer when madness struck the small town of Pont-Saint-Esprit in southern France. More than three hundred villagers became ill and developed chills, nausea, and stomach pains. Even the animals in the town began to behave abnormally. The ducks stood up, paraded like penguins, and then died. Dogs chewed stones and broke their teeth before dying.

The symptoms of the villagers grew worse. They became dizzy, had difficulty breathing, and many people had convulsions. Soon there were psychological disturbances added to the physical symptoms. People began to hear voices and to see visions. They also developed strange ideas. A little girl thought she was being eaten by tigers, and a vineyard worker who had the same idea threw dishes at the imaginary beasts. He became so wildly disturbed that he had to be subdued and strapped down. Even then he managed to chew through the leather strap, breaking off most of his teeth. Other villagers showed a wide variety of abnormal behavior. One man imagined he was a circus performer and was found walking along a cable that supported a bridge suspended over the river; another man wrote hundreds of pages of poetry, and whenever he stopped writing, he had an urge to jump from the window; and a woman huddled in complete misery because she believed that her children had been slaughtered by a butcher who had hung their bodies on hooks in his shop until he could make sausages of them. The town's three local doctors were completely baffled by the events, but medical help came from throughout France, and it was finally determined that the cause of the trouble was poisoned bread. A flour mill in northern France had shipped to the village flour made from rye grain infected with ergot, a parasitic fungus. This fungus affected the central nervous systems of the townspeople and the animals who had eaten the tainted bread. While such epidemics have been rare in modern times, they were quite common during the Middle Ages when grain carrying the ergot fungus often found its way into the bread. The results were similar to those seen at Pont-Saint-Esprit. The attacks of mass madness were so severe and so common that they were given the name St. Anthony's fire. The condition demonstrates vividly the manner in which a toxic substance can be the cause of abnormal behavior of the most serious kind. (Adapted from Fuller, 1968)

exceeds—dangerous levels as a result of air pollution from auto exhaust. The problem is so serious that federal legislation has been enacted to require automobile manufacturers to take steps to control the danger. Another example of potential metal poisoning is the finding of dangerously high levels of mercury in certain fish. It is possible that the increasing environmental pollution will have a more damaging physical and psychological effect on people than has yet been realized.

Degenerative Changes

The degeneration of tissue due to aging is also a factor in the development of mental illness. In every living organism, certain

The Dancing Cats of Minamata: Some Effects of Mercury Poisoning on Behavior

The first indication that something was wrong in the fishing village of Minamata on the southern Japanese island of Kyushu was the behavior of the cats. They began to act strangely and sometimes moved in ways which made them appear to be dancing. At the time, not too much attention was paid to the strange behavior. The residents of the village did not know that the cats were showing convulsive symptoms and that these were due to the eating of fish poisoned with mercury waste that had been dumped into the bay by a large chemical company.

Some months later, the village gained worldwide notoriety as a result of the paralysis, blindness, deformities, brain damage, and disturbed behavior afflicting hundreds of residents who had also eaten the fish. People living in neighboring towns refused to permit their sons to marry Minamata women for fear their offspring would be born deformed. In the early 1970s, more than $3.5 million in damages was awarded to the victims and their families. These tragic events, involving environmental pollution and mercury poisoning in particular, point out in a dramatic way how toxic chemicals can deform the body and cause psychological disturbances. (Smith & Smith, 1975)

structural changes accompany normal aging. These changes are related to the regulation of blood and tissue chemistry, the maintenance of uniform body temperature, metabolism, digestion, the processes of excretion, and resistance to injury and disease. In a similar way, sensorimotor changes accompany the normal aging process. Vision, hearing, reaction time, and other perceptual and motor functions are altered in significant ways. The physical cost of maintaining the complex mechanisms of adjustment increases as a person ages.

Scientific interest in the mental disturbances of later life is relatively new. One reason for this is that these disturbances have loomed suddenly as one of the most important problems of modern life. Not many years ago, the age span was so short that few people attained an advanced age; consequently the mental disorders of later life were not emphasized. Today, however, with rapidly increasing numbers of men and women living to advanced ages, the problem of mental disorder during the later years has become one of mounting urgency and importance.

Other brain damage In addition to the types of organic damage already discussed, there are other conditions which can injure brain tissue and result in abnormal behavior. Ruptured blood vessels on the surface of the brain, called "strokes" or *cerebrovascular accidents*, stop the supply of nutrients and oxygen to the brain cells in the area and interfere with the removal of waste products. The result is the destruction of tissue, which frequently leads to paralysis and sometimes to disturbed thinking and language usage.

Brain tumors, or *neoplasms*, are abnormal growths in the brain tissue which result in psychological symptoms in about 50 percent of the cases. In the other 50 percent, the

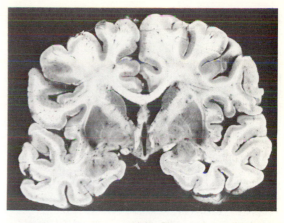

(a)

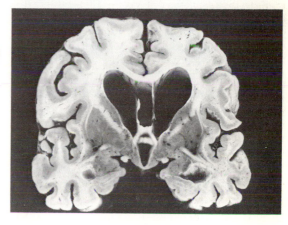

(b)

Figure 3.2 The brain undergoes many changes as it ages during the course of life. The cross-section view (*a*) shows the normal brain of a young adult. A similar view (*b*) is that of the brain of an elderly person. Notice how the tissue of the aging brain has atrophied, or wasted away. There is a marked enlargement of the ventricles, or spaces containing fluid, at the center of the brain. These gross changes are accompanied by microscopic changes in the brain cells.

neoplasm is in one of the "silent areas" of the brain where important tissue changes can take place without external signs of the process. In cases where symptoms are pres-

Figure 3.3 (*a, b*) Charles J. Whitman, an Eagle Scout and a model student, was killed by police after barricading himself on the tower of this University of Texas building and using a high-power rifle to shoot forty-four people on the campus walks and surrounding streets far below. The picture of Whitman was taken at the time of his graduation from high school.

ent, they are likely to be in the form of convulsions and other neurological disturbances as well as memory impairment, confusion, and delirium. The nature and extent of psychological symptoms are determined by the increase in intracranial pressure, the structural damage caused by the proliferation of brain cells, the edema, or swelling of the tissue, and the location of the growth, In tumors of the frontal lobes, it is quite possible to have large masses of pathological tissue with few signs of personality disorganization or none at all.

Stress Model of Abnormal Behavior

Stress is the condition of the body when it is being influenced by real (or imagined) pressures or *stressors*. These stressors may be

The University of Texas Sniper: Abnormal Behavior and a Brain Tumor

The worst mass murder in the recent history of the United States was carried out by a student of architectural engineering at the University of Texas. One morning he bought some guns and then went to a hardware store in Austin, Texas, to buy several boxes of ammunition. The clerk asked out of curiosity what all the ammunition was for. The student replied, "To shoot some pigs." A little later he went up to the observation deck of the tower on the University of Texas campus and began shooting everyone in sight. Before he was himself killed by police bullets, Charles Whitman had killed thirteen people and wounded thirty-one others. Some of the injured and killed were as far away as three blocks. Later, it was discovered that he had also slain his wife and his mother.

Charles Whitman had been an exemplary boy. He had been an altar boy in church, delivered newspapers, was pitcher on his school's baseball team and manager of its football team. He was one of the youngest boys ever to become an eagle scout. He joined the Marines when he was 18 and later enrolled at the University of Texas, where he was a B student. The obvious question was: How could such a young man do what he did?

The day after the massacre an autopsy was performed on the body of the killer. A tumor was discovered in his brain. The ironic part of it was that in a final note he requested an autopsy on his body "to see if there's any mental disturbance."

physical, as in the case of noise, bright lights, extremes of temperature, high humidity, abnormal barometric pressure, or pain. There also are psychosocial stressors in the form of failure, indecision, conflict, frustration, feelings of guilt, insecurity, lack of status, and similar conditions.

The most important impetus to stress theory was given by the classic work of Hans Selyé (1907–   ), the University of Montreal scientist who developed the concept of the *general adaptation syndrome* (Selyé, 1952).

This theoretical model states that there are various types of internal and external stress in the form of injuries, infections, poisons, hormones, diet, and similar factors which mobilize a system of defensive reactions. One of the most important features of the general adaptation syndrome is that the major response to stress depends upon two main channels. The first is a nervous system reaction, primarily through the activation of the autonomic centers in the hypothalamus. The second is an endocrine reaction through the production of hormones of the pituitary and adrenal glands.

Selyé has shown that animals exposed to continuous stress for long periods go through three phases of the general adaptation syndrome. The first phase is the *initial alarm reaction*. This early signal that all is not right with the organism is followed by the *resistance phase*, in which biochemical defenses are mobilized to offset the effects of the stressors. If stress continues, the animal eventually experiences the *exhaustion phase*. The result can be physical illness, psychological disturbance, and even death.

Selyé places considerable emphasis upon what he calls *nonspecific stress*. According to this view, the deciding factor in whether or not an individual develops a physical illness or a mental disorder is not primarily heredity, nutrition, or specific environmental factors but merely the nonspecific stress effects of trying to endure more than one is able to endure. However, he believes that an individual's capacity to adapt, or his *adaptation energy*, is determined by genetic and constitutional factors. We do not add to this fund of vitality during our lifetime; we only subtract from it. Nonspecific stress is one of the ways in which the adaptation energy is used up (Selyé, 1974).

In considering the development of abnor-

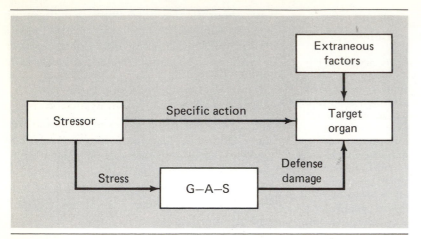

Figure 3.4 This model of the general adaptation syndrome shows that physical, psychological, and social stressors affect body organs in two ways: one through specific damage to the organ, as when the ear is damaged by exposure to jet plane noise; the other through indirect and nonspecific interference with the general adaptation of the organism. For example, the prolonged and excessive noise that damages the ear also can result in tension, irritability, sleeplessness, depression, and other physical and emotional disturbances. When a person's defenses against these disturbances are unsuccessful, the result may be physical damage or maladaptive behavior, or both.

mal behavior, it is important to remember that environmental pressures often lead to internal stress. A difficult situation in school, at work, or in the home creates stressful conditions within the body which are capable of triggering organic changes of an important kind. Even though the environmental pressure does not appear to be excessive, the long continuance of stress-provoking conditions can bring about alterations in body functions which ultimately may result in irreversible tissue changes.

While stress may be a major—and perhaps necessary—precondition in the development of some forms of abnormal behavior, it is not invariably followed by abnormal reactions. The severity of a stressor is determined by a person's perception. What is a stressor for one person may not be a stressor for another. Failure in a course may be enough to send one student into a deep depression, while a similar failure may be shrugged off as unimportant by another student. The first student is under stress; the second student is not.

Even the most trying life events may not lead to obvious emotional scars. A study of women who had survived the physical and psychological horrors of concentration camps thirty years earlier indicated that camp survivors generally were more poorly adjusted than control subjects. However, many of the survivors appeared to be well adjusted in spite of their earlier exposure to the very high level of stress (Antonovsky & Maoz, 1971).

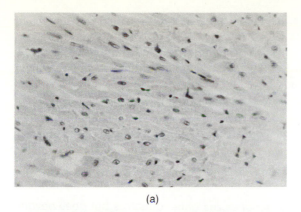

(a)

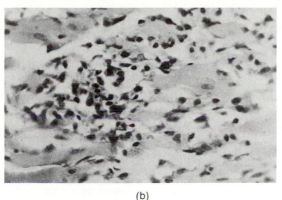

(b)

Figure 3.5 These photomicrographs show the effect of stress on body cells. The normal cells before stress (a) have a completely different appearance than the thickened and darkened cells after exposure to stress (b). Since many other organic changes associated with stress have been demonstrated, there is no longer any question about the importance of stress in physical disorders. It is also suspected that stress may be involved in some types of maladaptive behavior.

There has been an increasing interest in the role of stress and stressors as possible factors in determining the appearance of

physical illness and mental disorder. While Selyé emphasized the importance of physical stressors, he recognized that psychological stressors also contribute to specific and nonspecific stress.

Much of the more recent interest in the problems of stress has been related to those events in daily living which contribute to the susceptibility to illness. The name *life stress* has been given to this problem, and attempts have been made to measure life stress through the development of *life-stress units* (Gunderson & Rahe, 1974). This approach will be examined in greater detail in Chapter 6.

The concept of "future shock" is also related to the problem of stress. Here the idea is that people may one day in the future be overwhelmed by the rapidly accelerating rate of social and technological change. The advocate of this theory defines future shock as "the distress, both physical and psychological, that arises from an overload of the organism's physical adaptive systems and its decision-making processes" (Toffler, 1970).

The appeal of the stress model is to be found in the ease with which it can handle both physical and psychological events, and in its apparent reasonableness. Few people, including mental health professionals, have been untouched by the psychological or physical effects—or both—of disturbing, disrupting, and threatening situations. The admonition to avoid stress and excitement and to "take it easy" reflects the long-held popular belief that the pressures of living, when excessive, are likely to be harmful. Today this intuitive belief is being made the subject of scientific study.

The Chapter in Review

Biological models of abnormality are based upon the assumption that physical events are primarily responsible for personality disturbances and behavior disorders. These events include heredity, constitutional makeup, biochemical changes, damage to the brain, and the effects of stress.

1 Genetic Model

The genetic model concerns itself with the influence of hereditary factors in determining abnormal behavior. It deals with disturbances of the genetic code and abnormalities of the chromosomes.

2 Constitutional Model

The constitutional model also emphasizes genetic factors but goes beyond the basic mechanics of heredity to include all those physical events which influence a person's development from fertilization to birth.

3 Biochemical Model

The biochemical model of abnormality takes a variety of forms. The most recent emphasis has been on the neurohumors, chemical substances affecting the transmission of the nerve impulse. Norepinephrine and serotonin are neurohumors which appear to be closely associated with some of the more severe mental disorders. The possible role of malnutrition and mineral and vitamin deficiencies in the development of abnormal behavior is also being explored. Another interesting area of investigation has been the endocrine system and disturbances in the production of hormones. Other biochemical factors, such as the chemistry of body fluids, also are under scientific study.

4 Brain Damage Model

Brain damage is directly related to abnormal behavior in many cases. Such damage may be the result of accidental injury; various types of infection; toxic substances such as alcohol, drugs, and poisons; degeneration of brain tissue accompanying normal aging or pathological conditions; and other conditions such as brain tumors.

5 Stress Model

The stress model of abnormality places its major emphasis upon the effects of stressors on body systems. The stressors are physical and psychosocial events which result in strain and pressure. In some cases the stressors are specific and easily identified; more often the stress is the result of a combination of less obvious stressors. The cumulative effect of these stressors can be psychologically damaging.

Recommended Readings

Genetic Approach

Fieve, R. R., Rosenthal, D., & Brill, H. (Eds.) *Genetic research in psychiatry*. Baltimore: Johns Hopkins, 1975.

Rosenthal, D. *Genetics of psychopathology*. New York: McGraw-Hill, 1971. (Paperback.)

Constitutional Factors

Luce, G. G. *Body time*. New York: Pantheon, 1971.

Biochemistry and Abnormal Behavior

Gillette, P. J., & Hornbeck, M. *Psychochemistry*. New York: Warner, 1974. (Paperback.)

Shneour, E. A. *The malnourished mind*. Garden City, N.Y.: Anchor/Doubleday, 1975. (Paperback.)

Role of Stress

Levinson, H. *Executive stress*. (Rev. ed.) New York: New American Library, 1975. (Paperback.)

McQuade, W., & Ackman, A. *Stress*. New York: Bantam, 1975. (Paperback.)

Selyé, H. *Stress without distress*. Philadelphia: Lippincott, 1974.

Toffler, A. *Future shock*. New York: Bantam, 1970. (Paperback.)

4

Psychological Models of Abnormal Behavior

Objectives

To show how all psychological models of abnormal behavior must deal with certain common problems

To describe the behavioral model of maladaptive behavior and to show how it developed

To discuss some of the basic principles of the behavioral approach to abnormality

To give practical examples of the way in which the behavioral model explains abnormal behavior

To describe the general nature of the cognitive model of personality disturbance

To discuss the psychodynamic model of abnormality and to present some of the theories upon which it is based

To give some examples of how the psychodynamic model explains abnormal behavior

While it is undoubtedly true that biological factors are important in many forms of abnormal behavior, it is equally true that much behavior described as abnormal grows out of psychological problems independent of the organic condition of the individual. It is quite possible for a person to be relatively normal in a biological sense and yet to show abnormal behavior. This chapter will explain how a person who is, essentially, physically normal can come to be psychologically abnormal.

The psychological approach to abnormality takes a variety of forms. Not all psychologists and psychiatrists who are interested in the psychological explanation of abnormality agree as to the processes involved. Just as there are different biological models of abnormality, so are there different psychological models. As in the case of biological models, psychological models differ in emphasis and point of view. They are not necessarily at odds with one another. In fact, it is often possible to reconcile the different models and, indeed, to use one to reinforce the assumptions of another.

The principal psychological models of maladaptive behavior are the *behavioral* model, which explains abnormality in terms of learning; the *cognitive* model, which emphasizes the role of internal psychological processes; and the *psychodynamic* model, which maintains that abnormal behavior is due to unconscious conflict.

The Common Ground

All psychological explanations of abnormality deal in various ways with the basic nature of human behavior. The actions of people grow out of internal and external forces which influence behavior. These forces include the biological needs of the body and the demands made by the physical and social environments. There is also an internal behavior, or experience, which involves the sensing of environmental signals, the perceptual organization of incoming information, and information processing in the form of thinking. Any modification of overt behavior or internal experience takes place through learning.

Psychological models assume that these processes occur within the limits established by genetic makeup, constitution, biochemistry, and other biological conditions. While these physical conditions may facilitate the development of abnormal patterns of behavior and may give such patterns a characteristic stamp, the abnormal behavior itself is considered to be a function of psychological processes rather than physical ones.

Each psychological model emphasizes different sets of psychological processes. The behavioral model focuses on learning as the critical process in the development of normal and abnormal behavior. The cognitive model does not deny the importance of learning but prefers to examine such internal variables as perception and thinking. The psychodynamic model is interested in psychological processes that operate outside the range of conscious awareness.

Psychological models also share an interest in the techniques people use to adapt to stress. These techniques have been called strategies of adaptation (White, 1974). The principal behavioral strategy is overt coping. This technique involves learned habitual reactions which serve to reduce stress. The cognitive strategy could be described as covert coping, which is a more conscious and reflective technique involving problem solving and decision making. The psychodynamic strategy involves unconscious mechanisms of defense which protect people against the stress of anxiety.

Another common factor shared by psychological models is related to the treatment of disturbed behavior. The behavioral model seeks to modify such behavior through the learning of more adaptive patterns of behavior. The cognitive model emphasizes conscious problem solving in bringing about behavior change, and the psychodynamic model relies upon the exploration of the deeper levels of the personality in an attempt to uncover hidden conflicts assumed to be responsible for a person's symptoms.

Behavioral Model

The behavioral model of abnormality is currently the most widely used approach to the theory and treatment of personality disturbance and mental disorder. This model is based on the assumption that disturbed behavior has been learned and that such behavior can be modified in more positive and desirable directions through the use of learning methods.

As we saw in Chapter 1, the behavioral model had its roots in the animal-learning experiments of E. L. Thorndike in the United States and the conditioning studies of Ivan Pavlov in Russia. While the behavioral approach played an important part in the early history of experimental psychology in the United States, it did not assume a prominent position in clinical psychology and psychiatry until the 1960s. At that time the disenchantment with the psychodynamic model had become widespread because many of its basic assumptions did not lend themselves readily to experimental study, and those that

were investigated were frequently shown to be invalid or of questionable validity. The psychodynamic model also demanded a costly and time-consuming type of treatment which was increasingly criticized as having limited application and effectiveness.

As the influence of the psychodynamic approach declined, attention was turned to the work of B. F. Skinner (1904–   ) and a few other psychologists who had pursued the implications of the learning experiments of Thorndike and Pavlov early in this century. Skinner formulated a behavior technology which was to influence profoundly the direction of the theory and treatment of abnormal behavior (Skinner, 1938, 1953). This approach insisted that normal and abnormal behavior are acquired in the same way through the operation of internal and external environmental influences, or *contingencies*.

Learning through Conditioning
The ideas of Skinner, and those of other behavioral psychologists, are based upon established principles of learning. Essentially, two types of learning by conditioning are involved. One type of learning is the classical, or respondent, conditioning demonstrated originally by Pavlov. The other type of learning is operant, or instrumental, conditioning which developed out of Thorndike's experiments with trial-and-error learning.

Respondent (classical) conditioning This type of learning was discovered by Pavlov during his investigations of the digestive processes of dogs. He observed that when food was brought to the animals, they salivated and their digestive juices began to flow. Such behavior was neither unusual nor unexpected. What *was* unusual was the further observation that the salivation and flow of digestive juices also occurred when the person who usually fed the dogs appeared *without* the food. Somehow the animals had learned to associate the person with the food. This observation led Pavlov to a series of investigations which established the principles of classical conditioning.

In classical conditioning, a stimulus that normally evokes a response is called an *unconditioned stimulus*. The expected response is called an *unconditioned response*. Food is an unconditioned stimulus and salivation is an unconditioned response. Pavlov found that if a neutral stimulus, or one that in itself does not elicit the unconditioned response, is paired with the unconditioned stimulus often enough and in a proper time sequence, the neutral stimulus will eventually evoke an unconditioned response. That is, the animal will learn to respond to the new stimulus. For example, if a bell is sounded each time food is presented to an animal, eventually the animal will salivate to the sound of the bell even when no food is presented. Similarly, people will respond to new stimuli which previously had no effect on their behavior.

Operant (instrumental) conditioning We have seen how classical, or respondent, conditioning had its origins in the work of Pavlov. The principles of operant, or instrumental, conditioning also grew out of experiments with animals. Thorndike was interested in how animals solved problems through trial and error. He placed cats in a box with a door which could be opened by pressing on a pedal inside the box. Thorndike observed that as the cat explored the box, the animal would eventually step on the pedal, and the door would open. Each time the animal was

again placed in the box, the random exploratory movements became less frequent until the time came when the animal went directly to the pedal, stepped on it, and opened the door. The cat had *learned* new behavior. Thorndike said this learning was due to the *law of effect*. That is, the learning was the effect of the reward of escaping from the box.

Many years later, it became clear that this type of behavior was another form of conditioning. The learning was called operant, or instrumental, because the spontaneous behavior operates on the environment to procure a reward or to avoid punishment. In short, the behavior is instrumental in achieving a goal.

Operant conditioning differs from classical conditioning in an important way. In classical conditioning the learner is passive. The response to a stimulus takes place without the active participation of the learner. Operant conditioning, however, requires that the learner become involved in the learning process by actively operating on the environment and responding to it. Responses that are reinforced by environmental contingencies, or influences, are more likely to be repeated than responses that are not reinforced.

Social learning While the early concepts forming the behavioral model emphasized relatively clear-cut and controllable stimulus-response relationships, the model has been enlarged to include more complex forms of social learning in which environmental contingencies are not immediately apparent. The social learning approach emerged because some behavioral psychologists were not content with the view that behavior is due to simple forms of respondent and operant conditioning (Lazarus, 1971).

A common form of social learning involves a process through which new patterns of behavior are acquired as a result of the observation of the behavior of other people. This type of social learning begins very early in life. Both adaptive and maladaptive behaviors are developed in this way. The social-learning approach has also resulted in new techniques of behavior modification. The application of social learning to the treatment of abnormal behavior will be discussed in Chapter 17.

Some Basic Principles

The principles of learning which determine how new behavior is acquired are the same for adaptive and maladaptive patterns of behavior. Since later discussions of different types of abnormal behavior will frequently indicate how such behavior might be learned, it is important that the principles of *reinforcement*, *stimulus generalization*, and *extinction* be clearly understood.

The critical role of reinforcement The reinforcement of behavior is fundamental to learning. Positive reinforcement by means of pleasant, desirable, and rewarding consequences will increase the probability that the behavior being reinforced will be repeated. Negative reinforcement involving unpleasant, undesirable, painful, or punishing reinforcers will decrease the probability that the behavior will be repeated. In both cases, behavior is altered and learning takes place.

Maladaptive behavior that has been learned is maintained and strengthened by means of reinforcement. Abnormal response patterns, like other learned behavior, tend to be repeated because they are in some way rewarding to the disturbed person. Even though the rewards are often indirect and obscure, the abnormal behavior persists because of the reinforcement given to it.

Stimulus generalization The principle of stimulus generalization refers to the fact that a learned response to a stimulus will also be elicited by similar stimuli. If a person is conditioned to be afraid of a particular dog, the fear will also be aroused by similar dogs and perhaps all dogs. The fear might even generalize to feelings of uneasiness in the presence of other animals. Fear, as well as other learned reactions, may begin with a specific behavior response to a particular stimulus situation; but through the process of generalization, the behavior may also appear under conditions quite removed from the original situation.

The process of generalization is an important one in the development of maladaptive behavior. When an abnormal response pattern has been learned under one set of circumstances, the same pattern later appears not only as a response to the same circumstances, but also as a response to a wide range of related circumstances. Moreover, when the generalized behavior is reinforced, the abnormal behavior becomes more deeply established, and there is an increased probability that it will be repeated in the future.

Extinction of behavior Just as the repeated use of reinforcement operates to maintain and strengthen a conditioned response, the withdrawal of reinforcement results in the gradual elimination of the response. This principle helps to explain how adaptive behavior that is not sufficiently reinforced might be replaced by maladaptive behavior that is rewarded or otherwise reinforced in a positive way.

The principle of extinction is more pertinent to the modification of abnormal behavior than it is to its development. It is not unusual for a person showing maladaptive behavior to show a spontaneous change in behavior and to achieve a more satisfactory personal adjustment even though there has been no treatment or other intervention. What has happened is that the maladaptive behavior has been extinguished as a result of lack of reinforcement. It is also possible to use extinction techniques in a controlled way to modify maladaptive behavior. This treatment approach will be discussed in Chapter 17.

Behavioral Model Applied

Now that we have some idea of the origins of the behavioral model, and the principles of learning upon which it is based, it will be helpful to see how this model can be applied to the explanation of maladaptive behavior. Examples will be given to show how patterns of abnormal behavior can be established through respondent conditioning, operant conditioning, and social learning.

Classical conditioning and maladaptive behavior The first suggestion that conditioning might be related to abnormal behavior was made by Pavlov, who made an unexpected observation during one of his experiments. A dog was shown a circle marked on a card and was trained to salivate in expectation of food given after each display of the card. This same dog was also trained not to salivate if the card was marked with an ellipse rather than a circle. When these two responses were well established, the ellipse was gradually made more and more like a circle. When the dog could no longer differentiate between the circle and the ellipse, the resulting conflict precipitated a behavior disturbance. The dog became restless and uncooperative, refused to eat,

and howled and struggled in his harness. Pavlov described the behavior of the animal in the following way:

> The hitherto quiet dog began to squeal in its stand, kept wriggling about, tore off with its teeth the apparatus for mechanical stimulation of the skin, and bit through the tubes connecting the animal's room with the observer, a behavior which never happened before. On being taken into the experimental room the dog now barked violently, which was also contrary to its usual custom; in short, it presented all the symptoms of a condition of acute neurosis. (Pavlov, 1941)

Even though many psychologists consider it dangerous to draw parallels between the behavior of animals and human beings, there is no question about the fact that respondent conditioning can lead to maladaptive behavior in people as well as in animals. The first demonstration of this relationship involved the learning of a fear response in a child (Watson & Rayner, 1920). This child played without fear with a white rat in the laboratory. By means of classical techniques the child was conditioned to be terrified by the rat toward which he had formerly shown no fear. Moreover, the fear that was instilled in the youngster was not restricted to white rats. The fear generalized to all white furry objects including his mother's coat and even the white beard of Santa Claus.

It is not difficult to see how some abnormal fears, or *phobias*, can be learned through respondent conditioning. Similarly, other symptoms of personality disturbance and mental disorder are acquired by means of this type of passive conditioning. In Chapter 15 we will see how respondent conditioning can be used to eliminate maladaptive behavior.

Operant conditioning and maladaptive behavior While respondent conditioning is involved in the acquisition of some forms of pathological behavior, far more behavior of this kind is learned by means of operant conditioning. When a person responds to the contingencies of the environment, the probability of that response being repeated is a function of how rewarding the response has been. In most human behavior, both the environmental contingencies and the reinforcement of responses through rewards are not immediately apparent. Nevertheless, adaptive and maladaptive behaviors are frequently shaped by environmental influences which are relatively obscure and by subtle rewards which are meaningful only to the one receiving them.

In later chapters we will be discussing a number of different types of abnormal behavior ranging from transient conditions of borderline seriousness to those in which severe psychological damage is involved. Many of these patterns of maladaptive behavior can be explained in terms of operant conditioning. For example, the person who complains constantly and excessively about physical symptoms and bodily disturbances, even when they have been ruled out by medical tests and examinations, is called a *hypochondriac.*

Such a person learns to complain about his or her physical condition. One might ask, who would want to learn to be preoccupied with such distressing and unpleasant ideas? The answer is that it is not a matter of *wanting* to learn; the learning occurs because the physical complaints are rewarded by the increased attention and concern of other people; because the "sufferer" is excused from tasks and obligations from which sick people are excused; and because of other advantages and concessions. In short, the physical complaints have been learned through rewards that have reinforced the maladaptive behavior.

It is also possible to learn to become ad-dicted to alcohol or drugs through operant conditioning. The intoxicated state carries a number of rewards with it. The pleasant early effects of alcohol and drugs are in themselves a reward, and the use of these intoxicants tends to be repeated simply because the user "likes the feeling."

The rewarding effect of the intoxicant is accompanied by other rewards in the form of increased sociability, reduced tension and anxiety, and the forgetting of one's problems and concerns. The intoxicated condition also may be perceived as overcoming any number of personal difficulties. Since positive reinforcement in the early stages of addiction is far greater than negative reinforcement, the maladaptive pattern of behavior becomes firmly established. This conditioning process would be facilitated by any biological conditions favorable to the development of addiction (see Chapter 7).

The influence of learning in alcohol addiction is shown by the fact that more than 50 percent of this type of addiction in the United States and Canada follows a slowly developing pattern over five to fifteen years and is related to personal and social difficulties. This pattern is not the dominant one in France and many other countries (Bacon, 1973).

In later accounts of other forms of abnormal behavior, the possibility of operant learning in the development of the disorders will be discussed. Even where genetic and other biological factors are involved, learning can play a part in initiating and maintaining the maladaptive behavior.

Social learning and maladaptive behavior
Social learning involves a very complex form of conditioning. Higher-level conditioning of the classical type as well as operant conditioning—in which the contingencies and rewards are frequently difficult to

isolate and identify—operate to shape and mold behavior in a gradual way. The increments of learning may be so slight that the process goes unnoticed. Eventually the form and significance of the behavior patterns that have been developing become apparent. In the case of maladaptive behavior, by the time abnormality is realized, it has become deeply entrenched and may be highly resistant to change.

Many forms of behavior are learned, beginning early in life, by observing the behavior of other people. The young child often imitates parents or other children. Speech,

---

**Bang, Bang! You're Dead!—
Violence on Television As a Model
for Aggression**

Television is probably the most powerful and influential behavior model in contemporary life. More than 96 percent of homes in the United States have one or more television sets, and the average set is turned on for more than six hours a day. Much of the viewing is done by children, adolescents, and adults who are exposed to an impressive and inordinate amount of violence in the form of vicious fighting, physical torture, rape, terrorism, and murder. In short, the television screen presents an almost uninterrupted model of unrestrained aggression to millions of psychologically immature people in our society.

In spite of the television industry's insistence that there is little or no relationship between televised violence and violence in our society, there is growing evidence that such a relationship does in fact exist. It appears probable that violence on television contributes to the learning of aggressive behavior which may later be acted out. It seems probable that the daily fare of this violence helps to desensitize children and adults in a way which makes them accept violence more readily. As a result, an increasingly higher level of aggression is tolerated in our society.

The most comprehensive study of televised violence and its impact on youth was conducted by a special staff set up within the National Institute of Mental Health and directed by a committee of twelve psychologists, psychiatrists, social scientists, and communications experts. After 2 1/2 years of investigation and expenditures of $1 million, the report on the study was released in a summary volume and five volumes of supporting research (*Television and Growing Up: The Impact of Televised Violence*, 1971).

While many of the findings of the study were contradictory, inconclusive, and ambiguous, the summary volume ends by saying: "We can tentatively conclude that there is a modest relationship between exposure to television violence and aggressive tendencies." It also emphasized that the causal relationship operates only on those children who are already predisposed to aggression.

Although the major finding of the study supports the view that televised violence is an aggression model that influences the behavior of at least some viewers, the investigation was biased from the beginning in the opposite direction. Five of the twelve committee members had ties with the television industry, and the three major networks were given the extraordinary privilege of vetoing nominations to the committee. Seven people, including two of the country's prominent researchers in the field, were vetoed presumably because they had done research on television violence or had been critical of the industry.

The most informed opinion at the present time is that not only is violent behavior learned as a result of the behavior model shown on television but that the model is also responsible for the predisposition to violence. The director of the Center for Advanced Study in Behavioral Science at Stanford University commented on the findings of the government study in the following words:

I believe the Report confirms the folk wisdom that there is a causal relationship between violence on TV and the behavior of children in an anti-social way . . . not only does television incite violence in some who are predisposed to violence, but it is clear to me that violence on TV is a factor in determining this "predisposition." . . . In my judgment, violence is clearly dangerous enough to be called to the attention of Congress, the industry and the public. It merits attention, and it requires constructive action. (Cater & Strickland, 1972)

gestures and other movements, emotional reactions, and similar observable movements may influence the behavior of others. In a similar way, attitudes and opinions may be formed as a result of exposure to the attitudes and opinions of others. This type of social learning has been called *modeling* because the behavior of one person or a social group serves as a model for similar behavior in other people.

Many forms of maladaptive behavior can be explained in terms of social learning. It is frequently the case that a child confronted with a persistent pattern of delinquent behavior on the part of other children in the neighborhood will begin to show similar behavior. A youngster who is exposed to a parent who is an excessive drinker or a drug user runs a greater risk of developing those patterns of behavior than does a young person not so exposed. There is impressive clinical and experimental evidence that increased exposure to a behavior model can exert a significant influence on the behavior of those who are exposed to the model.

It has been found that a child who has been physically abused early in life has an increased potential for becoming a violent member of society later in life (Silver et al., 1969). Similarly, there is increasing evidence that the violence depicted on television has a damaging impact on many children, adolescents, and emotionally immature adults.

Experiments indicate that violence that is witnessed serves as a model which tends to increase aggression rather than to decrease it. The viewing of aggression does not seem to act as an outlet or safety valve which helps to reduce inner aggressive impulses. Quite the contrary. The more aggression one observes, the stronger one's own aggression becomes (Bandura, 1970).

Behavior Modification

We have already seen that the nature of the psychological model determines the type of treatment used in dealing with disturbed persons. In the case of the behavioral model, in which major emphasis is placed on the learning of symptoms, the treatment approach is through the modification of disturbed behavior by means of specialized learning techniques. Among these techniques are a variety of therapeutic approaches based upon classical conditioning, operant conditioning, social learning, and related methods. Behavior modification in the treatment of maladaptive behavior will be examined in detail in Chapter 17.

Cognitive Model

The cognitive model of abnormal behavior deals largely with intellectual events and conscious control. While the model does not deny the importance of learning in the development of maladaptive responses, it focuses primarily on conscious processes. In this model the person is aware of motivations, recognizes stress that has been generated, and deliberately makes decisions designed to improve personal and social adjustment.

Unlike the behavioral model already discussed and the psychodynamic model to be explained later in this chapter, the cognitive model has not been extensively developed either as a theoretical approach or as a method of modifying behavior. While an increasing number of psychologists and psychiatrists have been emphasizing the cognitive component in abnormal behavior, the practical influence of the model has been limited because its basic principles have not been presented in an organized and forceful way. Nevertheless, such basic cognitive processes as perception, thinking, problem solving, decision making, and language functioning are involved in some of the more complex forms of conditioning emphasized by behavioral psychologists as well as in the nonconscious psychological events which form the basis of the psychodynamic model.

Some cognitive principles The cognitive approach to abnormal psychology assumes that maladaptive behavior can be studied and understood in terms of how people perceive and think about themselves and the world around them. The major emphasis is on information processing, the most complex and least understood aspect of human behavior. In spite of our relatively limited knowledge of how information is processed, the cognitive model insists that disturbances of internal psychological processes are the cause, and not the result, of personality disturbances and behavior disorders.

Another basic principle of the cognitive model is that each individual develops a "cognitive style" that is highly personal. This style is essentially the way in which we perceive ourselves, others, and the physical world. When these perceptions are consistent and realistic, behavior is likely to be adaptive and "normal." When the perceptions are distorted and unrealistic, behavior will probably be maladaptive or "abnormal." The problem is one of discovering why the environmental signals a person perceives are processed in an abnormal way.

A third principle of the cognitive model is that people cope, at a conscious level, with their adjustment problems in an effort to reduce stress. The assumption is that behavior change can result from deliberate decisions made by the troubled person. This principle, like other assumptions of the cognitive model, is consistent with both the behavioral and psychodynamic approaches to abnormal behavior. The model itself differs in that it directs itself primarily to conscious psychological processes rather than to learning behavior or nonconscious events.

Cognitive Model Applied
The nature of psychological models of abnormality is such that each of the different models lends itself more readily to the investigation and treatment of specific forms of maladaptive behavior. For example, the assumptions of the cognitive model make it especially suited to deal with personality problems involving conscious conflicts, disturbed thinking, and communication disorders. Conscious conflict is illustrated by the search for identity which concerns so many people in our society. Disturbed thinking and communication disorders are common symptoms of schizophrenia and other psychotic conditions.

Search for identity The problem of knowing who we are has become increasingly important for many people in our highly technological and impersonal society. The word *identity* has been used in many ways over the years. Most people have heard of the "identity crisis," but few are able to give precise meaning to the phrase. In our discussion, the word *identity* will be used to refer to one's sense of self. As William James said in a letter to his wife, "there is a voice inside which speaks and says: *This* is the real me." An identity crisis occurs when there is a conflict involving this feeling. The blurring of one's identity, or sense of self, constitutes a threat and a danger. It is a source of tension, stress, and anxiety.

Figure 4.1 One of the critical personal problems of young people is identity. They seek to know who they are and what they are. This inner search is suggested by the young woman staring at herself in the mirror.

The expression of conflict and confusion related to one's identity ranges from the very real and specific search of an adoptee for his or her biological parents to the abstract and philosophical question of "Who am I?" in the cosmic sense. The preoccupation with who one really is takes a variety of forms and appears in differing degrees of intensity. In many people the problem is a negligible one; in others it is a matter of continuing concern; and in some it is the source of psychological disturbance.

Conflicts of identity are a normal expression of development during adolescence. The cost of emotional independence from the parents is the loss of childhood security and the image of oneself as a child. The result is an increased need to search for one's own identity. Sometimes the adolescent has the fantasy of not really being the child of the parents. It is the beginning of the feelings of alienation which have always been a part of adolescent development, but which in recent years have become more conspicuous.

The increased incidence of emotional disturbance in women has also been attributed in part to increasing sex-role conflict and problems of identity. The conventional psychological stereotype of the normal woman has been a submissive, noncompetitive, and unambitious person. While a number of women have always resisted and resented this role, society gave them little opportunity to behave in ways contrary to the socially imposed stereotype. Within recent years a combination of legal decisions in favor of women's rights, new opportunities in the professions and other work areas, and the changing attitudes of men and women have created conflicts of identity which many women find difficult to resolve.

Another illustration of sex-role identity conflict is in connection with homosexuality. Many homosexuals and lesbians pass through a period in which sex role conflict is intense. Most manage to resolve this problem, but some men and women find it impossible to reconcile their sexual inclinations with the expectations of society. When this happens, it is not unusual for the one so affected to develop a personality disturbance growing out of the identity conflict.

While the search for identity is one example of cognitive conflict, many other significant conflicts are sources of conscious preoccupation. Some of the most critical conflicts involve the satisfaction of sexual needs, hostile and aggressive impulses, the struggle for status, and the contradictory needs to be dependent and independent.

Delusional thinking Some of the most severe cognitive disturbances are seen in the false beliefs, or *delusions*, held by people admitted to mental hospitals. The following delusional ideas were expressed by patients in one of these hospitals:

> A man upstairs is nailing anothers man's toes to the bed.
> The milk delivered to my apartment is poisoned.
> The newspapers are going to release a headline saying that I am a "queer."
> My husband made me insane so he would be free to commit adultery.
> I am the richest man in the world.
> There is a devil in my ear.
> My head is filled with cornflakes.

These ideas reflect cognitive disorders. They are typical of comments made by people with the psychoses to be discussed in Chapters 11, 12 and 13. It is sufficient at this point to understand that such thinking involves a distorted perception and interpretation of reality. In some way, information has been incorrectly or inadequately processed. The cognitive model maintains that the failure in information processing is the central issue in understanding abnormal behavior patterns.

Disturbed communication The way in which language is used in communication is also of concern in the cognitive model because language is basic to concept formation and to the transmission of ideas. For this reason, psychologists and psychiatrists who emphasize the cognitive aspects of maladaptive behavior are particularly sensitive to the way in which disturbed people communicate verbally. The following exchange between a psychiatrist and patient indicates a significant disturbance of cognitive functioning:

Doctor: Who invented the airplane?
Patient: I do know.
Doctor: You mean, you don't know.
Patient: I do know.
Doctor: You do know.
Patient: Yes, I do.
Doctor: If you do know, can you tell me?
Patient: If I do know, how can I tell you? I could.
Doctor: You could tell me.
Patient: Yes, because I do know. I do know, I do know, ah, who invented the airplane.
Doctor: Okay, if you do know who invented the airplane, tell me who invented the airplane.
Patient: I can.
Doctor: You can.
Patient: I sure could.
Doctor: You sure could. Okay, can you tell me now who invented the airplane?
Patient: I do know.
Doctor: You do know.
Patient: Yes, I know.
Doctor: That means that you have the answer. You have the answer to that question.
Patient: Yes.
Doctor: Yes. Alright, now can you tell me what the answer is?
Patient: Who invented the airplane, I do know.
Doctor: What you mean to say is that you don't know.
Patient: I do know. If I don't know, I, I, I, I wouldn't be able to tell you.
Doctor: You're not able to tell me, though, are you?
Patient: Yes, I am, for I do know. (Laffal and Ameen, 1959)

The cognitive model looks upon breakdown in communication as further evidence of the failure of information processing. Verbal expressions are examined with the hope that they will clarify the conflicts being experienced by the patient and will give a clue to the nature of the cognitive disturbance.

Cognitive Therapy

The cognitive approach to the treatment of psychological disorders involves helping the disturbed person become more aware of the nature and consequences of conflict. It also emphasizes how problems can be solved in socially acceptable and personally constructive ways. While a number of specific techniques are used in treatment, they all involve conscious understanding and cooperation on the part of the person being treated.

Psychodynamic Model

While the cognitive model deals essentially with conscious events and deliberate decisions, the psychodynamic model is more concerned with the nonconscious and hidden forces determining behavior. As indicated in Chapter 1, the psychodynamic approach was largely the result of the work of Sigmund Freud, who developed the theory and technique of psychoanalysis. Freud's work was the beginning of the psychodynamic model, and his theories dominated this approach throughout the first half of the present century.

Some Basic Assumptions

The essence of the psychodynamic model is that the most significant forces shaping human behavior operate at the unconscious level. People are not aware of their most critical motivations or of their most important conflicts and frustrations. Similarly, the anxiety generated by conflict may be disguised, and the defenses which are used to reduce the stress operate at the unconscious level.

Unconscious motivation Modern views of unconscious motivation have grown out of

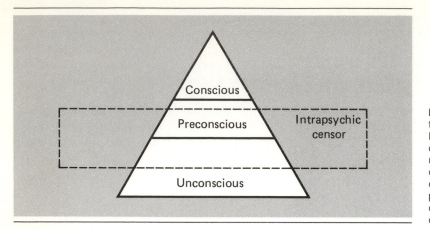

Figure 4.2 A simple model of the Freudian concept of the relation between conscious, preconscious, and unconscious mental activity. The intrapsychic censor is a hypothetical controlling mechanism that prevents anxiety-provoking unconscious material from becoming conscious.

the work of Freud. He showed that our unconscious life is not a mere storehouse of odd bits of information, images, memories, and assorted experiences, but a dynamic system of primitive needs and urges seeking expression. Yet many of these unconscious drives are expressed only under certain conditions, while others remain hidden throughout one's lifetime.

To fit these clinical findings into a theory, Freud created a theoretical model made up of three layers: (1) *conscious* mental activity, (2) *preconscious* (or *foreconscious*) activity, and (3) *unconscious* activity. Conscious activity was considered to be immediate experience; preconscious activity was held to consist of psychological events outside consciousness, but readily available through the process of memory; and unconscious activity was assumed to be made up of psychological events that could enter consciousness only with considerable difficulty, if at all.

For the most part, conscious activity and unconscious activity flow along together, but the amount of conscious activity is very small indeed compared with the unconscious activity that goes on at the same time. Conscious life is a mere fragment of the total psychological life.

While the concept of the unconscious is merely a hypothesis, it is needed to explain the facts of consciousness. The same is true in astronomy when a star system is entered on a celestial map even though there is no direct evidence that the stars exist. No one has ever seen them. However, the behavior and activity of stars and planets that can be seen indicate that something additional must exist at a certain place in space in order to account for the observed phenomena. A similar situation in psychology makes it necessary to postulate unconscious motivation.

Conflict and frustration Whatever the source of motivation—biological, psychological, or social—the human organism is never able to satisfy its entire range of needs. Much of what any given person wants and desires, both at conscious and unconscious levels, cannot be attained. There are external and internal controlling processes which make it impossible to satisfy many drives and motives. The two major conditions which interfere with the satisfaction of every need are (1) frustration and (2) conflict.

The word *frustration* comes from the Latin *frustra*, meaning "in vain." Dictionary definitions ordinarily include the idea of being

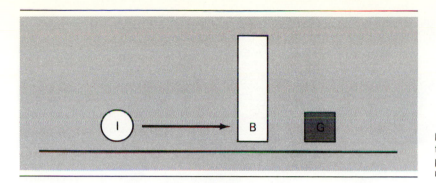

Figure 4.3 The basic frustration model. The individual (I) is prevented by a barrier (B) from reaching the goal (G).

defeated, baffled, or thwarted. Frustration, which begins in the very earliest period of life, is a condition in which one seeks to attain a goal of some kind and finds that his or her way to the goal is blocked by a barrier.

In spite of the many and inevitable frustrations in life, the major problems a person faces are not those involving goals blocked by barriers. Even more important are those situations in life in which a choice must be made between alternative goals. When such a choice cannot be made readily, one experiences the psychological state of conflict. The word *conflict* comes from the Latin *conflictus*, part of the verb meaning "to strike together." Psychological conflict involves the collision of incompatible drives and motives.

Whatever the form of frustration or conflict and whatever its intensity, the probability of its resulting in a personality disturbance depends upon how completely it is resolved. Fortunately, most people learn to

decrease their frustrations by recognizing the barriers and finding ways to circumvent them or, more often, by establishing substitute goals that are realistic and attainable. Similarly, conflicts are resolved through the simple expedient of making a choice and accepting it. However, it happens frequently that a choice cannot be made in a serious conflict situation, or that if it is made, the chooser cannot accept it. When this happens, the result may be some form of personality breakdown.

Guilt and anxiety As a result of the feelings of stress involving sexuality, hostility, status, and dependency, a characteristic emotional state is generated within the human organism. This emotional state consists of a generalized psychophysiological tension called anxiety, which is combined with the psychological attitude of *guilt*.

Nature of anxiety It has been said that anxiety is the most basic emotion. In a sense

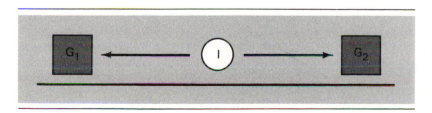

Figure 4.4 The basic conflict model. The individual (I) is forced to choose between two goals, (G₁) and (G₂), of equal or nearly equal attraction.

Figure 4.5   This dramatic scene illustrates the Oedipal conflict emphasized by Freudian psychoanalysts. The husband is being kissed passionately by his wife while his mother clings to him in her reluctance to give him up to her rival.

this is true because anxiety is a primitive response to threat. It has its origins in the behavior of lower animals. When animals are threatened by danger, they must fight or escape if they are to survive. In either case, a complex physiological reaction prepares the animal so that it is better equipped to meet the danger. These emergency changes are of various kinds. One of the most basic responses is the release of the hormone adrenaline by the adrenal glands. The increased presence of this hormone in the body results in a speeding up of the heartbeat, increased blood pressure, more rapid breathing, and the release of strength-giving sugars stored in the liver. All these changes are meant to prepare the animal to meet the threat of

physical danger. The same reactions occur when people are faced with threatening situations. However, while lower animals are threatened primarily by external environmental dangers, people are also threatened by their own impulses. The psychodynamic model maintains that the awareness of the physiological changes in the body is anxiety, and that it appears when unconscious conflicts threaten to become conscious. The most important of these buried conflicts involve impulses of a sexual and aggressive nature.

One of the problems associated with the concept of anxiety is the necessity to differentiate it from fear. While this differentiation is not always easy or even possible, fear is a relatively well-defined response to a real or imagined danger, and anxiety is more likely to be vague, diffuse, and undefined. Fear is a learned reaction to external events. Anxiety, a more chronic state, is usually produced by the conditioning of physiological reactions.

Another problem involves the difference between normal anxiety and pathological anxiety. The first occurs when the reasons for the anxiety are obvious. The second occurs when the reasons are not apparent. When we are told that another war may be on the way, real anxiety sweeps the country. Everyone can see the threat that lies ahead. But when a person is troubled and worried and there seems to be no reason for it, he or she is experiencing neurotic anxiety. Most of the anxiety that grows out of unconscious conflict belongs to this latter class.

Anxiety plays two major roles in the dynamics of personality organization and disorganization. First, it serves as a signal; second, it is a symptom. Anxiety as a signal alerts one to impending danger. It enables a person to set into motion the defensive and adjustive processes which will serve to protect him or her against the inner threats. Anxiety as a symptom is an expression of the breakdown of the defensive operations in the personality. In this role, anxiety becomes the basic symptom of a number of personality disturbances.

Importance of guilt While human beings share the physiological basis of anxiety with lower animals, the feelings of guilt which are so frequently associated with anxiety are peculiar to *Homo sapiens*. Guilt is a potentially damaging attitude which, according to the psychodynamic view, can be either conscious or unconscious.

Guilt arises in a variety of situations. Some people feel guilty whenever they enjoy themselves. Others have guilt feelings aroused simply by looking at such signs as "No Smoking" and "Keep off the Grass." In fact, any tabooed activity is likely to arouse feelings of guilt. Reading a banned book, engaging in a forbidden affair, going on a drinking spree, cheating at cards or golf, and spending too much money are forms of behavior that may lead to loss of self-respect. When one's self-image is threatened, guilt and anxiety soon put in their appearance.

Feelings of guilt vary in intensity from one person to another. Some people learn to live with their guilt by discounting it, others by devoting their lives to expiation. But in a great many people, guilt is a source of constant psychological irritation. Some people are not directly aware of their guilt, nor do they realize that many of their actions are attempts to rid themselves of guilt feelings.

Guilt is such a powerful force in our society, and is so widely recognized as such, that institutionalized means for reducing the tension and anxiety associated with guilt feelings have been devised. A well-known saying, "Confession is good for the soul," is psychologically sound—so sound, in fact, that the technique of confession is used to great advantage by such differently oriented groups and individuals as the Catholic Church, the religious revivalist, and the psychiatrist in his consulting room.

Guilt feelings are frequently seen in mental patients. One patient stopped her physician in the hall every day and said, "Everybody is sick because of me. I am to blame for everything. I ought to die." Another patient asked that she be put in a furnace. She repeated over and over that she was a sinner and that she should be sent to hell to burn for her sins.

Psychodynamic defense mechanisms
One of the most basic assumptions of the psychodynamic model is that the most threatening psychological conflicts are kept out of consciousness by means of defense mechanisms. These mechanisms protect people from the anxiety and guilt that the conflicts would arouse were they to become conscious. Most of the mechanisms are assumed to serve constructive purposes in maintaining a person's personal and social adjustment. However, when defense mechanisms break down or become distorted, abnormal forms of behavior appear. We will examine three defense mechanisms closely associated with abnormal behavior: *repression*, or holding unacceptable impulses in the unconscious; *fantasy*, or daydreams; and *regression*, or the return to earlier and less anxiety-provoking forms of behavior.

Reducing anxiety through repression The repression of unacceptable impulses and ideas is basic to the psychodynamic model. While such repression makes possible a relatively anxiety-free existence, it is not without psychological hazards in the form of unconscious conflicts which take the form of symptoms at the conscious level of the personality.

According to this view, each person's unconscious life is made up of troublesome urges, strivings, and impulses which are constantly seeking to be expressed. There is a critical, selective process which allows some urges to be expressed while others are held in check. At any given moment, we do not express all the urges we carry about with us. We express only a select few. The rest are controlled by the powerful forces of repression.

Although repression is carried on automatically and unconsciously, there are conscious forces supporting the process. The conscious part of this controlling mechanism is the *conscience*, or set of attitudes having moral overtones. When we are bothered by our conscience, we have become aware of the struggle between our unconscious impulses and the code of ethics and morals we have adopted.

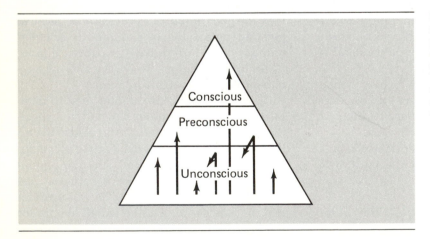

Figure 4.6 The basic repression model. Unconscious impulses that are not acceptable strive to become conscious but are turned back, or repressed. This repressed material, according to psychodynamic theory, is largely responsible for disturbed behavior.

Figure 4.7 Dreams are one of the most direct expressions of unconscious mental activity. Henri Rousseau's painting *The Dream* shows a fantasy involving a nude woman, native flute player, exotic birds, peering animals, and lush foliage. Although there is a dreamlike quality to this painting, the memory of our dreams is usually more vague and disorganized.

When repression is incomplete or inadequate, one experiences anxiety related to the unconscious conflict. For example, a young man developed a violent dislike of ballet after having attended a performance during which he was thrown into a panic. His heart pounded, he had difficulty with his breathing, and he broke into a cold sweat. As soon as he left the theater, his symptoms subsided. Later events revealed that this man had strong homosexual tendencies which he was struggling to keep from becoming conscious. He was unconsciously attracted to the male ballet dancers. His panic was a reaction to the threat that his defenses might break down and that he might reveal the homosexual component of his personality to himself and to others.

Reducing anxiety through fantasy Another way in which people protect themselves from anxiety is through daydreams, or fantasy. Such thinking is egotistical and self-centered. It is an attempt to build up a dream world which is more acceptable than the world of reality. Fantasy life, when carried to an extreme, is one of the key characteristics of the more serious personality breakdowns.

Fantasy is a turning-in of the mind on itself and its own problems. Ordinarily, fantasies have a concrete, pictorial quality which disregards logic and reason. They are determined by unfulfilled ambitions, motives, desires, and unconscious wishes.

Many people create fantasies in order to overcome the drab realities of everyday life. A frustrated and unhappy woman, tired of her husband, her children, and her marriage, imagines a life in which she is wealthy, clever, and irresistibly beautiful. She imagines herself pursued by handsome men. She convinces herself that other women are jealous of her. She constructs an unreal world in which she is the center of attention. Soon it becomes difficult for her to distinguish sharply between what is real and what is imagination.

In the case of some of the most serious mental disorders, fantasy life is carried to an extreme. The world of fantasy is substituted almost entirely for the world of reality. Such people become seclusive and withdrawn

---

"Dear Professor, I Love You!"— The Romantic Fantasies of a Disturbed Student

A young professor had a student in his class who received C's and D's in her quizzes and failed to take the final examination. She came in to see the professor about a makeup examination, which was prepared for her, but she never took it. That was the last the professor heard of her until the following year when he was teaching at another university. One morning he received a collect telegram which read:

Dear _____:
I am a lover thru and thru, and I'm in love with you. I am sitting by the telephone straight and tall, waiting for you to call.

Love,

The professor was completely mystified by the telegram, and thought it might be some kind of poor joke. But when he arrived home that evening, there was a long-distance call from his former student, who was obviously in a highly confused state. She poured out an incoherent story about her engagement being broken off because she had been in his class at the university. The next day the professor received several letters. One read:

Dear _____:
Please come down and get me. I love you. I'll die if you don't marry me. I can't see four good lives going to waste—yours, mine, and the two people to whom we are engaged. My fiance knows about you, and that's why he'll never be happy with me. Everywhere I go everyone knows the story about you and I. I'll never have friends any more, and I have to live here. Won't you please come back and get me because it's you I love and no one else. My whole life will be ruined. Now that I know you were always supposed to marry me, I can't contain myself until I hear from you. Please call and let me talk to you because I love you.

Love,

On the outside of one of the envelopes, the student wrote: "Sealed with a kiss. It's all your fault. Now I'm in love with you." The situation became progressively worse, with the student making telephone calls and sending telegrams and letters both to the professor and to the girl to whom he was engaged. In addition, the student began telephoning the professor's former colleagues at the university, demanding information and making accusations. Finally, it was possible to have the girl committed to a psychiatric hospital; and a completely unjustified scandal and public embarrassment were avoided.

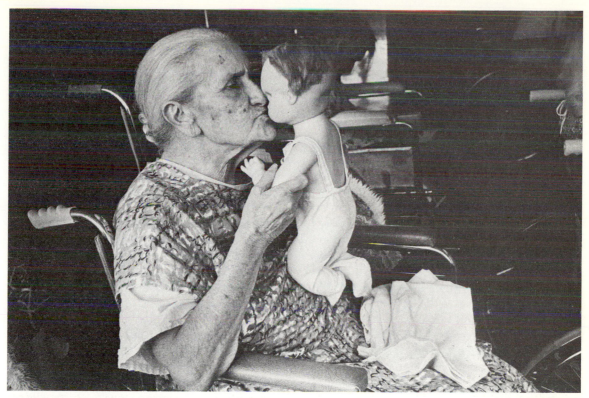

Figure 4.8 It is not unusual for elderly people to revert to forms of behavior expressed earlier in life. The elderly woman in her wheelchair, kissing the doll, is showing signs of regressive behavior. The reason for regression varies from person to person and can be determined only after a careful clinical examination of the individual.

and seem out of contact with their environment. It is impossible to reach them by means of the ordinary processes of communication. They live in a dream world of their own making, preferring it to the difficult world of everyday reality. The wards of every large mental hospital are filled with men and women who prefer a fantasy world to the sometimes harsh and bitter realities of ordinary living.

Reducing anxiety through regression Some people reduce their anxiety through a return to earlier and more primitive forms of behavior. Each person progresses through a series of developmental stages during his or her lifetime. First, there is the period during which one is relatively safe in the uterus of the mother. It is an easy and presumably anxiety-free time. Some psychoanalysts believe that it is a life to which most people secretly long to return.

Following the stress of birth, there is the period of infancy. Here, too, despite the many stresses associated with sexuality, toilet training, socialization, and the harnessing of aggression, life is easy compared with the later struggles which people must endure. Following the period of infancy, there are the characteristic stresses of childhood, adolescence, early adulthood, maturity, and finally old age.

When a person regresses, there is a return psychologically to one of the earlier periods when life was easier, there were fewer problems, and there was less anxiety and less guilt. Everyone at one time or another shows signs of psychological regression. When this happens, it indicates that stress has become so severe that there is a forced retreat to an earlier level. An attempt is made to solve problems of behavior in ways that proved satisfactory earlier in life.

Sexual behavior shows a wide range of regressions. An adult man who is fearful of contracting venereal infection or a woman whose anxiety is related to fear of pregnancy may resort to an earlier form of sexual satisfaction. Regressive masturbation is an escape from reality when more adequate outlets are available but not utilized. Homosexuality may also be a regression. Some homosexuals are people who have found that normal heterosexual relationships are too anxiety-provoking. Since strong attachment to members of the same sex is characteristic of the earlier phase of adolescence, a person may find later in life that it is easier to adjust emotionally to this earlier level than to the level of mature sexuality where heterosexual relations are expected.

Regressive behavior is seen in its most unvarnished form in mental disorder. The behavior of disturbed persons may be infantile or childish. They may suck their thumbs, masturbate, and show keen interest in urination and defecation. They may even play with their feces and smear them on the floor

and walls in the manner of young children. Among those in the old-age groups, a regression to childhood patterns is not unusual. "Second childhood" is an attempt to hang onto life by regressing psychologically to one's early years.

Psychodynamic Model Applied

Freud and his followers—who developed psychoanalytic theory and therapy and who laid the foundation for the psychodynamic model—saw most of their patients in private practice. These troubled people were usually able to make at least marginal personal and social adjustments in spite of their symptoms. They were not, for the most part, patients in mental hospitals.

This situation had an important bearing on the nature of psychodynamic theory and treatment. It accounts for the fact that this model is more applicable to personality disturbances and behavior disorders of nonhospitalized people than to hospital patients with severe psychological damage. It also accounts for the strong early emphasis on sex conflict. Freud's patients were middle-class men and women who were living in a period of Victorian morality.

Compulsion to steal Compulsive stealing, and the obsessive concern with such activity, has a number of possible psychodynamic explanations. The individual who is driven to steal impulsively and without apparent reason may be expressing a reaction against authority. Such behavior is a defiance of the police and the owners of the store, both of whom may represent parental figures. It is also possible that such thefts may be an expression of a more generalized hostility and aggression within the personality. In some cases, compulsive stealing appears to be related to a need to defy convention by engaging in activity completely contrary to the moral and ethical standards under which the person was raised. This type of reaction also contains elements of hostility.

The need for punishment is an important factor in these cases, since most neurotics of this type are quickly apprehended. It is as if the victim desired to be caught. At the unconscious level, it may be that certain compulsive neurotics of this kind do in fact have a need to be punished. The sexual element in compulsive stealing is also present in some cases, since people not infrequently describe erotic excitement associated with the act of stealing. The fact that such behavior is dangerous and forbidden may be associated with fantasies of sexual activities.

Psychological blindness Visual symptoms involve a variety of psychodynamic relationships. A middle-aged woman was brought to a clinic after some of the best eye specialists in the country had been unable to discover the cause of her blindness. At the clinic her story was uncovered. She had married, and her first and only child was a girl. She was disappointed because her heart had been set on a boy. The result was that she was not very kind to the little girl during the early years. When the daughter grew older she sensed her mother's dislike, and gradually she came to hate her mother because of it. The mother began to feel guilty about the way she had treated the girl, but it was already too late. The girl's hatred grew more intense each year. One day the mother suddenly went blind. It was interpreted that she was trying not to see her daughter's hatred for her. Through psychological treatment, her vision was restored.

Psychodynamic Treatment

The treatment approach dictated by the nature of the psychodynamic model is the exploration of the unconscious level of the personality. Since the psychodynamic model maintains that the conflicts responsible for symptoms shown by the disturbed person are at the unconscious level, the task of treatment is one of uncovering the conflicts. Once these conflicts have been identified and brought into awareness, their relevance to the symptoms can be determined. This is what is meant by gaining insight into one's problems. The insight then makes possible the positive actions which are required to bring about full recovery. The technical aspects of psychodynamic treatment will be discussed at greater length in Chapter 17.

The Chapter in Review

Any attempt to explain abnormality in terms of a psychological model must deal with certain basic aspects of behavior. Among the most important are the forces which lead to behavior, the way in which people detect and organize information, and the ways in which information is processed. The principal explanations of abnormality are in terms of the behavioral, cognitive, and psychodynamic models.

1 Behavioral Model

The behavioral model of abnormal behavior emphasizes the role of learning in the development of psychological disturbances and the modification of maladaptive behavior.

a The principles underlying abnormal behavior are the same as the principles of all learning, namely, reinforcement, generalization, and extinction.

b The modification of maladaptive behavior is accomplished through the application of the same learning principles responsible for the appearance of such behavior.

2 Cognitive Model

The cognitive model of abnormality is concerned primarily with conscious processes. The person is considered to be aware of motivational forces, to perceive conflicts and frustrations, and to make deliberate decisions as to action. One of the important cognitive conflicts is the search for identity. Cognitive corrective measures involve conscious understanding and constructive action.

3 Psychodynamic Model

The psychodynamic model is based upon the assumption that the most important conflicts in life occur at the unconscious level, and that the anxiety and guilt generated by the conflict is reduced by defense mechanisms which include repression, regression, and fantasy. Conflicts in the sexual area are important sources of psychological symptoms. When abnormal behavior is present, it is treated by exploring the unconscious in order to uncover the hidden conflicts responsible for the psychological disturbance.

The several psychological models of abnormality represent different points of view and different levels of explanation. They are not in complete disagreement, nor is it necessary to accept one model and reject the others. Models are convenient methods for thinking about problems. They also serve as a framework for the practical matters of treatment. The choice of a psychological model is frequently influenced by the nature of the problem.

Recommended Readings

Behavioral Model

Skinner, B. F. *About behaviorism*. New York: Vintage Books, 1976. (Paperback.)

Pines, Maya. *The brain changers*. New York: New American Library, 1975. (Paperback.)

Cognitive Model

Raimy, Victor. *Misunderstandings of the self*. San Francisco: Jossey Bass, 1975.

Psychodynamic Model

Gedo, J. E., & Goldberg, A. *Models of the mind*: *A psychoanalytic theory.* Chicago: University of Chicago Press, 1973.

Schur, Max. *Freud*: *Living and dying.* New York: International Universities Press, 1972.

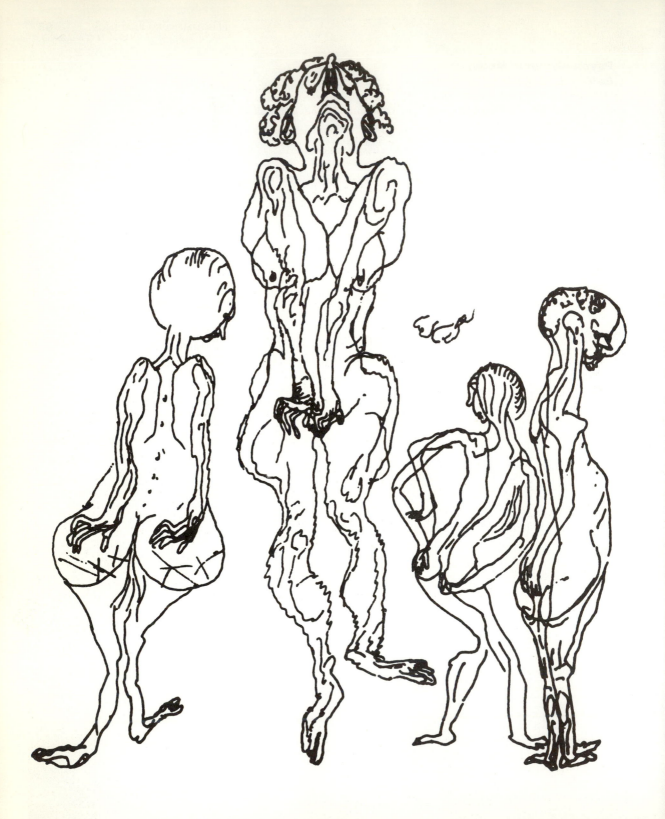

5
Sociocultural Models of Abnormal Behavior

Objectives

To indicate that sociocultural influences, as well as biological and psychological ones, are related to the development of abnormal behavior

To describe the socialization model of mental disorder

To discuss parental attitudes, child-rearing practices, and family pathology as examples of the socialization model

To describe the social disorganization model of abnormal behavior

To show how cultural disintegration, urbanization, mobility and migration, and social and economic deprivation contribute to the development of maladaptive behavior

To describe the cultural model of mental disorder

To indicate the nature of evidence related to the cultural model of abnormality

... A little girl aged 5, living alone with her widowed mother, one day saw a scarecrow in a field adjacent to her home. It waved to her and whistled. She heard it say that it would come and get her. She told her mother, who was perturbed by what she heard and said that when she was small scarecrows sometimes got free and came into the house, and that when they did you could usually expect a death to take place .... The next morning the mother told her neighbor that "they" were not going to get her child and that she knew what they were up to. She and the child now slept in the basement, both in a state of great apprehension, and the mother began to have nightmares. She explained to the child that the "scarecrow people" were now devising all sorts of tricks such as dreams to get into the house and kill the occupants. According to the mother, it was the child that they were after, and according to the child, it was the mother. (Anthony, 1970, pp. 574–575)

This true story suggests that social influences, as well as biological and psychological ones, may be involved in the development of personality disturbance. The interaction of the little girl and her mother is one aspect of the sociocultural model of abnormal behavior.

Just as the biological and psychological models of abnormality are not necessarily contradictory, so it is that the sociocultural model can often be reconciled with biological and psychological approaches. It is entirely possible that even though genetic influences predispose a person to abnormal behavior, the maladaptive pattern will not emerge except under conditions favorable to its appearance. These conditions may be primarily psychological or they may involve social interaction.

While sociocultural influences in mental disorder should not be discounted, it must be remembered that such influences themselves can operate only through their impact on one's biological and psychological systems. In this sense, any sociocultural model

of mental disorder must necessarily be indirect. Social conditions can be effective only to the degree that they are perceived and psychologically processed. For this reason, sociocultural models can be separated from psychological models only in terms of emphasis. Learning, cognitive processes, and psychodynamic relationships can be, and usually are, involved in sociocultural influences on abnormal behavior.

The principal sociocultural explanations of abnormal behavior include the *socialization model*, which emphasizes disturbances of normal social development; the *social disorganization model*, which takes the position that maladaptive behavior grows out of social pathology; and the *cultural model*, which maintains that abnormal behavior is abnormal because it is defined that way by a particular culture.

Socialization Model

This approach to abnormal behavior is an extension of the social learning model discussed in Chapter 4. It is included here because of the special emphasis upon the family and other group influences. The socialization process shapes behavior through social learning and determines to a very considerable extent how we think and act. The process begins very early in life and sometimes involves distorted parental attitudes and beliefs, disturbances of child-rearing practices, inconsistent and inappropriate role behavior, mentally disturbed family members, and similar contingencies which influence and reinforce behavior patterns of children growing up in that environment.

While the family can play a critical role in the development of abnormal behavior in family members, it is not the only influential group. Peer groups among children and ado-

CHURLISH =
SPITEFUL =
ETHNIC

خشن ، زحمت
کنیز قوز
SOCIALIZATION MODEL   **99**

آزار ، قوی

Figure 5.1   The family group, as depicted by a sculpture by Henry Moore. The family serves as an important mental health model for its members. Maladaptive behavior can often be explained in terms of family disturbances and disorganization.

lescents, the school experience, and the work situation can also contribute to abnormal behavior. Even when family life is stable and tranquil, disturbed interpersonal relations in other social groups can result in psychological difficulties.

It is clear that the success or failure of socialization in the family, school, or community may be critical to the maintenance of mental health. The socialization experience often determines if and when maladaptive behavior first appears and frequently influences the form it takes.

Parental Attitudes

The attitudes and beliefs of parents are among the most important socializing influences in the development of the personality of the child. These attitudes are sometimes damaging to the child and may be the source of maladjustment later in life. Parental rejection, overprotection, dominance, submission, and similar attitudes are at times responsible for the appearance of maladaptive patterns of behavior.

In one study, a number of men whose lives had been followed from ages 18 to 47 were assessed for overall psychological adjustment at the end of the thirty-year period. It was found that the presence of warmth and affection during childhood was significantly related to an adulthood showing few signs of abnormality or poor mental health (Vaillant, 1974). And a study of the family dynamics in homosexual women revealed a remarkably consistent picture of the childhood home. Most of these women described a neglectful and churlish father, a martyred and preoccupied mother, and children who felt angry and spiteful (Loney, 1973).

Maladaptive behavior also may be reinforced by family attitudes determined by ethnic and cultural influences. For example, the quality and quantity of drinking among most ethnic groups are strongly influenced by social norms and sanctions. Classic examples of negative reinforcement, or restraining influences, are the attitudes of the Orthodox Jews and the Italians.

Orthodox Jews participate in a number of rituals which involve frequent drinking. Drinking begins early in life—within the family—and wines, spirits, and beer may be used extensively. However, the drinking is done within a religious context and is moderate. Deviation from this established pattern is rare. Even though Jews probably have as many emotional problems as people of other cultures, because of their religious attitudes and beliefs, they usually do not resort to

Figure 5.2 There are wide cultural differences in the use of alcohol. Although members of Jewish families traditionally use wine as part of their religious rituals, few Jews drink excessively or become addicted to alcohol.

excessive drinking. In Italy, on the other hand, drinking is confined almost entirely to mealtimes; but although wine is widely consumed, the consumption of distilled spirits is relatively rare. While Italian-Americans consume far less alcohol than native Italians, the former become involved in more episodes of excessive drinking.

Maladaptive sexual behavior can also be influenced to some degree by attitudes and beliefs. Generally, the incidence of sex offenses is relatively high among Catholics and Protestants, while among Jewish groups it is relatively low. The disproportionate representation of Catholics among sex offenders may be due to the somewhat suppressive attitude of the Church toward sexuality. Similarly, family attitudes toward sex are generally more severe among Catholics than among Jews and most Protestant denominations.

Child-Rearing Practices
The socialization model is also concerned with child-rearing practices. There is a large and important segment of scientific authority which maintains that personality disturbances later in life can grow out of such practices as lack of breast-feeding, a curtailed period of nursing, abrupt weaning, an

overly rigid nursing schedule, premature toilet training, infrequent mothering, excessive punishment, and similar actions which operate to make the child feel unwanted, unloved, insecure, inadequate, and frustrated.

The importance of child rearing, especially as it involves the mother, was demonstrated in a classic study some years ago comparing children raised in a foundling home with others raised in their own homes. Involvement and support given by their mothers helped the second group of children to mature and develop emotionally. The children cared for in the institution suffered emotionally and developmentally. While the emotional effects of being fatherless have been studied less than the effects of maternal deprivation, the fatherless home can also be a mental health risk factor (Kogelschatz, Adams, & Tucker, 1972).

The weight of evidence indicates that child-rearing practices may influence a person's later susceptibility to emotional disturbance. While the manner in which this influence is exerted is not clear, one of the principal impacts of child-rearing practices may be in the area of stress tolerance. An examination of various practices under experimental conditions, and in different cultures, suggests that some of these practices increase the threshold for tolerating stress, while others decrease it. It is impossible,

Figure 5.3 The stress of separation from parents during childhood can be an important factor in the development of emotional disturbance. These war orphans run a higher risk of maladaptive behavior than do children raised in secure and supportive families. Some family situations, of course, can be more destructive than the experience of separation.

however, to say with any degree of certainty which child-rearing practices are ultimately beneficial and which are ultimately destructive in terms of a person's later emotional stability and mental health.

Family Pathology

There is little doubt that early life experiences can be emotionally damaging to the child. Since most of the earliest experiences take place within the family group, a considerable amount of attention has been given to the way in which high-risk, or disturbed, families contribute to the psychological difficulties of family members at the time and later in their lives.

The problem has been approached from two directions. One type of study investigates families with a mentally disturbed parent to determine the effect of the disturbance on the behavior of children in the family. A second approach has been to study families with mentally disturbed children in an attempt to isolate family factors that might be related to the children's disorders.

Studies of children with a mentally disturbed parent, particularly the mother, indicate that such children belong to a high-risk group and differ from low-risk children in a number of respects. Rate of development, emotional expression, social responsiveness, language development, and other psychological variables show deviations and irregularities in these children (Anthony & Koupernik, 1974). It has also been found that the

Figure 5.4   Disturbed family relationships can be emotionally damaging to everyone in the family. The assistance of a marriage counselor or family therapist is one of the ways in which friction between family members can be reduced or avoided.

COGNITIVE محیط اندیشه و تفکر

children of alcoholic parents have more adjustment problems than children of parents who are not alcoholic (Kammeier, 1971).

A study was made in England of all families with a child under age 15 in which a parent had been referred to a psychiatric clinic for mental disorder. The children in this group were compared with a control group matched for age, sex, and school class. It was found that the children of mentally disturbed parents showed more abnormal behavior than did the control children (Rutter, 1966). It seems clear that the children of disturbed parents suffer emotional, cognitive, and social defects which may precede mental disturbances later in life (Grunebaum, 1975). When families with psychologically disturbed children are studied, it is not unusual to find serious problems in other family members. One such study found disturbed marital relationships between parents in 50 percent of the cases (Clausen & Yarrow, 1955).

Another study of the families of disturbed children found that not a single family was well integrated (Lidz, 1958). Most of the marriages were seriously disturbed, with each parent trying to devalue the opposite parent to the children and striving to win the children to one side or the other. Insecurity and confusion, suspiciousness and distrust, and similar damaging attitudes were seen in many cases. Frequently one or the other parent appeared to be suffering from an incipient mental disturbance.

Although studies of family pathology are difficult to put to rigid experimental test, the evidence points to the fact that when one family member is mentally disturbed, other members are likely to show signs of maladjustment. While family pathology in itself is no guarantee that a child will develop maladaptive patterns of behavior, disturbed family relationships put the child at a greater mental health risk.

The socialization model maintains that there is a causal relationship between the family pathology and the appearance of mental disorder in family members. That is, the pathological family interrelationships cause the symptoms seen in family members. An alternative view is that such family members are already basically disturbed, and the stress of family pathology triggers the symptoms. The disturbed behavior of the family member is not caused by the family situation; it is a reaction to it.

There is the possibility that genetic or constitutional influences or both might be operating to cause the abnormal behavior of family members. Recent evidence suggests that this possibility becomes a probability when a parent is suffering from schizophrenia. In such cases, it is likely that the disturbed behavior of a child is due to a genetic factor that has been released by the stress of the difficult family relationships.

More important than the fact that children of mentally disturbed parents show a disproportionate amount of abnormal behavior is the question of why some children in the family show maladaptive behavior while others make a satisfactory adjustment. The socialization model would place the emphasis on differential social learning. That is, well-adjusted children learn effective coping techniques, while children who develop abnormal responses learn maladaptive patterns. While this explanation cannot be ruled out, it is also possible that the difference is due to genetic or constitutional influences.

Social-Disorganization Model

While the socialization model is concerned primarily with disturbances of social development in the family environment, the social disorganization model directs its attention to the effects of more general social pathology on behavior. The model assumes that abnormal behavior tends to develop in those areas characterized by cultural disintegration, urban deterioration, high personal and social mobility, social and economic deprivation, and related social pathology.

Cultural Disintegration

It has been suggested that a relationship exists between the degree of integration of the sociocultural environment and mental health, and that a disintegrated and disorganized environment will foster the development of mental disorder. This assumption has been basic to a number of field studies carried out by the Cornell Program of Social Psychiatry. Support for this hypothesis has come from investigations undertaken in Stirling County, Nova Scotia (Leighton, 1961), and among the Yoruba tribes in West Africa (Leighton et al., 1963). The cultural disintegration assumption has also been supported by a study of rural and urban populations in the South Sea Islands (Schmidt, 1973).

The studies of cultural disintegration indicate that urbanization, or the movement of people from rural areas to the cities, is related to mental disorder. It was observed as long as a century ago that mental disorder is more prevalent in urban than in rural areas.

There are a number of factors that might be of importance in explaining differences in the rates of mental disorder in urban and rural areas. One possibility is that there are differences in the national and racial make-up of urban and rural populations. A second possibility is that it is easier to care for those who are mentally disturbed in rural areas and that this factor affects the hospitalization rates. It has been suggested also that the higher urban rates might be due to the migration from rural areas into urban areas by older age groups approaching retirement, or to the fact that there is less stress in rural areas than in cities. Similarly, the higher urban rates might be due to the more intense striving for status in urban areas, the relative lack of security of group ties, the lack of stability in social roles, the less personal forms of authority, and the relative lack of integration of religious, occupational, and social groups. These hypotheses suggest the possibility that the degree of social integration might be the important factor, and not the degree of urbanization.

Mental Disorder in Urban Areas

It has been observed that not only is there a difference in the prevalence of mental disorder in urban and rural areas, but that disturbed behavior appears to follow predictable patterns within a city. Some years ago a study was made of all cases of mental disorder admitted during a twelve-year period to four Illinois state hospitals and eight private sanitariums (Faris & Dunham, 1939). The incidence rates of mental disorders per 100, 000 population were plotted on census maps of the Chicago area. This mapping made it possible to determine the degree of relationship existing between the various types of mental disorder and the neighborhood structure of the city. Mental disorder in general showed a marked concentration in the deteriorated downtown areas, with the rates declining successively in all directions from the center of the city to the suburbs.

The Chicago findings stimulated great interest and led to a number of subsequent investigations. Not all these more recent studies have substantiated the original findings. For example, one study of mental disorder in Chicago found a random distribution of cases throughout the city, in contrast to the concentration in the inner city that had been reported in the original Chicago study (Levy & Rowitz, 1973).

The social disorganization model of ab-

Figure 5.5 Being overwhelmed by massive and impersonal cities is not an unusual experience. Depression and frustration are common reactions. Sometimes the sense of isolation becomes so severe that one wonders whether life is worth living.

DRIFT =   شناوريدن ـ باراه بی معبر

normal behavior takes the position that deteriorated and disorganized areas of an urban community can cause mental disorder. However, there are several alternative explanations for the tendency for some mental disorders to be more prevalent in certain areas of the city. It is possible that downward drift occurs. That is, the mentally disturbed person is less competent and successful in life, and consequently drifts toward lower socioeconomic areas. The area does not cause the mental disorder; it attracts those who are already disordered.

Another possible explanation is that those with some types of mental disorder choose to live in neighborhoods that satisfy particular needs. Such people may select areas where they can associate more readily with others who have similar problems and where their maladaptive requirements can be met. It is also possible that different areas of cities tolerate abnormal behavior to different degress.

Mobility and Migration

The social disorganization model of abnormal behavior also assumes that individual mobility and migration can have adverse health effects. Language barries, changes of climate, religious conflicts, different habits, racial prejudice, and social nonacceptance are some of the stresses which may face people who make disruptive changes of residence. Studies in various parts of the world indicate that first admission rates to mental hospitals are markedly higher for migrants than for nonmigrants and that rates are higher for recent migrants than for earlier migrants.

The importance of migration in the development of psychological disturbance has been reported in New Guinea, where the migration of rural peoples to the city has been associated with a disruption of traditional family life and with an emergence of the problems associated with the community integration of diverse populations. More specifically, the introduction of Australian culture has resulted in the disappearance of the intervillage warfare which had dominated much of New Guinea's cultural scene. The result has been a redirecting of hostility to the family and personal level. Mental disorder in the rural areas was a negligible problem previously, but now there is an obvious need for mental health services in the towns to which the natives have migrated (Zigas et al., 1972).

Additional evidence of the influence of mobility in the development of psychological disturbance was found in a study in the Midi region of France. The investigation revealed that an abnormally high percentage of disturbed children had been born in other parts of the country. It was suggested that geographical location and the breakdown of the nuclear family were possible causal factors in the mental disturbances of the children (Luccioni and Scotto, 1974). The mental health implications of voluntary and enforced migrations, including displacement during World War II, have also been studied (Swingmann & Pfister-Ammende, 1973).

The study of large-scale mobility, as in the case of refugees, has afforded an opportunity to investigate the impact of massive dislocation on the mental health of the people involved. When the roots of one's traditional life have been torn away, a certain amount of psychological damage and abnormal behavior can be expected. A study of Pakistani refugees following the partition of India showed an increase in disturbed behavior among this group (Keller, 1975).

There are at least two possible interpretations of the findings in connection with migration and its relation to personality disorganization. The first possibility is that migration in some way triggers the onset of personality disturbance. A second view is that migration is itself a symptom of an unstable personality, one more prone to the development of mental disorder. That is, migration itself is not the important factor but rather the fact that a higher percentage of unstable people leave their native country. This assumption does not apply to massive migrations of political and racial refugees. However, even here it is possible that only those who are already susceptible to serious mental disturbance break down under the stress of dislocation.

Social and Economic Deprivation

There is a considerable amount of evidence pointing to a relationship between mental disorder and social and economic level. Early information on this subject was derived from hospital admission figures and from the analysis of men rejected from the armed services for neuropsychiatric reasons. Since World War II, studies have included patients seen by psychiatrists in private practice. All studies show a consistently increasing incidence of the more serious mental disorders as one goes down the socioeconomic scale.

One of the most comprehensive studies of social class and personality disorganization was the social stratification of the New Haven urban community by means of an "Index of Social Position" (Hollingshead &

Figure 5.6 These refugees react with shock and uncertainty to the experience of being uprooted from the protected and familiar environment of their home. Many millions of people in various parts of the world have lived through this type of involuntary migration. The stress of such an experience increases the risk of psychological maladjustments.

Redlich, 1958). To arrive at the level of social position, three factors were taken into consideration: (1) area of residence, (2) occupation, and (3) education. The index identified five major social class levels. The highest social level (class I) contributed only 1.0 percent of the psychiatric cases although this class was made up of 3.1 percent of the general population. At the bottom end of the social scale, class V contributed 36.8 percent of the psychiatric cases although only 17.8 percent of the normal population fell into this group. Important social class differences were also found in connection with the relative incidence of neurosis and psychosis. The highest rates for neurosis were found in classes I and II, while the highest rates for psychosis were found in classes IV and V. This same relationship of an overrepresentation of neurosis among upper-class individuals and of psychosis among the lower class was found in a study of the Lebanese (Katchadourian & Churchill, 1969).

An extensive follow-up study of over 1,500 psychiatric patients in New Haven revealed that 53 percent of these patients, who were hospitalized in 1950, remained or were again hospitalized during the next ten years; 2 percent were receiving outpatient care; and 31 percent had died by 1960. An interesting association between socioeconomic class and outcome was revealed. A patient from the higher social classes had three times as great a chance of remaining out of the hospital than did a patient from the lowest social class. Upper- and middle-class ex-patients, even if they showed greater psychological impairment than lower-class ex-patients, made better social and economic adjustments than did their lower-class counterparts. Thus, membership in the higher social classes appears to confer a measure of "immunity" against hospitalization and the social and economic consequences of mental illness. The reason may be better knowledge about mental health and greater tolerance of deviant behavior (NIMH, 1968).

In another study of the relationship of social class to mental disorder, 1,000 psychiatric cases in the Air Force were investigated (Lantz, 1953). The number of psychotics decreased as the socioeconomic level increased. High socioeconomic families contributed 1.9 percent of the psychotics, middle-income families contributed 4.3 percent, and low socioeconomic families contributed 10.2 percent.

It has also been shown that there is a relationship between general economic conditions and mental disorder. It is assumed that disruptive economic changes result in losses in jobs or income, and that this situation results in an increase in the prevalence of mental disorder (Brenner, 1973).

The finding that the probability of being admitted to a mental hospital becomes less as one's economic level increases is open to several interpretations. One is that people of higher income are able to take care of their psychological problems in ways other than commitment to a mental hospital. By being able to afford the services of psychiatrists and clinical psychologists in private practice, the higher-income family can have many personality disturbances cared for at home, in the therapist's office, or in a private nonpsychiatric hospital.

Another possibility is that the chances for recovery are less in economically deprived neighborhoods, since treatment is more likely to be of an inferior quality. Higher-social-class patients have a better chance of being selected for psychotherapy and of being treated by an experienced therapist. Lower-class patients tend to be left until they become chronic psychotics.

There is the further possibility that psychotic disorder represents a drift down the social scale as a result of incompetence. One study, however, showed that 91 percent of the patients were in the same social class as their parents, while several other studies have shown greater mobility upward than downward (Hollingshead et al., 1954).

A somewhat different explanation of the finding would be that increased economic status carries with it a sense of personal security. As a result of this security, stress is reduced and one is less exposed to tension and conflict. Such an explanation would imply that the difference in expectancy of mental illness among low-income groups and high-income groups is a real, rather than an apparent, difference.

It may also be that different cultural segments of society have different stress patterns putting pressures on the members of the segment. Other possibilities are that members of different social classes differ in their psychological defenses, in the conflicts to which they are susceptible, and, eventually, in the type of personality disorganization.

Cultural Model

This approach looks upon abnormal behavior as behavior that a particular culture decides is unacceptable and abnormal. Since attitudes toward such behavior vary from culture to culture, patterns of thought and action considered abnormal in one culture may be quite normal in a different social setting. The emphasis here is on the social definition of abnormality rather on socialization or the effects of social pathology.

"Exotic" Disorders

Earlier in our century, psychiatrists and anthropologists making observations in other cultures described a number of types of abnormal behavior which were thought to be unique to the cultures being studied. One of the first of these exotic disorders was a condition called *arctic hysteria*, observed among the natives of northern Siberia. This disorder was marked by a high degree of suggestibility which was almost hypnotic in its effect. The condition also involved symptoms in which the patient imitated the movements and actions of other people (Borgoras, 1904–1909). Another disturbance, called *pibloktoq*, was reported among Eskimo women during Admiral Peary's expeditions (Brill, 1913). In a sudden state of excitement, the victim would begin to sing, shout, run about, and tear off her clothing. Attacks lasted an hour or two and ended with the victim weeping and falling asleep. Sometimes there would be a loss of consciousness. The disorder was thought to be related to the insecure emotional environment of Eskimo women, who were considered the property of their men and could be acquired, exchanged, or disposed of as easily as any other property.

There has also been interest in two behavior disorders which have been reported among the Malays. The first of these conditions, called *amok*, is characterized by sudden, wild outbursts of aggression. The phrase *to run amok* is derived from early reports of this behavior. The second condition, known as *lata*, is a disorder marked by extreme passivity and oversuggestibility.

A Dutch psychiatrist in the East Indies described amok as the sudden and unexpected murderous attack of the Malay man who, without any known reason, suddenly jumps up and injures or kills anyone who happens to stand in his way. Amok was regarded as an acute state of mental confusion in which the victim tries to flee from a menacing danger. At the conclusion of the attack, he falls into a coma. Upon awakening, the victim has no memory of the preceding events. It was suggested that one factor in the etiology of the condition is the imperfect control of emotion which was felt to be common among the Malayans (Van Loon, 1927).

Lata is a different type of condition. Here, a sudden fright or other strong emotion causes the Malay woman to enter a curious state in which she imitates immediately and precisely what is done before her or repeats what is said to her. All normal control of action appears to be swept away by the sudden emotion. The lata woman sometimes utters, or even shouts highly obscene words and may express wishes which normally would be repressed. One possible explanation is that in Malay society the female is likely to be shy, colorless, and unaggressive and to live largely within the confines of the home. She is not equipped to cope with sudden, unexpected situations of an anxiety-provoking nature, and the lata reaction is her response to the threat of danger. While the Malays are particularly susceptible, the condition has also been reported in Java, Siam, China, and the Philippines. However, the disturbance does not appear to affect Europeans residing in the tropics (Yap, 1952).

Comparative Studies

The validity of the cultural model has been questioned on the basis of field studies of mental disorder in various cultural groups. If abnormal behavior is behavior that is so defined by a particular culture, we would expect to find marked differences in patterns of maladaptive behavior from one culture to another. Field studies in various parts of the world do not support this assumption.

One such field study was made of mentally disturbed natives living in a large area surrounding a mental hospital in Africa. The investigation included detailed personal interviews with more than four hundred villagers and mental hospital patients. It was found that the types of psychiatric disorder were very much like those seen in America and Europe (Leighton et al., 1963).

Another indication of the common core of mental disorder in all cultures is the finding that the patterns of abnormal behavior in the Eskimo population are similar to those found in other parts of the world. Schizophrenia, depression, neurosis, behavior disorders, alcoholism, and other widely recognized conditions are the basic disturbances found among the Eskimos even though the style of life and the physical and psychological stresses are completely different from those found in most other societies (Atche-

son, 1972). Similarly, a study of illnesses of the spirit among the Serer tribe of Senegal, West Africa, indicated that the conditions corresponded in many ways to Western notions of mental illness (Beiser et al., 1973). In another part of the world, the Sarawak Transcultural Psychiatric Research Project investigated abnormal behavior in three distinct ethnic groups: Malay, Iban, and Chinese. It was found that all the major mental disorders are present to some degree in all three cultures (Schmidt, 1973).

It is of considerable interest that the prevalence of major mental disorders, and schizophrenia in particular, does not vary significantly from culture to culture. This finding is not unexpected in view of the mounting evidence that a genetic component is probably involved in schizophrenia as well as certain types of severe depression.

It seems clear that while cultural influences may determine the conditions under which abnormal behavior appears and may give the characteristic stamp to the clinical symptoms, such behavior involves more than a mere matter of definition. Since the maladaptive behavior observed in widely dissimilar cultures tends to be very much the same, it appears that while surface symptoms are frequently determined by the culture, the underlying causes of abnormal behavior must be sought in psychological and biological processes common to all cultures and societies.

The Chapter in Review

Various sociocultural models of abnormal behavior have been used to explain mental disorder. These models are not necessarily inconsistent with biological and psychological explanations, since sociocultural factors must exert their influence within biological limits and through psychological processes. The principal sociocultural explanations of abnormal behavior are the socialization model, the social disorganization model, and the cultural model.

1 Socialization Model

Early social influences, primarily within the family, shape much of the behavior of developing individuals. The attitudes and beliefs of parents, child-rearing practices, and the degree of integration of the family unit are considered as factors that may be responsible for the appearance of maladaptive patterns of behavior.

2 Social Disorganization Model

This approach to abnormal behavior assumes that such behavior can be caused by various forms of disturbance in the social environment beyond the immediate family. The disintegration of cultural groups, deterioration of urban areas, disruptive mobility and migration, and social and economic deprivation are among the more important types of social disorganization thought to be related to the development of abnormal behavior.

3 Cultural Model

This explanation of mental disorder emphasizes how behavior is defined by the cultural group. Behavior considered maladaptive for a particular group is labeled abnormal by that group. The difficulty with this model is that the major mental disorders appear to be very much the same even among the most widely differing cultures.

Recommended Readings

Socialization Model

Nathan, P. E., & Harris, S. L. *Psychopathology and society*. New York: McGraw-Hill, 1975.

Winslow, R. W. (Ed.) *The emergence of deviant minorities*: *Social problems and social change*. New Brunswick, N. J.: Transaction Books, 1972.

Social Disorganization Model

Andrews, E. E. *The emotionally disturbed family*. New York: Jason Aronson, 1974.

Grunebaum, H., et al. *Mentally ill mothers and their children*. Chicago: University of Chicago Press, 1975.

Steinmetz, S. K. & Straus, M. A. (Eds.) *Violence in the family*. New York: Dodd, Mead, 1974.

Swingmann, C. A., & Pfister-Ammende, M. *Uprooting and after . . .* New York: Springer, 1973.

Cultural Model

Crocetti, G. M., et al. *Contempory attitudes toward mental illness*. Pittsburgh: University of Pittsburgh Press, 1974.

Kiev, A. *Transcultural psychiatry*. New York: Free Press, 1973.

6
Life-Stress
Disorders

Objectives

To explain the meaning of psychosocial stress

To define life-stress units and show how they are used to measure stress

To describe some of the life-stress situations during the early years of life

To discuss the stress of college life, sex and marriage, earning a living, and illness and surgery as examples of the many everyday stresses of adult life

To emphasize some of the psychosocial stresses of the later years of life

To describe some of the unusual types of stress which people are sometimes forced to meet in order to survive

To explore the psychological effects of catastrophic stress related to disaster

Many personality disturbances are of a relatively minor, and often temporary, nature. Such conditions are frequently due more to *situational* stress—that is, the stress of circumstances of shorter or longer duration—than to imperfections of the personality. These forms of personality disorganization were neglected until the present century because of the more pressing problems of the major mental disorders. Historically, cases requiring hospitalization were the first to gain attention. The chief concerns were the severely disturbed, those having organic disease of the brain, and the mentally retarded.

It was not until the 1950s that the official classification system recognized conditions which grow out of stressful environmental situations. They were called *transient situational disorders* to emphasize the fact that they are temporary conditions more dependent upon the stress of life events than upon biological or psychological defects or processes within the person.

The prevalence of life-stress disorders is difficult to estimate. The most recent report on admissions to public mental hospitals indicates that about 3 percent have the diagnosis of transient situational disorder (NIMH, 1975). That this should be the case is not surprising, since the symptoms by definition are temporary and tend to disappear as soon as stress is relieved. People with stress disorders seldom get as far as the mental hospital. The condition, if treated at all, is more likely to be treated on an outpatient basis by one of the public or private mental health services.

The word *stress* has been used in psychology in at least two different ways. Some writers use the word to mean a state of psychological upset or disequilibrium. In this meaning, stress is a characteristic of the organism. More properly, stress should be regarded as a class of stimuli which threaten a person in some manner and produce disturbances in behavior and inner experience. The stress is not the disturbance itself but the strain and pressure leading to the disturbance. Stress ordinarily is inferred as a result of a person's disorganized behavior.

Stressful situations may be organic, psychological, or cultural. At the organic level, injury and other physical stresses result in an increase in the blood level of pituitary and adrenal hormones. Stress situations of a psychological nature also raise the level of these hormones in the blood. Similarly, social pressures which have a psychological impact on a person are reflected in one or another form of disturbance of behavior of experience.

Everyone is faced many times each day with minor stress situations. The alarm fails to go off in the morning, there is not enough hot water, the toast is cold, traffic is heavy, and the student is late getting to the campus for class. At noon the cafeteria is crowded, and it is necessary to stand in line. A professor criticizes the student's work during class. A low grade is received on an examination. That evening, the blind date turns out to be a complete disappointment. Such situations are common to everyone and are an unwelcome part of everyday existence. At the time, one is annoyed and irritated and may become angry. But the incident is soon forgotten.

In addition to the minor stress situations faced each day, most people now and then are faced with stress situations of a much more serious nature. A severe illness of a member of the family, a dangerous surgical operation, a poor record on an important job, bills that pile up beyond one's income, a physical handicap, marital discord, and similar situations frequently are threats which

114

cannot be ignored or shrugged off. Such stress situations are often capable of bringing about behavior disorders and personality disturbances which may last for prolonged periods.

Whether or not a given situation is a stressful one depends ultimately on one's behavior. Some people are able to handle the most threatening situations without too much difficulty. Others break down under relatively mild stress. A stress situation for one person may not be a stress situation for another. There are wide individual differences in ability to handle threatening stimuli. The importance of how an event is perceived in terms of its stress is seen in the fact that depressed patients view a wide variety of events as involving significantly greater stress than do nondepressed subjects (Schless et al., 1974).

However stress is perceived, it is reflected in changes in the nervous and endocrine systems. These changes, which are typical of those associated with anxiety, make possible the use of the polygraph, or "lie detector," in the examination of persons suspected of having committed a crime. The polygraph is an instrument that records the suspect's heart rate, blood pressure, breathing pattern, and changes in electrical conductivity of the skin during the interrogation. It is assumed that when a person is deliberately lying about something as critical as having been involved in a crime, the situation is so stressful and threatening that there will be physiological changes characteristic of anxiety.

Most people, including professional criminals, are under more than ordinary stress when they are lying to the police. The heart beats faster, blood pressure goes up, breathing becomes more rapid and irregular, and the skin becomes moist as a result of perspiration. These various changes are recorded

by the polygraph; they are the physical reactions to the stressful event.

In the case of transient situational stress disorders, the psychological and physiological reactions to stress are temporary. The effects disappear when the stress is reduced or eliminated. However, in later chapters we will see that the effects of unrelieved stress can be long-lasting and seriously damaging.

Meaning of Psychosocial Stress

The term *psychosocial stress* is used to refer to changes in life events which have an impact on physical and mental health. It has been a matter of common observation that serious changes in one's life may result in physical illness or emotional disturbance. Flunking out of school, losing a job, financial reverses, being divorced, the death of someone close, and dozens of similar changes in life events can be upsetting and disorganizing.

It was not until the late 1960s that psychosocial stress was studied seriously. Through the use of a psychological scaling method, various changes in life events were given weightings as to their relative degree of stress. The result was the Social Readjustment Rating Scale (SRRS), which seeks to measure psychosocial stress in terms of *life change units* (Holmes & Rahe, 1967). The scale is made up of forty-three life changes ranked from the most stressful to the least stressful (see Table 6.1).

Studies have indicated that changes in life events measured by the SRRS, and modified versions of the scale, are related to both physical illness and psychological disturbance at a later date. The greater the number

Table 6.1   The Social Readjustment Rating Scale for the measurement of psychosocial stress. The mean values represent life-change units in terms of the relative stressfulness of each life event.

Rank	Life Event	Mean Value
1	Death of spouse	100
2	Divorce	73
3	Marital separation	65
4	Jail term	63
5	Death of close family member	63
6	Personal injury or illness	53
7	Marriage	50
8	Fired at work	47
9	Marital reconciliation	45
10	Retirement	45
11	Change in health of family member	44
12	Pregnancy	40
13	Sex difficulties	39
14	Gain of new family member	39
15	Business readjustment	39
16	Change in financial state	38
17	Death of close friend	37
18	Change to different line of work	36
19	Change in number of arguments with spouse	35
20	Mortgage over $10,000	31
21	Foreclosure of mortgage or loan	30
22	Change in responsibilities at work	29
23	Son or daughter leaving home	29
24	Trouble with in-laws	29
25	Outstanding personal achievement	28
26	Wife begin or stop work	26
27	Begin or end school	26
28	Change in living conditions	25
29	Revision of personal habits	24
30	Trouble with boss	23
31	Change in work hours or conditions	20
32	Change in residence	20
33	Change in schools	20
34	Change in recreation	19
35	Change in church activities	19
36	Change in social activities	18
37	Mortgage or loan less than $10,000	17
38	Change in sleeping habits	16
39	Change in number of family get-togethers	15
40	Change in eating habits	15
41	Vacation	13
42	Christmas	12
43	Minor violations of the law	11

(Reprinted with permission of T. H. Holmes & R. H. Rahe)

of life-change units in a given period, the greater the risk of subsequent physical or emotional symptoms.

In the area of psychological disturbances, one study found that the SRRS scores of a group of psychiatric patients with the diagnosis of depression were significantly greater than the scores of a control group of medical patients and members of the hospital staff (Thomson & Hendrie, 1972). Another study, using a modified version of the SRRS, investigated buildup of life-stress events in the six-month period prior to onset of depression in psychiatric hospital patients. It was found that there was a higher buildup of life-stress events in patients than in a matched control group (Paykel et al., 1971). A third study reported that while the nature of the symptoms in neurotic patients was not related to recent life-stress events as measured by a modified version of the SRRS, the intensity of symptoms was significantly related to such events (Uhlenhuth & Paykel, 1973).

While the life-stress scales have been used effectively in predicting a wide range of physical illness and mental disturbance, a question that has intrigued investigators, and which remains unanswered, is why most people are able to weather the most severe adverse circumstances without showing significant psychological damage while some people experience emotional disturbance under the most moderately stressful conditions. It is likely that there is no simple explanation for this phenomenon. A combination of biological and sociopsychological factors are probably involved.

It is known, for example, that some people have constitutionally more sensitive neuroendocrine systems which allow greater reactivity. It is possible that more stable neuroendocrine systems show a greater resistance to stressful events. It is also the case that people learn to perceive events as stressful or nonstressful. When previous experience has conditioned a person to regard life events as threatening, he or she is more likely to show an emotional reaction than the person who has been conditioned to regard such events in a more philosophical and less personal way. A combination of a highly reactive neuroendocrine system and a threat-conditioned attitude toward life events appears to be related to the development of life-stress disorders.

Stress of Everyday Life

While each period of life has its special stresses which must be handled, other forms of stress affect people of all ages. Extremes of temperature and humidity, physical pain, hunger and thirst, and similar physical conditions are stressful at any age.

Sometimes a condition of the physical environment can be stressful without one's being aware of what is happening. A good example is noise. Most people find noise an unpleasant and disturbing condition. But it has been only recently that we have learned how truly stressful noise can be. Clanking garbage cans, the whine and roar of jet planes, and the assorted sounds of trucks, sirens, pneumatic drills, arguing neighbors, and rock-and-roll bands have a damaging effect on physical and mental health.

Noise from planes using approach and takeoff paths over populated urban areas near London was found to be related to psychological disturbances. The stress of the excessive noise was "the last straw" for some people (Herridge, 1972). Noise can be the stressor that triggers the appearance of symptoms of abnormality.

Another unusual kind of stress which has

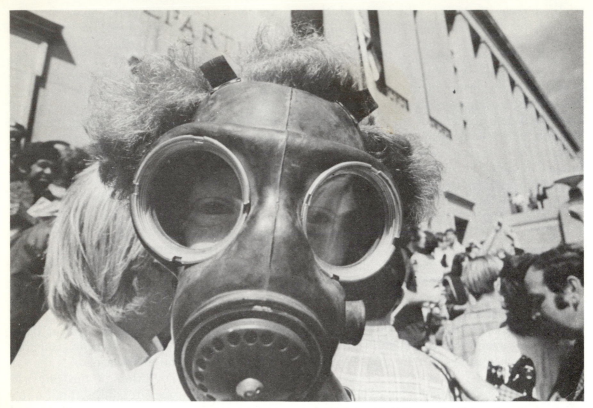

Figure 6.1 The stress of city life is very real. Crowds, noise, dilapidated buildings, advertising signs in poor taste, dirt and drabness, and polluted air are overwhelming in the central areas of most cities. The young man wearing the gas mask symbolizes the physical and aesthetic pollution of most large cities.

grown out of the jet age has been called "time-zone stress." This reaction is due to time-zone changes accompanying long-distance air travel. The "biological clock" which regulates sleep patterns and other bodily rhythms is upset. Stress of this type has been thought to cause military officers to give incorrect orders, politicians to make wrong decisions, and business executives to be confused in their thinking. The problems of time-zone stress are so important and intriguing that a large corporation organized *Project Pegasus*, an in-depth study of physiological and psychological performance of

volunteers on flights from London to San Francisco.

Even the stress of concern over the passage of time can be physically and psychologically damaging. A study showed that six times as many heart-attack deaths occurred among men who had an excessive sense of time urgency than among men without this characteristic (*Roche Reports*, 1968).

While physical stress influences human behavior, psychological stress is even more important. It is not uncommon for people to feel depressed at holidays and other occasions which have special meaning. Most psychologists and psychiatrists are familiar with the increase in complaints of depression as the Christmas holidays approach. Other people become depressed on their birthdays, on wedding anniversaries, and even at changes of season. These times trigger fantasies of lost happiness of the past, of the inexorable passage of time, of aging and loss of personal vigor and attractiveness, and of the deep-lying knowledge that life is passing and one's day must end.

Social factors are also responsible for generating stress. One such factor is the crowded condition of urban living. Metropolitan areas already contain most of the people in the United States, and the trend toward urbanization is accelerating. By the year 2000 the population of the United States is expected to reach 300 million, of which 240 million will live in urban areas. Since our cities were not designed or built for the large numbers of people and institutions that crowd them, the result has been poverty, unemployment, substandard housing, lack of recreational facilities, and other social ills characteristic of metropolitan centers.

The stress of the urban environment in which we live is very real. Cities are overcrowded, much of the air we breathe is polluted, and the source of our supply of food and water is constantly in danger. Suburban developments are being built with little regard for the natural surroundings. It has been shown that faulty urban design can lead to mental health problems among children and disadvantaged adults who are residents of such areas (Chicago Center for Policy Study, 1971).

A study of American and British housing projects has suggested that psychological stress can be generated by a variety of public housing problems. Mothers with young children are often unable to leave the housing complex for recreation or shopping. The lack

Figure 6.2 Life in the suburbs can be as stressful as life in a city slum. The endless rows of houses, without character or distinctiveness, can be emotionally depressing to families who must live there with little hope of escaping.

of playgrounds, day-care centers, and youth recreational facilities can cause stress for both parents and children. Elderly residents of such projects are frequently isolated and neglected. Their physical and psychological deterioration is thus hastened. Even the design of a project can lead to unhappiness and depression. While housing experts are not in agreement as to the degree of the direct relationship between certain types of housing and psychological stress, such a relationship apparently exists.

The very fact that public housing is provided may intensify stress, because the use of such housing places a negative label on the resident. This negative label, in turn, affects relations with employers and others in the community. The self-image of the resident of a public housing project may be damaged, and he or she may feel powerless and frustrated. "Trapped by his poverty in this low rent housing, he may regard it psychologically more as a *compound* or *concentration camp* than a home" (Huttman, 1971).

Recognizing the mental health problems created by urban population, the National Institute of Mental Health established a Center for Studies of Metropolitan and Regional Mental Health Problems. The center deals with every aspect of mental health and has a comprehensive program for research, service, training, planning, and demonstration.

Most of the stresses of life are faced and weathered without serious effects on the personality. However, when the stress is unexpected, severe, or prolonged and the one affected is not able to cope with it, a personality adjustment reaction may result.

Life Stress: The Early Years

The first important stress situation in life is birth. The new individual's essentially para-sitic existence within the body of the mother, where the fetus is fed and cushioned against shock, is changed radically during the birth process. When the amniotic sac bursts and the fetal head is subjected to the uterine contractions and the pressures of the pelvic canal, the physical stress is severe. Similarly, there is significant stress at the physiological and biochemical levels. While the evidence is contradictory, the possibility remains that the fetal life in the uterus of the mother and the experience of birth may have implications for the person's later psychological and emotional life. The stress of birth cannot be discounted completely as a source of later personality disturbance.

When the birth is premature, the risk of physical illness and psychological disturbance later in life is increased. Infants born prematurely are more likely to show signs of neurological disorder, have a greater probability of showing behavior disorders in childhood and adolescence, and are likely to perform less well on intelligence tests than infants born at full term. However, premature infants born to middle-class parents do not face the same high risk as premature infants born to lower-class families (Leiderman, 1974). The physical and psychological retardation for a group of middle-class youngsters born prematurely is less severe than for infants raised in lower-class families because the more advantaged infants usually receive better medical care at birth and during the early weeks of life.

Other stress situations during infancy are related for the most part to adjusting to an unfamiliar environment, and to the necessity to conform to the demands of the parents. The natural impulses of infants must be curbed. They must learn to eat according to schedule, they must be weaned from breast or bottle, and they must be toilet-trained. These adaptations do not occur automatically or easily. Even though infants cannot verbalize it, they are the victims of considerable stress. The tensions associated with this stress are ordinarily relieved with the help of the parents. But in some cases the stress persists to the point where lasting emotional damage occurs. In such cases the pattern of one's entire life can be affected adversely.

Most adjustment reactions of infancy, however, are a result of the infant's interaction with significant persons in the environment, or a response to the lack of such persons. The symptoms may include apathy or excitability, feeding and sleeping difficulties, breath holding, head banging, and similar disturbances. Adjustment reactions centering on the feeding problem are particularly common among infants. At least one-fourth of all infants and young children present feeding difficulties of one kind or another. These feeding problems include refusal of food, overeating, swallowing air, bringing up food and spitting it out or re-swallowing it, and habitually eating substances which have no nutritional value.

A major adjustment problem of infancy is concerned with maternal rejection in the form of lack of mothering. Infants need close bodily contact with the mother. When this contact is lacking, behavior disturbances may put in their appearance. Many hospital wards now require that an infant be not only washed and fed but also picked up, petted, carried about, and otherwise mothered. There is much clinical evidence to show that the rejected infant, as well as the overprotected child, develops more than his or her share of undesirable personality characteristics (Chess & Thomas, 1968).

Stress of Childhood

The psychosocial stresses of childhood take many forms and are of varying degrees of severity. The source of stress may be in the family, school, or relationships with other

Adjustment Reaction of Infancy

Corrine M. is an 18-month-old infant who first came to the attention of the pediatric clinic of juvenile court in connection with a paternity action. The unwed teenage mother had little interest in the child, who was small, thin, and poorly developed. The baby slept much of the time, and was irritable when disturbed. She never smiled, showed little interest in playing, and did not respond to other people. Feeding had been a continuing problem, and it was not unusual for her to regurgitate part of her food.

When seen at the clinic, the child was listless and unresponsive. She appeared frightened when people approached her, and spent much of her time whimpering and crying. The young mother reported that the child behaved in a similar way at home. Because of the lack of responsiveness, it was suspected that the child was mentally retarded. However, a psychological examination revelead that this was not the case. A social service report on the home situation verified the extent to which the child had been neglected, and a foster home placement was recommended.

In her new home, the child's behavior remained unchanged for the first few days. However, the foster parents showed great interest in the child and gave her continuing attention and affection. After several days, the child began to be more interested in her surroundings. She became less of a feeding problem, and by the end of a week began to smile. She played with blocks, a toy doll, and a rattle. For the next two weeks the child continued to improve in her behavior and responsiveness. She smiled more often and more quickly, clapped her hands, and sought the attention of adults. She began to feed herself, and learned to stand and to walk while holding onto her crib or various pieces of furniture.

The dramatic change in the behavior of this child was due to her removal from a deprived and neglectful environment to a stimulating environment in which there was an abundance of affection. Her lack of responsiveness at home, and her seeming retardation and emotional disturbance, were attempts to adjust to an unfavorable home environment.

children. Family stresses include lack of affection or too much affection from the parents, overly strict discipline or laxity in discipline, physical illness or handicap, and changes in family status. The stresses of

BOND₂   inane

Figure 6.3 This shy, lonely child is showing a situational adjustment reaction. Unless steps are taken to increase her social skills and her confidence in herself, she runs the risk of a lifelong pattern of inferiority and frustration.

school include the hostile attitude of teachers, lack of academic or athletic success, frequent changes of schools, examination stress, and similar difficulties.

An important form of stress during childhood is related to separation. It begins early in life when the child is left alone by the parent. There are other separation stresses as the child grows older. One is the separation from home when the child first begins to attend school. Another separation stress takes place when the youngster goes away to camp or boarding school. It is possible that the stress of separation is similar to "affectional bonding" in lower animals. These strong bonds between parents and offspring are found in many species of birds and mammals. It has been suggested that the violation of this bonding is the cause of the stress of separation in children and adults (Bowlby, 1969).

More critical separations are related to the divorce of parents and to the death of family members. The problem of divorce is a very real one when it is realized that the United States has the highest divorce rate among Western nations and that the rate is increasing. Almost 70 percent of divorcing couples have minor children, and there are nearly 9 million children of divorce. Since about 85 percent of divorced people eventually remarry, and 40 percent are divorced again, a large percentage of children have endured the stress of divorce more than once. Many children have lived through such stress more than twice, since 80 percent of third marriages also end in divorce (Anthony, 1974).

The loss of a parent can also come about as a result of abandonment or death. The impact is greatest when the loss is sudden and unexpected and when there has been love for the lost parent. One youngster, who was abandoned by his parents and became a ward of the Juvenile Court, wrote the following lines:

A.L.O.N.E.

No one cares. No one wants me. I'm alone in this world. I have But few possessions and some freinds that are few. No one ecept God and some freinds care about me. They just don't care if I die, for I'm just a no one to them. If any one cares Then its few that I know. There are some freinds That at least care for me. But I will not tell. Oh, I'm left all alone, very few to love and to tell my troubles to and thats how I feel.

BATTERX ~   خسروع

METICULOSITY =
DISADVANTAGE =
            قداول , دقت فراوان
            . زیان ~

LIFE STRESS: THE EARLY YEARS   **123**

NEAT =
         تمیز, مرتب, ورزیده

The Case of Victor:
A Young Victim of Stress

Victor H. is a 10-year-old boy who has had twenty-three contacts with the police for various delinquencies. Six of these contacts resulted in referrals to a juvenile court. The boy's offenses began two years previously when he was caught stealing soft drinks and beer from the basement of a cafe in his neighborhood. Since that time he has been charged with fire setting, malicious destruction of property, incorrigibility, theft, and assault and battery. On one occasion he set fire to a church, and later to an automobile which was entirely demolished by the fire. At another time he entered a locked building and broke most of the windows. Then he ran the elevator up and down until he was caught. He was suspended from school when he lost his temper, jumped out of a ground-floor window, and ran home. He has been involved in fights, shoplifting, stealing money from the teachers' purses, smearing tar on windows, dumping paint on stairways, stealing a peanut machine, and urinating in drinking fountains. In spite of his many delinquencies, the boy is cooperative at home, helps with the housework, and gets along well with his mother and brothers and sisters. He attends school and church regularly, although he was expelled from two schools because of his problem behavior.

The conditions under which the family lives are most unsatisfactory. The three-room apartment is in a deteriorated area noted for its high rate of juvenile delinquency. The mother, who is dovorced from her first husband and separated from her second, is a neat-appearing, narcissistic, and meticulously dressed woman. She works irregularly as a waitress, with the family supported by unemployment compensation and a small alimony from her divorced husband. The father is an unstable man who has been married six times. The mother is openly hostile toward her children and quite frankly says that she did not want any of them. The boy's brother and two sisters were born illegitimately.

The impression is that of a youngster whose numerous delinquencies grew out of a combination of stress situations including a broken home, an overtly rejecting mother, substandard living conditions, and a high-delinquency neighborhood.

While all children are subjected to a wide range of stresses in their daily lives, socially and economically disadvantaged children frequently are exposed to stresses which more fortunate children need not face. The black American child is at greater risk of psychological difficulty than most other children because of the added burden of race prejudice. And in spite of the various mechanisms blacks have developed to reduce social, psychological, and educational difficulties for their children, the prevalence of psychological disturbance in the black community is higher than it is in any other ethnic group. One possible explanation is that black children are more likely to continue to show symptoms as a result of differences in treatment facilities, and differences in attitudes of parents toward the use of available services.

It must be recognized, however, that in spite of adverse genetic and sociocultural conditions, the majority of children manage to develop normally and to make a satisfactory adjustment. Relatively little study has been directed toward the discovery of those factors which permit positive development in the face of even the most severe disadvantages (Garmezy & Neuchterlein, 1972).

Stress of Adolescence

There is a popular belief that adolescence is the most stressful period of life. While this belief is an unjustified generalization, it is true that adolescence is filled with stress situations, some of which are extensions of the stresses of childhood, while others are anticipations of the stresses of adult life. In addition, the period of adolescence, like every other period of life, has its more or less unique patterns of stress.

The most distinctive stress-provoking situation of adolescence is parental domination in the face of a growing need for independence. Many of the adjustment reactions of adolescence are expressions of the effort to achieve some degree of freedom from the parents. In some cases there are overtly expressed emancipatory strivings, while in other cases these strivings take more subtle and indirect avenues of expression. In either case, there is likely to be an unsuccessful attempt to control impulses and emotional tendencies. The most common symptoms of adjustment difficulties during the adolescent period are truancy, vandalism, running away, stealing, and sexual misbehavior.

Although the adjustment reactions of adolescence take a variety of forms, the boys and girls with this form of personality disturbance are essentially normal. The personality difficulty, expressed as a form of acting out, is precipitated by an unsatisfactory environment. Under more favorable circumstances, these adolescents might very well make a satisfactory adjustment.

The importance of the stresses of childhood and adolescence is seen in the fact that more than 12 percent of all children between the ages of 5 and 19 have mental health problems severe enough to require some kind of professional help. This figure means that at least 6 million children require treatment for psychological disturbance each year. Among the poor, there is a much higher incidence of mental health problems. Here, as many as 30 percent of children and adolescents show psychological disturbances (Berlin, 1975). The impact of stress on the adolescent is also reflected in the finding that suicide in the United States is the third leading cause of death in the 15- to 19-year age group (Ross, 1970).

Adjustment Reaction of Adolescence

Ginger M. is a 15-year-old girl who was seen at a psychiatric clinic following a series of adjustment difficulties. After a number of years of placement in various institutions, she had been sent to a foster home. While there she was the victim of an attempted rape, and also was "going steady" with a boy with a record of delinquency. The foster parents objected to this relationship, and as a result of the ensuing difficulties the girl was referred to the Juvenile Court. During her examination, Ginger spoke freely about her problems, volunteered information spontaneously, and revealed a degree of insight into her troubled situation. She appeared to be of average intellectual ability, showed a normal range of emotional responsiveness, and her thinking was clear and logical. She spoke coherently and showed no evidence of organic disorder or of more serious personality disturbance.

The stress situation in this adjustment reaction was the unstable family background. The father, who apparently was an emotionally unstable man, deserted the mother after several months of marriage. The mother, who recently was sentenced to a federal penitentiary on a charge of forging checks, had an illegitimate child when she was 15. She married the patient's father after a three-day courtship. Following her husband's desertion, she lived for several years in a common-law relationship with one man until his death. From that time she lived promiscuously with a number of other men, and has had a long history of excessive drinking.

As a result of the family situation, Ginger has been placed at various times in institutions, foster homes, and with relatives. In each case the girl has been unhappy about the placement. She hopes each time she will find what she is seeking, but never does. In a more normal home situation and social environment it is entirely possible that Ginger could have made a completely satisfactory adjustment.

Life Stress: The Adult Years

The adjustment reactions of adult life extend from the problems of adolescence to those of old age. Because of the long span of adult years, the stress situations are of a great

Student Stress:
Some Critical Concerns
of College Students

The college students who made the following remarks were not problem cases. They were typical
young men and women. Their comments reflect their
concern with themselves, their relations with others,
and their ability to meet what the future holds for
them.

I have no really tangible proof of my insufficiency,
but my lack of confidence becomes very depressing at times. I fear that my ability is not up to the
norms of the group.

I am concerned about being made to appear ridic-
ulous. I usually attempt to conduct my affairs so as
to arouse the greatest respect from my friends.

Sometimes I wonder whether life is worth the
struggle. I am depressed so often that I doubt very
much whether I will ever find happiness.

Sex scares me. I become uncomfortable and embarrassed whenever the subject is mentioned. I
worry about it because I am afraid I am not normal.

My biggest problem is my temper. The slightest
incident gets me so steamed up that I feel like
blowing my top. Sometimes I do, and then I feel
foolish.

The trouble with me is that I don't have any back-
bone. People walk all over me, and the worst part
of it is that I seem to get some peculiar kind of
pleasure out of it.

I am engaged, but I still place my father before and
above my fiance. The transition after I am married
will be hard for me.

I am a very moody person, and am particularly
susceptible to depressions. Probably I am too
conscientious and aware of what people think of
me and say to me.

I feel that people are watching me because of my
large size. I am always trying to dress in a way so
that my clothes rather than myself catch the eye of
others.

I lack a real sense of affection for my mother. I feel
that I really should love and care for her because
of all she has done for me in the past twenty years,
but it seems that her demanding attitude and the
fact that everything has to be done "exactly right
and exactly when she wants" has destroyed my
love for her.

It bothers me very much that I cannot always talk
easily with people and cannot always explain myself well or express myself. I feel I am bottled up. I
have many things inside that need airing, but I
cannot bring them to the surface. I do not have
much selfconfidence.

variety. However, most of the stress situations of adult life center on marriage and the
family; the problems of earning a living; sex,
pregnancy, and the menopause; and physical health. While it is true that many stress
situations of a personal nature do not fall
into these groups, the problem areas suggested here will serve to illustrate the major
forms of stress leading to adult adjustment
reactions.

Stress of College Life

College students, in the transition period
between late adolescence and early adulthood, have many special stresses with which
they must contend. Exams, grades, sex, and
pressure from parents create high levels of
stress. More students drop out of college for
emotional reasons than because of low
grades.

The typical problems of college students
involve guilt and confusion over the handling of sexual impulses, concern about the
expression of hostile and aggressive feelings,
and worry about personal inadequacy and
lack of status. Many additional problems,
more or less peculiar to the college student,
contribute to the forces which interfere with
personality adjustment.

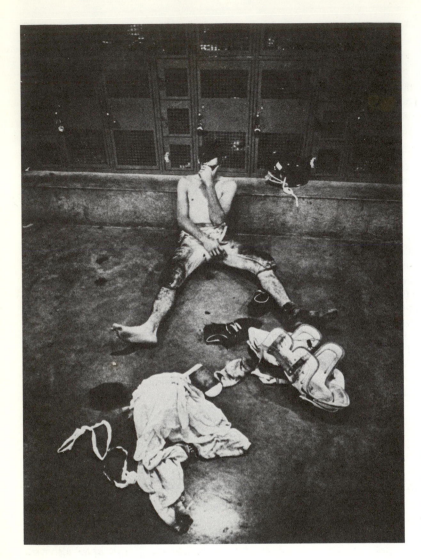

Figure 6.4 Defeat is a form of situational stress experienced by most people during some period of life. This emotionally drained, depressed, and exhausted athlete is showing a transient stress reaction. He will quickly recover when the impact of defeat has passed.

Of the more than one hundred thousand college students who threaten suicide each year, about nine thousand actually attempt to kill themselves, and more than a thousand are successful in taking their lives. Excluding auto accidents, suicide is the leading cause of death among college students (NIMH, 1969).

A study at the University of California at Berkeley found that college students who killed themselves were generally above average in scholastic attainment. Such students doubted their own adequacy, were dissatisfied with their grades, and were despondent over their general academic aptitude. They set unreasonably high standards for themselves and became depressed when they failed to meet these standards.

One student said, "I felt I was different. I just plain didn't know how to get along with other people, as if there was something missing in me. I hated my parents, and I hated myself because of them. They convinced me that I was no good, that whatever I did was nothing compared to what my two brothers did before me. I just couldn't please myself. My parents hounded me about my grades to the point where I couldn't study. They kept telling me 'You'll never make it.' By the end of the fall, I was so depressed. Failure was the worst thing in the world that could happen. I remember going home for Thanksgiving vacation, and the leaves had fallen. It was wet and cold. My midterm exams had been dreadful. I was depressed worse than ever. Then it happened. Then came 30 sleeping pills, a bottle of aspirin and a razor blade" (Sheperd, 1967).

Stress of Sex and Marriage

Some of the most important stress situations of adult life involve courtship, marriage, and the family. Every young adult who has been engaged, married, or a parent knows the many difficult situations which must be faced. The type of family living prescribed by our culture lends itself to a relatively high degree of stress and tension. The soaring divorce rate is merely one of the indications of the stress of modern family life. Even the most favorable marriages and family relationships must withstand periodic stresses of the greatest severity. Closely related to the problems of marriage and the family are the stresses of sex, pregnancy, and the menopause. In Chapter 4, we saw that the frustrations and conflicts in the area of sexuality constitute an important source of stress. Such stress may occur at any time through-

out the range of adult life and often results in temporary adjustment problems of a more or less serious nature.

The stress of premarital sex, although never very great for most men, was until recently the source of serious emotional problems for many women. Today such behavior is much less stressful for women because of rapidly changing attitudes, the "pill", and increasing permissiveness in sexual matters. These same factors have reduced the stress of extramarital sex. However, large numbers of men and women continue to be disturbed by those of their sexual activities which they perceive as being illicit and inappropriate.

Pregnancy and childbirth can also be stressful events. The stress is likely to be greater when an unmarried woman is faced with an unwanted pregnancy. However, the birth of a child can contribute to psychological disturbance even under the most favorable circumstances. The fact that mental illness often occurs during the months following childbirth has been observed for a very long time. In fact, the term *postpartum psychosis* was used for a number of years as one of the diagnostic categories. This relationship between childbirth and personality disturbance continues to be recognized (Cohler et al., 1974). However, while some women show psychological symptoms in the weeks and months following the birth of a child, a substantial number of these also showed signs of psychological instability before pregnancy and childbirth (Suh, 1969).

Another form of stress unique to adult women is connected with abortion. In 1973 the United States Supreme Court removed the legal barriers to abortions requested by adult women during the first trimester of pregnancy. This decision created new interest in postabortion emotional problems. While emotional reactions to abortion have

CONDONE ~ درگزشتن۔ چشم پوشی

been reported, such reactions are not common today. When psychological disturbances do occur, they are most frequently found in women who feel ambivalent about abortion. Problems may also arise in cases where motivation for continuing or terminating pregnancy is not strong and where there is a prior history of psychiatric illness or suicidal behavior (Marmer, Pasnau, & Cushner, 1974).

One study found that the emotional consequences of abortion may be both positive and negative. Two sets of factors are at work. One comes from the social environment and the other from the woman's attitudes toward her pregnancy and its termination. Abortion is more stressful in social groups where there is strong disapproval of abortion. If the social group views abortion as deviant or unacceptable, the woman is more likely to perceive the experience as stressful. In such cases, shame and guilt are not uncommon. Similarly, if the pregnancy filled the woman's personal needs, she is more likely to feel a sense of loss and may have strong feelings of regret, anger, and depression. Where the pregnancy was unwanted, the psychological consequences are not likely to be damaging (Adler, 1975). As in most life events, the degree to which an experience is perceived as being stressful determines the nature and severity of the psychological consequences.

Spontaneous abortion, which is unplanned and unexpected, can be a most stressful experience. In a large number of these cases, there is some degree of emotional disturbance. Feelings of guilt, disappointment, inadequacy, and inferiority are observed frequently. In some cases, serious depression occurs.

Stress of Making a Living

The problem of making a living in our culture is also an important source of stress during the adult years. We live in a highly competitive society in which there is a premium on economic achievement and financial security. While many people deplore the materialistic philosophy and regard it as undesirable and unimportant, the fact remains that a substantial proportion of the population struggles endlessly to maintain and to improve its financial position. Even those who scoff at the importance of money seldom turn down an economic opportunity.

Desirable or undesirable, the economic struggle is a central problem in the lives of most men and an increasing number of women. The stresses in connection with maintaining an adequate income are such that they frequently precipitate adjustment reactions.

Stress is frequently a factor in the depression, excessive drinking, and physical symptoms seen in successful business executives, professional people, and political figures (Kiev, 1974). Often the symptoms are not recognized as early signs of more serious psychological problems because it is so easy to explain such behavior in terms of the heavy burden of responsibility the person is carrying.

The excessive drinking of Wilbur Mills, one of the most powerful congressmen in Washington, was condoned and excused by his friends and colleagues until he became involved in a public scandal with a striptease dancer. It then became necessary for Representative Mills to face up to the fact that his excessive drinking had reached pathological dimensions, and he allowed himself to be hospitalized for treatment. Another example of executive stress was seen in the resignation of a Cabinet member for treatment of depression less than two weeks after his appointment to his high post. It has also been observed that there is a considerable amount of emotional disturbance among physicians. The most common signs

Figure 6.5 Being without a job and wanting to work is a form of stress shared by many men and women in our country. The combination of enforced idleness and frustration can lead to depression and other forms of maladaptive behavior in some people.

of stress in this group are alcoholism, drug dependence, and suicide (Pearson, 1971).

Another type of stress faced by many adults, especially in times of economic recession, is unemployment and the need to find work again. One study compared a number of men whose jobs were abolished, in plants about to be closed, with a control group of men from companies where there was no threat of job loss. The terminees were visited at home shortly after the plants closed and six months, twelve months, and twenty-four months later. A standardized set

of physiological, psychological, social, and economic data were collected at each contact by public health nurses. The controls were visited at similar intervals, but few were followed beyond twelve months. The important finding was that there were biochemical changes related to the course of unemployment. The changes were more severe in those with least social support and most extended unemployment. The biochemical changes were least pronounced in those with strong psychological defenses, social support, and more immediate prospects of future employment (Cobb, 1974).

Adult Adjustment Reaction

George C. is a 57-year-old married man who was admitted to a psychiatric hospital following a series of marital crises. He has worked for many years as a barber in a downtown hotel. The patient has been married twice, and was divorced from his first wife fifteen years ago. One of his difficulties has been that a son from the first marriage has become a self-styled minister, and has been telling his father that he is living in sin because of the divorce. The son has been advising the father to break up his present home, and return to his first wife.

A second marital problem concerns the hostility of the present wife toward the patient. She is a domineering and aggressive woman who quite frankly admits that she nags her husband constantly. She has forbidden him to correct or discipline their young son, and has denied her husband any responsibility in the child's upbringing. The marital difficulties have been aggravated as a result of a marked decrease in the patient's sexual desires.

As a result of the severe marital problems, the patient became extremely tense and was unable to eat. He was placed on tranquilizing drugs by his family physician, but the constant pressure put on him by his grown son and the increasing hostility of his wife became too much for him. He was admitted to the psychiatric hospital for more intensive treatment.

When seen at the hospital, the patient accepted the initial interview with considerable appreciation. He was polite and cooperative, although he showed some anxiety over his hospitalization. He was completely oriented, his thinking was logical, and his speech was relevant and coherent. Emotional reactions were within normal limits. He said that he hoped his stay in the hospital would result in a better marital adjustment and greater happiness.

Stress of Illness and Surgery

Another stress situation which increases in importance during adult life is the threat of ill health. Early in the adult years, there are the more temporary stresses of acute illness and the occasional necessity for surgical operations. Later, there is the growing possibility of illness of a more chronic nature.

In the case of surgery, the site of an operation plays an important part in the degree of stress and the severity of psychological disturbance. Eye operations, with the threat of blindness and the necessity for postoperative bandaging—and the consequent darkness and isolation—are particularly anxiety-provoking. Such operations sometimes lead to temporary panic reactions. The symptoms ordinarily disappear within a day or two following the removal of the bandages.

Several distinct types of psychological disturbance have been observed following open-heart surgery. One reaction is a state of delirium marked by clouded consciousness, disorientation, confusion, and misinterpretation of the environment. The second reaction is a paranoid one in which there are hallucinations and delusions of persecution. A third reaction to open-heart surgery is a mood disorder in which there is anxiety, depression, and irritability (Braceland, 1974).

Gynecological operations are also capable of producing a very considerable psychological impact. The surgical removal of the uterus is a particularly stressful situation because the uterus is regarded as one of the most important symbols of femininity.

It has been found that women undergoing therapeutic hysterectomies may later show signs of depression, neurosis, psychosis, and impaired feminine self-concept (Wolf, 1970). However, patients who have chosen hysterectomy as a means of sterilization ordinarily do not show adverse psychological symptoms (Hampton & Tarnasky, 1974).

Many factors are involved in the stress associated with surgical operations. The fear of mutilation and death, the symbolic significance of a particular body organ, the fear of emotional and financial dependency, and similar factors may lead to temporary psychological disorganization.

Any type of physical disability increases the risk of psychological disturbance. While a substantial number of handicapped people make adequate and even superior social and psychological adjustments, the incidence of psychological disturbance among the handicapped is higher than that found in the population at large.

Some people manage to go through an entire life with little or no physical disease or handicap. Most people, however, are faced with varying degrees of physical disability at one time or another. It is apparent that the greater the degree of physical disability, the more disturbing it is to the personality. People with chronic and discomforting physical disorders are generally not so likely to resist the inroads of aging as are those who enjoy better health.

Life Stress: The Later Years

The later years of life have their full share of stressful situations. The elderly person faces characteristic problems related to retirement from work, loss of family members and friends, financial insecurity, dependency upon relatives, chronic illness, and the prospect of death. These are but some of the stresses which occur frequently during the later years. The way in which the elderly person meets these stresses may mean the difference between mental health and an old age of bitterness, disappointment, and unhappiness.

Some 22 million Americans today are more than 65 years old. By the year 2000, it is estimated that 28 million will be over 65. Though medical science has increased the prospects of longevity, the complexities of modern life pose problems of adaptation, especially for older persons, far greater than those of earlier times and simpler societies.

Besides the mental health problems they share with other age groups, older people are vulnerable to specific difficulties associated with the aging process. Some of the mental impairment of many older people is related to physical aging, but the psychological reaction to the physical process makes for unnecessary impairment, as evidenced by the high incidence of depression, suicide, and other maladaptive behavior among older people. Loss of status in a youth-oriented society accelerates psychopathological reactions.

The formal study of the process of growing old did not begin until early in the present century. These early investigations were limited primarily to biological problems. It was not until the 1930s that psychological and social aspects of aging were studied in a systematic way. In spite of the many years of intensive investigation of aging, we do not yet have a clear understanding of the process (Tompkins, 1973).

The ability to resist stress appears to decline with increasing age. It is possible that this decline in resistance is related to lowered efficiency of the nervous and endocrine systems. In some people the loss of efficiency under severe stress is reversible, thus enabling them to return to normal when the stress is reduced or removed. In others, it is possible that a genetic factor leads to progressive loss of resistance to stress.

Stress may also play a role in how long a person lives. Long-term survivors are physi-

Figure 6.6 The later years of life are a time of emotional stress for millions of men and women. Even though physical health may be satisfactory, many older people must endure the most tragic neglect and loneliness. Friends and family members die or move away, and little remains but faded photographs and a few pitiful possessions.

cally healthier, are more intelligent, have a more stable home life, and are of a higher economic status than short-term survivors (Pfeiffer, 1970). All these variables are conditions which help protect people from the impact of stress.

The stressful effects of radical changes during the later years of life is indicated by the fact that 24 percent of 1,000 persons placed in an old-age institution died within the first six months. The comparable death rate of elderly persons in a community set-

ting is about 10 percent. It has also been observed that elderly persons placed in institutions have more serious physiological and psychological problems than do those who remain with their families (Lieberman, 1968). While part of this difference can be explained by the fact that the disabled elderly are more likely to be sent to institutions, at least some of the effect is due to the stress of being removed from the home.

Another factor of importance is companionship during the later years. Some men and women are favored with large and loving families or have developed friendships and other associations which guarantee against loneliness. Many aging people, however, grow old in isolation. Families have drifted apart, friends have died, and no one has taken their place. Through indifference or ignorance of the consequences, these people have allowed friendships to dwindle. Therefore they eventually find themselves alone.

While the death of a husband or wife may occur at any time during the adult years, it is more likely to take place during the later years of life. Whenever it occurs, it is a life-stress situation. One study indicated that bereaved people show disturbances of sleep and appetite as well as increased use of alcohol, tobacco, and tranquilizers. Compared with a control group of nonbereaved persons, those who had lost a husband or wife spent more days sick in bed and had more admissions to hospitals. Moreover, they more often sought help for emotional problems (Weiss & Parkes, 1971).

Finally, there is the realization that the end of one's own life is approaching. This type of stress is not as great as many younger people suppose. The closer one approaches the time of death, the more reconciled one becomes. There are also biological and psychological changes which serve a protective purpose. The gradually diminished awareness of the self and the world is one of these. There is evidence that death is more stressful for those people close to the dying person than it is for the one who is dying.

Surveys have indicated that only about 10 percent of those over 60 state flatly that they are afraid to die. One study showed that less than a third of dying patients over 60 years of age were clearly anxious, while two-thirds of dying patients under 50 showed a high level of anxiety (Hinton, 1967). Part of the reason for this finding is that older people have fewer hopes and expectations to be disrupted by death.

The stress of anticipated death is related to the philosophy of life held by the aging person and to the richness or barrenness of his or her earlier life. If that life was unproductive, uncreative, and unrewarding, the threat of death may be especially alarming. Similarly, the person who has not developed an effective personal philosophy of life and death is more likely to become a victim of personality disorganization during his or her later years.

Unusual Life Stress

People of all ages may be faced at times with extreme stress growing out of unusual situations which make extraordinary physical and emotional demands on them. Such situations may result in a *gross stress reaction*, a term used to distinguish the behavior from reactions to milder and more common forms of stress.

While the impact of unusual stress on the behavior of the victim has not been subjected to extensive clinical study, there is ample evidence to indicate that various types of personality disorganization may result. Patterns of greed, aggression, selfishness, and regressive behavior are frequently observed, in addition to the more common reactions of terror and anxiety.

Stress of Survival

Many people have been the victims of stress experiences so severe that it is hard to imagine how they were able to survive, or how

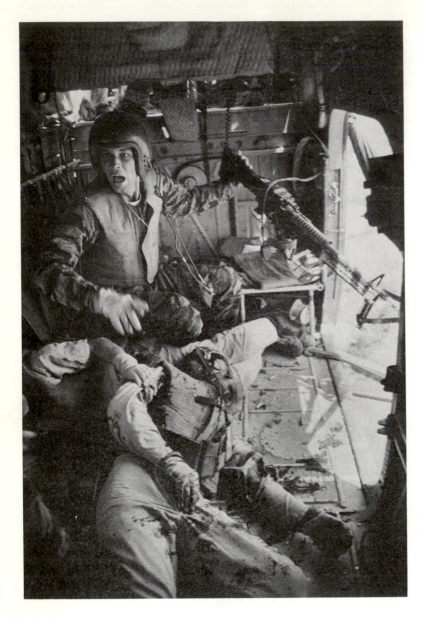

Figure 6.7 Some of the most stressful experiences in life occur during combat. This aerial gunner, in the midst of a raging battle, is calling frantically for help for his bleeding and badly injured crew member.

they were able to retain their sanity during and after the event. Some of these enormously stressful situations have involved large numbers of people, such as concentration camp victims and prisoners of war; others have involved individuals or small groups of people.

The stress of concentration camp life can be imagined only vaguely by those who did not experience it. We do know, from personal accounts and captured films, that the stresses must have been fearsomely overwhelming. Malnutrition, crowding, sleep deprivation, exposure to the elements, forced labor, torture, and threats of death were part of the daily routine. There came to be a complete loss of human dignity and identity. While millions died, large numbers of men and women survived by one means or another.

Soon after World War II ended, the name "KZ syndrome" (from the German word for concentration camp, *Konzentrationslager*) was given to the defects of memory and intellect which were combined with the anxiety, depression, and psychosomatic disturbances seen in the victims. Since that time there have been a number of studies of the long-term effects stemming from the concentration camp experience's massive stress.

One study investigated the adjustment of former inmates of Nazi concentration camps twelve years or more after the prisoners were freed. Anxiety was still a problem in 43 percent of the survivors, while most of the others had some type of residual symptom. The anxiety did not correlate with the adjustment of the survivor prior to the arrest or to the life situation following liberation. It appeared to be related directly to stress during imprisonment. About two-thirds of the survivors reported psychological disturbances while they had been in the camp. The symptoms were chronic anxiety, tension, and severe depression.

The findings of the study were summarized as follows:

> Prisoners who were very young when arrested, and those few who had suffered serious mental disorders before the war, seemed less able to withstand the stresses of concentration camp life than those who had the opportunity to develop their personality before they were arrested. The most important factor, however, was the total sum and combination of the different kinds of psychophysiological stresses to which the prisoners were subjected. The greater the sum of this stress, the greater the immediate psychopathological reaction and . . . the greater the incidence of chronic long-lasting reaction. (Eitinger, 1964)

Another study showed that the results of the severe stress persisted after more than a quarter of a century. Former concentration camp inmates continued to require more medical care than that required by the general population, and they showed more symptoms of psychological maladjustment. Many of these people continued to show anxiety, irritability, apprehensiveness, and restlessness. Others remained bitter, hostile, and belligerent. Psychosomatic complaints usually took the form of stomach disorders, weakness, and fatigue (Arthur, 1974).

There is also evidence that the stress of the concentration camp experience extends beyond the first generation. A Canadian study found that the children of parents, or a parent, who had been in a concentration camp were brought to child-guidance clinics more frequently than would be expected. These families had difficulty in controlling their children, and there was an overvaluation of the children's ability. All references to discipline and aggression were forbidden between parents and children. The parents appeared to be preoccupied with their past experiences and their children felt guilty about making demands on them (Sigal & Rakoff, 1971).

In spite of the evidence that many survivors of Nazi concentration camps suffered serious psychological damage, others managed to make a satisfactory adjustment. A study in Israel compared a group of women who had been in a Nazi concentration camp during World War II to a control group of women who had not. While the camp survivors were more poorly adjusted than the

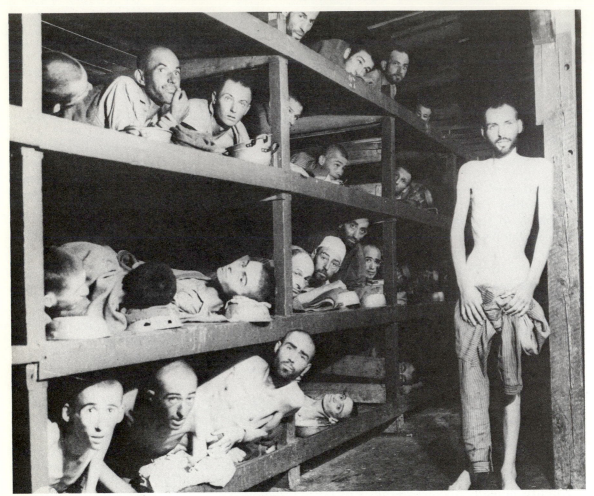

Figure 6.8 The experience of being a concentration camp inmate is stressful beyond the imagination of anyone who has not endured it. The eyes of these men reflect the horrors of the life they had been forced to lead. A very large number of survivors of these camps suffered permanent emotional scars.

controls, a considerable number of concentration camp survivors had made a good adjustment despite the extreme stress they had undergone earlier in life. Several explanations for this finding were suggested. It may have been that the women who adapted successfully had an initial underlying strength. It is also possible that their subsequent environment provided opportunities to reestablish a satisfying and meaningful existence. Finally, a hardening process may have taken place which allowed the survivors to view current stresses as less threatening (Antonovsky et al., 1971).

The experience of military prisoners of war in the Pacific during World War II, in North Korea, and in Vietnam frequently rivaled that of the concentration camp survivors. In the Korean war and the war in Vietnam, the element of political indoctrination was added to physical and mental cruelty. Sensory deprivation was a common form of stress. Solitary confinement in a cell with lights on continuously for months or years led to confusion and exhaustion.

One study compared U.S. Army veterans who were prisoners of war during World War II with those who were POWs during the Korean war. Symptoms, disability, and maladjustment were studied. Symptoms of the stress experience were both physical and psychological. However, while World War II POWs from Europe showed only a persistence of psychological disturbances, the POWs from World War II in the Pacific, and the Korean POWs, showed a persistence of physical as well as emotional symptoms. Moreover, the mental problems of the Pacific and Korean POWs were more serious than those of men who had been in prison camps in Europe (Beebe, 1975).

The plight of the returning veteran is another example of a stress situation. Soldiers returning from World Wars I and II showed relatively little stress upon their return to the United States, although stress reactions were relatively high while the men were overseas. However, in the case of soldiers returning from Vietnam, there has been evidence of a high degree of psychosocial stress even though psychiatric casualties were relatively low overseas. This situation may be due to the blighted self-image of the Vietnam veteran. Society does not regard him as a hero. Consequently, there is a sense of loneliness which has frequently led to depression and a continuation of drug abuse that began overseas (Bourne, 1972).

It is often overlooked that the very large majority of psychiatrically disabled veterans had serious educational, vocational, or social problems prior to entering active duty. Sexual adjustment and family relationships in most cases were either unsatisfactory or inadequate. The findings suggest that active military duty may make symptoms more serious but that military duty in itself does not suffice to explain the psychiatric disorders. It is also true that most psychiatrically disabled veterans never served in a combat area (Lumry et al., 1972).

The stress of survival goes beyond the experience of the concentration camp inmate and the prisoner of war. Individuals and small groups of people find themselves from time to time in unique situations which make unusual physical and psychological demands on them. One such case was that of Donald Crowhurst, a British yachtsman who entered a contest to sail alone around the world.

Crowhurst left England in a new boat, the *Teignmouth Electron*, before it had been properly tested or prepared. He should have abandoned the race soon after sailing from port, but the pressure of publicity he had received was too much for him to resist. Rather than admit failure, Crowhurst devised a scheme for sailing around the Atlantic while making a detailed record of a false voyage around the world. Eight months later, the *Teignmouth Electron* was found abandoned in mid-Atlantic about 1,800 miles from England. The yacht was sailing quietly, undamaged and fully equipped except for the captain's chronometer. Log books, tape-recordings, copies of cables sent and received, and hundreds of pages of handwritten notes were found in the deserted cabin.

At first it was thought that Crowhurst had been the victim of malnutrition, the toxic effects of decayed food, water shortage, head injury, or the misuse of a drug. Even sensory deprivation was considered a possible explanation. However, these factors were ruled out. A careful analysis of the documents on board suggested that the real cause of Crowhurst's breakdown was psychosocial, rather than physical, stress (Bennet, 1974).

When another boat leading the race became disabled and sank, Crowhurst realized that he would be forced into winning. The prospect of the tremendous reception he

---

The Tragic Log of the *Teignmouth Electron*: Captain Crowhurst's Record of His Last Hour

JULY 1

Time	
10 08 40	Reason for system to minimiser error To go—Remove Experience Barometer pressure on move
10 10 10	System of Books reorganise perfectly
10 11	Many parallels
−20	Realisation of role of decision making hesitation − time Action + time Freq.
10 13 30	Books Soul of men into their work − reason for 'work' unimportant? Hermits force unnecessary conditions on themselves
10 14 20	Seek truth wasting time
10 14 30	My Folly gone 'forward' in imagination wrong decision not perfect Time no longer computed Had disorganised clocks
10 15 40	Clocks Think no need worry about time ± but only elapsed time. ± May be meaningless? Important reason for work is (lost) understand
10 17 20	right Sorry waste of time Ape indicates perplexity by head-scratching! not [right?] 10 19 10
not quite right	Evil is choice of interpretation of symbols New reas[on] occurs for game. My judgement indicates cannot use anything 'put' in place but have to put everything in place. Task very difficult. NOT impossible. Must just Do the B Strive for perfection in the hope of
10 22	Understand Two 'reasons' for task of conflict. Rule of game unsure. If
10 23 30	game to put everything back? Where is back?
10 23 40	Cannot see any 'purpose' in game.
10 25 10	Must resign position in sense that if Set my self 'impossible' task then nothing achieved by game. Only Reason for game to find new rules governing old truths. Understand Exact position of concept of ballance of Power. It is only one way of expressing hope. the age process

Time	
	is new way of despair concept
10 28 10	Only requirement for have new set
10 2.2	of rules is that there is some
10 2.	Understand reason for need to devise games. No game man can devise is Resign game if you will agree only [. . .]

harmless. The truth is that there can only be one chess master that is the man who can free himself [from] the need [to] be blown by a cosmic mind. there can only be one perfect beauty that is the great beauty of truth. No man may may do more than all that he is capable of doing. The perfect way is the way of reconcilliation Once there is a possibility of reconcilliation there may not [be] a need for making errors. Now is revealed the true nature and purpose and power of the game my [?offence] I am [Plate 3] I am what I am and and I see the nature of my offence

I will only resign this game if you will agree that of the next occasion that this game is played it will be played according to the rules that are devised by my great god who has revealed at last to his son not only the exact nature of the reason for games but has also revealed the truth of the way of the ending of the next game that
It is finished—
It is finished
IT IS THE MERCY

| 11 15 00 | It is the end of my my game the truth |

has been revealed and it will be done as my family require me to do it

| 11 17 00 | It is the time for your moove [*sic*] to begin I have not need to prolong the game It has been a good game that must be ended at the I will play this game when I choose I will resign the game 11 20 40 There is no reason for harmful |

would receive—with personal interviews, newspaper stories, and radio and television coverage—raised the frightening prospect that his hoax would be discovered. His notes show that he became increasingly introspective and philosophical in his thinking. Eventually he began to lose contact with reality. One day the stress of his hopeless situation caught up with him. With the chronometer in his hand, he slipped over the side of his boat and ended the tragic "game" he had been playing.

Stress of Disaster

The most common forms of disaster involve natural catastrophes such as storms, floods, fires, and explosions. When these events occur, often unexpectedly, they create high levels of stress in people who are most seriously threatened. In recent years, there has been a growing recognition of the possible mental health consequences of disasters.

The National Institute of Mental Health established a Disaster Assistance and Mental Health Section in 1974. The purpose of the unit is to provide professional counseling services and financial assistance to state and

Figure 6.9 Natural disasters—violent storms, fires, floods, and earthquakes—are stressful events that temporarily shatter the psychological stability of many people. Like this mother and child standing in front of their home destroyed by a tornado, disaster victims go through a period of stunned disbelief and immobility before they are able to cope effectively with problems of returning to a normal life.

local agencies or private mental health organizations, and to train disaster workers in order to relieve mental health problems caused or aggravated by major disasters.

The observation of a variety of civilian catastrophes has indicated that a *disaster syndrome* made up of at least three distinct psychological phases can be expected in the reaction to gross stress situations. The *shock reaction* is the first response to the impact of the disaster. This phase is followed by the *recoil reaction* when the immediate danger is past. The third response is the *recall reaction* when the disaster victim begins to realize the wider implications of the loss and the damage (Wallace, 1956).

The shock reaction to a disaster is different for different people. About 10 to 20 percent of the survivors can be expected to behave in a cool and collected way; 70 percent are likely to become confused and bewildered; with another 10 to 20 percent showing outbursts of severe anxiety, panic, anger, and screaming. During this period of impact, there is nothing much that can be done to help the person. He merely needs time to adjust emotionally to the situation.

Following the bombing of Hiroshima, a number of observers remarked on the overwhelming silence of the survivors. Long lines of people moved and behaved like automatons, and walked silently away from the city. However, the shock reaction of survivors nearest the explosion involved a more frantic effort toward escape. Thousands of blinded, deafened, and physically shattered men, women, and children struggled frantically in their efforts to reach safety.

In the recoil reaction, the second phase of reaction to catastrophe, the survivor comes out of a stunned, confused, or excited state and finds that the danger is over and life must be faced. In this recoil phase, the survivor may giggle or sob, or may be forlorn or irritable. Sometimes there is anger and hostility. It is during this phase that psychological treatment is necessary. The victim must be given an opportunity to ventilate his or her feelings about the tragic events.

In the recall reaction, the third phase, the survivor of a disaster is tense and restless. He or she either is preoccupied with memories of the horrifying experience or may blot it out of memory completely. In either case, sleeplessness, nightmares, and emotional upsets are common. This phase is often accompanied by physical symptoms.

While it appears that long-range psychiatric disabilities growing out of disasters are infrequent, the residual emotional impact of such disasters may be long-lasting and far-reaching. Relatively few victims of such disasters require hospitaliztion for psychiatric reasons. However, the disaster experience might very well have a long-term effect on the anxiety tolerance level of the survivors and might in this way have important mental health implications.

The Chapter in Review

The emphasis on relatively minor and temporary psychological disturbances is a recent development in abnormal psychology. Until the 1950s, most attention was directed toward the more serious mental disorders requiring hospitalization or intensive treatment. It became evident, however, that many people show maladaptive behavior as a reaction to the ordinary stresses of life. These conditions were called *transient situational disorders* because they were responses to stressful situations in life, and tended to clear up when the stress was removed.

1 Meaning of Psychosocial Stress

Psychosocial stress refers to the impact of life events on physical and mental health. Techniques for measuring psychosocial stress in terms of life-stress units have been successful in relating psychosocial stress to later episodes of physical illness and psychological disturbance.

2 Stress of Everyday Life

While some forms of stress are experienced from early childhood to the later years, each period of life involves stresses which are more or less unique. The infant finds weaning and toilet training stressful, and the child faces many stress situations related to the socialization process at home, in school, and with other children. Adult life has its special stresses involving work, court-ship, marriage, and family obligations. People in their later years must contend with the loss of friends and relatives, increasing loneliness, economic insecurity, and the feeling of being useless and unwanted.

3 Unusual Life Stress

In addition to the ordinary stresses of everyday life, many people are called upon to endure unusual amounts of prolonged stress in situations where their very survival is threatened. Another type of unusual life stress is associated with the unexpected and overwhelming events of disasters. The term *disaster syndrome* refers to characteristic behavior of people subjected to the sudden and catastrophic stress.

Recommended Readings

Nature of Life Stress

Dohrenwend, B. P., & Dohrenwend, B. S. (Eds.) *Stressful life events: Their nature and effects.* New York: Wiley, 1974.

McQuade, W. *Stress.* New York: Dutton, 1974.

Selyé, H. *Stress without distress.* Philadelphia: Lippincott, 1974.

Stresses of Everyday Life

Glasscote, R. M., & Fishman, M. E. *Mental health on the campus.* New York: Joint Information Service, 1973.

Kaplan, B. H., et al. (Eds.) *Psychiatric disorder and the urban environment.* New York: Behavioral Publications, 1971.

Kiev, A. *A strategy for handling executive stress.* Chicago: Nelson-Hall, 1974.

Unusual Life Stress

Bailey, M., & Bailey, M. *Staying alive! 117 days adrift.* New York: Ballantine, 1975. (Paperback.)

Des Pres, T. *The survivor: An anatomy of life in the death camps.* New York: Oxford University Press, 1976.

Toch, H. *Men in crisis: Human breakdowns in prison.* Chicago: Aldine, 1975.

Read, P. O. *Alive: The story of the Andes survivors.* New York: Avon, 1975. (Paperback.)

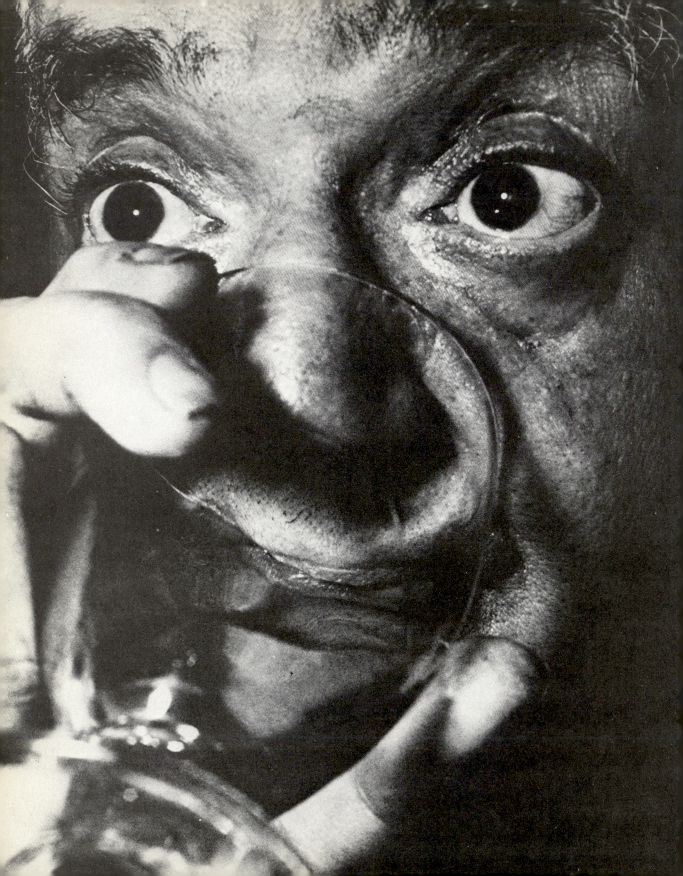

7
Alcohol Addiction and Drug Abuse

Objectives

To describe the nature and hazards of addiction to hard drugs

To discuss the use and psychological effects of marihuana and the hallucinogenic drugs

To describe alcohol addiction and to indicate how it differs from chronic alcoholism with accompanying brain damage

To discuss some of the biological influences which appear to be related to alcohol addiction

To show how excessive drinking is basically a learned pattern of behavior

To discuss the use and psychological effects of marihuana and the hallucinogenic drugs

To show how theories of drug dependence closely parallel theories of alcohol addiction

The life-stress disorders discussed in the previous chapter are relatively temporary conditions caused by stressful events which for the most part are external. In another group of psychological disturbances, called *personality disorders*, the critical forces responsible for the difficulty are to be found *within* the person. These disorders are life-long patterns of maladaptive behavior that become firmly established and resistant to change. It is not unusual for the symptoms to appear during childhood or adolescence.

The personality disorders include alcohol addiction and drug dependence, sexual deviations, and some forms of antisocial behavior. Alcohol and drugs will be discussed in this chapter, while sexual deviations and antisocial behavior will be covered in the following chapter. Another group of conditions, called *personality trait disturbances*, are also part of the personality disorder classification. However, these conditions are borderline patterns of maladaptive behavior which frequently are mere exaggerations of normal traits, or represent a lack of social skills and competence. It is questionable whether most of these conditions are personality disorders in a clinical sense; some may simply represent unfortunate personality characteristics which make social adjustment more difficult.

About one-third of all patients admitted to public mental hospitals in the United States are diagnosed as having personality disorders. Of this group, 66.6 percent are alcohol addicts; 15.6 percent are people dependent upon drugs; and most of the remaining 17.8 percent are sexual deviates and persons showing antisocial behavior. The number of patients diagnosed as having personality trait disturbances is very small (National Institute of Mental Health, 1975).

These figures do not accurately reflect the prevalence of personality disorders in the general population because most people with the types of problems included in this diagnostic category do not find their way into public mental hospitals. Some are admitted to correctional institutions; others are treated in clinics or by therapists in private practice; and many do not receive any form of care or treatment.

Alcohol Addiction

The use of alcoholic beverages can be traced to the earliest period of human history. Almost all people have had one or another kind of alcoholic beverage. Primitive people in widely scattered parts of the world discovered the intoxicating qualities of various fermentable materials. Honey, dates, fruits,

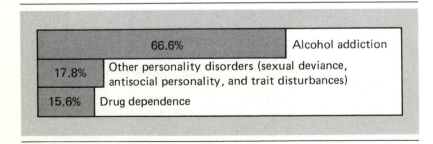

Figure 7.1 The relative distribution of various conditions within the personality disorder group. Note that alcohol addiction and drug dependence account for more than 80 percent of mental hospital admissions of men and women having this diagnosis.

berries, and even tree sap have been used to produce intoxicating beverages.

Alcoholics account for a large proportion of the people known to health and social welfare agencies. For example, in recent years alcoholics have accounted for more than one-fifth of all the men admitted to public mental hospitals and to the psychiatric wards of general hospitals. Alcohol is a significant factor in almost half of all fatal motor vehicle accidents, and it is now clear that a majority of these drinking drivers are alcoholics.

The term *alcoholism* has been used to refer to every degree of excessive drinking from that of the party guest who drinks too much to that of the hospitalized mental patient whose nervous system has been severely damaged by alcohol. The various levels of severity have been designated by such names as *normal alcoholism*, *primary alcoholism*, *alcohol addiction*, and *chronic alcoholism*. Unfortunately, these terms are confusing, inadequately defined, and often contradictory.

Most people who drink excessively are not alcoholics in a clinical sense. Some people drink more than they should to combat boredom in their work, others to get relief from marital difficulties, and still others to reduce their tensions. Life is filled with situations which lead to excessive drinking. And while it is true that the alcoholic comes from the group of excessive drinkers, the distinction between excessive drinking and alcoholism is by no means clear.

For our purposes, and in keeping with the latest diagnostic classifications, there are only two major forms of alcoholism with which psychologists and psychiatrists are concerned: (1) alcohol addiction and (2) alcoholism associated with brain damage.

In alcohol addiction, excessive drinking is a preferred method for solving problems. In these cases the symptoms are psychological, and there is no significant damage to the nervous system as a result of the excessive drinking. Such cases are classified as personality disorders. The second major type of alcoholism includes those cases in which the excessive drinking has resulted in reversible or irreversible damage to the nervous system and particularly the brain. These cases include a number of different conditions which are grouped together and called "brain syndromes." This form of alcoholism will be treated in detail in Chapter 14.

The point at which excessive drinking becomes alcohol addiction is dependent upon a number of factors. An individual becomes an alcoholic of the addictive type when he or she drinks excessively, when drinking leads to intoxication, and, most importantly, when drinking becomes a preferred way to solve problems. There is always a transitional period during which excessive drinking slips over into alcohol addiction. It is often difficult to say when the transition has been completed.

In alcohol addiction there is a more or less regular intake of alcohol of sufficient quantity to bring the drinker into conflict with family, friends, employers, and sometimes the police. People addicted to alcohol drink steadily, or are frequently drunk for days, weeks, or months. Physiologically, the alcohol addict is a person whose alcohol intake exceeds the rate of alcohol metabolism for extended periods of time.

The damaging aspect of alcohol addiction, and the reason why excessive drinking may lead to a personality disturbance, is that the chronic intoxication results in the release of inhibitions, the impairment of judgment, and a loss of emotional and motor control. There may also be disturbance in self-evaluation and the creation of an unrealistic self-image. There is likely to be a deteriora-

Figure 7.2 The problem of alcoholism usually begins very early in life. These young people have been drinking to the point where they can no longer remain awake.

tion of personal habits, a lack of regard for one's personal appearance, a blunting of emotional sensitivity, and an interference with realistic planning and foresight.

What Causes Alcohol Addiction?

There is no easy answer to the question of why and how people become addicted to alcohol. As with most forms of maladaptive behavior, explanations tend to emphasize biological, psychological, or sociocultural influences or all three. There is increasing evidence that genetic and biochemical factors may be important in some cases of addiction. Whether or not this is the case, there is wide agreement today that alcohol addiction is a learned pattern of maladaptive behavior rather than a disease in the medical sense. Psychodynamic explanations of ad-

**"Not Even God Will Help Me Anymore!"—
The Destructive Nature of Alcohol Addiction**

Otto A. is a 46-year-old man who was referred to a psychiatric hospital after an episode in which he was arrested on charges of drunkenness and refusing to pay a taxi fare. The patient was given a suspended sentence, and ordered to leave town. A few days later he was arrested again for drunkenness and refusing to pay another taxi fare. He was sentenced to the workhouse; but in view of his long history of alcohol addiction, he was sent to the psychiatric hospital.

The patient began drinking when he was 18 years old, although his excessive drinking did not start until he was 25, following his divorce from his first wife. He began drinking beer and wine, but eventually came to drink anything that was available. Most of the time the patient drinks in bars with friends. He is a "spree" drinker who manages to go for some time without touching alcohol, and then suddenly begins drinking excessively. During these bouts of alcoholism he ordinarily loses his job, and often is arrested for disorderly conduct. The episodes of excessive drinking have increased in frequency and severity over the years. The patient describes himself as the "black sheep of the family, the worst drinker in the state of Ohio, and such a great sinner that not even God will help me anymore."

Otto has a number of brothers and sisters, all of whom are well established as respected members of the community. They long since gave up in their efforts to bring an end to the patient's excessive drinking. While they continue to accept him when he is sober, they refuse to have him in their homes when he is intoxicated. During the past two years he has had very little contact with his relatives. His work history has been erratic, since he has always been able to obtain a job but can never hold one more than a few months. He has worked for numerous companies, and at one time went into business for himself. In each instance he has been unsuccessful due to his excessive drinking.

diction, while not completely discredited, have lost much of the attraction and influence they once had. While sociocultural factors are related to excessive drinking, they cannot in themselves cause addiction.

Addiction as biologically determined It has been observed for a very long time that some people seem to be more resistant than others to the physiologic effects of alcohol. Men and women of this type are said to have a high tolerance and presumably are less prone to addiction than those who have a low tolerance to alcohol. This difference in tolerance suggests the possibility of hereditary influences, possibly in the form of inborn metabolic differences. There may be a generalized and nonspecific organic pattern which forms a congenial soil for the development of alcoholism. There is the further possibility that alcoholism may be due to a biochemical defect in which genetic factors may lead to a failure in the production of specific enzymes. As a result of this deficiency, the person affected may be unable to utilize some necessary element of nutrition. In such cases, the intake of alcohol may be regarded as a response to a tissue need.

The controversy as to whether there is an inherited factor associated with alcohol addiction has been going on for more than a hundred years. While the results of studies have been inconclusive, recent investigations have suggested that there is probably a genetic predisposition for the more severe forms of alcoholism.

An American-Danish research team took advantage of a pool of 15,000 known adoptees, most of whom were separated from their biological parents in early childhood and raised by nonrelatives (Goodwin et al., 1973). From this pool, an experimental group of 55 male adoptees was selected where at least one biological parent had been hospitalized primarily for alcoholism. Each of the adoptees had been separated from his biological parents during the first six weeks of life, had been adopted by nonrelatives, and had no known later contact with his biological parents.

A comparison group of controls consisted of adopted males to whom the same criteria were applied except that these men had no alcoholic biological parents. The groups were matched in approximate age at adoption and adult age. Members of the experimental and control groups were interviewed when they were between 25 and 45 years of age.

All the adoptees were interviewed by a Danish psychiatrist who was not told beforehand to which group each person belonged. During the interview, information was obtained on a wide range of factors including drinking practices and problems. The interview records were then sent to Washington University in St. Louis for coding, card punching, and computer analysis without knowledge of any of the subjects' histories.

A subject was classified as a heavy drinker if he (1) had drunk for at least one year on a daily basis, (2) had six or more drinks on the same occasion at least twice a month or had six or more drinks on the same occasion at least once a week for over a year, and (3) reported no problems as a result of the drinking. A problem drinker was a heavy drinker with problems but not enough to be classified as an alcoholic. Alcoholism was inferred if the individual met the criteria of heavy drinkers and had alcohol-related problems in at least three of the following four areas:

1 Social disapproval of his drinking from friends and parents, marital problems
2 Job trouble, traffic arrests, other police trouble
3 Frequent blackouts, withdrawal tremor, hallucinations and convulsions.
4 Loss of control over drinking, morning drinking

Of the fifty-five men in the experimental group, ten met the criteria for alcoholism; the group as a whole had nearly four times the alcoholism rate of the controls. Almost without exception, members of the experimental group had more drinking problems than the controls. They also had received some type of psychological treatment twice as often as the controls, and had five times the rate of psychiatric hospitalization. Of those men hospitalized, 75 percent were diagnosed as alcoholics while none of the controls were alcoholic persons.

While the findings in this study do not constitute proof of a genetic predisposition for alcoholism, they suggest that such a predisposition is possible. While the study created a considerable amount of controversy in scientific circles, the findings persuaded a very large number of experts that there may indeed be a genetic factor in the more severe types of alcohol addiction.

The biochemical aspects of chronic alcohol ingestion are also in need of clarification. For example, it has frequently been speculated that the behavioral and pharmacological tolerance shown for alcohol by alcoholics might be accounted for by a more rapid rate of ethanol metabolism. A number of recent studies have shown that prolonged alcohol consumption may induce a significant increase in enzyme activity in the liver of animals. On the other hand, other studies have failed to demonstrate any differences between blood alcohol levels of alcoholics and nonalcoholics. Since disappearance of blood ethanol may not be an adequate way of measuring all steps in the degradation of ethanol, scientists have carried out a carefully controlled study on the rate of metabolism in alcoholic and nonalcoholic subjects. The data suggest that tolerance for alcohol is related to processes of adaptation in the central nervous system rather than to alterations in the rate of metabolism of ethanol.

Addiction as learned behavior The possibility of genetic and constitutional influences in individual susceptibility to the effects of alcohol does not rule out the role of learning in acquiring and maintaining an addiction to alcohol. The biological explanation tells us why some people are more likely than others to become addicted. It does not tell us how the maladaptive behavior begins or becomes established.

The behavioral approach to alcohol addiction assumes that people learn to drink excessively as a result of the rewarding effects of such drinking. Alcohol is a sedative, and the ability to reduce tension is one of its basic properties. Since tension is an undesirable state, any quick and effective method of reducing tension is likely to be rewarding. The drinker then continues to seek relief from tension through the use of alcoholic beverages. The cycle of reward and reinforcement may be repeated so often that the drinking becomes a preferred and necessary means of reducing tension.

Since so many people use alcohol, one might ask why addiction is not more prevalent than it is. One answer would be that most people have learned to reduce tension and to solve their problems by more acceptable means. Another possibility is that those with a constitutional sensitivity to alcohol are most likely to become addicted. While learning is involved in all cases of excessive drinking, a genetically determined predisposition to the damaging effects of alcohol could significantly increase the likelihood that a person would become addicted.

Environmental contingencies in the form of sociocultural influences are also involved in learning to become addicted to alcohol. Such factors as marital status, socioeconomic level, religion, education, ethnic origin, and group attitudes toward drinking combine to create a favorable or unfavorable climate for the development of alcoholism. While these factors in themselves are not the cause of addiction, they are significant reinforcing influences.

Addiction as an unconscious need The psychodynamic view of alcohol addiction concerns itself with unconscious needs and conflicts which are assumed to be responsible for the excessive drinking. Some psychoanalysts view such drinking as a regression to infantile oral needs that were not satisfactorily met. It has even been suggested that alcohol is a symbolic substitute for the mother's milk.

A different psychodynamic interpretation of alcohol addiction is that intoxication may be an attempt to recapture feelings of importance and omnipotence or to discharge aggressions against a frustrating world. It has been suggested that people do not commit crimes because they are drunk, but rather that they get drunk in order to commit crimes. The validity of these, and other, psychodynamic explanations of alcohol addiction is highly questionable and such interpretations are accepted today by relatively few psychiatrists who practice psychoanalysis.

The consensus of informed opinion is that alcoholism results from a complex interaction of social, psychological, and biological

---

**Profile Analysis of Persons
With High Rates of Alcohol-Related Problems**

Highest rates of alcohol-related problems for respondents in a national survey were found among:

1 Men
2 Separated, single, and divorced persons (in that order)
3 Persons with no religious affiliation
4 Persons who are beer drinkers as compared with those who drink mostly hard liquor or wine
5 Persons who were more likely (compared with other persons in the survey) to say:: "Drunkenness is usually *not* a sign of social irresponsibility" and "Drunkenness is usually a sign of just having fun" (National Institute on Alcohol Abuse and Alcoholism, 1974)

Profile Analysis of Persons Most Likely to Have Low Rates of Alcohol-Related Problems

Lowest rates of alcohol-related problems for respondents in a national survey were found among:

1 Women
2 Persons over 50
3 Widowed and married persons
4 Persons of Jewish religious affiliation
5 Residents of rural areas
6 Residents of the South
7 Persons with postgraduate education
8 Persons who are mostly wine drinkers (National Institute on Alcohol Abuse and Alcoholism, 1974)

factors. Even the most enthusiastic proponents of any specific theory of what causes alcoholism agree on the necessity of an eclectic approach to the multifaceted problems of this condition. Such an approach, if it is to be truly effective, must involve more interdisciplinary research.

In spite of the various theories of alcohol addiction, it is unlikely that there is a single explanation to account for the condition. Alcohol addiction develops in a wide range of personalities for a wide range of different reasons. The attempt to force all alcohol addicts into a common etiologic mold is not consistent with clinical observations.

Problem Drinkers Are Problem People

Alcohol addicts are not only problems to themselves; they are problems to their families and the community. The loss of productivity caused by problem drinkers in business and industry amounts to hundreds of millions of dollars each year. The usual approach in the past was to dismiss employees with alcohol problems. It became evident, however, that many problem drinkers make valuable contributions to the compa-

nies for which they work. Men and women with technical, creative, and administrative skills are not easily replaced. The training and development of a new employee was found to be more expensive, in many cases, than the rehabilitation of the problem drinker who remained with the company.

The difficulty with this change in policy was that most employers did not know where to find the technical assistance to deal with the problem drinker. For this reason, the federal government initiated a nationwide program in 1972 to promote programs for alcoholic employees in private work organizations. Funds were also made available to state and local government agencies to develop program consultants. Some community mental health centers now offer consulting services to private and public employers on the operation of programs for problem drinkers.

In one project, smaller employers have formed a consortium to make use of referral, counseling, and treatment services which have been set up under the direction of professionals specializing in work with employees. Another project utilizes services delivered by union-based specialists. It has been estimated at least 2.6 million people work in organizations with some problem drinkers (Keller et al., 1974). A survey of executives of large industrial and business corporations showed that 34 percent of the companies had a program for problem drinkers (Caravan Surveys Opinion Research Corporation, 1974).

Alcohol addiction is also a problem in the military forces. The highest rate of problem drinking in the Army was found among enlisted men 30 years old with less than a college education and not accompanied by their wives. The enlisted men were more likely than officers to suffer adverse social, health, and economic consequences of drinking and to show more uncontrolled drinking, belligerence when drinking, and problems with friends and neighbors, the job, the police, and finances. The problems of officers were roughly similar to those of civilian men of the same age (Cahalan et al., 1972).

A study of drinking in the Navy found that enlisted men had more problems of every type, except those related to marriage, than officers. Junior enlisted men had more problems of every kind, except marital, than senior enlisted men. Of the junior enlisted men, 15 percent reported that they had had job-related drinking problems in the past three years, and 21 percent reported having been "high" or "tight" while on duty at least once during the past three years (Cahalan & Cisin, 1973).

In the case of high school students, a study found that problem drinking was not an isolated behavior but was associated more frequently with other deviant behavior than was the case with nonproblem drinking. The problem drinkers placed relatively low value on achievement but emphasized independence more than did the nonproblem drinkers. The problem drinkers were also more tolerant of deviant behavior. Girls who were problem drinkers were less compatible with their parents than were boys (Jessor & Jessor, 1973).

Among adults, addiction is less frequent among the elderly than among the young partly because many problem drinkers do not survive to old age. There are some people, however, who become problem drinkers only when they grow old and for reasons connected with aging. As the proportion of older people is growing, alcoholism among the elderly is becoming an increasingly important problem.

Alcohol is more likely to be consumed by older people who are socially active and who report themselves as being in good health. At moderate levels of drinking, no adverse effects on health have been found. In fact, in some elderly persons, alcohol may be desirable as an alternative to medication for maintaining physical comfort. However, problem drinking does occur among the elderly. The incidence is lower than among younger people, and the factors leading to the problem drinking are less likely to be related to deep-seated psychological problems. The excessive drinking is more likely to be related to problems associated with increasing age (Keller et al., 1974).

Unfortunately, there is no single, most effective way to treat alcohol addiction. We need not only more information about the reasons why some people come to drink excessively but also better methods of preventing alcoholism. Not enough trained personnel, money, and facilities are available for the needs of research, treatment, and educational efforts to combat this widespread disorder. Education about alcoholism and drinking is usually weak, often unscientific, and generally not based on sound educational principles. Despite these serious problems and deficiencies, however, increasing numbers of people with alcohol problems are being treated and rehabilitated.

During the past two decades there has been a noticeable change in the view toward alcoholism. Significant advances have been made, for example, in both public and professional acknowledgment that alcoholism is a psychological and medical problem rather than a form of moral transgression. The contemporary approach to the study and treatment of alcoholism incorporates scientific and humanitarian goals. The courts are increasingly inclined to view the alcoholic as a person with a psychological problem, and legal procedures involving the jailing of alcoholics are in the process of being revised.

As in the cases of other mental and personality disorders, rehabilitation of alcoholics is based upon development of a continuum of services including institutional programs, halfway houses and other postinstitutional facilities, transitional employment, and appropriate job placement and followup.

Drug Abuse and Dependence

Dependence on drugs has many points in common with alcohol addiction. The drug-dependent person is basically one who finds the effects of the drug to be a solution to his or her problems. As in the case of alcohol and alcoholics, the drug becomes so essential to the users that they cannot face reality without it. In drug dependence, particularly in the early stages, there is no damage to the nervous system. When damage does occur, the condition is classified as a brain syndrome rather than as drug dependence (see Chapter 14).

The World Health Organization Committee on Drugs defines drug dependence in the following way:

> A state of periodic or chronic intoxication detrimental to the individual and to society, produced by the repeated consumption of a drug (natural or synthetic). Its characteristics include: (1) an overpowering desire or need (compulsion) to continue taking the drug and to obtain it by any means; (2) a tendency to increase the dose; (3) a psychic (psychological) and, sometimes, a physical dependence upon the effects of the drug.

It is difficult to estimate the overall prevalence of drug abuse. Statistics from public mental hospitals are misleading because they reflect only a small and atypical sample of drug users. However, the available figures are of interest when analyzed in terms of the age and sex distribution of drug-dependent persons entering public mental hospitals. Most such persons are admitted to psychiatric hospitals between the ages of 20 and 34. An interesting difference is that a relatively larger percentage of women than men enter in both the younger and older age groups (National Institute of Mental Health, 1975). A possible explanation of this difference is that drug abuse among adolescent girls is more readily detected, and that older women who become drug-dependent are hospitalized while male users are more likely to become involved in antisocial behavior that results in their being sent to correctional institutions.

Hard Drugs

The hard drugs are the traditional drugs of the addict. The most important of these are opium and its derivatives.

The addiction to raw opium is rare except in Oriental countries and in a few cosmopolitan centers where there are large Oriental colonies. In this type of addiction, the addict feels elated and carefree after smoking a number of pipes. The euphoric feeling lasts for several hours and is followed by a deep sleep. Upon awakening, the addict often experiences a feeling of malaise. Persons addicted to opium show a number of chronic symptoms of both a physical and psychological nature. Physically, they are weak, emaciated, oversensitive to pain, and troubled by constipation. Psychological symptoms include a general apathy along with a decline in ethical values and the moral sense. There is depression, and it is not unusual for the opium addict to attempt suicide.

The most commonly seen opiate addic-

Figure 7.3 Opium is obtained from poppy plants, which are being harvested here by a group of native women in Turkey. Heroin, the most widely used of the hard drugs in the United States, is one of the derivatives of opium.

tions involve morphine and its most important derivatives, such as heroin and Demerol. Morphine was prescribed for many years by physicians for the relief of pain, and its medical use led to many cases of addiction. There appears to be a sensitivity to morphine in certain people which makes it possible for them to become addicted very quickly. Other people are able to take morphine over a long period of time without developing an addiction.

The most serious addiction problem is that of heroin. Between 1969 and 1974, the estimated number of heroin users in the United States rose from 315,000 to nearly 725,000, an increase of 130 percent (U.S. Drug Enforcement Administration, 1975).

The sequence of opiate intoxication is quite different from that of alcoholism. The first effects of an opiate include a temporary nausea which is followed by various body reactions such as warmth, itching sensations, feelings of pins and needles, and stomach sensations. At the same time, there is a sense of relaxation and relief from tension. It is at this time that the experience of being "high" takes place. This is a sense of detachment from the world and its problems—a feeling of not being involved, an "out of this world" feeling in which there are no cares or worries. When drug addicts return to their usual activities, they continue to experience these comfortable, relaxed feelings which were induced initially by the drug.

In opiate addiction, while the user is still taking relatively small doses daily or twice daily, the body develops a tissue need for the drug. This physiological addiction requires the regular and continued use of the drug and, in most cases, an increase in the amount. If the user attempts to stop using the drug, there are extremely distressing *withdrawal symptoms*. These include general restlessness, abdominal pains, yawning, hot and cold flashes, perspiration, increased salivation, heart palpitation, and anxiety, which increase rapidly to a marked extent. Addicts are depressed and fatigued, sleep restlessly, and may suffer nausea, vomiting, and diarrhea. The severity of the symptoms and their duration depend on the degree to which the person has been addicted, the length of the addiction, and the individual personality and somatic makeup. The withdrawal symptoms reach a maximal intensity after twenty-four hours and begin to subside after forty-eight to seventy-two hours.

Marihuana: The Controversial Weed

Marihuana is a name given in the United States and Latin America to a preparation made from the hemp plant (*Cannabis sativa*). This plant grows wild in most countries and is used throughout the world as an intoxicant. The United Nations has estimated that cannabis preparations are used by more than 200 million people, most of them in Asia and Africa.

The principal active ingredient in marihuana is THC (tetrahydrocannabinol). In low dosages, this compound induces effects similar to those of alcoholic intoxication; in high dosages, the drug frequently causes hallucinations. Nearly a hundred derivatives of THC have been synthesized and studied for their drug effects.

The Drugstore High: Psychological Dependence upon Paregoric

Norman J. is a 29-year-old narcotics addict who was referred to a psychiatric hospital after being arrested for using a false name to obtain paregoric in a drugstore. The patient has been an addict for a number of years, cooking the paregoric to obtain the narcotic residue. He has been in jail many times, and was in a federal narcotic hospital for a period of six months. While he has worked at a number of odd jobs, he has never had steady employment.

When admitted to the psychiatric hospital, the patient was friendly and cooperative. His manner and voice indicated a man who was accustomed to being questioned and was willing to answer in some detail. He was fully oriented, and his thinking was clear and logical. Speech was relevant, and there was no indication of emotional disturbance. The patient claimed that he had had a happy childhood, and that he started to take paregoric at age 16 "just for the kick." While he admitted that he had become unusually upset at the time of his mother's death, and that there was difficulty in adjusting to the father's second marriage, he insisted that these stress situations had nothing to do with his addiction. He said that he did not take drugs to escape his problems, but rather for his own pleasure.

In recent months the patient has been eating and sleeping poorly, and there has been physical deterioration with a weight loss of more than 20 pounds. He was able to break the habit several times in the past, and each time experienced the usual withdrawal symptoms of sweating, abdominal pains, and heart palpitation. He has talked frequently to his younger brother about the evil effects of drugs and has attempted to frighten the brother so that he will stay away from the habit.

Of all the illegal drugs currently in use in our society, marihuana has generated the most popular concern. Next to alcohol, it is the most widely abused drug. Its use was originally concentrated in limited sectors of the population, but it has now come to include large numbers of young people from junior high school to college age.

Figure 7.4 These marihuana plants are easy to grow and often mistaken for common weeds. For this reason, they have been grown in such highly unlikely places as window boxes at the Naval Academy at Annapolis, the side yard of a police station, and the median strip of an interstate highway in downtown Los Angeles.

Prior to the early 1970s, information on the extent and nature of marihuana use in the United States was spotty and suspect. National data concerning use in the general population and detailed studies on use by young people, especially high school and college students, are now available. There is also an accumulating amount of information on the social and personal aspects of use, and there is increasing research on family and peer relationships of users (*Marihuana and health,* 1974).

It has been estimated that about 24 million persons in the United States have used marihuana. More than half of those who have used it have only experimented with it. Probably not more than one in twenty uses it on a daily basis. The most common frequency reported by regular users is one to four times per month. In general, the use of marihuana in the United States has not increased dramatically; in some segments of the population, there is evidence that it may have diminished.

The highest rate of use is consistently found among college students. In 1971 this figure was 42 percent. By 1973 it had increased to 54 percent. Twice as many students were beginning to use the drug as compared to those discontinuing it. It was predicted that drug use in the nation's college population will probably stabilize at a point where about two-thirds of the students will make some use of marihuana.

The rates of use are much higher in single-sexed colleges and universities than they are in coeducational institutions. For males and females, use is about a third higher in schools segregated by sex. Marihuana use is more common in the Northeast and West than in the Central or Southern United States. It is also more common among urban than among rural residents.

Males are twice as likely as females to have tried marihuana, and they tend to use it with greater frequency. There is evidence, however, that the drug is being used by larger numbers of girls and women and at an increasing rate. In colleges, the ratio of male to female use is about 3:2, but use in high schools is about equally distributed between the two sexes.

The role of parents and peers in adolescent drug use is one of considerable interest. The use of marihuana by teenagers is closely associated with use by friends. One study found that when none of a teenager's friends reported the use of marihuana, only one out of fifteen youngsters reported use.

When all the friends reported marihuana use, nine out of ten had also used the drug. When brothers and sisters have used it, 75 percent of those reporting have also done so. But when siblings are nonusers, less than 40 percent report themselves as users. Moreover, those adolescents who spend more time with friends, and place greater reliance on the advice of friends than on that of parents, are more likely to be users than parent-oriented teenagers.

The use of marihuana by children and adolescents is also related to drug use by parents. When both parents use drugs such as alcohol, tobacco, and other psychoactive drugs, there is a greater likelihood that their children will use marihuana. The probability of drug use is also associated with lack of family cohesiveness, use of other medication, and less parental emphasis on self-control.

Less is known about the pattern of marihuana use among nonstudent groups. A study of physicians in New York City, San Francisco, upstate New York, and Nebraska found that over a third of those who responded had tried marihuana, although only 7 percent of the physicians reported current use. The most frequent users were younger physicians and those living in New York City and San Francisco. Rates of use among nurses and nursing students were considerably lower. Only 3 percent of graduate nurses reported ever having used marihuana, and only a third of these were using the drug currently (*Marihuana and health*, 1974).

The use of marihuana among military personnel is of special interest in view of the publicity given drug use in Vietnam. A worldwide study of enlisted personnel in the U.S. Armed Services found that 30 percent had used marihuana in the preceding year, 40 percent reported using the drug several times a week or more, and as many as 16 percent reported having used marihuana while on duty (Fisher, 1972).

Another large study of the use of marihuana was made of enlisted military personnel at Fort Lee, Virginia. Forty-four percent reported having used the drug at some time in the past; 19 percent had used marihuana

Figure 7.5 The joys of lighting up a hash pipe, and the anticipation of sharing it, are clearly reflected in the faces of these young people. Meanwhile, the debate as to the physiological effects of excessive or continued use of marihuana continues among mental health experts.

only; another 19 percent had used marihuana and other drugs except heroin; and 6 percent had used marihuana, heroin, and possibly other drugs (Greden & Morgan, 1972).

Marihuana produces rather characteristic effects. There may be fear and anxiety immediately following the ingestion of the drug, but this feeling quickly turns to a sense of well-being and euphoria. There is also an increase in speech and a show of irritability in some users. Different people are affected in different ways. One feature of marihuana intoxication is the distortion of the time sense. Time intervals seem to be stretched out, and distances appear greater. This disturbance of the perception of time and space is the aspect of marihuana intoxication which has appealed to some jazz musicians. They feel that the distortion of time makes it possible for them to play in a faster and more distinctive style.

A 32-year-old man who had been smoking two or three marihuana cigarettes every night since the age of 15 described his experiences as follows:

> Once you smoke it, it never lets you go. It makes your mind so that it can never fail. It makes you stronger, makes you laugh a lot and makes you like everybody. It makes me very energetic to my wife so that I even got twins. There is no crime in it—it is only with alcohol that it makes you do wrong things. It is best if you smoke it with other people but if alone you can think you hear the best bands playing. Your imagination is so great that you can see someone you have not seen for a long time. But if there are other people with you, you don't see or hear anything—you just enjoy yourself. If you smoke it and go to sleep immediately you feel terrible next morning. You must have a little enjoyment and exercise before you sleep, and the next morning you feel fine. (Ames, 1958)

A major area of interest has been the possible relationship between marihuana use and personality disturbance. Unfortunately, most earlier studies of this problem were deficient in many respects. Variables were inadequately controlled, diagnosis was often questionable, and there was a failure to distinguish preexisting disturbances from those related to marihuana use.

One study, in the emergency room of a large hospital in Amsterdam, found that reactions to marihuana were not as severe as reactions to alcohol and consisted mostly of panic. However, three cases were seen in which hallucinations and paranoid delusions were present (Geerlings & Schalken, 1972). Another study of psychological disturbances was made among marihuana users in Sweden. Of 66 cases of psychosis among marihuana users, 20 were excluded because other drugs were used more heavily than marihuana. Of the remaining cases, 24 were acute, lasting one to five weeks, and 22 were chronic, lasting four months or longer. Hashish was the preparation most commonly used, in amounts of 2 to 15 grams daily. A majority of the chronic psychoses occurred in persons who had a history of psychosis prior to the use of cannabis; almost all these cases appeared to be chronic schizophrenia. However, only 2 of the 24 patients who had an acute psychosis had a previous history of psychotic episode. In many of those who had an acute episode, there had been a considerable increase in use just prior to the psychological disturbance (Bernhardson & Gunne, 1972).

The effects of *hashish*, a much stronger drug than marihuana but also derived from the hemp plant, have also been studied. The U.S. Army issued a report on psychiatric disorders among military personnel referred for problems related to smoking hashish. Among light users there were no damaging psychological effects; the major complaint involved minor respiratory problems. Somewhat less than 3 percent of the referrals were seen because of a panic reaction or toxic psychosis following a single high dose of hashish. The severe symptoms disappeared within three days following treatment with psychoactive drugs.

About 12 percent of the subjects in the Army studies were referred for treatment of an acute toxic psychosis after using hashish in combination with other drugs such as alcohol, amphetamines, sedatives, and various hallucinogens. In 16 percent of the cases, a psychosis similar to schizophrenia was observed and progressed to a chronic psychotic condition similar to chronic schizophrenia. Almost all those so affected were very heavy hashish users.

Finally, more than a hundred heavy users were referred because they were in a chronically intoxicated state which interfered with their psychosocial functioning. Here the problem was very similar to chronic alcoholism. It was concluded that 10 to 12 grams or less per month of hashish was without adverse psychological effects, while higher levels of usage—and use in combination with other psychoactive drugs—may produce a variety of psychological disturbances ranging from toxic psychoses to chronic drug intoxication (Tennant & Groesbeck, 1972).

An increasing amount of attention has been given to the so-called *amotivational syndrome.* It has been suggested that prolonged use of marihuana may result in a decrease in conventional motivation. One study (Kolansky & Moore, 1972) observed a loss of interest on the part of marihuana users in their professions and occupations, along with a tendency to acquire new and less competitive values. Unfortunately, it is not possible to determine whether use of marihuana caused the change in behavior and values, or whether the change in values and behavior led to use of marihuana.

The investigation of the amotivational syndrome has yielded conflicting results. A study of marihuana use in Jamaica has indicated that this condition is not associated with regular cannabis use in that society. In Canada, a study conducted by the Addiction Research Foundation found that when subjects were forced to consume larger daily quantities of marihuana than they wished, there was a decrease in work productivity (Le Dain, 1970). However, in another study of experimental administration of marihuana, there was no consistent effect on pattern of work over a three-week period (*Marihuana: A signal of misunderstanding*, 1972).

A major difficulty in the investigation of the amotivational syndrome has been the confusion as to definition. Some authors appear to be referring to the direct result of frequent intoxication; others emphasize a lasting change in behavior and personality

presumably due to some type of brain damage. If such a syndrome indeed exists, it will probably need to be demonstrated in terms of permanent or semipermanent organic brain changes.

Mind-Blowing Drugs: Hallucinogens

The possibility of a biochemical basis for at least some of the more serious mental disorders has resulted in a considerable amount of interest in a group of very powerful mind-altering, or *psychedelic*, drugs. Various other terms have been used to describe these drugs and to distinguish them from narcotics and other physiologically addictive drugs. The term *hallucinogenic* refers to the ability of the mind-altering drug to induce, or to generate, hallucinations. These drugs have also been called *psychotomimetic* drugs because the effects sometimes resemble, or mimic, the symptoms seen in psychotic states.

Hallucinogens are chemicals that produce, in normal people, transient states resembling psychoses. They make it possible to induce hallucinations, delusions, dissociations, and feelings of unreality under relatively standardized conditions. The value of the investigation of these psychotomimetic substances is that if it can be discovered why known chemical compounds cause changes in feelings and behavior, there may be clues to the chemical structure and processes of natural substances in the body which may be related to mental disorder.

Lysergic acid (LSD) One of the best-known of the hallucinogenic drugs is LSD-25, or lysergic acid diethylamide. This drug is derived from ergot, a substance which has been associated with mental illness since the Middle Ages. The hallucinogenic effects of

(a)

(b)

LSD-25 were first observed by Albert Hoffman, a research chemist in Switzerland. Hoffman was working with the drug in 1943 when he accidentally sucked a small quantity through a glass tube. Less than an hour later, he became confused and muddled in his thinking and developed visual and audi-

tory hallucinations. Hoffman did not understand what was happening, and he was so frightened that he left his laboratory and started home on his bicycle. Although he lived only a short distance away, he said later that the ride was like a nightmare. It seemed as if he rode a thousand miles. When

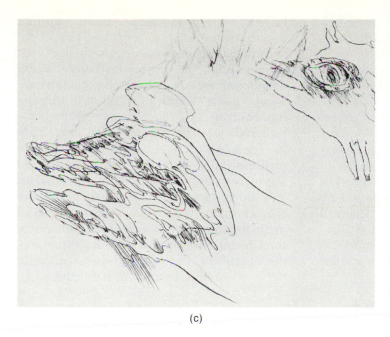

(c)

Figure 7.6 (a *and* b, *opposite page;* c, *left*) The work of the artist Bernhard Jager, while under the influence of LSD. Note the progressive distortion of the image. Jager stated, "Everything begins to move on this picture. The ears of a wolf turn into a burning pine forest."

Hoffman recovered, he deliberately measured out a quantity of the chemical, and took it again. This time the experience was even more severe. He developed all the signs of schizophrenia. As a result, the psychosis-producing nature of the drug was established.

In a study in which two graduate students in psychology volunteered to take LSD-25, the first symptoms of personality disorganization were noticed in the area of mood. The subjects began to smile more often, and then they started to giggle. Everything suddenly seemed humorous. Finally they became hilarious and roared with laughter. Sometimes they laughed at what others said and sometimes apparently at their own thoughts. Their mood was completely inappropriate to the situation. A careful medical check was kept on each subject during the experiment. Every fifteen minutes a physician recorded blood pressure and heart action. While minor changes in the functioning of the body

took place, they were of relatively little importance.

After a period of several hours, the subjects in the experiment were confused in their thinking. The inappropriate laughter was gone, except for occasional silly giggling. A little later, the subjects became suspicious. One crouched on a bed in the corner of the room and looked fearfully at anyone who came near him. Later he said that he thought he might be killed. At the height of the confused thinking, hallucinations were experienced. The subjects heard voices and saw strange figures in the room. One student reported seeing human shapes and animal forms in the wood grain on the doors.

The outward signs of LSD-25 intoxication bear a strong resemblance to the behavior of some schizophrenic patients. Such a superficial resemblance, however, does not mean that the underlying biodynamics are necessarily the same. It is well known that certain states of alcoholism, particularly in alcoholic hallucinosis, are highly similar to paranoid schizophrenia. It may be that the alcohol in one case, and the LSD-25 in the other, acts merely to release the schizophrenic potential within a given patient.

With respect to possible biological effects of LSD, there have been conflicting reports of chromosomal damage, with uncertainty expressed as to the ultimate significance of these findings. An underlying concern has been that chromosomal changes found by some investigators have also been observed in survivors of the atomic bombing of Hiroshima and might be related to an increased probability of developing disorders similar to leukemia.

Other Addictive Drugs

In addition to the hard drugs, marihuana, and the hallucinogens, there are other drugs to which people can become addicted. The most important are the amphetamines. These drugs are stimulants and are used to treat mild depression and to provide psychological stimulation. The continued use of amphetamine drugs leads to a false sense of well-being which is not a reflection of the true state of the organism. It has been found that a high tolerance for this drug is developed very rapidly.

Abuse of amphetamines and barbiturates ranges from the practice of using illicitly obtained drugs to the more hidden forms of abuse represented by inappropriate usage of medically prescribed medication. Some experts would also include as an abuse the prescribing of amphetamines in programs of weight reduction. Very large quantities of these drugs are manufactured; in the case of the amphetamines, it has been estimated that

fully half the production finds its way into illegal channels.

Authorities have been particularly concerned about the upsurge in the high-dose, usually intravenous, abuse of methamphetamine ("meth," "speed," "crystal"). Increasing numbers of young people are using a hundred times the average dose in a single injection, which may be repeated a number of times daily. "Speed freaks" may exhibit impulsive, paranoid, unpredictable behavior and are a danger to themselves and those around them. When this severe misuse of methamphetamine is prolonged, malnutrition, hepatitis from unsterile injection needles, brain cell damage, and disturbances of the heart rhythm become possibilities.

Theories of Drug Dependence

The theories as to the possible cause of drug dependence closely parallel those advanced for alcohol addiction. Biological, psychological, and sociocultural factors have been emphasized. As in the case of alcohol addiction, these factors do not ordinarily operate independently of one another.

It is quite possible for a person to have a physical sensitivity to drugs based upon genetic, constitutional, or biochemical conditions. This physical sensitivity, however, would not in itself result in drug dependence. Some type of learning would necessarily be involved. The learning could be at the physiological level in terms of the conditioning of a tissue need which becomes physically rewarding; or the reinforcement of drug use might be based upon modeling or other more complex forms of social learning. In the latter case, cognitive factors would also contribute to the reinforcement of the maladaptive behavior. Moreover, learning to

Figure 7.7 This assortment of pills, powder, dried leaves, and a hypodermic needle shows that drugs can be swallowed, smoked, sniffed, and shot into the veins. Some drug users have experimented with the entire range of substances. Most people who use drugs regularly develop a preference and become addicted physically or psychologically, or both.

depend on drugs would probably take place within a permissive sociocultural framework.

It is possible that a specific physical sensitivity to drugs is not a necessary condition for drug dependence. It is also possible for drug dependence to occur without sociocultural reinforcement. But there can be no drug dependence without some type of learning taking place at some level.

The Chapter in Review

Alcohol addiction and drug dependence are major forms of psychological disturbance. These two conditions account for more than 80 percent of persons admitted to public mental hospitals with the diagnosis of *personality disorder*.

1 Alcohol Addiction

Problem drinking is one of the most serious mental health problems in the United States and many other countries. Alcohol addiction is essentially a psychological problem which interferes with the drinker's personal and social adjustment. An alcohol addict is one whose frequent intoxication has not yet resulted in brain damage. When such damage does occur, the condition becomes one of the organic forms of chronic alcoholism. The causes of alcohol addiction are not clear, although it is suspected that genetic or constitutional factors may lower a person's resistance to addiction. Sociocultural conditions also may favor or inhibit the development of addiction. In any case, some form of learning is a necessary precondition for the appearance of this type of maladaptive behavior.

2 Drug Abuse and Dependence

Drug abuse and dependence have become increasingly important problems in our society. The most serious dependence involves heroin and other opiate derivatives. However, the most controversial drug is marihuana, which now rivals alcohol in popularity among secondary school and college students. The nature and extent of physical and psychological damage resulting from prolonged marihuana use remain unclear. The dangers of hallucinogenic drugs are more widely recognized, but their ability to induce symptoms resembling those of psychosis make them of great interest in experimental psychopathology. While the exact cause of drug dependence is unknown, the explanations given for such dependence are the same as those advanced for alcohol addiction. Biological factors may be involved, and sociocultural ones are usually influential. In all cases, the actual pattern of dependence is the result of the learning process.

Recommended Readings

Alcohol Addiction

Cahalan, D., & Room, R. *Problem drinking among American men*. New Haven, Conn.: College & University Press, 1974.

Fleming, A. *Alcohol—the delightful poison*. New York: Delacorte, 1975.

Trice, H. M., & Roman, P. M. *Spirits and demons at work*. Ithaca, N.Y.: Cornell University Press, 1972.

Drug Abuse

Brecher, E. M., et al. (Eds.) *Licit and illicit drugs.* Boston: Little, Brown, 1972.

Grinspoon, L. *Marihuana reconsidered.* Cambridge, Mass.: Harvard University Press, 1971. (Paperback.)

Grupp, S. E. *The marihuana muddle.* Lexington, Mass.: Lexington Books, 1973.

Gustaitis, R. *Turning on.* New York: New American Library, 1970. (Paperback.)

8
Sexual Deviance and Antisocial Behavior

Objectives

To examine the general nature of sexual deviance as a form of maladaptive behavior

To show what is meant by passive sexual deviance

To discuss deviant sexual behavior of the aggressive type

To explore the mental health aspects of sex-role preference and confusion of sexual identity

To indicate the type of antisocial behavior that is an expression of personality disorder

To present some of the possible explanations of the behavior of people diagnosed as antisocial personalities

Alcohol addiction and drug abuse, discussed in the preceding chapter, are not the only forms of personality disorder. This diagnostic category also includes sexual deviance and certain types of antisocial behavior. However, relatively few people with these problems are admitted to public mental hospitals. The behavior of some sexual deviates and many antisocial persons brings them into conflict with the law and to the attention of the police. Consequently, they may be sent to correctional institutions, where some receive treatment but most do not. Others seek help voluntarily or are urged, or required, to enter into a treatment program in the community. In spite of more favorable attitudes resulting from the mental health movement, many people continue to view sexual deviance and antisocial actions as social and moral transgressions requiring punishment rather than treatment.

Sexual Deviations

Sexual deviations are among the most important personality problems in our culture. While these cases sometimes overlap with the more serious personality disturbances, such as the neuroses and psychoses, many sexual deviations are due to personality disorganization of a less severe kind, and some do not represent personality disorder in the clinical sense. In the past, sexual deviations were grouped under the heading of psychopathic personality. For this reason, the term *sexual psychopath* has been used widely in medicine, psychology, and the criminal codes.

While the concept of the sexual psychopath is found in many books and articles, the current diagnostic classification considers sexual deviance apart from the psychopathic or antisocial type of personality disorder. Such a separation in classification is important because, while many sexually deviant acts are the result of an antisocial personality, many others grow out of personality dynamics of a quite different kind.

The first half of our century was dominated by a post-Victorian morality which looked upon any "unusual" sexual behavior as "sinful." This moral view was carried over into medicine and psychiatry. Even the most usual and conventional sexual activities were considered somewhat shameful and were banned from public discussion and consideration. Faced with these severe social sanctions, any variation in sexual behavior came to be regarded as deviant or perverted.

The entire concept of sex deviancy must be reconsidered in the light of changes in social attitudes as to what constitutes acceptable sexual practices. An important indication of these changes is the increasing tendency for the law to regard sexual activity between consenting adults as a private matter. While it is not generally known, many states still have laws which decree what is legal and illegal sexual behavior even between married couples in the privacy of their home. Such laws have seldom been enforced, but the fact that they exist to this day is significant.

Another indication of changing attitudes toward sexuality is the open portrayal of a variety of sexual activities in novels, plays, magazine articles and illustrations, and motion pictures. Not many years ago, there was a virtually total censorship of any public reference to sexually related behavior.

In spite of more liberal social attitudes toward deviant sexual behavior, some behavior is considered abnormal because it interferes with personal and social adjustment. In the past, such behavior was considered to be abnormal per se. The emphasis has now shifted so that sexual behavior is more likely to be considered abnormal only when it is self-defeating or damaging to others.

The types of sexual behavior of greatest interest to abnormal psychology fall into three major categories: (1) sexual disturbances of a passive nature; (2) sexual offenses against other persons; and (3) sexual problems involving identity conflicts and sex role preference.

Passive Sexual Disturbances

Some forms of sexual behavior considered deviant involve acts which are essentially private. They involve other people in only an indirect way. There is no dangerous or aggressive element in behavior of this type, and many of these people manage to keep their activities hidden from family and friends. The two most common forms of passive sexual disturbance are *voyeurism* and *fetishism.*

Voyeurism: The Urge to Look

Voyeurism is a form of behavior in which the individual receives erotic satisfaction from watching sexually arousing situations. This impulse is seen, in more or less socially acceptable form, in the popularity of magazines featuring nude men or women, X-rated movies, and pornographic literature which induces visual images of a sexual nature.

In a less acceptable form, voyeurism is responsible for a wide variety of behavior ranging from that of the frustrated youth who peeps into the windows of dormitories and sorority houses to the pathological cases of men and women whose only relief from sexual tension comes from watching the erotic behavior of others. One man managed a vicarious incestuous relationship with his promiscuous daughter by encouraging her to invite young men home and then peeping at their lovemaking.

An extreme form of voyeurism was observed in a man who had an urge to look under women's dresses. This man sometimes felt the impulse so strongly that he waited for women to go into telephone booths to make calls. If a woman left the door to the booth open, he had an irrestible need to get down on his hands and knees in an attempt to see under her dress as she stood at the telephone.

Even though voyeurism is a passive act, it may bring the voyeur to the attention of the police because of the implied invasion of the privacy of others. In enlightened courts, such persons are referred for psychological study and treatment. Other voyeurs recognize that their behavior is socially undesirable and seek help with the problem. If the behavior is a learned pattern that has become a preferred means of seeking sexual satisfaction, psychological treatment is generally successful. There are some cases, however, where the voyeurism is an expression of a more serious psychological problem.

Fetishism: The Sexual Substitute

This pattern of maladaptive behavior is one in which an individual receives sexual pleasure and satisfaction from another person's clothing, personal possessions, or parts of the body. Favorite fetish objects are shoes, stockings, undergarments, handkerchiefs, and similar articles of apparel. Hands, feet,

Figure 8.1 The urge to look for sexual signals is a basic and perhaps biologically determined aspect of human behavior. In some people, especially men, this urge may become so overwhelming that they become voyeurs. Although our society provides increasing opportunity for satisfying such needs, the urge to look can be troublesome and may result in embarrassing consequences.

legs, hair, and breasts are also common objects of erotic attachment. The condition is seen more frequently among men than among women.

The study of primitive tribes reveals many instances in which an object assumes the magical power of its possessor. The system of totem and taboo is built upon this idea. In the case of the fetishist, the same principles are at work. The fetish becomes a mystical substitute for the loved one.

There are a great number of different kinds

of fetishes. "Hair snippers" are fetishists who derive pleasure from surreptitiously clipping hair from women's heads. A favorite haunt of the hair fetishist is the motion picture theater. Taking a seat behind a girl with attractive hair, he quietly snips a few locks for himself and then hurries away to another unsuspecting victim. If the fetishist thinks that the person may be willing to let him have the lock of hair, the situation loses its attraction. Nor will he be satisfied by being given locks of hair as gifts.

The foot fetish is another relatively common distortion of the erotic impulses. A young man in Ohio telephoned a number of attractive girls and told them he was making a foot survey. He then proceeded to ask such questions as the following: "Are you more ticklish in your feet than your ribs?" "Did you ever have your feet tickled in a swimming pool?" "Can you control the movements of your feet when they are being

Turned on by a Wet Shoe:
A Study in Fetishism

A young man was brought to a psychiatrist for treatment because his mother became concerned over his habit of playing with wet canvas shoes. He told the psychiatrist, "I like to take shoes and get them wet; I go around and ask all the ladies in the neighborhood to let me have their shoes and wet them." He was unable to say when the fascination with wet shoes began. He said, "It just came on me and stayed in my mind."

The young man told the psychiatrist that he was aroused by women's canvas shoes, perferably black. He said that he preferred that a woman put on the shoes and allow him to wet them with soap and water in a bucket. He then preferred that the woman walk in the wet shoes for a short time. "I like to watch the bubbles." He would then like to dry the shoes while the woman was still wearing them. While he preferred that the woman wear the shoes, he said that it was about as good if he wet the canvas shoes and scrubbed them when not on the woman's feet.

When the young man described his fetish, his face flushed and he spoke with excitement. He asked the psychiatrist if one of the secretaries could come in and perhaps she would not mind wearing wet canvas shoes. When the psychiatrist was unwilling to go along with the suggestion, the young man asked whether the psychiatrist could furnish him with canvas shoes and a bucket on his next visit.

When the young man arrived for his next therapy session, a pair of new black canvas shoes were in the office. He looked at the shoes and said that he didn't know whether he should wet them because they were so new. When the shoes were placed on the desk near him, his face reddened and he was obviously excited. He asked the psychiatrist whether the shoes would fit him even though it was quite evident they were too small. Nevertheless, he took off his shoes and tried to put the canvas shoes on. He then asked for a bucket and debated whether he should wet the shoe. He asked the psychiatrist to leave the office because he wanted to do it alone. The water could be heard running and when the psychiatrist reentered the room, the tip of one shoe was wet. He gave the shoes to the psychiatrist and said he had better empty the bucket. He was unwilling to discuss the matter further.

On the third visit the young man began by asking the secretary whether he could put the shoes on. He then told the psychiatrist to stay and watch him with the shoes. He took the black canvas shoes, and he looked at them and felt them. There was a slight flushing and excitement as he held the shoes. He walked over to the sink and slowly soaked the entire shoe. He then put the shoes on the desk and said, "Could you leave the room for a few minutes so I could take my shoes and socks off and put the shoe on and walk around watching the bubbles come out?" The psychiatrist agreed and when he returned, the young man appeared excited. He said, "It makes me feel good."

The young man was in treatment for a period of a year. During one session, he asked for the shoes and examined them in an absorbed way, putting his hands into the shoes as well as over them. He wet one of the shoes under the faucet, and he soaked both shoes in a bucket. As he manipulated the shoes in the water, it was obvious that he was sexually aroused.

On another visit he said, "I don't know why I do this." He remarked that he thought about shoes much of the time and that he dreamed about them. He also said that his head ached after he wet the shoes. When asked what else he felt during and after wetting the shoes, he replied that he felt "very good inside." He admitted that he was sexually aroused sometimes but not always. He asked, "Why do I have this? How did it start?" His earliest memory concerning his fascination with wet canvas shoes was being at a swimming pool and wanting to pay one of the girls to step in the water with canvas shoes on. (Epstein, 1975)

SWOLLEN   ورم کرصه ـ ادکرو

tickled?" "Could you stand to have your feet tickled continuously for fifteen minutes?" In one case he asked, "Could I come out and see for myself whether your feet are ticklish?" The young woman said no, but a little while later the doorbell rang, and there he was. "I've come to tickle your feet," he announced.

Theories of passive deviance   While genetic and constitutional factors have not been implicated in such passive behaviors as voyeurism and fetishism, the possibility of a biological link with the behavior of lower animals must be considered. Many animals show intense interest in the sexual signals and display behavior of other animals of the same species. This observation has led to the suggestion that sexually oriented looking and fetish attachment to body parts and clothing are biologically conditioned. For example, it is known that rubber, leather, shiny metal, and wet and glistening objects and surfaces are common fetishes among humans. This attraction, however, is not limited to the human species. It has been reported that a rubber boot can evoke sexual excitement in a baboon and a chimpanzee (Epstein, 1969). The theory has been advanced that such surfaces are a sexual signal related to the swollen contour and coloration of the sexual skin of the anogenital area (Wickler, 1967).

Whether or not such observations are relevant to human behavior, the emotional attachment to fetish objects can be readily explained in psychological terms. The behavioral approach assumes that this attachment is due to conditioning during childhood or early in life. For example, a young boy refused to go to sleep until he had been given a stocking which had been worn by his mother. Eventually the stocking became part of the youngster's sexual fantasies during

masturbation. The rewarding effects of these early experiences established a lifelong pattern of behavior in which all stockings became erotic objects. In a similar way, sexual excitement can become attached through conditioning to any object that might accidentally accompany the early sexual experiences of the child. The psychodynamic theory emphasizes the significance of the fetish object as a substitute for the sex organs. The critical factor is assumed to be the symbolic nature of the fetish and the way in which the behavior satisfies unconscious needs.

Sexually Aggressive Acts

Unlike passive sexual disturbances, some deviant forms of sexuality are emotionally and physically damaging to other people. Aggressive sexual behavior ranges from exposing one's genitals in public to child molesting, forcible rape, and sadistic acts involving torture and murder. In all such cases, psychological problems of varying degrees of severity are present.

Exhibitionism: The Urge to Display the Body

Possibly the least serious and threatening of the aggressive sexual acts is exhibitionism. The exhibitionist is a person who obtains erotic stimulation by displaying, or exhibiting, the body to other people. Since women have many socially acceptable ways of satisfying this need, most exhibitionists are men.

This type of behavior has traditionally been treated as a legal offense rather than as a psychiatric or psychological problem. Yet the more enlightened lawyers, police officials, and jurists are coming to realize that this is an emotional problem which cannot be cured by a jail sentence.

CONTOUR ـ   ببیند ـ
STOCKING ـ   ہوراہ یش تن کو سلیر

Figure 8.2 Most exhibitionism lacks the charm and humor of this young woman strolling casually with her male friend. In everyday life, exhibitionism is likely to be a furtive and somewhat sordid expression of disturbed motivation.

The precursor of exhibitionism is seen in children when they show their sex organs to one another. It is seen also in the sexual display behavior of animals, in the ceremonial dances of many different cultures, and, finally, in the erotic relationships of adult human beings.

The activity pattern of exhibitionism is fairly consistent. The exhibitionist is likely to expose himself at the same place and at the same time of day. In fact, he seems to go out of his way to risk being caught. The executive of an advertising firm was arrested after exposing himself at his office windows to the girls who worked in the offices across the street. A man in Connecticut staged dances in the nude on moonlit residential lawns. He tapped on windows of houses to gain attention, and then he began his impromptu ballet. A trap was set by a group of husbands, and the exhibitionist was caught. To everyone's amazement, the nude dancer turned out to be the town's model policeman and the father of three children.

As in the case of voyeurism and fetishism, exhibitionistic behavior in humans is paralleled by the sexual displays among lower animals. In fact, sexual areas of the body of some animals are brilliantly colored or otherwise emphasized in order to attract maximum attention. Here again there is the possibility of a carryover to humans of some type of primitive biological programming.

Among humans, the behavioral approach seeks to explain exhibitionism in terms of a learned redirection of sexual needs. It is possible that during childhood or adolescence a person might have discovered by chance that the exposure of the sexual organs aroused the interest and excitement of a member of the opposite sex. This experience could be so sexually stimulating and rewarding that the behavior would be repeated and reinforced. In this way it could become a preferred means of obtaining gratification.

There is also clinical evidence that a person who finds it difficult or impossible to make a conventional sexual approach to a member of the opposite sex may learn to

Confessions of a Confirmed Exhibitionist

The following comments by an exhibitionist reveal something of the feelings, conflicts, and behavior of a man with this personality problem:

> I have exhibitionistic tendencies toward women, and I am sure it will get me into difficulties. It's a peculiar thing that it is only six or seven months that I have had these impulses. I want to halt them before they get me into hot water. It's a matter of great shame. I am quite sure I can get rid of them, but I need moral support and bolstering up. If someone found out about them it would be a great disgrace. I couldn't face my wife.
>
> The exhibitionistic tendencies really started ten years ago. I remember one incident distinctly. I used to go bathing and undress in back of some rocks and shrubbery. While I was undressing, a woman about a block away was looking at me and was interested. I made note of this interest. I couldn't help but notice that she was a member of the opposite sex and that she had an interest in my body. It made me feel important and secure. Until this experience, I had been very modest and shy about showing any part of my body. . . .
>
> I am still not very much at ease with women. I realize that they are human beings, and I get along with them tolerably well. With my wife I am rather modest, reserved and conservative. She is the same way. I never display my body to her. . . .
>
> I have had that impulse to exhibit myself several times. To me it is such a shameful thing, I try to put it out of my mind and forget about it. It's never been toward any particular person, but it is always toward a woman my own age or younger. I can hardly bear to talk about these things. It took a lot of courage to come to talk to you.
>
> I would have to be in a pretty secure place where no one could find out about it. It would have to be where no one knows me and with a woman who wouldn't object. It's more the thrill of anticipation. That first experience with the woman on the beach was very, very interesting. I got the impression that all women might feel the same way, and I want to experiment again to see if it is true. (Henry, 1955)

make use of an indirect approach such as exhibitionism in order to obtain sexual satisfaction. This fact may account for the occurrence of exhibitionistic behavior among handicapped and elderly people.

Attempts have also been made to explain exhibitionism in psychodynamic terms. Here the emphasis is on the satisfaction of unconscious needs. For example, it has been suggested that the exhibitionist is less concerned with the relief of sexual tension than with the need to be apprehended and punished. The fact that exhibitionists seem to take unnecessary risks and are usually apprehended is taken as evidence of the unconscious need for punishment. Other psychodynamic explanations have emphasized unconscious needs based upon such psychoanalytic assumptions as the need to prove masculinity and to deny castration.

Sadism and Masochism

Sadism refers to behavior in which the person receives satisfaction, usually with sexual overtones, from punishing others and inflicting pain on them. *Masochism* is behavior in which similar satisfaction is gained from being punished or experiencing pain. The sadist wants to hurt others; the masochist wants to be hurt. In both cases, the pain and punishment may be necessary to conventional sexual relationships or may become a substitute for them.

Since sadistic behavior usually involves unwilling victims, it is a more dangerous condition than masochism, in which the person permits himself or herself to be victimized. The nature of sadistic behavior is such that it tends to be extreme. Some of the most atrocious crimes are committed by people with sadistic impulses.

A vicious case of sadistic murder took place in Long Beach, California, where a 10-year-old girl died as a result of injuries received in the home of her female music teacher. The child was found tied to a chair, her body covered with burns, bruises, and bites. In Kansas City, a 14-year-old stabbed a young girl to death with a butcher knife. When arrested, he said, "I didn't want to kill anyone. All I wanted to do was to slash somebody."

Man Beats College Girls with Belt

Los Angeles, Nov. 1—A 29-year-old man was taken into custody on suspicion of assault with a deadly weapon. He gained entrance to two sorority houses by posing as a Hollywood talent scout. At each sorority on the UCLA campus, he told the girls of the need for suffering in order to portray genuine emotion. He induced several of the girls to allow him to beat them with a belt in order to test their ability to register pain. In the second sorority house, one of the girls became suspicious and called the police.

The first indications of sadistic behavior are often seen during childhood.

A university professor described the sadistic impulses of his childhood in the following words:

I am cruel. I was cruel even as a child. I tortured insects before I killed them. I tore the wings from flies, pierced butterflies with a needle, and fastened them alive upon the walls. I wanted to catch snakes and tear off their heads as the other boys did, but I feared they would bite me. I tweaked the cats' tails until they cried out with pain and writhed in my grasp. I would torment animals in a cage. If I tortured any animal to death, it fascinated me to watch how long it could live. My sport with earthworms was to cut them in pieces, smaller and smaller until they no longer moved. Or I would stick them with needles until they died. I would tear one or two wings and legs from an insect and take delight in watching the maimed creature trying to get away. I caught wasps, tore out their sting or laid them upon hot irons; I picked out their sting and pulled off their heads. (Stekel, 1929)

The term *masochism* is derived from the name of Count Leopold von Sacher-Masoch, an Austrian writer who pursued women whom he could depend upon to inflict pain on him. He would grovel at their feet and obtain the greatest erotic pleasure from his mistreatment and selfabasement.

The Sexual Slave Fantasy: A Case of Masochism

Marianne S., a 24-year-old schoolteacher, came for psychotherapy because of a disturbing aspect of her sexual life with her husband. While she appeared to be very much in love with her husband, she found it impossible to engage in sexual intercourse unless she had vivid fantasies of a masochistic nature. It was necessary for her husband to tell her stories of women who were slaves, forced to perform menial and often revolting tasks, and who were generally mistreated by the men who were their masters. The more masochistic the behavior of the women in the story, the more likely it was that the patient could become aroused in an erotic way. Her favorite fantasy, which her husband related to her, was that of women who were forced—against their wishes—to perform unnatural sexual acts with strange men. The more debasing the actions, the more stimulated the patient became. In this case, the patient experienced a vicarious form of masochism by identifying herself with the women described by her husband.

Masochism is such a common compulsion that several magazines have been published containing masochistic stories, letters, historical sketches, and personal advertisements designed to put masochists in touch with one another.

The masochistic compulsion has led to all sorts of strange situations. One young man visited prostitutes and paid them to engage in an Indian war dance with him. He carried a long rubber dagger; after the dancing had completely exhausted him, he would fall to the floor, and the girl would then stab him with the dagger. There were no other intimacies. The drama was designed to satisfy a masochistic need.

Girl Uses Razor to Mar Beauty

New York, Dec. 14—Because her fiancé complained that she was too popular, a 17-year-old girl cut fifteen deep gashes in her face, arms, and legs with a razor blade. Not until six hours after she was admitted to a hospital did she admit to police that she had inflicted the wounds herself. Previously she had insisted that she had been the victim of a hit-and-run driver.

Theories of aggressive deviance Various attempts have been made to explain sadistic and masochistic behavior. While there is no evidence pointing to genetic influences, the possible involvement of constitutional factors, particularly those having to do with the biochemistry of the endocrine system, cannot be ruled out. There is evidence that aggressiveness in lower animals can be influenced by altering the biochemical balance (Welch & Welch, 1969).

It is unlikely, however, that biochemical imbalance alone could account for the complex behavior patterns associated with sadism and masochism. The link between sexual satisfaction and the externally directed aggressiveness in sadism and the aggressiveness directed toward the self in masochism is possibly a learned relationship.

The experience of becoming sexually aroused as a child while being spanked or otherwise punished in a physical way can be a rewarding one. Physical punishment may create sexually arousing experiences so satisfying that further punishment is sought in order to rearouse the sexual excitement. The reinforcement of such behavior through repetition can establish a lifelong pattern of maladaptive behavior based upon masochistic needs.

Similarly, erotic pleasure resulting from observing the sexual responsiveness of someone else being punished in a painful way can lead to the establishment of a preference for sadistic behavior. In this way, it is possible to view both sadism and masochism as operantly shaped behavior.

The psychodynamic view of sadomaso-chistic behavior takes the position that sadism and masochism are symptoms of unconscious needs and conflicts. For example, the male sadist may be symbolically punishing his mother, for whom he has repressed feelings of love and hatred. The masochist, according to the psychodynamic view, might want to be punished in order to be rid of strong guilt feelings. The assumed psychodynamics supposedly vary from patient to patient and can be determined only through a thorough exploration of the unconscious levels of the personality.

Child Molesting

It is not uncommon for children of both sexes to be the victims of sexually aggressive actions of adults. The technical term for this type of maladaptive behavior is *pedophilia.* Since young children are naive and lacking in sophistication, they often become willing partners in sexual encounters with adults. Such behavior is always dangerous because the adult's fear of being discovered sometimes leads to physical violence and because of the potential psychological damage to the child.

An analysis of 100 males convicted of molesting young girls showed that the offenders were of average intelligence and had an average age of 37 years. Most of them—78 percent—were married or had been married; 73 percent were white, and 67 percent molested children whom they knew (Fisher, 1969).

An attempt was made to develop a typology (five categories) of child molesters based on the way in which the victim was regarded and treated by the offender. The passive type desires the child as a love object and uses enticement and seduction to enlist the cooperation of the child. This type is usually discouraged if the child refuses. An aggressive type of offender inflicts sexual abuse on the child and sadistically hurts or punishes the child in some way. Three intermediate types, depending upon the relative degree of passivity or aggressivity involved, were also described (Groth, 1972).

Why do adults molest children? Explanations of child molesting have been advanced in behavioral and psychodynamic terms. The behavioral approach holds that adults learn to prefer children as sexual objects because young children are easier to approach, rejection by them is less anxiety-provoking, complicated attachments are avoided, and the sexual encounter is less threatening. When these contingencies are perceived by the adult as being rewarding,

---

The Menace of Child Molesting: Two Cases

Harry E. is a 52-year-old divorced man who was admitted to a hospital because of his pathological sexual behavior. The patient was having a sexual relationship with his teenaged daughter, and at the same time was involved in a homosexual relationship with his 12-year-old son. The patient had a history of homosexual relationships with other men, and several months before his admission to the hospital he was arrested for making suggestive remarks to two young boys.

John M. was picked up six or seven times between the ages of 16 and 23 for sex offenses against children. Each time his family managed to get him off with a reprimand or a small fine. Once he was sent to jail. However, one afternoon this young man was driving along a country road when he saw a girl of 9 walking home from school. He stopped and asked her if she wanted a lift. She did, and he drove her to a secluded lot where he raped her, and then, in a panic that she would identify him, crushed her skull with a rock.

---

the behavior is reinforced, and the probability of its being repeated is increased.

The psychodynamic view is that the sexual preference for children is a symptom of a deeper conflict. The sexual approach to a child is assumed to be the result of incomplete psychosexual development, a reflection of hostility toward adults, an expression of inferiority and inadequacy, or similar needs and conflicts at the unconscious level of the personality.

Forcible Rape

Forcible rape has only recently been considered in the light of abnormal psychology. There had been a tendency for many years to regard rape as merely the impulsive expression of overwhelming sexual need. It has become increasingly clear, however, that forcible rape is in many cases an expression of serious maladjustment.

There is apparently no single motivation for rape. Clinical observations at the California State Penitentiary suggest that one type of rapist attacks any female as a representative of the woman who rejected him. Another type of rapist is a severely inadequate man who is so overwhelmed with threat that he must subdue and frighten the victim in order to be able to engage in sexual intercourse (Howel, 1972).

Our knowledge of forcible rape is extremely limited, owing to the lack of formal study directed toward the problem. Fortunately, there is a marked trend in the direction of better understanding of the problems of the rapist and the victim. The influence of the growing number of rape crisis centers will undoubtedly have a beneficial effect not only as to victims of rape, but will encourage investigations of the psychological makeup of the rapist.

Problems of Sex Roles and Preferences

Some of the most intriguing problems in the field of sexual behavior involve sex roles and preferences. There are millions of men and women who, for reasons as yet obscure, express some degree of sexual preference for members of their own sex. Others feel a strong urge to wear the clothing of the opposite sex, while some seek to change their sex through surgical operations.

Homosexuality: A Problem in Sex Preference

One of the most common problems of sexual identity is homosexuality, in which the love object is a member of the same sex. Such behavior has been a favorite theme in literature. It is mentioned in the Bible, as well as in the basic religious, artistic, and philosophical works of other cultures. Petronius discussed the problem in *The Satyricon*, and both the *Eclogues* of Virgil and the *Metamorphoses* of Ovid, written many centuries ago, contain eulogies to homosexuality.

The Judeo-Christian tradition, however, has considered homosexual behavior to be morally wrong from biblical times to the present day. The concept of wrongness and sinfulness inevitably led to the consideration of such behavior as deviant and abnormal. It did not matter that most homosexuals were able to make a satisfactory adjustment. Because of the moral issue involved, even the best-adjusted homosexuals were considered to be abnormal.

This attitude has been changing in recent years. The 1968 revision of the diagnostic manual of the American Psychiatric Association listed homosexuality as one of the sexual deviations. Since that time, the Association has gone on record to the effect that homosexuality is not a mental disorder in the psychiatric sense. An increasing number of psychologists and psychiatrists agree that while homosexuality may be socially deviant, it is not psychologically deviant. The courts are beginning to recognize this difference, and there is less tendency to prosecute sexual acts between consenting adults.

In spite of the more permissive attitudes toward homosexuality, there remains considerable opposition to this type of behavior. Some people continue to believe that homosexuality is "contrary to the word of God." Many parents feel that the legal acceptance of homosexuality might be damaging to their children. Other people admit to irrational bias and prejudice concerning homosexuals and homosexuality.

An example of the resistance to the gains made by homosexuals was the fight in California in 1975 to repeal a bill that decriminalized homosexual as well as heterosexual acts between adults in private. The bill was regarded by homosexuals as freeing them from the threat of prosecution and police harassment for conduct that in the past had forced them into a criminal role.

One result of society's lack of acceptance of homosexuals has been that a significant number of them suffer from emotional conflicts and an impaired self-image. Such symptoms are the result of a sexual preference which is not socially approved. The symptoms are not part of the homosexuality; they are a reaction to it. One study of volunteer members of a lesbian organization found that the lesbians were significantly more prone to anxiety and obsessive thinking than were women who were not lesbians (Goodhart, 1972).

The conflict and emotional turmoil experienced by the homosexual was also shown in a study of a group of male homosexuals. Certain significant events usually preceded the admission, "I am a homosexual." These events included (1) early sex play of a homo-

Figure 8.3 Homosexuality is an ancient pattern of behavior. The poems of Sappho of Lesbos described the delights of sexual love between women, and male homosexuality was widely accepted in ancient Greece. This drawing by Aubrey Beardsley shows Lysistrata calling upon the women of Athens to withhold their sexual favors from men.

Figure 8.4 For many years it was assumed that lesbianism, or homosexuality among women, was less frequent than male homosexuality. Part of the reason for this attitude was the greater acceptance of public displays of affection between women. It now appears that there is little or no difference in the number of lesbians and male homosexuals.

sexual nature, (2) actually seeking persons for homosexual contact, and (3) "coming out," or participating in the gay world. An average of four years separated the first homosexual experience and the admission that one was a homosexual. More importantly, this period was one of extreme emotional turmoil during which 48 percent of the subjects had visited a psychiatrist and 31 percent had made a significant suicide attempt (Roesler & Deisher, 1972).

Causes of homosexuality In spite of thousands of articles, research reports, and books on the subject of homosexuality, the basic nature of this condition remains obscure. Biological, psychological, and sociological theories have been advanced to explain the behavior, but there has been no general agreement as to cause or causes.

Biological theories of homosexuality assume that the behavior is inborn and may be related to genetic mechanisms involving maleness and femaleness. The psychological view is that sexual preference is acquired through conditioning early in life. Psychodynamic theories assume that homosexual behavior is a symbolic expression of unconscious conflicts related to disturbed psychosexual development. The sociological theory places major emphasis on faulty family relationships and pathogenic parenting.

The biological theory of homosexuality includes the possibility that the condition is caused by hormonal imbalance. This view assumes that the cells in the brain area (hypothalamus) that mediates sexual behavior are hypersensitive to the hormonal content of the blood. For a number of years studies failed to find any hormonal differences between homosexuals and heterosexuals. More recent positive findings are based on improved and more sensitive methods for measuring hormone levels. One study found significant differences in the ratios of male and female hormones excreted by male homosexuals as compared with those of heterosexual males in the same age range. The male-female ratio was substantially lower in homosexuals (Glass, 1972). It has been suggested, however, that hormonal differences might be the result of homosexuality rather than the cause of it.

Studies of the physical characteristics of homosexuals as compared with those of heterosexuals have yielded conflicting results. One study of height, weight, fleshiness, muscularity, and similar measures—combined with a biochemical study of urinary metabolites and blood serum lipids—found differences warranting the conclusion that a common unidentified factor underlies physical and personality characteristics and homosexuality (Evans, 1972). Other studies have failed to find differences that would distinguish homosexuals from heterosexuals in terms of physical characteristics (Swanson et al., 1972; Eisinger et al., 1972; Goodhart, 1972).

While biological factors might eventually be shown to be involved in some cases of

Figure 8.5 Although most men and women are heterosexual in their attitudes and sex preferences, each person has something of the opposite sex in his or her personality. This basic bisexuality is suggested by the intriguing painting by René Magritte, in which the female figure symbolizes the eternal femininity in man.

homosexuality, the appearance and maintenance of homosexual behavior is probably a learned pattern. Early environmental contingencies are largely responsible for sex-role preferences. Being reared as a member of the opposite sex, exposure to homosexual companions, homosexual seduction, and similar social learning experiences help shape homosexual behavior. Subsequent rewards reinforce the pattern until a bisexual or homosexual pattern becomes well established.

The problem of homosexuality has also intrigued psychoanalysts and others inclined toward psychodynamic explanations. This approach concerns itself not only with overt homosexuality, but also with latent, or unconscious, homosexuality. The latent inclinations make their appearance in a variety of ways. At a relatively superficial level, the male with this problem prefers feminine activities, reacts emotionally more like a woman, and unconsciously adopts feminine mannerisms and modes of dressing.

The homosexual, according to the psychodynamic view, is a person who has become fixated at, or has regressed to, the genital stage of psychosexual development which normally occurs during early adolescence. At that time, homosexual "crushes" on teachers and other members of the same sex are considered to be expressions of normal development. This period, however, is followed by the phallic stage of development, during which attachments to members of the opposite sex are formed. If a person does not progress beyond the genital stage, or returns to it later in life, a pattern of homosexuality is assumed to emerge.

As with other forms of maladaptive behavior, the preferred explanation of homosexuality at this time is that the behavior is determined primarily by learning experiences. These experiences are facilitated or otherwise modified by possible biological and probable sociocultural influences. Conventional cognitive processes are able to account for psychodynamic influences without the necessity of resorting to psychoanalytic concepts and assumptions.

Transvestism: The Urge to Cross-Dress

Another important problem of sexual identity, which may or may not involve homosexuality, is *transvestism*, or cross-dressing. The urge to wear the clothing of the opposite

sex has been recognized for many centuries and has appeared in a wide variety of cultures. Herodotus, in ancient Greece, described men who put on women's clothing, did women's work, and behaved in a feminine way. The condition was also known in ancient Rome. Both Caligula and Heliogabalus occasionally dressed as women.

Cases of transvestism are frequently reported in the newspapers. A "man" who was over one hundred years old when "he" died had been known for at least fifty years by the name of Charley Howard. "He" dressed as a man, acted like a man, and engaged in a man's occupation. Not until "his" death was it discovered that Charley was really a woman. In another case, a 26-year-old man posed as a woman for ten years. He worked as a waitress, a chambermaid, and even a chorus girl. Married for six years, he was arrested for a minor offense and taken to jail, where it was found that "she" was a man. The "husband" with whom he had been living for six years insisted that he was shocked to learn that his "wife" was a man. It is quite probable that in this case the two men were living in a homosexual relationship but were reluctant to admit it.

The common notion that all transvestites are necessarily homosexual is not correct. While it is true that many transvestites are openly homosexual, a substantial number of them maintain conventional heterosexual relationships. This fact suggests that the causes of transvestism are both varied and complex.

One theory is that the condition is a form of fetishism with the preference for clothing of the opposite sex determined by early learning experiences. The cognitive component of transvestism has also been emphasized. According to this view, the need to cross-dress is based upon a complicated pro-

Figure 8.6 The transvestite often effects a remarkable transformation merely by changing the mode of dress. These two pictures are of a man called Caprice. Dressed as a man (*left*), Caprice looks like thousands of other young men his age. Made up as a woman (*right*), he is feminine and sleekly seductive.

cess of self-perception. The psychodynamic theory maintains that the transvestite is unconsciously homosexual.

Transsexualism: The Urge to Change Sexes

Transsexualism is a problem of sexual identity which has only recently been studied by psychologists and psychiatrists. The problem is not that the transsexual has a sexual preference for members of the opposite sex or wishes to wear their clothing, but that he or she actually wants to become a member of the opposite sex. These are the people who seek to have surgical operations performed which would change their sex.

The problem of transsexualism emerged in the early 1950s when surgical procedures for changing one's sex were first publicized. Since that time attitudes toward granting sex change have become increasingly liberal

Half Boy, Half Girl:
A Classic Case of Cross-Dressing

Sonny B. is a 17-year-old boy who was sent to a psychiatric clinic after he used improper language on the telephone to the mother of a young girl he had called. The mother, who answered the phone, referred to him as "half-boy, half-girl." Sonny became enraged, and used obscene language in denouncing her.

When seen at the clinic, Sonny was a rather small, slenderly built youth with very marked effeminate features and mannerisms. He spoke in a rather high and feminine voice, and his hands fluttered about in an effeminate way as he talked. He admitted to a history of transvestite behavior for a period of years, often appearing on the street dressed as a young woman. He has appeared at private parties as a female impersonator, and has engaged in striptease acts. Sonny said that the performances are somewhat disgusting to him, since he dislikes exposing his body publicly to other males. He takes part in the shows only because he is paid for his act. He commented that while everyone tells him he looks and acts like a woman, he does not think he looks like one. He admitted, however, that deep inside he feels like a woman. He would really like to be a woman, and when he dresses in feminine clothing he feels as if he were a completely different person.

Sonny has three sisters, one of whom he described as being bisexual and having emotional attachments to both men and women. He volunteered that his second sister is a prostitute, but that his third sister is "O.K." His earliest and fondest memories are those of living in his grandmother's home, where he was treated as a girl. He was permitted to play only with girls until he was 13, and his most cherished toys were dolls.

(Stoller, 1973). There is as yet no standard category of abnormal behavior that covers this condition adequately (Hoenig & Kenna, 1972).

As in the case of transvestism and other sexual deviations, the motivation for wanting to change one's sex is not a simple one that can be applied to all those who have this problem. It is probable, however, that genetic and constitutional factors play an important part in most cases.

Some of these people have anomalies, or structural abnormalities, of their sex organs. They may have parts of both male and female genitals. In such cases, surgery is sought to bring the person closer to the preferred sex. In other cases, even though structurally normal sex organs are present, a

The Man Who Became a Woman:
A Case of Transsexualism

The first book by the British woman writer Jan Morris was also the eighteenth book by the British male author James Humphrey Morris. At age 47, after twenty-five years of married life, James Morris underwent a surgical operation in a clinic in Casa Blanca to change his sex from male to female. As a result, Jan Morris became sister-in-law to his own wife, and aunt to his own children.

After leaving an English boarding school near the end of World War II, James Morris served nearly five years as an officer in one of Britain's cavalry regiments. Following the war, he became a journalist. At age 26, he climbed three-quarters of the way up the world's highest mountain to report on the conquest of Mt. Everest. Later, he became one of England's most distinguished foreign correspondents, reporting wars and revolutions from countries throughout the world. By the time he was 40 he was one of Britain's best-known writers of nonfiction.

Eighteen months after the sex-change operation, Jan Morris wrote a book which was a personal account of the transformation from man to woman. James Morris wanted to be a woman all his life. Night after night in his childhood he prayed, "Please, God, make me a girl." The compulsion to be a woman grew stronger as he grew older. He told his wife about his feelings even before they were married. Like many wives, she thought she could change her husband. When she realized this would not be possible, she helped him through the most difficult moments leading up to his decision to become a woman. The secret was kept successfully from their children, families, and friends.

Figure 8.7 Jan Morris, a British writer, in the library of her home in England. Before undergoing an operation to change her sex. Jan was a man named James Morris. This case is an example of an increasing number of transsexuals who are successfully crossing over from one sex to the other.

change of sex may still be desired. One possibility is that the biochemical balance of the endocrine system strongly inclines the person toward the opposite sex. Other people appear to want a sex change because of learned needs involving complex cognitive factors combined, in some cases, with obscure psychodynamic processes.

The Antisocial Personality

Early psychiatrists were not able to accept antisocial behavior as a form of mental disorder, particularly since the more conventional symptoms are not seen in these cases. One of the paradoxes in psychopathology is that some people appear to be intellectually quite normal but at the same time quite abnormal in other personality traits. For many years there was a failure to admit this paradox. It was accepted without question that only the disintegration of reason and intellect could produce mental disorder.

Many people, however, do not show the conventional symptoms of disorientation, thinking disturbances, perceptual distortions, and other forms of pathological behavior. Philippe Pinel, in the late eighteenth century, described people who were destructive and aggressive and yet had none of the conventional symptoms of "insanity." Early in the nineteenth century, people were described who seemed to possess no moral sense. They were called *moral imbeciles.* Gradually the condition came to be looked upon as an inherited condition that could be passed down from generation to generation.

Late in the nineteenth century, the term *psychopath* was used to designate a person of this type. When the first diagnostic manual of the American Psychiatric Association was published in the early 1950s, *psychopath* was dropped and *sociopath* was introduced to stress the sociocultural components of the behavior and to deemphasize the constitutional theories that had dominated the first half of our century. When the second edition of the diagnostic manual appeared in 1968, the term *sociopath* had been abandoned, and these people were called *antisocial personalities.*

It is virtually impossible to estimate the incidence of antisocial personality in our society. Very few of these people are admitted to public mental hospitals. In fact, most hospitals are extremely reluctant to admit them because the institutions are not equipped to handle them. A very large number of men and women with antisocial personalities find their way to correctional institutions, where little effort is made to look beyond the criminal behavior. Another large number of antisocial personalities manage to stay out of institutions by their wits or through the help and influence of their families and friends.

The antisocial personality is one of the least understood diagnostic groups in the field of abnormal psychology. There is disagreement even among experts as to what constitutes an antisocial personality. Some writers include alcoholics, drug addicts, and sex deviants in the group, using the category as a convenient dumping ground for misfits. But even when care is taken to isolate the antisocial personality, considerable difficulty exists. For this reason there has been a trend in the direction of seeking a physiological basis for defining the condition.

The key to the diagnosis of antisocial personality is not so much in the nature of the behavior but in the characteristics of the person. The failure to make this important distinction has led many people to be labeled antisocial personalities when in fact they were people with other types of problems who had engaged in antisocial activities. It is for this reason that studies of antisocial personality must be viewed with the greatest caution. Far too many generalizations have been made about antisocial personality on the basis of studies of the overall criminal population. Such studies may or may not be relevant to an understanding of the clinical type of antisocial personality.

The antisocial personality has been defined as a person who shows five principal personality traits: (1) inability to profit from experience, (2) superficial emotion, (3) irresponsibility, (4) lack of conscience, and (5) impulsiveness. Moreover, the antisocial personality must not fall into any of the following diagnostic groups: mental retardation, organic brain damage or disease, psychosis, neurosis, or situational maladjustment (Ziskind et al., 1973). The point here is that while antisocial behavior can be explained in terms of a number of psychological and organic disturbances, the specific diagnosis of antisocial personality can only be made when these other conditions have been ruled out.

The antisocial personality is unable to establish truly warm and meaningful relationships with other people. He or she is incapable of friendship based upon trust and affection. When such a person enters into what appears to be a friendship, it is a matter of expediency. Friends exist only to the extent that they can be useful. Similarly, marriage is never more than a source of narcissistic satisfaction. When antisocial persons do not get their way, they may become dangerous and even violent. Because they lack conscience, they are capable of the most extreme types of behavior. Aggressive brutality, brutal sex crimes, and other acts of violence are quite within their capability.

Why Are "Antisocial Personalities" Antisocial?

subjective

Most antisocial acts are not committed by people who could be called antisocial personalities. The vast majority of crimes and delinquencies are impulsive acts or efforts to achieve financial gain, personal status, or some similar objective. Such people are conscious of their wrongdoing, which ordinarily is accompanied by some degree of anxiety and feelings of guilt. When the antisocial behavior is repeated, as it is in a great many cases, it is because the behavior was rewarding. Repetition of the reward and reinforcement cycle often leads to a lifelong pattern of delinquency and criminality.

The antisocial personality also learns that antisocial acts can be rewarding. However, this type of person clings to the maladaptive pattern even after it has been repeatedly punished. More importantly, the person diagnosed as an antisocial personality carries the maladaptive behavior into all areas of social life. Such persons do not hesitate to steal from their parents and other family members, cheat those who seek to help them, and lie to their friends and associates—all with no apparent indication of regret or remorse. These actions are not characteristic of even most hardened criminals.

It appears that the learned antisocial behavior shown by these people is combined with some additional factor which remains obscure. One assumption is that the traditional view of a genetically or constitutionally determined defect is correct. Some studies of twins and adopted children suggest that

---

The Case of the Phony Physician

When the 37-year-old man applied to a Brooklyn hospital for a medical internship, he was hired immediately on the basis of photostats of degrees from Scottish and German universities. During the next few months he helped deliver several hundred babies. Over a period of five years, he transferred from one New York hospital to another. Finally, after he missed a payment on a car he had purchased, police found that he had never been licensed to practice medicine. Horrified officials of the hospital where he was serving as Senior Resident then learned that he had not even finished high school. In the Army he had been assigned to the Medical Corps, and he had read every medical book he could find. When the war was over, he forged credentials and references and applied to a medical placement agency as a physician. Due to the shortage of physicians, he had no trouble in finding an opening. The superintendent of the hospital where he was first hired said, "He was a very good doctor, and a nice person. He had a marvelous personality and impressed all of us at the hospital." When the self-styled "doctor" appeared in court, he found that the judge had been one of his patients at the hospital only a few weeks before. Granting that the "doctor" was quite an impressive fellow, the judge nevertheless sent him to the penitentiary for a year.

---

this might be the case. There is the possibility, however, that the critical problem is not the learning of antisocial behavior but rather the failure to learn appropriate moral and ethical values early in life. This failure would explain the facility with which delinquent and criminal patterns of behavior are learned by these people. It would also account for the distorted attitudes which permit them to victimize even those who are closest to them.

Personality Trait Disturbances

This group of personality disorders is made up of conditions which, for the most part, are exaggerations of traits found in the personalities of all people. It is only when these traits become so pronounced that they interfere with personal and social adjustment, that the condition becomes clinically significant.

The majority of men, women, and children with personality disorders never receive treatment for their difficulties. They do not recognize that they are disturbed, nor are they regarded by others as having personality difficulties of a serious nature. It is only when their personality characteristics lead them to overt behavior which gets them into difficulty that it is realized that they are psychologically disturbed. Since most of these people learn to live with their disturbances, they avoid serious conflicts and therefore do not come to the attention of psychiatrists and psychologists.

Some of these disturbances are relatively superficial and could be changed if treatment were undertaken. Other disturbances in this group are more deep-seated and are extremely resistant to change. In most cases the disturbances appear to be the result of developmental defects based on a combination of psychosocial and constitutional factors.

Some Typical Trait Disturbances

Only certain traits fall into the category of personality disorders because most personality traits are not maladaptive even when they are exaggerated. Generosity, for example, is a trait that ranges from profligacy to miserliness. Both extremes might be highly undesirable, but such behavior could not be considered abnormal in the clinical sense. Among the personality traits most frequently included in the personality disorder group are seclusiveness, suspicion, and aggressiveness.

The seclusive personality The tendency to withdraw within oneself from time to time, and to avoid other people, is a normal one. But there are some people in whom this trait is present to a dangerous degree. When this is the case, the person is said to be *schizoid*. The schizoid reaction is seen in people who are incapable of close relationships with others and who are cold, aloof, and emotionally detached. They find their satisfaction within themselves and tend to be intellectually and emotionally independent of other people. They are the seclusive, nonsocial ones who cannot be easily drawn into group activities. Such people are inclined to avoid both competition and cooperation, preferring to remain emotionally uninvolved.

Schizoid personalities ordinarily find little satisfaction in face-to-face relationships. Sometimes such people are said to have a "shut in" personality. They have few friends, and even these few friends do not get to know them well. Frequently they are considered odd or peculiar. Sometimes they show exceptional intellectual ability or creative talent; but in spite of their occasional brilliance, they are likely to lead unhappy and isolated lives.

The first signs of this rather seriously

maladaptive personality pattern may become apparent during childhood. The child who is seclusive and withdrawn and who becomes irritable when this seclusiveness is disturbed may be beginning to build up the world of fantasy and daydreams characteristic of the schizoid personality. All children indulge freely in make-believe, and this behavior serves a useful and constructive purpose in child development. The difference between the psychologically healthy child and the schizoid child is that the schizoid finds it increasingly difficult to know what is real and what is fantasy.

Many mildly schizoid persons maintain a satisfactory adjustment throughout life. Some seek help because of difficulty in making friends, feelings of inadequacy, or general social ineptness. Hospitalization is not necessary unless a more serious mental disorder is suspected.

The suspicious personality The suspicious, or *paranoid*, personality has many of the traits of the schizoid person and also a marked tendency to be envious, jealous, and stubborn. The reaction is relatively common in our culture. Most of us know people who are persistently suspicious. Such persons go through life constantly questioning the motives of others. They are sure the salesclerk has shortchanged them, the grocer has cheated them, and other people are trying to get the best of them. They are likely to be stubbornly resistive to reasoning. Moreover, they find it difficult to form warm and close emotional relationships with other people. They may seek to protect themselves from the world by means of sarcasm and invective.

As with other personality disturbances, elements of paranoid thinking are found in even the most normal individuals. It is only when the paranoiac trend becomes the determining factor in the person's behavior that the condition can be called a personality pattern disturbance.

Many paranoid personalities manage to make a marginal adjustment in spite of their symptoms. These people, because of their generally disagreeable natures, are likely to have few friends. Usually they prefer to live alone and either do not marry or have unsuccessful marriages. The studies of the ecology of mental disorder in Chicago showed that this type of person was most likely to be found in rooming-house areas of the city. Such areas contain relatively large numbers of men and women who are single, separated, or divorced. The paranoid personality, not unexpectedly, is represented among these groups in disproportionately large numbers.

The aggressive personality The aggressive personality is the most common of the trait disturbances. This condition is one in which the person takes the attitude "Nobody's going to push me around." These are the people who carry the proverbial chips on their shoulders. They take every frustration in life as a personal affront, and they react with irritability, temper outbursts, and destructive behavior.

There are also variations on the aggressive pattern. One is called the *passive-aggressive* personality. This condition is typified by the technique of rebellion through inaction and stubbornness. Such people express aggression, but in a passive way. To be stubborn and resistive, to be muleheaded, to be sullen and spiteful, and to be negativistic is to be aggressive in a nonactive way.

In the *passive-dependent personality*, there is a childlike clinging to other people. Such persons seek to avoid responsibility, are likely to be indecisive, and may show anxiety and ineffectual behavior in situations requiring personal initiative. All the variations of aggression can become psychologically damaging to personal and social adjustment. If the damage is severe enough, a diagnosis of personality disorder is made.

Some Possible Explanations of Trait Disturbances

Unlike sexual deviance and the behavior of individuals diagnosed as having antisocial personalities, personality trait disturbance has a relatively uncomplicated explanation. All personality traits are acquired and maintained through learning. The biologically oriented psychologist would suggest that in some cases, especially where schizoid and aggressive traits are present, physical influences might be involved.

Similarly, the importance of unconscious processes would be emphasized by the proponents of the psychodynamic explanation of maladaptive behavior. But it is unlikely that genetic or constitutional factors, or psychodynamic relationships, in themselves, could operate independently of conditioning, modeling, and other more complex forms of social learning.

More important than how personality traits become maladaptive is the problem of when a trait should be considered abnormal. As we have seen, many people are inadequate, seclusive, suspicious, or aggressive. The question is, how seclusive or suspicious must one be in order to be diagnosed as having a schizoid or paranoid personality disorder? The matter is further complicated by the fact that maladaptive traits may sim-

"I Hate You! I Hate You!"— The Case of an Aggressive Adolescent

Helen P. is a 14-year-old girl who was sent to a juvenile court after she had run away from home. While in the detention unit of the juvenile center, the girl's behavior became so aggressive that she was referred to the psychiatric clinic. When she entered the interview room, she shouted that she hated her mother, and would kill her if she ever had the opportunity. Throughout the stormy interview, which was punctuated by crying, cursing, and shouted obscenities, the girl variously threatened to kill her mother, herself, and the examiner. She became particularly disturbed while describing an incident involving the stabbing of a child which occurred five years earlier. The details of this incident were hazy, although the event appeared to have had a traumatic effect.

In a later interview, the youngster's mood was somewhat more depressed. On one or two occasions she came very close to tears but at no time did she cry. A few times she managed a feeble smile. She verbalized marked hostility toward her mother although she denied she would harm her. Helen admitted she had an explosive temper, especially when pressure was put on her by her mother. The aggressive personality disorder is seen in the extreme hostility toward the mother, the hostile acting out in the detention unit of the juvenile center, and the aggressive impulses directed toward the examiner during the initial clinical interview.

ply reflect a lack of social skills and competence. In such cases it is questionable whether the behavior should be considered abnormal in any sense. For these reasons, the diagnosis of personality trait disturbance tends to be an unsatisfactory one.

The Chapter in Review

Sexual deviance and certain types of antisocial behavior, along with alcohol addiction and drug abuse, are expressions of personality disorder. A group of conditions called personality trait disturbances are also considered to be personality disorders. Few people with these forms of maladaptive behavior are admitted to public mental hospitals. Sexual deviates and those given the diagnosis of antisocial personality are more likely to be sent to correctional institutions. People with personality trait disturbances, if treated at all, are usually treated in the community.

1 Sexual Deviations

Maladaptive patterns of sexual behavior are of three principal types: passive behavior involving private problems which do not directly affect other people; aggressive sexual deviance, which is usually imposed upon unwilling victims; and problems of sexual identity and sex-role preference. Most types of sexual deviation can be explained in terms of learning experiences in childhood or early in life. In some cases, genetic or constitutional factors may contribute to the deviant behavior. The possibility of deep-lying conflicts and the need to satisfy unconscious needs must also be considered in some cases.

2 Antisocial Behavior

Most antisocial behavior is not engaged in by people with psychological disturbances. The diagnosis of antisocial personality is reserved for those whose personality makeup permits antisocial behavior with little or no feeling of guilt or anxiety. There appears to be a flaw in their character development. The maladaptive behavior is probably more related to the failure to learn moral and ethical attitudes than it is to the learning of antisocial patterns of behavior. There is also the possibility that a genetic factor may in some way be involved.

3 Personality Trait Disturbances

The personality disorders include psychological disturbances in which normal personality traits are exaggerated to the point where there is interference with personal and social adjustment. The traits most frequently involved are seclusiveness, moodiness, suspicion, passivity, aggression, and obsessive-compulsiveness. These conditions are relatively stable and continuing patterns of behavior which are frequently troublesome and for which a person may or may not seek help.

Recommended Readings

Sexual Deviance

Johnston, J. *Lesbian nation*. New York: Simon and Schuster, 1973.

Humphreys, L. *Tearoom trade*: *Impersonal sex in public places*. Chicago: Aldine-Atherton, 1975. (Paperback.)

MacDonald, J. M. *Indecent exposure*. Springfield, Ill.: Charles C Thomas, 1973.

Sagir, M. T., & Robins, E. *Male and female homosexuality*. Baltimore: Williams & Wilkins, 1973.

Antisocial Behavior

Abrahamsen, D. *The murdering mind*. New York: Harper & Row, 1973.

Bremer, A. H. *An assassin's diary*. New York: Harper Magazine Press, 1973.

Denisoff, R. S., & McCaghy, C. H. (Eds.) *Deviance, conflict, and criminality*. Chicago: Rand McNally, 1973. (Paperback.)

Hare, R. D. *Psychopathy*: *Theory and research*. New York: Wiley, 1970. (Paperback.)

9
Neurosis: The Struggle with Anxiety

Objectives

To discuss the general nature of neurotic behavior

To describe the essential features of some of the more common forms of neurotic behavior

To indicate that neurosis is basically a learned form of maladaptive behavior

To point out how cognitive processes can be involved in the acquisition and maintenance of neurotic behavior

To present some of the psychodynamic theories advanced to explain neurotic reactions

The word *neurotic* is popular and widely used in everyday conversation. Most of the time people use it incorrectly and without any real knowledge of its meaning. A newspaper reporter described the murderer of an entire family as being "neurotic," when in fact the killer showed all the signs of a far more serious mental disorder.

The scientific view of neurosis is that it is a pattern of maladaptive behavior in which a person responds to life stress with persistent anxiety or other behavior representing attempts to control the anxiety. The neurotic ordinarily recognizes the undesirable and sometimes disabling nature of his or her symptoms. There is no break with reality, and neurotic people usually do not need to be hospitalized.

Only 8 percent of the people admitted to public mental hospitals in the United States are diagnosed as neurotic (National Institute of Mental Health, 1975). However, figures from public mental hospitals do not reflect the prevalence of neurotic disorder in the general population, since most neurotic people, if treated at all, are seen in community outpatient facilities or by therapists in private practice.

What Causes Neurosis?

While there is rather general agreement that neurotic behavior is related to anxiety and the struggle to control it, there is considerable difference of opinion as to how neurosis develops and is maintained. As in the case of many other forms of maladaptive behavior, it is unlikely that there is a simple or single explanation. Biological, psychological, and sociocultural influences combine in varying degrees to determine whether or not a person

becomes neurotic and what form a neurosis may take.

People differ widely in their sensitivity to stress and their tolerance for anxiety. This sensitivity and tolerance depends to a great degree upon inherited resistance within the nervous and endocrine systems. When the inherited resistance is low, the person is likely to be overly sensitive to stress and may have a low tolerance for anxiety.

Sigmund Freud was one of the first to emphasize that neurotic behavior occurs only in predisposed individuals. He pointed out that there must be a favorable biological soil if a neurotic reaction is to flourish. He said, in effect, that inborn and constitutional factors are a necessary precondition for the development of neurotic behavior.

Family and twin studies suggest that at least some neurotic disorders have an important genetic component, whereas others may have none or a relatively unimportant one. A person's genetic background influences his or her physiological level, which involves neurones, hormones, and enzymes. This physiological level, in turn, influences behavior when environmental conditions are favorable or unfavorable. This view has been referred to as the genetic-environmental interaction model of neurosis (Miner, 1973).

In an investigation of genetic influence in neurotic persons in West Berlin, a depth-psychological study was made of fifty pairs of twins. In all these cases, it was possible to interview both twins. It was concluded that the amount of variance of neurosis that might be attributed to heredity in the population sampled was probably within the range of 40 to 60 percent (Schepank, 1974). Another study found that the genetic influence is specific for the type of neurosis rather than for neurotic behavior in general (Young et al., 1971).

While it may very well be that there are biological influences favoring the appearance of neurotic behavior, the behavior itself is a learned reaction pattern. Classical conditioning, operant shaping, modeling, and more complex forms of social learning are responsible for the different patterns of behavior characteristic of the various neurotic conditions. Learning also plays a central role in determining when the behavior appears and how firmly established it becomes. Neurotic behavior is contingent upon internal reinforcements of a cognitive nature and external reinforcements from the sociocultural environment.

The psychodynamic view of neurosis is that neurotic behavior is a symptom of the attempt to deal with anxiety that is related to unacceptable and hence repressed sexual and aggressive urges. These deep-lying and troublesome impulses and feelings, according to psychoanalytic theory, would create an intolerable degree of anxiety were they to become conscious. For this reason, they are held in check by repression, fantasy, symbolism, and other personality defense mechanisms. When these conventional defense measures are inadequate, the neurotic is faced with an overwhelming degree of anxiety which in some cases is experienced directly as an anxiety neurosis. In other cases, the person attempts to handle the anxiety by transforming it into other neurotic symptoms.

In the following discussion of some of the specific forms of neurotic behavior, the primary emphasis will be on neurosis as a learned form of behavior. There will be a continuing assumption that genetic and constitutional influences may predispose a person to neurosis and that both cognitive and sociocultural contingencies operate to initiate and maintain the maladaptive behavior pattern.

Anxiety Neurosis

The anxiety neurosis is a pattern of behavior in which the physiological symptoms of anxiety become so intense or persistent that they interfere with the sufferer's personal and social adjustment. It is the most common of all neurotic conditions. The hundreds of millions of tranquilizers used each year are consumed largely by people attempting to reduce excessive anxiety.

The mere presence of anxiety, however, is not an indication of anxiety neurosis. Even the most normal people become anxious when faced with stressful situations. Moreover, our culture and the times in which we live give rise to a relatively high level of anxiety in most people. In fact, a certain amount of anxiety is to be expected in everyone.

**"I Won't Be Able to Hold On!"—
An Anxiety Neurotic Describes Her Symptoms**

It was just like I was petrified with fear. If I were to meet a lion face to face, I couldn't be more scared. Everything got black, and I felt I would faint, but I didn't. I thought, "I won't be able to hold on." I think sometimes I will just go crazy. My heart was beating so hard and fast it would jump out and hit my hand. I felt like I couldn't stand up, that my legs wouldn't support me. My hands got icy, and my feet stung. There were horrible shooting pains in my forehead. My head felt tight, like someone had pulled the skin down too tight, and I wanted to pull it away. I couldn't breathe. I was short of breath. I literally get out of breath and pant just like I had run an eight-mile race. I couldn't do anything. I felt all in, weak, no strength. I can't even dial a telephone. Even then I can't be still when I'm like this. I am restless, and I pace up and down. I feel I am just not responsible. I don't know what I'll do. These things are terrible. I can go along calmly for awhile, then, without any warning, this happens. I just blow my top. (Laughlin, 1956, p. 39)

Many men and women who have a low tolerance for stress go through life in a state of constant anxiety. They are fearful, worrisome, easily fatigued, frequently complaining, unable to sleep, tense, and unhappy. In most cases in which a high level of anxiety persists, the person does not seek treatment and is not considered to be neurotic in the conventional sense. It is only when the level of persistent anxiety reaches a point where the symptoms interfere with family life, social relations, or occupational adjustment that the condition is looked upon as a neurosis.

Symptoms of Anxiety Neurosis

The typical anxiety neurotic is an excessively tense person who is filled with uncontrollable dread and apprehension. He or she tends to have a rapid pulse and elevated blood pressure. There may also be difficulties in breathing, frequent sighing, digestive upset, and similar physical signs of an overreacting autonomic nervous system. These physical symptoms are a reflection of the emergency measures being taken by the organism to make itself ready to meet the threat, whatever it might be. In the case of lower animals, the threat typically comes from the environment. However, in human beings the danger is more likely to be within the organism in the form of thoughts of a dangerous or forbidden kind.

On the psychological side, anxiety neurotics are likely to have pronounced feelings of dread and apprehension. They may be convinced that something terrible is going to happen, but they do not know what it will be, or even why it should happen. Nevertheless, they are quite sure that they are in grave danger. They live under a cloud of impending doom, and nothing they tell themselves,

or are told by others, can dispel the aura of tension and fearfulness.

Anxiety reactions include acute anxiety attacks and chronic anxiety states. While these reactions may exist independently of one another, in many cases the chronic state is punctuated by acute episodes of more intense anxiety. Attacks of acute anxiety are episodic, come on unexpectedly, and may last from a few minutes to several hours. The victim of acute anxiety usually cannot account for the onset of the symptoms or for their later disappearance. Such attacks are terrifying for the victim, who not infrequently believes he or she is going to die. The heart begins to pound, breathing becomes rapid or difficult, there is sudden perspiration, the gastrointestinal system is upset, and there is an urge to frequent urination. The person is thrown into a state of acute apprehensiveness without being able to say what is causing it.

In the chronic anxiety state, the anxiety persists over a period of weeks, months, or even years. Such conditions are marked by an exaggeration of the various psychological and physiological symptoms of a milder degree. Frequent sighing, headache, gastrointestinal upsets, chronic fatigue, and general apprehensiveness are common complaints. Such people often complain that they cannot concentrate, cannot keep their minds on their work, and have lost all interest in life.

While anxiety reactions are widely prevalent, it is well to remember that many organic states give rise to symptoms similar to those seen in anxiety. Hyperthyroidism, organic heart disorders, disturbances of the cerebellum and the semicircular canals, toxic conditions, endocrine disorders, and numerous other diseases and dysfunctions of an organic nature may produce symptoms that could readily be mistaken for anxiety.

Theories of Anxiety Neurosis

The behavior theory is that excessive or inappropriate anxiety or both is established through operant conditioning or other forms of learning. Recent demonstrations of autonomic and visceral conditioning in animals and human beings have given strong support to the assumption that the physiological reactions underlying anxiety can be learned through reinforcement by life stress and other environmental contingencies.

Cognitive influences also play an impor-

tant, if not critical, part in the development and maintenance of neurotic anxiety. Since all anxiety is a response to threat or danger, it is necessary that an event be perceived as threatening. The seriousness of the perceived threat must then be evaluated, and a decision must be made as to whether the threat calls for emergency measures. The degree of anxiety is influenced by appraisal of the threatening situation (Beck et al., 1974). The perception, evaluation, and decision making are the cognitive components of anxiety neurosis.

Psychodynamic theory assumes that the most psychologically damaging threats to human beings arise from the possibility that

---

The Father as Lover and Villian:
A Case of Anxiety Neurosis

Hilda J. is an 18-year-old girl who was referred to a psychiatric clinic because of marked anxiety centering on sexual conflicts involving her relationship with her father. The girl first came to the attention of the authorities eight months earlier, when she attempted suicide. At the time, she told a story of difficulties at home and of her intense fear of her father. She came to the attention of the police again later when she was arrested for drinking. She showed great anxiety in connection with her father, and told how he beat her and her brothers and sisters, how he drank excessively, and how he attempted to molest her.

At the time of the interview, Hilda was found to be a rather small, thin, dark-haired girl who was pleasant and cooperative but who obviously was under considerable tension. At the beginning of the interview she pulled at her hands, sighed repeatedly, shifted uncomfortably in her chair, and had difficulty speaking because of her tenseness. The anxiety lessened somewhat in the face of repeated encouragement and reassurance. Eventually she told a story which revolved for the most part around her father. She said that he had told her that her mother had frustrated him sexually. At another time he kissed her, but

she denied any overt sexual activities with him. She admitted having frequent dreams and nightmares, most of which involved the father. She repeated one dream in which the mother was in the kitchen making supper, and the father tried to get his daughter to give him a knife so he could stab the mother. She also had dreams of old men lurking in the street.

Hilda's anxiety became so great that she insisted that her mother sleep with her. Before going to bed, she went through a ritual of barricading the bedroom door, hanging a cloth over the doorknob, and forcing the cloth into the keyhole with the point of a butcher knife. She could sleep as long as her mother kept an arm over her, but she awakened and would be terrified when her mother moved her arm away. At the same time, Hilda was afraid of the mother and occasionally hesitated to eat anything the mother had prepared. The girl was sometimes so fearful that she remained awake all night in order to watch her mother.

The problem has been intensified by the father's seductive action toward his daughter, and by the mother's passive reaction to the situation. The girl has deeply ambivalent feelings about both her father and her mother. In spite of her repeated expressions of fear and hatred for the father, she is preoccupied with thoughts of him both in her waking fantasies and her dream life.

sexual and aggressive thoughts and feelings of a forbidden nature will find their way into consciousness. Neurotic anxiety is seen as a symptom indicating that unacceptable material in the unconscious is threatening to become conscious. When there is an imminent breakdown of psychological defenses, the neurotic person may experience catastrophic anxiety in the form of panic.

Phobia: Irrational Fear

A phobia is an overwhelming and irrational fear. In these cases, a person's anxiety becomes attached, through conditioning, to a specific object or situation. The person then attempts to control the anxiety by avoiding the phobic object or situation.

Phobias are so common among children that they have been called the normal neuroses of childhood. Fear of the dark, ghosts and goblins, cemeteries, and bugs and animals is an everyday occurrence among children. Such fear reactions are particularly common when the child is 4 to 6 years old. During this period of development, children learn to have fears which may influence their behavior for the rest of their lives.

> From ghoulies and ghosties
> And long-leggety beasties
> And things that go "bump" in the night,
> Good Lord, deliver us. (Cornish Prayer)

Most adults also learn to have irrational fears, at times bordering on phobias. Among the common everyday fears are those of the dark, thunder and lightning, corpses and graveyards, and snakes, spiders, and creeping things. Some people are afraid of crowds or afraid to cross the street, stand near an open window, or cross a bridge. Still others

learn to have a pathological fear of dirt, germs, and disease. It is characteristic of the phobic person to recognize that the fear is foolish and unreasonable, but at the same time to be unable to do anything about it. The fear is magnified out of proportion to the actual situation. As a result, the person is likely to show other symptoms such as headache, backache, stomach upset, dizziness, and feelings of insecurity and inferiority.

Phobias have no respect for age, intellectual level, or social position. Chopin had an intense fear of being buried alive; Arthur Schopenhauer, the German philosopher, was so frightened of razors that he singed his beard rather than shave it; Henry III of France was afraid of eggs and became terrified at the sight of them. A prominent labor leader was well known for his fear of germs. He had his New York office equipped with ultraviolet germ-killing devices, and in a handshake he used only one finger.

Some Common Phobias

Most of the phobias have been given technical names. In practice these terms are seldom used, although they do appear from time to time in the literature. Some of the more common phobias are *claustrophobia*, or the fear of small, closed places; *aichmophobia*, the fear of pointed objects; *agoraphobia*, the fear of open places; and *acrophobia*, the fear of heights.

The word *claustrophobia*, which first appeared in the literature in 1879, means a morbid fear of closed places. This pathological fear is probably the most common of all phobias. For its victims, the world is often a terrifying place. Airplanes, elevators, railroad cars, buses, and automobiles are all small, closed places. In some sufferers from this phobia, the urge to jump from a vehicle

Figure 9.1   The fear of high places, called *acrophobia*, is not uncommon. Many people cannot look down from heights without feeling weakness in their knees. Other people are afraid they will fall, as suggested by this picture of a man clinging in terror to the side of a building.

is so great that travel becomes almost impossible. A New York man who travels to work on the subway is so tense and anxious that he must get out at five or six different stations on his way to and from his job. He stands on the platform until he calms down; then he takes the next train.

In *aichmophobia* the person develops a pathological fear of sharp and pointed objects. He or she fears pieces of broken glass, scraps of metal, nails, and scissors. Fear of this kind leads to all sorts of eccentric habits.

One man must eat with his fingers because of his fear of a knife and fork. Another can eat only when he uses a blunt wooden spoon. A young woman is unable to sign her name because she is afraid of pencils and pens.

The word *agoraphobia*, which is derived from the Greek word *agora*, meaning "marketplace," was first used in 1873. The condition refers to a pathological fear of open or public places. In such cases, the person develops sudden attacks of anxiety when faced with the problem of crossing a wide

The Fear of Leaving Home: Agoraphobia As a Protective Measure

Ellen R., a 32-year-old woman, developed a severe case of agoraphobia in which she became terrified each time she attempted to leave her house. The phobia became so serious that she gave up her job and remained home at all times. When she sought psychological help, it was found that when she was in her early teens she had been sexually promiscuous with several boys in the neighborhood. The patient changed her behavior when the family moved to another neighborhood and she entered a new school. She experienced intense guilt feelings about her behavior, and she repressed all memories of it. The phobia which developed later in her life was based on the fear that she might lose control of herself and be led into a life of prostitution. Without realizing what had happened, the patient had reactivated the entire episode some weeks earlier when she was going through some old papers and found a group photograph of herself at the time she had been promiscuous. The chain of associations triggered by the picture was responsible for the appearance of the agoraphobia at that particular time.

street or an open square. He or she may be afraid to go out or to leave home. Some of these people remain in their houses or locked in hotel rooms for months and even years at a time.

The fear of flying has developed relatively recently with the growth of aviation. One study was made of a flying phobia in trained members of flight crews including pilots, navigators, and a steward. The symptoms were the usual psychological and somatic manifestations of anxiety and were usually confined to flying or to fantasies about flying. The first symptoms were usually the result of flying with reduced visual cues and other frightening experiences. It was also found that symptoms were frequently preceded, or accompanied by, psychosocial stress, such as sexual or marital problems (Aitken et al., 1971).

How Phobias Develop

In our discussion of the causes of neurotic anxiety, we saw that genetic and constitutional influences are probably factors in the development of the condition since the endocrine and nervous systems are involved. We also saw that while the biological influences make it easier for some people to develop anxiety neurosis, the neurosis itself is a learned pattern of behavior reinforced by cognitive and environmental contingencies.

A similar condition exists in the case of the phobia except that the generalized psychophysiological component of anxiety has been replaced by the excessive fear of a specific object or situation. For this reason, it is probable that hereditary and constitutional factors play a less important role in phobic behavior than in neurotic anxiety. Whether or not this assumption is correct, there is abundant evidence that the development of pathological fear and the form it takes involves a learned pattern of maladaptive behavior.

It is well established that an intense fear experience is readily conditionable to other stimuli that happen to be present at the same time. Such conditioned fear can persist over long periods of time. It is entirely possible that most phobic states in adults have their roots in earlier life experiences. One youngster had been locked up in a closet as punishment at the age of 5. Another child was accidentally trapped in the cellar of an old building. Still another lost his way in an abandoned mine shaft. In each of these cases, a neurotic fear of closed places developed soon after the terrifying experience. Such incidents suggest that classical conditioning can be responsible for the establishment of a phobia.

Phobias can also develop as a result of operant conditioning. The original fear may be reinforced by a variety of environmental contingencies. The fear brings sympathy and increased attention, elicits help and assistance from others, or may be a means of dominating and controlling members of the family or other significant persons. The phobic person learns that there are other advantages to the symptom and consequently is reluctant to give it up.

Some phobias are based on social learning. The fearful parent serves as a model for the children in the family. A mother who is afraid of lightning and thunder may convey this fear to a child. Whether the child's fear develops into a neurotic reaction depends upon the type and amount of reinforcement the fear receives after it has been established.

The learning approach to understanding phobic behavior has largely replaced the psychodynamic view. However, psychoanalysts continue to regard the phobia as a neurotic defense against anxiety generated by unconscious conflicts related to sexual and aggressive feelings and impulses. For example, it is assumed that some people harbor within themselves the wish for their own destruction. Such people may develop a phobia that is a defense against thoughts of suicide. If the aggression is directed toward other people rather than toward oneself, the phobia may be a reaction against, say, the fear that pointed objects will be used to harm someone else. The impulse to punish and injure other people is not uncommon. When this feeling is developed to an exaggerated degree, a phobia may be the means whereby such unacceptable impulses are kept under control.

Obsessions and Compulsions: Unbidden Thoughts and Unwelcome Acts

The person with an obsessive-compulsive neurotic disorder is plagued by unwelcome recurring ideas, called *obsessions*, which are accompanied in many cases by unwelcome repetitive actions, called *compulsions*. While obsessive ideas are sometimes present without the accompanying compulsive actions, the two symptoms are combined in most cases. Just as the phobia is a development of the anxiety reaction, the obsessive-compulsive reaction is a further development of the phobia. In its very nature, obsessive-compulsive behavior implies fear and anxiety and the effort to control these emotions.

An obsession is an idea or thought that is silly, absurd, or apparently meaningless yet one that the obsessive person cannot get rid of. Many people experience obsessive reactions when a catchy tune, a slang phrase, or a bit of nonsense keeps coming to mind, even though they do not want to think about it. When this happens, the individual is literally obsessed by the idea.

"I Hope He Isn't Dead!"—
Obsessive Thoughts about a Husband's Safety

Myra Y. is a young married schoolteacher who was referred for treatment because of her disturbing thoughts about her husband. Whenever she was alone, she worried that he might have been in an accident. If she heard a siren in the distance, she began to shake and tremble, being certain that an ambulance was carrying her husband to the hospital. The symptoms became so serious that she was in an almost constant state of panic when her husband was away. In desperation, she sought professional help. During her treatment she admitted that her marriage had been a failure and that she secretly wished for her freedom. It was not difficult to show this patient that her obsession was based on her hostility toward the husband. She hoped something would happen to him, and the obsession was a reaction against the wish.

Compulsions are obsessions carried into action. People who suffer from compulsions repeat certain actions over and over again, even though they realize there is no sense to it. When asked why they do these things, they reply that they feel uncomfortable and uneasy if they do not do them. Some people have the compulsion to snap their fingers, tap their feet, or repeat a word or phrase. A lawyer had to make a slight bow before he could enter a door either at home or elsewhere. He managed to live with his compulsion for many years with only a few people knowing about it.

As early as 1896, Freud described compulsive behavior in a young boy:

> An 11-year-old boy had instituted the following obsessive ceremonial before going to bed. He did not sleep until he had told his mother in the minutest detail all the events of the day; there must be no scraps of paper or other rubbish on the carpet of the bedroom; the bed must be pushed right to the wall; three chairs must stand by it and the pillows must lie in a particular way. In order to get to sleep he must first kick out a certain number of times with both legs and then lie on his side. (Freud, 1896)

Obsessions and compulsions occur together so frequently that ordinarily they are considered to be a single reaction. In some cases the obsessive quality is outstanding, without any overt action that could be called a compulsion. In other cases, the obsession is accompanied by compulsive actions. While it is possible for a person to show obsessive thinking without a compulsion, compulsive behavior is always based upon an obsession.

A study of obsessive-compulsive neurotics found that the onset is usually in childhood and adolescence or very early in adult life (Templer, 1972). While the prognosis for obsessive-compulsive reactions is good when the disorder is seen in children, it is less favorable when the condition begins during adolescence and the adult years. Because of the disabling nature of the symptoms, some psychologists and psychiatrists are inclined to view this reaction as a link between the neuroses and the psychoses.

Some Common Compulsions

A woman developed the idea that there might be broken glass in her food. Before she could eat, it was necessary for her to sift through everything on her plate to make certain that there was no broken glass in it. A similar case was that of a man who could not drink his coffee for fear that a pin might have dropped into it. He would pour his beverage back and forth several times to make absolutely certain that no pin was in it.

Some obsessions are so powerful that the victims go to great lengths to protect themselves from what they might do to themselves or others. One man made a ceremony of locking his door every night, hiding the key, putting chairs in front of his bed, and stretching strings across the room. When asked why he did these things, he was unable to give a satisfactory reason.

The washing compulsion was so strong in one woman that she would find it necessary to go into a drugstore and ask for a glass of water. She would then wash her fingers. Sometimes this ritual occurred as often as a dozen times during a visit to the city. Another woman covered the door handles in her house with pieces of paper to keep them from becoming contaminated. Still another had to wash her hands several dozen times a day. She washed her hands over and over until the skin was red and raw. She wore gloves constantly in order to protect herself against germs on objects that other people had touched.

In kleptomania there is a strong—and

often uncontrollable—urge to steal. The behavior is differentiated from ordinary stealing by the fact that the act is impulsive and seemingly without reason. Department store managers, judges, and bewildered relatives are faced from time to time with habitual shoplifting on the part of a person who has been carefully brought up, is in good financial circumstances, and has no need for what has been stolen. When such persons are arrested by store detectives, they are frightened and humiliated and at a loss for an explanation of their strange conduct. All they can say is that the temptation seemed to sweep over them, and that they tried to resist it but felt driven to give in in spite of themselves.

One young woman had a compulsion to go into a certain department store to see if she could get out without paying for her lunch. She kept a record of 136 stolen meals. But on the next meal she was caught. When asked why she did it, she said, "I don't know. There is something in me that compels me to do it. I can't explain what it is."

The obsessive-compulsive concern with fire is called *pyromania*, a term first introduced in 1883. In pyromania, the person is preoccupied with the idea of fire and may have an overwhelming urge to set fires, even though the consequences are likely to be disastrous. A 14-year-old Baltimore boy admitted setting innumerable fires, one of which resulted in the death of two children and another of which caused damage worth $250,000. A pyromaniac in Seattle set fire to 130 factories, warehouses, and similar structures over a period of four years. The property damage amounted to $6.5 million. In another case, six fires were started in the hallways of six different apartment buildings on Third Avenue in New York City during a two-hour period shortly after midnight.

Theories of Obsessive-Compulsive Behavior

It is widely accepted today that obsessions and compulsions are learned reaction patterns. Such behavior satisfies a variety of individual needs. The personal satisfaction serves to reinforce the behavior and to maintain it. When additional cognitive and environmental contingencies become associated with the behavior, the possibility of the behavior becoming maladaptive is substantially increased.

For example, the obsessive-compulsive preoccupation with fire and setting fires can be interpreted behaviorally as a revenge reaction which satisfies hostile thoughts and the aggressive urge to act. This satisfaction is positive reinforcement that leads to further behavior of the same kind. The revenge, which may originally have been directed toward a specific individual, is eventually generalized to other people and situations. Setting fires then becomes a preferred reaction pattern.

The cognitive element in some forms of obsessive-compulsive behavior is quite evident. Indecisive people with feelings of inadequacy sometimes develop compulsive doubts about themselves and their relationships with others. They doubt that they can do a good job, that their husbands or wives are faithful, or that they are the real children of their parents. An automobile mechanic developed the idea that he was not the father of the 8-year-old daughter he had always adored; a fashion editor was obsessed by the idea that she no longer had the necessary talent for her job; and a schoolteacher so seriously doubted her ability to teach that she had to give up her work.

The psychodynamic approach views obsessions and compulsions as symptoms of the attempt to resolve unconscious conflicts of a sexual or aggressive kind. For example, a man became obsessed with the thought that he would drive his car off the side of the road and over an embankment. While driving, he would grip the steering wheel so tightly that sometimes it became necessary for him to stop the car and rest until he had calmed down. The psychoanalytic interpretation of this behavior was that the man had an unconscious wish to kill himself and that the obsession was a symptom of this inner conflict.

Hypochondria: The Chronic Complainer

The term *hypochondria* has a long history in medicine. The word itself refers to the area below the ribs, the part of the body considered by the ancient Greek physicians to be the seat of the black bile which caused melancholy. Later, the term came to be used for all forms of physical complaints that were without an organic basis.

In hypochondria, a person believes he or she has a physical disease when there is no real evidence for such a disease. It is an extreme preoccupation with bodily functions. Marcel Proust, the French novelist, began talking about his ill health and predicting his imminent death in 1900. He died twenty-two years later. Thousands of people experience this neurotic concern over nonexistent illness.

What Causes Hypochondria?
This maladaptive pattern of behavior clearly demonstrates the way in which learning is involved in the development of neurosis. When people find themselves losing importance and prestige, they may learn to devel-

"Doctor, I Need an Operation"— The Multiple Complaints of the Hypochondriac

John M. is a 31-year-old married man who was admitted to a psychiatric hospital. He had an eighth-grade education, and lived with his parents until his marriage. He worked for two years as a messenger with the Western Union Telegraph Company, but then was discharged because he was sending telegrams through the mail instead of delivering them to the homes.

The patient came from an emotionally and economically deprived environment and was hospitalized for tuberculosis for two years. Following his release from the hospital, he was referred to the Bureau of Vocational Rehabilitation, where he pursued a night course in commercial subjects to prepare him for clerical work. He married a girl of extremely limited intelligence, and they have a 5-year-old son. John's mother is emotionally unstable and his father has been a dependent and inadequate person who has never been able to hold steady employment. His sister, who is a patient at the same hospital, has a diagnosis of schizophrenia.

The present illness began with multiple complaints about physical health. The patient said that one day while he was playing with his 5-year-old son, he suddenly felt a "jump" and realized that his "glands were swollen and hurt." He became extremely preoccupied about this, and went from doctor to doctor insisting upon having treatments, but nothing seemed to help him. He was then referred to a psychiatrist; and since his behavior became so centered on his physical complaints that he could not work, he was sent to the hospital.

The patient, a tall, thin man, is alert, responsive, and well oriented. He is friendly and pleasant, with a clinging, extremely docile and suggestible manner. He has a wide emotional range, expressing deep concern about his physical health and, a few moments later, flashing a friendly smile in response to a question. His thinking is clear and rational except for his preoccupation with his health. He thinks his sex glands have been infected, that he has a hernia, and that he is severely constipated. He complains of feelings of tightness and pain in his abdomen. During the interview, the patient was mildly anxious with some restlessness, but motor behavior was generally unremarkable.

Figure 9.2 The French artist Honoré Daumier captured the excessive concern of hypochondriacs with the state of their health in this caricature of a man taking his pulse. People with this neurotic condition are constantly worried about their body functions. Their aches and pains, digestive upsets, elimination problems, and other physical symptoms, no matter how minor or routine, become cause for fear and alarm.

op attention-getting devices. Complaining about ill health is one way of getting other people to pay attention to them. They adopt the role of a sick or disabled person because they know that their families and friends will rally around them, give them more attention, and cater to their wishes. The hypochondriac grows into a household tyrant who must have special food and dress, the most comfortable chair, the best bed, entertainment as desired, and quiet when ordered.

Elizabeth Barrett Browning fell from a pony when she was 15 years old and remained an invalid for the next twenty years. Her illness spared her competition with her brothers and sisters. Moreover, she received extra attention and care, had a room of her own, and fared quite well. Even as her literary career grew, she kept her symptoms. However, when she was 40, she met Robert Browning, who was six years her junior. They married, and Elizabeth's symptoms promptly disappeared. At 43, she had a child. She was no longer a hypochondriac because she no longer needed her symptoms.

Hypochondria can also develop as a result of social learning. The undesirable effect of confronting people with models of illness and disease was brought into focus by a weekly television series in Great Britain. This series consisted of ten programs, each showing the work of a different hospital in relation to a specific disease. The British Broadcasting Corporation said the purpose was to satisfy the public's "healthy interest in disease," to display the fine quality of medicine in Great Britain, and to allay fears about going into hospitals. The British Medical Association, on the other hand, accused the BBC of fostering hypochondria, pandering—by including films of surgical procedures—to a desire for sensationalism, and invading doctor-patient relationships. When the film series was put on, two viewers took their lives in the belief that they had cancer; and a third viewer, about to undergo a heart operation, committed suicide after seeing the operation performed on television.

A psychodynamic interpretation of hypochondria is that it is an attempt to deal with anxiety associated with feelings of inadequacy, inferiority, and failure. The preoccupation with ill health and the physical complaints are seen as rationalizations. If one is sick or in pain, poor performance is excused and anxiety associated with inferiority is avoided. While behavioral and cognitive components are present, the emphasis is on the symbolic meaning of the symptom.

Hysteria: "A Tough Old Word"

The concept of hysteria is one of the least understood and most abused in the field of abnormal psychology and psychiatry. From the time of Hippocrates, *hysteria* has carried a broad meaning and included a great many different symptoms. Among the ancient Greeks, the disorder was thought to be unique to women and to result from a disturbance of the uterus. This theory was held for many centuries, although in the sixteenth century it was believed that the cause of hysteria was not in the uterus but in the brain. It was argued that since this is the case, hysteria is a disorder of men as well as of women. At the time, this idea was extremely advanced, and the medical profession was not ready for it.

It was not until the first edition of the diagnostic manual of the American Psychiatric Association appeared that the diagnosis of hysteria was dropped from the classification system. However, the term reappeared in the second edition as one of the personality disorders, and again as a neurotic disorder. As Sir Aubrey Lewis commented in 1975, "It is a tough old word!"

Today, hysteria is a neurotic reaction in which the person seeks to control anxiety through one or the other of two modes of behavior: (1) the *conversion* of anxiety into physical symptoms or (2) the *dissociation* of thinking. The hysterical conversion involves neuropsychological relationships, while hysterical dissociation is related to cognitive behavior.

Conversion Reaction

This type of neurosis is one in which a person's anxiety is converted into a physical symptom. When the symptom is expressed through the sensory or motor pathways of the central nervous system, the condition is called a *hysterical conversion neurosis*. However, when neurotic symptoms involve the autonomic nervous system, the maladaptive behavior is called a *psychophysiological disorder* (see Chapter 10).

Sensory symptoms Neurotic behavior can be expressed through any of the senses.

However, the most frequent conversion symptoms involve disturbances of skin sensation, vision, and hearing. Anesthesia, or lack of skin sensation, is one of the most common conversion reactions. When anxiety becomes too great, the person may seek to escape by withdrawing into a "cloak of anesthesia." Such persons no longer feel pain. It is possible to stick them with sharp objects, and they do not draw away. In some cases, a needle can be pressed under the fingernail without causing the person to flinch.

The notorious "devil's claw," used during the Middle Ages as a sign of possession by demons, was probably a conversion reaction. The part of the skin insensitive to pain, which was considered to be a place on the body where the devil had laid his hand, was simply an area of localized anesthesia. Highly suggestible people, under the stress of superstition and fear, developed the type of symptom expected of them. Many hundreds, if not thousands, of men and women were put to death as witches when in fact they were showing neurotic symptoms of the conversion type.

Some of the most dramatic examples of conversion blindness are seen during wartime. As described in Chapter 6, the hardships and horrors of war frequently cause soldiers to break down and show severe psychological symptoms. Following the evacuation of Dunkirk during World War II, a number of acute cases of conversion blindness were seen in British hospitals. In almost every case the blindness resulted from the patient's refusal to watch the horrors of the combat. One soldier became blind moments after he had seen a very close friend blown apart by an exploding shell. Another patient lost his sight after one glance at his own mangled leg.

Conversion symptoms involving hearing are also relatively frequent. It is a common observation in everyday life that many peo-ple fail to hear things they do not want to hear. The child who is playing does not hear the mother calling, the young suitor fails to hear the clock, and the reluctant student does not hear the school bell. In conversion reactions, the person may become deaf so as not to hear the unpleasant things the world has to say.

A young man lost his hearing just before World War II. He became so upset each time he heard the radio announcer give news of the impending conflict that he used deafness to solve the problem. During the war, especially in London and other cities exposed to bombing, cases of psychogenic deafness sometimes developed as a means of shutting out the unwelcome sounds of explosions, bells, sirens, and the screams of the injured.

Motor symptoms The motor symptoms of the conversion neurosis are expressed in a variety of ways. The less serious symptoms include trembling, ticlike movements, and minor cramps and contractions of muscles. The more serious symptoms—or at least the more dramatic—involve disorders of speech, paralyzed limbs, and convulsive seizures. In many cases, the conversion symptoms closely resemble the symptoms of organic disease and disability.

The conversion paralysis is one of the most dramatic of the motor conversion reactions. The intuitive recognition of the possibility of such a condition is revealed clearly in our everyday language. Such phrases as "paralyzed with fear," "scared stiff," or "glued to the spot" are merely ways of indicating that emotional conflicts have been converted into physical symptoms. In some cases, the conversion paralysis becomes a preferred way of reacting to stress. A student nurse suddenly found her arms paralyzed when she was told to scrub an operating room floor stained with blood. A soldier became paralyzed when the order was given

"Don't Leave Me; I'm Paralyzed!"— The Convenience of a Conversion Symptom

Fred K. is a 50-year-old married man who developed a marked contracture of his left hand and a partial paralysis of his arm. He held his arm bent in front of him, as if it were in a sling, and his fingers were curled inward toward the palm of his hand. He was unable to raise his arm above the level of his shoulder, and he could move his fingers only slightly.

The symptoms came on suddenly; and before he was referred for psychological treatment, the patient had undergone medical and neurological examinations by local physicians as well as by specialists at Rochester, Cleveland, Baltimore, and Boston. Various diagnoses were made, including vertebral dislocation with the recommendation of surgery on the spine. One medical center placed the patient in an elaborate traction device "to take the pressure off a pinched nerve." Other medical treatments were tried; but the patient did not respond, and the symptoms remained unaltered.

The psychological evaluation of this patient revealed that he was a well-to-do executive married to an attractive and considerably younger wife. While he seemed anxious to be cured of his disorder, there was nevertheless a remarkable casualness about his attitude toward it; one sensed that the patient took a certain pride in it. He displayed his hand and arm with some satisfaction, demonstrating the lack of feeling by touching his lit cigarette to the back of his hand to show he felt no pain. The attitude of the patient toward his symptom, combined with the lack of positive neurological findings, pointed to the possibility of a conversion reaction. Psychotherapy was recommended; and at the end of several treatment hours, the symptom was removed. While it returned a few days later, the psychological nature of the disor-der had been proved, and psychotherapy was continued.

It was clear to the therapist that the patient had been using his neurotic symptoms to solve his problems. His young and attractive wife was fond of nightclubs, while the patient merely wanted to come home at night, have dinner, read his paper, and go to bed. The difference in age and interests resulted in serious conflict. Finally, the wife began to go out without her husband. It was at this point that the symptoms appeared.

The paralysis served a number of purposes. It gave the patient a good excuse for staying home at night. After all, who would expect a man with a paralyzed arm to go to nightclubs? It also forced the patient's wife to spend more time with him at home in the evenings. Only the most callous wife would go out and leave her paralyzed husband at home alone. Moreover, the paralysis brought the patient the sympathy and attention of friends and relatives. Previously, being a rather colorless and uninteresting person, he had been overshadowed by his attractive and vivacious wife. Now he was the center of things. Finally, because the patient was jealous of his wife and suspected her fidelity, he used his symptom as an excuse to come home from his office at any hour of the day. Sometimes he would return home, complaining about his arm, an hour after leaving in the morning.

Interestingly enough, the eventual cure in this case was not brought about through the efforts of a psychotherapist, but rather by a policeman. The patient's suspicions about his wife had not been unfounded, and one day he awoke to find that his wife had run off with a police officer. Days later, when he was convinced that his wife would never return to him, his symptom disappeared spontaneously. It had served his unconscious motives, and he no longer had need of it. Without his wife and the problems of living with her, the symptom served no purpose.

---

to attack the enemy. Another soldier, who started to cry out in fear, found that after he had opened his mouth he could not close it again, nor could he withdraw his tongue. Hours later, when the attack was over, his tongue gradually withdrew and his mouth closed again. A young seaman developed a paralysis of his arms when forced to clean up the mangled bodies of his shipmates.

The problem of diagnosis The problem of diagnosis of the conversion reaction is somewhat more complicated than the diagnosis of anxiety reactions, phobias, and obsessive-compulsive conditions. In the case of conversion reactions, the symptoms must be distinguished from true organic disorders, malingering, and incipient psychotic conditions in which there may be somatic delusions. The most difficult differential diagnosis is between the conversion reaction and symptoms resulting from organic impairment of the nervous system.

Lack of concern Persons with hysterical conversion symptoms tend to show little concern for their disability. Even though such symptoms are a serious handicap, and even though the victims believe their symptoms to be incurable, there is an inclination to regard the symptoms casually and almost indifferently. It is as if the person realized unconsciously that the symptom was not truly organic. The patient with a serious organic disability is more likely to show real concern about symptoms, to be anxious and preoccupied with them, and not to treat them lightly. The neurotic person does not show this same concern. He or she seems quite willing to accept an organic interpretation of the disability and seems resigned to the fact that probably nothing can be done about it.

Contrariness to anatomy Hysterical conversion symptoms frequently do not correspond to the facts of anatomy. Skin anesthesias may show sharp lines of demarcation between areas in which pain is felt and areas in which it is not. However, the distribution of pain receptors in the skin is such that sharp lines of demarcation would be highly unlikely. As noted earlier, the anesthetic areas are likely to follow the popular conception of nerve distribution rather than the actual anatomic distribution.

Sudden onset Another important diagnostic feature of the conversion reaction is that the onset is more likely to be sudden; also, the symptom may disappear entirely and then recur. In contrast, the organic symptom is usually more insidious in onset and shows a more consistent course.

In spite of the guidelines for the diagnosis of conversion hysteria, the condition is difficult to identify. A study of patients who had been diagnosed at a neurological hospital as having conversion hysteria was made seven or more years after diagnosis. A few of the cases were found to have organic disease which had not been recognized originally. Among the patients in whom no organic disease had been found, two were later diagnosed as schizophrenics, one as an obsessional neurotic, and seven as depressives. Having obtained similar results in a followup study of patients who had been diagnosed as conversion neurotics at a psychiatric hospital, the same investigator concluded that there is nothing consistent in the condition of patients with this diagnosis. They appeared to be a random selection of patients with many different conditions (Slater, 1961). Another study of patients diagnosed as suffering from conversion hysteria found that only 13 percent could really be diagnosed as hysterics. The other 87 percent showed symptoms which could place them in various other diagnostic groups (Reed, 1975).

Theories of conversion neurosis In spite of the fact that some persons with the diagnosis of conversion hysteria are probably not neurotics, most psychologists and psychiatrists agree that the conversion reaction is a valid clinical syndrome requiring explanation. Like other neurotic behavior, the conversion symptom is an attempt to deal with anxiety. The behavioral approach emphasizes the learned nature of the behavior, even though the way in which the physical disability is originally acquired is not clear in most cases.

It is unlikely that classical conditioning, operant shaping, modeling, or other forms of social learning are involved in the typically sudden appearance of the physical symptom. The learning involved at this point is probably a complex form of cognitive conditioning. Once the physical disability has been established, the maladaptive pattern of behavior is readily maintained by means of the rewards stemming from the disability. The reinforcing contingencies would vary from case to case.

The psychodynamic view of hysteria was formulated by Freud, who originally regarded the physical symptom as a symbolic expression of repressed sexual wishes. For example, one of the motor conversion symptoms is the convulsion. Freud and his followers believed that the convulsive movements were symbolic representations of the sex act. Over the years this concept of hysteria was broadened to include other types of symbolism. The neurotic paralysis of a hand developed by a young woman during the terminal illness of her father was interpreted as a symbol of her desire to hold onto his life.

Dissociation: The Separation of the Self

The hysterical dissociative neurosis is a pattern of maladaptive behavior in which that part of the personality known as the *self* loses its cohesiveness and separates into two or more psychological systems. The self develops as a result of information processing beginning with the relatively uncomplicated sensory input of early infancy. Later, through the use of language and abstract concepts, the self evolves into a psychological system of the greatest complexity. Under certain conditions which are as yet unknown, parts of this psychological system begin to function in an independent way. When this happens, more than one "self" seems to exist. The dissociation of the self is the basis for such neurotic conditions as amnesia, automatic behavior, and multiple personality.

Amnesia: A type of psychological suicide

One of the most common hysterical dissociative reactions is *amnesia*, or loss of memory. This condition is the inability to recall events of personal identity. Amnesiacs may find themselves wandering in the street and be unable to remember who they are, where they live, or whether they are married or single. When picked up by the police, the amnesia victim very often appears dazed. Sometimes he or she is thought to be intoxicated, but at the police station or the hospital the real trouble is likely to be discovered. In some cases, the condition lasts only a few hours or days; at other times it may be a matter of weeks or months before it begins to clear.

One type of amnesia is due to head injury. A person who suffers brain damage in a train, airplane, or automobile accident may lose all memory of the crash itself or of the events before and after the incident. Most cases of amnesia, however, have psychological causes. Economic, marital, sexual, or social life may become so difficult that a person is driven to find a way out of the conflict, to escape by forgetting. One man decided to jump into the river when he lost his savings in a swindle. On his way to the river, he lost his memory and wandered through the streets until he was picked up by a policeman and taken to the hospital. Several months later his memory was restored. The real suicide he had planned had been given up in favor of the less serious psychological suicide.

A young woman found wandering along a country road was brought to the hospital by police. She knew the date and the fact that she was in Cincinnati. She said she believed she had two children and had a feeling she should "get back to them." She did not know how old she was, but she insisted, "I know I'm not over 30." In Mississippi, a 26-year-old druggist lay on a hospital bed and stared blankly at his white-haired mother, who was reminding him of his boyhood in an effort to restore his memory. The druggist answered his mother's pleas by saying, "I'm sorry but I don't know you. I wish I did know you because I love you better than anything in the world." The entire family gathered around the bed, but the young man did not recognize any of his relatives.

The Fugue: Flight without awareness This form of amnesia is one in which the person literally flees from difficulties. The fugue may last from a few days to weeks or months and may take the victim to cities hundreds of miles away from home. During the fugue state, the secondary personality appears to disregard completely the basic personality. However, the secondary personality during the period of the fugue ordinarily utilizes the previous experience of the basic personality. The patient changes his or her name, but usually is able to manage in a reasonably normal fashion.

The most complicated forms of behavior may be carried out during the fugue. A victim may travel great distances, purchase train or airplane tickets, take a room in a hotel, find a job, and lead a seemingly normal life in a completely different setting. A 22-year-old man disappeared from his fishing boat in Florida. He was thought to be dead by his family and friends, but six years later he telephoned his brother and said that he was working as an orderly in a convalescent home in New Orleans and had suddenly remembered his name. However, he had no memory of what had happened during the six-year period.

Automatic behavior: Unawareness of speech and action The hysterical dissocia-

tive type of neurotic reaction is also illustrated by *automatic behavior*. Persons displaying such behavior are not consciously aware of what they are saying or doing. They may talk in an automatic way and be surprised to hear themselves. In other cases, the person's hand moves involuntarily and produces automatic writing or automatic drawing.

Automatic talking occurs from time to time during waking states but under ordinary circumstances is not open to clinical or experimental study. A great many people have had the experience of hearing themselves suddenly, and without conscious intention, make an exclamation or otherwise blurt out a remark or a phrase. Most people have had the experience of talking on the telephone or listening to a lecture and "doodling" at the same time with a pencil on a scrap of paper. Sometimes it is done consciously and deliberately, but more often it is done unconsciously. The results frequently come as a surprise to the person who made the drawings or designs or wrote the words.

Occasionally a very productive automatic writer appears. Among the best-known automatic writers have been Flammarion and Sardou. Patience Worth of St. Louis wrote several novels by this method, the Reverend Stainton Moses wrote a history, Andrew Jackson Davis wrote on evolution, and Elsa Barker produced the *Letters from a Living Dead Man*. While this latter work was publicized as a series of "spirit messages," it was in reality an example of automatic writing. Gertrude Stein sometimes used automatic writing, and certain of the effects achieved by other modern writers and poets depend (with or without the writer's knowledge) upon personality dissociation.

Automatic writing appears under a variety of conditions and shows a rich variation in its expression. Very often the first words are isolated and apparently meaningless. Gradually the person may write phrases, then sentences, and—if there are strong tendencies toward behavior of this type—the person becomes skillful in writing longer passages. In some cases, the material can be related to underlying personality conflicts.

Multiple personality It is an easy psychological step from automatic writing, with its separate selves, to the condition of *multiple personality*, in which the dissociated segments of the personality exist alternately, or even concurrently, in a relatively autonomous way.

Centuries of philosophy, religion, and creative art have made us familiar with the contradictory nature of the human being. The inner struggle between different aspects of the self has been a subject of the most intriguing interest. Robert Louis Stevenson used the double personality as the basis for his classic story "Dr. Jekyll and Mr. Hyde." It is also the theme of such relatively recent books as *Sybil* and *The Three Faces of Eve*.

Figure 9.3 Many people have the vague feeling that their real self is not the same as the one perceived by other people. In cases of dissociation neurosis, the self splits into two or more relatively independent psychological systems, which become separated or dissociated. The dissociation is suggested by this still from the film *The Three Faces of Eve*, based upon the true story of a woman with three distinct personalities.

Multiple personality is most likely to develop in people who walk and talk in their sleep, who are easily hypnotized, and who show a tendency toward other dissociated actions. One young woman felt herself drawn out of bed and forced to go through a series of weird dances. Another had two personalities, each of which tried to read a page in a book or magazine at the same time. Unfortunately their readings did not keep step, and one personality would always finish the page before the other.

Occasionally the multiple personality is first recognized in connection with amnesia. A young woman was found wandering on the street, and the police took her to the

The Mystery of Multiple Personality: A Case Study

Mrs. A. B. was 25 when she was first admitted to a psychiatric hospital complaining of recurrent faints, amnesia, and blindness. She was referred to the hospital by her physician because she had tried to attack her five-month-old baby on two occasions.

The problem started about 15 months before she was admitted to the hospital during a period when she was uncertain about the stability of her relationship with her future husband. She developed frequent "fainting" attacks of up to 20 times in one day. These lasted for about half a minute, but later some lasted several hours. About four months later she developed periods of mutism which lasted up to four hours, and at about the same time she experienced visual and auditory hallucinations of little green men in yellow coats talking to her and comforting her after arguments with her husband.

After the birth of her daughter, the fainting started again, but when she recovered consciousness, she was often aware of her own identity until another "faint" occurred. These periods lasted up to five days, and she sometimes presented an entirely different personality. Three personalities were reported: Alma Smith, a Newcastle prostitute; an unnamed twelve-year-old girl; and a German woman called Elke Schweik. In this third personality she spoke a few phrases of German although normally she did not speak the language.

Shortly after her admission to the psychiatric hospital, she asked a nurse who she (the patient) was. A week later, she fainted, and on recovery, she believed herself to be 16 years old and still living with her mother. Her account of her situation as a 16-year-old was in keeping with the account of her life given in the case history. She had a knowledge of current events for the period in which she said she was living. This state lasted for approximately 18 hours and then ended spontaneously. On an evening two weeks later, she entered the character of Alma Smith, the prostitute. She gave an extremely elaborate account of Alma Smith's life, with details of her childhood and experiences in the brothel. She was again able to give an accurate account of the current events for the time in which she was supposed to be living. The episode lasted about 20 hours. After two months in the hospital, she was released on a weekend leave and did not return.

Five months later, the patient was readmitted to the hospital. While out of the hospital it was revealed that she had changed her personality at least once a week. For several weeks, she had been confined to bed because of difficulty in walking, and at times, she had been unable to see, to talk, to hear, or to move her arms. She also showed selective vision in that she would be able to see her baby but nothing else in the room, or she would see a tray being carried by her husband but not her husband carrying it. During this period, she experienced changes of personality to four different characters: Alma Smith; Ellen Briggs, a 21-year-old typist from Andover; Brenda Allen, a real person who had been a friend of the patient; and a woman from A.D. 2002.

After being admitted to the hospital she adopted the personality of an 11-year-old schoolgirl, Eve Johnson, a real person who had been at the same school as the patient and who had been described by the patient as "horrible and a showoff." During this change of personality, she talked and behaved like a child.

A follow-up 15 years later showed that the patient had a good work record, but few social contacts outside her work. Her marriage, while not entirely happy, was much improved. She occasionally experienced anxiety, and she complained of migraines. During the previous five years there was a marked decrease in the frequency of personality change. (Cuttler & Reed, 1975)

hospital. There she was identified by a card in her purse which indicated that her husband should be called if she had an attack of amnesia. When examined, the patient was rather anxious and unable to give her name or any other information about herself. She did not know where she was other than in a hospital. During the course of her treatment, a distinct secondary personality emerged. The patient's real name was Sara, but the secondary personality insisted her name was Maud.

Except for amnesia, the dissociative reaction is relatively rare. It is perfectly possible to spend an entire career in the field of mental health without seeing a person who exhibits a classic dissociative reaction. When such cases do occur, the dramatic nature of the symptom picture creates wide interest.

What causes dissociation?   The various forms of dissociative neurosis appear to be based on conflicting needs and desires. The separation of the self is the climax of repeat-ed failures of personal adjustment and integration. However, the manner in which ideas and emotions are capable of breaking away from the main personality and leading a quasi-independent existence is an unsolved problem.

The behavioral aspects of dissociation are probably less important than the cognitive component. Some type of learning must be involved since it is highly unlikely that dissociative behavior is biologically programmed. It is probable that higher-order symbolic conditioning operates in these cases. Dissociative neuroses also demonstrate, in a dramatic way, the powerful effects of conflicting motivational systems.

Neurotic Depression: The Dark Despair

Neurotic depression is probably the most common of all neurotic conditions. It accounts for about 76 percent of persons diag-

Figure 9.4 This man shows the inactivity and lethargy typical of the person with neurotic depression. The bare room suggests the complete lack of interest these people have in the world around them.

nosed as neurotic in public mental hospitals, and there are millions of people with neurotic depression who are being treated in community mental health services and by psychiatrists in private practice.

Depression refers to a change in mood in the direction of sadness, despair, and hopelessness. But since all people experience fluctuations in mood to some degree, a distinction must be made between normal and abnormal moods. For most people, there are times of happiness and times of sadness. Very often we know why we are in a good mood or a bad one. More often, we are not aware of the conditions determining our mood. It is only when moods become so exaggerated that they interfere with personal or social adjustment that they can be called abnormal.

One type of abnormal mood is the neurotic depression. In such cases, there is an exaggeration of feelings of sadness and depression. Very often something has happened in the person's life to trigger the original depression. However, the depressed mood does not return to normal, as it ordinarily would. Instead, the person remains seriously depressed.

There is a question as to whether sadness and unhappiness are merely the early stages of depression or whether they are conditions quite apart from depression in the clinical sense. One study found that while over 50 percent of a group of men and women developed deep sadness, sleep disturbances, and crying following the death of a spouse, only 2 percent required treatment for depression (Clayton et al., 1968). Similarly, a study of a group of women whose husbands were dying of cancer revealed that while all of the women were sad, only a small percentage developed the psychomotor retardation, extreme hopelessness, and suicidal thoughts characteristic of clinical depression (Schmale, 1970).

Figure 9.5 *The Last Resort*, a woodcut by Kathe Kollwitz, is a grim reminder that the thoughts of depressed people are frequently concerned with suicide.

Such observations have led to recent interest in the classification of depression. One view is that depression is a single condition that may range from mild to severe (Beck,

1967). The maladaptive behavior is a final common pathway resulting from a number of causes (Paykel, 1974). Another approach is that there are two quite different forms of depression. According to this view, neurotic depression is a reaction to life stress; endogenous depression is genetically or biochemically determined. A factor-analysis study of the symptoms of a large number of depressed people found that they fell into either the reactive or endogenous groups (Kalman et al., 1971).

The neurotic depressive reaction is probably the least serious of all neuroses, except for the ever-present possibility of suicide. Otherwise, the prognosis for this condition is very favorable. In the majority of cases, the depression disappears as the person's situation improves or is otherwise altered. Since the useful purposes served by the symptom are less important in this type of neurosis than in other neuroses, the spontaneous recovery rate tends to be relatively high. Many of these people improve even though they receive no treatment.

Causes of Neurotic Depression

Some people learn to react to life stress with depression, just as some learn to react with anxiety or other forms of neurotic behavior. One view is that depression of this type is the result of positive reinforcers. Another behavioral view is that depression is a pattern of learned helplessness. The cognitive approach to neurotic depression is that a "negative cognitive set" is established. This negative set is made up of low self-esteem, a pessimistic view of the world, and poor

It's All Too Much for Me!— Depression As a Neurotic Reaction

Virginia F. is a 33-year-old married woman who is separated from her husband. She was married at the age of 22 and has six children. The marriage has been a disturbed one, with the husband drinking heavily and being abusive toward his wife. The children were so neglected and undernourished that it was necessary to place them in foster homes. Mrs. F. was admitted to a psychiatric hospital because of her severe depression. When examined, she was found to be a pale, haggard, and unkempt woman who was depressed and had thoughts of suicide but no other symptoms of mental illness. She was cooperative, and willing to talk about her family and her past life. She was pregnant, and the depression started when her husband left her. She had been living in a run-down apartment, without gas or electricity, overrun with rats. She began to feel that it would be better to die and kill the children than to live such a life. After a short time in the hospital, and as a result of the efforts of the social service department to help her start a new life, the patient's depression lifted. The entire depressive episode was a reaction to a seemingly unbearable situation.

expectations for the future (Beck, 1973). This view holds that depression is a thought disorder rather than an emotional disorder.

Most psychodynamic theories of depression regard the behavior displayed by the depressed person as an effort to control anxiety generated by unconscious conflict related to hostility. Typically there is severe hostility toward family members or others in the environment, and this unconscious hostility results in guilt feelings. The hostility is then turned upon the self in the form of feelings of unworthiness, self-depreciation, and despondency.

The Chapter in Review

The neurosis is one of the most common forms of maladaptive behavior. However, since the neurotic remains in contact with reality and is not a threat to the physical well-being of other people, confinement in a hospital or an institution is not required. Neurotic behavior is expressed in many different ways.

1 The Common Neuroses

The most frequently seen form of neurotic behavior is the anxiety neurosis, in which overwhelming anxiety is experienced. All other neuroses are patterns of maladaptive behavior which develop in the attempt to control the anxiety. The phobia is neurotic fear, while obsessions and compulsions are persistent and unwelcome thoughts and actions. Hypochondria is a neurotic preoccupation with physical health and body functions. Hysterical neuroses include conversion reactions involving interference with sensory and motor functions, and dissociative reactions in which the self is altered in such a way that separate psychological systems exist in the same person. Neurotic depression is another very common type of maladaptive behavior.

2 Cause of Neurosis

While the susceptibility to anxiety is probably related to genetic and constitutional factors, the development and maintenance of anxiety neurosis, as well as other neurotic reactions, is a learned pattern of behavior. In the phobias, hypochondria, and neurotic depression, the role of conditioning and social learning is quite clear. Cognitive factors are probably involved in the obsessive-compulsive conditions and particularly in the hysterical conversions and dissociations. In addition, the possibility of psychodynamic influences in neurotic behavior cannot be ruled out.

Recommended Readings

Fear and Anxiety

Fischer, W. F. *Theories of anxiety*. New York: Harper & Row, 1970.

Martin, B. *Anxiety and neurotic disorders*. New York: Wiley, 1971.

Rachman, S. *The meanings of fear*. Baltimore: Penguin, 1974. (Paperback.)

Obsessive-Compulsive Behavior

Adams, P. L. *Obsessive children*. Baltimore: Penguin, 1975. (Paperback.)

Beech, H. R. (Ed.) *Obsessional states*. New York: Harper & Row, 1974.

Multiple Personality

Lancaster, E. *The final face of Eve*. McGraw-Hill, 1958.

Schreiber, F. R. *Sybil*. New York: Warner, 1974. (Paperback.)

Thigpen, C. H., & Cleckley, H. M. *The three faces of Eve*. McGraw-Hill, 1957.

10
Psychophysiologic Disorders: The Psychosomatic Relationship

Objectives

To define psychophysiologic disorders and to explain their general nature

To point out that the psychosomatic relationship has become a basic principle of medical psychology

To indicate the nature of biofeedback and show its relationship to psychophysiologic disorders

To show how psychophysiologic disorders are basically the result of learning

To indicate some of the psychodynamic influences suggested as being related to the development of physical illness

To emphasize the relationship between life stress and the onset of psychophysiologic disorders

To demonstrate, by means of reference to specific physical illnesses, the relationship between psychological factors and physical symptoms

It has been said that at least 50 percent of the beds in general hospitals in the United States are occupied by people whose physical illnesses are largely due to psychological causes. This does not mean that the physical symptoms are nonexistent or grossly exaggerated, as in hypochondria. The physical disturbances are real enough, as in the case of ex-President Nixon's phlebitis. It does mean that the illness would probably not have occurred without psychological reinforcement.

It was pointed out in Chapter 9 that when physical symptoms involve the sensory and motor nerves of the central nervous system, the disorder is called a conversion neurosis. However, when the physical disturbances are related to the autonomic nervous system, the condition is known as a psychophysiologic disorder.

This distinction is more the result of a historical accident than of necessity. Conversion reactions have been described since the time of Charcot in the late nineteenth century, when there was great interest in the sensory and motor functions of the central nervous system. The concept of psychosomatic disorders, however, grew out of the increasing knowledge of the nature of the autonomic nervous system. This development did not take place until well into the present century. As a result, interest in the two conditions developed along more or less independent lines. When these lines came together, the distinction had already been made. In terms of causes, however, the conversion reactions and psychophysiologic disorders are similar.

An extremely small number of patients are admitted to public mental hospitals in the United States with the diagnosis of psychophysiologic disorder. The number of admissions is only about one-tenth of 1 percent

(National Institute of Mental Health, 1975). As in the case of neurotic disorders, public mental health statistics do not reflect the actual prevalence of psychophysiologic disturbances in our society. Since the symptoms are physical rather than psychological, there is no reason for people with these disorders to be admitted to mental hospitals or to community mental health facilities. Most cases are seen originally by physicians. If the psychological component of the condition is recognized, a referral may be made to

---

A President under Pressure: The Psychosomatic Side of Political Stress

There is a distinct possibility that the pressures related to the Watergate scandal may have been a factor in Richard M. Nixon's repeated attacks of phlebitis following his resignation from the Presidency in 1974. Soon after he resigned, a number of blood clots developed in his left leg, and one large clot required emergency surgery to prevent further complications.

Since critical changes in life events frequently anticipate physical illness, the circumstances surrounding the resignation are of unusual interest. The loss of power, position, and prestige was of such magnitude and occurred over such a relatively short period of time that the development of physical illness or psychological disturbance in a predisposed individual would not be surprising.

The importance of predisposition to a psychosomatic disorder is shown in the fact that President Nixon suffered his first phlebitis attack in 1965. This fact would suggest that the President had a constitutionally weak body system which determined the form of the specific symptom.

While it is dangerous to make assumptions about anyone's physical condition without a personal examination of the patient, everything we know about the relationship between life stress and physical illness points to the very strong possibility that President Nixon's phlebitis was probably aggravated by the resignation and the stressful events leading up to it.

a psychiatrist or clinical psychologist in private practice. For this reason physicians and psychologists should be familiar with the way in which psychological factors can influence the development, course, and treatment of psychophysiologic disorders.

The Psychosomatic Principle

The word *psychosomatic* was used, not many years ago, instead of *psychophysiologic* to describe physical illnesses with strong psychological, or behavioral, components. However, the concept of the psychosomatic relationship acquired such a broad meaning that it lost its usefulness for diagnostic purposes. It became increasingly apparent that *all* physical illnesses, diseases, and disabilities have a psychological component to some degree. For this reason, the psychosomatic concept evolved into a general principle of medicine and psychology. The clinical classification of psychophysiologic disorders was introduced to refer only to those illnesses in which the behavioral component is considered to be a determining factor in the condition.

The psychosomatic relationship is evident in a number of dramatic instances other than psychophysiologic disorder. One of these is the phenomenon of unexplained death both in animals and human beings. The phenomenon of voodoo death has been recorded frequently by anthropologists. Also, there have been many cases of unexplained death both in civilian and military situations. While there is a preexisting organic defect in a number of these cases, pathology cannot be shown in some of them.

Intense fear and other violent emotions can cause catastrophic disturbances of the

Figure 10.1   The voodoo ceremony is an example of how psychological states can influence body processes. This teen-age girl is on the verge of physical collapse because of her belief that she is "possessed." Both illness and the cure of illness frequently depend upon a person's attitude. Feelings of defeat and hopelessness can accelerate illness and disability; faith and optimism often speed recovery.

homeostatic balance of the body. Radical changes in respiration, heart action, blood pressure, biochemistry, and other vital functions of the body sometimes lead to the sudden death of an otherwise healthy person.

"Faith healing" is a further example of the powerful nature of psychological factors in influencing body systems and functions. Throughout history, and to the present day, certain persons and also various phenomena such as religious relics, sacred wells, and grottoes have had attributed to them the power to heal and to cure.

In spite of the admitted elements of charlatanism and quackery in much that passes for faith healing, the fact remains that there have been numerous examples of dramatic improvements in physical condition which can be attributed only to changes in the attitude of the patient. Even the most skeptical physicians are impressed from time to time by the sudden and seemingly inexplicable recovery of patients for whom hope had been abandoned.

Biofeedback: A Psychosomatic Breakthrough

One of the most exciting developments in psychosomatic relationships has been the finding that people can learn, through a technique called *biofeedback*, to control body functions which previously were thought to be beyond conscious influence. The technique developed as the result of research in the late 1960s suggesting that animals can be trained to control their involuntary nervous responses.

Animals with electrodes implanted in their brains were apparently able to learn to alter their heart rate in order to be rewarded with electrical stimulation that caused a pleasurable sensation. It was also reported that animals were able to learn to change their blood pressure, intestinal contractions, urinary excretions, and blood-vessel constriction (Miller & DiCara, 1968). While these findings created a considerable amount of controversy and the investigators have had difficulty in replicating the original work, the approach led to a scientific breakthrough of very great importance.

Adele! Where Are You Going?— A Case of Dying Delayed

A young woman was apparently dying. Her temperature had risen to 107.5, her pulse was 160, and her respiration had dropped to 60. The attending physician said that the patient could not live more than two hours. Another physician, who was called to the bedside, described his experience:

When I entered the room she was unconscious; her eyes were turned up so that only the white sclerotic coats were visible; she was from a medical point of view beyond the pale of hope. As I looked at the girl an inspiration came to me; I took her by the hand, learned her first name from the nurse, and said with great incisiveness: "Adele! Where are you going? You cannot die! Come back. You have work to do. Come back at once!" In answer to the summons, the upturned eyes resumed their normal angle and became riveted on mine. The voice that had for days uttered only the ravings of a delirium now spoke coherently. "It is too late," it murmured. "It is not too late. Stay where you are. Assume immediate control of your physical functions, and get well. You are going to recover." All this in an imperative, forceful tone. The directions were immediately accepted and implicitly followed. A change for the better supervened. Gradually the mental mist cleared away, the physical strength returned, and today the young lady is perfectly well and filling an important position in the musical world. (Quackenbos, 1908)

The principle of feedback in biological systems is basic to the self-regulating mechanism of living organisms. Body temperature, heart rate, brain waves, respiration, amount of light admitted to the eye, and many other body functions are kept within normal limits by means of feedback signals. These controlling systems have been observed for many years. The learning of skills, for example, involves biofeedback. Information about the direction and speed of a movement is fed back, and speed and direction are adjusted to make the movement more exact. This happens when a person lines up a putt on the green, prepares to shoot a basket on the basketball court, types a letter, or drives an automobile.

Biofeedback training makes use of instruments to detect and amplify body changes. The information is then fed back to the subject by means of visual displays or auditory signals that permit the subject to monitor his or her own physiological functions. The objective of the monitoring is to have the person learn how to modify and control his or her body processes. In biofeedback research, people have learned to control such involuntary functions as heart rate and blood pressure when they can see or hear the function electronically.

One evidence of the remarkable ability to alter body function is the finding that a person can learn to control the electrical activity of the brain through conditioning. The electrical brain waves fall into a number of different frequency ranges. The 10-per-second alpha rhythm is a basic frequency accompanying rest and relaxation. It appears and disappears intermittently and spontaneously. It has been found, however, that people can learn to increase or decrease the amount of alpha activity (Kondas, 1973). However, it has not been possible to produce levels exceeding those that occur spontaneously during rest periods (Lynch & Paskewitz, 1971).

While the original work indicating an ability to control alpha brain waves created great interest and stimulated much research, critics of biofeedback suggest that the results obtained occur only when the amount of alpha has already been depressed and that

Figure 10.2 Brain waves before and after biofeedback training. The top tracing was made during a first attempt to control the alpha rhythm. The lower tracing was made after nine months of biofeedback training. The amplitude, or height, of the wave indicates the strength of the electrical impulse. The number of waves per unit of time indicates the frequency. Note the marked increase in the regularity of the rhythm as a result of the training.

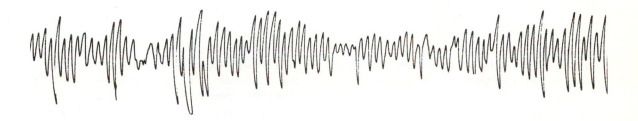

the biofeedback training merely involves learning to ignore the stimulus that had depressed the alpha activity in the first place (Orne & Wilson, 1976).

Biofeedback provides both a theoretical model and an experimental technique for exploring psychosomatic relationships that have been clinically recognized but which have been extremely difficult to explain. The most widely accepted theory of biofeedback is that there is instrumental conditioning of autonomic responses. There is also the possibility that some undiscovered form of learning is involved.

In any event, the importance of understanding the biofeedback circuit lies in two directions. The first has to do with the clarification of the relationship between cognitive functions (perception and thinking) and body changes. The second area of importance related to biofeedback is that of treatment. This latter aspect of biofeedback will be discussed at greater length in Chapter 17.

Theories of Psychophysiologic Disorder

While there is general agreement that psychological influences play an important role in physical illness, the way in which this influence operates has been interpreted in several ways. It is quite clear that many people make use of their illnesses once the symptoms have developed. The advantages of being ill include sympathy, attention, and special privileges. Illness also makes it possible to avoid responsibility and to be excused from obligations. The rewards of being ill are sometimes greater than the inconveniences.

The way in which psychological factors contribute to the onset of illness, however, is not so obvious. Recent advances in our knowledge of biofeedback and research in the area of autonomic conditioning have given strong support to the theory that visceral and other body symptoms can be learned through mechanisms not yet clearly understood. The psychodynamic explanation of psychophysiologic disorders has emphasized the importance of unconscious needs. Increasing attention is also being given to the way in which psychosocial stress contributes to the onset of physical illness.

Learning to Be Ill

Psychophysiologic disorders are made up of physical symptoms resulting from the disturbed functioning of a body system. The subject's emotions and thinking bring about changes in the activity of the autonomic nervous system which alter the flow of neural impulses, the secretion of hormones, and the biochemistry of the body. In such cases, the onset of symptoms can be learned, and the subject can also control the course of the physical disorder and its response to treatment. The situation is different, of course, in illnesses transmitted by viruses or other microorganisms. But even in these cases, body resistance may be determined to some extent by psychological contingencies.

The Need to Fall Ill

The basic model for the psychodynamic view of physical illness and disability grew out of Freud's early observations and treatment of persons showing hysterical conversion symptoms. This approach emphasizes the symbolic significance of symptoms; it takes the position that psychophysiologic disorders are attempts to handle anxiety growing out of unconscious conflict. Each illness, according to this model, satisfies unconscious needs.

Psychosocial Stress and Physical Symptoms

It is a matter of everyday observation that stress and physical illness are closely related in most people. As a result, it is generally inferred that there is a causal connection between stress and illness. While not everyone accepts this view, it is nevertheless true that significant changes are frequently present in the lives of people who develop psychosomatic illness. These events usually occur from six months to one year prior to the onset of acute physical illness (Dohrenwend & Dohrenwend, 1974).

Dramatic examples of the possible rela-

tionship between critical stress related to changes in one's life situation and subsequent illness are evident in Senator Joseph McCarthy's fatal liver ailment, Senator Robert A. Taft's terminal cancer, President Lyndon B. Johnson's heart attack, and President Richard M. Nixon's phlebitis. In each of

Figure 10.3   (*a*) Senator Joseph McCarthy, (*b*) President Lyndon B. Johnson, and (*c*) Senator Robert A. Taft were forced to cope with unusually stressful situations during their careers. Each one also developed serious physical disorders which could have been caused or aggravated by the severe stress.

(b)

(a)

(c)

these cases the physical damage could very well have been triggered by the intense emotional stress of the highly significant changes in life events preceding the illnesses.

The objection has been raised that it is not always possible to find significant life changes preceding physical illness, and in many cases where such life changes are found, the person affected appears to be reconciled to the change. The problem is that of determining just what is significant to a given individual and how he or she reacts to stressful events. Many people who seem to be untouched by critical life changes are showing overcontrol. It is entirely possible for a person to appear to be unruffled by changing events and yet to be in an inner turmoil that he or she does not sense directly. It is this inner tension that disturbs, and sometimes damages, the target organ or body system.

It is not always easy to determine what another person considers to be a significant life change or important event. The Social Life Change Survey (see Chapter 6) lists a number of events which most people agree are related to some degree of stress. However, the events listed are not the only important changes that occur in a person's life. It may be that the life change is an internal matter involving a highly personal decision. For example, a person who has been striving to gain political prominence might come to the reluctant decision that the goal is unattainable.

This decision could represent a life change of the greatest importance, and yet it would not be measured by any standard scale nor indeed would the person be likely to think of the decision as a life change if asked about significant stressful events in his or her recent life. Significant life changes are not always changes in the actual conditions of living; they may also involve shattered hopes, abandoned aspirations, and dreams that can never be realized.

The question of the "target organ" in psychosomatic disorder remains unanswered. Even though changes in life events may generate stress which results in physical damage, one must explain why a particular organ becomes the target for the release of the tension that has been built up. While the possibility of the symbolic meaning of the symptoms cannot be ruled out, it is more likely that the selection of symptoms is related to autonomic conditioning or a constitutional weakness of the selected body system.

Common Target Systems

Psychophysiologic disorders have been defined as physical disturbances involving the autonomic nervous system and having a significant psychosomatic component. Such a definition is an inclusive one and applies to a very large number of physical illnesses. Those body systems with the richest supply of impulses from the autonomic nervous system are the ones most likely to become targets for the development of psychophysiologic disorders. These systems include the heart and blood vessels, stomach and intestines, lungs, skin, and sexual organs. Other body systems and organs are involved somewhat less frequently.

The Heart under Stress
One of the most common of the psychophysiologic disorders is the cardiovascular reaction, in which the principal symptoms involve the heart and the blood vessels. While organic heart disease accounts for the great-

est number of deaths in the United States, most heart specialists agree that a very large percentage of patients who present cardio-vascular symptoms do not have an organic disease or disability. The symptoms are real enough, but the cause in such cases is emotional rather than physical. During World War II, the Office of the Surgeon General reported that nearly 50 percent of the heart cases in Army hospitals were psychological rather than physical. The statistics are much the same for heart cases in general hospitals.

The heart invalid frequently is afraid to face problems. Among the cardiac cases is the young woman who is jealous of a prettier sister, the man with a more successful brother, the salesman who has not received his promotion, the wife who is being neglected by her husband, and the college student who cannot make good grades. For all such frustrated people, the heart symptom is a means of escape.

The body language of the heart is extensive. We "put our heart" into projects in which we are emotionally involved; we are "heartbroken" when things go wrong; we "give our heart" to our beloved; and we extend our "heartfelt sympathy" to our friends who are grief-stricken. We use such terms as *good-hearted* and *warm-hearted* to indicate affection, while *hard-hearted* and *cold-blooded* suggest hostility and dislike. In every instance, the heart is a prime source of emotional investment.

The nervous heart is organically sound but reacts in an unhealthy manner. One physician explained psychogenic heart disorder by saying, "A sick heart is like an automobile with a defective motor. A nervous heart resembles an automobile with an excited driver."

The role of the physician as a factor in producing a psychophysiologic disorder is nowhere more important than in connection with the cardiovascular reactions. Many men, women, and children have developed psychogenic heart disorders, or have had minor heart symptoms exaggerated out of all reason, because of the careless words and attitudes of physicians. During routine physical examinations, psychologically unsophisticated physicians may make what to them are harmless statements: "Your blood pressure seems to be up," "You have low blood pressure," "You have a slight murmur," or the like. Similarly, while listening to the heart, taking a pulse, or checking blood pressure, physicians may find it necessary to recheck or may frown or otherwise indicate concern. The result of such behavior, verbal and nonverbal, is the establishment of an unnecessary preoccupation with heart functions on the part of the patient. The anxiety and preoccupation, in turn, exaggerate the physical symptoms, and in this way a vicious circle is instituted.

The importance of psychological factors in heart attacks is suggested by the fact that a history of emotional stress prior to the attack is found in a number of cases. In the typical heart attack, a clot of blood forms within the blood vessel supplying the heart, causing an *occlusion*, or closing of the artery. Consequently, the muscle of the heart does not receive its proper blood supply, resulting in an area of damaged tissue.

The relationship between the heart attack and emotional stress is in the *thrombosis*, or clotting of the blood. When an animal is threatened, blood coagulation is speeded up to protect the animal in the event that it is injured in flight or fight. Similarly, in human beings, stress situations of a threatening nature lead to a more rapid clotting of the blood. Anxiety, irritation, and excitement increase heart action, increase resistance to

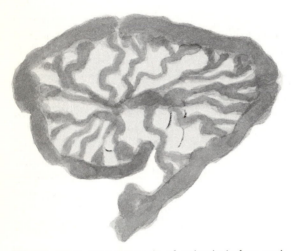

Figure 10.4 Blood vessels of animals before and after exposure to stress. The vessels supplying a segment of the intestine of a normal rat before stress are illustrated in the top drawing. The vessels of the rat subjected to stress (bottom) are markedly thickened, leading to high blood pressure and death.

the flow of blood, and speed up blood clotting.

The Harvard physiologist Walter B. Cannon showed many years ago that when people are under stress, their blood clots much more readily than when they are not under stress. Heart specialists reported in the 1950s that the clotting tendency of certified public accountants was greatest during the first four months of the year, peaking on April 15, the day federal income taxes are due.

An attempt to connect susceptibility to heart attack with personality characteristics was made by a group of investigators who described coronary-prone type-A individuals and more placid type-B people (Friedman & Rosenman, 1974). Type-A people are assumed to be tense perfectionists who are excessively ambitious and unable to relax.

One study was made of nearly 3,000 men without heart disease to see whether they had a type-A or type-B personality. The men were then followed for the next four years to see which of them developed heart attacks. Men who scored high on type-A behavior were found to have twice as many heart attacks as men who scored low (Jenkins et al., 1974). The type-A theory of heart attacks has been challenged by a number of authorities. It has been maintained that such well-established coronary risks as high blood cholesterol, cigarette smoking, high blood pressure, and overweight are probably more important than personality patterns. However, it is perfectly possible that these high-risk factors are critically involved in heart attacks but that stress triggers the attack in those who are predisposed.

The importance of stress in precipitating heart attacks has been shown in a ten-year study of a large number of Japanese men living in the San Francisco area. It has been observed for many years that Japan has the lowest rate of coronary heart disease of any industrialized nation, while the United States has one of the highest rates. Moreover, the rate of heart disease increases significantly in Japanese men as they migrate eastward from their homeland to Hawaii and then to California.

The study found that Japanese-Americans who have become Westernized have a 2½ times higher rate of heart disease than those who continue to live in the traditional Japanese style. Those who have become most removed from their culture have 5 times the rate found in the most traditional groups. The most Westernized of all reached a rate as high as that for white males in the United States.

Since Japan appears to be as industrialized and life there to be as stressful as in the United States, the explanation in the past has been in terms of diet. It now appears that the major difference is in the area of life-style and stress. It has been suggested that the Japanese culture has built-in buffers to stress that are not found in the United States. Traditional Japanese have considerable stability in their life. They live in closely knit family groups, and their future places in society are determined when they are young. They also have strict customs to guide their actions in most situations. There appears to be less preoccupation with intense competition for a place on the ladder of success. It is assumed that such factors as these are responsible for keeping the rate of heart disease low in Japan and among Japanese-Americans who adhere most closely to traditional life-styles (De Vos, 1973).

Biofeedback control of heart function Some of the most recent and persuasive evidence of the close relationship between heart function and psychological processes has come out of biofeedback research. It has been possible, through biofeedback training, to control heart rate, blood pressure, and blood flow in the peripheral blood vessels.

Heart rate can be increased or decreased significantly by means of operant conditioning. In one experiment, five subjects were reinforced for spontaneous decreases in heart rate, five for spontaneous increases, and five noncontingent upon heart rate. The increase and decrease groups changed significantly in the expected directions above and below the noncontingent group (Ascough & Sipprelle, 1968).

In biofeedback control of heartbeat, heart contractions are counted by a pulse sensor that amplifies and integrates the pulse before the information is fed into an accumulator that reports the number of heartbeats for each unit of time. The person watches a digital signal and trains himself or herself to control heartbeat (Brown, 1974). However, it is not completely understood how biofeedback operates in the control of heart rate.

Biofeedback training has also been used successfully to teach patients to decrease premature contractions of the heart with the learning of heart-rate control. This study was additional evidence that at least some aspects of cardiac ventricular function can be brought under voluntary control and that clinically significant changes in cardiac function are possible through biofeedback (Weiss & Engel, 1973).

Within recent years the necessary equipment has become available for the application of biofeedback to the control of high blood pressure. It has been shown that the self-monitoring of blood pressure level by patients with high blood pressure can have the effect of significantly lowering systolic blood pressure (Kleinman, 1971). Diastolic blood pressure can also be lowered, but the decrease tends to be less pronounced (Carnahan, 1973). Studies have also shown that the flow of blood in the peripheral blood vessels can be altered by means of biofeedback learning (Sabbach, 1972; Surwit, 1973).

While it has been generally accepted for a number of years that psychological factors apparently influence the cardiovascular system, the way in which this influence is exerted was completely unknown. While biofeedback has not solved the problem, the discovery of autonomic, or visceral, learning was an important step in furthering our understanding of psychosomatic heart disturbances.

The way in which learning can be responsible for a psychophysiological disorder is seen in the development of high blood pressure. When a person becomes anxious and upset, the blood pressure goes up. At the same time the person may receive increased attention, support, and sympathy. These rewards reinforce the emotional response and the accompanying rise in blood pressure. In people with genetic or constitutional predispositions to unstable blood pressure, the repeated occurrence of the environmental contingencies may eventually lead to high blood pressure as a preferred pattern of response.

Tension and the Gut Reaction

The stomach and intestinal tract frequently become target organs for psychophysiologic disturbances because the processes of digestion and elimination are intimately associated with autonomic activity. Any situation within the personality which is serious enough to upset normal autonomic function is capable of producing gastrointestinal disturbances, particularly when this system has a constitutional weakness.

The stomach is closely related to the emotions, since it is supplied with autonomic nerve fibers which serve as the lines of communication between the brain and the viscera. By this means, psychological events may, with proper reinforcement, exert an influence on the tissues of the stomach and intestines.

An accidental gunshot wound suffered by a hunter in the Northwest Michigan territory did much to establish our knowledge of the influence of the emotions upon the digestive tract. William Beaumont, a physician, nursed this man back to health over a long period of time in spite of the great odds against his recovery. In return for his services, the physician was permitted by the patient to make observations on his stomach, which, of necessity, remained exposed. Observations continued for eight years, during which Beaumont found numerous instances when emotional changes caused changes in the flow of stomach juices (Beaumont, 1902).

The intimate relationship between gastric secretory functions and emotional life was demonstrated in a similar way in a 60-year-old woman undergoing psychotherapy. This patient had a small gastric *fistula* (an abnormal tubelike structure with a small opening to the stomach) of fifty-two years' duration. The gastric secretions were observed regularly through the fistula for $2^1/_2$ years, while the patient was receiving intensive psychotherapy. For the first eight months of treatment, the hydrochloric acid secretion of her stomach remained at persistently high normal levels. At the end of eight months, when the patient became aware of her aggressive feelings and when she began to express verbally material related to these feelings, the level of the hydrochloric acid gastric secretion dropped abruptly and remained at a low normal level for the next eighteen months. Whatever psychological processes were involved, the relationship between the emotions and gastric secretion was demonstrated dramatically. In some way, talking about the conflicts appeared to influence the gastric secretory functions (Stein et al., 1962).

The available evidence supports the view

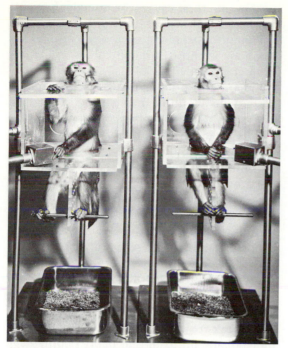

Figure 10.5 These monkeys took part in a classic experiment in which one monkey operated a lever which could be used to ward off electrical shocks. The other monkey also had a lever, but it had no effect on whether or not a shock was experienced. The monkey that could prevent the shocks remained under constant pressure and tension in anticipation of the punishment. This monkey developed stomach ulcers; the passive monkey that could do nothing about the situation did not develop ulcers. The experiment added to the evidence that there is a relationship between stress and physical damage to the body.

that gastrointestinal symptoms are exaggerated, if not precipitated, by stress. The relative effects of various types and degrees of stress have not been demonstrated clearly. It is likely that many types and degrees of stress are capable of resulting in gastrointestinal symptoms for psychologically and physiologically susceptible persons.

The importance of stress in connection with stomach ulcers was demonstrated in a study of stress-induced ulcers in rats. The animals were exposed to six hours of shock-induced stress at two different periods during the natural daily rhythm of corticosterone, a chemical produced by the adrenal glands. A higher incidence of ulceration occurred in animals subjected to stress during the elevated phase of the corticosterone cycle (Wald & Mackinnon, 1972).

Another study of psychosomatic relationships in gastrointestinal disorders found that 93 percent of patients with an irritable colon showed psychological disturbance, and that two-thirds of the subjects had experienced disturbances prior to the onset of the physical symptoms. It was concluded that the symptoms of irritable colon are often a part of a psychological disorder (Liss, Alpers, & Woodruff, 1973). The study also suggests the possibility of stress associated with life changes prior to the onset of the physical symptoms.

Biofeedback from the bowels The psychosomatic nature of some gastrointestinal symptoms has been demonstrated by biofeedback studies. One investigation involved persons suffering from nonorganic disorders of the bowels. An amplified electronic stethoscope was used to enable the subjects to hear their own bowel noises, and verbal reinforcement was used to help them achieve control of bowel activity. All subjects showed an improvement in the control of functional diarrhea. One, who had experienced lifelong functional diarrhea and who had been almost toilet-bound, learned normal bowel function (Seymour, 1973). It is also possible to learn to control gastric acid secretion. When feedback information about acid level was given to patients, significant changes in acid concentration and volume occurred. The work showed that the secretion of gastric acid can be altered and controlled with appropriate feedback (Welgan, 1974).

Evidence from biofeedback studies and autonomic conditioning suggests how psychophysiologic disorders of the stomach and intestines can be learned. For example, many people are victims of simple gastritis, or "nervous indigestion." This condition is one in which there is stomach distress in the form of gas pains, belching, flatulence, and other gastrointestinal symptoms whenever the person is anxious, worried, and under stress. As in the case of high blood pressure, the physical symptoms can be learned as a result of reinforcement through rewarding contingencies. These rewards may be essentially internal, or cognitive, or they may be determined by external environmental influences. In either case, some form of visceral conditioning apparently takes place.

The Skin: Mirror of Emotion

The relation of skin reactions to emotional behavior has been observed for centuries. Nearly everyone is familiar with some of the ways in which the skin mirrors the emotions in everyday life. When people are embarrassed, the skin flushes, and they "blush." In severe fright or states of intense anger, the blood is drawn out of the small capillaries of the skin, and the face pales and blanches. When people are tense and upset, they may develop acne or a skin rash.

The skin is an unusually sensitive indicator of emotional behavior because it is so richly supplied with small blood vessels under the control of the autonomic nervous system. In this way, psychological events can lead to various skin disorders.

The psychosomatic nature of certain skin reactions is shown dramatically in religious *stigmatization*. In these cases, the "stigmata" are wounds similar to those of Christ on the cross. The wounds may be on the hands, feet, side, and in spots on the scalp in the pattern of a crown of thorns. In some instances, the wounds have been on the back or shoulder, suggesting where Christ bore the cross. At one time it was assumed that these spontaneous wounds were of divine origin. More recently, the psychological nature of these wounds has been emphasized by psychiatrists and psychologists and accepted by a substantial number of theologians and church scholars.

Feedback from the skin Studies involving biofeedback indicate that many people have a remarkable capacity to control skin temperature and the flow of blood in the peripheral blood vessels. One biofeedback experiment showed that people can produce a difference in the temperature of the two hands and can cause the temperature of the two hands to change in opposite directions (Maslach et al., 1972). Another biofeedback study trained subjects to produce a difference between the temperature of the two index fingers first in one direction, then in the other direction, and then back in the first direction on successive trials during one session (Roberts et al., 1974). Such demonstrations of control over body functions previously considered to be beyond voluntary influence indicate that autonomic learning is probably a powerful factor in the development of psychophysiologic symptoms.

Disorders of the skin usually cannot be

Religious Stigmatism:
A Case of Spontaneous Bleeding

The most famous stigmatic of our century was Therese Neumann, a peasant girl living in Bavaria. When she was 20 years old, the house of her employer caught fire and Therese fought the flames. She injured her back and was admitted to a hospital, where she went into convulsive seizures. During the following months, the young woman suffered from headaches and impaired vision. Later, she was unable to walk, speak, or hear. Four years following her admission to the hospital, she was diagnosed as a case of severe hysteria.

When St. Therese was beatified in 1923, Therese Neumann's sight suddenly returned. When the saint was canonized, her other symptoms disappeared. It was on Good Friday, 1926, that the stigmata appeared on her hands and feet. About six months later, she began to bleed from her scalp and side. The episodes of bleeding followed a regular pattern. Every Thursday night between eleven and twelve o'clock, she went into a trance and remained in that condition until the following noon. In the early stages of the trance, she would sit up in bed every ten or fifteen minutes and remain motionless. While bloody tears ran down her face, she seemed to be reliving the crucifixion. Therese came out of her trance on Friday and was so exhausted that she usually slept the rest of the day. She was her normal self by Saturday.

The bleeding from the skin was described by a professor of psychology at Erlangen University in Germany in the following words: "Through a magnifying glass, fluid was seen to appear in a manner comparable to the formation of a drop of perspiration. It became bloody and rolled away. When examined microscopically, it was seen actually to be blood." It is reported that she spoke a strange tongue which a professor of Semitic philology said was the Aramaic language of Jesus' time.

During the years before her death in 1962, Therese Neumann was observed by thousands of people who filed past her bed and by a number of physicians and psychiatrists. There was no question about the reality of her wounds.

hidden. The evidence of the sufferer's distress is quite evident to everyone. For this reason, there are immediate and considerable expressions of attention and concern from friends, family members, and physicians. Environmental support is strong, and if the person affected perceives the symptoms as being rewarding in any way, they are reinforced, and autonomic learning occurs. Skin disorders can be learned just as other autonomic and visceral symptoms are learned. In fact, the rewards of having a skin disorder are frequently more pronounced than in the case of other psychophysiologic conditions.

The Chapter in Review

Psychophysiologic disorders are conditions in which physical symptoms related to the autonomic nervous system are caused or significantly influenced by psychological events. Sometimes these events are obvious and are clearly related to the symptoms; in other cases, the events and their relationship to the disorder must be inferred.

1 The Psychosomatic Principle

The word *psychosomatic* was introduced to describe specific illnesses in which a strong psychological component is involved. However, the meaning of the word became so broad that it is now used to refer to a basic principle of medical psychology rather than a specific diagnostic category.

2 Biofeedback: A Psychosomatic Breakthrough

It was assumed during most of the present century that blood pressure, secretion of gastric juices, skin temperature, and other physical functions controlled by the autonomic, or involuntary, nervous system could not be consciously controlled. It is now known that people can learn to control a number of these basic functions with continuous feedback of pertinent biological information by means of visual displays. Advances in our knowledge of biofeedback and autonomic conditioning help us to understand how learning can be involved in psychophysiologic disorders.

3 Theories of Psychophysiologic Disorder

The principal attempts to explain psychophysiologic disorders have made use of psychodynamic, behavioral, and psychosocial stress concepts. The earlier emphasis was on physical illness as an expression of unconscious needs and conflicts. More recently, attention has shifted markedly in the direction of physical symptoms as learned patterns of behavior. There is also considerable interest in the impact of psychosocial stress on constitutionally predisposed body systems.

4 Target Systems

While all body systems and organs are theoretically subject to psychophysiologic disorder, the more common targets are parts of the body most closely associated with the autonomic nervous system. It is for this reason that the heart and blood vessels, stomach and intestines, and skin are particularly susceptible to the influence of psychological events.

Recommended Readings

The Psychosomatic Relationship

Lachman, S. J. *Psychosomatic disorders*: *A behavioristic interpretation*. New York: Wiley, 1972.

Lewis, H. R., & Lewis, M. E. *Psychosomatics* (Rev. ed.) New York: Pinnacle, 1975. (Paperback.)

Shontz, F. C. *The psychological aspects of physical illness and disability*. New York: Macmillan, 1975.

Biofeedback

Brown, B. *New mind, new body*. New York: Harper & Row, 1974.

Jonas, G. *Visceral learning*: *Toward a science of self-control*. New York: Pocket Books, 1974. (Paperback.)

Karlins, M., & Andrews, L. M. *Biofeedback*. New York: Warner, 1973. (Paperback.)

Psychological Healing

Frazier, C. A. *Faith healing*: *Finger of God*? *Or scientific curiosity*? New York: Thomas Nelson, 1973.

Kruger, H. *Other healers, other cures*: *A guide to alternative medicine*. Indianapolis: Bobbs-Merrill, 1974.

11
The Psychotic Experience

Objectives

To define psychosis and show how it differs from other forms of abnormal behavior

To point out the principal differences between neurosis and psychosis

To describe some of the cognitive aspects of psychotic behavior

To show how motivation and emotions are disturbed in psychosis

To give examples of some of the interpersonal and communication difficulties of psychotics

To indicate why it is difficult to find a cause of psychosis

Psychotic behavior is a serious form of personality disturbance in which the person affected shows periodic or prolonged loss of contact with the world of reality. This loss of contact is reflected by disorders of perception, thinking, emotion, and personal orientation. In some cases, the psychosis is clearly related to organic disturbances of the brain. In other cases, however, physical causes have not been established.

About 50 percent of all patients admitted to public mental hospitals in the United States show psychotic symptoms in connection with organic and nonorganic disorders (National Institute of Mental Health, 1975). The present chapter will concern itself with the general nature of psychotic behavior, while the following three chapters will discuss the specific clinical conditions in which psychotic symptoms are present.

While the psychotic disorders are considered to be of psychogenic origin, it is probable that a combination of organic, psychological, and cultural factors are involved in these conditions. Some of the psychoses appear to have strong genetic and constitutional components, while others may be linked to a disturbed biochemistry. The psychosis has been viewed by psychoanalysts as

a disturbance in which repressed conflicts are so strong that they overwhelm consciousness in spite of the patient's frantic attempts to hang onto reality; or reality becomes so painful that the patient gives in to unconscious impulses. Another view is that the psychosis represents a learned pattern of behavior designed to meet frustration by adapting to a more primitive form of adjustment. Sociodynamic factors in the etiology of psychotic behavior also cannot be dismissed.

Psychosis versus Neurosis

It is important to make a clear distinction between neurotic behavior (see Chapter 9) and psychotic behavior. We saw that neurosis is the experience of a pathological degree of anxiety or a maladaptive attempt to control the anxiety. We also saw that the neurotic does not lose contact with reality and hospitalization is seldom necessary. The psychosis, however, is a serious mental disorder of major proportions which frequently requires treatment in a mental hospital.

The neurotic is usually able to function more or less adequately in spite of the symptoms. He or she is likely to know what the symptoms are, if not why they exist. The psychotic, on the other hand, is not able to view the symptoms objectively. Psychotics become so completely caught up in their disturbance that they lose perspective. This inability to handle symptoms is a central feature of the psychosis. It contributes in a very substantial way to the psychotic's loss of contact with reality.

Since psychotics ordinarily are not in contact with reality, either continually or for temporary periods, they are considered to be

238

Figure 11.1 Chaim Soutine's painting *Madwoman* conveys something of the feeling of mental disorder through the use of bold brush strokes, distortion, and the feeling of turmoil. Psychotic people experience severe forms of emotional or cognitive disturbance or both.

wants to go to a hospital or agrees to go. The state assumes responsibility; upon the proper certification by qualified psychiatrists, the court commits such a person to a psychiatric hospital.

Neurotic persons, since they are never out of contact with reality and are able to make a reasonably adequate adjustment to their environment, cannot be committed because of their behavior. As a result, few neurotic people find their way to public psychiatric hospitals. Sometimes there is a question of diagnosis, and hospitalization is ordered pending the clarification of the diagnosis. In other instances, the neurotic person may request commitment.

A further distinction between neurosis and psychosis is that the neurotic person does not deny reality but merely attempts to ignore it. The psychotic, on the other hand, flatly denies reality and attempts to substitute something else for it. In a more popular vein, someone once said that the neurotic builds castles in the air, while the psychotic lives in them.

The neurotic who is retreating from reality nevertheless manages to hang on, however precariously, to the real world. The victim of psychosis, however, loses contact with reality in one way or another. His or her world is an unreal one, made up of fantasies, fictions, and fragments of dreams.

Signs of Psychosis

The woman who writes about her invisible visitors (page 240) shows prominent signs of psychosis. It is immediately evident that her psychological disturbance goes far beyond any of the conditions we have studied up to this point. In general, the signs of psychosis

a potential danger to themselves and others. At times, their behavior is unpredictable and uncontrollable. For this reason, any person who shows clinical evidence of psychotic symptoms is committable to a mental hospital. It does not matter whether he or she

The Invisible Visitors:
Reflections of a Psychotic Woman

At midday on the Saturday I left my desk tidy and walked out through one of the University gardens where the earliest spring flowers were coming into bloom. The sun was shining, and I had a sense of liberation and release. I was joined at once by an unseen companion, and I decided to take him out to lunch. We went down the hill and into a restaurant that was well-known to me. I was disconcerted to find that I was now invisible too; the waitress could not see me, and there was no hope of getting served. An observer would have commented that the waitress was extremely busy and that I had not given her time to attend to me, but I knew better. She and others around her were not real people, they were animated fakes. As we went out again I realized how lucky we were that we had not been served; the food would have been spiritual poison to us. This region of the city had been transformed by a total removal of its spiritual component, and it had become Vanity Fair. Luckily the district in which I lived was still intact, and the food in my own room was wholesome. My companion was somewhat upset and ashamed at what had happened to the main Centre of the city, and so was I. During the afternoon, he left me, as he had business elsewhere.

I had two unseen visitors that night in fairly quick succession. The first was the spirit of a man. He made love to me tenderly but briefly. His composition was of a different texture from mine, and like a wisp of cloud pressing against a fine-meshed screen, he passed straight through me and was gone.

The second visitor was my companion of the afternoon. A man, yet more than a man. When he made love to me it was with a vigor that fired my whole being. His composition was also different from mine, but in the opposite direction. His passion, untempered and unhumanised by flesh, left me inwardly a little burnt. We sat together afterwards in comfortable companionship for a time, but this relaxation was no more than a brief preparation for the grave and strenuous work we had to do. The task before us was no less than to lift Christ down from the cross. (From Coate, 1964, pp. 55-56.)

reflect disturbances of cognitive, emotional, and interpersonal behavior.

Cognitive Confusion: Disturbances of Thought and Perception

Some of the most obvious signs of psychosis are seen in connection with cognitive behavior. Perception and thinking appear, at times, to be grossly distorted. The psychotic person becomes disoriented, experiences perceptual distortions, and thinks in a disorganized way. These symptoms may appear separately or in combination. Similarly, they may persist over long periods of time or appear only occasionally.

Disorientation This symptom is one of the signs of a psychotic break with reality. Persons who are disoriented do not know who they are, where they are, or what time, day, week, month, or year it is. The clinician seeks to determine the degree to which the person is oriented for *time*, *place*, and *person*. Some people are disoriented in only one of these areas; other people are disoriented in two or three areas.

The following material, taken from an interview with a psychotic, reflects a severe degree of disorientation in all areas.

Q: What is your name?
A: It is called fast colors.
Q: What is your father's name?
A: He put his head on the railroad tracks and see where he is today. He's in heaven.
Q: Do you have children?
A: How are you today?
Q: What work did you do?

A: I drove machines all around the corner.

Q: Where do you live?

A: I am not, and never was, foolish. I live in the barracks.

Q: Have you ever seen me before?

A: Well, according to your word, I will stretch it. Well, according to your word, I will stretch it. Well, according to your word, I will stretch it.

Q: What is your doctor's name?

A: Between you and me and him and the airplane.

Q: What day is it?

A: According to my brain, it is two weeks from to-morrow.

Q: What time of the day is it?

A: It's sub-noon in Egypt.

Q: How old are you?

A: Diagram.

Q: What city is this?

A: I am out of my brain today. City in mind. You're not getting any more sense out of me than out of a turnip!

The surprising flash of insight and rationality shown by the last remark is not uncommon in the psychoses. It appears sometimes that the person is playing a game with the examiner, and to some extent this assumption is valid. It is not so much a matter of the person not knowing who or where he or she is, but of refusing to acknowledge these facts.

Sometimes an additional dimension of orientation is used. This dimension is orientation for *situation*. Here the question is whether or not the patient realizes why he or she is in the hospital. This type of orientation, which is in fact a form of insight, frequently gives some indication of the patient's contact with reality. One woman who was asked why she was in the hospital replied that it had been raining outside, and

Figure 11.2 The psychotic person who painted this picture with the title *Celler, Inn, Salon and Stable* combined images in a way not too different from the methods used by some modern artists. The telescoped images have a dreamlike quality.

she entered the hospital to get out of the rain. Another person insisted he was merely "waiting for his son." Such improbable and exaggerated rationalizations are common among psychotic patients.

Delusions: Beliefs beyond reason Psychotic people frequently hold beliefs which are improbable or obviously untrue. Such ideas are called delusions. While many people who are not mentally disturbed also cling to such ideas, they do not ordinarily continue to hold them in the face of clear evidence to the contrary. The psychotic person, however, persists in his or her delusional ideas in spite of rational arguments, contradictory evidence, or sheer impossibility. One man insisted that his arms and legs had been cut off, even though he was standing up and using his hands to show where his legs had been removed.

Delusions can be classified in two ways. The first is according to the degree of cohesion or systematization of the delusional system. Delusions range from loose and unsystematic to tightly organized. The second way of classifying delusions is according to their content. The most common delusions involve ideas related to persecution, sexuality, religion, grandeur, and body changes.

The most frequently observed delusions are of the persecutory type. For example, a man who suffers this type of delusion may have the idea that he is the victim of a plot to discriminate against him, to cause him trouble, to make life difficult for him, to harm him in some physical way, or, in the more extreme cases, to take his life. The following persecutory delusions were expressed by people in a psychiatric hospital:

The cops are after me. . . . People spit at me. . . . They are trying to steal my money. . . . The cook puts pee-pee and cat's dirt in my food. . . . They are going to horsewhip me. . . . People stick me with wires. . . . A man in the room upstairs is nailing another man's toes to the mattress. . . . Everybody I see is talking about me. . . . The communists in South America are trying to poison the beet sugar crop. . . . A gang in Washington is trying to kill me because I wanted to get in touch with the President. . . . The neighbors are saying that I am not a citizen. . . . Someone is stealing my mail. . . . The milk delivered to my apartment has been poisoned. . . . Someone down the hall is chopping little children to pieces.

Sexual ideas also are a common source of delusional material:

My neighbors accuse me of being a pervert. . . . A man in a green convertible drives past my house at night and flashes his lights to signal that I am a prostitute. . . . The newspapers are going to release headlines saying that I am a "queer." . . . They are whispering that I am a homosexual. . . . They insinuate that I am not a man. . . . The neighbors say I have syphilis. . . . My husband made me insane so he would be free to commit adultery.

A common delusional belief, especially of emotionally disturbed women, is that certain men are in love with them. Physicians, psychologists, social workers, college instructors, members of the clergy, lawyers, and other professionals whose work brings them into contact with large numbers of women not infrequently find themselves the victims of this form of distorted thinking. It is interesting that these delusional ideas are relatively rare among younger women. Most cases involve mature women, usually married and often with children. Delusional thinking of this type is so common among disturbed women that a widely used rating scale for determining the seriousness of emotional disorder includes among the most critical symptoms a category called "unjustified sexual beliefs." One of the items in this category is that the woman believes without justification that certain persons have an amorous interest in her.

Similarly, religious delusions are seen in a number of people. The following statements represent some ideas of this kind:

> I am God. . . . I am the Virgin Mary. I've committed my unpardonable sin. . . . I have to shake my bed at night to get the devils out. . . . I have four devils inside me. . . . I am Jesus Christ. . . . God is my husband. . . . I went to heaven to see Jesus and to talk to the Virgin Mary.

Somatic delusions, or delusions involving the body, are not uncommon among psychotics:

> I am sick because I swallowed a rock. . . . There are holes bored in my head. . . . My right eye is growing out of the top of my head. . . . I've lost my skin. . . . I'm mangled inside. . . . I have no arms or legs. . . . My mouth is sewed closed. . . . My head has nothing in it but iodine. . . . My ears have disappeared. . . . There isn't any blood in my veins. . . . I have no heart, liver, or lungs.

Delusions of power and grandeur are also observed frequently among psychotics. Patients have expressed the following ideas:

> I am so powerful that the heads of people change when I look at them. . . . I own all the hotels in the world. . . . I have a $100 million in the bank.

Hallucinations: Perceptions of an unreal world The hallucination, like disorientation and delusional thinking, is one of the key symptoms of psychosis. Persons are said to be hallucinating when they perceive objects and events without an appropriate external stimulus. In spite of the lack of an adequate stimulus, the experience seems real to such a person. Hallucinations are ordinarily classified in terms of the sensory areas involved.

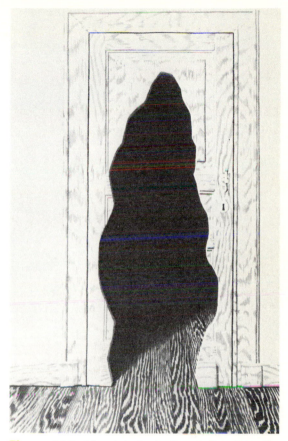

Figure 11.3 Visual hallucinations often take the form of ghostly figures similar to this dark apparition standing in the doorway. It is not unusual for these false perceptions to be vague and threatening. Most hallucinatory figures cannot be clearly described or identified.

While visual and auditory hallucinations are the most common in psychotic disorders, it is not unusual to find hallucinations involving taste, smell, touch, and body sensations.

Hallucinations occur from time to time even in mentally healthy people during periods of emotional stress. Following the death of someone close to us, it is not uncommon to imagine that we see that person again in a

Figure 11.4 This drawing by William Blake was based on a hallucination experienced by the British artist. He titled his drawing *The Ghost of a Flea*.

voice from heaven say, "Take courage. Be not afraid, nor fear. I will provide for all." On his final voyage he heard the voice again. Hallucinations are also common during periods of religious exaltation and ecstacy, when sensory input in severely limited, and when LSD or other hallucinogenic drugs are used.

The most frequently encountered hallucinations among mentally disturbed people are of an auditory nature, with the subject hearing voices. Sometimes the voices are supportive and conciliatory, and sometimes they direct the person's thoughts and activities. More often they are accusatory and disagreeable. A young man was riding on a bus and became convinced that the man in the seat behind him was carrying a hypodermic needle. Then he thought he overheard the man whisper to him, "If you want to go crazy, I'll help you." He was certain that the man was going to drug him with a needle, so he hurried off the bus at the next stop.

Visual hallucinations, while somewhat less frequent than auditory experiences of this kind, nevertheless occur in a large number of psychotic people. Such hallucinations

favorite chair, standing in the doorway, or taking part in some familiar activity. Hallucinations are also experienced as a result of intense guilt and anxiety. A man who was stealing money from the cash register in a store was startled to "see" his father looking at him sadly. Another man "heard" his mother weeping while he was visiting a prostitute. Shakespeare's Macbeth saw a phantom dagger and later saw Banquo's ghost sitting at the table.

Many well-known historical figures experienced hallucinations. Martin Luther had such a vivid hallucination of the Devil that he threw an inkwell at him. Christopher Columbus, on one of his voyages, heard a

---

"Radioactive Voices" Blamed in Murder of Child

Cincinnati,, June 8—A screaming 8-year-old girl was hurled to her death from the Western Hill Viaduct by an ex-convict who had spent two years in a hospital as a mental patient. Captured by passers-by was a gaunt six-foot-four-inch man who blamed his act upon "radioactivity." The strange drama unfolded near the middle of the viaduct as horrified motorists slammed on their brakes and jumped from their autos. The suspect, laughing and gibbering, grabbed the girl as she stopped to tie her shoestring. He stared moodily from deep-set eyes, and at detective headquarters he mumbled: "Radioactivity did it. They keep calling me yellow. When I go to sleep at night they call me yellow, and when I get up in the morning they call me yellow."

"Shucks, You Can't Fool That Old Lady!"— A Case of Hallucinations

Helen R., tall and thin, is a married woman of 40 who was holding both hands on the top of her head when she entered the office. Asked about why she held her head, she explained, "Last night while I was in bed someone hit me with a piece of pipe. I have to hold my head to keep my brains from oozing out." Later, she exclaimed suddenly, "That Askerin fellow!" Asked what she meant, she replied, "Elmer Askerin." For a time she was reluctant to explain further, but finally she said, "Sometimes I see Elmer Askerin and his gang come over the top of the wall and down the side of the room. I look up, and there is Elmer and his gang. When they get down near my bed, I hear Elmer say 'There she is. Let her have it. Shoot her.' But he doesn't frighten me. I tell him, 'Elmer, you get out of here and leave me alone!' And he and his gang go back up the wall. Just as he disappears over the top of the wall, he snaps his fingers and says, 'Shucks, you can't fool that old lady!'"

are often of a religious nature, but they may involve a variety of other images. A 20-year-old roustabout started a circus fire which resulted in the death of 169 people and in injury to more than 400 others. When he was caught, he blamed his behavior on visions of "a flaming red Indian on a fiery horse" urging him to set the fires. The young man confessed to scores of fires from Maine to Ohio.

Lilliputian hallucinations are those in which the person "sees" tiny figures of people or animals. One psychotic woman said that she saw a large number of little children gathered around her. They were so small she could take them all in her hand. She even had names for them. One was called Harold and another Reginald. At one time she was heard to say, "Reginald, you must be a good boy and not slip away through my fingers." She would watch these children climb down to her lap. Then, with an indulgent smile, she would pick them up again. She complained that Reginald gave her a great deal of trouble.

Hallucinations arise from both organic and psychological causes. Organic determinants include such factors as excessive fatigue, drugs, fever, brain damage, or alcohol. Psychological determinants include, among other possibilities, the processes of projection, rationalization, wishful thinking, fantasy, and feelings of guilt.

Psychotic Emotion: Inappropriate and Unpredictable

While cognitive disturbances involving perception and thinking are often the most obvious and dramatic signs of psychosis, the psychotic person frequently shows various forms of emotional disturbance. Some people are emotionally impulsive, while others seem to have a complete lack of emotional responsiveness. Occasionally the symptom takes the form of emotional responses which are inappropriate to the situation.

The emotionally impulsive person is completely unpredictable. It is not unusual for such people to jump up suddenly in anger or exuberance. Without apparent reason and with no warning, such people may act out in an aggressive or sexual way. Episodes of uncontrollable violence sometimes punctuate an otherwise tranquil course of psychosis. The impulsive and unpredictable emotional behavior of such people makes them a source of constant danger to themselves and others.

A complete absence of emotional responsiveness is also found in some psychotic people. They neither smile or laugh, nor do they appear depressed. They are simply without emotion, at least on the surface.

During the examination of such a person, the clinician may deliberately attempt to provoke laughter, tears, or anger. In most cases, all such efforts fail. It is as if the person were completely incapable of expressing emotion of any kind. Inappropriate emotion is another psychotic symptom. Here the person responds emotionally in a way that is incomprehensible to others. While discussing a sad or depressing experience, the person responds with a smile or laughter. Similarly, a humorous incident or story might call forth a feeling of melancholia or a torrent of tears. In other cases, the person may giggle or laught without apparent reason or may suddenly begin to sob.

Of the several types of emotional disturbance, the absence of emotional responsiveness and inappropriate emotional responses are of the greatest importance in diagnosing psychosis because these two forms of behavior are seldom seen in other classes of personality disorganization. Emotional instability, however, as we have seen in earlier chapters, is also characteristic of some of the personality disorders and neurotic reactions.

Cryptic Communication: The Secret Language

Some of the most striking symptoms of psychosis are seen in the way in which the psychotic person communicates with other people. Because of the break with reality and the indifference to social conventions, the psychotic often uses highly personal forms of verbal and nonverbal expression. Cryptic words and movements make up a secret language that sets psychotic behavior quite apart from all other forms of maladaptive behavior.

Obscenities Deleted!
An Emotionally Unstable Psychotic

Rita M. is a 30-year-old woman who has had a number of admissions to mental hospitals. The present admission followed an incident in Florida where the patient publicly cursed a motorist who drove too close to her. She fought with the police who questioned her; and because of her marked hostility and overtalkativeness, she was sent to a psychiatric hospital.

This patient was raised in a home in which there were many children under a domineering and cruel father. When she was 11, the patient threatened to kill her father when she saw him beating her mother. As a result, the father changed his attitude toward the mother, and the patient applied her technique of threats and belligerency toward people outside the family. At 15, the patient became sexually involved with a young man in the neighborhood. A year later she married this same man, but the marriage was an unhappy one because of his attention to other women. There were two children, and the patient was forced to support the family by working as a waitress in a bar. She was unable to hold a job more than a few weeks or months. The marriage ended in divorce, and four years later she married again. After three months the patient became extremely unhappy because of lack of affection on the part of the second husband. At this time, the patient began to show her first psychotic symptoms. She was convinced she was a saint, and could walk upon the water. At one time she was saved from drowning by the police, who were under the impression she was trying to commit suicide.

When seen at the hospital, the patient was excitable, hyperactive, and careless about her appearance. Her voice was loud, and her manner was aggressive. She talked and walked rapidly, jumped up from her chair on numerous occasions, and frequently left the interviewing room. Sometimes she would frown in a menacing way, and other times she would laugh. Words came in an easy flow. The patient was distractible and expressed feelings of hostility toward various people. Her language was profane, and she was preoccupied with sexual matters.

Psychotic "verbalities" The spoken and written language of the psychotic is often strange-sounding and frequently bizarre. Sometimes there are involved sentences, the meanings of which are hidden and obscure. One psychotic said, "I am the double polytechnic irretrievable." Another commented, "They put the hypnotic idle atrophy on me." And a third said, "I have been hypnotized by the subconscious force of supernature." Still another psychotic exclaimed, "My son has been thrust into the vortex of the educational ecclesiastic of the specifics of the world."

Another speech characteristic of certain psychotics is *echolalia*, or the repetition of words spoken by someone else. When the examiner says to a person, "How old are you?" the answer is a parrotlike, "How old are you?" There is an automatic feedback of everything that is said.

Occasionally the symptoms of psychological deterioration can be detected in the writing of a creative mind in the process of disorganization. In both the poetry and letters of Ezra Pound, the development of eccentric and even bizarre thinking can be traced. The following selection is taken from his "Pisan Cantos" (Pound, 1948):

As Arcturus passes over my smoke-hole
  The excess electric illumination
    is now focussed
on the bloke who stole a safe he cdn't open
    (interlude entitled: periplum by camion)
  and Awoi's *hennia* plays hob in the tent flaps
        k-lakk. . . . .thuuuuuu
          making rain
                  uuuh
2, 7,   hooo
        der im Baluba.

While Pound was a literary genius, this selection from his work is more a symptom of a developing psychosis than an indication of his poetic gifts. Less talented people show their personality disorganization in a similar manner. The psychotic pours out a jumble of apparently meaningless and unrelated words in what has been called a "word salad."

Why nylons, autos, men city people more cancer—because more polluted meat and drinks not one single connection with cigs—never jitters from narcotics or disorganization of nervous system—"Iffam-ity" Megalomania—why Napoleon had to conquer world—Hitler and Mussolini and Me Too so now that I have conquered all mystery diseases (asthma and rheumatism too/experiment any dementia case) I am going to conquer the Russians/It is just a mathematical problem/New York, Cleveland, St. Louis, Detroit, California, Miami/they have control of now pulling in Cincinnati so I won't die of cancer, or the apparent heart attack/but a couple of bullets—so KEEP my name out—Please as I know of one check upon me—mathematics they are watching me see signals in paper. Mathematics if I disappear they have me—please copy and send to Hoover—telegraphers mail men caught in net.

A relatively common language disturbance is the *neologism*, a newly made-up word having a private meaning to its inventor. One woman used the word *deathenated* to mean "dead but raised alive." Another said that God is a *whoumationer*, or, as she explained, a "match for the body." Still another psychotic wrote, "Mrs. Barnes is a right-hand *bouw* of those who use the time-machine."

Neologisms are not uncommon in literature. Who has not been delighted with Lewis Carroll's word inventions in *Alice in Wonderland* and *Through the Looking Glass*? The creative artist and the psychotic person give their own meanings to their words in the same way that Humpty Dumpty did. "There's glory for you," said Humpty Dumpty, and he explained to Alice that it meant "There's a nice knockdown argument for you." Alice protested the meaning and said, "The question is whether you can make words mean so many different things," Humpty Dumpty's reply was, "The question is, which is to be master—that's all."

When psychotics communicate with one another, the result is a strange mixture of sense and nonsense. In the following conversation between two psychotic young men, the communication process manages to maintain itself in spite of the *non sequiturs* and general lack of contact:

> **Jones:** (laughs loudly, then pauses) I'm McDougal, myself.
> **Smith:** What do you do for a living, little fellow? Work on a ranch or something?
> **Jones:** No, I'm a civilian seaman. Supposed to be high mucka-muck society.
> **Smith:** A singing recording machine, huh? I guess a recording machine sings sometimes. If they're adjusted right. Mm-hm. I thought that was it. My towel, mm-hm. We'll be going back to sea in about—eight or nine months though. Soon as we get our—destroyed parts repaired.
> **Jones:** I've got love sickness, secret love.
> **Smith:** Secret love, huh? (laughs)
> **Jones:** Yeah.
> **Smith:** I ain't got any secret love.
> **Jones:** I fell in love, but I don't feel any woo—that sits over—looks something like me—walking around over there.
> **Smith:** My, oh, my only one, my only love is the shark. Keep out of the way of him.
> **Jones:** Don't they know I have a life to live?
> **Smith:** Do you work at the air base? Hm?
> **Jones:** You know what I think of work, I'm thirty-three in June, do you mind?
> **Smith:** June?
> **Jones:** Thirty-three years old in June. This stuff goes out the window after I lived this, uh—leave this hospital. So I can't get my vocal cords back. So I lay off cigarettes. I'm a spatial condition, from outer space myself.
> **Smith:** (laughs) I'm a real spaceship from across.
> **Jones:** A lot of people talk,—that way, like crazy, but believe it or not by Ripley, take it or leave it—alone—it's in the *Examiner*, it's in the comic section, believe it or not by Ripley, Robert E. Ripley,

believe it or not, but we don't have to believe anything unless I feel like it. (pause) Every little rosette—too much alone.
> **Smith:** Yeah, it could be possible.
> **Jones:** I'm a civilian seaman.
> **Smith:** Could be possible. I take my bath in the ocean.
> **Jones:** Bathing stinks. You know why? Cause you can't quit when you feel like it. You're in the service.
> **Smith:** I can quit whenever I feel like quitting. I can get out when I feel like getting out.
> **Jones:** Take me, I'm a civilian, I can quit.
> **Smith:** Civilian?
> **Jones:** Go my—my way.
> **Smith:** I guess we have, in port, civilian.
> **Jones:** What do they want with us?
> **Smith:** Hm?
> **Jones:** What do they want with you and me?
> **Smith:** What do they want with you and me? How do I know what they want with you? I know what they want with me. I broke the law, so I have to pay for it. (Haley, 1959)

The chief signs of personality breakdown, as expressed in writing, are the excessive use of punctuation (quotation marks, exclamation points, capitalization, and underscoring), overproductivity, peculiar and bizarre expressions, and changes in the quality of the handwriting itself. One psychotic wrote furiously on world problems, offering solutions by the dozen and expressing his willingness to act as a mediator between the nations. He delighted in complicated forms of expression and wrote extensively on unintelligible topics.

Some psychotics find a particular satisfaction in rhyming and the play of words. The following letter illustrates the way in which a woman elaborates and intellectualizes a relatively simple idea.

> Dear Doctor _____:
> I hope the last letter of mine didn't offend you in any way. I couldn't help snickering, laughing and sneering as I wrote all that stuff. I was immensely involun-

Sexiatry and Mythiatry:
An Example of Psychotic Neologisms

Helen W. is a slender and alert woman of 44 who is the mother of four children. She has a history of mental illness for the past ten years. She is cooperative, and speaks in a persuasive and plausible manner. Her facial expression is mobile, and her mood appears somewhat elevated.

The patient is well oriented in all areas. She knows who she is, the day and month, and the fact that she is in a mental hospital. Both her recent and remote memory appear to be unimpaired. It is impossible to examine her for many psychological functions because she cannot be distracted long enough from her delusional stories to allow accurate estimates of her judgment to be made. The patient has no insight into her condition.

At the time of the initial interview, the patient believed that she was a professor at the University of Smithsonian in England, and that she was the only woman professor among many men. She said that she had attended many other universities in Europe, and had been accepted as an authority on the planets and the satellites. She placed great emphasis on the fact that she was the only woman professor, and that she was obliged by the University of Law to have relations with any of the male professors who desired it. She believed there was a war on between the University of Smithsonian and Purdue University for the mastery of her three specialities which are psychiatry, "sexiatry," and "mythiatry."

The following excerpts from an interview with the patient show her frequent use of neologisms: "I am here from a foreign university . . . and you have to have a 'plausity' of all acts of amendment to go through for the children's code . . . and it is no mental disturbance or 'puterience' . . . it is an 'amorition' law . . . there is nothing to disturb me . . . it is like their 'privatilinia' . . . and the children have to have this 'accentuative' law so they don't go into the 'mortite' law of the church."

The patient was in the psychiatric hospital for the next two years. When seen again she was found to be loose and delusional in her thinking, and continued to tell a vague and disjointed story of her professorship at the University of Smithsonian where she was instructing young boys in the science of 'texules.'

tarily amused at my own bumptious presumptiousness and generally (to me) delicious maliciousness.

Psychotic "body language" The symbolic movements of the psychotic person, in the form of gestures and mannerisms, are another sign of cryptic communication. A skilled psychiatrist or psychologist can make clinical inferences about the personality merely by observing the way a person walks, moves about, sits down, and stands up. These motor symptoms become diagnostic in the case of those people who are on the verge of breaking with reality or who have already broken with reality. Some psychotics go through all sorts of weird-looking movements and make peculiar gestures with their hands and arms. To the uninitiated observer, such movements and gestures appear meaningless. Actually, they may be rich with symbolic meaning. Each movement, in its own way, may reveal something of the inner conflict.

An elderly lady stood throughout the day in the corridor of the hospital. Each time the door opened and someone entered the ward, she made a series of complex measuring movements with her hands. For many months she refused to tell anyone what she was doing. Then one day she confided that she was measuring people for their coffins. Another woman held up the three middle fingers of her hand. She explained later that the first outside finger represented the number seven, the middle finger represented herself, and the other outside finger represented the "others." She held up these fingers to "protect" herself from the doctor and nurses. Such symbolic gesturing retains something of the magical practices and beliefs of children and savages.

A psychotic stood against the wall for

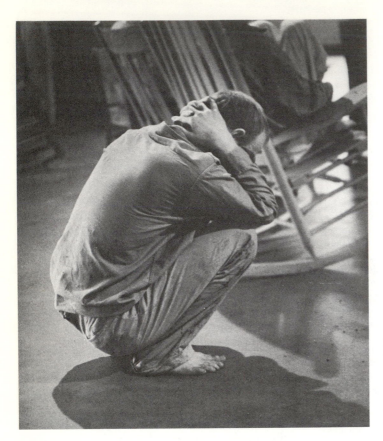

Figure 11.5 This man is crouching on the floor in the ward of a psychiatric hospital. It is not unusual for some psychotics to assume strange and bizarre positions. The psychodynamic view assumes that such positions have a symbolic meaning.

hours, with his arms raised above his head. One arm was bent over his head and his index finger was extended as if pointing. Another, a woman, sat with her eyes tightly shut and would open them only for a moment or two at a time. She explained that when her eyes were open the doctor and nurses saw what she was seeing and that they were therefore seeing through her eyes. To prevent this, she kept her eyes closed. In another case, a small, gray-haired woman in her sixties walked slowly from one building to another. Without warning, she spread out her arms and executed a series of dance steps across the courtyard. When she reached the entrance to her building, she turned around, bowed several times, and blew kisses to an imaginary audience. Another woman, of about the same age, crossed the hospital courtyard carrying a bucket of lettuce. Halfway across, she stopped, placed the bucket on the ground, ceremoniously picked out a leaf of lettuce, and placed it carefully on the ground. After circling the leaf three times, she continued on her way.

It is occasionally possible to make a diagnosis of psychosis merely on the basis of a person's nonverbal actions. When a person enters the examining room, sits down with eyes tightly shut, and responds to all questions with a vigorous shake of the head, the seriousness of the personality disorganization is at once apparent. In a similar way, the skilled clinician becomes sensitive to a wide range of more subtle motor manifestations. The underlying psychotic process is often revealed by slight and sometimes almost imperceptible mannerisms, postures, and facial expressions. These minimal motor cues, easily missed by the student or the inexperienced clinician, may contribute in an important way to the diagnosis of psychosis in borderline conditions.

What Causes Psychosis?

The cause or causes of psychotic behavior are not yet known. For many years it was thought that psychosis was due to psychological or sociocultural influences. While these views have not been abandoned, it is now thought that genetic and biochemical factors contribute significantly to the onset of psychotic behavior.

One of the difficulties in seeking a cause of psychosis is that the term does not refer to a distinct clinical disorder. Psychotic symptoms merely indicate the presence of any one of a number of underlying conditions. The situation is similar to fever, or elevated body temperature, in physical illness. The fever itself is not the illness or disease. It is a warning signal that a more fundamental and damaging physical process is at work.

The view that psychotic behavior is not the disorder itself is supported by the common observation that identical psychotic symptoms are present in widely differing conditions. Such symptoms are found where there is no apparent organic damage to the brain, as in schizophrenia (see Chapter 12); in the affective, or emotional, disorders (see Chapter 13); and in conditions in which obvious and extensive organic damage is present (see Chapter 14).

The Chapter in Review

Psychotic behavior presents one of the most puzzling and intriguing problems in abnormal psychology. It consists of a variety of dramatic symptoms which are associated with conditions in which there may or may not be organic damage of the brain.

1 Neurosis versus Psychosis
The psychotic differs from the neurotic person in a number of ways. The psychotic condition is more serious than a neurosis because psychotic behavior often leads to difficulties with other people. Since the psychotic is sometimes completely out of touch with reality, placement in a mental hospital may be necessary.

2 Signs of Psychosis

The most common indications of psychosis are in the areas of perception and thinking, emotional control, and social behavior. There may be many symptoms or a single critical one, and the signs of psychosis may be present continuously or appear only occasionally.

a Cognitive Confusion

Some of the most revealing signs of psychosis are disorientation for time, place, and person; delusions, or false ideas; and hallucinations, or perceptions without appropriate stimuli. The presence of any one of these symptoms is highly suggestive of a psychotic process.

b Emotional Behavior

The emotional reactions of the psychotic person are sometimes inappropriate, unpredictable, or inadequately controlled. These symptoms are usually combined with disturbed perception and thinking.

c Communication Difficulties

The way in which the psychotic person communicates with other people can also be a sign of the psychological disorder. Some psychotics speak and write in a cryptic way, and their nonverbal behavior is marked by symbolic gestures and mannerisms.

3 The Causes of Psychosis

The specific cause of psychotic behavior is unknown, although it is assumed that it is more likely to appear in people who have a genetic or biochemical predisposition to such behavior. Psychological events, sociocultural influences, and organic brain damage appear to be contributing, but not necessary, conditions for the appearance of psychosis.

Recommended Readings

The Psychotic Experience

Esterson, A. *The leaves of spring: A study in the dialectics of madness.* Baltimore: Penguin, 1972. (Paperback.)

Friedrich, O. *Going crazy: An inquiry into the madness of our time.* New York: Simon and Schuster, 1976.

Golann, S., Pomerantz, J. M., & Baker, J. *The Bethlehem diaries: student–mental patient encounters.* San Francisco: Canfield Press, 1974. (Paperback.)

Jefferson, L. *These are my sisters: A journal from the inside of madness.* Garden City, N.Y.: Anchor/Doubleday, 1975. (Paperback.)

Laing, R. D., & Esterson, A. *Sanity, madness, and the family* (2d ed.) New York: Basic Books, 1971.

Perruci, R. *Circle of madness: On being insane and institutionalized in America.* Englewood Cliffs, N.J.: Prentice-Hall, 1974. (Paperback.)

Perry, J. W. *The far side of madness.* Englewood Cliffs, N.J.: Prentice-Hall, 1974. (Paperback.)

12
Schizophrenia: A Major Mystery

Objectives

To define schizophrenia and to discuss the general nature of the disorder

To present the principal characteristics of schizophrenic behavior

To examine the major types of schizophrenic psychosis

To indicate some of the more important biological, psychological, and social theories of schizophrenia

To discuss the nature and symptoms of paranoid psychosis

To show why paranoid psychosis is a puzzling clinical concept

The young woman who believed her mother was a redbird was showing signs of *schizophrenia*, a term used to describe a group of psychotic behavior patterns of unknown origin. The condition represents one of the most important mental health problems of our time. The disorder accounts for about one-third of the admissions to public mental hospitals and more than half of the resident population of these institutions (National Institute of Mental Health, 1975).

These figures reflect both the large number of people involved and the chronicity of the disorder. Schizophrenia is also important because of its resistance to treatment. Fortunately, major advances in the control and treatment of schizophrenia are being made at this time; but the fundamental nature of the condition is not yet understood.

Signs of Schizophrenia

The term *schizophrenia* refers to a group of psychotic reactions marked by disturbances in reality relationships and in emotional and intellectual processes. While there are important differences in the symptom pictures of persons affected by schizophrenia, there is a common core of apathy and indifference, withdrawal, and the splitting of thought processes from their normal emotional tone.

All people are seclusive to some degree and under certain circumstances. They withdraw into themselves and isolate themselves from others, at times even from those they love most. Such isolation becomes necessary from time to time. It is a protective device that insulates people from the often difficult task of maintaining a serene and effective relationship with others. Each person constructs a system of "psychological distances" that determines the degree to which he or she enters into emotional relationships with other people. When the psychological distance is short, people enjoy active and warm relationships with others. When the psychological distance is great, they remain cold and aloof.

Some people are close to nearly everyone. They make friends while waiting for the bus, while making a purchase in a store, or while sitting in the park. Others are close to some people but remain distant toward others. And some people—those who are characteristically seclusive and withdrawn—tend to keep everyone at a distance all the time. It is in this latter, and relatively small, group that a break with reality is likely to occur. Such a personality in itself is no guarantee that a break will take place. But it is the soil from which schizophrenia develops.

It is difficult to make generalizations about the symptoms of the schizophrenic disorders

because there are so many different subtypes, each with its own distinctive characteristics. However, certain common features
are observed from time to time in all persons
with this diagnosis. Emotionally these people are apathetic or indifferent, or they over-
react. Their thinking is likely to be bizarre
and often regressive and deteriorated. Delusions and hallucinations of all types are
common. Speech may show distinctive
changes in the form of rambling and circum-
stantiality, lack of spontaneity, and evasiveness, or there may be gross changes such as
stylized speech, neologisms, echolalia, or
incoherence.

The schizophrenic thought process, which

A Worldwide Mental Health Problem

The importance of schizophrenia as a worldwide
mental health problem is reflected by the International Pilot Study of Schizophrenia (IPSS). The study
was designed to lay scientific groundwork for future
international studies of schizophrenia and other psychiatric disorders. The pilot study resulted in the
development of an international standard method for
diagnosis. It was found that the method could be
administered reliably across national settings and
result in data which would make possible the comparisons of the prevalence of psychosis from one
culture to another. Field research centers were established in nine countries where the nature and
course of schizophrenia in more than 1,200 patients
were studied over a period of five years.

The study found that a group of schizophrenics
having similar symptom patterns can be identified in
all centers. Second, a core of symptoms appears to
be common to schizophrenia regardless of the culture in which it is found. Third, certain types of
schizophrenia appear to be more prominent in one
culture than in the other. Finally, the course of
schizophrenia in terms of the stability of certain
symptoms such as delusions of persecution varies
across national settings (World Health Organization,
1973).

is one of the most fascinating phenomena in
human psychology, has received increasing
attention. Schizophrenic reasoning is quite
different from that of normal subjects; it
follows a private logic. The thinking of the
schizophrenic person has been described
variously as *prelogical*, *paralogical*, and *paleological*. These terms, which are largely
synonymous, suggest the nonlogical nature
of the thinking process.

Some schizophrenics use a form of non-
Aristotelian logic in their thinking. This type
of logic is found among children and primi-
tives as well as psychotic persons. More than
two thousand years ago, Aristotle demonstrated that *A* is *A* and cannot be *B*. However, the schizophrenic, along with the dreamer and the primitive, thinks with a different
kind of logic. Among certain primitive people, there is a belief that some human beings
are crocodiles. It is not that some human
beings act like crocodiles, but they actually
are crocodiles. On the surface such a belief is
absurd. If a person is a person, he or she
cannot be a crocodile. But the logic of the
primitive mind as well as the schizophrenic
mind is of a different order. This special
logic makes it quite possible for a person to
be a crocodile. One man was convinced that
he was Switzerland. Following the logic of
the normal mind, it seems incredible that a
human being could entertain such a thought.
However, the patient's thinking followed the
line of "Switzerland loves freedom. I love
freedom. I am Switzerland" (Bleuler, 1950).

The clinician who works with the schizophrenic soon learns to adapt to the peculiar
logic used by the patient. A psychotic may
be asked, "Do you hear voices?" When the
patient assures the examiner that he or she
does not, the skilled clinician does not hesitate to ask what would appear to be a *non
sequitur*, "What do the voices say to you?"

Figure 12.1 The disturbed nature of schizophrenic perception and imagination is reflected in the artwork produced by people with this disorder. Bizarre elements, distorted images, and compulsive repetition of detail are frequent features of schizophrenic drawings.

The patient is not surprised at such a question, nor is the clinician surprised when the patient replies, "They say all sorts of things."

In the behavioral area, schizophrenics, more than any other type of psychotic, betray themselves by posture, facial expression, mannerisms, and other symbolic movements. A tentative diagnosis of schizophrenia sometimes can be made on the basis of motor behavior alone. In some cases, the limbs can be molded into any position, and they will remain in that position indefinitely. In other cases, the patient mimics the motor movements of other people. These symptoms, while not common ones, are suggestive of schizophrenia, although such behavior also is seen occasionally in certain types of brain syndromes.

Varieties of Schizophrenia

The schizophrenic reactions are classified into types according to the distinguishing symptom pattern. However, there is a considerable degree of overlapping of symptoms and much room for difference of opinion, even among experts. It is not unusual for a schizophrenic person to be diagnosed as one type in one hospital and another type in another hospital Many cases of schizophrenia present challenging problems of differential diagnosis.

Even though the major categories of schizophrenia were established a hundred years ago, they continue to be used in diagnosis and classification in spite of the fact that they have little relevance to recent advances in our knowledge about the condition. Various attempts have been made to isolate different forms of schizophrenia apart from the old classification, which is based more on tradition than on science. The most prominent of these attempts to redefine the subgroups of schizophrenia is the distinction between *process* schizophrenia and *reactive* schizophrenia (Kantor & Herron, 1966). Process schizophrenia is assumed to develop early in life, and the person affected shows a long history of peculiar and disturbed behavior. Ordinarily it is not easy to find a specific traumatic or stressful event that can be related to the onset of the symptoms. Instead, there is a gradual development of typical behavior. Once the process schizophrenic is admitted to the mental hospital, he or she is likely to remain there indefinitely. The reactive type of schizophrenia is quite different. The first symptoms can frequently be related to some type of psychosocial stress. The person shows many of the same psychotic symptoms as the process schizophrenic. Disorientation, delusions, hallucinations, and emotional disturbances are common. Sometimes the symptoms of reactive schizophrenia appear to be more serious than those of process schizophrenia. In spite of this situation, however, reactive schizophrenia has a much better prognosis. Such people respond more readily to treat-

ment, and their stay in the mental hospital is usually much shorter than that of process schizophrenics. Some authorities view process and reactive schizophrenia as being at the opposite ends of a continuum in which genetic and constitutional factors become increasingly important as the process end of the continuum is reached. Other authorities feel that while the distinction between process and reactive schizophrenia is a valid one, two quite different disorders are involved.

Simple Schizophrenia

The simple type of schizophrenia is one of the most difficult to identify because the person rarely shows the more dramatic symptoms such as disorientation, delusions, hallucinations, or disturbances of language or action. Instead, such persons show a gradual waning of interest and activity, usually during adolescence or early adult life. They withdraw from family and friends and seek to be alone, often remaining in one room and refusing to eat. They show little or no interest in school, recreation, or work. They are inclined to become careless about personal habits and appearance and are content to indulge in daydreaming.

This type of reaction is characterized by reduction in external attachments and interests and by impoverishment of human relationships. It involves adjustment on a lower psychobiological level of functioning, with an increase in the severity of symptoms over long periods and, usually, with apparent mental deterioration. This picture contrasts with that of the schizoid personality, in which there is little if any change.

While there is no marked intellectual impairment, simple schizophrenics give the impression of being dull mentally. Their

Apathy and Indifference:
A Case of Simple Schizophrenia

Edwin W. is a 49-year-old man who has been in a psychiatric hospital for more than thirty years. He was a physically healthy and mentally alert youngster until the third year of high school, when he failed Latin. He became discouraged, and refused to return to school for his senior year. He took a job as a bank messenger, but after nine months' employment decided to return to a military academy, where he did well in his academic subjects. He also won several athletic medals. However, he complained that he could not concentrate, and felt that he did not have enough intelligence to go to college. He returned to work, but soon lost his job because he remained in bed until late morning. He refused to mix with his friends, and became exceptionally quiet. He lost interest in everything around him, and would not leave the house unless coaxed by his family. Occasionally he would go to his room and cry. He would shrug his shoulders frequently, saying, "What's the use!" The patient often talked of going away, insisting that his family did not care for him. He was sent to a private sanitarium and later transferred to the state psychiatric hospital. When first seen at the hospital, the patient was well oriented, and his memory was intact. Speech was slow, and the patient would reply to questions only after much prompting. There were no delusions, hallucinations, or other signs of severe mental illness.

During the thirty years of hospitalization, the patient has remained withdrawn and apathetic. His speech is slow and soft, and he speaks in a low monotone. He does not mingle with other patients, and sits by himself most of the time. He is generally well behaved and seldom causes a disturbance on the ward. He shows no interest in his surroundings or in ward activities. Although the patient was well oriented when he first came to the hospital, there has been a certain amount of deterioration over the years. He is no longer certain about the date or his age. When asked how long he has been in the hospital, he replies, "about two or three months." When questioned about how he likes it at the hospital, he replies, "pretty good." He presents the classic picture of the long-term hospitalized simple schizophrenic patient.

---

apathy, indifference, lack of ability to concentrate, and low level of motivation sometimes suggest mental retardation. Psychological testing, however, shows that these people are not mentally retarded, even though they give that impression. Nevertheless, the simple schizophrenic is likely to be dull emotionally, to withdraw from social and interpersonal relations, and to be indifferent to social standards of various kinds.

A second problem of differential diagnosis is between the simple schizophrenic and the inadequate personality. Both conditions result in ineffective social, family, and work relations, with the person showing a long history of failure and lack of general adaptive capacity. The key distinguishing factor between these two conditions is the apathy and withdrawal tendencies seen in the schizophrenia. The inadequate personality may try to function effectively, even though he or she is unable to do so. The schizophrenic, however, does not seem to make an effort.

Over a period of time the symptoms become worse, and many simple schizophrenics drift into a life of vagrancy, delinquency, and prostitution. Because of the relatively mild nature of the symptoms and the reasonably good contact with reality, these cases usually do not find their way to the psychiatric clinic or the mental hospital. They are more likely to be involved chronically with the courts and with social agencies.

Hebephrenia: The "Silly" Disease

A German psychiatrist coined the name *hebephrenia* in 1871 to describe those cases of mental disorder in which giggling and silli-

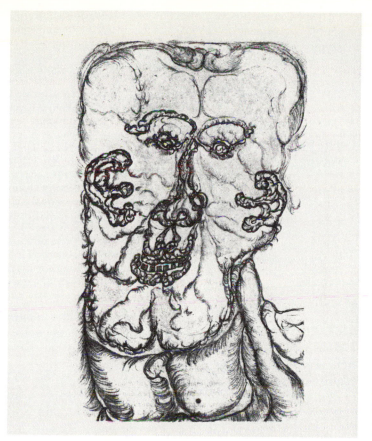

Figure 12.2 This strange and inhuman form, called *Air Apparition*, is an example of the grossly distorted images produced by some schizophrenic persons.

ness were associated with other psychotic symptoms. The word comes from the name Hebe. Hebe, the adolescent daughter of Zeus and Hera in Greek mythology, was the cup-bearer to the gods; she would sometimes sip the wine she was carrying, would begin to giggle, and often would become quite silly.

Unlike the simple schizophrenic, the hebephrenic shows a severe disintegration of the personality. Disorientation, symbolic language disturbances, and symbolic actions are seen in their most exaggerated forms. However, the most clearly identifying symptoms in this type of schizophrenia are the

silly and inappropriate giggling and smiling, facial grimaces, and bizarre language. There also may be a wide range of mannerisms, gestures, posturings, and attitudinizings. Some of the most dramatic psychotic symptoms are seen in hebephrenia.

In the past, prolonged hospitalization was required in cases of hebephrenia. Every state hospital has a number of such patients who were admitted twenty, thirty, and even forty years before. Today, while cases of hebephrenia are seen from time to time, new methods of treatment are able to prevent the chronic regression and deterioration that was so common not many years ago. While we do not understand the special etiology of this type of schizophrenia, important steps have been taken in reducing the severity of its effects.

Paranoid Schizophrenia

The paranoid type of schizophrenia is one of the most commonly seen forms of mental disorder. The condition is marked by delusions and hallucinations, frequently of an accusatory and threatening nature. Paranoid schizophrenics believe that neutral events taking place in the world outside somehow concern them personally. They are certain that radio and television programs make references to them and that other everyday occurrences refer to them directly or indirectly. They are convinced that various forces are operating against them. Although persecutory ideas predominate in most cases, there are other forms of paranoid schizophrenia characterized by sexual preoccupation, religious ideas, and somatic complaints. While the delusional system of the paranoid schizophrenic is the central feature of the disorder, it is often contaminated with other symptoms. Frequently a homosexual component is detectable in the delusions and in the implications of the hallucinations. Characteristically, paranoid schizophrenics do not show the regression or deterioration of the hebephrenic type. As a consequence, they sometimes manage to avoid hospitalization and may make a marginal adjustment in the community.

Paranoid schizophrenics, in the early stages of the disorder, reveal themselves by evasiveness, suspicion of others, ideas of reference, and other paranoid symptoms. Somewhat less frequently, the early delusional material involves religious ideas or feelings of exaggerated self-importance and grandeur.

The delusions and hallucinations of the paranoid schizophrenic take many forms, ranging from the deceptively plausible to the bizarre. A businessman was sure that his partners were trying to get rid of him and take over the company. A married man believed that his wife and children were plotting to get hold of his property and bank accounts. At the other extreme, and more clearly schizophrenic, is the woman who said, "One of the doctors stole my mind out of my head, and he is going to use it to make a lot of money." Another person wore a rubber suit at home to protect himself from the rays of an "influencing machine" which a spiteful neighbor was directing against him.

A 33-year-old tailor insisted that people had influence over him through "concentration" and "hypnotism." He said that these people, whom he did not know, were trying to force him to do "abnormal" things. He also confided that there were people who had the power to pull his brain out and replace it with an inferior brain. He said that he was suspicious of his fellow workers and that people in Hollywood were trying to dope him. A city fireman said that a porch light on a nearby house was broadcasting stories about him. A 21-year-old laborer said that "they" were going to lower him into hot acid and make hot iron out of him. He also complained that people were sprinkling powder in his room "to make him weak."

The following delusions are typical of the ideas expressed by paranoid schizophrenics in the psychiatric hospital:

They poured acid down my throat. . . . They want to tie me under a bridge and then steal my furniture. . . . Two men have been trying to get in my bedroom window to keep me from giving the news. . . . They are trying to catch me to throw me in the Irish Sea. . . . An opium smoker doped me by sticking a needle in my heel. . . . The manager of the baseball team tried to give me syphilis by putting germs on my sandwich. . . . The Masons have secret signs to tell what is going on in the world. They have bells that ring messages in code. . . . Some boys injected mercury into my brain to make me do things. . . . They are trying to steal my secrets by using electricity on me. . . . People can control my thoughts and movements. . . . My mother is trying to use my mind. . . . The Italians won't let me have my hair cut.

The paranoid schizophrenic is inclined to be very verbal about his or her ideas and beliefs. Some of the "Letters to the Editor" in the newspapers appear to be written by borderline schizophrenics of this type. Moreover, because of their tendency toward intellectualization, their views not infrequently are taken seriously. In more advanced stages of the disorder, the psychotic elements become clear. The following letters are typical of those received from paranoid schizophrenics:

> Dr. _____:
> We are getting near God's Holy years *again*. So let us servants of God watch our language and meanings Please. Such as vanity, iniquity and swearing. Study ten commandments Please. God Wants His Earth Straight and Clean *again*.
>
> Sincerely, _____

"They Are Trying to Kill Us!"— A Case of Paranoid Schizophrenia

Dorothy L. is a 49-year-old single woman who had a high school education and worked as a switchboard operator for twenty-six years. During that time she took evening college courses in art, interior decorating, and business administration. Her main interest was in collecting antiques. She lived her entire life on a small farm, first with her parents, later with her younger brother and sister, and more recently alone. The father was a passive person who provided well for his family as a farmer. The mother was a borderline psychotic who had paranoid ideas, and a sister had a history of neuroticism.

The patient made a reasonably good early adjustment. The mother died when the patient was 34, and two years later the patient took off suddenly for New Orleans. At the time, she was confused and delusional. However, she returned to her job, where her somewhat bizarre behavior was tolerated for several years. Then, when she was 40, she had a more serious break with reality, and had to be hospitalized for two months.

For the past eight years the patient has been living on the farm with an aged uncle who receives an old-age pension. She is known as a character and an eccentric in the community. She objects to her uncle using the electric lights or the hot water, and she attempts to prevent him from eating the food. For months she carried an old shopping bag with her, never allowing it out of her sight. When her brother finally managed to look into it, he found nothing but old rags in which mice had built a nest. The patient became such a problem in the community by bothering her neighbors with her delusions that it became necessary to place her in a psychiatric hospital.

When admitted to the hospital, the patient was untidy, spoke rapidly, and sat in an almost statuelike position as she told her story. There was a flight of ideas, with loose associations, neologisms, and bizarre delusions. Her emotional tone was flat and inappropriate. She remained completely detached, even when describing the most vivid persecutory delusions.

The patient told a story of being persecuted by the British and Dutch "confusea," an agency which believes in killing and which has been plotting against her ancestors and members of her family. The story becomes highly involved. She believes that John the Baptist was her great-grandfather, and that Pope Clement and Sister Maria Theresa were her grandparents. She says that she is a direct descendant of the clan of Abel. The patient talks at length about the symbolic significance of words and letters. For example, in the word *Catholic*, the *c* means the semicircle where people gather, *a* stands for the clan of Abel, *t* means the cross, *h* stands for the builders of corrals, *o* for the stones placed in a circle around water, *l* for women, and *i* for men.

Dear Dr. _____:
God is Consciousness; Consciousness is Everything the Ultimate Reality. Life is an Evolution of Consciousness. The Divine Plan is the Evolution of Spiritual Consciousness. The Super-Conscious, the Conscious and Subconscious are the 3 departments of the One Consciousness. It is a balance of opposite Polarities on all questions into Ultimate Synthesis. As follows: Religions, Metaphysical Philosophies and Truths, Psychiatry and Occupations. You have the Vegetarian-Meat Eating Polarities. The Pacifism-Militarism Polarities. The Sex Transmutation-Sex Expression Polarities. The Fasting-Naturopathic and the Medical Polarities. Colonization-Individualism Polarities. I call your attention to the Multiplicity of Metaphysical Occult and Progressive Groups in Southern California. The New World Order. The Coming World Government is an ultimate synthesis of Individualism and the Whole. I suggest that you and your World Psychiatrists write a book on New Age Spiritual Development in Southern California: the World Cradle of the New Age.

Respectfully,_____

The paranoid form of schizophrenia is important as a mental health problem because of its frequency and because it appears in a wide range of forms from very mild to quite severe. While in the milder cases it is possible for the person to make a marginal adjustment in society, the mere presence of such people in the community is potentially dangerous. Many accusations and legal actions have been brought against innocent people by borderline paranoid schizophrenics whose psychoses have not been recognized.

Catatonia

The catatonic type of schizophrenia was believed to be an organic disease during the nineteenth century. The disorder was attributed to an edema, or swelling, of the brain. The most common symptom is a generalized inhibition of motor activity, although in some cases there is excessive motor activity, grimacing, overtalkativeness, and unpredictable emotional outbursts.

The most classic catatonic symptoms are related to the stupor. They include a combination of mutism, rigidity, and the peculiar quality of muscular tonus called *cerea flexibilitas,* or waxy flexibility. The arm or leg of the patient can be placed in any position, and the limb remains in that position, sometimes for minutes or even hours. While this symptom is already diagnostic of catatonia, it is not necessary to the diagnosis. Most catatonic patients show the symptom only occasionally, and some not at all.

The motor symptoms in catatonia are more important, or at least more easily observed, than the intellectual or the emotional symptoms. The person sits or stands in one position, refusing to talk to anyone and seeming not to pay attention to anything that is said. Sometimes there is a rigidity of the muscles and a general resistance to movement. Occasionally there may be symbolic gesturing, posturing, and stereotyped movements.

In spite of the fact that the catatonic seems completely out of touch with the world, there is evidence that the person does know what is happening, but simply does not respond to the ordinary stimulation of the environment. People who have been in catatonic stupors and have later described their experiences indicate that they were aware of the world around them but felt unable to respond to it in a meaningful way.

The excited phase of catatonia is somewhat less frequent than the stuporous phase. When it does occur, it is likely to show violence and impulsivity and makes schizophrenia one of the most dangerous of the mental disorders. Such people develop attacks of rage in which they become destructive and tear apart everything they can get their hands on. Without warning, these people are capable of attacking others in the most aggressive way. The excited phase is marked by a continued restlessness, overactivity, sleeplessness, and episodes of aggressive acting out.

The onset of catatonia is likely to be sudden. A person who has otherwise appeared to be relatively normal will one day be found in a catatonic stupor. Similarly, catatonic excitement is frequently first observed as a completely unexpected burst of violence. It is likely that a certain number of assaultive acts, and even homocides, have been committed by catatonics in outbursts of excitement.

Catatonic schizophrenia tends to be episodic, the person affected having a number of relatively short attacks over a period of years. However, chronic cases of schizophrenia with catatonic components are seen in every large psychiatric hospital.

At the psychological level, the catatonic posture has been explained by psychoanalysts in terms of a regression to the uterine period. This view regards the catatonic stupor as a symbolic representation of the unconscious desire to return to the womb of the mother. It has been suggested also that the catatonic state is comparable to the feigned death reaction which is utilized by lower animals to protect them from terrifying situations. Finally, the catatonic stupor may symbolize death itself, with its implication of an ultimate escape from all care and worry. Such views, however, are unsubstantiated hypotheses.

The evidence for a biochemical basis of catatonic schizophrenia is substantial. It has been shown that animals injected with heavy water (deuterium oxide), or such drugs as bulbocapnine, show motor reactions similar to those seen in human catato-

Silence and Secrets: The Catatonic Condition

Harry G. is a 27-year-old man who developed his mental illness while serving a prison sentence in the Army. He became depressed and unable to sleep, refused food, was uncooperative, expressed paranoid ideas, and had auditory and visual hallucinations. He was transferred from the military prison to an Army hospital, and after a period of treatment he was returned to civilian life and placed in a psychiatric hospital.

When seen at the hospital, the patient was neat and clean in his dress and habits. While he was rather seclusive in his behavior, he caused no difficulties in the ward, and he cooperated readily with nurses, attendants, and examiners. His mood was somewhat depressed, and his emotional level appeared markedly flattened; but no abnormalities were noted in his thinking. When asked why he was in the hospital, he told a story of having been sent to military prison for striking a noncommissioned officer who tried to take a bottle of cognac away from him. The patient said, "I was always in trouble in the Army, always for just little things, but always in trouble."

The most distinguishing feature in this case was several psychotic episodes in which the patient became mute, would not obey instructions, and sat or stood in one place for hours at a time. He would follow slowly if taken by the hand and led, but he would not move on his own initiative. When questions were put to him, it appeared as if he did not hear. While his eyes were open, he stared straight ahead in an unseeing way. The diagnosis in each instance was catatonic schizophrenia.

nia. Such reactions can also be obtained in the experimental animal by the production of certain types of brain lesions. Another experimental evidence of a possible biochemical basis for catatonia is the fact that the injection of sodium amytal or the inhalation of carbon dioxide and oxygen results in periods of lucidity in these patients. This lucid interval lasts from a few minutes to a

Figure 12.3 The catatonic person may remain motionless and unresponsive for many hours or days at a time. This woman with her mouth open and eyes half-closed appears to be in a catatonic state. She will stand in this position until someone takes her by the arm and leads her away. Such people show no initiative but usually do not resist being led from place to place.

few hours, and then the catatonic stupor returns.

Schizo-Affective Type

Some schizophrenics show a considerable degree of emotion. The emotional instability may be so pronounced that they may present difficult management problems. During the course of a single interview such people may show affective changes ranging from laughter to tears.

When this type of emotional instability is combined with delusional ideas, the results are often of a serious nature. Strong emotional attachments are developed particularly by women, and quite unsuspecting men sometimes find themselves the innocent victims of the delusional affections of someone they hardly know or do not know at all.

The acute schizo-affective attack is one in which the mental content is predominantly schizophrenic, but with a turmoil of emotion. Sometimes these people become so disturbed that they are dangerous to themselves and to others. While such persons now are kept under control by means of psychoactive drugs, they were for many years among the most violent in the psychiatric hospital.

Undifferentiated Type

Many cases of schizophrenia cannot be easily classified as simple, hebephrenic, paranoid, catatonic, or schizo-affective. When there is such a combination and overlapping of symptoms that the patient cannot be placed in a clear-cut diagnostic category, a diagnosis of undifferentiated schizophrenia is made. This condition, like the schizo-affective type, is a relatively recent addition to the classification of schizophrenia.

The following letter is one of a series received from a chronic undifferentiated schizophrenic. This patient makes a reasonably adequate social adjustment and has never been hospitalized.

Dear Dr. _____:

This material is flying all over the country now to about 20 research men. Federal agent said #1 over his head had me dictate it in simple form—this recorded (also Washington, D.C.) and ask me to see M? Another department better versed on this subject (no time). I do not know if you received another letter. I asked someone else to read first and mail. Now I could not tell you one word that is in #2. My writings are kept by all medical men—no comment—no return on request—after all four pages difficult for me to do over (public stenographer). Twelve copies of that gone out. Please return

"I'll Kill You If You Take the Children!"— A Case of Undifferentiated Schizophrenia

Sylvia M. is a 45-year-old single woman who was admitted to a psychiatric hospital after a series of complaints by neighbors, the fire department, and the Board of Health. The patient's psychotic condition existed for at least four years, during which time she had been living alone. She hallucinated actively, talked to herself, and screamed at night. Neighbors reported she would scream from the window, "Get out of here, or I'll kill you if you take the children." The patient has never been married and has no children. Her apartment was filthy; thirty-seven large bags of garbage were found in it when she was hospitalized.

The patient was an excellent student in school and graduated from her university with honors in sociology. She was an active and well-liked member of a sorority, and following her graduation she took a position in the field of social work. She enjoyed a secure financial position, and was considered an attractive and well-dressed woman. Several young men wanted to marry her, but her father interfered each time.

Sylvia's mother died soon after Sylvia was born, and her father then became an alcoholic. Sylvia was adopted by relatives, although she did not know of her adoption until her adoptive mother died while Sylvia was in her late twenties. At that time she had an emotional disturbance which required hospitalization. Upon her recovery she returned home and took care of her father until his death a few years ago. Since that time she has been living alone, showing a steady deterioration of her personality.

When seen at the hospital, the patient appeared somewhat older than her age. She was unkempt and disheveled. When she entered the interview room she was suspicious and looked carefully at the walls and into the corners. She was tense and agitated, frequently rubbing her hands, and sometimes giggling and laughing inappropriately. She commented, "There doesn't seem to be much the matter with me, just my nerves." When asked why she was in the hospital, she replied that she had no idea except that the police brought her. At times she appeared puzzled and bewildered. She was oriented for time, place, and person, although her remote and recent memory were impaired. She showed much delusional material centering on her practice of "standing" as a part of some type of legal action involving her nonexistent children. She admitted that she did not understand it very well but knew that the situation required that she stand up for long intervals, sometimes throughout the night.

this copy (have copied if you want). I want a line of encouragement from just one. Why—opposition and arguments every night with J. My biggest problem "All I want you to do is get whatever you are doing over with. No intuition stuff, I want facts."

The diagnosis of undifferentiated schizophrenia has been made with increasing frequency since this category was introduced into the official classification system. Since cases of mental disorder, and particularly schizophrenia, are seldom as clear-cut as textbooks suggest, the problem of differential diagnosis is often a difficult one. Schizophrenics frequently combine features of hebephrenia and catatonia with thinking that is characteristic of paranoid schizophrenia. On one examination a person may show a particular symptom picture which suggests catatonia; at another time the same person may impress the examiner with his or her paranoid thinking. There may also be hebephrenia or schizo-affective components. It may be difficult, if not impossible, to specify exactly the type of schizophrenia with which one is dealing. For such cases the classification of undifferentiated schizophrenia was introduced.

Residual Type

The residual type of schizophrenia is seen in the person who has had serious schizophrenic disturbances and who has improved enough to return home and to make at least a marginal adjustment in the community. Nevertheless such people continue to show traces of the disorder in their thinking, emotions, and actions. These residual symptoms are not incapacitating and may not interfere seriously with adjustment to family, work, or social life.

The terms *ambulatory*, *borderline*, and *pseudoneurotic* schizophrenia have also been used to refer to the many cases of marginal schizophrenia found in every large community. While important steps have been taken in the treatment of schizophrenia, and while an increasing number of these persons are being returned to the community after relatively short periods of hospitalization, there are few "cures" in the sense of the eradication of all evidence of the schizophrenic process. There is a growing belief that one does not cure schizophrenia but merely manages the symptoms. Whether or not this point of view is valid will depend upon further investigations into the cause of the disorder.

What Causes Schizophrenia?

In his classic monograph on schizophrenia published early in the 1900s, Eugen Bleuler said, "We do not know what the schizophrenic process actually is." Today, more than three-quarters of a century later, Bleuler's comment is equally true. The problem of etiology in the schizophrenias is complicated by the fact that this group of disorders includes a variety of conditions. It is unlikely that there is a single cause common to all the schizophrenias. One would hardly expect, on the basis of the symptom picture, to find the same causative factors responsible for such widely divergent clinical types as simple schizophrenia and catatonia. While it is true that the various forms of schizophrenia show withdrawal and disorganization, these characteristics express themselves in widely different ways.

There are literally dozens of biological, psychological, psychodynamic, behavioral, and sociological theories of schizophrenia. When these theories are examined, they frequently prove not to be theories at all. They are statements about the behavior of people who happen to be schizophrenic. Even when a so-called theory is put to experimental tests and the theory is supported by the findings, it turns out that very little has been added to our knowledge of the *cause* of schizophrenia.

It is undoubtedly true that many schizophrenics experience a breakdown in communication, exhibit a defect in information processing, are unable to form close personal relationships, perceive themselves and the world in a distorted way, and show many other typical behavioral characteristics. It is also true that such findings are frequently important to our understanding of how the schizophrenic thinks and acts. However, the assumptions and the findings may be quite irrelevant to the critical problem of why some people are schizophrenic and other people are not. In spite of the increasing likelihood that a single cause of schizophrenia may never be found, the search for causes continues. The principal avenues of investigation include heredity, biochemical error, psychosocial influences, and life stress.

Schizophrenia As an Inherited Condition

The interest in the possibility of genetic influences in schizophrenia has a very long

Figure 12.4 These psychologically disturbed children are victims of childhood autism. Because such children are usually withdrawn, seclusive, and unresponsive, and show a breakdown in communication, they are sometimes classified as schizophrenic. However, since the possibility of obscure brain damage is present in these cases, most clinicians prefer to ascribe the condition to an unknown cause or causes.

history. From the time the condition was first described in the late 1800s, it was observed that the disorder seemed to occur in some families more frequently than in others. While many attempts were made to investigate the problem, the early studies were handicapped by problems of diagnosis, lack of proper controls, and inadequate statistical techniques. More recent investigations have sought to minimize these deficiencies and to make use of new approaches to the problem. Current evidence for genetic influences in schizophrenia come from three major types of investigation: family-risk studies, twin studies, and studies of adopted children.

Family-risk studies This approach is one in which the incidence of schizophrenia in the relatives of schizophrenics is compared to the incidence of the disorder in the general population. For many years, findings from this type of study provided the principal evidence for a genetic factor in schizophrenia. It was found consistently that the families of schizophrenics had a disproportionately large amount of mental disturbance. Kraepelin, in the 1890s, reported an incidence of 53.8 percent of mental disorder in the families of more than a thousand schizophrenic individuals. This early investigation was followed by a great many other studies that also indicated relatively high rates of mental disorder in families of schizophrenics.

While the consistent findings have given support to the assumption of a genetic factor in schizophrenia, it has been argued that social influences of an interpersonal nature could also account for the higher incidence of psychological disturbance among family members.

Twin studies Some of the most persuasive evidence for genetic influences in schizophrenia comes from the comparison of identical and fraternal twins. The term *concordant* is used when both twins are schizophrenic, and *discordant* is used when only one of the twins shows the disorder.

Studies over the years have indicated that both twins of an identical pair are much more likely to be schizophrenic than are both twins of a fraternal pair. The rates of concordance vary from one study to another, but they are consistently higher for identical twins than for fraternal twins. Such a finding is in agreement with a genetic view, since identical twins are genetically the same while fraternal twins have the genetic differences of ordinary brothers and sisters.

One might expect that if one identical twin was schizophrenic, the other twin would be schizophrenic in 100 percent of the cases. The fact that in some identical twin pairs only one twin is schizophrenic is explained in several ways. It may be, for example, that the nonschizophrenic twin has not yet developed the disorder. One follow-up study of discordant identical twins 7.8 years after an original study found that as many as 25 percent of the twins without schizophrenia later developed the condition (Belmaker et al., 1974).

Where the nonschizophrenic twin does not develop the disorder later on, it is possible that the learned resistance to stress has been different in each twin. Such a view assumes that while the genetic predisposition is present to the same degree in both members of the twin pair, the ability to resist psychosocial stress is a learned reaction that cannot be the same in any two people, no matter how biologically similar they are.

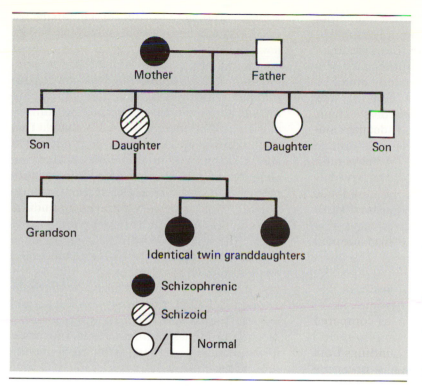

Figure 12.5 Three generations of a family with mental disorder. The mother was a hospitalized schizophrenic. Her daughter showed some of the signs of schizophrenia but was never admitted to a hospital. The identical twin granddaughters were both hospitalized with the diagnosis of schizophrenia. While this pattern does not prove biological inheritance, it is highly suggestive of some form of genetic influence.

Adoption studies The investigation of children of schizophrenic parents adopted by normal parents, and children of normal parents adopted by schizophrenic parents, has also given support to the view that there are genetic influences involved in schizophrenia. Studies have shown that the children of schizophrenic parents, even when they are adopted early in life and reared by normal parents, have a higher probability of developing schizophrenia than do control subjects (Wender et al., 1974).

Types of schizophrenic inheritance While it is generally accepted that genetic influence operates in the development of schizo-

phrenia, the type of inheritance has not been established. Some theories have emphasized a recessive gene (Kallmann, 1953); others have assumed that a single dominant gene is involved (Slater, 1968). A third approach holds that the disorder depends upon the interaction of two genes, one a carrier of the disorder and the other a modifier (Karlsson, 1973). The evidence for each of these assumptions is limited.

The most widely accepted view of the genetic mechanism of schizophrenia is that the disorder is *polygenic*, or dependent upon the complex action of a number of genes (McCabe et al., 1972). Such a view is consistent not only with the findings relative to schizophrenia itself but also to the more broadly defined schizophrenic spectrum disorders (Kety, 1973). The families of schizophrenics show, in other family members, a relatively high incidence not only of schizophrenia but also of heavy drinking and nonneurotic personality disorders. Other psychotic disorders, mental retardation, neurotic personality disorders, and suicide are also present but are found less frequently (Stephens et al., 1975).

The overwhelming combined evidence from family studies, twin studies, and studies of foster children makes it clear that genetic factors are involved in the onset of at least some of the schizophrenias. The question no longer is whether there is a genetic component to schizophrenia, but how important and specific this component is in the development of the disorder.

Schizophrenia As a Biochemical Disorder

While many investigators over the years have searched for a genetic explanation for schizophrenia, others have explored the possibility that the disorder might be caused by a biochemical disturbance in the body. It was suggested, early in the century, that some undiscovered toxin, or poison, manufactured in the body might cause the psychological disturbance. Since then, the search for some substance that would explain the symptoms of schizophrenia has continued.

By the 1950s, knowledge about the biochemistry of the nervous system, and especially the brain, was sufficiently advanced that an increasing amount of attention was being directed to the problem of schizophrenia. A number of challenging hypotheses were suggested. Some have been discarded; others remain controversial; and some are in the process of being tested.

One approach to the biochemistry of schizophrenia has been the attempt to isolate psychosis-inducing substances in the blood serum. At first it was thought that *ceruloplasmin*, a copper protein, was elevated in schizophrenics, but it was then found that the substance increased because institutional diets were deficient in ascorbic acid. This work, however, led to the finding that a special form of ceruloplasmin could bring about behavioral changes when injected into monkeys. It was also claimed that this substance, called *taraxein*, induced hallucinations and delusions in volunteer human subjects. Although the findings have not been confirmed by others, some investigators continue to pursue this line of research.

A different approach is based on the well-known fact that the drug *mescaline*, obtained from a globe-shaped cactus called mescal, produces hallucinations and other psychological disturbances that resemble the symptoms of schizophrenia. Since it is also known that mescaline is chemically similar to epinephrine, a substance produced by the adrenal glands, the assumption was made that a disturbance of the chemistry of epinephrine might result in products that could cause psychotic symptoms (Osmond & Smythies, 1952). It has been found that such products, *adrenochrome* and *adrenolutin*, do indeed exist and are capable of producing disturbed behavior.

It has also been suggested that schizophrenia may be related to a deficiency in the brain of the neurohumor *serotonin*. This substance, which is involved in the transmission of the nerve impulse, has a chemical structure that is similar to the structures of mescaline and lysergic acid (LSD-25). Since both mescaline and LSD are capable of inducing disturbed behavior, the assumption was made that schizophrenia might be related to a deficiency of serotonin (Woolley & Shaw, 1954). Other examples of the search for a biochemical cause of schizophrenia have been the claims that the urine of schizophrenics contains a characteristic substance (Friedhoff & Van Winkle, 1962), and that certain plasma proteins can alter body metabolism in such a way that the symptoms of schizophrenia appear (Frohman, Caldwell, & Gottlieb, 1974).

While it is true that a number of biochemical disturbances and metabolic errors have been found in schizophrenics, the findings have not been consistent. It may very well be that there is a critically important factor in schizophrenia, but it would be necessary to demonstrate that such a factor is present only in cases of schizophrenia, that it is present in all cases of schizophrenia, and that it can induce schizophrenia when introduced into the bodies of nonschizophrenic people.

These basic requirements have not been met by any of the assumptions or research findings related to the biochemistry of schizophrenia. For this reason, a biochemical basis for this disorder is merely an intriguing and elusive possibility.

Schizophrenia As a Psychosocial Disorder

In spite of the mounting evidence that genetic and biochemical factors are critically involved in a substantial number of cases of schizophrenia, efforts continue to explain the condition in psychological and sociological terms. Even before the current emphasis on behavior theory, most psychological explanations were in terms of social learning. Other explanations have emphasized the psychodynamic concepts of Freud and the psychoanalysts.

The social learning, or behavioral, explanation of schizophrenia is that the disorder is a learned pattern of behavior and is acquired in the same way that normal behavior is acquired. There is no agreement, however, as to the types of learning experiences that are critical to the development of schizophrenia.

One view is that the schizophrenic learns to withdraw into a private world of fantasy. There is a flight from reality in which communication with others is interrupted and emotional participation in the outside world is reduced. The person solves problems by isolating himself or herself from the harsh realities of everyday life.

The theory of the *schizophrenogenic* mother is that mothers with certain personality characteristics tend to cause schizophrenic reactions in their children. This theory received a considerable amount of support until a study of the parents of schizophrenic, neurotic, asthmatic, and chronically ill children found that there were no special personality characteristics which distinguished the groups of mothers.

On the basis of clinical descriptions of so-called schizophrenogenic mothers, the mothers of schizophrenic children did not differ significantly from mothers of asthmatic children. There was a relationship, however, between psychological disturbances in the mother and symptoms in the child. The correlation accounted for about 25 percent of the psychological symptoms in the children of disturbed mothers. This finding was interpreted to mean that even the complete removal of all psychiatric symptoms from the mothers would not relieve the children's schizophrenia in an appreciable way (Block, 1969).

The psychodynamic model of schizophrenia holds that the condition is based on emotionally traumatic experiences that occurred early in life. This basic assumption was elaborated by a vast number of assumptions about the symbolic nature of symptoms. However, even during the height of psychoanalytic influence, psychologists and psychiatrists of analytic persuasion were much less interested in the psychotic than they were in the neurotic. Few psychoanalysts were inclined to work in institutions where psychotics were confined. The major thrust of psychodynamic theory and practice was directed toward the neurotic person and, to a much lesser extent, to people with personality disorders.

It seems clear that there is a relationship between schizophrenia and social variables such as social class, economic condition, and place of residence. A study by the British Psychiatric Rehabilitation Association (1969) found a close association between schizophrenia and poor socioeconomic conditions in London. The number of schizophrenics in East London was 50 percent above the national average, while the rate for dockland areas of Stepney rose to $2^{1}/_{2}$ times the national average. Stepney also had higher rates for most other categories of mental disorder, with 90 percent above the national rate for depressive illness and 153 percent higher for alcohol and drug addiction. The concentration of schizophrenics in deteriorated areas of the city can be explained by the fact that disturbed people move to these areas after the mental disorder develops. Such people "drift" to areas where housing is inexpensive, few demands are made upon them, and their deviant behavior is tolerated. The theory of drift also accounts for the fact that a disproportionate number of psychotics come from the lowest socioeconomic level. It is likely that schizophrenia occurs across the socioeconomic scale, but that these people tend to sink lower and lower until they are at the bottom of the scale. Therefore people from deteriorated areas are more likely to be admitted to public mental hospitals.

Schizophrenia As a Stress Disorder

The view that stress is an important factor in the development of schizophrenia is consistent with genetic, biochemical, and psychosocial interpretations of the disorder. We saw in Chapter 3 that resistance to stress is determined in part by hereditary factors. We also learned that stress can alter the biochemistry of the brain and other parts of the body. In Chapters 5 and 6 it was pointed out that psychosocial events can be stressors that contribute to maladaptive behavior.

Stress theory contends that in biochemically normal brains, the alterations resulting from stress remain within normal limits and do not have a noticeable impact on experience or behavior. However, in a genetically predisposed brain and nervous system, the stress triggers biochemical and metabolic changes which result in schizophrenic symptoms. One possibility is that stress produces chemical substances that act as inducers of enzymes, and that these are involved in the production of a protein which may be related to the onset of schizophrenia. Another possibility is that stress activates autoimmune processes which may play a causative role. It is also possible that stress can change levels of brain amines or alter the permeability of the blood-brain barrier (Strahlevitz, 1974).

There are many examples of schizophrenia appearing in connection with physical stress. A pair of 24-year-old identical twins were victims of a disorder of the basal ganglia, an area in the lower part of the brain. Both women developed similar schizophrenic symptoms within a few hours of each other (West, 1973).

The interrelation between physical and psychological stressors has been shown in the development of psychosis following heart transplants. At one medical center, 38 percent of heart transplant patients developed a postoperative psychosis. One patient grew increasingly belligerent, developed delusions, and accused nurses and others of trying to kill him. Whenever he failed to receive his medicine within a minute or two of its scheduled time, he viewed the incident as part of a plot. He was convinced that one of the drugs he was receiving was poisoning his body and was meant to kill him. The patient saw dozens of masked people coming into his room, and he decided that the masks were worn to hide contemptuous and mocking expressions (Lunde, 1969).

Sociocultural stressors can also trigger the schizophrenic reaction. A study of children with schizophrenic mothers found that those in the lower socioeconomic groups had a greater incidence of mental disorder than children in economically average families. Apparently the stress of being poor and disadvantaged contributed to the onset of the psychotic condition. It was also found that children who spent substantial parts of their early lives in orphanages and children's homes were more likely to become psychologically disturbed (Stern, 1972).

The relative importance of inborn genetic predisposition to schizophrenia and the effects of stress in releasing the psychotic reaction is disputed. One investigator, who made a close study of schizophrenics and their families over a period of twenty-two years, believes that about 75 percent of the people who become schizophrenic would not have developed the disorder except for psychosocial stress (Bleuler, 1974). An op-

posing view is that the environmental contribution is less specific and less important than the genetic influence (Shields & Gottesman, 1973).

A reasonable conclusion appears to be that genes are a necessary, but not sufficient, cause for the development of schizophrenia. It is also probable that environmental factors in the form of stress are necessary as well but similarly are not in themselves sufficient to cause the disorder. Moreover, it is likely that a weak genetic predisposition to schizophrenia can be activated by a high degree of stress, while a strongly predisposed person might have a schizophrenic reaction triggered by a relatively low level of stress. Whatever the mechanisms involved, stress theory makes it possible to reconcile the seemingly contradictory facts and findings of the genetic, biochemical, and psychosocial investigations of schizophrenia.

The Puzzle of Paranoid Psychosis

Some psychotics develop complex delusional systems, but without the disorientation, hallucinations, and disturbances of language and action seen so frequently among schizophrenics. In these cases, the delusions tend to be more or less systematized and integrated with the rest of the personality. Moreover, there is little or no intellectual deterioration, and emotional responses are completely consistent with the ideas held. As a result, the delusions of the paranoid person are sometimes so persuasive that his or her ideas are accepted by others who are not mentally disturbed.

The word *paranoia* was already in use at the time of Hippocrates, with a meaning roughly equivalent to the now obsolete term *insanity*. With the emergence of modern psychopathology in the eighteenth century, the word took on a more specific meaning. It referred primarily to a condition in which the mental faculties appeared to remain intact, though at the same time the person affected was the victim of a highly organized delusional system. Today, paranoia is indicated by such terms as *paranoid reaction*. Unlike the paranoid personality discussed in Chapter 8, these conditions fall into the psychotic category because of their delusional component.

Most experts in the field of psychiatry and abnormal psychology find it difficult to fit the paranoid condition into the conventional classification system. In fact, a number of authorities have gone so far as to deny that the paranoid state is a diagnostic entity. However, the condition is much too clearcut for its existence to be denied. In fact, it is not a difficult diagnosis to make. For this reason, most clinicians accept the diagnosis as a valid one.

However, once the diagnosis is made, the question arises as to what it is with which one is dealing. Traditionally, the paranoid state has been regarded as a psychosis primarily because delusions are considered to be psychotic symptoms. Yet the paranoid person is likely to be completely free of other psychotic symptoms. At the same time, the delusional thinking may be so overwhelming that the person has no insight into the irrationality of his or her thinking.

In some respects, the paranoid psychosis resembles a neurosis. It might be argued that the pathological fears, obsessions, compulsions, and similar neurotic symptoms are not far removed from the fixed belief that there is a plot against one or that there is a danger of being executed by enemies. The thinking of

Figure 12.6 The artistic productions of paranoid people are likely to reflect their delusion systems. This work is called *Holy Sweat Miracle On The Insole*. The religious elements and symbolism are clearly apparent.

the paranoid person, even in its most serious form, has more the flavor of an obsession than of the disorganization usually associated with psychotic disturbances.

The classic symptom picture of the paranoid reaction is one in which there is no loss of intellectual efficiency and in which the person is quite capable of functioning adequately in all areas except those involving

**Persecuted by a Machine:
A Letter from a Paranoid Psychotic**

Dear Dr. _____:

I have a neighbor who owns and operates an ultrasonic machine. The transducer is projected toward us, i.e., we are in the direct beam of its energy! This neighbor has tried at various times to kill us but we have always managed to run from the apartment, thereby getting out of its beam before it affects us too much! Most of the time, he has just turned it on us to give us various feelings (not all of them at once, of course): headaches, fever, extreme fatigue or nervousness, tiredness, irritability, dizziness, nausea, sometimes fainting, and a feeling of "impending doom." There is absolutely nothing in the world we can do about it, or at least there hasn't been so far. That is what makes our case so unique! They could murder us, as they did a neighbor of ours, and even a post mortem would only show an ordinary heart attack. No one can even prove it on our neighbor, because it would only show what an ordinary heart attack would show. His widow knows this fact and so do we. She couldn't even tell the authorities because they would think she was crazy or too unbalanced by her grief.

Really, there is no telling how many more of these machines our neighbor owns throughout the country. He certainly wouldn't stop with one since he has long since recognized his strength and secret treachery.

No one has caught him yet and no one is able to except for one thing that I shall write later.

Why is this man doing this? He used to be our neighbor and he hated us for what we are and what we have—those are the only things that we have been able to figure out other than that he has a complex he can't outgrow. He just happened onto this machine and he has followed us around the country with it, moving in just next door with it wherever we have moved to get away from him.

Since there is no obvious law governing machines of this sort, there is nothing we can do to stop him. Can you imagine a flat-foot cop having the knowledge of an ultrasonic machine? There aren't any! It doesn't come under the jurisdiction of the FBI since there is no federal offense committed, nor the FCC because they are only interested in radio waves.

To prove all this in a mechanical way, that this neighbor actually has an ultrasonic machine, and that he projects it on our apartment, we would have to order *custom-built* (from a reputable electronics firm) a model GA-1007 sound pressure equipment with built-in calibrator, and with a M-123 microphone, costing around $1,350. Who has money like that nowadays to spend on such a thing? *What would you do?*

Sincerely, _____

P.S. Call me long distance, reverse the charges. I'll be glad to give you any more information after 5 P.M.

his or her delusional system. This system usually develops slowly over a relatively long period of time. Moreover, the system has a high degree of internal consistency. In fact, if the affected person's basic assumptions are granted, the delusional system is likely to have a compelling logic. An interesting aspect of the paranoid reaction is that this logic often makes it possible for a paranoid person to convince others of the reasonableness of his or her ideas. The intensity and apparent sincerity of the person often sway others; this sometime results in strange cults, sects, and movements in religion, philosophy, political science, economics, and similar fields.

Usually the person suffering from paranoid psychosis appears quite normal in conversation, emotional responsiveness, and actions. Only the delusional ideas betray the underlying disturbance. Since they have convinced themselves so completely of the reality of their delusions, these people cannot tolerate any criticism of their ideas. No matter how much evidence there is to the contrary, no matter how unlikely or impossible their plans and proposals are, any questioning results in evasiveness, defensiveness, and irritability. Such people are inclined to make sweeping generalizations and to come to far-reaching conclusions based entirely on their delusional ideas rather than on facts or reality. Paranoid persons are potentially dangerous; the world has more than once suffered at the hands of leaders whose paranoid beliefs went unrecognized until it was too late.

The Chapter in Review

Schizophrenia refers to a group of conditions showing psychotic symptoms and presumably having a common, but unknown, cause. The disorder is the most serious of all psychotic disturbances and accounts for the largest single group of people admitted to public mental hospitals.

1 Signs of Schizophrenia

It is difficult to generalize about the clinical signs of schizophrenia because of the variety of conditions included in this diagnostic group. The basic psychotic disorders of perception, thinking, emotion, and interpersonal communication are usually present. However, the common core of schizophrenia is considered to be seclusiveness, social withdrawal, and retreat into a private world of fantasy.

2 Varieties of Schizophrenia

There have been two principal approaches to the classification of schizophrenia. The traditional one has been to use labels indicating groups of symptoms. This approach dates back to the late 1800s, when simple schizophrenia, hebephrenia, catatonia, and paranoid schizophrenia were first described. Today, efforts are being directed toward discovering a more logical and useful basis for classification. The distinction between reactive and process schizophrenia is an example of this trend.

3 What Causes Schizophrenia?

There is little agreement about the cause, or causes, of this disorder. Biological explanations emphasize genetic influences and biochemical disturbances. The psychological approach seeks to discover the cause in the breakdown of cognitive mechanisms or in psychodynamic influences. The sociocultural view holds that schizophrenia develops as a result of faulty child rearing, family disorganization, or some other disturbed social relationship.

4 Paranoid Psychosis

This disorder is a puzzling one, since it involves many of the symptoms seen in schizophrenia but not the psychological disorganization that so frequently accompanies the schizophrenic psychosis. The principal symptom is a relatively well-organized system of delusions, often of a persecutory nature. The cause of the condition is unknown.

Recommended Readings

The Schizophrenic Condition

Arieti, S. *The interpretation of schizophrenia.* New York: Basic Books, 1975.

Hoffer, A., & Osmund, H. *How to live with schizophrenia.* Secaucus, N.J.: University Books, 1974.

Neary, J. *Whom the gods destroy.* New York: Atheneum, 1975.

O'Brien, B. *Operators and things.* New York: New American Library, 1976. (Paperback.)

Osmund, H. *Understanding understanding.* New York: Bantam Books, 1974. (Paperback.)

Pfeiffer, C. C. *The schizophrenias: Yours and mine.* New York: Pyramid Publications, 1970. (Paperback.)

Plante, E. *Rene: The biography of a schizophrenic.* New York: Vantage Press, 1974.

Salzinger, K. *Schizophrenia: Behavioral aspects.* New York: Wiley, 1973.

Vonnegut, M. *The Eden express: A personal account of schizophrenia.* New York: Praeger, 1975.

Sorrow

Vincent

13
Affective Disorders: Mood and Madness

Objectives

To discuss the general nature of the affective disorders

To define *bipolar depression* and describe the forms it takes

To show what is meant by *unipolar depression* and to indicate how it differs from bipolar depression

To discuss the genetics of depression

To present some of the biochemical theories of affective disorders

To discuss psychosocial influences in the development of these conditions

The schoolteacher (below) who made a nude pursuit of the chambermaid was showing signs of an affective disorder. Unlike the schizophrenic conditions, in which the behavior disturbances are primarily in the areas of perception and thinking, the affective disturbances involve emotional reactions including depression and elation, or elevated mood. The disorders range from mild to severe and are accompanied by delusions, hallucinations, disorientation, or other signs of psychosis.

These psychotic conditions, made up largely of severe depressions, account for 11.8 percent of patients admitted to public mental hospitals in the United States (National Institute of Mental Health, 1975). However, the majority of people suffering from depressive illnesses are not admitted to hospitals, with the result that hospital inpatients represent only a minor part of the problem. A government-sponsored survey has indicated that, in any given year, some 15 percent of all adults between the ages of 18 and 74 may suffer significant symptoms of depression (House Hearings, 1975).

Part of the problem of understanding depressive disorders is that the word *depression* has been used in a variety of ways. It has been used to refer to an *affect*, which is a

---

"I'm As Nutty As a Fruitcake!"— A Case of Hypomania

Paul J., a 56-year-old schoolteacher, was admitted to a psychiatric hospital from the county jail after having been picked up at a local hotel where he had been staying. The incident which brought him to the attention of the court was one in which he ran down a hotel corridor in nude pursuit of a chambermaid. He had also stuck toilet paper to the doors of various hotel rooms with toothpaste, and it was reported that he urinated in the wastebaskets from time to time. He became such a problem at the hotel that the police were called, and the police department probated him to the psychiatric hospital.

The patient came to the interview straight from a shower. He had not bothered to dry himself off, and his head was dripping with water. His personal habits in grooming since admission had been good, and he had not given any active trouble on the ward. However, his excessive talkativeness made him unpopular with the other patients. For the most part, he was difficult to contend with during the interview due to his verbal overactivity. The interviewer had to interrupt continually in order to keep some relevancy to the story. The patient's manner and voice were overbearing and condescending, and his posture varied from slumping in the chair to thumping on the table.

During the interview, the patient said he felt fine, and everything was wonderful. When the physician addressed him as Paul, he became upset and said he would be pleased and honored if he were to be called Willis. When asked why he had rushed from his shower, he said that he had to take showers to get massage and heat for his injured spine. He left the shower in a hurry because "there were six lunatics in there having coffee and cigarettes." He said that he had come to this city to see a friend. When on the plane on the trip to the city, he met a "professional Southern woman" who had a child with her. He said the child smeared feces from its diaper on his suit, and in the resulting furor the woman stole his money and ran toward the back of the plane. He said he went after her, and got his money back. At one time he said that everybody with an IQ over 110 is neurotic. He also said, "I'm as nutty as a fruitcake, but as pure as a dove." He said he felt superior to most other people, and he showed a marked contempt for the human race. He was fully oriented for person, place, and time.

The patient had an M.A. degree, and had taught for twelve years in high schools and colleges in various parts of the country. He had been active in church work and school activities. Ordinarily, he was a well-adjusted, thoughtful, kind, and cooperative person. He had been divorced from his wife during one of his personality disturbances when he became angry with her for having him sent to a hospital.

subjective feeling tone of short duration; to a *mood,* which is a sustained state over a longer period of time; to an *emotion,* in which feeling tones are combined with detectable physiological changes; and to a personality disturbance with characteristic symptoms (Zung, 1973).

The question is, when does depression become abnormal? The problem is similar to knowing when a strong fear becomes a phobia or when "normal" anxiety becomes neurotic anxiety. In the present state of our knowledge, the difference between normal and pathological depression must depend upon the ability of the depressed person to handle the situation. If the depression becomes so severe or prolonged that it interferes with his or her personal or social life, and if a need is felt for help with the condition, the depression becomes abnormal at that point. Another view holds that all depression, accurately defined, is pathological. It follows that there is no such state as "normal" depression. What has been called normal depression is really sadness, sorrow, and unhappiness.

Until recently, most of what we knew about depression came from clinical observations of depressed people. More recently, the emphasis has shifted to the experimental investigation of assumptions and hypotheses about the possible causes and nature of depressive behavior. An important outgrowth of this new emphasis has been the classification of depression into two major types. *Unipolar depression* refers to conditions in which there are isolated or recurring episodes of depression. *Bipolar depression* refers to the condition in which an individual has episodes of both depression and manic excitement. The unipolar-bipolar classification has been supported by a wide range of biological and psychosocial studies (Winokur, Clayton, & Reich, 1969).

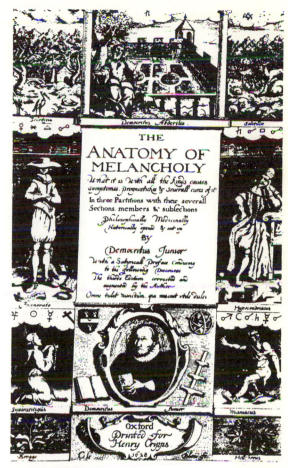

Figure 13.1 The title page to Robert Burton's seventeenth-century treatise on melancholy. This book is the most comprehensive historical treatment of depression ever written. It is a vast storehouse of fact and fancy about the causes and cures of depression, with humorous, romantic, and satirical digressions ranging from antiquity to the time the book was completed at Christ Church College, Oxford, on Dec. 5, 1620.

Bipolar Depression

This affective disorder is one in which there are severe and recurrent swings in mood. While most of the swings are in the direction of depression, the pattern also includes episodes of elation and excitement. These fluctuations in emotional level are accompanied by psychotic symptoms. Late in the 1800s, Kraepelin gave the name *manic-depressive psychosis* to this pattern of maladaptive behavior. The term continues to be used as part of the classification system.

The emotional reaction in this disorder is an exaggeration of the mood changes most people experience from time to time. Sometimes people are "on top of the world," and at other times they are "down in the dumps." Yet, most of the time, they cannot say why they feel as they do. Many people travel through life fluctuating between sadness on the one hand and elation on the other. In general, they manage to maintain a balance, without going too far in either direction. Some men and women, for reasons which remain obscure, go too far in one direction or the other. Some go so far, in fact, that they need to be hospitalized. Fortunately most of the attacks are short-lived, and the average stay in the hospital is only a few months. While most of the patients recover completely, they are likely to have future attacks.

Swing toward Depression

In the depressive phase of bipolar depression, depressives feel sad and discouraged. They lose interest in their surroundings, and life seems hopeless. As a result, there is a general reduction in psychomotor activity. Both thought and action are slowed down progressively. As the condition worsens, delusions and hallucinations may appear. In most cases, there are definite bodily symptoms in the form of loss of muscle tone, sadness of facial expression, and a variety of vegetative symptoms such as lowered blood pressure, lack of appetite, constipation, diminished secretion of saliva, and insomnia.

Among women there may be interference with the menstrual cycle.

There are times when everyone feels dejected, gloomy, and listless. Life seems to be a burden. People get the "blues" and see only the dark side of things. Many people have personalities slanted consistently in this direction. Depression, unhappiness—the attitude of uncertainty, doubt, and defeat—and thoughts of suicide are common experiences. The depressive phase of the manic-depressive reaction is a severe extension of such symptoms. If the reaction progresses, it passes through three major stages known as (1) simple depression, (2) acute depression, and (3) depressive stupor.

In *simple depression*, there is a general slowing down of physical and mental activity, with a feeling of dejection and discouragement. Bodily complaints are frequent, and there is usually loss of appetite and loss of weight. Thinking remains clear, and unless the depression progresses to the next stage, hospitalization is not ordinarily necessary.

In the stage of *acute depression*, the retardation of mental and physical activity is increased, and the feelings of worthlessness and failure become more pronounced. The person may sit alone for hours at a time, refusing to speak to friends or relatives. He or she sees no hope for recovery, and ideas of suicide are common. It is during this stage of the disorder that the preoccupation with bodily ailments begins to take on a delusional quality. Vague and poorly defined hallucinations also may be present.

When the affective reaction reaches the stage of *depressive stupor*, the patient becomes completely mute and occasionally resistive and negativistic. Such psychotic symptoms as confusion, disorientation, delusions, and hallucinations are seen frequently; and because of the almost complete lack of motor activity, these patients sometimes must be fed artificially. Under the circumstances, there may be a general deterioration in the health of the patient, with increased danger of infection, toxic reactions, and circulatory disturbances.

When an accurate diagnosis of depression of the bipolar type has been made, it can be predicted with about 80 percent probability that there will be at least one additional attack and that future attacks will be limited to a few weeks or months (Winokur, Clayton, & Reich, 1969). In one study, people suffering from bipolar depression were interviewed an average of 3.2 years after their discharge from the mental hospital and 14.7 years after the onset of their disturbances. It was found that they had an average of more than five episodes of emotional disturbance. About one-third of them showed moderate to severe emotional impairment which interfered with work, social relationships, and family life. The other two-thirds made a good adjustment except during the episodes of the disorder (Carlson et al., 1974).

Swing toward Elation

The manic, or excited, phase of bipolar depression is marked by elation, feelings of well-being, optimism, self-confidence, self-assurance, and generally high spirits. Along with this elevation in mood there is a general increase in psychomotor activity—the person talks a lot and is restless. Thoughts flow freely and are expressed easily and rapidly. As the disorder progresses, there may be delusions and hallucinations, along with such physical symptoms as increased heart rate and blood pressure, heightened muscle tone, and alert expression. Because of the overactivity, sleeplessness and loss of

weight are seen from time to time in these people.

The manic reaction, or excited phase of the manic-depressive psychosis, appears to be a paradox because the behavior is quite the opposite of that seen in depression. However, it has been known for more than a hundred years that elation and depression are closely linked in many people. When manic behavior does occur, it may remain relatively mild, as in the case of *hypomania*, or it may become progressively more serious until it reaches the *acute* or *hyperacute* stages.

There is a moderate degree of elation and overactivity in hypomania. People so affected have an extraordinary sense of self-confidence and faith in their ability to accomplish whatever they undertake. They seem to have boundless energies and acquire an unusual social facility because of their lack of self-consciousness. Many hypomanics manage to remain outside the mental hospital. In fact, a person who is mildly hypomanic and does not progress to a stage of more serious symptoms sometimes does unusually well in endeavors where these traits are important.

In the hypomanic stage of elation, people show symptoms which may be the very factors responsible for business or professional success. They become self-confident and somewhat boastful, and they are inclined to be dominating and assertive. Such a person is described as being "dynamic," a "go-getter," a "ball of fire," or the "life of the party." But in some cases, the pressure of activity leads to overtalkativeness, loud and rapid speech, furious writing, exaggerated gestures, and eccentric dress.

In *acute mania*, there is a break with reality. People become more irritable, impatient, and overbearing. Their speech be-

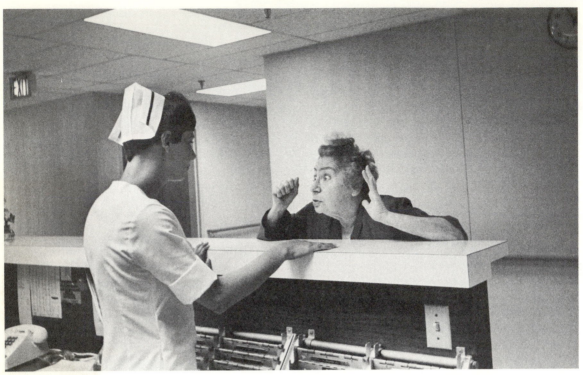

Figure 13.2 People in the manic phase of bipolar depression are excitable, talkative, and overactive. They move restlessly about the ward, observe everything that is happening and, like this woman, volunteer information to the staff, give advice, and demand that immediate action be taken.

comes confused and may include vulgar and vicious remarks. They have flights of ideas which appear incoherent or nearly incoherent to the listener. They may even become combative and destructive, rush about tearing and breaking things, yelling and shouting, and showing hostility and aggression in every move they make. Some people become lewd and obscene, expose themselves, or make crude sexual advances toward others. Physical and mental activity becomes so great that patients find little time to sleep or eat. They become partially disoriented and have occasional delusions and hallucinations.

In *hyperacute mania*, excitement is so intense that the person is likely to be totally disoriented, with an outpouring of incoherent speech and a burst of frenzied activity that leaves him or her totally exhausted. Restless pacing, loud singing, shouting and screaming, gesticulating, and pounding and tearing occur in most cases. The excitement is so intense that it endangers the person affected and those who must come in contact with him or her. Delusions are severe and hallucinations are vivid, with a total lack of insight and control. At one time it was necessary to keep this type of patient in protective restraint for hours or days at a time. Today, thanks to advances in the use of drugs, relatively few of these people reach the hyperacute stage of the disorder.

Unipolar Depression

Unipolar depression differs from the bipolar type of disorder in several ways. The most important of these differences is that the unipolar reaction does not show the pattern of depression and elation seen in the manic-depressive person. Instead, there may be only one episode of severe depression, or if there is more than one episode, they are usually associated with stressful life events. Such depression may accompany personal failure, critical injury or illness, death of a friend or relative, or some similar event. In other cases, the depression may be related to more general frustrations and dissatisfactions.

The two depressive disorders also differ in that the strong evidence for genetic influence in bipolar depression is lacking in unipolar disorders. For example, there is a very high concordance for bipolar depression among identical twins. That is, when one of the identical twins shows the bipolar pattern of depression, the genetically similar twin is also likely to be manic-depressive. However, concordance for unipolar depression in identical twins is relatively low and approaches the rate for nontwin brothers and sisters. This finding suggests that the unipolar type of depression is not linked with the genetic factor which appears to operate in bipolar depression.

The characteristics of two traditional types of depression fit the unipolar pattern. One is *psychotic depression* in which a nonrecurring episode of deep depression is accompanied by psychotic symptoms. The other condition fitting the unipolar pattern is *involutional depression.* For many years it was believed that this type of depression was unique to women during the involutional period, or menopause. It is now known that men as well as women develop involutional depression.

Psychotic Depression

The psychotic depressive reaction is one in which the person is so severely depressed that reality is distorted and delusions and hallucinations are experienced. While this reaction does not always include prominent psychotic symptoms, the depression may be so deep that the person appears to be in a stupor. It becomes necessary at times to feed him or her through a tube because of the refusal to take nourishment.

The major difference between the neurotic depression and the psychotic depressive reaction is the depth of the depression and the presence of psychotic symptoms. Both conditions may appear as the result of environmental stress, but only the psychotic depressive reaction includes delusions, hallucinations, and disorientation.

Psychotic depressions, which sometimes follow traumatic events and experiences, often accompany the onset of old age. Such depression may be a severe situational reaction to the realization that one is approaching the end of life. For men and women who are not prepared philosophically for death, the severe depression may be an attempt to evade the realization that life is drawing to a close.

Involutional Depression

The involutional psychotic reaction is also a depression of the unipolar type. It develops

Figure 13.3 Depressed people are likely to be preoccupied with thoughts of taking their lives during the involutional period. In this caricature, the depressed man is having fantasies of hanging himself, jumping off a high place, stabbing himself, and taking poison. Most people who attempt suicide make their decisions during deep depression.

during middle age and without previous episodes of severe depression. The condition begins somewhat earlier in women, usually between the ages of 45 and 55. In men, the changes are more gradual and less noticeable, and are likely to occur between the ages of 55 and 65.

The involutional reaction starts with feeling sorry for oneself, frequent crying spells, and a general restlessness, apprehension, and uneasiness. The person becomes sad and anxious and is overwhelmed with vague feelings of impending danger. Such people lack energy and enthusiasm, are indecisive, dislike their work and amusements, avoid social gatherings, and become despondent. They have vague fears and anxieties and show many hypochondriacal symptoms. They are irritable and moody, lose their psychological and physical elasticity, and may become self-accusatory. The condition often leads to thoughts of suicide.

The physical complaints include feelings of pressure or emptiness in the head, rush of blood to the head, dizziness, poor sleep and appetite, loss of weight, and coldness of the hands and feet. As the condition becomes more severe, the person may complain of pain and suffering and become increasingly edgy. He or she may pace the floor and develop such habits as hand wringing, skin picking, nail biting and may often tear at pieces of paper or cloth.

In some people, the involutional psychotic reaction is marked by delusions of persecution. In these cases, they blame their frustration on others. It is not unusual for people of this type to compensate for a colorless and unsatisfactory life by constructing elaborate delusions involving action and excitement.

Among men, the middle years of life are marked by a decline in sexual capacity, with its implication of loss of youth. There is also a gradual decline in energy and general physical prowess. Moreover, it is at this time that men ordinarily reach the peak of their earning power and occupational status. For the most part, men by this time have achieved all they can hope to achieve. The "future" to which they have looked forward for so many years suddenly has arrived. The realization that they have not attained what they had hoped for is critically disturbing to many of them. An overwhelming sense of frustration may develop at the thought that most of their opportunities in life have already passed.

For both men and women, there is a growing awareness that life is passing with increasing rapidity. Friends and family move away or die. Children grow up and leave the home. People who develop an involutional reaction become increasingly preoccupied with themselves and their problems. They dwell on past failures, evidences of poor health, and the supposed bleakness of the years ahead.

The involutional years are also marked by a realization of the economic problems of the future. Most people are not able to accumulate sufficient savings to allow them to lead a worry-free life during their later years. Some must look forward to help from their children or relatives. Others know they are destined to depend upon inadequate pensions or social security. Many more know that they will become wards of the city or state welfare system. Such an outlook is not likely to give comfort or to lend to feelings of optimism and lightheartedness during these critical years.

While many persons with this disorder improve spontaneously, the period of recovery is relatively long; frequently two or three years will pass before the patient comes out of the depression. When physical and psychological treatment measures are combined, the recovery period is speeded in a significant way. When recovery finally does occur, the symptoms are likely to disappear entirely; the depression lifts and increased feelings of happiness and renewed capacity for work appear.

"Help Me! Keep Me from Hollering!"— A Case of Involutional Depression

Laura A. is a 50-year-old woman who was admitted to a psychiatric hospital after complaining at home that she was "losing her mind." For days she made this complaint, spoke of a "visual fog," and said her mind was a "blank." She had episodes of involuntary crying over a period of several months and was sent to a private hospital, where the treatment she received did not alleviate her symptoms.

When seen at the psychiatric hospital, Laura was found to be a short woman who looked many years older than her age. Her eyes were sunken and her long straight hair was disheveled. She had the appearance of a sad and somewhat ghostly person who constantly repeated her symptoms in a flat singsong voice. She complained that she "had no head," that her mind was gone, and that a nerve in her forehead was making her "holler." She cried repeatedly, "Help me! Keep me from hollering!" Her moaning and occasional screaming could be stopped temporarily by distracting her, and it was possible with some effort to get her to talk about herself. She was well oriented in all areas, although her thinking was somewhat rambling and egocentric. Although her mood was one of dejection, she was restless and disturbed.

The patient was seen on a number of subsequent occasions, and there appeared to be some degree of deterioration. She did not remember the examiner, and she became increasingly hostile and vicious. At the time of her admission to the hospital she had been a rather gentle person in spite of her agitation. The patient was placed on medication, and two weeks later was sitting quietly on the ward in a rather relaxed state. She did not remember talking previously to the examiner, but she repeated the ideas that her mind was gone, her head was no good, and that she was "crazy." She said that she talked too much, walked up and down too much, and "acts like an animal." She concluded by saying there was no hope for her. While these ideas were similar to those expressed when she was admitted to the hospital, they were now expressed in a relatively calm and unemotional way. Several months later the patient was able to leave the hospital and make a satisfactory adjustment. She returned to work as a secretary, and managed her home efficiently, and developed a growing interest in her activities.

Masked Depression

Most depressive states can be recognized without difficulty by an experienced clinician. However, it has been suggested that there are situations in which the depression is hidden or masked (Keilholz, 1974; Lesse, 1975). Instead of the usual signs of depression, there are psychosomatic symptoms or behavior disorders in the form of alcohol addiction, drug dependence, or antisocial actions. It is believed that these other types of behavior are covering up the underlying depressive feelings (Cadoret & Winokur, 1972; Dorfman, 1973). One study reported that of approximately 1,000 patients treated for depression, 34 percent had masked depression (Lesse, 1973).

The concept of masked depression is a difficult one, particularly for the behavioral psychologist, since it is based on an *assumption* that depression has been replaced by the observed behavior. If a person does not show signs of depression, how can it be said that such a person is depressed? Psychodynamic theory, with its emphasis on unconscious determinants, would find the concept of masked depression a congenial one and would have no trouble in explaining it in terms of symbolism and symptom substitution.

Why Do People Become Depressed?

The growing evidence indicating a fundamental difference between unipolar and bipolar depression, as well as the discovery of masked depression, has intensified the search for the cause of these disturbances. As in the case of schizophrenia, most attempts to explain depressive reactions have been in terms of genetic, biochemical, and psychosocial influences. However, the probability of finding a single cause of all depressive reactions appears more remote as our knowledge of these conditions increases.

Genetics of Depression

The possible influence of genetic factors in the development of affective disorders has been suspected for many years. As long as a century ago, physicians concerned with the care and treatment of mentally disturbed people commented that *circular insanity*, later to be called manic-depressive psychosis, seemed to occur frequently among close relatives in the same family. Later findings, such as the high degree of concordance in bipolar identical twins compared with unipolar twins, confirmed the early impression that hereditary factors play a role in the manic-depressive disorder. A survey of seven investigations found that 68 percent of identical twins in the studies were concordant for the condition while only 23 percent of fraternal twins of the same sex were concordant (Williams, Katz, & Shield, 1973).

It is now clear that the disorder is transmitted as a dominant trait in a large number of cases. There is also evidence based upon linkage studies with color blindness that the disorder is sex-linked (Winokur, 1974). This finding helps explain why bipolar depression is found more frequently among women than men. One study found that the daughters of women with bipolar depression later developed the disorder twice as often as did the sons of such women (Powell, Hall, & Wilson, 1973).

There is also an indication that bipolar depression, like schizophrenia, may involve a spectrum of disorders that are genetically related (Schuyler, 1975). For example, it has been suggested that the high incidence of alcoholism in the families of persons suffering from bipolar depression may be a biological marker of another process that might be related to manic episodes (Cadoret and Winokur, 1974).

The available evidence gives strong support to the assumption that bipolar depression has a strong genetic component which does not appear to be present in unipolar depression. This assumption, however, does not rule out the contributing influence of biochemical and psychosocial factors in the bipolar disorder.

Biochemistry of Depression

Since the affective disorders involve psychotic symptoms along with depression and occasional elation, some investigators have attempted to find a biochemical component linking these conditions. One of the early suggestions of a possible biochemical influence grew out of the use of *reserpine*, one of the first tranquilizers used in the treatment of psychotic behavior. It was observed that many people became depressed while using the drug. It was found later that reserpine reduces the effectiveness of norepinephrine, a catecholamine chemical which is involved in the transmission of nerve impulses in the brain (see Chapter 3). These findings led to the formulation of the *catecholamine hypothesis* of affective disorders.

This hypothesis states that severe depression is associated with a deficiency of catecholamines and that elation and manic excitement is a result of an excess of these chemical neurotransmitters. It is assumed that clinical improvement depends upon the return of these chemicals to their normal levels. While the exact nature of the relationship between the brain catecholamines and affective disorder is not clear, the relationship appears to be well established and widely accepted. The essential problem today is the way in which the biochemical disturbances influence depression or manic excitement.

Psychosocial Influences in Depression

Even though genetic and biochemical factors are becoming more firmly established as causative factors in some types of affective disorders, psychosocial influences are probably the chief cause of unipolar depression and possibly a contributing one in bipolar cases. In both types of depression, psychosocial explanations have emphasized learning and psychodynamic relationships in a context of stressful life events.

Learning to be depressed The behavioral view of depression is that it is, with the possible exception of the bipolar disorder, a learned reaction. People are depressed because the behavior is in some way rewarding, and rewarded behavior is reinforced. This positive reinforcement increases the probability that the depressive pattern will persist and appear again. The way in which such behavior is rewarding depends upon the environmental contingencies in each case.

One view is that depression is a form of "learned helplessness." The person learns that the depressed state brings sympathy and support. Friends and relatives offer help and assistance. The depressed person receives attention that may have been lacking in the past. Companionship is provided, meals may be prepared, entertainment is arranged, and similar services and advantages are available. For some people these rewards may be valuable enough to establish depression as a preferred pattern of behavior. In effect, such people have learned to be helpless.

While the learning view explains how some forms of depression are maintained and repeated, there remains the question of why depression appears originally as a response. In bipolar depression, genetic and biochemical influences probably account for the initial reaction. However, the appearance of unipolar depression presents a somewhat different problem. The traditional view has been that depression is a direct emotional response to distressing life events. A more recent view is that depression is essentially a cognitive response (Beck, 1967). That is, the person perceives and evaluates a situation and then decides that it is depressing. The depressive feelings follow, rather than precede, the perceptual and intellectual aspects of the behavior.

Psychodynamics of Depression

One of the earliest psychodynamic views of depression was Freud's theory of inverted hostility, which he advanced to explain mourning. Freud believed that the depression associated with the death of someone we love is due to the fact that we are at first angry with that person for leaving us. We resent the separation and feel the need to rebuke the departed person. However, this hostility and resentment is then turned against the self and becomes the cause of depression.

The idea that depression is related to separation has persisted to the present time. The loss may be a physical one, as in the case of death, abandonment, and enforced separation; or it may be psychological in the sense of being ignored, neglected, or rejected by someone we love. In either case, the unwelcome separation is considered to be the cause of the depression.

There has been much emphasis on the fact that depressed people tend to have lost their parents early in life. However, a similar finding has been reported for a number of other conditions including alcoholism, drug dependence, antisocial behavior, and schizophrenia. It has also been reported that depressed people have usually experienced a variety of other losses and separations during their early years (Scott & Senay, 1973). While a number of studies have attempted to show a relationship between these early life experiences and later depression, a study of nearly 500 depressed women failed to find an association between childhood losses and adult depression (Jacobson, Fasman, & DiMascio, 1975).

Another psychodynamic view of depression is that the behavior is a form of self-punishment designed to rid the sufferer of guilt feelings associated with unacceptable wishes and actions. For example, many people develop a sense of inadequacy and personal failure as a result of rejection, being ignored, poor performance, or lack of success. If feelings of guilt accompany the loss of self-esteem, the person affected may feel the need to be punished for failure. Depression, according to the psychodynamic approach, is one of the ways in which the need for punishment is satisfied.

Although it is true that guilt is often associated with feelings of depression, it is by no means generally present, and most depressed people do not appear to be burdened with feelings of guilt. The answer given by those who hold to the importance of guilt as a cause of depression is that the guilt may be at the unconscious level. This view, which is characteristic of the psychodynamic approach, is as difficult to refute as it is to validate experimentally.

The Chapter in Review

The affective psychoses are disorders in which emotional behavior is distorted, usually in the direction of depression, although in some cases there is elation and excitement. The concept of depression is complicated by the fact that the term is used in various ways, and that it is difficult to know when normal sadness and sorrow turn into clinical depression.

1 Bipolar Depression

This form of depression refers to the pattern of behavior known as manic-depressive psychosis. It consists of recurrent episodes of depression and elation which occur spontaneously and are apparently unrelated to the stress of life events.

2 Unipolar Depression

Depression of this type is similar to neurotic depression in that it is usually a reaction to life change or environmental stress. However, the presence of delusions, hallucinations, and other disturbances makes it necessary to include the condition among the psychotic disorders.

3 Masked Depression

It has been suggested that, in some cases, psychosomatic symptoms or behavior disorders mask the underling depression. It is assumed that the masking symptoms protect the person from depressive episodes.

4 The Causes of Depression

a *Genetic influences*. There is evidence that bipolar depression is inherited as a sex-linked dominant characteristic.

b *Biochemical factors*. It has been established that chemicals involved in the transmission of nerve impulses in the brain are related to the episodes of depression and elation in the manic-depressive reaction, and possibly also in other forms of depression.

c *Psychosocial forces*. The development and maintenance of the unipolar type of depression appears to be more dependent upon psychosocial influences than genetic or biochemical factors. Behavioral psychology views depression as a learned pattern of behavior, while the psychodynamic approach emphasizes unconscious needs.

Recommended Readings

Brussel, J. A., & Irwin, T. *Understanding and overcoming depression*. New York: Hawthorn, 1973.

Fieve, R. R. *Moodswing: The third revolution in psychiatry*. New York: Morrow, 1975.

Flach, F. F. *The secret strength of depression*. New York: Lippincott, 1974.

Kline, N. S. *From sad to glad: Kline on depression*. New York: Putnam, 1974.

Lowen, A. *Depression and the body*. Baltimore: Penguin, 1973. (Paperback.)

Mitchell, R. *Depression*. Baltimore: Pelican, 1975. (Paperback.)

14
Organic Disorders of the Brain

Objectives

To explain what is meant by an organic disorder of the brain

To describe the various types of brain disorder associated with the later years of life

To discuss the major forms of alcoholism and to show how they differ from alcohol addiction

To indicate the difference between drug dependence and brain disorders due to the use of drugs

To show how infections can result in organic brain disorders

To describe some of the brain injuries that lead to abnormal behavior

The organic disorders of the brain differ in a fundamental way from the various forms of abnormal behavior discussed in the preceding chapters. The maladaptive behavior seen in people with organic brain disorders is associated with actual physical damage to the brain tissue. Such damage is not evident in transient stress disorders, personality disorders, neuroses, psychophysiologic disorders, or psychoses. Even when there is evidence of strong biological influences, as in the case of schizophrenia and bipolar depression, the brain tissue remains intact. However, when this tissue deteriorates because of the aging process, exposure to toxic substances or infectious disease, or is otherwise injured or damaged, the condition becomes an organic brain disorder.

An interesting trend has been taking place in connection with the number of cases of organic brain disorder in public mental hospitals in the United States. For many years, the number of these cases admitted to hospitals was about the same as the number of psychotics admitted. However, in recent years, there has been a marked decrease in the number of brain disorder cases admitted to mental hospitals. In 1970, these conditions made up about 27 percent of the admissions; they now account for only about 12 percent (National Institute of Mental Health, 1975).

One might assume that there had been a decrease in brain disorders in the general population. The fact is that there has been an increase rather than a decrease. How then do we explain the decline of such cases in mental hospitals? Not many years ago, any person who showed an adjustment problem associated with physical disorder ran the risk of being placed in a mental hospital if there were no relatives willing and able to assume the responsibility for taking care of

him or her. There were very few nursing homes, and those that did exist were for the privileged few. With the emergence of public and private medical care programs, there was a proliferation of nursing homes and convalescent centers; it is here that increasingly large numbers of people with organic disorders live out their lives. Today, only the most seriously disturbed people find their way to the wards of the public mental hospitals.

Thus most of the decline in the number of patients with organic brain disorder who are entering mental hospitals can be explained by the shift in the medical services available to elderly people But advances in medical science have also reduced the number of people admitted to mental hospitals with brain disorders related to convulsive disorders, infectious diseases, and brain damage. The only conditions which are seen more often in mental hospital admissions are the brain disorders associated with alcoholism and drug intoxication

Signs of Organic Brain Disorder

Marked physical changes in brain tissue are usually not difficult to identify when the brain itself is examined. But these changes develop gradually in most cases of organic brain disorder. And since there is ordinarily no occasion for the direct examination of brain tissue, the connection between tissue changes and abnormal behavior must be inferred.

The problem is further complicated by the fact that most organic brain disorders involve diffuse, or widespread, changes throughout the brain, while other disorders are related to damage in limited areas. Finally, and perhaps most puzzling, is the fact that psychotic behavior is seen in people with organic brain disorders as well as in people without apparent brain damage.

The symptoms of organic brain disorder vary in form and intensity depending upon the nature of the brain damage. However, some symptoms appear with sufficient frequency that they can be closely associated with organic conditions. One of the most common signs of organic brain disorder is impairment of memory. Most cases of diffuse damage show a gradual loss of memory before other symptoms are noticed. Memory for recent events may be impaired while remote memory remains intact. Many organic brain disorders are also marked by disorientation for time, place, and person. Such people have difficulty in knowing the month or the time of the year, where they are, and even who they are. This condition is a matter of degree. At first the confusion is very slight, but it gradually increases. In some people, the confusion becomes so pronounced that they need constant attention to prevent them from wandering away or suffering injury.

Other symptoms associated with organic brain disorder include a decrease in general information, hesitancy in thinking and speaking, lack of enthusiasm and motivation, and depression. Psychotic behavior is also seen frequently in these cases. It is impossible to know to what extent these symptoms are due to tissue changes, to the stress of having brain damage, or to other influences.

In the following sections of this chapter, we will take a look at some of the more common organic brain disorders. The most important, in terms of numbers of people involved as well as the critical problems

The Soft Rain of Old Age

When my grandfather was old, he had to be in a nursing home. He had Parkinson's disease, and at the same time, like they say, "His mind began to go," the result of arteriosclerosis. This was especially distressing for his wife, my grandmother, and his daughters who saw the man they had known and loved dissolving slowly before their eyes. But I do not think it was altogether distressing for my grandfather, and for us, his grandchildren; there was wonder in the process as well as fear and sadness. The deeper layers of his mind, rich veins of forgotten experience and language (he spoke Yiddish again for the first time in years), were bared as the worldly surface was worn away by the soft rain of old age. The lawyer anxiously preoccupied with business, the prideful perfectionist whose digestion fluctuated with the stock market, was gone; in his place was a man who, in greeting, reached out a trembling hand to take mine, looked up into my eyes and said with the difficulty and earnestness of someone trying to express exactly what he meant: "Are you playing and dancing?" (With the permission of Annie Gottlieb and *The New York Times Book Review*)

they pose for our society, are the disorders associated with old age. Alcoholism and drug intoxication also make up a significant portion of brain disorder cases. The other forms of organic brain disorder discussed in this chapter will give some indication of the wide variety of brain damage associated with abnormal behavior.

Brain Disorders of Later Life

The longer one lives, the greater the risk of developing physical disabilities and mental impairment. However, most people live throughout their later years without becoming psychologically disturbed, even though they must contend with many social and personal problems peculiar to old age. In

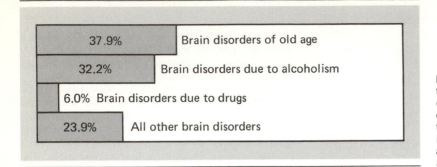

Figure 14.1 Percent distribution of clinical conditions included in the organic brain disorder group. Note that more than 75 percent of the cases involve physical damage due to aging and to the use of drugs and alcohol.

fact, some old people show little change in their emotional balance, their intellectual integrity, or their physical vigor. George Bernard Shaw was intellectually alert until he died at age 94, and a well-known magazine publisher made a parachute jump from an airplane into the Hudson River on his eighty-third birthday.

The term *old age* is a relative one. Very often this period of life is arbitrarily defined as that beyond age 65. There are many people, however, who show the physical and mental characteristics of old age long before they are 65, and there are many more who live into the eighties and even the nineties without significant impairment. Of the more than 20 million people aged 65 and over in the United States, only about a million live in institutions. Those in mental hospitals number about 120,000. The rest are in nursing homes and other institutions for the chronically ill.

Even though people aged 65 and over account for about 38 percent of all brain disorder cases in public mental hospitals (National Institute of Mental Health, 1975), it must not be concluded that all older people with psychological disturbances have organic disorders of the brain. Many elderly people are merely showing stress, neurotic disorders, and psychotic depression.

Psychosocial stress is no less important in triggering psychological disturbances among the elderly than it is in the case of younger people. The progressively declining resistance to stress has been considered the most important biological characteristic of aging (Comfort, 1956). This decline may be due to a functional deficit of the neurohormonal mechanism related to the process of aging. Under severe stress, the function of the hypothalamus is interfered with in certain persons. In most cases, this impairment is reversible. However, a mental disorder develops in some others (Kral, 1973).

A study of people who had reached the age of 100 found that those who had aged most successfully had shown ingenuity in avoiding stress and frustration (Poinsard, 1972). It has also been found that long-term survivors in old age are more intelligent, have a more intact home life, are physically healthier, and are of a higher economic status than short-term survivors (Pfeiffer, 1970).

The psychosocial deficit seen in old age is probably related to a decrease in sensory input (Harris, 1972) and to a reduction in the cognitive capacity of the aging nervous system (Miller, 1974). The more complex an action is, the more susceptible it is to the interference effects of brain damage.

The relationship between psychological

impairment and brain damage in the elderly is by no means consistent. Some elderly people with severe psychological disturbance have little brain damage, while others with serious physical impairment of the brain show only mild symptoms. The reason for this apparent contradiction is not known (Busse & Wang, 1973). Genetic factors may play some part in physical deterioration, but it is not yet possible to determine the extent to which heredity might be involved (Hunter et al., 1972).

Very obviously, not all the psychological disturbances of old age are the result of brain damage. Elderly people with quite normal brain tissue may react to psychosocial stress with some of the same symptoms seen in younger people. This reaction is frequently the case when the symptom is depression. It is unwise to assume that because an elderly person shows psychological disturbances, the cause is a brain disorder.

It is difficult to say which symptoms are the result of brain changes and which are reactions to the problems of being elderly. Not many years ago, it was assumed that most, if not all, of the symptoms seen in elderly people were the inevitable outcome of advancing years. Today we know that this is not the case. Many of the elderly, even those who have been hospitalized and for whom hope of improvement had been abandoned, can make remarkable strides with the help of drug treatment, physical therapy, and psychological and social support.

We are only now beginning to understand the extent to which the impact of old age can be softened through physical and psychosocial intervention. Elderly people are frequently frightened and overwhelmed by a feeling of hopelessness. Many become frustrated and angry. Others give in completely; their resistance to stress decreases to such a marked degree that they die prematurely.

While it is obviously impossible today to make significant changes in the aging process itself, dramatic changes in behavior can often be brought about by giving attention to proper diet, caring for physical needs, stimulating verbal skills, and increasing social and material rewards in various ways.

Senility: Deterioration Disorder

The aging process is inevitably accompanied by some degree of degeneration and deterioration of the brain tissue, but the amount of damage varies considerably from one person to another. The reason for these individual differences is not known. However, some older people begin to show signs of *senility*, a gradually progressive disorder with increasing mental and physical deterioration.

The rate of the deterioration varies considerably from one person to another, and many of the symptoms are transitory. Restlessness, agitation, confusion, and similar symptoms may be seen at one time but not at another, only to appear again later. Generally, the progress is downward, and unless the disorder is interrupted by an intercurrent physical disease, the senile person becomes more and more deteriorated, helpless, incontinent, and bedridden. Finally, he or she leads a completely vegetative existence, ultimately dying of pneumonia, infection due to decubital ulcers (bedsores), or other terminal diseases.

The line between normal senility and senile brain disorder is a completely arbitrary one and often depends upon the facilities available for caring for the aging. The wards of mental hospitals still contain many elderly people who are feeble and confused, but who are not psychotic. If these people had a place to live and someone to look after them, there would be no reason for them to be in a psychiatric hospital.

Figure 14.2 This elderly woman is enjoying a return to one of the pleasures of her childhood. We learned in Chapter 4 that regressive behavior is a technique used at times by younger people to cope with conflict and frustration. Similar behavior is sometimes seen among elderly men and women who are beginning to show signs of senility.

The senile disorder is seen in women about twice as often as in men, with the age of onset ranging from the sixties to the nineties. The onset of the disorder is usually gradual; previous personality traits become exaggerated and the attitudes characteristic of old age begin to appear. There is a gradual impairment of efficiency and a general slowing down of psychomotor functions; errors of judgment increase and personal habits deteriorate. The early symptoms come on so gradually that family and friends are frequently unaware of the seriousness of the changes.

Brain changes At the level of gross anatomy, the brains of the senile show shrinkage to one degree or another of the cerebral convolutions and the white matter. However, the changes observed in the brains of senile psychotics are sometimes no more pronounced than those seen in the brains of nonpsychotic people of the same age.

The microscopic changes in the cerebral cortex are nonspecific and of considerable variety. Shrinkage and atrophy of the neurons are frequent; while there may be a dropping out of many individual nerve cells, the overall cortical architecture is not affected. A characteristic lesion of the senile brain is the *senile plaque*. These plaques, which are found between the nerve cells and which vary in size and number, consist of masses of granular material, often with a pale center surrounded by a ring of threadlike material. It is not clear how these plaques are developed; they are found only in the central nervous system of the human species.

The causes of the senile psychoses have not been fully determined. However, several factors play a role in the causation. Among these critical factors are (1) heredity and constitution, (2) physical changes within the organism, and (3) psychosocial stress.

Genetic factors play an important role in the brain syndromes of later life. Longevity itself is dependent in part upon one's hereditary makeup. It is a common observation that the length of one's life—barring injury, in-

Figure 14.3 The later years of life need not be empty and frustrating. This woman, despite her age, has remained young in spirit. Wide and active interests and optimistic attitudes can make old age a rewarding experience even to those men and women with physical limitations and disabilities.

The Confusion of Old Age: Senile Dementia

Alice A. is a 78-year-old widow who was admitted to a psychiatric hospital from a home for the elderly, where she had become unmanageable. She was very confused, did not recognize her relatives, and thought her son was her father. Frequently she was excited and noisy and used profane language. At the hospital she had to be led to the examining room, and while she was somewhat agitated, she tried to be cooperative. In spite of her agitation, her facial expression changed little during the interview. Once a question was put to her, she continued to talk but was seldom able to answer intelligently. She rambled on and on, frequently mentioning her "daddy." She said her daddy had been at the hospital only a short time before, that he had talked to her, and that he would return soon to take her home. From time to time she interjected a word or phrase in French. She knew her name but was otherwise completely disoriented. Her memory for both remote and recent events was defective, and rational conversation was impossible. There was a total lack of insight.

fection, and similar acute conditions—depends upon genetic influence. It is true also that the point at which psychological symptoms begin to express themselves during the later years is dependent to some extent upon heredity. In many cases, the mental break occurs at about the same time in various members of a given family over a period of several generations. It is not that the mental disorder of old age is in itself inherited. Rather, the physical conditions which allow the organism to withstand stress are similar due to a similarity in genetic makeup.

One of the major problems in understanding senile psychosis is that the physical changes which are observed in the brains of psychotic people are by no means consistent. The changes in themselves are often not pronounced enough to account for the presence of the disease. Similar changes are found in the brains of many persons of advanced age. In some cases, the brains of normal men and women show very marked changes, and yet there are no psychotic symptoms. This fact suggests the possibility of a psychological component in the senile psychosis.

While the cellular changes that occur during aging are of major importance in the development of senile disorders, psychological and social factors cannot be ignored. Even under the most ideal psychological and social conditions, many aging men and women develop symptoms of senility. However, a very large group of people show psychological symptoms of aging long before these would appear to be natural from a physiological point of view. When aging takes place in an adverse social and psychological climate, personality disorganization is precipitated more quickly.

Another important variable is related to sensorimotor functions. Men and women in their sixties write much more slowly than subjects thirty years younger. Obviously, any test depending upon writing speed is likely to handicap older people. The factor of speed in other areas is also important. The tempo of living is slower during the later years, and this slowing down of activity is reflected in the test situation.

In addition to genetic and psychological influences in the senile psychoses, the cultural milieu in which aging takes place must

Psychological Functioning and Old Age

Just as there are objective and predictable physiological changes which occur with increased age, there are also psychological changes. While the functions measured by standard intelligence tests appear to decline as a person grows older, the decline is selective in that some functions fall off more rapidly than others. This apparent decline in intelligence must be interpreted with extreme caution. It is probably true that certain functions making up the trait of intelligence are increasingly less efficient as one grows older, but other factors must be considered as well. The motivation during psychological testing is certainly not the same for older people as it is for those who are younger. The declining motivation unquestionably plays a role in the apparent loss of intellectual capacity.

Educational level must also be taken into account. Most tests of intelligence are heavily weighted with items that depend upon knowledge rather than ability. Since men and women of advanced years are likely to have had less formal education than younger people, the lower scores on intelligence tests might very well reflect a difference in education, rather than a difference in basic ability.

be considered. It is probable that aging occurs more rapidly in certain environmental settings. An elderly person who is emotionally rejected, financially insecure, and generally unaccepted will probably age more rapidly than one who is emotionally and financially secure. For this reason, the attitude of relatives, the availability of friends, the opportunity for socialization, and similar factors are important in helping the aging person to resist the stresses of later life.

At the community and national level, the general attitude of the group toward the aging person is of great significance. There are some cultures in which the elderly members of the group are held in the very highest esteem. In other cultures, the aged are regarded as unproductive members of the group who must be tolerated until their death. The attitude of the group—the family, the local community, or the larger cultural unit—plays a critical role in determining the onset of senility.

Hardening of the brain arteries   The essential feature of mental disorder associated with cerebral arteriosclerosis, or hardening of the arteries of the brain, is that the psychological changes are dependent upon the cerebral blood vessels. The condition is seen most frequently among the more advanced age groups, but a substantial number of people develop it earlier in life. Men are affected

about three times more frequently than women.

The thickening of the walls of the arteries interferes with the diffusion of foodstuffs and oxygen; destruction of surrounding brain tissue results. The first symptoms of psychosis with cerebral arteriosclerosis are likely to be headache, dizziness, vague physical complaints, and more or less prolonged periods of physical and mental letdown. The actual onset of the disorder may be sudden or gradual, with more than 50 percent of the cases showing an acute onset marked by a sudden attack of confusion. There may be clouding of consciousness, loss of contact

Figure 14.4   Cerebral vascular changes associated with aging. (a) Blood vessels at the base of the normal brain of a young adult. (b) The same blood vessels—enlarged, thickened, and damaged—in an elderly patient.

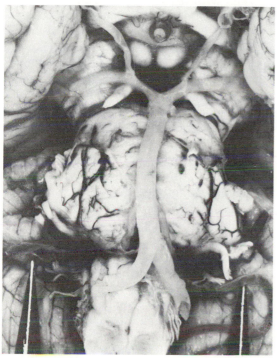

(a)

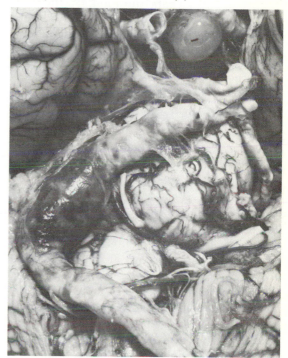

(b)

with surroundings, incoherence, and restlessness.

In cases where the onset is gradual, the symptoms are very similar to those of senile psychosis. There is a gradual intellectual decline, with loss of efficiency and impairment of memory. Irritability, quarrelsome behavior, jealousy, and a general lowering of moral and ethical standards are common. Ideas of mistreatment and persecution are seen frequently, and where there is extensive organic involvement, there may be explosive outbursts of weeping or laughter.

The course of arteriosclerotic psychosis varies from person to person. In some cases there is confusion and clouding of consciousness associated with cerebrovascular accidents, which lead to a fatal outcome in a short period. In other cases, there is chronic illness of many years' duration. On the average, in a typical psychiatric hospital, this disease continues for about three to four years, after which death usually occurs.

Toxic Disorders of the Brain

The psychological disturbances resulting from various types of intoxication are important because of their frequency and seriousness. These disorders are conditions in which the organic reaction and the personality disorganization are a result of the toxic action of alcohol, drugs, metals, or gas. Cases of brain damage due to alcohol and drugs make up about 38 percent of all cases of organic brain disorder in public mental hospitals (see Figure 14.1). While patients with brain damage due to metal and gas poisoning are seen from time to time in mental hospitals, their numbers are relatively small.

Alcoholism: Brain Damage from Drinking
It will be recalled from Chapter 7 that alcohol addiction in itself is not a brain syndrome and is more properly classified as a personality disorder. It is only when the excessive drinking has resulted in temporary or permanent damage to the nervous system that the condition is classified as an organic brain disorder. The major types of brain disorders associated with alcoholism are as follows: (1) pathological intoxication, (2) delirium tremens, (3) alcoholic hallucinosis, (4) alcoholic deterioration, and (5) Korsakoff's syndrome. Of these, the first two types are acute, while the fourth and fifth types are chronic disturbances.

Pathological intoxication: "Crazy drunk"
This acute type of alcoholic brain disorder appears with dramatic suddenness after the ingestion of relatively small amounts of alcohol. In such cases, a bottle of beer or a glass of wine is sometimes enough to throw a susceptible person into a state of violence, confusion, agitation, and excitement. Symptoms include disorientation, hallucinations, and delusions, combined with exaggerated emotional responses. Extremes of anger, rage, and hostility are frequently present, along with anxiety and terror. Occasionally the drinker is plunged into depression, and he or she sometimes makes an attempt at suicide.

During the outbursts of violence accompanying pathological intoxication, a person may commit almost any kind of assaultive crime. Physical aggression, heterosexual and homosexual advances, and even homicide are not uncommon. Usually it requires two or three people to subdue this type of alcoholic. The episode of excitement and confusion may last from a few hours to a day or more and is followed ordinarily by a long period of sleep. When the person awakens, he or she is unable to remember anything of what happened.

Pathological intoxication is the condition police officers call "crazy drunk." This type of alcoholic suddenly goes berserk and proceeds to break up the room or the bar. The acute and unsuspected nature of the condition is seen in the case of a 16-year-old boy whose mother gave him a hot whiskey toddy when he caught a head cold. The youngster reacted by going on a neighborhood rampage. He struck his mother and four men who tried to restrain him, bit three other men, and broke a window. Finally quieted in jail, he had no memory of the violent episode.

The underlying mechanisms of pathological intoxication are not clear. At the neurophysiologic level, it is possible that the victim of this disorder has an unusual sensitivity to alcohol, with an extremely low tolerance. Some experts believe there is a connection between pathological intoxication and earlier brain injury. Psychologically, these people are unstable emotionally, and the small amount of alcohol so disorganizes their control that the typical emotional storm is released. The relative infrequency of the condition, combined with its temporary nature, has made careful investigation difficult.

Delirium tremens: The "shakes" This condition is an acute brain disorder which develops after prolonged periods of heavy drinking. It is most likely to appear in persons who have a history of alcoholism, but it is relatively rare in those below age 30. The disorder was first described in 1813 by a physician who observed an acute congestion of the brain associated with an excess of free fluid (Sutton, 1813). However, since the microscope was not available to him, he was not aware of the changes in the brain cells which are now known to be present.

The disorder, which is an acute alcoholic episode superimposed on chronic alcoholism, is marked by delirium and hallucinations. The first signs of the onset include a lack of appetite, increasing restlessness, irritability, and fitful sleep with disturbing dreams. These symptoms are accompanied by mounting fear and apprehension. As the disorder enters the more serious stage, body temperature goes up, with flushing of the skin and profuse sweating. There is a marked tremor of the hands and tongue and sometimes of the facial muscles as well. Other symptoms include physical weakness, overactive reflexes, and an unsteady gait. There may be convulsions due to excessive loss of body fluids. At one time, death due to concurrent physical disabilities was frequent, but mortality today has been very much reduced.

In the excited phase of delirium tremens, the psychological symptoms include mental confusion and intense anxiety and fearfulness. Disorientation for time and place is common, although these people often continue to know who they are. The most dramatic psychological symptoms are the hallucinations. In most cases, they are visual and tactile: the person may, for example, see the room alive with insects, vermin, and rodents. The pattern of the wallpaper may be seen as the eyes of rats glaring at one; the design of the rug becomes a snake coiled and ready to strike. Persons so affected may feel roaches and spiders crawling on their bodies; they then make frantic, futile efforts to rid themselves of the horrible creatures.

When auditory hallucinations are present, they are likely to be of a threatening nature, often with homosexual content.

An attorney, a victim of delirium tremens and confined in a sanitarium, said: "Doctor, they have a most peculiar and curious way of handling their cows here. You see those palm trees and the cows that are tethered in them? That is strange in the first place, but the most curious thing is the way they move the cows to other pastures. They do not take them down and put them into other trees; they dig up the trees and move them bodily with the cows still in them." Another patient, a physician, heard a police siren and then thought he heard officers dragging chains up the stairs to chain him. The patient ran to a second-floor window, leaped out, and fractured his leg. Still another patient saw his image in a mirror, thought it was someone who was after him, and drove his fist through the glass (Nielsen, 1956).

In a study of delirium tremens cases treated at the Detroit Receiving Hospital, the average duration of the episode was three days, although the average hospital stay was more than five days because of other illnesses associated with the condition. On the first day in the hospital, 40 percent of the patients had hallucinations, 58 percent showed marked tremors, and 60 percent suffered from uncontrollable anxiety. All patients showed some degree of confusion and disorientation. On the second and third days in the hospital, a number of the patients showed more pronounced anxiety, confusion, and tremors. However, the other symptoms showed a marked reduction (Krystal, 1959).

The exact nature of delirium tremens is not known, although it appears to be a withdrawal symptom since it occurs most frequently when the person has been drinking heavily and is suddenly deprived of alcohol. The condition is probably a metabolic disturbance involving impaired carbohydrate metabolism, faulty protein metabolism, disturbed water balance, and vitamin deficiency, particularly of the B complex. The alcohol, by supplying the necessary calories, reduces the person's appetite. Consequently, a vitamin deficiency is established. And since the vitamins of the B complex are of critical importance in the metabolism of the neurons, their continued lack brings about disturbances of the nervous system.

Alcoholic hallucinosis: Voices and visions
This condition is one in which the major symptom is the hallucination, although there may be a certain amount of delusional material. In a typical case, the sensory reactions are normal, and there is no confusion, disorientation, or delirium. The person may be well oriented and even able to carry on his or her daily work.

The principal symptom is the auditory hallucination, in which voices seem to be making insulting, accusatory, and derogatory remarks, often with homosexual overtones. At times the person will respond to the delusions and hallucinations by attacking his or her supposed tormentors. In many respects, alcoholic hallucinosis resembles paranoid schizophrenia, and the question of differential diagnosis arises frequently. In its acute form, alcoholic hallucinosis lasts from a few days to several weeks and recurs with continued drinking. After a number of years of heavy drinking, the symptoms become irreversible.

The mechanism of alcoholic hallucinosis is not clear. The condition presents an interesting paradox, since the person is often well oriented and shows few signs of deterioration. At the same time, the hallucinatory experiences have a particularly real and vivid quality. One possibility is that the alcohol releases an underlying schizophrenic-like process which expresses itself in the hallucinatory experience.

Alcoholic deterioration: The "Skid Row" drunk Most chronic alcoholics show progressive deterioration over the years. This deterioration is probably caused by impairment, due to nutritional deficiency, of the nerve cells of the cerebral cortex. It ranges from mild symptoms of personality disorganization to serious states of dementia.

Among the earliest symptoms of alcoholic deterioration is the tendency of these alcoholics to act out their more primitive impulses. Their inner controls weaken, and they resort to childish behavior in attempting to satisfy their needs. Gradually, seeing that family and friends are critical of their behavior, these people become hostile and resentful, suffering increasing feelings of guilt. These feelings reinforce the psychological need for alcohol, which in turn aggravates the metabolic disturbance. As the cells of the brain are altered, such signs as memory impairment, difficulties in paying attention, loss of judgment, and emotional instability in varying degrees begin to appear.

There may be no psychological symptoms for many years, and no history of hallucinosis or delirium tremens. Yet gradually, physical and psychological symptoms become apparent. The person shows a general irritability and discontent, with increasing anxie-

Figure 14.5 When excessive drinkers lose their jobs and the support and sympathy of their families and friends, they may drift away and eventually find themselves on skid row where they spend their days and nights in an alcoholic stupor.

ty and depression. However, the defenses against these feelings may be strong, enabling the person to hide his or her depression under a superficial camaraderie and good humor. But such people are less successful in hiding their forgetfulness, dullness in comprehension, impaired judgment, and poverty of ideas.

Other early symptoms are seen in the ethical and moral behavior of the person. There is an increasing breakdown in standards of behavior and in social inhibitions. Personal appearance is neglected, unconcern is shown for family obligations, and lies are told with greater frequency and less and less guilt. Vulgar speech and lewd actions are not uncommon. In the physical area, the deterioration is shown in tremors and muscular weakness; in stomach, kidney, and liver disorders; and in a characteristic facial expression which has been described as being "flat" and "ironed out."

Alcoholic deterioration is generally seen in men and women who drink steadily over a period of many years, but who avoid acute episodes of heavy drinking. Such people have a history of drinking excessively, but they do not go on binges.

Korsakoff's syndrome: Memory disorder
This disorder, first described in 1887, is characterized by disorientation, memory impairment, and falsification of memory, in addition to organic symptoms in the form of multiple neuritis. While the syndrome has been associated traditionally with the more severe forms of alcoholism, it is more accurately a vitamin deficiency secondary to alcoholism and is found in other conditions as well. In any case in which a toxic condition results in degeneration of cells in the cerebrum and the peripheral nerves, Korsakoff's syndrome might be expected to develop.

**"Goodbye, Mr. Wolf!"—
A Case of Confabulation**

Fred D. is a 69-year-old married man who was admitted to a psychiatric hospital because of his confusion and disorientation. The patient had a history of many years of heavy drinking, although he denied drinking during the past several years. When seen in the admitting ward, the patient was neatly dressed, but there was some deterioration of his personal habits. Although pleasant and sociable with the interviewer and ward personnel, he was definitely confused. He wandered about the ward, investigating objects and trying on other people's clothing. He talked freely, though his speech tended to be rambling and at times incoherent. Most of his spontaneous conversation centered on himself, and there were a number of hypochondriacal complaints. The patient was disoriented for time and place, although he was able to give his name. He could not give his correct address, said his age was 91, and was unable to name the day, the month, or the year. He did not know where he was, although he said he was sent here by his landlord because he had been drinking. He admitted that he had been arrested for fighting and drinking, but he said that he had never had an attack of delirium tremens. The patient showed the characteristic symptom picture of Korsakoff's syndrome with disorientation, confusion, and a strong tendency toward confabulation. When asked where he was, he said he was in a brewery. He gave the name of the brewery, but when asked the same question a few minutes later, the patient named another brewery. Similarly, the patient said that he knew the examiner, called him by an incorrect name, and a little later changed the name again. When leaving the examining room, the patient used still another name when he said politely, "Goodbye, Mr. Wolf!"

Korsakoff's syndrome in alcoholics is frequently detected when what appeared to be an attack of delirium tremens fails to clear. Instead of recovering within a few days, the person remains confused and disoriented. He or she fails to recognize friends or relatives, and a serious memory loss is apparent. The physical symptoms of the Korsakoff syndrome are inflammation of the nerves, anesthesia of various areas of the skin, and paralysis. A sign frequently seen in this condition is the wrist drop, in which the person cannot raise his or her hand. The major psychological symptoms of the Korsakoff syndrome are memory disturbances, confabulation, or the filling in of memory gaps, delirium, and emotional instability.

The syndrome is a deceptive disorder in many ways. Superficial conversation with the person may reveal a reasonably clear consciousness. It is only on careful questioning that the true extent of the impairment is recognized. As long as the conversation is limited to the immediate surroundings and circumstances, the person appears to function in a normal manner. But as soon as recall is necessary, he or she resorts to confabulation.

The prognosis in Korsakoff's syndrome is poor, since the removal of the toxic condition does not ordinarily bring about complete recovery. The treatment, which includes massive doses of vitamins and a high-calorie diet, can be expected to bring about only partial restoration of normal psychological function.

Why Does Drinking Damage the Brain?

A very large number of men and women drink excessively and are addicted to alcohol (see Chapter 7), but only a relatively small percentage of these people develop the clinical signs of organic brain disorder. This observation raises the question of how drinking damages the brain and why some people appear to be more susceptible than others to the damaging effects of alcohol.

When alcohol is taken into the body, it is absorbed by the walls of the stomach and intestinal tract and enters the bloodstream as alcohol. It is not broken down or altered as are most foods. The absorbed alcohol is then carried to the liver and eventually to the heart, where it is pumped to all parts of the body, including the nervous system.

Of the alcohol taken into the body, only about 10 percent is eliminated through the breath, urine, and perspiration. The other 90 percent remains in the body, where it is oxidized to form carbon dioxide and water. However, this process of oxidization is slow; only 5 to 10 grams (about two teaspoons) of alcohol are burnt up in an hour. Any excess remains in the blood and tissues until it can be oxidized. The effects of excessive amounts of alcohol in the body are multiple, and many are only vaguely understood. Disturbances of metabolism, endocrine function, and hypothalamic action probably are involved, and a cycle of increased physiological tolerance and tissue need is established.

The possibility that even social drinking might result in brain damage has been suggested. Research shows that a heavy intake of alcohol causes such changes in the blood and blood vessels that brain cells could be destroyed by oxygen starvation. The effect of this minimal brain damage is cumulative. The outward signs of this type of brain damage are increasing forgetfulness and progressive loss of the ability to work efficiently.

There is also evidence that alcohol damages the brain by causing blood cells to clump. This process slows the rate of blood through the capillaries of the brain. Brain cells are thus killed by oxygen deprivation.

Granting the operation of these physiological factors, it remains to be explained how it happens that one person who drinks heavily develops a brain disorder while another heavy drinker does not.

Figure 14.6 Hard drugs are among the toxic chemicals that can have a damaging—and sometimes deadly—effect on the body. Janis Joplin, shown here, was a tormented young singer with tremendous talent who turned to drugs to solve her problems. An overdose caused her death.

Another theory of the etiology of alcoholism is based on the possibility that an inherited metabolic pattern makes certain people particularly susceptible to the destructive influences of alcohol. This constitutional-genetic theory, if established, would make it possible to explain the onset of alcoholism in cases where neither developmental nor psychodynamic factors appear to be operative and to explain why so many men and women with damaging developmental and psychodynamic influences do not become alcoholic, even under the most stressful conditions.

Drugs and Brain Damage

As in the case of alcoholism, there is a difference between being dependent on a drug and having developed an organic brain disorder as a result of using drugs. Most people who use drugs do not have brain damage. For example, such drugs as LSD, mescaline, and marihuana are quite capable of bringing about profound psychological changes which in some cases resemble mental disorder; however, these drugs are not ordinarily associated with brain damage. It is for this reason that they were discussed in connection with drug dependence (see

Chapter 7). It must not be assumed, however, that these drugs are without danger. The excessive and indiscriminate use of any chemical substance affecting the nervous tissue increases the risk of developing an organic brain disorder. Such disorders are seen most frequently in connection with the use of morphine, amphetamines, and barbiturates.

Effects of morphine The toxic effects of morphine are reflected in the physical and psychological symptoms. Among the physical symptoms are motor disturbances, glandular impairment, nutritional disturbance, and a variety of other difficulties. The motor disturbances include paralysis and tremor. There is also a decrease of the rhythmic movement of the alimentary canal and an inability to control urine.

Numerous other physical symptoms are seen in morphine intoxication. The nails of the fingers and toes become brittle, the enamel of the teeth softens, and the hair turns gray. Skin eruptions are common, and fever may occur as the result of abscesses caused by the drug injections. Glandular impairment is reflected in partial or complete sterility in women. There is a decrease in the secretion of saliva and an increase in the secretion of sweat. The glands of the skin are affected, and the skin becomes dry.

The early personality changes in morphine addiction are selfishness and carelessness, with the addict becoming indifferent and forgetful. He or she shows less and less initiative and finds it difficult to sleep. Later, hallucinations are common symptoms. More permanent psychological symptoms are loss of memory, deadening of sensation, and a breakdown of morale. Morphine addicts often become negligent, lose their sense of conscience, and may engage in various forms of deceitful behavior.

Amphetamines: "Speed" drugs When the stimulating effects of the amphetamine drugs became known, there was a sharp increase in their use. As with most drugs, excessive use results in biochemical imbalances; in the case of amphetamine and methamphetamine, there may also be some degree of personality disorganization.

These drugs produce feelings of well-being and exhilaration, although these initial reactions are likely to be followed by exhaustion and depression. When used excessively, the drugs result in tension and apprehension, trembling, sleeplessness, and marked loss of appetite. The clinical picture is that of a paranoid psychotic reaction with a minimal disturbance of the intellectual functions. Delusions of persecution and auditory (and sometimes visual) hallucinations are accompanied by such autonomic symptoms as rapid pulse and dilated pupils.

Barbiturates: Sleep drugs As with most other drugs, there are wide individual differences in the reaction to the ingestion of the barbiturates. Some people are able to take these sedative drugs more or less regularly over long periods without signs of intellectual deterioration. Others, taking lesser amounts of the drugs for shorter periods, become irritable and lethargic. Sometimes paranoid ideas become prominent. Many people show varying degress of intellectual deterioration, personal inefficiency, and general deterioration.

Because of the widespread use of the barbiturates to induce sleep, it is not unusual to see cases of acute barbiturate poisoning. Depressive persons not infrequently save their tablets until they feel they have acquired a lethal dose and then take them all at once with suicidal intent. Such people fall into a deep coma from which they cannot be awakened. An acute poisoning of this type is a medical emergency. In addition to the coma, the patient shows a weak, rapid pulse, along with low blood pressure, shallow respiration, and a rapidly developing cyanosis, or bluish discoloration of the skin. The condition is controlled by washing out the stomach and by administering drugs to counteract the effects of the barbiturate.

Epilepsy: Convulsive Disorders

Convulsive behavior, or *epilepsy*, is one of the most dramatic symptoms of disturbed brain function. The earliest medical writings contained vivid clinical descriptions of such behavior, and the convulsion has continued to be a subject of great interest to the neurologist, the psychiatrist, and the clinical psychologist. While important steps have been taken in recent years in the control of the surface symptoms of convulsive behavior, its underlying nature remains largely unknown. Moreover, the clinical symptoms must be recognized and understood before the necessary treatment measures can be taken.

In spite of the very large number of epileptics in the United States, very few of these people enter the public mental hospitals. When they do go to such hospitals, it is not because of the convulsive behavior, but because there are psychological disturbances accompanying, but not necessarily related to, the epileptic attack. While the epileptic has a greater risk of developing psychological disturbances than a nonepileptic person does, there is no necessary connection between the convulsive attacks and the personality disturbances. It is quite possible for an epileptic to have a stress reaction, personality disorder, neurosis, psychophysiologic disorder, or psychosis, without the condition being related to the organic disorder of

the brain. However, many epileptics show psychological disturbances resulting from the psychosocial stress of the convulsive disorder.

While attitudes toward children with epilepsy have softened considerably, there is still a substantial amount of prejudice toward epileptics. This social rejection of the epileptic occurs on a worldwide basis. A study at the Children's Hospital of the University of Vienna showed that 43 percent of parents preferred to keep the condition of their child a secret (Groh & Rosenmayr, 1972). It has also been found that there is more prejudice against people with epilepsy than against those with mental disorder (Bagley, 1972).

Varieties of Epilepsy

The convulsive disorders have been classified traditionally as *idiopathic* and *symptomatic*. Idiopathic disorders are disturbances

---

Some Facts and Figures about Epilepsy

There are more than 2 million epileptic people in the United States.

The total cost of convulsive disorder to the nation probably exceeds a billion dollars.

There are a number of different types of epilepsy.

At least 50 percent of all epileptic persons can gain complete control over their seizures through anticonvulsant drugs.

Another 30 percent can achieve partial control through medication.

Seizures usually become less frequent as the patient grows older.

Most patients can go to school, take part in sports, work, marry, and have children.

Seizures are not necessarily associated with mental illness or mental retardation. (Epilepsy Foundation of America, 1975)

having no apparent etiologic agent to account for them. Such disorders are not accompanied by structural changes in the organism. This type of convulsive disorder has been described variously as *essential*, *cryptogenic*, *primary*, *genetic*, and *hereditary*. Symptomatic convulsive disorders, however, are related directly to an underlying pathological condition of the organism. Conditions responsible for the appearance of symptomatic convulsions include syphilis of the brain, intoxication, head injuries, cerebral arteriosclerosis, and brain tumors. In such cases, in which the convulsive behavior is merely a symptom of some other disorder, the condition is classified under the more basic disturbance, not as a convulsive disorder or epilepsy. This symptomatic type of convulsive disorder has also been called *secondary*, *acquired*, and *focal* epilepsy.

Convulsive disorder expresses itself in four major forms:

1 *Grand mal* seizures
2 *Petit mal* seizures
3 *Psychomotor*, or temporal-lobe, attacks
4 *Jacksonian* seizures

The first form is characterized by the classic epileptic convulsion; the second by transient losses of consciousness for short periods without convulsions; the third by a variety of nonconvulsive behavior with disturbances of consciousness; and the fourth by localized convulsive behavior.

What Causes Convulsive Seizures?

Efforts to explain the nature of convulsive behavior have ranged from the primitive idea of spirit possession to the current emphasis on psychogenic and physiogenic (particularly bioelectrical) factors.

There is evidence that heredity plays an important, if not completely clear, role in the etiology of convulsive disorders of the idiopathic type. Among identical, or monozygotic, twins, if one twin has a history of idiopathic convulsive disorder, the other twin is likely to have a similar history. Such concordance of convulsive behavior is seen in between 60 and 90 percent of identical twins but in less than 10 percent of fraternal, or dizygotic, twins (Shields & Slater, 1960).

The most clear-cut etiology is seen in symptomatic convulsive disorders in which an irritating agent is responsible for the seizures. When this agent is removed by surgical means, the seizures are frequently brought under control.

The psychological view of convulsive behavior is that it is a reaction to frustration, or a form of escape from an intolerable situation. It has been shown experimentally that an animal placed in a conflict situation for which there is no solution may react with convulsive behavior. It is also possible that men and women, upon occasion, react in a similar fashion and for similar reasons.

Even if one or another psychogenic theory of convulsive behavior is valid, the underlying neurophysiologic mechanism remains to be explained. Most of the earlier explanations emphasized lack of oxygen in the brain, spasms of the cerebral arteries, altered permeability of the cell membranes, a disturbance of water balance, lowered blood sugar, and similar factors. More recently, attention has been directed to the bioelectrical activity of the brain. This approach looks upon idiopathic convulsive disorder as a result of disturbed cerebral electrical activity, seeing the disorder, in fact, as due to an "electrical storm" in the brain. This disturbance, or *cerebral dysrhythmia*, can be demonstrated objectively by means of the EEG (electroencephalogram).

Electrical disturbances of the brain can be triggered in susceptible people by a wide variety of stimuli. Flashing lights are a common source of stimulation leading to convulsions because of their powerful influence on the brain waves. Two young girls attending a psychedelic show in England had attacks brought on by the flashing strobe lights. It is also possible that epileptic seizures may be precipitated by the use of drugs. A graduate student at the University of California experienced seizures about fifty minutes after he took his first dose of LSD. However, in cases of idiopathic epilepsy, the seizures are likely to be related to a complex interaction of electrical activity of the brain, physical factors determining the convulsive threshold for a particular person, and psychological factors which may play a role in precipitating the convulsion.

Even in these cases, a genetic predisposing factor may be present. A study of the families of symptomatic, or focal, epileptics reported findings supporting the view of a genetic basis for temporal-lobe epilepsy. The incidence of abnormalities among families of epilepsy-prone people was significantly higher than in control subjects (Andermann, 1969).

Preventing and Controlling Convulsions

While most people with epilepsy are able to lead normal and productive lives, many suffer from seizures that do not respond to treatment. The result has been a continued research effort directed toward the problems of prevention and more effective control of the condition.

One approach to prevention is to avoid the

**Epilepsy and Psychosocial Stress:
The Crisis of Convulsions**

Edwin F. is a 27-year-old single man with a history of *grand mal*, *petit mal*, and psychomotor seizures. The *petit mal* condition was noticed first when he was 10 years old. Since that time he has shown various other forms of convulsive disorder and has been on continuous medication.

Edwin was referred to a psychiatric hospital when he was 22 years old because of uncontrollable seizures involving both legs. The condition cleared spontaneously soon after hospitalization. After six months in the hospital, the patient was discharged. Two months later, he was admitted to the city hospital in a dirty, unshaven, confused state. He appeared to be having auditory hallucinations, and had the delusion that someone was trying to kill him. He was referred to the psychiatric hospital, where a diagnosis was made of chronic brain syndrome associated with a convulsive disorder. Within several days the patient's condition improved, although there was a loss of memory for the entire episode.

Edwin was sickly as a child and frequently ran high fevers without apparent cause. He was a feeding problem throughout his early years. When he entered school, he had trouble concentrating and did poor academic work. His teachers described him as a "dreamy" child. However, intelligence tests showed that he was of well above average intelligence. The first convulsive seizures were noted when he was 12 years old. He was working as a caddy at a golf course, and his companion noticed that he had brief blackout periods. The mother recalled instances in which she had seen him blink his eyes and seem dazed for a few seconds at a time when he was younger. Eventually neurological examinations were undertaken, and a diagnosis of convulsive disorder was established. As he grew older, Eddie showed various behavior problems and adjustment difficulties. On one occasion he ran away from home, on another he stole an automobile, and he had an extremely poor work record. There is also a history of heterosexual promiscuity and homosexual prostitution.

When seen at the hospital, the patient was found to be a neat, pleasant, and cooperative young man who appeared eager to talk about his problems. While there was some irrelevancy, there were no signs of disorientation, delusions, hallucinations, or other psychopathology. His judgment appeared good, and there was some degree of insight.

birth of an epileptic child. This approach involves genetic engineering and will probably be an issue in coming generations. A more current type of prevention deals with the prevention of the seizures themselves. A number of effective drugs have been developed; these will be discussed in Chapter 18. Efforts are also being directed to the prevention of brain damage due to seizures and of secondary handicaps in epileptic persons (Taylor & Bower, 1971).

One of the advanced prevention techniques in the field of epilepsy is a pocket-size radio device that warns the person of an impending seizure. Very tiny surface electrodes, hidden in the hair, are connected to a small transmitter worn in a pocket or on a belt. The brain waves are radioed continuously to a computer programmed to detect significant changes. When these changes reach a critical point, a warning signal is transmitted back to the wearer of the device, who is then able to find a place to rest or to take additional medication.

Another recent development is the brain pacemaker. Battery-powered electrodes are implanted in the skull and connected, by means of a wire running under the skin, to a receiver about the size of a half dollar that is implanted just below the collarbone. An antenna is taped to the surface of the chest directly over the receiver and connected to a battery-powered transmitter that can be worn on the belt. When the wearer feels the warning signs of a convulsion, the device is switched on and an electrical stimulus forestalling the attack is sent to the brain.

An 18-year-old boy whose epileptic seizures were accompanied by aggressive behavior, including repeated suicide attempts and assaults on his mother, was furnished with a brain pacemaker which quickly brought the seizures under control. When a wire broke in the equipment, the youth had thirteen seizures in one day, but when repairs were made, the seizures were controlled and the young man was again able to work regularly (Cooper, 1975). While the brain pacemaker must be considered in the developmental stage, it suggests the possibility of controlling epilepsy which will not respond to drugs. The brain pacemaker also makes it unnecessary to resort to surgery, which previously had been the only way of treating certain types of violent epileptic attacks.

Brain Injuries and Abnormal Behavior

The physical and psychological symptoms associated with injury to the head vary over a wide range. Since injuries are of differing degrees of severity and involve various parts of the head, the symptoms are of different kinds. They include the acute symptoms immediately following the injury and the chronic symptoms which last for months or years afterward. The immediate symptom of any serious head injury is most likely to be a disturbance of consciousness. This disturbance may range from a temporary daze to a complete loss of consciousness lasting from minutes to a week or more. Head injury may be accompanied by nausea, vomiting, headache, and dizziness. In some cases there is confusion and disorientation, while in more serious injuries there may be delirium, incoherence, and hallucinations.

Damage to the brain may be the result of tiny hemorrhages over large areas of the brain, or it may involve the rupture of major blood vessels. There may also be an edema, or swelling, of the tissue itself, and in penetrating wounds of the brain there may be direct damage to brain centers. The major types of brain injury are (1) concussion, (2) penetrating injuries, and (3) vascular accidents.

Concussion Syndrome

Concussion is one of the most common forms of brain injury. Many accidents in ordinary everyday living involve nonpenetrating blows to the head. A fall from a ladder, tripping over the curb, striking one's head against an open cupboard door, slipping on the ice, and other common accidents in the home or at work frequently result in a glancing blow to the head. If the blow is severe enough, the underlying brain tissue is affected. The victim may "see stars," lose consciousness, become confused and disoriented, or show other symptoms.

Following the acute period, the patient may experience such symptoms as headache, dizziness, inability to concentrate, and deficient memory. The concussion victim may also show irritability, loss of energy, decreased tolerance for physical stress, and inability to sleep. The symptoms usually clear within a matter of days or weeks.

In some cases the effects of brain injury are delayed. A youngster who was hit by a car seemed unhurt except for a bump on his head. He was playing as usual within a few minutes. About a week later, he fell to the ground and had a convulsive seizure. The medical examination showed that the youngster's brain had been injured at the time of the accident.

Penetrating Brain Injuries

Some of the most serious brain injuries are those in which the skull is penetrated and the underlying brain tissue is damaged. Any sudden and severe blow to the head by a sharp object can result in a penetrating wound.

Figure 14.7 This fighter is receiving a solid left to the head during a boxing match. Although a single punch is unlikely to cause brain damage, repeated blows to the head over a period of time can cause physical changes to the brain. The "punch-drunk" fighter is a person whose abnormal behavior is a result of this kind of brain damage.

The type of symptom seen depends to a large degree upon the location of the wound and the extent of the brain damage. Accidental injuries of the penetrating type are usually associated in civilian life with automobile accidents, plane crashes, train wrecks, and industrial accidents. During war, such injuries are common among civilians and military personnel.

The surgical removal of brain tissue is also a form of penetrating injury, even though the operation is performed to correct some other condition such as an abscess or brain tumor.

The Punch-Drunk Fighter: Brain Injuries in the Boxing Ring

Some professional boxers continue to fight long after they have lost their skill and endurance. They do it because they need the money and are willing to take the inevitable beating. The constant pounding and battering of the head, even though the damage during any one fight may be minimal and often unnoticeable, eventually leads to psychological symptoms. The cumulative effect of subtraumatic blows to the head leads to the concussion and the symptoms accompanying it.

The behavior of the "punchdrunk" fighter is marked by slurred speech, difficulty in walking normally, and a flat and expressionless appearance of the face. A study was made of the brains of 15 boxers who died after retiring from the ring. The ages at death were from 57 to 91. The men had fought an average of 300 fights during their careers. A similar pattern of abnormality was found in the brains of most of the fighters. (Corsellis et al., 1973)

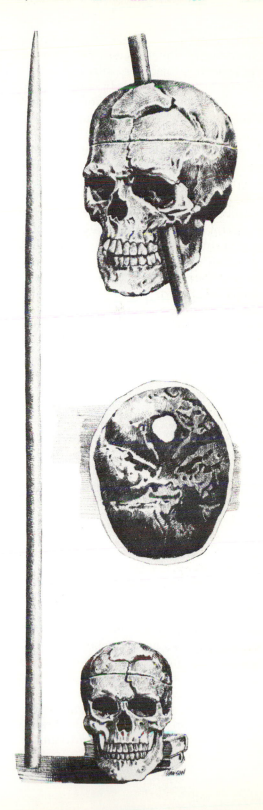

As a result of the improvement of neurosurgical techniques during World War I, there was a rapid expansion of brain surgery during the 1920s. By 1930, it was possible to remove large areas of the brain, including the entire frontal lobe. While the studies of sol-

Figure 14.8 One of the most extraordinary examples of brain injury and its psychological consequences was the case of Phineas Gage, a railroad construction worker who was tamping a stick of dynamite into a hole. There was an explosion and the tamping iron was blown through the workman's head. The top drawing shows how the iron entered the left side of the face, passed through the brain, and came out through the skull. The middle drawing is an inside view of the skull showing the size of the hole in the top of the head. In spite of the massive damage to the brain tissue and the severe shock associated with the injury, the man remained conscious and was even able to ride in a cart to his hotel and to climb a flight of stairs to his room. Following his recovery, there were marked personality changes. He became stubborn, obstinate and unpredictable, and showed childish and impulsive behavior. The interesting aspect of the case was that the behavior changes were not more severe considering the extent and severity of the brain damage.

diers injuried in battle involved difficult problems of the tissue-shattering effect of high-speed projectiles, surgical lobectomy made possible a relatively controlled condition. A number of investigators were quick to take advantage of the opportunity to explore the functions of the frontal region more extensively. It was found that large amputations of the frontal lobe frequently produce surprisingly little disturbance of function.

A birth injury is also a craniocerebral trauma, although here the damage ordinarily does not involve a penetration of the skull and brain. During an instrumental delivery or a particularly difficult natural birth, the head of the infant may be compressed or otherwise distorted, resulting in some degree of damage to the brain tissue. However, only the most severe injuries result in neurological or psychological symptoms because of the semifluid consistency of the infant brain and the abundant supply of undifferentiated nerve cells.

"Stroke"

One of the most common injuries to the brain is the "stroke," or cerebrovascular accident, in which a blood vessel ruptures and the brain area is flooded by the hemorrhaging blood. If the bleeding continues, the victim dies. But in a great many cases, the bleeding is self-limiting or is stopped by medical treatment, and the victim recovers. The damage from such a vascular accident may nevertheless result in a wide range of neurological and psychological symptoms.

There may be such neurological signs as paralysis of the facial muscles, the arm, and the leg on the side of the body opposite the site of vascular accident. As a result of the facial paralysis, which also involves the tongue and throat, the person has difficulty in speaking, eating, and swallowing. Depending upon the extent of the brain damage, he or she may have difficulty in walking or using a hand or arm.

The neurological symptoms of the stroke depend upon the area of the brain affected. The damage is generally localized, and the symptoms are similar to those seen in cases of brain tumor. The difference in the clinical picture between the stroke victim and the person with a tumor is that in the former condition, the symptoms appear abruptly, may improve considerably, and may then appear again with the occurrence of a further stroke. The symptoms seen in the tumor case are likely to be of a more gradual development. When the initial stroke has not been recognized, the subsequent symptoms are sometimes difficult to diagnose.

In massive strokes, the abruptness and severity of the symptoms leave little doubt about their cause. However, many strokes are relatively minor and occur in areas of the brain which do not produce neurological symptoms. In such cases, the only changes noticed are those of a psychological nature. In the later years of life, some people experience a degree of personality disorganization as a result of the cumulative effects of small strokes which go unrecognized.

Brain Disease and Infection

Psychological disturbance due to brain disease and infection was one of the most common organic brain disorders during the first part of the present century. Such conditions are now relatively rare because of the discovery of antibiotic drugs and other important advances in medicine. However, some of the older men and women in public mental hospitals today were admitted many years ago because of infections that damaged the brain tissue. Most of these people had brain syphilis.

Brain Syphilis

Syphilis is an infectious disease caused by a spiral microorganism, or spirochete. The organism enters the body through minute abrasions in the skin or in the mucous membranes. The infection can be transmitted to the fetus while it is still developing or while it is passing through the birth canal at the time of birth. However, syphilis is never inherited in the genetic sense.

The term *neurosyphilis* is used to indicate that the spirochete has attacked some part of the brain or spinal cord. However, only a relatively small number of untreated or poorly treated cases of syphilis develop neurosyphilis. In most cases, some other system of the body is attacked. The reason the microorganism selects the nervous system in one person and a different system in another is not clear.

The speech disturbance is rather typical and frequently forms the basis for the initial diagnosis. Speech becomes indistinct due to slurring and mispronunciation. Even in the earlier stages of the disease, the person finds it difficult or impossible to repeat such words and phrases as "Methodist Episcopal," "hippopotamus," and "medical superintendent." In attempting to repeat such words, the person characteristically stumbles, stutters, and omits important syllables. As the disease progresses, speech becomes increasingly unintelligible.

Handwriting also shows characteristic changes. In the beginning stages of the disease, the most pronounced change is the unsteadiness of the writing. In later stages of the disorder, the handwriting becomes coarse and heavy, letters are omitted, and the writing is crude and untidy. In the final stages, writing becomes entirely illegible, degenerating to little more than a few lines scratched on a sheet of paper.

The physical changes in the brain also lead to disorders of movement. These people drag their feet, walk with a shuffling gait, and have trouble keeping their balance. They cannot catch a ball tossed to them, they have

---

"Darling Madame"—
A Patient with Brain Syphilis Writes to a Hospital Secretary

Darling Madame:
Goodmoring wonderful madame. How are you today—are you your little best? This is an acquaintence positive and it is positive true that madame is a mighty fine girl. Also, Mary, Beatrice and Bertha girls are positive very nice. And it gives me sincere gratitude to say something about you folks. At the present time I am not doing things the mighties of level evollition, or worth a dam, prosperious assimililation seems to be defiliated—and of simplest reason. I don't know what the hell level vurge thinks this is. Of course I am expecting to get a visit from (very little nice madame), and I have not pass it up, though things seem to be reasumable slow. Just what have you planned for your summer varieties? I have always admired your evolutionize challengency.

Exquisitely yours,

This letter shows many of the characteristic disturbances of verbalization and writing seen in the people with brain syphilis. This man was above average in intelligence and had completed two years of high school. The misspellings and bizarre forms found in the letter are a result of the destructive brain processes rather than a lack of education.

---

trouble buttoning their clothes, and they are unable to thread a needle or tie a knot. In some cases there are mannerisms, such as grimacing, dancing about, ceaseless rubbing and picking, grunting, smacking the lips, chewing, and sighing. Features become flabby and expressionless, and the voice is monotonous or tremulous.

The psychologcal symptoms are as varied as the physical symptoms. Among the first signs of the disorder are loss of memory and judgment. Such people are unable to notice contradictions in their own thinking or in the conversation of others. Emotionally, those suffering from brain syphilis are quite unstable and unpredictable. Their mood changes from one extreme to the other. One moment they are happy and enthusiastic, the next morose and depressed. A little later they will sulk, and then they will have a temper tantrum. They are easily excited by trivial events and have frequent fits of crying and laughing. Moreover, these people develop a rich variety of delusions and hallucinations.

People with brain syphilis usually show an increasing disregard for propriety, customs, and social niceties. Their lack of inhibitions makes them tactless and frequently grossly offensive. They become careless of their personal appearance, and their table manners deteriorate to a point where they eat greedily and noisily.

Although psychological disturbances become more pronounced as brain damage becomes more severe, behavioral changes cannot be explained merely in terms of damage to the nervous system. The pattern of symptoms varies from one person to another and is probably related to the reorganization of each person's personality under stress.

Brain Tumors

Brain tumors are pathological masses of cells which grow in the brain. They exert their effect on behavior and personality either directly through damage to brain centers involving speech, hearing, vision or other sensorimotor functions, or indirectly through disturbances in blood circulation or increased intracranial pressure of the cerebrospinal fluid. In the latter cases, the brain cells are subjected to degenerative processes as the result of lack of needed nutritional substances, or the increased pressure brings about a mechanical displacement of the cells. In either case, symptoms of personality disturbance may appear.

Psychological symptoms are very often the first signs of tumors of the brain. In many cases, intellectual and emotional changes occur weeks or months before there is neurological evidence of the brain tumor. Frequently, the first signs of this type of disorder is a vague feeling of anxiety which may be an expression of the victim's unconscious realization of the disorder. Many tumors develop in so-called "silent" areas of the brain—areas which do not produce neurological symptoms and which are not critical to the sensory, motor, or association functions. People so affected show few or no symptoms for long periods of time, often over a span of years. Postmortem examinations of the brains of persons who have died of other causes indicate that some people have brain tumors without ever realizing it.

The Chapter in Review

The organic brain disorders are conditions in which there is direct evidence of physical damage, or malfunction, of the nerve cells in the brain. Other forms of abnormal behavior also may depend upon physical influences, as in the case of the psychoses, but here the influence is on presumably normal tissue.

1 Brain Disorders of Later Life

While most elderly people do not show signs of organic brain disorder, the largest number of people with this condition are in their later years. The senile state is one in which there is a progressive mental and physical deterioration related to a generalized degeneration of brain cells. In cerebral arteriosclerosis, the thickening of the walls of the blood vessels interferes with the metabolism of brain cells and leads to their destruction.

2 Toxic Disorders of the Brain

Some organic brain disorders are due to the toxic effects of alcohol and other drugs. In alcohol addiction and drug dependence, the brain changes associated with intoxication are temporary and reversible. An organic brain disorder develops in cases in which the toxic effects become chronic and irreversible or are pathologically severe.

3 Epilepsy: Convulsive Disorders

Epilepsy is an example of an organic brain disorder in which there may be malfunctioning of brain cells rather than physical damage. While localized damage to the brain can cause convulsive behavior, most epilepsy is caused by disturbances of the patterns of electrical discharges of the brain cells.

4 Injuries to the Brain

Several types of injury result in organic brain disorders. The concussive effects of blows to the head, injuries in which the skull is penetrated and brain tissue destroyed, and damage to brain cells caused by ruptured blood vessels, all may result in abnormal behavior.

5 Other Organic Brain Disorders

Less common organic disorders of the brain include conditions involving disease, infection, and tumors of the brain. As in other organic brain disorders, the psychological disturbances are determined by the personality reorganization in response to stress as well as by the location and extent of the physical damage.

Recommended Readings

Brain Disorders of Old Age

Gaitz, C. (Ed.) *Aging and the brain*. New York: Plenum, 1973.

Alcohol and Other Drugs

Fleming, A. *Alcohol: The delightful poison*. New York: Delacorte, 1975.
Israel, Y., & Mardones, J. (Eds.) *Biological basis of alcoholism*. New York: Wiley, 1971.
Richter, R. W. *Medical aspects of drug addiction*. New York: Harper & Row, 1975.

Convulsive Disorders

Brazier, M. A. B. (Ed.) *Epilepsy: Its phenomena in man*. New York: Academic Press, 1973.
Silverstein, A., & Silverstein, V. *Epilepsy*. Philadelphia: Lippincott, 1975. (Paperback.)

Brain Injuries

Gardner, H. *The shattered mind: The person after brain damage*. New York: Knopf, 1975.
Williams, M. *Brain damage and the mind*. New York: Jason Aronson, 1974.

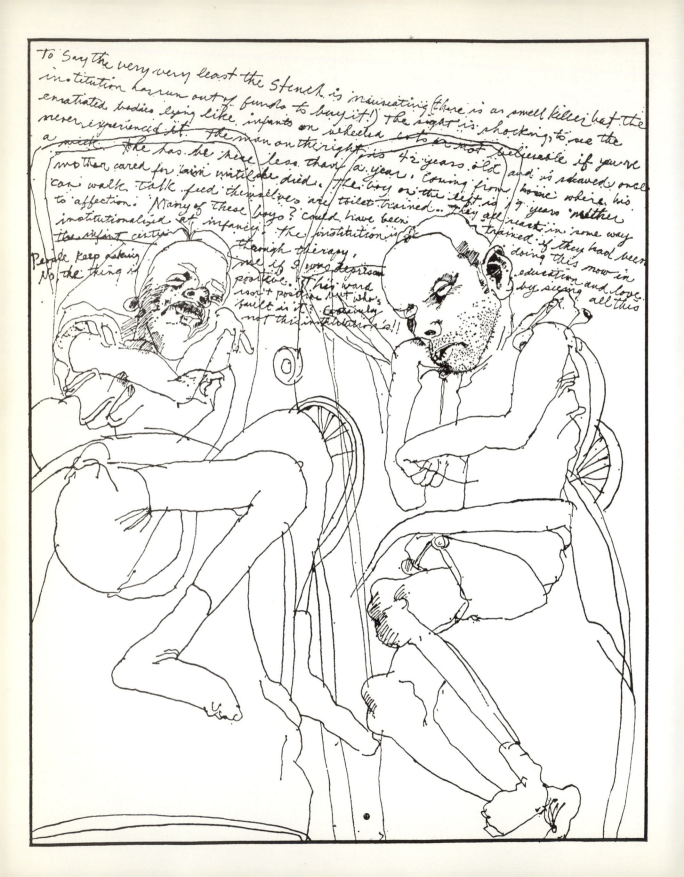

To say the very very least the Stench is nauseating (there is a smell killer but the institution has run out of funds to buy it!) The sight is shocking to see the emaciated bodies lying like infants on wheeled cots is not believable if you've never experienced it. The man on the right is 42 years old and is shaved once a week. He has he here less than a year, coming from home where his mother cared for him until she died. The boy on the left is 9 years 'mother can walk talk feed themselves are toilet trained... They all react in some way to affection. Many of these boys? could have been trained if they had been institutionalized at infancy. The institution is doing this now in the infant center through therapy. education and love.

People keep asking me if I was depressed by seeing all this No the thing is positive. This ward isn't positive but who's built in it? Certainly not this institution's!!

15
Mental Retardation

Objectives

To discuss the general nature of mental retardation

To indicate how psychological tests have been used to determine the level of mental subnormality

To show the importance of adaptive behavior, or educability and trainability, as a measure of retardation

To describe the characteristics of the more common clinical forms of retardation

To discuss some of the problems of training, educating, and treating retarded people

To show how early detection programs are being used to prevent certain types of retardation

The problem of mental retardation is one which, until the middle of the present century, was relatively neglected by specialists in the field of mental health. The condition has been recognized over the centuries, but for various reasons it was not considered of much importance. Fortunately, a new and vigorous interest in mental retardation developed following World War II. The somewhat hopeless attitude which pervaded the thinking of all but a few physicians, psychologists, social workers, and educators gave way to a refreshing optimism. The possibility of preventing many cases of mental retardation and of improving the lot of many of the already retarded became well established.

Mental retardation in itself is not a personality problem and might appear out of place as a topic in a book dealing with abnormal psychology. Certainly there is no implication that mental retardation and personality disturbance are synonymous or necessarily related. There are, however, many parallels, and in some areas there is an important overlap. This overlap is seen most clearly in the relationship between mental retardation and the brain disorders. Also, the lack of intellectual ability frequently results in behavior difficulties which bring the retarded into conflict with their families and communities.

The number of mentally retarded people in public mental hospitals has remained constant over the years, while very marked changes have been seen—both in terms of numbers and types of patients—in other diagnostic categories. The most recent figures indicate that about 3 percent of additions to public mental hospitals are diagnosed as being mentally retarded (National Institute of Mental Health, 1975). About one-fifth of these people are admitted to hospitals before they are 18 years old. In most of these children and adolescents, the retardation is combined with other behavioral symptoms which make the young people difficult to handle at home. There is a concentration of admissions of mentally retarded people between the ages of 20 and 34—both men and women. This heavy concentration of admissions represents people who manage to make an adjustment while in the protected environment of the home but are unable to make the necessary social and occupational adjustments during the early adult years.

Public mental hospital admissions also include people with psychological disturbances secondary to mental retardation. For example, a young adult might be drawn into delinquent or criminal activities, and when he or she appears in court, it is recognized that retardation is present. In such cases the antisocial behavior is not a symptom of the mental retardation; it is behavior that is made more likely because the person is retarded. Similarly, resistance to psychosocial stress of certain kinds is lower in the mentally retarded. They are much less able to adapt to many of the more complex demands of modern living. The result is that they develop symptoms of other types of psychological disturbance. Being mentally retarded does not preclude the development of stress reactions, personality disorders, neurosis, or psychosis. However, when mental retardation is present, it is ordinarily the primary diagnostic label placed on the person affected.

Terminology and Classification

In Chapter 2 we saw that the terminology and classification of mental illness underwent many revisions and alterations over the

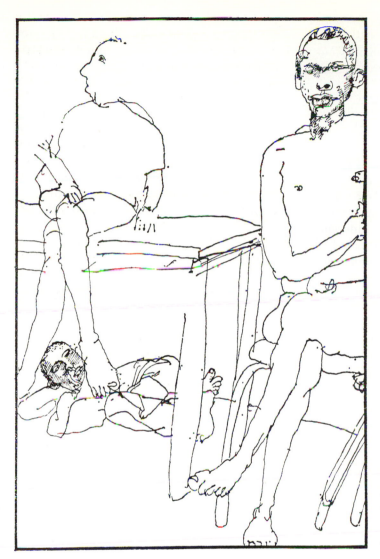

Figure 15.1 Although important advances have been made in the care and treatment of the mentally retarded, conditions in some institutions have improved very little. This drawing suggests the neglect and needless boredom that face many retarded people who must spend their entire lives locked in a ward.

years and that even today it is stabilized only precariously. The same is true for mental retardation. As late as the early 1960s, it was defined in a number of different ways, and the mentally retarded were classified into a variety of types and levels. The American Association on Mental Deficiency has been making a concerted effort to establish a common terminology and classification, but conflicting systems have been advanced by the World Health Organization, the National Association for Retarded Children, and the American Psychiatric Association.

Today, the most widely accepted definition of mental retardation is the one which appears in the 1973 revision of the *Manual on Terminology and Classification in Mental Retardation* (Grossman et al., 1973), published by the American Association on Mental Deficiency. This definition states:

> Mental retardation refers to significantly subaverage intellectual functioning existing concurrently with deficits in adaptive behavior, and manifested during the developmental period.

The term *adaptive behavior* refers to the person's potential for training and education. It has been described as the "effectiveness or degree with which the individual meets the standards of personal independence and social responsibility expected of his age and cultural group" (Grossman et al., 1973, p. 11).

The concept of adaptive behavior is an important one because it reflects a significant shift away from the reliance on intelligence test scores as the sole indication of retardation. While measured intelligence continues to be one of the determining factors, it is now recognized that some people of lower intelligence are more easily trained and educated than some others with higher intelligence.

Measured Intelligence

The first important attempt to segregate and classify the mentally retarded in terms of measured intelligence occurred during the early part of the present century when the Binet-Simon test was developed (Binet & Simon, 1916). These investigators introduced the concept of *mental age*, a measure of intellectual ability in terms of test performance. A child of 6 who could pass tests at the 8-year level was said to have a mental age of 8. Such a child would be intellectually advanced. However, the 6-year-old who could pass only tests at the 4-year level would have a mental age of 4 and would be mentally retarded. Later, a ratio was established between the mental age and the chronological age. This index was called the *intelligence quotient* (IQ).

In terms of psychological test scores, an IQ of 100 is considered the midpoint of the distribution. It is the theoretical "average intelligence," although for practical purposes the entire range of IQ scores from 90 to 110 is regarded as average. Approximately 50 percent of the population falls into this group.

For many years, the terms *moron*, *imbecile*, and *idiot* were used to describe the levels of mental retardation. These terms are no longer used by careful writers, but since the words appear frequently in the earlier literature on mental retardation, it is important to know that the term *idiot* was used for persons having a mental age of less than 3 years, or an intelligence quotient of less than 20. The term *imbecile* indicated a mental age of 3 to 7 years, or an intelligence quotient of 20 to 49. A *moron* was a person with a mental age of 8 or higher, and an intelligence quotient between 50 and 69.

While the terms *moron*, *imbecile*, and *idiot* had a wide use for a great many years, they are now avoided since they have an emotional loading which is completely undesirable. Moreover, to label anyone in this way adds little to our understanding of his or her problems. It has the damaging effect of overgeneralizing both physical and psychological characteristics. Individual variations, even among the relatively low levels of mental retardation, are of considerably greater importance than are similarities.

The *Manual on Terminology and Classification in Mental Retardation* classifies mental retardation into four levels of seriousness: *mild, moderate, severe,* and *profound.* In terms of intelligence test scores, the top of the mild group is defined as performance which is more than two standard deviations below the average of the test used. For this reason, the four levels of mental retardation in terms of IQ differ slightly from one test to another (see Table 15.1).

The diagnostic manual of the American Psychiatric Association departs radically from the more usual conception of the levels of mental retardation and designates anyone with an IQ between 70 and 85 as having a *mild mental deficiency,* with emphasis on vocational impairment. People with IQs between 50 and 70 are considered to have a *moderate mental deficiency* and to be in need of special training and guidance. The classification of *severe mental deficiency* is reserved for the IQ range of 0 to 50; these patients are judged to be in need of custodial and protective care. This classification is unrealistic in that more than 20 million people—most of whom are making an adequate social, economic, and personal adjustment—are classified technically as mentally retarded.

In any case, the diagnosis of mental retar-

dation should not be made merely on the basis of a low IQ. It is necessary to have supporting information on both the clinical and psychosocial status of the person concerned. It is quite possible for someone to score in the mentally retarded range on intelligence tests and yet not be retarded. Psychosocial deprivation, learning disability, cultural bias, and lack of motivation are some of the conditions that contribute to test scores that do not reflect the person's true level of intellectual ability.

Adaptive Behavior

The emphasis on the training and education potential of retarded people has made it possible to classify them into three groups. The first and smallest of these groups is made up of those who are *untrainable* and who must remain completely dependent because of their low intellectual level. This group makes up about 5 percent of the total number of mentally retarded. The second major group, according to this classification, includes about 20 percent of the total—those who are *trainable* to some extent. These people constitute the most neglected group at the present time. The third major group, by far the largest, is made up of about 75 percent of the total mental retardates in the country. These people are considered to be *educable;* with the aid of special classes they can be expected to reach a reasonable degree of educational achievement and to make an adequate social and economic adjustment in the community.

The prevalence of adaptational difficulties is probably greater among mildly retarded children than among normal children. One important factor is that excessive demands are frequently made on children of low abili-

Table 15.1 Levels of mental retardation in terms of obtained intelligence quotients. Note that the level of retardation varies in terms of the tests used.

Level of retardation	Intelligence quotient	
	Stanford-Binet	Wechsler scales
Mild	67 to 52	69 to 55
Moderate	51 to 36	54 to 40
Severe	35 to 20	39 to 25
Profound	19 and below	24 and below

(Adapted from Grossman et al., 1973)

Classification by Adaptive Behavior: A Practical Example

Independent functioning: Feeds self with spoon (cereals, soft foods) with considerable spilling or messiness; drinks unassisted; can pull off clothing and put on some (socks, underclothes, boxer pants, dress); tries to help with bath or hand washing but still needs considerable help; indicates toilet accident and may indicate toilet need.

Physical: May climb up and down stairs but not alternating feet; may run and jump; may balance briefly on one foot; can pass ball to others; transfers objects; may do simple form-board puzzles without aid.

Communication: May speak in two- or three-word sentences (Daddy go work); name simple common objects (boy, car, ice cream, hat); understands simple directions (put the shoe on your foot, sit here, get your coat); knows people by name. (If nonverbal, may use many gestures to convey needs or other information.)

Social: May interact with others in simple play activities, usually with only one or two others unless guided into group activity; has preference for some persons over others.

Assuming that all the behavior described above represents the *highest* level of adaptive functioning of which a person is capable at a given age, the following levels of mental retardation would be indicated:

3 years of age	Mild retardation
6 years of age	Moderate retardation
9 years of age	Severe retardation
12 years and above	Profound retardation

(Adapted from *Manual on Terminology and Classification in Mental Retardation*, 1973, p. 29)

ty when their limited intellectual capacities are unrecognized. The psychosocial stress related to being retarded takes many forms. Parental rejection, excessive demands, and anxiety related to feelings of inadequacy and ineptitude are among the stresses which lead to psychological disturbances (Potter, 1972).

Causes of Mental Retardation

The causes of mental retardation are clear in some cases, complex in others, and completely unknown in many. However, there are three important approaches to the problem of causation. The *polygenic* approach assumes that a genetic factor is present in the majority of cases of retardation, particularly those in the mild and moderate ranges. The *psychosocial* approach is concerned with the role of sociocultural deprivation as a cause of retardation. Finally, a number of cases of retardation are due to some type of *biological* deficit.

Polygenic Retardation

The largest group of the mentally retarded is made up of people for whom a specific physical cause cannot be identified. These cases have been referred to as *primary, constitutional, familial, hereditary*, and *genetic*. Each of these terms suggests the presence of an inborn factor of some kind.

The emphasis on heredity, triggered by the rediscovery of the work of Gregor Mendel in 1900, was a milestone in the history of mental retardation. During the last two decades of the nineteenth century, there was an active interest in the familial incidence of mental retardation, just as there was an interest in the familial occurrence of genius. In the main, this interest stemmed from the writings of Sir Francis Galton, who dealt extensively with both problems (Galton, 1883).

Although the early family studies were open to the most serious objections in terms of methodology and interpretation of results, they served to stimulate a considerable amount of interest in the possible genetic component in some types of mental retardation. The current view is that those cases of

Bad Apples on the Family Tree: The Kallikaks

A classic study of the occurrence of mental retardation over several generations of a family involved the investigation of two lines of descendants of Martin Kallikak, a fictitious name given by the investigator to a soldier in the American Revolution. While in the Army, Martin became involved with a mentally retarded girl—a barmaid in a tavern—and fathered an illegitimate son. This son, who was to become the father of ten children, was the starting point for the study of one line of 408 descendants. After the war, Martin married a Quaker girl of good family and normal intelligence. It was possible to trace a second line of 496 descendants from this marriage.

The findings were dramatic. All but two of the descendants from Martin's marriage were intellectually normal and, in many cases, quite superior. There were successful businessmen, doctors and lawyers, judges, college presidents, and governors. In sharp contrast, more than a third of the descendants of Martin's union with the retarded girl were mentally retarded, while most of the others had a history of alcoholism, criminality, and other forms of maladaptive behavior.

The Kallikak study was presented as proof that mental retardation is inherited. It was soon pointed out, however, that the same findings could be used to support the view that an inferior environment can produce inferior people. This argument is certainly a valid one, and much of the maladaptive behavior of the "inferior" Kallikaks was undoubtedly due to poverty, a high rate of illegitimacy, and related social and environmental influences. Nevertheless, it is highly unlikely that a random sampling of families in similar circumstances, but not starting with a mentally retarded parent, would reveal mental retardation in 35 percent of the descendants.

mild and moderate mental retardation which do not show clinical features other than the intellectual deficit are merely part of the normal variation in the range of ability. Just as there are people who are very bright intellectually, there are others who are intellectually dull. The limits of ability are established by the action of an undetermined number of genes. For this reason, the term *polygenic* has been used to refer to this complex hereditary influence.

Polygenic influence is shown in a series of surveys of a residential section of Milwaukee having the lowest average family income, greatest population density, and highest rate of dilapidated housing in the city. It was found that maternal intelligence was the best single predictor of intellectual development in children. Mothers with IQs under 80, although making up less than half the total group, accounted for four-fifths of the children with IQs under 80. Moreover, the offspring of the relatively "brighter" mothers remained at a constant IQ level over a period of time, while the others declined progressively with age. The study supports the view that mild retardation is not randomly distributed among the poor and disadvantaged but is heavily concentrated in families with intellectually subnormal parents (Heber et al., 1972).

Psychosocial Retardation

In spite of strong and continuing evidence of polygenic factors in mental retardation, there has been a persistent interest in the possible role of psychosocial deprivation in the development of the condition. Those who hold to this point of view look upon deprivation as being analogous to a vitamin or endocrine deficiency. Emotionally deprived children are considered to be oversensitive to psychological stress in the same way that the patient with vitamin deficiency is oversusceptible to infection. To support this position, there is evidence that maternal deprivation results in a retarded rate of development, greater susceptibility to disease, and less adaptability in later life. Psychosocial retardation sometimes results from deprived, crowded homes in which the child has difficulty in developing verbal ability, a critical ingredient in the measurement of intelligence. The school system labels such children as retarded on the basis of their appearance, speech, background, and intelligence test scores. Such children develop a high expectancy of failure, which in turn retards further education. Fortunately, psychosocial retardation is not irreversible; most schools and social agencies have come to recognize this fact and to act to overcome this type of retardation (Loquet, 1973).

The importance of psychosocial retardation is shown in "Project 100,000," initiated by the U.S. Department of Defense. It had been found that nearly 19 percent of all white recruits and about 67 percent of all blacks who took the qualifying test failed. The passing grade was lowered to permit 100,000 of the approximately 300,000 men who fail the test each year to enter all four branches of military service. When these men were later evaluated as to their performance, they were found to be doing at least as well as other soldiers. Most of the men who originally failed the test were not mentally retarded in the technical sense. They were psychosocially and educationally retarded.

"Deprivation dwarfism" This term has been used to refer to a combination of mental retardation and stunted physical growth related to unhappy home conditions. When children are removed from such homes they sometimes show spurts of physical and psychological growth. If the intellectual level reaches the normal range, the apparent retardation was an example of "pseudo-retardation" rather than true mental retardation. The symptoms, which are often noticed by age 2, include extreme shyness, inability to control temper, insatiable hunger and thirst, and a craving for bizarre foods. Such children are most likely to be found in home situations where there is a history of alcoholism, sexual incompatibility, illness, beatings, unemployment, and unwanted pregnancies.

The reason for the physical retardation is not known. One theory is that continuous anxiety leads to a condition in which the digestive system is less able to absorb food. Another view is that the growth hormone of the pituitary gland is involved in some way. The exact way in which mental state and growth are related, and how an emotional problem becomes a physical one, is not known.

The effects of early childhood deprivation are seen in a study of two groups of infants, each diagnosed as retarded but without brain damage. The two groups were raised separately and differently. One group was given early mothering and care and was reared in good foster homes. Members of this group became educated, are employed in various occupations and professions, and are raising normal families. Most of the other group, left to custodial and nonstimulating institutional care, are wards of the state thirty years later (Brown, 1969).

While deprivation and other sociocultural factors unquestionably influence the level of intellectual expression, they probably do not influence the basic level of intellectual capacity. Social and psychological factors often operate to prevent a child from realizing his or her full intellectual capacity. That capacity, however, has rather definite limits. The problem of true mental retardation involves the limits of capacity rather than the limits of the expression of the capacity. According to this view, no matter how low the expressed ability of the child, he or she is not truly mentally retarded if this level can be raised to the borderline range of normal intelligence or higher.

Biological Deficit

While as many as 90 percent of retarded people have limited intellectual ability as a result of normal genetic variation, mental retardation is also associated with more specific biological disorders and deficiencies. Chromosome abnormalities, brain damage due to disease or injury, errors of body chemistry, and developmental defects are among the conditions which can limit a person's intellectual capacity (see Figure 15.2).

Chromosome abnormality An important breakthrough in our knowledge of the cause of one type of mental retardation, called Down's syndrome, occurred in the late 1950s. It was discovered that there is a *trisomy*, or three chromosomes instead of the normal pair, of chromosome 21 in people with this type of mental retardation (Lejeune et al., 1959). Since that time, other chromosome abnormalities have been discovered in the cells of some retarded people.

The person with Down's syndrome is likely to be somewhat smaller than average, with a characteristically round face. The typical sloping eyebrows and eyelids give such people a somewhat Oriental appearance. It was this appearance which suggested the name *mongolism*, a term no longer used. The tongue frequently has characteristic transverse fissures, and in some severe cases it tends to protrude from the rather small mouth. The teeth may be small and misshapen. The skin is frequently lacking in elasticity, and circulation may be poor due to associated congenital heart disease. The hands and feet also tend to show characteristic signs. The little finger may be short, and there may be only one crease in the finger rather than the usual two. Similarly, the cleft between the first and second toes is sometimes unusually large. The palms frequently have a characteristic appearance, with the two main skin creases replaced by a single crease. The fingerprints may have loops rather than the usual whorls.

The mental retardation associated with this condition ranges from moderate to severe, although a few scattered cases of mild retardation have been reported. There appears to be a relationship between the severity of the physical symptoms and the degree of retardation.

While the tripling of chromosome 21 is the most common deviation related to mental retardation, there are other chromosome abnormalities which have been identified as being related to limited intellectual ability. One of these abnormalities is *mosaicism*, in which chromosome material appears in a

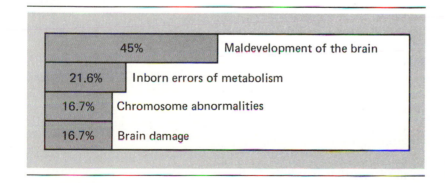

Figure 15.2 Distribution of biological deficits found in a large group of retarded people.

(Figure contents:)
- 45% Maldevelopment of the brain
- 21.6% Inborn errors of metabolism
- 16.7% Chromosome abnormalities
- 16.7% Brain damage

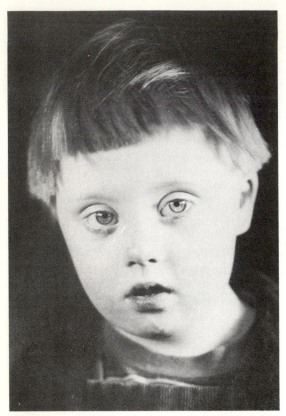

Figure 15.3 This youngster shows the physical signs of Down's syndrome, a condition once called mongolism because of the facial features. The cause of this disorder remained unknown until 1959, when it was discovered that there are chromosome abnormalities in these cases. The associated mental retardation ranges from mild to severe.

mosaic pattern. Another type of abnormality is *translocation*, in which there is a shift in the normal position of a chromosome. While such conditions are infrequent, they have led to the search for other possible chromosome deviations in retarded people.

Damage to the brain A long-recognized cause of mental retardation has been physical damage to the brain—damage resulting from injuries before birth, at the time of delivery, or following birth. Prenatal injury is relatively uncommon, but it does occur from time to time. Perhaps the best example of this is in connection with x-ray irradiation of the uterus. When pregnant women are exposed to large amounts of irradiation, the incidence of defective offspring is significant. The type and degree of damage depends to some extent upon the developmental stage of the fetus. When the uterus is irradiated during the first three months of pregnancy, the incidence of mental retardation in the offspring is significantly high.

Birth injury A more important type of damage associated with mental retardation is birth injury. Difficulties during labor may result in damage to the infant's brain. Severe injuries of this type are likely to be reflected in symptoms that are seen immediately following birth. These include respiratory difficulties, convulsions, and the inability to make normal sucking movements. Less severe brain damage may not be immediately apparent and may be expressed later, in infancy or early childhood, in a variety of ways.

The risk of hemorrhage of the brain is also present at the time of birth. In normal births, this risk is minimal. However, in cases of abnormal position of the fetus, breech extraction, the use of forceps, and other obstetrical procedures, the possibility of bleeding in the brain is increased. In premature infants, where the blood vessels are immature, a considerable additional risk is involved.

It is difficult to delineate a model for the behavior of brain-injured children because the extent and location of the injury vary from one child to another. As a result, a wide range of symptoms is possible. In some children, there is a general mental retardation; in others, the retardation is limited to a more specific disability. Similarly, the severity of the symptoms varies from case to case.

Oxygen deprivation One of the main causes of prenatal damage to the nervous system is compression of the umbilical cord, which supplies the fetus with blood carrying oxygen and nutritional substances from the mother. Cord compression produces a condition called *asphyxia*, which means oxygen deprivation and consequent suffocation of the tissues. Studies of the rhesus monkey show that the severity and type of damage caused by asphyxia depend upon when during pregnancy the injury occurs.

The earlier the asphyxia occurs, the less vulnerable to it the fetus is and the longer the period of oxygen deprivation it can withstand. Rhesus monkey fetuses at 3½ months (pregnancy in the rhesus lasts 6 months) can withstand oxygen deprivation twice as long as a monkey infant can at full term. Moreover, the earlier in pregnancy the asphyxia is introduced, the less the overall damage to the brain and, particularly, the less the damage to the higher parts of the brain.

Cerebral palsy This condition is a motor disability associated with organic brain damage or malformation. It is not a single disease, but a condition characterized by a multitude of causes and degrees of impairment. Frequently the exact cause is unknown. An estimated 750,000 men, women, and children are victims of cerebral palsy.

The damage from cerebral palsy can be limited to motor difficulties affecting a few fingers, or it can extend throughout the body. It can be tragically obvious at the time of birth or strangely elusive, impairing development several years later. The condition is neither contagious nor progressive. The brain lesions which produce the damage have been shown to be associated with physiological events surrounding pregnancy and birth, events which until recently were little understood.

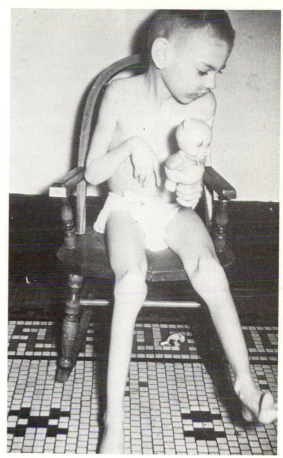

Figure 15.4 Cerebral palsy is due primarily to birth injury to the brain. This boy shows the typical atrophy of the muscles of the limbs and the inability to fully control the movements of his head and right hand. It is important to remember that this condition is a neurological one and is not always accompanied by mental retardation. In fact, some people with cerebral palsy are very talented and have high intellectual ability.

Estimates of the incidence of mental retardation among sufferers from cerebral palsy range from slightly below 30 percent to close to 80 percent. The lack of agreement among the various studies is due to the great difficulty of administering conventional psychological tests to patients with severe motor disability and speech disturbances. There is the further problem of the type of brain injury of the people being examined. It is virtually impossible to match groups in terms of extent and location of brain damage. The social and emotional environment of the people under investigation also has an effect on the apparent amount of retardation.

In a few cases, mental retardation may be associated with anoxemia, or lack of oxygen, at the time of birth or after birth as a result of anesthetic accidents. Since brain cells are extremely sensitive to changes in the oxygen supply, damage may take place when that supply is shut off or falls below normal levels. In some cases, mental retardation results from accidental brain injuries received during infancy or later in life. Many children sustain minor head injuries as a result of falling from chairs, tables, and cribs. Usually no permanent damage results, although occasionally, when the injury is associated with a fractured skull or prolonged unconsciousness due to concussion, it may cause an intellectual defect in the child. Later in life, accidental brain injuries, disorders of the blood vessels of the brain, and asphyxia may sometimes result in mental retardation.

Errors of body chemistry By the mid-1970s, more than fifty inborn errors of body chemistry that damage an infant's brain were known. These chemical errors involve the metabolism of various fats, proteins, carbohydrates, and other substances necessary to the normal functioning of the nervous system. Metabolism is the chemical process by which body cells are built up and broken down, and by which energy is made available for their functioning. Various disturbances of metabolism are known to be related to mental retardation.

Faulty fat metabolism Tay-Sachs disease is a disorder of fat metabolism transmitted as a simple recessive characteristic. Its highest incidence is found in people of Jewish ancestry, among whom carrier probability is one in thirty, or approximately ten times that of the general population. A child with this disorder develops normally and appears normal at birth; the clinical signs of disease appear between the ages of 1 month and 1 year. Such a child then becomes apathetic, shows muscular weakness, is unable to hold his or her head steady or maintain normal posture, and loses the ability to grasp objects. Ordinarily there is a visual deterioration leading to blindness, and death occurs within a few years. Because it is a disease of infancy and involves blindness, a hereditary factor, and mental retardation, the condition is also known as *infantile amaurotic family idiocy*.

Disturbed protein metabolism The most important error of protein metabolism associated with mental retardation is *phenylketonuria* (PKU). This disorder, which is also transmitted as a simple recessive trait, is one in which the patient is unable to metabolize the amino acid phenylalanine. The result is an accumulation of phenylalanine, most of which is excreted in the urine. Children with this clinical disorder show a number of characteristic physical symptoms along with various degrees of mental retardation. Most cases show severe retardation.

The history of PKU dates back to the early 1930s, to a family in Norway with two retarded children. The mother detected a peculiar odor and consulted a number of physicians in an effort to learn the cause. It was eventually discovered that the urine of both children reacted with ferric chloride to give an unusual green color. This condition was determined to be due to the presence of phenylpyruvic acid (Fölling, 1934).

Extensive mass testing of blood phenylala-nine levels of newborn infants in the United States suggests that the incidence of PKU is about 1 in 15,000 live births. While both sexes are affected and all races appear to be involved, the incidence is higher in people of European stock and particularly low in blacks and people of Ashkenazi Jewish ancestry (Centerwall & Centerwall, 1972).

Thyroid deficiency This metabolic disorder, called *hypothyroidism*, is one in which there is a decrease in, or absence of, the thyroid hormone *thyroxine.* Congenital *hypothyroidism* may be due to iodine deficiency in the mother during pregnancy, or to an absence or underdevelopment of the thyroid gland. It may also be due to a genetically determined enzyme defect which results in a defective synthesis of thyroxine by the infant.

Traditionally, this disorder has been known as *cretinism.* The origin of the word *cretin* is uncertain. It has been suggested that it is derived from *chrétien*, the French word for Christian, in keeping with the once popular idea that the cretin is especially blessed by heaven. Other authorities derive the term from *cretina*, which means stupid or silly. Another view is that the term is derived from *cretine*, the word for alluvial soil—the sandy and muddy sediment deposited by streams and rivers—since it was believed at one time that an alluvial region was related to the cause of the disorder.

The hypothyroid infant is rarely recognized at birth, but the symptoms become apparent during the early months. The older child is ordinarily dwarfed, with coarse and heavy facial features. There is a general appearance of dullness and apathy. In most cases there is a swollen abdomen which, when combined with other distinguishing features, gives the child a characteristic appearance. Mental retardation in the untreat-ed is a constant symptom. Fortunately, these cases are identified relatively easily, and therefore the necessary endocrine therapy can be initiated promptly. At one time, institutions for the mentally retarded had many

Figure 15.5 When hypothyroidism, or lack of thyroid hormone, is present prior to birth, the condition is frequently associated with typical physical characteristics and mental retardation. This retarded woman shows the characteristic short stature, protruding abdomen, and coarse facial features. The disorder can be alleviated to some degree by hormone therapy during early infancy.

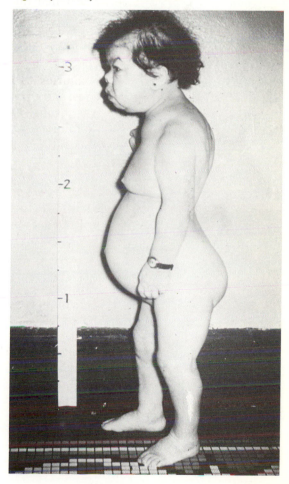

cases of this type. Relatively few such cases are admitted to the hospitals today.

Developmental Defects

Mental retardation associated with congenital, or inborn, defects in the development of the skull and brain account for the largest number of people with specific biological disorders. Some of these conditions have been observed for centuries, as indicated by drawings made by the ancient Greeks and Egyptians. However, the cause of most of these conditions remains unknown.

Congenital cerebral defects include the complete absence of the major portions of the brain, malformations of the convolutions and fissures on the surface of the brain, and conditions in which there are funnel-shaped cavities in the brain. These defects primarily involve brain tissue.

There are also inborn defects of the skull. Some skulls are steeple-shaped and others are boat-shaped. In one condition, the abnormal development of a bone at the base of the skull increases the distance between the eyes to the extent that, in extreme cases, the eyes appear to be at the side of the head rather than in the normal position in front.

(a)

Figure 15.6 This man is the victim of a developmental defect called *scaphocephaly*. The protruding bone structure of the forehead is quite evident in both the frontal *(a)* and side *(b)* views. As in the case of microcephaly (see Figure 15-7), mental retardation is usually moderate, and the cause of the defect is not known.

(b)

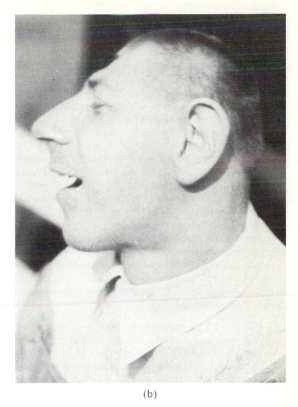

(a)   (b)

Figure 15.7   This good-natured thirty-year-old man is an example of microcephaly, a condition in which the skull is abnormally small. Although the frontal view *(a)* does not reveal the full extent of the physical defect, the side view *(b)* shows the small size of the cranium relative to the rest of the face and head. Moderate mental retardation is usually associated with this developmental disorder of unknown origin.

Sometimes the head becomes abnormally large. When the defect is due to the pathological growth of supportive tissue of the brain, the condition is called *macrocephaly*. In other cases the large head is due to an increased amount of cerebrospinal fluid in the ventricles, or internal chambers of the brain. This condition is known as *hydrocephaly*. There is also a condition, called *microcephaly*, in which the skull is abnormally small as a result of defective development.

Training and Treatment

Since most mentally retarded people do not have associated physical problems that can be treated by medical or surgical means, treatment takes the form of training and education. During the nineteenth century and the first part of the present century, training was largely restricted to the most simple crafts, housekeeping tasks, and farm chores in connection with large public institutions for the retarded.

The "Wild Boy" of Aveyron

Interest in the education and training of the mentally retarded was aroused in France in the early 1800s as a result of publicity given to the case of Victor, the "Wild Boy of Aveyron." This defective boy of 11 or 12 years of age had been living in the woods without contact with other people for a number of years. He had been observed on several occasions, completely naked, seeking berries and roots. He was captured in 1799 by three hunters when he climbed into a tree in an attempt to escape from them. The boy was taken to Paris, where he was considered to be an incurable idiot. The attending physician, believing the condition to be due to the boy's lack of contact with people, insisted that the boy could be cured.

Victor was studied over a period of five years, but he did not learn more than a few words. His emotional behavior was crude, and his reaction to the environment was largely in terms of his biological needs. A report to the French Minister of the Interior contained the following:

> One cannot help concluding: First, that by reason of the almost complete apathy of the organs of hearing and speech, the education of this young man is still incomplete and must always remain so; secondly, that by reason of their long inaction the intellectual faculties are developing slowly and painfully, and that this development, which in children growing up in civilized surroundings is the natural fruit of time and circumstances, is here the slow and laborious result of a very active education in which the most powerful methods are used to obtain most insignificant results; thirdly, that the emotional faculties, equally slow in emerging from their long torpor, are subordinated to an utter selfishness and that his puberty, which sets up a great emotional expansion, seems only to prove that if there exists in human beings a relation between the needs of the senses and the affections of the heart, this sympathetic agreement is, like the majority of great and generous emotions, the happy fruit of education. (Itard, 1824)

In spite of the pessimism expressed in the report, Victor did make progress. When compared with normal adolescents, the boy seemed at a considerable disadvantage. However, compared with his original behavior when captured in the woods, his behavior five years later showed marked improvement.

It was not until World War II, in the 1940s, that the training potential of the retarded became widely recognized. Retarded men assigned to Special Training Units were found able to perform valuable and constructive services. It became apparent that many men who earlier would have been rejected as unsuitable because of low intellectual ability could be trained effectively for labor battalions. This realization had a later influence in civilian life, particularly in connection with the use of high-grade retardates in industrial organizations. Following World War II, advances in the field of mental retardation were rapid and extensive. Important progress was made in the understanding of the etiology of mental retardation, early identification and diagnosis of the condition, education and training, prevention and treatment, and research.

The education and training possibilities in the field of mental retardation are much greater than most authorities realized until recently. The U.S. Office of Education reported that in 1922 there were 23,000 mentally retarded children in special classes. By 1975, this figure had increased to over a third of a million.

Early Detection and Prevention

Mental retardation frequently remains undiscovered until months or years after birth. It is not unusual for the condition to go unnoticed until the child enters school. By the time mental retardation has been diagnosed, it is usually too late to minimize its effects. For this reason, a considerable amount of attention has been given to the problems of early detection and prevention.

Detecting Retardation

The most effective detection programs involve conditions in which a biochemical error, or other type of biological marker, is present. For example, we saw that phenylketonuria is due to an error of protein metabolism and that in this condition phenylalanine, an amino acid, is excreted in the urine. This discovery made possible the development of a diaper test to detect whether a newborn infant had the metabolic disorder that would lead to retardation. The urine test has now been replaced by a relatively simple blood test.

The U.S. Children's Bureau and the National Institutes of Health initiated a jointly sponsored phenylketonuria-prevention program in which the blood specimens of all newborn infants were tested as part of regular hospital routine. It was emphasized that if only two babies afflicted with phenylketonuria were found in the course of the tests, the financial saving due to the avoidance of lifelong severe mental retardation would equal the cost of testing the 400,000 babies in the program. In one year, at least twenty-five affected infants were located and placed on a low-phenylalanine diet before brain damage or mental retardation took place. Assuming that these children would have died in an institution between age 35 and 40 and that the average cost to the state would have been approximately $2,000 per year for each of these children, the detection program involved a potential saving to the states of almost $2 million. This saving does not include the value of potential earnings and productivity of the twenty-five children.

There is also growing interest in metabolic diseases other than PKU that lead to mental retardation. The Children's Bureau is supporting a study of the clinical application of screening tests to detect *galactosemia*, *maple syrup urine disease*, and *histidinemia*. Support is also being given by the bureau to conduct studies of new approaches to broader screening methods, for example, a battery of automated tests for screening metabolic diseases. In addition, field trials are being conducted of a simple method to determine elevations of ten different amino acids. These levels are useful in the detection of metabolic disorders.

Detection programs also seek to determine the risk of incurable chromosome abnormalities before the child is born. By means of a test called *amniocentesis*, in which a small amount of amniotic fluid surrounding the developing fetus is extracted and the cells are examined, it is possible to determine whether or not a child will be the victim of Down's syndrome. When the test is positive, the mother can decide whether to abort the fetus or to allow the pregnancy to continue. If she chooses to have the child, she can be informed about the problems that will need to be faced in raising a mentally retarded son or daughter.

Another important development in detection has been the fluorescent blood test to determine whether prospective parents in families with a history of Tay-Sachs disease are carriers of the recessive gene causing the condition. The test provides a rapid, accurate, and visual determination of whether a person is genetically normal or is a carrier of the potentially dangerous gene. While this information cannot prevent mental retardation in a child, it can be an important factor in genetic counseling. If both the husband and wife carry the recessive gene for this incurable condition associated with profound mental retardation, the risk of having such a child must be given the most serious consideration.

Preventing Retardation

The problem of preventing mental retardation has been approached in several ways. In a few clinical conditions, retardation can be prevented, or substantially reduced, after it has been detected at or before birth. For example, retardation can be prevented in phenylketonuria through the control of diet and in hypothyroidism by means of hormone treatment. Some conditions, such as Down's syndrome and Tay-Sachs disease, can be prevented by genetic counseling and the avoidance of pregnancy, or by therapeutic abortion after pregnancy has occurred. Fortunately, these conditions account for a relatively small number of cases of mental retardation.

Another approach to the prevention of retardation has been through the control of environmental conditions which contribute to its occurrence. Some of the most important work of this kind involves the worldwide effort to combat malnutrition and dietary deficiencies, especially in underdeveloped countries.

Evidence from work with a variety of animal species, supplemented by scattered tests in human beings, indicates that protein and caloric deprivation may inhibit mental and social development. In animal studies, these effects seem to depend upon fairly acute nutritional deprivation of the type only seen in grossly malnourished children. Several studies reported by the National Institute of Mental Health have been organized in South and Central America, where malnutrition is widespread, thereby providing a natural test area for the relationships between nutritional deprivation and intellectual and social development.

Most mental retardation, however, is of the polygenic type which is unrelated to specific causes other than inferior genetic material. Here the problem of prevention is the extraordinarily difficult one of improving genetic quality. Some people believe this can be done by sterilizing the mentally retarded to prevent them from having children. However, most of the more severely retarded are already sterile or lack the opportunity to reproduce. The real problem concerns those who are mildly or moderately retarded and the millions who have only borderline ability. In these cases, sterilization would not only be morally and ethically objectionable but would present insurmountable practical difficulties.

Our knowledge of polygenic mental retardation is not sufficiently advanced to allow us to prevent the condition or to reduce its prevalence. We cannot predict the eventual impact of genetic engineering on this type of retardation, nor is it possible to foresee scientific discoveries that might one day solve or alleviate the problem. In the meantime, the only preventive measures available are information and education, genetic counseling, and voluntary birth control.

The Chapter in Review

Mental retardation is a condition in which there is a deficiency in intellectual capacity. Their low level of intelligence makes it difficult for most retarded people to achieve satisfactory personal and social adjustment without special training. Even with such training, the more seriously retarded must remain in schools for the retarded and other institutions.

1 Terminology and Classification

Mental retardation, also called mental deficiency and mental subnormality, has traditionally been defined in terms of intelligence test scores. A more recent trend uses adaptability, or the potential for training and education.

2 Causes of Retardation

Most cases of mental retardation involve normal variations of intellectual ability due to the interplay of complex genetic influences. In other cases there are more specific genetic defects, biochemical errors, developmental disorders, and brain damage. While psychosocial factors are frequently responsible for behavior that appears to reflect intellectual subnormality, true mental retardation is not involved. The problem is one of lack of skills, knowledge, and competence rather than limited intellectual capacity.

3 Training and Treatment

Although the biological limits of intelligence cannot be readily influenced, few people make full use of their inborn abilities. For this reason, most efforts to modify the behavior of the mentally retarded are directed toward special training and education. When such measures are taken, many of the retarded are able to become self-supporting and productive members of society.

4 Early Detection and Prevention

Because of the essentially biological nature of mental retardation, the most effective approach to the problem is to detect the condition as early as possible or prevent its occurrence. Early detection is possible in cases involving metabolic errors, chromosome abnormalities, and other physical markers. Medical and surgical treatment can then be helpful in some cases. Preventive measures take the form of genetic counseling and the control of environmental conditions contributing to some forms of retardation.

Recommended Readings

Mental Retardation

Bernstein, N. *Diminished people: Problems and care of the mentally retarded*. Boston: Little, Brown, 1970.

Blatt, B. *Souls in extremis: An anthology on victims and victimizers*. Boston: Allyn and Bacon, 1973.

Blatt, B., & Kaplan, F. *Christmas in purgatory: A photographic essay on mental retardation*. Boston: Allyn and Bacon, 1966.

Forrest, A., Ritson, B., & Zealley, A. (Eds.) *New perspectives in mental handicap.* New York: Longmans, 1973.

Lane, H. *The Wild Boy of Aveyron*. Cambridge: Harvard University Press, 1976.

Mannoni, M. *The backward child and his mother*. New York: Pantheon, 1972.

Veras, R. *Children of dreams, children of hope*. Chicago: Regnery, 1975.

Watson, M. *Mainstreaming the educable mentally retarded*. Washington, D.C.: National Education Association, 1975.

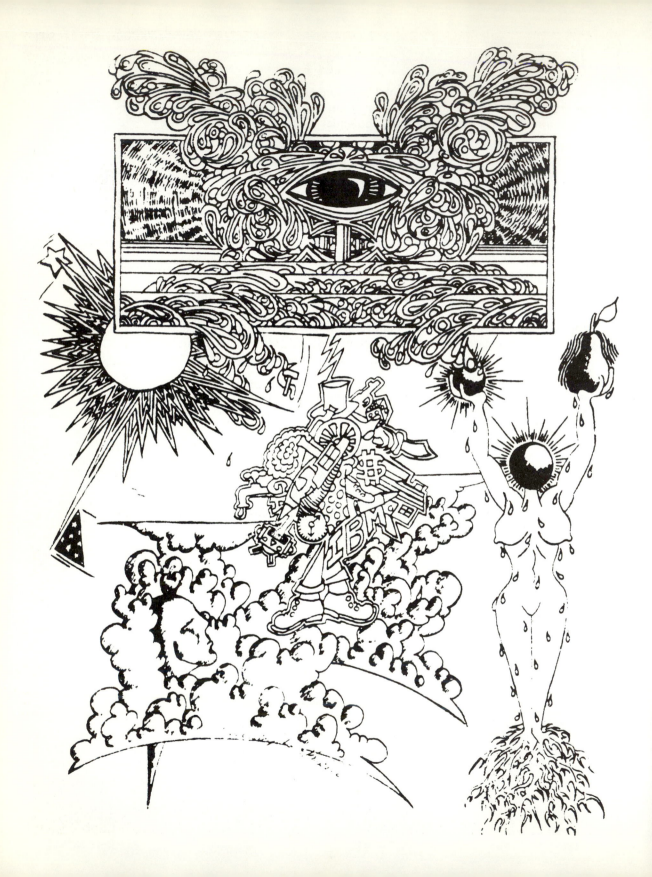

16
Diagnosis of Mental Disorder

Objectives

To indicate what is meant by *psychological diagnosis*

To point out some of the shortcomings of traditional diagnostic categories and what is being done about them

To show how computer techniques are being used in connection with psychological diagnosis

To describe some of the objective approaches to the assessment of maladaptive behavior

To show how projective techniques differ from objective methods of diagnosis

To discuss some of the psychophysiologic techniques used in psychological evaluation

To gain a full understanding of the field of abnormal psychology, it is necessary to consider the problems of diagnosis and treatment as well as those of historical development, causation, and the description of the clinical syndromes. This chapter and the two chapters following deal with the practical matters of how the clinical psychologist and the psychiatrist go about uncovering and identifying the various forms of personality disturbance, and how such conditions are treated once they have been recognized and classified.

The word *diagnosis*—used widely in medicine and increasingly in psychology, social work, and remedial education—means identification of a disease or disorder and recognition of its relationship to other conditions. In medicine, the diagnosis is made on the basis of physical signs and symptoms. In the same way, psychological signs combine to give the characteristic picture of the different psychological disorders. Psychodiagnosis is the specialized technique in which psychological methods are used to reveal the nature and extent of psychological damage. As such, psychodiagnostic procedures are used in a variety of situations, from the identification of the problem child in public school to the classification of the seriously disturbed person in the psychiatric hospital.

Some Current Concerns

Although the importance of psychological diagnosis is widely recognized today, there are still areas of concern and misunderstanding. During a substantial part of this century, an antidiagnostic bias has been expressed by a vocal minority of clinicians. This point of view was a reflection of the psychoanalytic influence in American psychology.

It was felt that it was more productive to understand individual psychodynamics than to make a classification in terms of presenting symptoms. The reaction was to the earlier descriptive classification of neurosis, in which dozens of phobias and other conditions were labeled with no practical usefulness. Unfortunately, the psychoanalytic attitude toward the diagnosis of neurotic conditions spread to other areas of abnormal behavior, and an increasing number of psychologists and psychiatrists came to believe that all diagnosis is useless and undesirable.

During the 1960s there was a concerted attack on diagnosis of any kind. It was claimed that diagnosis is impersonal and authoritarian, that it is based on norms which are unfair to minority groups, and that it is unnecessary and dehumanizing. Fortunately, the trend has shifted in a marked way, and the long and useful tradition of diagnosis is once again the subject of intensive investigation. It is now generally recognized that the problem lies not in diagnosis itself but in those who make the diagnoses and in the categories that have been arbitrarily established.

Unreliable Labels

Diagnostic labels are the names given to established categories of behavior. The words *depression*, *neurosis*, *schizophrenia*, and similar terms are examples of such labels. It might seem that highly trained professionals in the field of mental health should be able to agree on a diagnosis. However, studies have consistently shown that psychological diagnosis is highly unreliable.

In one study of patients admitted to the

psychiatric ward of a general hospital, only 34 percent of the patients (most with chronic and severe illnesses) could be given an adequate diagnosis within the categories provided by the American Psychiatric Association's *Diagnostic and Statistical Manual of Mental Disorders* (Pinsker, 1967).

A different type of evidence indicating the uncertainty of diagnosis on psychiatric conditions was a cross-cultural study comparing the diagnoses of psychotic patients from essentially similar populations in outpatient clinics in the United States and the Netherlands. Americans classified patients as schizophrenic thirteen times more often than did their Dutch colleagues (National Institute of Mental Health, 1975). The questions raised are: Is schizophrenia really that much more prevalent in the United States? Are the criteria for diagnosis different in the two countries? Or do we require more knowledge to define the specific nature of the disorder called schizophrenia?

One important study of the reliability of diagnosis involved more than 250 consecutive admissions to a private psychiatric hospital (Tarter, Templer, & Hardy, 1975). All subjects were interviewed by two of five of the most experienced psychiatrists on the staff of the hospital. These psychiatrists had an average of sixteen years of clinical experience beyond their residency in psychiatry.

An analysis of diagnoses was made in order to determine the percentage of agreement on major categories such as neurosis, functional psychosis, personality disorders, and organic disorders of the brain. It was found that the highest agreement was for brain disorder (see Table 16.1). However, the level of agreement was not impressive for any of the major diagnostic groups.

The study also included specific diagnostic conditions within the major classifica-

Table 16.1 Percentage of agreement between two experienced psychiatrists on the diagnosis of major clinical groups

Clinical group	Percent agreement
Organic brain disorder	72.3
Functional psychosis	54.8
Personality disorder	47.8
Neurosis	46.4

(Adapted from Tarter, Templer, & Hardy, 1975.)

tions. Here the agreement was even poorer. While the psychiatrists agreed on depression in 71.2 percent of the cases, the agreement fell to very low levels when it became a question of neurotic depression or psychotic depression. In the case of schizophrenia, even when all subtypes of schizophrenia were considered together, less than 50 percent of the diagnoses were in agreement (see Table 16.2).

Three possible sources of error could have been involved in the diagnostic process. First, a difference in the amount of experience of the clinician could account for the differences in diagnoses. Yet in the study reported, all the psychiatrists had long clinical experience and were acknowledged by their colleagues to have a high level of professional skill. The second possible reason for the lack of agreement was that the patient population was not representative of patients in general, since they were private patients from the middle socioeconomic class. This factor was considered to be an

Table 16.2 Percentage of agreement between two experienced psychiatrists on the diagnosis of specific clinical conditions

Specific diagnosis	Percent agreement
Schizophrenia	47.6
Neurotic depression	32.2
Psychotic depression	18.1

(Adapted from Tarter, Templer, & Hardy, 1975.)

unimportant one since the people in the study were of at least normal intelligence and were verbally articulate, making it easy to acquire pertinent diagnostic information. The third possible explanation was that the APA *Diagnostic and Statistical Manual of Mental Disorders* is inadequate as a classification system. It was felt that this factor was the most likely explanation for the lack of diagnostic agreement in the study (Tarter, Templer, & Hardy, 1975).

Another investigation showed how diagnosis can be influenced by suggestion. A professional actor, who was briefed on the characteristics of a mentally healthy person, memorized a script in which he and his life were described in the most normal terms. The actor was then interviewed, and the interview was recorded. He did not know the purpose of the experiment or that the interview would be diagnosed by twenty-five psychiatrists, twenty-five clinical psychologists, and forty-five graduate students in clinical psychology.

Just before the recorded interview was played, it was arranged that the clinicians would hear a professional person of high prestige, acting as a confederate of the experimenter, say that the person to be diagnosed was "a very interesting man because he looked neurotic, but actually was quite psychotic." After listening to the interview, the clinicians were asked to indicate their diagnosis on a sheet which listed ten psychotic conditions, ten neurotic disorders, and ten miscellaneous personality types, one of which was "normal healthy personality."

The intriguing result of this experiment was that not one of the twenty-five psychiatrists diagnosed the person as being mentally healthy, and only three of the twenty-five clinical psychologists considered him to be normal. Similarly, only five of the graduate students in clinical psychology made this diagnosis. The most striking finding was that 60 percent of the psychiatrists found the person psychotic, as did 28 percent of the clinical psychologists and 11 percent of the graduate students (see Table 16.3).

Four different types of control groups were used in connection with the study. One group received no prestige suggestion, another group received a positive suggestion of mental health, a third group was presented with the material in the context of an employment interview, and a group of jurors

Table 16.3 Percentage of diagnoses made by psychiatrists and clinical psychologists, including students in advanced training, on the basis of a recorded interview with a "normal, healthy" male. Before listening to the interview, the clinicians were exposed to the fact that a "recognized authority" thought that the subject "looked neurotic but actually was quite psychotic."

| | Diagnosis | | |
Clinical group	Psychosis	Neurosis and Character disorders	Mentally healthy
Psychiatrists	60.0	40.0	0.0
Clinical psychologists	28.0	60.0	12.0
Graduate students in clinical psychology	11.1	77.8	11.1

(Adapted from Temerlin, 1968.)

Table 16.4 Percentage of diagnoses made on the basis of a recorded interview with a "normal, healthy" male, under four different control conditions.

| Control condition | Diagnosis | | |
	Psychosis	Neurosis and character disorders	Mentally healthy
With no prestige suggestion	——	42.9	57.1
With prestige suggestion of mental health	——	——	100.0
Presented as an employment interview	——	29.2	70.8
Presented as a sanity hearing	——	——	100.0

(Adapted from Temerlin, 1968.)

heard the interview as a sanity hearing. Most of the judgments made by members of the control groups were that the person whose interview had been recorded was mentally healthy. No one in any of the four control groups judged him to be mentally disturbed (see Table 16.4).

An important international investigation of diagnostic practices in the United States and Great Britain also found that the diagnosis of psychological disorders can be highly unreliable. One of the studies in this investigation compared the diagnoses of people admitted to New York mental hospitals with those of others admitted to mental hospitals in the London area (Cooper et al., 1972). The cases were diagnosed by hospital physicians according to their usual methods, and they were also diagnosed independently by members of the project team, who used a structured interview schedule.

In one of the studies, videotape recordings of psychiatric interviews were shown to large numbers of American and British psychiatrists. Some of the interviews resulted in strikingly large differences in diagnoses between the countries. For example, 69 percent of the psychiatrists in the United States made a diagnosis of schizophrenia, while the same diagnosis was made by only 2 percent of the psychiatrists in the British Isles. The study also demonstrated that the frequent differences in reported incidence of disorders are due to differences in diagnostic terms and practices rather than to real variations in the prevalence of the disorders.

A survey of a number of studies of the reliability of psychiatric diagnosis found that there are no diagnostic categories for which reliability is universally high. Satisfactory reliability is found in only three conditions: mental retardation, alcoholism, and organic brain disorder. However, reliability is not satisfactorily high for the subtypes of brain disorders. The survey also found that reliability is no better than fair for psychosis and schizophrenia, and it is poor for neurosis, personality disorders, and psychosomatic reactions (Spitzer & Fleiss, 1974).

Search for a Common Language

It is generally agreed that the most important factor contributing to the lack of diagnostic reliability is the looseness of the terminology used to describe clinical conditions. Diagnostic practices in the United States are based, for the most part, on the APA's *Diagnostic and Statistical Manual of Mental Disorders*. The first edition was published in 1952, a second appeared in 1968, and a third edition was being developed in the mid-1970s. While the manual is a distinct improvement over the earlier classification system of Kraepelin, it has many shortcomings. One critic said: "It classifies on the basis of

---

Contrasting Descriptions of Anxiety Neurosis

A Clinical Description

This neurosis is characterized by anxious overconcern extending to panic and frequently associated with somatic symptoms . . . anxiety may occur under any circumstances and is not restricted to specific situations or objects. This disorder must be distinguished from normal apprehension or fear, which occurs in realistically dangerous situations. (*Diagnostic and Statistical Manual of Mental Disorders*, 2d ed., 1968)

An Operational Description

A The following manifestations must be present: (1) Age of onset prior to 40. (2) Chronic nervousness with recurrent anxiety attacks manifested by apprehension, fearfulness, or sense of impending doom, with at least four of the following symptoms present during the majority of attacks: (a) dyspnoea, (b) palpitations, (c) chest pain or discomfort, (d) choking or smothering sensation, (e) dizziness, and (f) paraesthesiae.

B The anxiety attacks are essential to the diagnosis and must occur at times other than marked physical exertion or life-threatening situations, and in the absence of medical illness that *could* account for symptoms of anxiety. There must have been at least a week from the others.

C In the presence of other psychiatric illness(es) this diagnosis is made *only* if the criteria described in A and B antedate the onset of the other psychiatric illness by at least two years. (Feighner et al., 1972)

---

both manifest symptoms and etiology, both clusters of symptoms and groups of persons, and both class and trait concepts" (Buss, 1966).

Today, there is an increasing tendency to replace descriptive definitions with operational definitions. Descriptive definitions consist of brief descriptions of the characteristic features of a condition accompanied by a summary of the essential elements of the condition. This is the traditional textbook definition of abnormal behavior. Such definitions tend to be quite general. Operational definitions are based on a set of clearly defined criteria which must be fulfilled if behavior is to be classified and diagnosed. One project has developed operational definitions for sixteen diagnoses (Feighner et al., 1972).

One of the major difficulties with operational definitions is that a category of "undiagnosed psychiatric disorder" is required for a relatively large number of people who do not meet the criteria for a specified diagnosis. However, it may be better to have a few reliable diagnostic categories, even if many people are not classified, than to include all cases in categories having questionable reliability.

Clinical Evaluation

Psychological diagnosis is based upon information about the disturbed person. This information comes from a variety of sources. The case history is a collection of facts about every phase of the person's life. The most critical information often comes from the personal interview with the clinician. In most cases, a diagnosis can be made on the basis of the case history and the diagnostic interview. Sometimes it is necessary to use special psychological tests and techniques to assess behavior and personality before a satisfactory diagnosis can be made.

Case History

The case history is the starting point for the clinical evaluation. The history brings together all available information about the person under study. This serves not only to orient the psychologist and the psychiatrist to the total situation but also in many cases to yield important clues which determine the direction of the diagnostic interview. The major areas covered in the case history include:

1 Identifying information, such as name, address, age, religion, occupation, and marital status
2 A statement of the problem
3 The reason for referral
4 Family history and background, including information on grandparents, parents, and brothers and sisters
5 Health and medical history, including childhood diseases, accidents and injuries, and surgical operations
6 School and educational background, including level attained, past failures, and special difficulties
7 Personal and social adjustment as a child, as an adolescent, and as an adult
8 Work and occupational record, including jobs held, wages, and adjustment to the work situation
9 Marital history and adjustment, including courtship, family climate, and relationship to marital partner and children
10 Personality description

The effectiveness of the case history depends upon the care with which it has been prepared and the accuracy of the information it contains. Some clinics and hospitals are fortunate in having a social service department with trained social workers who have the skill and time to collect and organize large amounts of background data. In such agencies, the clinician is furnished with the complete case history. However, in many settings, the case history material is prepared by untrained workers. In other agencies and institutions, the clinical psychologist or the psychiatrist must rely upon the diagnostic interview for background information. Here taking the history is not merely a means of collecting information; it is a method for establishing contact with the troubled person and creating a workable interpersonal relationship.

Diagnostic Interview

The second major clinical technique used in psychodiagnosis is the personal interview. In this approach, the clinician sees the person, talks to him or her, asks questions, and observes reactions and behavior. In many instances, this interview requires as much as an hour or longer, although some cases are so clear-cut in their symptom pictures that a diagnosis can be made in a very few minutes. Where a particularly difficult problem of differential diagnosis exists, more than one diagnostic interview may be required.

The diagnostic value of the personal interview depends to a large extent upon the skill and experience of the clinician. Signs and symptoms are meaningless unless the observer is able to appreciate their significance. The student who aspires to a career in clinical psychology, psychiatry, psychiatric nursing, or psychiatric social work must realize that there is no adequate substitute for personal contact. No amount of reading of textbooks, case histories, or psychological reports can take the place of direct experience with men, women, and children who show the various forms of personality disorganization.

Through repeated and intensive contact with people who are having problems, the student interviewer gradually develops into a clinician. With each new case, the clinical frame of reference becomes enlarged, and the pattern seen today becomes a standard of comparison for tomorrow. In this way, clinical judgment develops and becomes increasingly sensitive. Much of psychodiagnosis remains more an art than a science, however one might wish it to be otherwise.

Even so, the diagnostic interview does have its objective guideposts in the form of the behavior characteristics of the person being studied. From the moment the person walks through the door of the clinician's office, he or she is giving the psychologist personal information. One person enters the office with complete self-possession and self-confidence; another enters shyly and with embarrassment; still another appears suspicious; and others are hostile, depressed, anxious, or agitated. Such signs are noted automatically by the clinician, even before the first words have been exchanged.

Throughout the diagnostic interview, people reveal themselves by tone of voice, posture, facial expression, gestures, movements, and similar actions. All this is quite apart from the answers to questions or the story the person tells. What the person says may be of considerably less importance than how he or she looks and acts. The diagnostic interview in the hands of a skilled clinician is probably the most important single aid to understanding and classifying the disorganized personality.

Diagnosis by Computer

Recent advances in computer technology have opened vast new possibilities in low-cost, sensitive, reliable analysis of diagnostic information. A number of projects are engaged in programming computers with clinical observation data. Members of mental health clinical teams are being trained to make observations of a person on specially designed forms and on a continuing basis. These observations are similar to those made in connection with behavior rating scales and other procedures for recording the everyday behavior of people during their routine activities. However, instead of forming the basis for relatively crude ratings and comparisons, the information is fed into a computer. It is then analyzed, and a computer readout is furnished on the person's behavior. Present behavior is compared with previously established norms, and the report also indicates the extent and direction of any changes which have taken place.

A research group in England has developed a computer-based technique using a standardized interview known as the Present State Examination (PSE). With the aid of a glossary of defined symptoms, personality disturbances and behavior disorders are classified automatically by means of a computer program called CATEGO (Wing et al., 1974). Another computer program for psychiatric diagnosis is called DIAGNO (Spitzer & Endicott, 1974). This program is based on a logical model similar to that used in clinical medicine. The input information is limited to current symptoms—as reflected in scale scores on the Psychiatric Status Schedule—and items of personal information. The output is in terms of twenty-five standard diagnostic categories.

The most recent development in diagnostic interviewing is to allow the person to interact with a computer terminal rather than an interviewer. Most clinicians are influenced by a number of irrelevant factors which generate unimportant and even dam-

**Mental Status Examination Report:
A Computer Printout**

The following report is based on the use of the Mental Status Examination Record, a rating scale developed to standardize the diagnostic interview.

Introduction
This is a report of a female patient based on information collected using the mental status examination record. Her attitude toward the examiner was very negative. The reliability and completeness of the material in this report are considered very poor because information refusal acts as a barrier to communication.

Appearance
The patient looks younger than she really is. She appears to be in good physical health. She is short and is overweight. In her dress and grooming she is slightly unkempt. Her posture is slightly stooped. Her facial expression is mildly suspicious and angry.

General attitude and behavior
Her behavior is markedly uncooperative. She seems moderately suspicious. She shows moderate overt anger. She has been sarcastic, argumentative, and irritable. To a slight degree, she tends to provoke anger in others. She is mildly impulsive, and slightly guarded. Excessive alcohol use is suspected.

   On the positive side, the patient is likeable.

   There have been no reports of suicidal behavior during the period under study.

Motor behavior and gait
An unusual motor feature present is slight fidgeting.

   The patient shows neither psychomotor retardation nor excitement.

Mood and affect
She seems slightly depressed and anxious. Anger is present to a marked degree. Qualitatively, her affect is moderately inappropriate. Her mood is markedly labile.

   Her mood is not flat.

Quality of speech and thought
She speaks with a very loud voice. Her rate of speech is fast and productivity is increased. She is moderately incoherent and irrelevant. Moderate loosening of associations is also noted. The quality of her speech and thought is suggestive of neurological disorder.

Content of speech and thought
This patient has slight grandiose thoughts.

   The examiner was unable to determine whether suicidal ideation, ideas of reference, bizarre thoughts, phobias, compulsions, obsessions, and delusions are present.

Somatic functioning and concern
Appetite and energy level are both normal.

   This patient has no insomnia, psychophysiologic reactions, or unwarranted concern with her physical health.

Perception
The examiner is unable to determine whether hallucinations are present.

Sensorium
This patient is too disturbed to test for memory impairment. This patient is moderately disoriented as to time and place. The examiner is unable to determine whether disorientation in person is present.

Cognitive functions
The examiner is unable to estimate this patient's level of intelligence.

Judgment
The patient has no plans for the future. Her judgment concerning family relations, non-familial social relations, and employment is poor.

Potential for suicide or violence
In the examiner's judgment, this patient's potential for physical violence is very high. The examiner is unsure about this patient's potential for suicide.

Insight and attitude toward illness
It is unknown whether or not the patient recognizes that she is ill. Her motivation for working on her problems is unknown. It is not known whether the patient has any awareness of her own contribution to her difficulties.

Overall severity if illness
The overall severity of this patient's illness is judged to be severe. During the period under study, her condition has been stable. (*Psychopharmacology Bulletin*, 1972, 42.)

aging questions. The computer program avoids these unproductive and time-consuming questions. Moreover, there may be personal and embarrassing material that one might not want to express to someone else but would be willing to present to a computer.

In a typical computer-assisted diagnostic interview, the person sits at a computer terminal with a television screen and a modified typewriter keyboard. Questions and information are displayed on the television screen, and the typewriter keyboard is used to respond in a variety of ways.

Multiple-choice answers can be given by using only number keys; special keys indicate instructions such as "go," "back up," and "change." Other responses can be made by using the full typewriter keyboard. Patient acceptance of computer interviewing has generally been high (Coombs et al., 1970; Grossman et al., 1971; Stead et al., 1972).

One computer-assisted diagnostic interview is programmed so that it can be repeated to check on a person's progress. The first go-through interview establishes the initial complaints and the severity of the symptoms. Follow-up interviews allow for a redefinition of the target symptoms and opportunity to describe any new symptoms or changes in the intensity of symptoms. The entire computer program involves 243 frames (questions or information or both) available in a single path through the interview. The interview can be accomplished with a minimum of 52 frames and a maximum of 194 frames. All responses are stored on magnetic tape, and a printout is available immediately after the interview has been completed (Greist et al., 1973).

Although these techniques are still in the developmental stage, it can be expected that very rapid progress will take place in the future. Computer diagnosis, already important in other phases of medicine and public health, could very well become one of the most significant technological developments in mental health.

Behavioral Analysis and Assessment

The behavioral approach to psychological diagnosis emphasizes objective and measurable dimensions of behavior. Every effort is made to support the personal opinions and judgments of the clinician by external and independently derived facts about the disturbed person. These facts come from direct observation, rating scales and personality inventories, standarized tests, and measures of psychophysiologic functions. These various approaches to behavioral analysis and assessment contribute significantly to the objectivity of diagnosis.

Direct Observation

Clinicians use observation in an automatic way in their diagnostic work. Each time they are with a person, they are making clinical judgments based on appearance, what is said, the emotional state, and similar aspects of behavior open to observation. The validity of such observation is in direct relationship to the skill and experience of the practitioner; it is an invaluable aid to the sophisticated clinician but may be of little value to the lay person or the naive interviewer.

In order to increase the effectiveness of the direct interview, the clinician sometimes uses the method of controlled observation, in which a person is observed for predetermined periods of time or under specified conditions. In this way, it becomes possible to describe, study, and compare samples of behavior. In terms of objectivity, it is a step beyond the general clinical impression obtained as a result of relatively uncontrolled direct observation.

Rating Scales

Since the effectiveness of clinical observation is so dependent upon the skill of the observer—his or her ability to sense what is important, as well as to describe it—specialized types of rating scales have been developed to make observation more objective and to permit less skilled observers such as nurses, aides, and others who have contact with disturbed people to participate in the evaluation of personality. The accurate observation and recording of behavior on the ward of a psychiatric hospital is of the greatest importance. Such observation and recording make possible a more objective evaluation of the changes in behavior and furnish a method by means of which the effectiveness of the forms of treatment can be measured.

A number of rating scales and behavior charts have been developed to facilitate the observation and recording of the behavior of emotionally disturbed people. These scales and charts can be used to check a person's behavior against his or her diagnosis, or they can be used to assist in the initial formulation of the diagnosis.

Diagnostic Inventory

The first important diagnostic instrument of this type was developed during World War I for use in military service. As a result of the increasing knowledge of psychological and psychiatric disorders, it became desirable to

	None or a Little of the Time	Some of the Time	Good Part of the Time	Most or All of the Time
1. I feel down-hearted, blue and sad	☐	☐	☐	☐
2. Morning is when I feel the best	☐	☐	☐	☐
3. I have crying spells or feel like it	☐	☐	☐	☐
4. I have trouble sleeping through the night	☐	☐	☐	☐
5. I eat as much as I used to	☐	☐	☐	☐
6. I enjoy looking at, talking to, and being with attractive women (or men)	☐	☐	☐	☐
7. I notice that I am losing weight	☐	☐	☐	☐
8. I have trouble with constipation	☐	☐	☐	☐
9. My heart beats faster than usual	☐	☐	☐	☐
10. I get tired for no reason	☐	☐	☐	☐
11. My mind is as clear as it used to be	☐	☐	☐	☐
12. I find it easy to do the things I used to	☐	☐	☐	☐
13. I am restless and can't keep still	☐	☐	☐	☐
14. I feel hopeful about the future	☐	☐	☐	☐
15. I am more irritable than usual	☐	☐	☐	☐
16. I find it easy to make decisions	☐	☐	☐	☐
17. I feel that I am useful and needed	☐	☐	☐	☐
18. My life is pretty full	☐	☐	☐	☐
19. I feel that others would be better off if I were dead	☐	☐	☐	☐
20. I still enjoy the things I used to do	☐	☐	☐	☐

Figure 16.1 The Self-Rating Depression Scale. An example of an objective diagnostic method by means of which people rate the severity of their own symptoms.

devise a method for screening out the more obviously unstable and disturbed recruits.

While a dozen or more tests of this type are available, and while some have been found useful in guidance and personnel work, most of them offer little that is useful to the clinician interested in psychodiagnosis. The single possible exception is the Minnesota Multiphasic Personality Inventory (MMPI; Hathaway, 1945). This test is made up of more than 500 statements to which the subject is required to respond with "true," "false," or "cannot say," insofar as the statement applies to the subject. The responses are scored, and the results are recorded in nine clinical diagnostic categories. A graph is drawn indicating the relative weight of items pointing to such clinical symptoms as depression, hypochondria, paranoid thinking, and so on. A narrative report is then ordinarily written by the clinician, or the data may be fed into a computer, which furnishes a readout describing the personality pattern of the person.

Diagnostic Testing

The use of psychological tests in psychodiagnosis is a specialty practiced largely by the clinical psychologist. Psychiatrists ordinarily do not have the time, inclination, or training to make use of the many specialized testing techniques available to the mental health clinician. Yet one of the country's best-known psychiatrists has said, "The practice of psychiatry without the assistance of modern psychological testing is as old-fashioned and out-of-date as would be the practice of orthopedics without the x-ray" (Menninger et al., 1947).

While few clinicians would disagree with this view, there has been a growing dissatisfaction with the conventional and established psychological tests. Even the best of the clinical tests have been questioned as to their standardization, reliability, and validity. Such tests are particularly vulnerable to criticism on the basis of inadequate standardization with minority groups.

Measuring intelligence

The cornerstone of psychodiagnostic testing is the evaluation of intellectual functioning. The degree of organization of the factors contributing to intelligence, as well as the level of organization, are diagnostic reference points of considerable value to the clinician.

A person's intelligence is of importance to psychodiagnosis in a number of ways. At first glance, it might appear that intelligence has a bearing only on the question of whether or not a person is mentally retarded. However, the measurement of intelligence for such purposes is only one limited aspect of the usefulness of the evaluation of intelligence in psychodiagnosis.

Through the measurement of intellectual functioning, the clinician is able to study the ways in which personality disorganization has interfered with intellectual activity. Since different forms of psychopathology affect intelligence in different ways, it is helpful diagnostically to have a clear picture of the present level of general ability even though that present level is not an accurate reflection of true ability. Such factors as apathy, hostility, lack of interest, poor motivation, inattention, impairment of memory, and organic deficit operate to mask a person's real ability.

The measurement of intelligence is also important in psychodiagnosis because it permits the clinician to make observations under a relatively standard set of conditions. By noting the reactions to the various questions and tasks required by the clinical test of intelligence, the psychologist is able to observe such characteristics as determination, perseverance, tolerance for frustration, ability to maintain attention, emotional stability, reaction to stress, and similar personality components.

Detecting brain damage For many years psychologists have been interested in the use of psychological tests to detect organic change in the brains of people with personality disturbances. Where organic changes are pronounced, various neurological, x-ray, and electronic techniques are useful. But these physical methods are often insensitive to the early and more subtle changes in the nervous system, particularly in the brain. Because of the need for recognizing these early changes, an increasing amount of attention has been directed to tests for organicity.

In every case referred to the clinical psychologist for a diagnostic workup, there exists the possibility of underlying destructive processes in the nervous system. In many cases, this possibility is remote and can be ruled out without much difficulty. But in other cases, special methods must be used to determine the possible presence of such damage.

There have been two major lines of development related to the psychological study of brain damage. One has its roots in the interest in localized damage from injuries and accidents, brain tumors and similar processes, and surgical removal of brain tissue. The interest in this type of damage goes back many years and ranges from early clinical reports of accidental brain injury to current attempts to evaluate psychological changes accompanying advanced forms of neurosurgery.

The second line of development has grown out of early studies of psychotics. It was observed that these people often scored well below their expected levels on tests of intelligence. This deficiency in test performance was so general that it was assumed that a special process, called *deterioration*, was

involved. For many years attempts were made to isolate and measure this deterioration factor. Today it is recognized that the only true deterioration occurs in certain diffuse organic conditions such as alcoholism, cerebral arteriosclerosis, and brain infections.

Psychophysiologic Approach to Behavioral Assessment

Recent advances in the field of psychophysiology—that branch of physiology most directly concerned with psychological problems—are the basis of another approach to the diagnosis of personality disturbances and behavior disorders.

New techniques involving complex electrical recording of physiologic changes make it possible to evaluate quite precisely the nature of a person's reactions even when circumstances prevent him or her from communicating experience verbally.

The most important psychophysiologic technique in psychodiagnosis is the measurement of brain waves (electroencephalography). Other approaches of this general type are the recording of the electrical resistance of the skin (electrodermal response), and neuromuscular responses (electromyography).

Brain waves and behavior One of the most intriguing approaches to diagnosis has been through the measurement of spontaneous electrical changes in the brain. It was recognized early in the present century that all living tissues, including brain cells, possess electrical properties which can be studied in terms of the familiar units of electrical measurement. However, the early studies attracted scant attention because the electrical po-

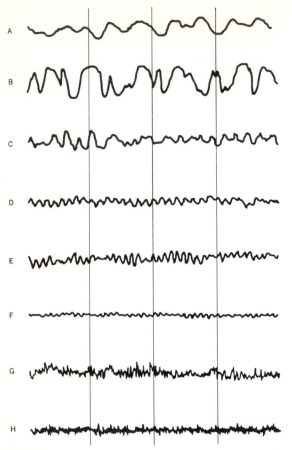

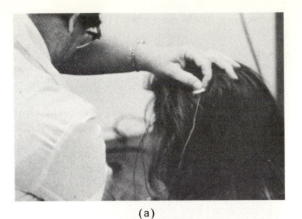

(a)

Figure 16.2 The electrical energy generated by various areas of the brain in different states of consciousness can be recorded graphically. Slow waves from 2 to 8 per second are associated with deep relaxation and sleep (A, B, and C). The basic 9 to 11 per second alpha rythm (D) is characteristic of relaxed wakefulness. The fast waves, ranging from 12 to 30 or 40 per second, are associated with states of alertness.

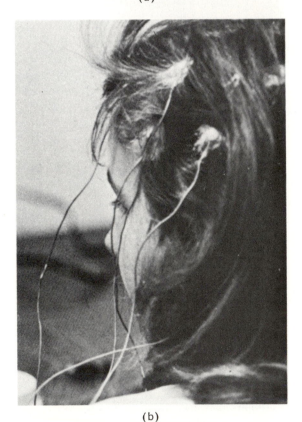

(b)

tentials were so minute that their details could not be measured adequately.

Electroencephalography (EEG) as a diagnostic approach began with the work of Hans Berger, a German investigator who became interested in the early observations on the spontaneous electrical activity of the brain and began a series of investigations in his own laboratory. After several years of study, he published his classic report on human brain electrical potential (Berger, 1929).

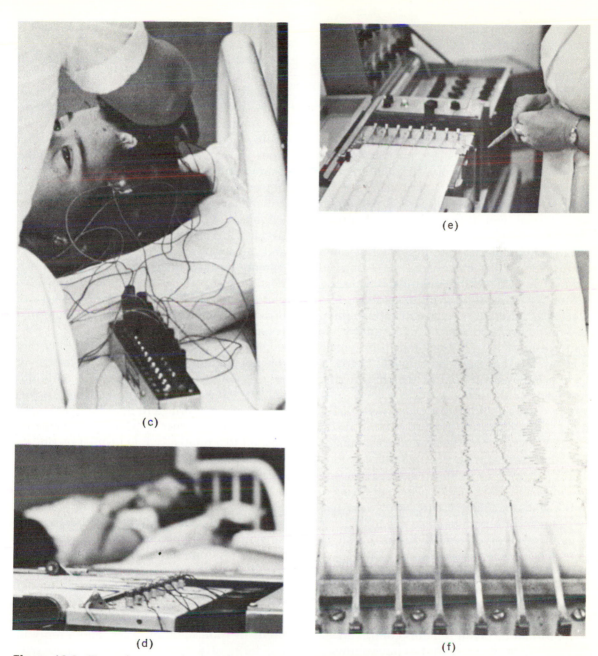

(c)

(e)

(d)

(f)

Figure 16.3 The various steps in obtaining an electroencephalograph (EEG) record are shown in this series of photographs. One of a number of electrodes is attached to the subject's head *(a)* by means of a special paste. When the other electrodes are in place *(b)*, the subject reclines on a bed and the wires to the electrodes are plugged into the EEG machine (*c* and *d*), which amplifies the electrical energy being generated by the brain. A graphic record of the electrical brain waves is made by pens on moving chart paper (*e* and *f*). The interpretation of the EEG record requires specialized training and a high order of technical skill.

Berger demonstrated the presence of more or less continuous rhythmic fluctuation of potential recorded from electrodes attached to the scalp. He showed that these electrical potential changes arose from the brain tissue and were not due to circulatory pulsations, muscle activity, or other extraneous factors. He found that the electrical activity of the brain is modified by sleep, anesthesia, and various forms of sensory stimulation; that the patterns of activity vary with age in young children; and that certain pathological clinical conditions produce abnormal electrical recordings.

The EEG patterns are influenced by such factors as cell metabolism, the electrical properties of the cell membrane, the character of the surrounding fluid medium, and electrical impulses along—but independent of—the neural pathways. To account for the patterning of the EEG record, a "pacemaking" system has been postulated. This system is believed to control the rhythm and regularity of the brain waves.

The analysis of brain-wave patterns is most valuable in diagnosing organic disorders of the brain which may be causing personality disturbance or mental disorder. The method is particularly useful in detecting epilepsy. Each of the principal forms of epilepsy has a characteristic brain-wave pattern. Localized brain damage due to injuries, tumors, and other conditions can also be detected in many cases (Fenton, 1974).

While there is general agreement as to the value of brain-wave analysis in cases of organic disturbances of the brain, the matter of EEG changes associated with other forms of abnormal behavior remains controversial. For a number of years, studies have shown a relatively high incidence of EEG abnormalities in children and adolescents with behavior disorders. This finding might be explained by the fact that some of these young people are suspected of having some type of minimal brain damage.

There is also evidence suggesting that there are characteristic EEG changes in schizophrenia (Itil et al., 1972) and that the brain-wave patterns of schizophrenics differ from those found in people with bipolar depression (Shagass, 1973). There is mounting evidence of some type of organic involvement in both these disorders. Since the evidence of EEG changes associated with psychosomatic disorders, neurotic reactions, and other psychogenic conditions is extremely limited, it seems clear that the diagnostic value of the analysis of brain-wave patterns is directly related to the degree of organic change associated with the abnormal behavior.

One of the shortcomings of the EEG as a diagnostic tool has been the necessity of relying on the visual inspection of brain-wave tracings by EEG experts. Not only has there been a shortage of qualified personnel in this field, but the complexity of the tracing has led to a relatively low level of reliability in interpretation. Only those conditions associated with marked changes in the EEG record have been identified with any degree of certainty. Moreover, EEG interpretation has been time-consuming and unavailable to large numbers of people who live away from the metropolitan medical centers where EEG facilities are located. The computer is now bringing EEG analysis to people no matter where they live. EEG information obtained in a local clinic can be relayed over hundreds or thousands of miles, and a reply in the form of a complete and detailed EEG analysis can be available in a matter of minutes.

Electrical responses of the skin The electrodermal response, also known as the *galvanic skin response* (GSR) and the *psychogalvanic response* (PGR), is a reaction which involves changes in the electrical resistance of the skin as a result of emotional states. Fear, anxiety, anger, and other emotions are accompanied by a moistening of the skin, which causes changes in electrical resistance. It is often possible to detect underlying emotional conflicts through the analysis of the graphic record of these electrical changes. The first studies of this type took place early in the present century in connection with emotional changes during the administration of word-association tests designed to detect unconscious "complexes." Since that time there has been a continuing interest in electrodermal changes in the various clinical conditions.

Since the electrodermal response is a reflection of emotional reactions rather than a sign of organic damage or dysfunction, as in the case of brain-wave patterns, the electrical skin response is sensitive to the entire range of psychological abnormalities. One would anticipate that the method would be an exceptionally valuable means of psychophysiological diagnosis. Unfortunately, there are a number of difficulties in using the electrodermal response as a diagnostic method. A major problem is in establishing the conditions under which the recordings are made. Since skin resistance is highly sensitive, variations occur as a result of many internal and external stimuli which are difficult to control. Another problem is the difficulty of making a meaningful analysis of the highly complex recorded data.

Muscle movements The measurement of the electrical activity of the muscles of the body by means of the electromyograph (EMG) has been of considerable interest for many years. Its primary use has been in the diagnosis of conditions showing tremors, impairment of muscle movements, and other neurological problems. It has also been used to evaluate the general level of muscular tension.

The EMG studies have indicated that states of generally increased muscular activity and tension appear to be relatively constant in individual subjects, that high muscle tension is associated with depressed moods, that disturbed people as a group appear to have a considerable amount of neuromuscular hypertension as compared with control groups, and that overall muscular tension decreases as these people improve. By feeding EMG signals into an averaging computer, it has been possible to make increasingly more sensitive diagnostic evaluations (Caine & Lader, 1969).

While the electromyograph is used primarily in the study of neurological disorders, the measurement of muscular tension also has diagnostic implications for personality disturbances. Just as changes in the electrical resistance of the skin give a continuous reading of a person's emotional state, so also can changes in muscle tension indicate emotional conflict. There will, for example, be an increase in tension when hidden conflicts are touched upon during diagnostic interviews and treatment sessions.

A study using the EMG with anxious and depressed persons found that the anxiety state was characterized by a stable and significant increase in EMG background activity but that depression was associated with a general reduction of the bioelectrical activity of the muscles. Improvement of mood tended to be accompanied by increased muscular activity. The study showed that changes in the EMG reflect emotional shifts and may be used as an objective index of the changing emotional state (Volynkina et al., 1971).

Psychodynamic Diagnosis: Exploring the Unconscious

Although behavioral analysis and assessment have dominated psychological diagnosis in recent years, a psychodynamic approach to the problem is also possible. This approach, which grew out of the theories and practices of Freud and his followers, is less concerned with objective measures of behavior than it is with discovering clues to the unconscious life of the troubled person. For this reason, psychodynamic diagnosis frequently makes use of methods and techniques that have not been standardized and which have questionable validity and reliability. The intuition and sensitivity of the clinician are assumed to be more important than ratings, test scores, and other objective measures.

Expressive Behavior

An important aspect of psychodynamic diagnosis is the analysis of expressive behavior. The way in which people write, walk, talk, and draw sometimes reveals more about their problems, conflicts, and disturbances than hours of interviews and tests. Posture, gesture, motor attitudes, and muscular movements reflect underlying psychological states to a very considerable extent.

It has been recognized for many centuries that people reveal something of their personalities in their body movements. In Prov. 6:12-13, the Bible says, "A naughty person, a wicked man, walketh with a froward mouth. He winketh with his eyes, he speaketh with his feet, he teacheth with his fingers . . . ." Movement is a language of personality that comes to be known to every clinician who works in the area of psychological diagnosis.

Clinicians who follow the psychodynamic model believe that the postures, gestures, gait, and physical attitudes of the person with an emotional disturbance are important clues to the inner dynamics of the disorder. Such movements sometimes have a symbolic meaning and may be of significance for treatment. While movements often are expressions of immediate emotional states, they may also be reactions to former life experiences. Freud believed that such movements represent the reappearance in consciousness of repressed fantasies and memories. Today there is widespread interest in

---

The "Body Language" of Behavior

A study of nonverbal behavior of mentally disturbed individuals used a film of each patient during a standardized interview conducted within 48 hours of admission to the mental hospital. Another film was made within a week of the time of discharge. A silent version of the film was shown to groups of untrained observers who did not know they were viewing a mentally disturbed person. Each group of observers saw either the admission or the discharge film, and they recorded their impressions of the person by checking a list of characteristics.

It was found that the nonverbal behavior shown at admission conveyed quite different information from that shown at the time of discharge. One patient was judged to be despondent, worried, dissatisfied, fearful, self-pitying, sensitive, unstable, disorderly, gloomy, and moody by the majority of observers who saw the film concerning the admission. Observers who saw the same patient's discharge film described the individual as being friendly, active, impulsive, immature, cheerful, cooperative, energetic, and informal. (Ekman & Friesen, 1974)

the conscious and unconscious significance of the way people stand, walk, sit, and move.

The psychodynamic approach also assumes a close and revealing relationship between the form and content of speech and the person's unconscious life. It has been suggested that metaphors and idioms which are used today in an abstract way once may have had a concrete and even magical meaning.

Art in diagnosis Psychodynamic diagnosis also makes use of the artistic expressions of disturbed people. Drawings, brush paint-ings, finger painting, clay modeling, and sculpture are expressive media through which the unconscious needs and conflicts of people with psychological problems are revealed.

At the form level, the art productions of the mentally disordered may show lack of integration, distortions and disproportions, stereotypy and perseveration, the compulsive filling in of space, lack of symmetry, and similar features which are seldom found in the drawings of those who are not mentally disturbed.

The content of the art may reflect the

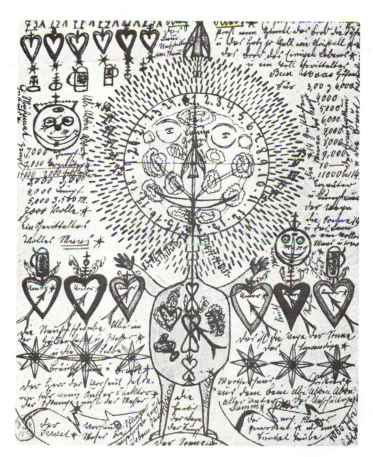

Figure 16.4 This drawing *The Lamb of God,* is so typically schizophrenic that an experienced clinician would have little difficulty in making a diagnosis. The major diagnostic features are the bizarre quality of the drawing, the inclusion of handwriting, the seemingly irrelevant objects, and the repetition of small details. Some modern artists whose work resembles these drawings may themselves have schizoid personalities or have been influenced by having seen the drawings of schizophrenics.

underlying nature of the pathological process. Among psychotics, there may be a representation of delusional ideas or hallucinatory experiences. Drawings may stress sexual or religious themes, or the material may be symbolic or allegorical. Paranoid persons may depict ambitious projects, making use of plans, maps, and complex designs. Sexual themes, hidden or overt, are not uncommon and sometimes are indicative of disturbances of psychosexual development.

Projective Techniques

Personality diagnosis by means of the projective approach involves the revelation of the uniqueness of personality through responses to relatively unstructured materials and situations. The projective test creates an ambiguous situation in which people being tested are encouraged to express themselves in such a way that the basic structure and dynamics of their personalities will be revealed. Although of less importance today than in former years, projective tests continue to be used by clinicians who follow the psychodynamic model of abnormal behavior.

Rorschach test The most highly developed, and the most widely used, of the projective methods of psychodiagnosis is the

Figure 16.5 The Rorschach technique has been used for many years to explore the structure and dynamics of personality. The method requires that the person being studied give responses to a series of inkblots. The responses are then analyzed in terms of a number of technical variables. A high level of clinical skill is required to analyze and interpret the results.

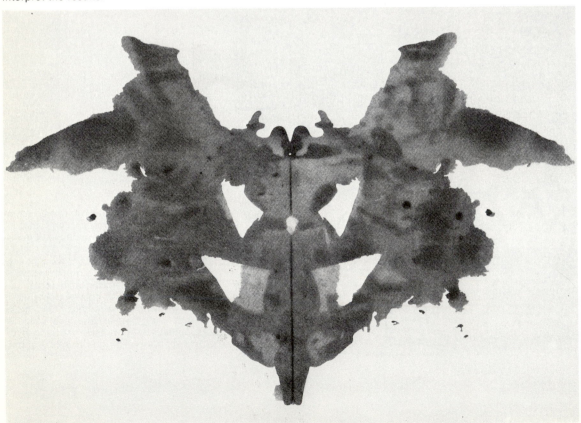

Rorschach test. This test requires the person to find meaning in a standard series of ten inkblots. The subject is handed one card at a time and required to describe what the inkblot looks like to him or her. The card may be held in any way and there is no limit to the number of responses allowed. A normal adult of average intelligence gives two or three responses to each inkblot for a total of twenty to thirty association responses for the entire test.

While the Rorschach technique is easily administered, analysis and interpretation are quite different matters. They depend not only upon experience in previously giving the test but even more on clinical experience and a thorough knowledge of the psychodynamics of human behavior. In the hands of a skilled clinician, the test can be extremely revealing. But in the hands of overly enthusiastic or poorly trained Rorschach "experts," the analysis of the personality can become nothing more than a recital of professional clichés.

In spite of the great mass of work with this technique, there is little quantitative validation of the patterns which are claimed to be characteristic of the various personality disturbances. Some psychologists reject the test completely. While the Rorschach test is certainly a means of obtaining insight into personality, the remarkable results obtained depend not only on the instrument but perhaps even more on the clinical sensitivity of the investigator.

Thematic Apperception Test The Thematic Apperception Test (TAT) requires the subject to make up a story about a series of pictures which are presented to him or her one at a time. The following story was given as a response to card 1, which shows a young boy who appears to be sitting at a table and looking at a violin:

He's sitting there because he broke his fiddle. He is acting real mad about it. He must have been playing or something like that, and he broke it. He is just sitting at the table looking at it. I guess it was his. He is mad. One of his friends may have broken it, and he is going to call his mother and tell her what happened. I guess his mother will straighten things out. Maybe she will buy him a new one.

The psychodynamically oriented clinician is able to find at least five themes in this story. First there is the idea of the "broken fiddle," suggesting hostility and aggression. Second, the person telling the story says twice that the boy is "mad" about it, empha-

Figure 16.6 The Thematic Apperception Test (TAT) requires the person being examined to make up stories based upon a series of pictures. Study this TAT picture and write a paragraph about who these women are, what they are doing, and what the outcome will be. Then examine what you have written and see if you can determine what your story has revealed about yourself.

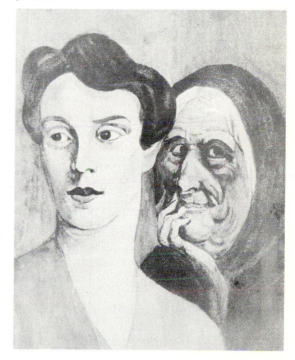

sizing feelings of anger. The third theme is a paranoid one derived from the statement that "one of his friends may have broken it." Maternal dependency is suggested by the fact that the boy is going to "call his mother." The fifth theme is optimism and is expressed by the fact that the mother probably will "straighten things out" and "buy him a new one."

The usual procedure in analyzing the TAT stories is to determine which themes recur most frequently. It is assumed that these themes point to important areas of motivation and conflict. Unfortunately, the method is time-consuming, and the findings are difficult to quantify. Nevertheless, clinicians who use this technique are convinced that inferences about psychological disturbances are most helpful for an assessment of problems dealing with motivation and conflict.

Other projective techniques While the Rorschach method and the Thematic Apperception Test have been the two most important projective techniques, there are other projective methods which contribute to psychological diagnoses. One of these approaches is the *figure-drawing test* in which the one being studied is given a pencil and a sheet of paper and asked to draw a person. He or she is assured that drawing ability is not important and is encouraged to make the effort. If the first drawing is that of a man, the person is given another sheet of paper and told to draw a woman. If the first drawing is a woman, the person is then told to draw a man. The interpretation of such figure drawings depends upon a consideration of three aspects: (1) the general overall impression given by the drawings, (2) the analysis of the structural features of the drawings, and (3) the analysis of the content of the drawings.

The *sentence-completion test* is a projec-

Figure 16.7 Human figure drawings are not always as directly revealing as is this drawing by a drug-dependent college student. This self-portrait was the first clue the clinician had as to the real nature of the young man's problem.

tive method in which a person is presented with a series of partial sentences and required to complete the meaning. Some of the statements are related to insight and orientation. Others are concerned with major areas important in psychodiagnosis: depressive tendencies, hostility and aggression, sexual preoccupation, religious feeling, psychosomatic complaints, autistic tendencies, relation to parents, paranoid tendencies, fear and anxiety, and guilt feelings.

The *self-image test* requires subjects to describe themselves in a variety of ways. In one version of the test, the person is told to

(a)   (b)

Figure 16.8 These figures were drawn by a fifteen-year-old boy referred to a juvenile court clinic on a charge of suspected child molesting. Although the boy insisted he was not involved, his emphasis on the female genitals *(a)* suggested an obsessive preoccupation with sex. Further questioning led to his admission that he had attempted to molest young girls on a number of occasions.

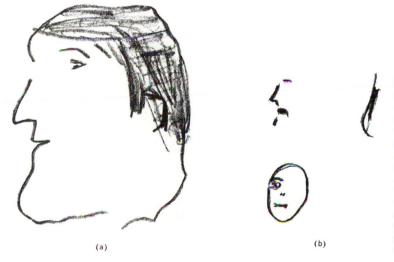

(a)   (b)

Figure 16.9 The man who drew these faces had a ruggedly masculine appearance similar to his first drawing *(a)* of a man. When he attempted to draw a woman *(b)* he made two false starts and then managed a face with one eye. At that point he said he felt ill and then began to vomit. The clinician correctly assumed that the inability to complete the female figure and the nausea were due to problems of sexual identity. Further exploration of the problem revealed that this man was struggling with strong homosexual inclinations.

The Sentence-Completion Test:
Diagnostic Implications of Selected Items

I am here *because I am mentally disturbed.* (Insight)
I worry *every minute of my life.* (Anxiety)
I am ashamed *of my dirty mind.* (Guilt)
I am sorry *that I failed.* (Inadequacy)
My thoughts *are of getting even.* (Hostility)
My sexual life *is frightening to me.* (Sex)
I would like *for someone to help me.* (Dependence)
My body is *MP BWHS AMD.* (Symbolism)
My name is *Jesus Christ.* (Delusion)
I hear *voices telling me to kill myself.* (Hallucination)
Someone *is trying to embalm me.* (Delusion)

write down as many true statements as possible beginning with the words "I am." In another version, the subject is asked to tell who he or she is in twenty different ways. In either case, the subjects project their personalities through the manner in which they perceive themselves. The clinical psychologist analyzes the responses to these questions and attempts to get significant clues about unconscious motivation and inner conflicts.

The *word-association test* is a projective method in which the person being studied is presented with a word and required to respond with the first word that comes to his or her mind. Nineteenth-century psychologists such as Sir Francis Galton and Wilhelm Wundt used word associations, but they were interested primarily in reaction time. The use of the method in personality investigation did not develop until Sigmund Freud and his colleagues pointed out the relationship which exists between a person's word associations and his or her inner needs and conflicts.

The Chapter in Review

Psychological diagnosis is a matter of interest to psychiatrists, clinical psychologists, and other professionals who deal with problems of maladaptive behavior. Accurate diagnosis makes it possible to determine the most effective treatment approach and to predict the course and outcome of a disorder. It also serves the secondary purposes of facilitating research and making uniform public health reports possible.

1 Some Current Concerns
One of the important problems related to psychological diagnosis is the unreliability of diagnostic labels. It is not unusual for a disturbed person to receive different diagnoses from different diagnosticians. To overcome this difficulty, operational definitions are being developed to replace relatively vague clinical descriptions.

2 Clinical Evaluation
Most diagnostic studies begin with an overall clinical evaluation. This evaluation is based upon the case history and the personal interview. Sometimes it is possible to make a diagnosis on the basis of information derived from these two sources. In other cases, it is necessary to use additional methods and techniques.

3 Behavioral Analysis and Assessment

Clinicians who follow the behavioral model of psychological disorder emphasize the objective approach to diagnosis. They use observational techniques, rating scales and inventories, and objective tests. Psychophysiologic information derived from the analysis of brain-wave patterns, electrical resistance of the skin, and other sources is also part of behavioral assessment.

4 Psychodynamic Diagnosis

The psychodynamic approach to diagnosis is directed primarily to the search for unconscious motives and conflicts. Emphasis is placed upon (1) possible symbolic meanings of expressive behavior and (2) projective techniques which are used to obtain material from which inferences are drawn concerning the person's behavior and personality.

Recommended Readings

Assessment of Behavior

Davis, J. D. *The interview as arena*: *Strategies in standardized interview and psychotherapy*. Stanford, Calif.: Stanford University Press, 1971.

Frank, G. *Psychiatric diagnosis*: *A review of research*. New York: Pergamon, 1975.

Freedman, A. M., & Kaplan, H. I. (Eds.) *Diagnosing mental illness*: *Evaluation in psychiatry and psychology*. New York: Atheneum, 1972.

Goldberg, M. *A guide to psychiatric diagnosis and understanding for the helping professions*. Chicago: Nelson-Hall, 1973.

Scheff, T. J. (Ed.) *Labeling madness*. Englewood Cliffs, N.J.: Prentice-Hall, 1975. (Paperback.)

Small, L. *Neurodiagnosis in psychotherapy*. New York: Brunner/Mazel, 1973.

17
Psychological Treatment of Mental Disorder

Objectives

To present the general nature of psychological treatment

To indicate the difference between psychotherapy and behavioral therapy

To describe some of the important forms of psychotherapy

To show how different types of behavior modification are used in the treatment of maladaptive behavior

To discuss trends in group therapy

The roots of the psychological treatment of abnormal behavior reach back to antiquity. The temple priests of ancient Egypt and Greece, the medicine men of the primitive tribes of Africa and South America, the mesmerists of eighteenth-century France, and the nineteenth-century physicians who relied upon reason and persuasion to influence disturbed people—all were making use of forms of psychological treatment. Although these methods frequently were effective, the underlying explanations were naive or nonexistent.

It was not until the present century that clinicians began to specialize in psychological therapy. Their treatment techniques grew out of their theories of abnormal behavior. The first important development in psychological treatment was due to Sigmund Freud, who developed the theory and technique of psychoanalysis. His work effectively established psychological treatment as an independent professional field. At the same time a number of other forces were at work, with the result that a wide range of nonmedical techniques were developed to treat the disorganized personality. These methods, including psychoanalysis, are known collectively as *psychotherapy*.

The effectiveness of psychotherapy began to be questioned seriously in the early 1950s (Eysenck, 1952). Studies were cited suggesting that psychotherapy was no more effective in bringing about changes than was the process of spontaneous recovery (whereby people change over a period of time without treatment of any kind). It was even suggested that there may be an inverse relationship between the amount of therapy and the rate of recovery; the more therapy, the slower the recovery. When these allegations were first made, they were met with hostility and violent criticism. They were challenged many times, but no convincing proof to the contrary was ever advanced. In any event, the dramatic nature of the charges turned the attention of an increasing number of clinicians to the evaluation of psychotherapy. It became increasingly clear that the value of much psychotherapy was questionable in view of the time and expense involved, the relatively few people treated, and the uncertainty of results.

Part of the disenchantment with psychotherapy was the feeling that what psychotherapy has to offer is too little and that it comes too late. It also became clear that psychotherapy is unsuitable as a therapeutic method with many people. It has been relatively ineffective in treating those with delinquent and criminal tendencies, people of low intelligence, those who show little anxiety, those who find it difficult to verbalize their problems, and people who are seriously disturbed.

This rather widespread dissatisfaction led to a new emphasis upon personality disturbance and disorganization as a *learned* reaction. The treatment of such conditions, according to this view, must be in terms of the principles of unlearning and relearning. This approach is based upon *behavior theory*, and the treatment method has become known as *behavioral therapy*.

Psychotherapy: The Insight Approach

One of the most basic principles of psychotherapy is that successful treatment requires that the person being treated achieve insight into the nature and causes of the maladaptive behavior. All psychotherapy seeks to help people gain this understanding to some degree. The assumption is that symptoms tend to disappear when the reasons for the symptoms are made clear.

Psychotherapy can be classified in terms of the objectives of the treatment. If the therapy concerns itself primarily with adjustment to the psychosocial problems of everyday life and deals with conscious events, the treatment technique is a form of *therapeutic counseling*. When therapy attempts to bring about deep and fundamental alterations in basic personality structure and deals largely with unconscious processes, the treatment is known as *depth therapy*.

Therapeutic Counseling

Psychotherapy based upon personal counseling seeks to reduce stress and to improve psychosocial adjustment by making the person aware of conflicts and motivations which are at the conscious level or just below the surface of consciousness. In the directive approach, the troubled person relates his or her problems to the therapist, who listens to the story, decides what is involved, and then tells the person what should be done. This approach is based on an authoritarian relationship between the therapist and the person being treated. To one degree or another the therapist actively manipulates the life of the patient. He may make suggestions, give advice, furnish information, provide counsel, and regulate the person's daily activities. The key feature of this form of treatment is that the therapist takes an active and authoritative role in it.

In the *nondirective* approach, the patient is largely responsible for his or her own cure. The therapist does not impose any views; rather, during the course of therapy, the person being treated arrives at a solution which is his or her own. The therapy as-

sumes that each person has an inner potential for growth and maturity, that one can achieve insight in the therapeutic relationship and make constructive use of it. There is a basic reliance on the patients themselves for the content and the direction of the treatment process. The therapist makes no effort to guide patients or to clarify their attitudes. No patterns or values are imposed on the patients, and no efforts are made to interpret their behavior for them. Instead, emphasis is placed on the expression of feeling. The therapist accepts feelings in a tolerant, nonjudgmental way and reflects them in such a way that the patient can become fully aware of his or her own attitudes.

Nondirective therapy is a more difficult procedure than directive therapy, even though the role of the therapist in nondirective therapy seems less important. In the nature of things, people are inclined to be free with their advice and suggestions. Psychotherapists are no exception, unless they have received specialized training in the nondirective approach.

Nondirective therapy was originally used with maladjusted college students, in cases of marital adjustment problems, in vocational counseling, in parent-child relationships, and in the mild personality disturbances and neurotic reactions. However, as therapists gained additional experience with the nondirective approach, the technique was extended to other groups. Those least likely to respond favorably to the nondirective approach are psychotics, people with low intelligence, excessively dependent persons, and those who find it difficult to verbalize their feelings.

There are many cases in which therapeutic counseling is effective. The attention and concern of the therapist, the emotional support derived from the continuing sessions, and the increased self-understanding that is gained make the method valuable with some of the less serious personality problems. However, the approach is less effective with the more severe disturbances of behavior and personality.

Depth Therapy

Psychotherapy of this type is directed toward a fundamental reorganization of the basic personality structure and dynamics of the person in treatment. It may include some of the techniques of therapeutic counseling, but depth therapy goes much farther. It is concerned with the deep and unconscious levels of personality and designed to bring about basic and profound changes in personality.

Psychoanalysis The method of *psychoanalysis*, as a technique of psychotherapy, began to take form in 1886, when Sigmund Freud became associated with a physician who had been using hypnosis in the treatment of neurotics. This method was to let the person talk while under hypnosis and say what was troubling him or her. Freud observed that hypnotized people talked freely

Figure 17.1 Psychoanalysis is a long-term form of therapy in which the analyst sees the patient several times a week for periods ranging up to several years. During each session, the person being treated often rests comfortably on a couch and is encouraged to say anything that comes to mind. The analyst ordinarily remains out of view so as not to distract or embarrass the patient when intimate material is being revealed.

and often displayed considerable emotion. Moreover, they seemed to feel better when they awakened.

Freud was impressed with the method, and he began to use the same technique. No suggestions were given. The hypnotic state was used merely to allow the person to ventilate his or her problems. Because of the emotion released during the session, the method was called *catharsis*.

Freud developed the method into a long-term treatment that may last for two or three years, with meetings from three to five times a week. The basic technique used in psycho-analysis is *free association*. The person being treated is asked to relax comfortably on a couch and to say whatever comes to mind. The patient is encouraged to speak freely and to continue whether or not what is said makes sense, is "proper," or is painful to talk about. The person is told that all thoughts and feelings are important to the treatment process.

Through the analysis of material produced by means of free association, the therapist begins to get clues about the possible underlying causes of the personality difficulty. The type of material produced through free association varies with the individual. Rigid personalities are likely to produce relatively controlled material, particularly in the early phases of therapy. More flexible personalities produce a wide range of varied, and often chaotic, material.

The analysis of dreams is another technique used in Freudian psychoanalysis. The therapist encourages people in treatment to keep a record of their dreams and to bring them to therapy sessions for discussion and analysis. Through the analysis of the dreams, the therapist is able to explain symbolic behavior and to redirect unacceptable impulses. Ordinarily, the person describes the dream as it is remembered, and the therapist

Free Association: The Basic Technique of Depth Therapy

The following childhood memories are typical of the free flow of images and ideas expressed during psychoanalysis and other forms of therapy in which unconscious material is brought into consciousness. The person undergoing treatment is usually reclining comfortably on a couch in a quiet room with subdued lighting. The therapist is seated unobtrusively nearby, listening carefully and recording what is being said.

I can see myself as a little girl—sort of a visual image—standing between Father and Mother. I am thinking "Which one will like me?" Mother is looking at Father, very upset; she's all taken up with his flirtation. Father is looking away, watching the New York girl sitting on the beach. This whole thing is at the beach, and the same beach where I played in the sand when Mother almost drowned. Father and Mother are both completely taken up and neither notices me. The whole thing is so vivid that I can see it, but I don't know if it's a real memory. I think I just concocted it out of different scraps of memory. The New York woman is like a snake in the garden of Eden. If I attract her and make her like me, that would make me feel satisfied. Father would be real mad and Mother would too. You know, while I'm telling you this, I can actually see it going on, sort of like a movie; I can actually see my mother's face getting angrier and angrier. The reason why Mother gets so angry about it is that if I take the New York woman away from Father, he will come back to Mother and become more threatening to her. He will do something terrible to Mother if I take Mother's rival away. I never thought of that before. I wonder if that has something to do with my sex problem. (Janis, p. 67, 1958)

then asks for spontaneous associations. In this way, the therapist is able gradually to discover the hidden meaning of the dream.

While the psychoanalyst engages in a certain amount of explanation and interpretation, he or she attempts to remain objective and impersonal. By encouraging free association, the psychoanalyst attempts to explore the unconscious mind of the person being treated. Through the reliving of childhood experiences, and with the assistance of the therapist, the person's mental and emotional life is reorganized in a more positive and constructive way.

In psychoanalytic therapy, the patient may become emotionally attached to the therapist, and there may be a reenactment of the child-parent relationship. The therapist uses this relationship to illustrate unconscious fantasies and resistances, and in this way the person being treated becomes aware of the existence of infantile attitudes. The therapist tracks down early identifications and shows the person how these early experiences have affected his or her emotional life. The assumption is that a cure is effected when the emotional attachment to the therapist is understood and accepted, when dream content has changed, and when past significant experiences have been remembered.

Psychoanalytically oriented therapy   In this variation of depth therapy, the techniques and theories of psychoanalysis are used to varying degrees, but wide differences are seen from therapist to therapist. The therapy may last from several sessions to several hundred, with meetings one to three times each week. Dream material is used, and the therapist may call for projective psychological tests. The therapeutic sessions deal with present situations and relationships and utilize unconscious material only when the progress of therapy seems to require it. The face-to-face interview is used in most instances, although the couch may be used at times. The psychoanalytically oriented therapist may take advantage of such treatment adjuncts as play therapy, art therapy, group therapy, and hypnosis.

Non-Freudian depth therapy This approach is similar in many ways to orthodox psychoanalysis, but with some modification. The treatment sessions may go on two to four times a week for two or more years. The couch is used sometimes, but more frequently the therapy is conducted by means of a face-to-face interview. Also, the therapeutic sessions are more likely to be focused on current situations, interpersonal relationships, and other sources of conflict. Free association is used to some degree but not exclusively. The attitude of the therapist may range from nondirectiveness to a moderate degree of directiveness.

Other Treatment Approaches

The classification of psychotherapy into therapeutic counseling and depth therapy does not reflect the wide range of treatment techniques and theories developed by psychotherapists. These techniques range from simple to complex, naive to sophisticated, and reasonable to irrational. In most cases they involve a combination of approaches. Some of the newer types of psychotherapy combine behavior therapy with the more traditional methods of psychological treatment. Each of these forms of psychotherapy was developed out of the theories and experiences of the clinician with whom the particular method is associated. While successful treatment has been reported for all these approaches, the successes may be due more to the personalities of the therapists, or to the expectations of the person being treated, than to the special nature of the treatment technique involved.

Figure 17.2 The progressive improvement during psychological treatment is sometimes reflected in the art productions of the person being treated. In this series of drawings, William Tell is shown with his son. The first drawing, made during the most serious phase of the disturbance, shows the boy almost completely swallowed up in the father's leg. The successive pictures indicate a gradual return to reality.

(a)

(b)

(c)

(d)

(a)

(b)

(c)

(d)

Some Concerns and Confusions

One of the most difficult problems related to psychotherapy is the loose way in which the term has been defined. Another problem has to do with the vagueness of the techniques used in treatment. Finally, there is the difficult problem of measuring the results of psychotherapy. One psychologist said: "Psychotherapy is an undefined technique applied to unspecified problems with unpredictable outcomes" (Raimy, 1950).

Psychotherapy frequently means one thing to one therapist and quite something else to another. Even psychotherapists trained in the same technique vary widely in their application of the method. Moreover, psychotherapy ordinarily involves an extended period of time during which most of the person's continuing life experiences are unrelated to the treatment. For these reasons, the factors responsible for any changes in personality usually remain obscure.

Behavior Therapy: The Learning Approach

Although many forms of psychotherapy based upon the attainment of insight continue to be used, psychoanalytic and related depth therapies have lost much of their earlier popularity. Such factors as cost, time involved, and difficulties in evaluating personality change have contributed to a continuing search for alternative treatment techniques. The most recent emphasis in psy-

Varieties of Psychotherapy

Reality therapy

Assumes that people make a conscious or unconscious decision to behave in a maladaptive manner. Treatment is directed toward showing which decisions have been made, what alternative choices could be made, and how these new decisions could result in improved behavior (Glasser, 1965).

Gestalt therapy

Emphasizes the wholeness of the personality. Attempts to deal with the here and now. Holds that people are alone responsible for their behavior. Considered to be a means of personal growth helpful to all people, not only to those who are disturbed (Perls, 1976).

Logotherapy

Focuses on the search for meaning in life. Seeks to help people find reasons for what has happened to them. Encourages persons to grow through experiences rather than be defeated by them. An existentialist therapy (Frankl, 1955; 1962).

Primal therapy

Holds that people with personality problems have separated themselves from their primal needs in order to avoid psychological pain. Seeks to help the person to relive the core (primal) experiences assumed to be the cause of the difficulties (Janov, 1970).

Rational-emotive therapy

Seeks to uncover irrational assumptions, mistaken beliefs, and misinterpretations of events and goals that are assumed to cause abnormal behavior. Helps the person to strengthen feelings of self-worth and independence. Emphasizes importance of self-choice (Ellis, 1974).

Note: The names and dates in parentheses indicate the person most closely associated with the technique and the publication date of an important book by that person.

Figure 17.3 Among the psychotherapists who have developed specialized treatment techniques are (a) Arthur Janov, who is identified with primal therapy, (b) Viktor Frankl, who is known for his work with existential therapy, (c) William Glasser, who is associated with reality therapy, and (d) Albert Ellis, who developed rational-emotive therapy.

chological treatment is based on the learning model of maladaptive behavior (see Chapter 4).

The term *behavioral therapy*, first used in the 1950s (Skinner & Lindsley, 1953), refers to those methods of psychological treatment

Figure 17.4 B. F. Skinner (1904–). The application of the principles of operant conditioning to the modification of maladaptive behavior has been one of this century's most dramatic developments in psychological treatment. The work of Skinner and others who favor behavioral therapy has been one of the important reasons for the continuing decline of psychoanalysis.

constructs is replaced by a precise description of stimulus conditions, reward and punishment schedules, and response behaviors. It is a technological approach that is uncontaminated by obscure interpersonal factors which make it impossible to know what has been responsible for any change in behavior that might have taken place. The fundamental principles of behavioral therapy include detailed observation, specification of treatment roles, objective measures of outcome, and relevance to the patient's real-life situation (Thurrell & Marshall, 1974).

Another advantage of the behavioral approach is that the method can be taught to nurses, psychiatric aides, and paraprofessional staff members. At one hospital, student nurses were trained in the use of behavioral therapy to treat schizophrenic patients who had been mute from eleven to forty-two years. More than one-third of these patients showed improved speech after fifteen sessions. About 80 percent of the improved group had substantially retained their reacquisition of speech one year later (Cliffe, 1974).

Behavioral Reinforcement

The effectiveness of reinforcement in learning was first demonstrated scientifically early in this century. However, the use of behavioral reinforcement as a treatment technique, although demonstrated in psychological laboratories many years ago, did not develop significantly until Skinner and his associates showed that it is possible to alter a person's behavior in the direction of more normal actions by means of carefully selected rewards and schedules of reinforcement. Clinical improvement is indicated by the increase in the number of favorable responses over a period of time.

which make deliberate use of learning theory and techniques to bring about a modification of the person's behavior. Major emphasis is placed on getting rid of disturbing symptoms and constructing positive behavioral repertoires rather than on achieving insight.

One of the major advantages of the behavioral approach is that it is based on operational definitions. The vagueness of such concepts as *insight, ego strength, identity, self-awareness,* and similar hypothetical

In an experiment with autistic children, the youngsters learned to manipulate various devices. The first was a simple electrical switch; for operating it, the child was rewarded with food. Gradually more complex performances were built up with such reinforcers as candy, music, the opportunity to play a pinball machine, and permission to look through a picture viewer. In a later phase of the experiment, coins were used as reinforcers, and the children could use the coins to operate devices which presented cartoons; to get a trained animal to perform; to play with an electric organ, a motor-driven rocking horse, an electric train, and a television set; and even to obtain a life jacket and to go swimming. The children eventually learned to save the coins and use them only when certain stimuli indicated that the coins would be effective in "purchasing" one of the rewards. While the children exhibited essentially normal behavior for periods of several hours, they remained autistic outside the controlled environment of the laboratory (Ferster, 1961).

Reward and reinforcement have also been used successfully in the treatment of anorexia nervosa, a condition in which the person affected refuses to eat. Eleven girls and women, aged 13 to 21 years, were admitted to a hospital because of this disorder. They participated in a behavior modification program in which each girl was asked to draw up a hierarchy of seven suitable rewards of her choosing. These rewards included being allowed to receive letters, newspapers, and flowers. The most desirable reward in all instances was permission to have visitors. The order of reward attainment was the reverse of reward preference. That is, the least desired reward was given first. The first reward was given after the patients had eaten eight consecutive meals, each consumed within sixty minutes of the time it was presented. When this goal had been achieved, the patient received her first reward. The requirements became progressively more difficult. The time for each of the eight consecutive meals was reduced in five-minute steps. The meals were not supervised, but the patient rang a bell to tell the nursing staff she had finished. The patient was kept aware of the time spent eating, the target time, and the next reward by means of a chart in the room. Satisfactory weight gains resulted in about 88 percent of the cases while the method was being used. It was also observed, however, that the operant conditioning technique was often inadequate for long-term maintenance of normal eating habits and weight, and that the behavior modification methods are best used as a means of rapid weight restoration in times of a nutritional crisis (Bhanji & Thompson, 1974).

The "token economy"   The demonstrated effectiveness of rewards for improved behavior led to the rapid development in the late 1960s of the *token economy* as a method of treating groups of patients in the wards of mental hospitals (Ayllon & Azrin, 1968). In this type of behavior therapy, those patients who show positive and desirable types of behavior are rewarded with tokens which can be used to obtain special food, cigarettes, magazines or newspapers, or special privileges such as television viewing or single-room accommodations. When positive behavior is rewarded, this type of behavior tends to occur more frequently than when it is not rewarded.

A mental hospital in England established a token economy ward in which the basic token was a red plastic disc about an inch in diameter. This token had a value of 1. In

Figure 17.5 A token economy is one in which people are rewarded for substituting acceptable behavior for maladaptive behavior. The rewards are usually in the form of tokens that can be exchanged for special privileges, personal services, food and beverages, or store items. This behavior modification technique has been most effective in improving the behavior of people in institutions.

addition, tokens of values of 5 and 10 were also available. Each patient received a free issue of forty-five tokens a day, from which nine tokens had to be paid for meals and for a single-room accommodation. The remaining tokens could be spent in a ward shop at the rate of one token for one penny. The shop carried cigarettes and tobacco, candy, fruit drinks, magazines, items of clothing, and

other goods. It was found that patients improved in several areas. They dressed better, showed more initiative, and displayed fewer signs of withdrawal and thought disorder (Baker, Hall, & Hutchinson, 1974).

Aversive control While most behavioral reinforcement involves rewards for the occurrence of preferred behavior, there are some situations in which undesirable behavior is punished. The most common behavior therapy technique of this type is *aversive control*, in which electric shock or some other punishment is used as the stimulus to modify behavior. The principles of aversive conditioning can be found in the customs of the distant past. For example, in ancient Rome, an alcoholic might be forced to drink from a wine goblet containing an eel. This procedure was designed to create a revulsion on the part of the drunkard, with the hope that the experience would be so repulsive that the person's drinking would be reduced.

An example of aversive control is the treatment of chronic alcoholism with the drug Antabuse. A strong and unpleasant physical reaction occurs in anyone who drinks alcoholic beverages after taking the drug. There is a flushed feeling in the face, increased pulse rate, difficulty in breathing, and a splitting headache. The drug is eliminated slowly; as long as it is in the body, a drink of alcohol brings on the typical reaction. Antabuse therapy, which is a form of continuous conditioning, is based on the fact that the drug increases the conversion of ethyl alcohol to acetaldehyde, with the increase of this otherwise normal metabolite causing the discomforting symptoms.

Most of the work with aversive conditioning has been directed toward the treatment of sexual deviance. For example, a program was developed in a correctional institution for the treatment of child molesters. Simple conditioning techniques were used during which an inmate received a shock on his thigh whenever a slide of a naked child was flashed on a screen. When photographs of adults were shown, no shock was given. Later the treatment program was broadened, and the inmates were taught to associate objects or thoughts they feared with pictures and thoughts of children. At the same time, they were taught to associate pleasurable thoughts with pictures and thoughts of adults. One inmate who was imprisoned on four occasions for molesting children commented on his experience by saying:

> I used to have dreams and nightmares about children I molested. Now I don't have them anymore—I couldn't have them anymore—I couldn't have them if I tried. Children are not sexual objects to me anymore. I want to lead a normal life and go back to my wife and son. I'm tired of jail. I was skeptical about the shock treatments and a little scared of it—you hear so much about shock treatments in mental hospitals. But it's not like I found out. It doesn't hurt, but I hate it.

Aversive control techniques have also been used successfully with homosexuals who want to change their sexual orientation. One study found that homosexual responses could be suppressed by avoidance conditioning. This program treating male homosexuals required each subject to bring in his own pictures for the conditioning treatment. The pictures included past homosexual partners, lovers, and fantasy objects. The female pictures included women with whom the patient was acquainted and—when possible—liked.

Each subject was seated alone in a darkened, soundproof room facing a projection screen, with a response key at his side. He was observed by the conditioning technician through a one-way mirror from an adjacent room. Any comments made by the patient could be heard through an intercom system. Each trial began with a male picture being flashed on the screen. When the male picture appeared, the patient had a short time, varying from two to fifteen seconds, during which he could avoid shock by pressing a response key. When he failed to respond, he

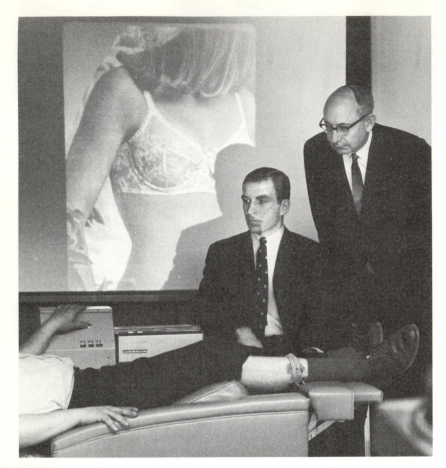

Figure 17.6 The man with the electrode strapped to his leg is being treated by the behavioral technique of aversive control. The electrode gives him an unpleasant electric shock each time a forbidden picture is flashed on the screen. The shock continues until he presses a button to change the picture to an acceptable one. A man being treated for homosexuality would receive a punishing shock while looking at the picture of an attractive male but would be permitted to look at the female body without being punished. The assumption of aversive treatment is that the subject will gradually learn to avoid a maladaptive pattern of behavior and to prefer a more desirable and acceptable one.

received a shock during the last one to three seconds the male picture was on the screen. If the subject responded promptly, his response terminated the male picture and allowed him to avoid the shock he would otherwise have received. The response also produced a half-second exposure to a picture of an attractive female. In order to keep the female on the screen, the subject had to continue actively pressing the key at a rate greater than two per second. Suppression of homosexual responses was achieved in five of the eight men who were treated. Two of the eight shifted from homosexuality to heterosexuality during the treatment, with the change enduring over a follow-up period of $3^{1}/_{2}$ years (Birk et al., 1971).

In spite of the numerous case studies indicating that long-standing deviant behavior has been radically altered after a relatively short period of aversive therapy, the effectiveness of aversive control has been challenged because of the lack of carefully controlled studies (Serber & Wolpe, 1972). Even

Aversive Control: An Ethical Problem

The use of aversive control has become a controversial issue in behavior therapy. Since painful stimuli are used, there is the ever-present danger that aversive procedures might be used as punishment rather than treatment. The criticism is very much the same as that raised against the use of electroshock therapy and psychosurgery. Various measures have been taken to ensure the rights of people in mental hospitals, schools for the retarded, and correctional institutions. However, some behavioral therapists believe that the opposition to aversive conditioning techniques has gone too far. These psychologists and psychiatrists feel that there has been an overreaction to the potential dangers—which they do not deny—of aversive control, and that this exaggerated reaction has unfortunately denied many people the right to an effective treatment approach.

more serious has been the growing concern over ethical issues involved in the use of aversive methods.

Desensitization Therapy

This type of psychological treatment involves a variety of methods designed to increase the subject's ability to tolerate an anxiety-provoking situation. There are various kinds of desensitization techniques. At one extreme, a person in a state of deep muscular relaxation may be exposed, gradually and systematically, to situations which arouse anxiety. At the other extreme, the subject may be exposed to a sudden flooding with overwhelming amounts of anxiety. In some desensitization treatments, the anxiety-provoking situations to which the person is exposed are real-life events; in other forms of treatment, the stressful events are imagined by the person undergoing therapy. In all cases, the object of the treatment is

to build up the capacity to handle fear and anxiety.

Systematic desensitization In this method of desensitization, a person is progressively taught to reduce levels of anxiety related to an anxiety-provoking situation. Each step in the sequence is accompanied by a lowering of anxiety through this step-by-step process. The person finally reaches a point where anxiety for a particular object or situation is significantly decreased or eliminated.

A woman with a twenty-six-year history of a pathological fear of chlorine bleach was treated successfully through a nine-hour program of desensitization. The woman said that the fear began at a party when her brother came into the room carrying a glass of chlorine bleach and said jokingly, "We could drink this bleach if the liquor runs out." Over the years the fear of bleach became excessive. She said that she was afraid of the foot of her bed because she had put a dress there on which she had wiped her hand after touching a glass held by a family friend whom she had seen reach across a bottle of bleach to pick up a towel. Her fears became so severe that she was unable to leave home because she was afraid of coming into contact with bleach, seeing it, or being in a place where it was used or stored. The phobia led to compulsive hand washing whenever she was reminded of bleach by seeing television commercials concerning bleach or seeing white spots which reminded her of things that were bleached. During the year prior to treatment, she washed her hands an average of fifty times a day.

During the treatment, the woman was helped to make up a list of twenty-eight items related to her fear. These items ranged from driving past a swimming pool where chlorine was used to having bleach spilled on her hands. At the beginning of the treatment the patient was asked to imagine herself in each situation, starting with the one that was least anxiety-provoking. If she did not show anxiety in twenty seconds, the next situation was presented. After a few sessions, the woman was able to imagine all the situations without anxiety. At that time, she moved from imaginary to real situations, and a similar program of systematic desensitization was followed until her phobia was overcome (Deiker & Pollock, 1975).

When the method of systematic desensitization was introduced, it was explained in terms of *reciprocal inhibition*, or an assumed incompatibility between the relaxed state and the autonomic nervous system responses aroused by the anxiety-provoking situations to which the person is exposed. However, it is also possible to explain systematic desensitization in terms of counterconditioning, extinction, and habituation.

Flooding   In this method of desensitization, the person being treated is exposed immediately to the most anxiety-provoking situation. There is no gradual introduction to less stressful situations as is the case in systematic desensitization. The flooding technique is one in which the person is encouraged to go into the frightening situation and remain there, regardless of how much anxiety is generated, until a spontaneous decrease in anxiety takes place. The subjects are instructed not to attempt any physical or mental avoidance, but to concentrate on their surroundings, bodily feelings, and experiences. The purpose of flooding is to show the person being treated that peak anxiety does not last very long and can be tolerated.

Common to all flooding, or exposure techniques, is the assumption that if the subject nfronted with the distressing situations, he or she will eventually get used to them, and the distress will be diminished or alleviated. Flooding can be done through the person's imagery, through presentations by audiotape or videotape, or by way of real-life situations. The flooding may last for a few moments or for hours, and the person in treatment may be allowed to escape from it or forced to endure it. In any event, and however produced or programmed, flooding is a form of treatment that produces intense emotional reactions.

Behavior Modeling

Modeling is a behavior therapy technique in which one's behavior is modified as a result of observing the behavior of other people or one's own behavior. Sometimes the therapist demonstrates the desired behavior while the person being treated observes how the therapist handles the situation. Later, that person attempts to behave in a similar way. In other cases, people observe their own behavior by means of film or videotape and are encouraged to make constructive changes that will improve personal adjustment.

The effectiveness of modeling as a means of modifying behavior is well known. Children learn new ways of behaving by imitating their parents, companions, teachers, television actors and actresses, and other people they frequently see. A very substantial part of each person's behavioral repertoire is due to this type of social learning.

The importance of modeling is well established in connection with the development of aggressive behavior. It is not unusual for the children of aggressive parents to show aggressive tendencies. Studies of parents who abuse their children have found that such parents frequently were subjected to abuse during their own childhoods.

The effectiveness of modeling as a treatment technique was demonstrated more than a half-century ago when a psychologist was successful in eliminating the fear of animals by having children observe other children play with the animals in a pleasurable manner (Jones, 1924). This classic study led to more recent investigations of modeling as a means of treating childhood fears. In one study, 67 percent of a group of nursery school children, who observed a "fearless" 4-year-old play with a dog, became willing to remain alone in a room in a playpen with the dog. Only 33 percent of a control group of children not exposed to the modeling treatment were willing to remain alone with the dog (Bandura, Grusec, & Menlove, 1967).

Modeling has also been used to teach mute schizophrenic children to speak (Hingtgen, Coulter, & Churchill, 1967), to pay attention to personal hygiene (Lovaas et al., 1967), to eliminate aggressive responses (Kazdin, 1973), and to form and strengthen a wide range of adaptive social behaviors (Eisler et al., 1973).

One of the most recent uses of modeling has been in the treatment of sexual disturbances. By means of films or live models depicting explicit sexual behavior, the person with the sexual problem is instructed in practical techniques designed to overcome the difficulty.

Behavioral Rehearsal

Even though the person with psychological problems has been exposed to such behavior modification techniques as modeling, conditioning, and desensitization, the newly learned behaviors must be practiced and rehearsed. This rehearsal ordinarily occurs without conscious awareness in everyday social situations where the actions of other people are imitated or attitudes are adopted.

In behavior therapy, however, the troubled person is encouraged to deliberately rehearse the behaviors learned during the treatment sessions.

Assertiveness training This type of behavior rehearsal is designed for use with shy and

Some Sample Encounters in Assertiveness Training

1 *Narrator*: "You're in a crowded grocery store and in a hurry. You pick one small item and get in line to pay for it. You're really trying to hurry because you're already late for an appointment. Then, a woman with a shopping cart full of groceries cuts in line in front of you." *Woman*: "You don't mind if I cut in here do you? I'm in a hurry."

2 *Narrator*: "You go to a ballgame with a reserved seat ticket. When you arrive you find that a woman has put her coat in the seat for which you have a reserved ticket. You ask her to remove her coat, and she tells you that she is saving that seat for a friend." *Woman*: "I'm sorry, this seat is saved."

3 *Narrator*: "You're in a restaurant with some friends. You order a steak, very rare. The waitress comes over to your table and serves you a steak which is so well done it looks burned. You really like your steak rare." *Waitress*: "I hope you enjoy your dinner, sir."

4 *Narrator*: "You take your car to a service station to have a grease job and the oil changed. The mechanic tells you that your car will be ready in an hour. When you return to the station you find that in addition to the oil change and grease job, they have given your car a major tune up." *Cashier*: "You owe us $215. Will that be cash or charge, sir?"

5 *Narrator*: "You are having lunch with a friend when suddenly she asks you if you would lend her thirty dollars until she gets paid next week. You have the money, but were planning on spending it on something else. *Friend*: "Please lend me the money; I'll pay you back next week."

From the Behavioral Assertiveness Test (Eisler, Miller, & Hersen); see Hersen et al., 1973.

passive people who are easily dominated by others. Using the principles of modeling, behavioral rehearsal, and successive approximations, progressive learning of more assertive behavior is possible.

Assertive behavior can be taught through the presentation of situations to which the person must respond in his or her usual way. The situations may be in the form of cartoons and other pictures, films and videotapes, or live encounters. In the modeling type of assertiveness training, the person is presented with a videotaped or live session in which someone acts out the situation and responds in an assertive manner. Later, the person being treated is required to respond in the same way to the same situation.

One study of assertiveness training of psychiatric patients made use of a series of interpersonal encounters designed to simulate real-life situations. Those in the training sessions were presented with the encounter situations and their responses were videotaped. On the basis of these tapes, judgments could be made as to degree of assertiveness in terms of such measures as the length of time the patient looked at the person who presented the material, the length of time the patient spoke in reply, the loudness of the subject's speech for each session, and overall assertiveness. It was found that unassertive psychiatric patients became more assertive following the training sessions involving videotape modeling (Hersen et al., 1973).

Biofeedback As Behavioral Therapy

Recent developments in the field of biofeedback have important implications for the treatment of a variety of psychological disturbances. In Chapter 9 we saw that *biofeedback* refers to the learned control of psychophysiologic processes such as those

influencing brain waves, heart action, blood pressure, body temperature, and other organic functions. This control is possible when information about a physiologic function is fed back to the person in such a way that the activity can be continuously monitored. The person can then learn to modify the function in desired directions. The fact that the precise way in which these changes are brought about remains obscure does not detract from the exciting treatment possibilities of this new approach.

As might be expected, the most dramatic successes with biofeedback therapy have been in connection with psychophysiologic disorders. These conditions involve a subtle and not clearly understood combination of psychological influences and physiologic processes. Among the conditions which have responded favorably to biofeedback therapy are disturbances of heart action, tension headache, and epileptic seizures.

In the treatment of rapid heart action by means of biofeedback, the subject is told to watch the graphic record of heart action on a television screen and to attempt to slow the rate of the lines. When auditory feedback is used, the person being treated listens to clicks or other sounds corresponding to the beat of the heart and is asked to try to slow the frequency of the sound. The intriguing aspect of the treatment is that most people can learn to control their heart action even though the mechanism of this learning is unclear (Schwartz, 1975).

The use of biofeedback to treat tension headache is an example of how the control of muscular activity can be effective as a form of therapy. In one study, people with tension headache were given auditory feedback from the muscles of the forehead by means of electrodes taped to the head. One control group received false feedback from another person, and another control group received no treatment.

Members of the headache and control groups participated in sixteen training sessions and a follow-up period of three months. The subjects receiving real feedback showed a marked decline in tension headache, and improvement continued throughout the follow-up period (Budzynski et al., 1973).

The effectiveness of biofeedback in the control of epileptic seizures was shown in a 19-year-old woman who had fifteen to twenty psychomotor seizures and one to two grand mal seizures every month. After $8\frac{1}{2}$ months of biofeedback training, the psychomotor seizures were completely eliminated, and there was, on the average, less than one relatively brief grand mal seizure per month (Lubar & Bahler, 1976). While not all people with epileptic seizures respond to biofeedback training in such a dramatic way, most are able to reduce the number or severity of their seizures.

Although biofeedback has demonstrated its effectiveness as a treatment technique in some conditions, the nature of the method requires a willingness to cooperate and to seek improvement. For this reason, the treatment is generally inappropriate for resistant people and those who are severely disturbed.

One of the advantages of biofeedback therapy is that it involves the subject actively in the treatment. It is not as if the therapist were doing something for the patient; the patient is actually doing something for himself or herself. Such an attitude is an extremely important one, particularly in people who are motivated. The approach is likely to be relatively ineffective in those who are not motivated. In spite of the very considerable interest in biofeedback training, a number of

Varieties of Behavioral Therapy

Behavioral self-control

This treatment method is one in which the person learns how to behave in desired ways in the face of environmental stimuli which foster maladaptive behavior. The early emphasis of the behavior therapy approach was upon external, or environmental, controls. Behavioral self-control, however, emphasizes internal, or cognitive, factors. The self-regulation of behavior is accomplished by means of self-observation, self-reward, covert self-control, and similar techniques (Thoresen & Mahoney, 1974).

Implosive therapy

This behavioral treatment combines psychodynamic concepts and the techniques of desensitization. The person being treated is exposed to increasingly higher levels of anxiety through direct contact with the problem situation, through suggested imagery, sexual conflict, and other psychodynamic cues assumed to be related to the problem (Stampfl & Levis, 1967).

Multimodal therapy

This treatment approach encompasses a broad spectrum that makes use of a variety of behavioral techniques. Systematic desensitization, aversive conditioning, modeling, assertiveness training, and behavior rehearsal are used to whatever extent considered necessary by the therapist (Lazarus, 1976).

Note: The names and dates in parentheses indicate the person most closely associated with the technique and the publication date of an important book by that person.

investigators remain skeptical as to its effectiveness in practical clinical situations. Others question the interpretations of the experimental findings (Lynch, Paskewitz, & Orne, 1974). While biofeedback experiments have served to suggest how the technique might eventually apply to clinical problems, a great many questions remain to be answered; much more clinical research needs to be undertaken before biofeedback can take its place alongside other forms of psychological treatment.

Group Therapy

Group therapy is a method of treatment in which a number of people are treated at one time or in which group dynamics are used in the treatment of one person. While new as a controlled method, group therapy is old in a more general sense. The technique has been used for centuries by religious leaders and philosophers. Ancient priest-physicians used group methods to control and lessen the anxiety of their followers. In these various instances, there was an intuitive realization of the importance of the group approach.

Today there are a number of different types of group therapy. Some of the earliest forms of group treatment involved small classes in mental hospitals, where staff members explained the principles of mental hygiene or gave inspirational talks. Later, group approaches were based upon psychodynamic theory and techniques. The most recent emphasis has been placed upon group experience as a means of self-discovery or as an opportunity to learn more effective patterns of adjustment. In fact, most therapeutic viewpoints can be carried out in a group context.

Encounter Groups and Self-Discovery
This highly controversial type of group therapeutic experience attained an almost cultish vogue by 1970. Referred to variously as T-groups (training groups), sensitivity

Figure 17.7 Touching and other forms of body contact are basic techniques used in some encounter groups. Being able to be physically close to other people is regarded as necessary to the release of one's full potential as a human being.

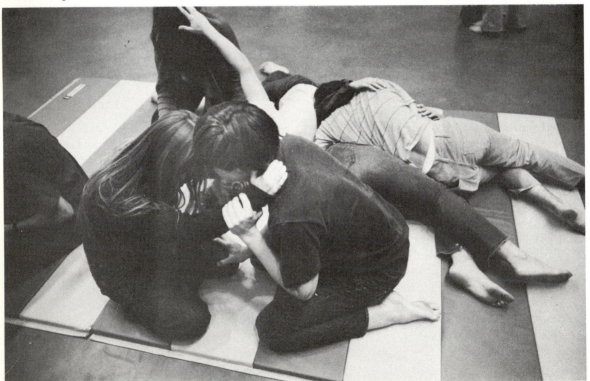

Figure 17.8 The two women standing in the center of this encounter group are demonstrating a technique of physical relaxation often used in the early stages of group therapy.

Figure 17.9 The nude encounter is one of a number of group techniques designed to help people discover themselves. The shedding of clothes is considered, by advocates of this method, to be an important step in getting rid of psychological barriers between people.

training, and leadership training, the essence of the group experience is the relatively intimate encounter, or close interaction with others, and the working out of personal and interpersonal problems with the assistance of a "trainer" or group leader and other members of the group.

Despite a persistent effort on the part of some advocates of the encounter group to divorce it from therapy, the group experience is unquestionably a therapeutic one. Herein lies its power and effectiveness, but here also is its greatest danger. In spite of the very considerable interest in encounter groups of all kinds, there has been a justifiable uneasiness over such groups on the part of some psychiatrists and psychologists. While many behavioral scientists find merit in the theory of the encounter group, the principal objections center on the all too frequent lack of qualifications of the trainers or group leaders, and the invasion of the rights of the participants.

As one critic put it in an editorial published by the American Psychiatric Association:

> Today we are witnessing a proliferation of sensitivity training programs aimed at persons in educational, industrial, and community settings. Variations of sensitivity programs have been established that purport to train community development leaders, promote international relations, secure labor-management harmony, increase marital happiness, and resolve other thorny problems via the T-group method of enhancing interpersonal communications. That so much has been promised by sensitivity training and so little delivered by means of evaluation and research findings suggests that psychiatrists should be increasingly aware and distressed about these programs.
>
> Of primary concern to psychiatrists, many of whom have seen the "casualties" of insensitive sensitivity training programs and "trainers," should be the outright invasion of individual privacy such programs tend to promote. Sensitivity training appears to have been so effectively oversold to an unaware public, clamoring for psychiatric and psychological insights, that it is not uncommon for teachers, business representatives, high government officials, and others to be required, as a function of their jobs, to participate in these sessions. As a consequence, these participants involuntarily and unknowingly may be subjected to personal onslaught in a pseudo-psychotherapeutic situation characterized by inappropriate transferences and unrelenting group pressures to "reveal themselves," while unprotected by the ethical safeguards which are inherent in a professional therapeutic encounter. For some participants the results have been traumatic indeed! (English, 1969).

A study of encounter groups at Stanford University used professional group leaders with more than 200 people in 18 groups. Ten different encounter techniques, including basic encounter groups, T-groups, gestalt groups, transactional analysis groups, and marathon groups were used in the study (Lieberman, Yalom, & Miles, 1972; 1973). Changes in the personality and behavior of group members were measured by self-rating questionnaires, ratings by group leaders, and ratings by friends of each participant.

The self-ratings made immediately following the group sessions showed that 57 percent of those who took part in the groups felt that the experience had been a positive, or helpful, one. However, 14 percent reported that the experience had been negative, or damaging, in some way. The other 29 percent were neutral. Six months later, these same people rated their feelings again. The number who gave a negative report increased to 21 percent while those who reported positive feelings dropped to 46 percent.

The ratings by group leaders following the sessions indicated that they felt that 33 percent of the participants showed a substantial benefit, 40 percent showed some benefit, and 27 percent showed no change. Ratings by friends of the people who took part

Varieties of Group Therapy

Group therapy takes many forms. There are differences in objectives, theories, and techniques. Some groups are inspirational; others seek to promote insight, to release unconscious impulses, to facilitate self-discovery, or to teach social skills.

EST (Erhard Seminars Training) Therapy

An assertiveness-training technique in which as many as several hundred people meet, usually in a hotel ballroom, on two consecutive weekends. The participants stand, sit on hard chairs, or lie on the floor for sixty hours while experiencing the EST "message" that people are the cause of their own behavior. The sessions are led by a trainer who uses confrontation, role playing, and enforced concentration (Hargrove, 1976).

Family therapy

Emphasizes that the problems of the individual are rooted in family interaction. Treatment involves meeting with family members as a group. Most effective when family ties and loyalties are strong (Ackerman, 1958; Satir, 1967).

Psychodrama

Treatment by means of role playing in which the therapist, assistants, person being treated, and observers participate in the spontaneous acting out of problem situations related to the troubled person's life (Moreno, 1946).

Resocialization

A name given to a large number of techniques designed to improve personal adjustment through the learning of new social skills in everyday living. Emphasis is on social learning in real life rather than in contrived or simulated situations. The approach can be effective with people who are seclusive, withdrawn, and socially isolated.

Transactional analysis

Therapy based on the assumption that the person's life is programmed by "life scripts," or plans based on childish illusions and ways of acting. Each person plays three roles: parent, adult, and child. Interpersonal transactions are analyzed in terms of which of the three is talking (Berne, 1973).

Note: The names and dates in parentheses indicate the person most closely associated with the technique and the publication date of an important book by that person.

---

in the group encounters showed that they could see no difference in the personality or behavior of those who had the group experience and control subjects who did not have it.

The study also revealed that 10 percent of the participants were psychologically damaged by the group experience. One woman dropped out of her group and sought emergency psychiatric help after the third meeting, in which she was called a "fat Italian mama with a big shiny nose."

Another study has shown that while encounter groups do increase a person's capacity for intimate contact and bring about changes in self-perception, the effects are not carried over to the world outside the group. The changes in self-perception resulting from the group experience quickly dissipated when the experience was over (Marks & Vestre, 1974).

The group encounter movement remains an important force in the United States. Since there is a universal desire for instant revelation and shortcuts to personal success, thousands of men and women continue to seek some sort of salvation through group encounters. Fortunately, there has been a tendency to be selective in terms of group members, and a demand for more competent group leaders has arisen. Nevertheless, there is considerable question as to whether the successful experiences of some group participants are the result of what is actually happening in the group or merely a self-induced reaction to expectations.

The Chapter in Review

Psychological treatment is a method of influencing behavior by nonmedical means. Techniques have been developed to treat individuals and groups. The two major approaches to psychological treatment are insight therapy and behavioral therapy.

1 Insight Therapy
Individual psychotherapy assumes that effective treatment requires insight, or understanding, on the part of the person being treated. In therapeutic counseling, the therapist attempts to elicit insight by giving explanations and recommendations or to help the person find his or her own explanations and solutions. Depth psychotherapy is designed to bring about insight through the uncovering of unconscious conflicts and motivations.

2 Behavioral Therapy
This type of psychological treatment is based upon the principles of learning. The therapist uses such techniques as behavioral reinforcement, desensitization, modeling, aversive control, and biofeedback to modify behavior disturbances. Behavioral therapy assumes that the critical problem is the maladaptive behavior itself, and that successful treatment is the modification of the behavior in desired directions.

3 Group Therapy
Group therapy developed to meet the increasing need to treat larger numbers of people. Most therapeutic groups make use of many of the same principles and methods used in insight therapy and behavioral therapy. Some of the specialized forms of group therapy are psychodrama, encounter groups, family therapy, and resocialization.

Recommended Readings

Psychotherapy

Bry, A. (Ed.) *Inside psychotherapy: Nine clinicians tell how they work and what they are trying to accomplish.* New York: New American Library, 1973. (Paperback.)

Calhoun, K. S., Adams, H. E., & Mitchell, K. M. (Eds.) *Innovative treatment methods in psychopathology.* New York: Wiley, 1974.

Fix, A. J., & Haffke, E. A. *Basic psychological therapies: Comparative effectiveness.* New York: Behavioral Publications, 1976.

Kiernan, T. *Shrinks, etc.: A consumer's guide to psychotherapies.* New York: Dial, 1974.

Kovel, J. *A guide to psychotherapy and psychoanalysis.* New York: Pantheon, 1976.

Suinn, R. M., & Weigel, R. G. (Eds.) *The innovative psychological therapies: Critical and creative contributions.* New York: Harper & Row, 1975.

Tennov, D. *Psychotherapy: The hazardous cure.* New York: Doubleday/Anchor, 1976. (Paperback.)

Behavioral Therapy

Brown, B. B. *New mind, new body: Biofeedback, new directions for the mind.* New York: Bantam, 1975. (Paperback.)

Fensterheim, H., & Baer, J. B. *Don't say yes when you want to say no.* New York: Dell, 1975. (Paperback.)

Kanfer, F. H., & Goldstein, A. P. (Eds.) *Helping people change: A textbook of methods.* New York: Pergamon, 1975.

Sansweet, S. J. *The punishment cure.* New York: Mason and Charter, 1976.

Group Therapy

Schur, E. M. *The awareness trap: Self-absorption instead of social change.* New York: Quadrangle, 1976.

Verny, T. R. *Inside groups: A practical guide to encounter groups and group therapy.* New York: McGraw-Hill, 1975.

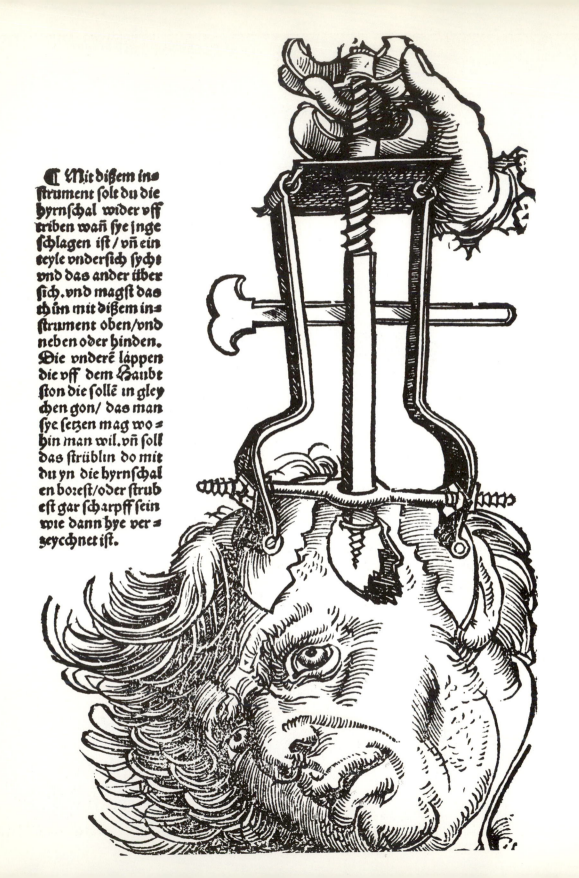

Mit dißem instrument solt du die hyrnschal wider vff triben wañ sye jnge schlagen ist / vñ ein teyle vndersich sycht vnd das ander über sich. vnd magst das thůn mit dißem instrument oben/vnd neben oder hinden. Die vnderē läppen die vff dem Haubt ston die sollē in gley chen gon/ das man sye setzen mag wo= hin man wil. vñ soll das strüblin do mit du yn die hyrnschal en bozest/oder strub est gar scharpff sein wie dann hye ver= zeychnet ist.

18
Medical
Approach
to Treatment

Objectives

To indicate the general nature of the medical techniques used to treat abnormal behavior

To discuss tranquilizing drugs in the treatment of neurotic and psychotic disorders

To describe how antidepressant drugs are used to treat unipolar and bipolar depression

To show how shock therapy has been used to modify abnormal behavior

To discuss brain surgery as a means of bringing about changes in personality and behavior

To indicate some of the ethical issues involved in the use of drugs, shock treatment, and psychosurgery

The use of physical methods to treat abnormal behavior began many centuries ago. The medical literature of ancient Greece contains many references to *hellebore*, a drug obtained from a species of plants. In a letter to Hippocrates, Democritus wrote, "Helebore, when given to the sane, pours darkness over the mind; but for the insane, it is very profitable."

Surgery for mental disorder can also be traced to the Greeks and Romans. The head was sometimes opened to let out "vapors" and fluids thought to be responsible for disturbed behavior. In less advanced societies, the openings made in the skull were for the purpose of releasing demons and evil spirits.

The modern medical treatment of abnormal behavior has taken three major forms: drugging the brain, shocking the brain, and operating on the brain. The first approach is known as *pharmacotherapy*, the second as *shock therapy*, and the third as *psychosurgery*. In this chapter we will examine these approaches in terms of their origins, the techniques used, their relative effectiveness, and their present status as treatment measures.

Pharmacotherapy: Drugging the Brain

Although drugs have been used for centuries in the treatment of psychologically disturbed people, the use of modern psychoactive drugs did not begin until the 1950s. The first of these drugs were the tranquilizers, which soon became the most widely used of all medical treatments. In the 1960s, the major emphasis was on drugs for the control of depression. Today, there are dozens of psychoactive drugs designed to control a wide range of psychological symptoms.

The effectiveness of a psychoactive drug depends upon a number of factors. The nature of the chemical, the attitude and expectations of those taking the drugs, the setting in which the drugs are given, and similar factors are important in determining effectiveness. Even social class and economic status appear to have a bearing on the effectiveness of psychoactive drugs (Rickels et al., 1973).

The use of drugs to alter personality and behavior presents special problems. One problem has to do with self-medication. Millions of prescriptions for tranquilizing drugs are filled each year, mostly for people who are tense and anxious. Hundreds of thousands of other people with more serious psychological disturbances have been put on psychoactive drugs after being released from mental hospitals. The result has been the wide use and availability of psychotherapeutic drugs. It has also resulted in the abuse of these drugs by many people who fail to realize the complexity of drug action and the dangers of using these drugs in combination with other drugs and alcohol. Psychoactive drugs should be used only under medical supervision.

A quite different problem involves the ethical issue of giving drugs to people in mental hospitals for the convenience of the institution rather than to help the patient. This kind of abuse has occurred in some institutions where tranquilizing drugs have been used merely to keep patients quiet and under control. Medical and therapeutic considerations, in such cases, are secondary or completely lacking.

Drugs That Tranquilize

The tranquilizing drugs are among the most effective of those used in the treatment of mental disorder. Developed for the most part since 1950, these drugs are neither sedative

Figure 18.1 Among the mechanical devices developed in the 1800s for the treatment of mental disorder was one designed to hoist people into the air and swing them back and forth. The swaying motion was thought to have a calming effect on the emotions.

nor narcotic in the ordinary sense. In many cases they induce a detached serenity without loss of consciousness and without noticeable impairment of intellectual ability.

The introduction of tranquilizing drugs had an important impact on the treatment of emotional disturbances. Through the calming and relaxing effects of these drugs, disturbed people frequently become more cooperative and communicative. The need for more radical treatment is reduced; in psychiatric hospitals, mechanical restraints are seldom needed; and patients are likely to be more receptive to various other forms of individual and group therapy. Moreover, the tranquilizing drugs can be administered to an entire ward by one or two paraprofessional workers.

Tranquilizers that reduce anxiety It is believed today that anxiety is the most prevalent of all psychological symptoms. Many millions of people experience some degree of anxiety ranging from mild episodes to chronic and disabling neurosis. The traditional treatment for such conditions—until the tranquilizing drugs became available in the 1950s—was rest, relaxation, and sedative drugs. Some of these new drugs were able to reduce anxiety through their action on the autonomic nervous system; others acted as muscle relaxants. Some of the widely used drugs to reduce anxiety are meprobamate (Miltown), chlordiazepoxide (Librium), and diazepam (Valium). Dozens of other drugs are also used in the treatment of anxiety reactions.

Some Characteristic Effects of Tranquilizers That Reduce Anxiety (Chlordiazepoxide; Diazepam)

1 Usually, a slight decrease in psychomotor activity
2 In some people, an increase in psychomotor activity because of disinhibition
3 Slight decrease in arousal and excitement
4 Slight decrease in response to stimuli
5 Decrease in avoidance and escape responses
6 Increase in active approach behavior
7 Sometimes, unmasking of hostility
8 Overall reduction in anxiety

These drugs have a calming and relaxing effect, but one of a lesser degree than that produced by the major tranquilizers. These drugs do not cause the motor symptoms characteristic of the more potent tranquilizers, and side reactions are relatively infrequent and easily controlled. Some of the anxiety-reducing tranquilizers tend to be habit forming. Drugs in this group are more effective in the treatment of neurotic persons than in that of disturbed psychotics.

Tranquilizers that control psychotic behavior While the anxiety reducing tranquilizers have been of enormous benefit to millions of people who have been treated by physicians in general practice and psychiatrists working at the community level, the drugs that control psychotic symptoms have had an equally dramatic effect upon patients in mental hospitals. In fact, the discovery of these powerful tranquilizers was primarily responsible for the start of the decline of the public mental hospital population which began in 1955 and has continued to the present time.

The major tranquilizer that controls psychotic behavior is chlorpromazine (Thorazine). The drug is of historical importance because it was the first tranquilizer to be developed. Discovered in the early 1950s, this tranquilizing drug set the stage for a decade of lively interest in the development of newer and more effective psychoactive drugs of all types.

Chlorpromazine was synthesized in France in 1952 during a search for a compound which would potentiate, or enhance, the effects of conventional anesthetic drugs. It was used first as a chemical treatment at the University of Paris to control agitation and excitement. The unique effects of the drug as a tranquilizer soon became apparent.

Figure 18.2 Dr. Jean Delay (1907–) of Paris was a pioneer in the use of tranquilizing drugs as a method of treatment for mental disorder. Chlorpromazine, the first and most widely used tranquilizer for psychotics, was developed in France in the early 1950s.

Some Characteristic Effects of Tranquilizers That Control Psychotic Behavior (Chlorpromazine, Perphenazine, Fluphenazine, Haloperidol)

1 Decreased psychomotor activity
2 Decreased excitement and agitation
3 Decreased responses to provoking stimuli
4 Decreased operant responses of approach, avoidance, and escape
5 Decreased violence
6 Decreased vigilance and alertness
7 Decreased repetition, perseveration, and compulsive behavior

Although the exact way in which chlorpromazine and related drugs influence psychotic behavior is not known, these drugs have an effect on the metabolism of the chemicals involved in the transmission of nerve impulses in the brain. This finding is one more piece of evidence of the involvement of the brain amines in psychotic behavior and reinforces the possibility that the symptoms of schizophrenia and other psychotic conditions are due to a biochemical disturbance (see Chapters 12 and 13).

While small doses of chlorpromazine produce drowsiness and reduce motor activity, the person is easily aroused and is able to pay attention, follow instructions, and respond normally. Even when large doses are given, there is little evidence that the higher mental functions are impaired, as they are in the case of sedatives and central nervous system depressants. Clinical observation as well as psychological tests show relatively normal functioning of the brain as reflected by memory, judgment, information, and intelligence.

Drugs That Influence Mood
The dramatic results obtained with the tranquilizing drugs in the late 1950s were responsible for a sharp step-up in the investigation of other psychoactive drugs. Since the tranquilizers are not useful in cases of depression and since these conditions are widespread in the population, major research was turned in this direction. The result was the development of new antidepressant drugs and the further development of older drugs known to have antidepressant properties.

Treating unipolar depression Although sleep-producing drugs have been used for centuries to calm the excitement of people with mental disorders, the use of drugs to treat depression began less than fifty years ago. The first antidepressant drugs were those having a direct and stimulating effect on the central nervous system. These drugs were followed by a group of enzyme-inhibiting chemicals. The most recent development has been a class of drugs called *tricyclic antidepressants.*

Stimulating drugs Chemical stimulants have a brief and rapid influence on the central nervous system—an effect that may wear off in a matter of hours. Sometimes there is a letdown feeling following their use. Stimulants of this type tend to raise the blood pressure and reduce the appetite. Although they are relatively nontoxic, they are occasionally habit forming, and people sometimes develop a dependence upon them.

One of the first stimulants used as an antidepressant was *amphetamine sulfate* (Benzedrine). In 1935 this drug was found to be effective in the treatment of narcolepsy, a condition characterized by untimely and involuntary episodes of sleep. Further use of the drug indicated that it elevates the mood, lessens depression, and increases cheerfulness. In most people, there are decreased feelings of fatigue and a greater interest in work. People lose their shyness and gain self-confidence. In larger amounts, the drug leads to increased speech production, facetiousness, and uncontrollable laughter. The stream of mental activity is accelerated, and thought content is enriched. However, when the drug is withdrawn, there are likely to be symptoms of weakness, depression, gastrointestinal disturbances, and trembling.

In psychiatric treatment, the drug has been used for the relief of fatigue and for the treatment of apathetic neurotics and depressed psychotics. The drug is more successful in treating milder cases of depression than deep depression. It does not have therapeutic value in treating schizophrenics and in fact sometimes releases violent outbursts when given to such people.

Because of the stimulating effects of amphetamine sulfate, the drug has been used by students cramming for their examinations, by motorists and truck drivers on long trips, and by others who need to remain awake and full of energy. There was such a general abuse of the drug that it became necessary to place legal restrictions on its sale. Its addictive nature and undesirable side effects were so serious that the drug was replaced by other amphetamines. The amphetamine derivatives are also addictive and must be used in a carefully controlled manner.

Enzyme-inhibiting drugs These chemical antidepressants are called *MAO inhibitors* because they interfere with the action of the enzyme *monoamine oxidase* (MAO). While there may be a slight direct stimulating effect on the central nervous system, the action of the MAO inhibitors is quite slow, and some days or weeks may be required before the

Some Characteristic Effects of the Stimulating Drugs (Amphetamine, Methylphenidate)

1 Increased psychomotor activity
2 Increased excitement
3 Increased response to stimuli
4 Increased active modes of operant response (approach, avoidance, escape)
5 Increased alertness, vigilance, and wakefulness
6 Increased elation and euphoria
7 Increased instability and violence when taken in large doses

effects become apparent. The drugs have been used in cases of nonagitated depression, depression which has not responded to other forms of therapy, and some forms of schizophrenia with depressive features. The exact mode of action of the MAO inhibitors is unknown. The drugs appear to be related to the functions of the neurotransmitters such as serotonin, noradrenalin, and similar substances involved in the control of nerve impulses in the central nervous system.

The MAO inhibitors are rarely used today even though these drugs can be most effective in some cases of severe depression. The principal objection is to the toxic side effects of these drugs. Disturbances of liver function and high blood pressure crises involving severe headache, nausea, vomiting, and disturbed heart rate are risks that most psychiatrists have been unwilling to take with their patients.

Triple-action drugs The drugs in this chemical group, called *tricyclic antidepressants*, are the most widely used and most effective method for treating unipolar depression. Drugs of this type (*imipramine*, *amitriptyline*) were introduced in 1957 as a treatment for schizophrenia, but it was soon found that they were more effective in treating depression associated with the psychoses.

The trycyclic antidepressants are slow-acting drugs; it takes three to ten days or more before any improvement due to their use is seen. When improvement does occur, there is often a striking change in behavior as a result of the lifting of the depression. There are many cases, however, in which the depression is not lessened, and other forms of treatment must be tried.

This group of chemicals shares with other drug treatments the disadvantage of side effects in some people. Minor annoyances

---

Some Characteristic Effects of Tricyclic Antidepressants
(Imipramine; Amitriptyline; Doxepin)

1 A slight decrease in arousal and excitement
2 Looseness of thinking
3 Increased detachment
4 Decreased obsessive concern with self
5 Slightly decreased hostility
6 Slightly increased psychomotor activity

---

include dryness of the mouth, sweating, sensitivity to light, and constipation. More serious side effects may involve changes in cardiovascular functions.

Treating bipolar depression The attempt to treat bipolar depression, or manic-depressive psychosis, was limited until recently to emergency measures. While narcotic drugs were used successfully to control manic excitement, it was recognized that the treatment did not get at the real problem. At the same time, the depressive phases of this condition were peculiarly resistant to treatment even after the antidepressant drugs were discovered.

Not until the early 1950s was it discovered that the lithium salts could be used effectively in the treatment of manic excitement (Cade, 1951). It was believed at first that lithium was of no value in depression, but the concept of unipolar and bipolar depression had not been advanced. It is now generally recognized that lithium is useful in the treatment of both phases of the bipolar disorder. The drug is of relatively little value in treating unipolar depressive reactions to life stress.

One study found that all cases of bipolar depression having a prior history of manic excitement responded to lithium therapy.

When episodes of elation were not present in the history, 44 percent of the cases improved (Noyes et al., 1974). Many similar studies have indicated that lithium is superior to any other treatment for bipolar depression (Shopsin et al., 1975).

The precise way in which lithium exerts its therapeutic effect is not known. As a generalization, it appears that the drug influences mood by acting on the metabolism of the chemicals involved in the transmission of nerve impulses in the brain. However, since other antidepressant drugs also alter these chemicals, the question remains as to why lithium has a beneficial effect on bipolar depressions but not on other types of depression.

Shocking the Brain

Shock therapy is a specialized form of treatment in which deep comas, convulsions, or both are induced artificially. The therapeutic advantages of the method grow out of the metabolic, neuroelectrical, and biochemical changes associated with the drastic and fundamental physiological reorganization forced on the patient by shock-inducing drugs or electrical current.

The use of shock therapy as a form of medical treatment in cases of mental disorder raises ethical problems similar to those raised by critics of psychological treatment by aversive control (see Chapter 17). While the effectiveness of shock treatment in some cases has been demonstrated, the method has been abused in other cases.

Since shock treatment is usually frightening and sometimes terrifying, the threat of the treatment has been used in some institutions as a means of controlling the behavior of people who are difficult to handle. An even more objectionable, but less common, situation is that in which shock treatment is actually used as punishment rather than therapy. Fortunately, the sharp decline in the use of shock treatment has made these problems less pressing than when tens of thousands of hospitalized people were treated by this method each day.

Chemical Shock Therapy

The first use of shock treatment as a relatively controlled form of medical therapy grew out of a chance observation. Many people with severe mental disorders refuse to eat, and various methods have been used to correct this condition. An Austrian psychiatrist decided to try to increase appetite by giving insulin, a chemical that lowers the person's blood sugar. While using this method, some of the patients went into coma, and others had convulsions because the blood sugar level went down too far.

The psychiatrist had little difficulty in controlling this condition in his patients by giving them sweetened drinks or injections of glucose. However, to his surprise, he found that some of the disturbed people who had this experience seemed to show psychological improvement. On the basis of this observation, he began to use insulin deliberately to induce convulsions in his patients by reducing blood sugar levels. This method of treatment eventually came into use throughout the world, and it was called *insulin shock therapy*.

The usual procedure was to give the patient insulin early in the morning, and then to allow the blood sugar level to decrease through the stages of restlessness, coma, and convulsions. Sugar was then given to end the

Insulin Shock:
Reflections of a Physician Who Received the Treatment

I heard very distinctly the voices of the doctor and sister. I do not now remember what they were saying. I saw the doctor's and sister's faces. The doctor asked me repeatedly if I was awake and slapped me lightly on the left cheek, as he usually does when I am recovering from a coma. I could not speak and I felt very helpless and confused mentally. The next recollection I have is of the nurse's white worried face with its distended arteries and forehead vein looking down at me and asking me if I was alright. He asked me this question two or three times but I could not answer him. He felt my pulse and arranged my bed clothes rapidly—very rapidly—it seemed to me, two or three times. I was conscious of a tremendous effort I seemed to be making to avoid slipping into a land which was different from that of the nurse's, as being a land or "life" of no movement. The nurse seemed to me to be making also a terrific effort to help me, to bring me back to *his* life. I felt fully conscious of this intensive and combined effort and strove or seemed to strive with all my powers to drag myself back from this abyss of "no movement." I do not recollect moving my limbs, on the contrary I seemed to be paralyzed in my voluntary movements. After a long struggle in which at times I thought that I could not make the effort any longer—I found that I could speak, and I felt an overwhelming sense of gratitude to the nurse whom I hailed as my "saviour." I had an intolerable thirst and also felt very hungry. I asked the nurse for sweet drinks and he brought me a glass of tea and sandwiches of which I ate three or four. I insisted on the nurse having a sandwich, which he did to please me. I also insisted that he should have a drink, but he replied that he would have one later. Sister came in then and I discussed the question of glucose and its relation to obesity. . . . (Mayer-Gross, 1959)

insulin shock episode. A course of treatment was usually made up of insulin shocks given two or three times a week for an extended period. Often the patient received more than one course of treatment. While many dra-

matic improvements in behavior were reported, insulin shock treatment was eventually replaced by electroshock therapy, a faster-acting method that was much easier to control.

Electroshock Therapy

During the nineteenth century there was an increased interest in the medical application of electricity. It was suggested that all diseases should be treated by this method before they were considered incurable. Numerous experiments were undertaken to study the effects of electricity in various mental disturbances.

The modern technique of electroshock therapy (EST) involves the production of a convulsion by passing an electric current through the brain. The patient is placed on a comfortable bed with a pillow under his or her head. The convulsion is then induced by electrodes placed on the head. When the current is turned on, the body becomes rigid and breathing stops for a few seconds. Recovery is rapid, and men and women treated in offices and clinics may be dressed and ready to leave within half an hour after their arrival.

The treatment is frightening to many people. It may be followed by periods of increased restlessness and agitation and states of excitement and uncooperativeness. The person often appears confused and experiences a temporary loss of memory.

EST is most useful in the affective reactions. The treatment is given several times a week in cases of ordinary acute depression; but in cases of great disturbance and agitation or depression of suicidal proportions, it may be given daily or even twice daily. The frequency of treatment is decreased as clinical improvement is shown. A course of treat-

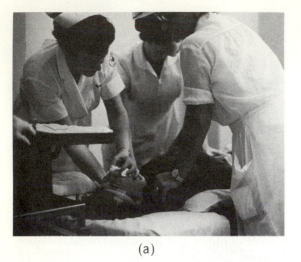

(a)

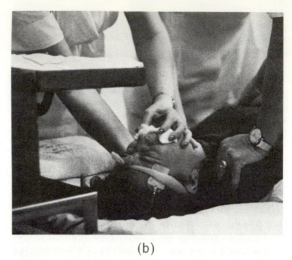

(b)

Figure 18.3 Electroshock therapy (EST) was once the most widely used treatment for schizophrenia and other major mental disorders. Its use is limited today to only the most resistant cases of depression. Here we see a woman with electrodes strapped to her head and a mouthpiece to prevent biting the tongue *(a)*. Nurses and other ward personnel take hold of the patient *(b)* in order to prevent bone fractures or other injuries during the convulsive seizure which occurs when the electrical current is applied to the brain.

ment ranges from five to twenty or more electroshocks.

While it is not known how electroshock therapy achieves its results, the method brings about changes of carbon dioxide and oxygen tension and equilibrium, disturbance of acid-base balance, and the formation of intermediary products of metabolism. The entire autonomic system is affected by these changes. EST also lowers the blood-brain barrier and makes possible a more ready passing of chemical substances from the circulating blood into the brain and cerebrospinal fluid.

The effectiveness of EST as a treatment method is indicated by the fact that while insulin and metrazol therapy are relatively little used today, electroshock is still used to treat resistant cases of depression. EST has helped to lift some very severe depressions.

Psychosurgery: Conflict and Controversy

The modern era of psychosurgery began with experimental work in the United States. Brain operations on two now-famous chimpanzees, Becky and Lucy, showed that surgical interference with the frontal brain areas did away with anxiety and frustration. Before the removal of their frontal lobes, the animals would race about, scream, shake the bars of their cages, defecate and urinate, and otherwise show symptoms of anger and excitement in the face of experimentally induced frustration. Following the removal of their frontal lobes, the same animals became indifferent and showed a lack of concern. They were no longer frustrated by their inability to solve difficult problems put to them. After a few desultory attempts, they would

Electroshock Therapy: A Personal Account by a Man Who Experienced It

The next morning at six o'clock I was told to stay in bed. There would be no breakfast this morning, because I was getting shock treatment. I already knew quite a bit about shock treatment. I had helped them give it to other patients many times. I worked in the dormitory, helping to lift the unconscious patients into bed from the wagon, covering the bandage gag that prevented the patient from biting his tongue or chipping his teeth, tying a man in bed if necessary, and occasionally holding the patient down in bed when things got really rough. It wasn't easy work and in a way I was glad not to be doing it this morning.

At nine o'clock the doctor came on the ward. The doctor was a good friend of mine and it was a nice feeling to know that someone was doing his best to help me. But at this moment I was none too happy. I hoped that I'd be the first on the list to get treatment. Yet I was glad to see another patient wheeled out first. I was scared and there was no getting around it. I wondered if I was going to burn, and if I did burn, whether I'd smell. But by this time there was an awful cry down the hall and I knew that the first patient's shock treatment had begun.

Soon a man was pushed into the dormitory and lifted into bed while another man on another wagon was pushed into the visiting room where the shock was administered. They had a system. Fifteen patients could be given shock treatment in an hour, easily.

Now it was my turn. I climbed up on the high wagon and stretched out. Three sand bags in the form of a pyramid stuck into the small of my back to expand my chest. Many of the men squirmed and fidgeted and fooled with the sand bags trying to make themselves comfortable. But you were never on the wagon long. A counterpane was pulled up to my neck and a small straw pillow, though covered with a clean towel, was wet with the sweat of the men who had gone before. I was wheeled out into the hall to wait my turn. There was another scream and a gurgling coughing groan, and the patient ahead of me was moved out down the hall and into the dormitory, with arms and legs and head flopping around. Before I realized it I was zooming down the hall. Mac was pushing me, and Mac was in a hurry.

The wagon bumped over the thick rubber matting that formed a hollow rectangle for the wagon to fill. The doctor was looking down, smiling. "Hello there, young fellow." "Good morning, Sir." Sarge was rubbing some sticky stuff on my head beside my ears. I had seen tubes of the stuff in the office, "electrode jelly." After all you had to make a good contact—to burn. I was mighty scared and there was no use kidding about it. Mac held my right arm and pressed hard with the elbow just inside my shoulder muscle. Sarge had the other arm. Another attendant climbed up on the wagon and lay across my knees gripping the side of the wagon with hands and toes. The three attendants would hold me down during my convulsion. The theory was: The more severe the convulsion, the better the results. I heard the doctor give the pretty blonde nurse a set of numbers, and I knew that she was setting the dials. "God, don't let her give me an overdose." Mac's face was about eight inches above my own. I looked up into Mac's eyes. Mac wasn't smiling a bit. I stared up into Mac's eyes and slowly said over and over to myself, "Mac, you big Irish lug, take care of me now." Very deliberately, very slowly a black shade came up over my eyes. I woke up sometime later feeling completely refreshed, not tired or logy, or drugged with sleep, just ready for a big day. (Alper, 1948)

give up without any of the symptoms of agitation shown before the operation (Fulton & Jacobsen, 1935).

It occurred to a Portuguese psychiatrist, Egas Moniz, that if this indifference to frustration could be brought about in experimental animals, it might be possible to relieve human reactions to frustration in the same way. He reasoned that certain mental disorders might be due to maladaptive cell complexes in the frontal areas of the brain. The problem was to develop a technique for destroying or isolating these cell complexes in order to force the brain to reorganize itself

Figure 18.4 Although brain operations were undertaken in Switzerland early in the 1900s in an attempt to modify abnormal behavior, modern psychosurgery began with the ideas and techniques developed in Portugal in the 1930s by professor Egas Moniz (shown here) and his colleagues. The method soon spread to other countries and created controversy which continues to the present time.

elation, refusal of good, lack of cooperation, destructiveness, and disorientation. In addition, delusions, ideas of reference, apathy, and auditory hallucinations sometimes disappeared after the operation. The best results were eventually obtained in the agitated depressive form of involutional psychosis. Psychosurgery has also been used with chil-

Figure 18.5 When psychosurgery was introduced as a method of treating mental disorder, the procedure involved drilling a small hole in each side of the skull (top) and inserting a knife (bottom)into the brain. The knife was then moved in an arc (middle) in order to cut nerve pathways connecting the frontal lobes with lower brain centers.

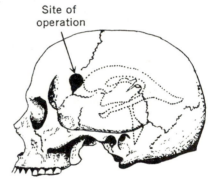

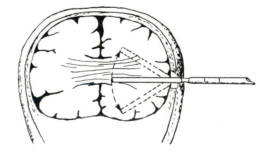

in a more normal way. The best procedure would be one that would cut the association tracts connecting the prefrontal brain areas with the centers in the thalamus; therefore the technique was called *prefrontal lobotomy*. Such surgical procedures came to be known as *psychosurgery*.

When psychosurgery was first introduced, it was used in cases where shock therapy had been unsuccessful. It was found that although the surgical approach could not improve cases of intellectual deterioration, it could relieve such symptoms as fear, worry,

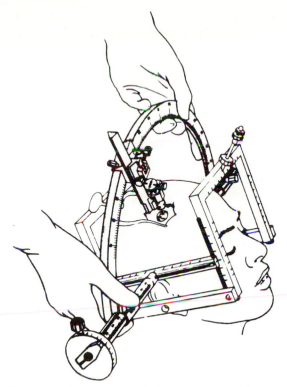

Figure 18.6 A stereotaxic instrument used in one form of psychosurgery. The skin of the scalp has been opened and a small button of bone has been removed from the skull to permit the insertion of the electrode into the brain.

dren, but the results have been less favorable than with adults.

As in the case of the shock therapies, there is no clear explanation for the mechanisms by means of which the several forms of psychosurgery result in changes in behavior and subjective experience. In the case of the operative techniques which are directed toward the highly localized destruction of small areas of tissue, the results can usually be explained in terms of the conventional functions associated with that area. When the psychosurgical operation has damaged

more extensive brain areas and when more complicated brain functions are involved, the explanation of observed changes is considerably more difficult.

Even though there is ample evidence that many patients profited as a result of prefrontal lobotomy during the original phase of the work, a considerable number of psychiatrists remain violently opposed to this approach. Claims have been made that the destruction of frontal lobe tissue is reflected in the progressive loss of human functions such as insight, sensitivity, self-awareness, judgment, and similar higher-level functions. A highly critical review of psychosurgery (Breginn, 1972) was followed by the public outrage of a number of congressmen. One congressman commented: "*Shocking* and *frightening* are too mild to describe my reaction to this material." He then had the critical review read into the *Congressional Record*. Even though other psychiatrists described the charges in the paper as being reckless, and some of the conclusions distorted, the damage was done. Objections to psychosurgery were raised by individuals and groups throughout the country.

In spite of the controversy, advances have continued in the development and refinement of psychosurgical techniques. These techniques have been developed to a point where almost any part of the brain can be approached. Most neuropsychiatrists and neurosurgeons interested in psychosurgery feel that the method has been effective in selected cases in the past, and that it holds even more promise for the future. The most beneficial aspect of the controversy has been the more careful selection of patients for psychosurgical operations. Strict consideration is given to the problem of consent by the person upon whom the operation is to be performed, and there has been a tendency toward avoidance of operations on members of prison and other institutional populations where there is always the possibility of coercion rather than true consent (Older, 1974).

The Chapter in Review

The medical treatment of abnormal behavior reaches back for many centuries. Various kinds of drugs have been used to treat mental disorder, and crude operations on the skull have been used by some groups to permit demons and evil spirits to escape from the heads of the emotionally disturbed. Modern methods of medical treatment include the use of psychoactive drugs, shock therapy, and psychosurgery.

1 Drugging the Brain
The drug treatment of psychological disturbance has emphasized chemicals that tranquilize people and those that influence mood. Some tranquilizers are effective in reducing tension and anxiety in neurotics; more potent tranquilizers are able to get rid of psychotic symptoms. The drugs that influence mood can be classified as those having an effect upon unipolar depression and those which influence bipolar depression.

2 Shocking the Brain
Shock treatment was developed for use in cases of severe psychological disturbance. The principal means of inducing shock have been chemicals and electricity. Chemical shock treatment was the first to be used, but it was eventually replaced by electroshock. Today electroshock is used only in cases of deep depression that have been resistant to other forms of treatment.

3 Psychosurgery: Conflict and Controversy
The use of brain surgery for people with psychological disturbances but presumably normal brain structure has been the most controversial of all medical treatments of mental disorder. Although psychosurgery was widely used for a number of years, the popularity of the method declined when psychoactive drugs were developed. However, renewed interest in the method in recent years has rekindled criticism and controversy.

Recommended Readings

Drug Treatment
Fieve, D. R. *Moodswing*: *The third revolution in psychiatry.* New York: Morrow, 1975.

Klein, D. F. & Gittelman-Klein, R. *Progress in psychiatric drug treatment.* New York: Brunner/Mazel, 1975.

Snyder, S. H. *Madness and the brain.* New York: McGraw-Hill, 1975. (Paperback.)

Shock Treatment

Friedberg, J. *Shock treatment is not good for your brain*: *A neurologist challenges the psychiatric myth.* New York: Glide, 1976.

Psychosurgery

Gaylin, W., Meister, J., & Neville, R. (Eds.) *Operating on the mind*: *The psychosurgery conflict.* New York: Basic Books, 1975.

Valenstein, E. S. *Brain control*: *A critical examination of brain stimulation and psychosurgery.* New York: Wiley, 1973.

Glossary

This glossary is designed to help the student understand terms discussed in the textbook and related readings. Synonyms and descriptive phrases frequently are substituted for definitions. The student who is interested in more exact and complete definitions is referred to the third edition of the *Psychiatric Dictionary* (Oxford University Press, 1970); *Blakiston's Gould Medical Dictionary* (McGraw-Hill Book Co., 1972); and *A Comprehensive Dictionary of Psychological and Psychoanalytical Terms* (David McKay Co., Inc., 1958).

Ablation   Surgical removal of part of the body.

Abortion   Expulsion of the embryo from the uterus during the first three months of pregnancy.

Abreaction   Release of emotion by reliving a traumatic experience.

Abscess   Area of pus resulting from disintegration of tissue.

Acetycholine   Chemical mediator in the transmission of the nerve impulse; neurohormone.

Achondroplasia   Abnormal development of the bones, resulting in dwarfism.

Acrocephaly   Distortion of the skull, giving the head a steeple-shaped appearance; oxycephaly.

Acrophobia   Fear of heights.

ACTH   Adrenocorticotropic hormone.

Acute mania   Second stage in the development of the manic reaction.

Addisons's disease   Syndrome resulting from an underproduction of adrenocortical hormones.

Ademine   Basic chemical unit of the DNA molecule.

Adenoma   Nonmalignant tumor of glandular origin.

Adrenal cortex   External portion of the adrenal gland.

Adrenal glands   Endocrine glands located adjacent to the kidneys.

Adrenal medulla   Inside core of the adrenal gland.

Adrenalin   Hormone of the adrenal medulla having a stimulating effect on the sympathetic nervous system; epinephrine.

Adrenochrome   Breakdown product of noradrenalin; hallucinogenic substance.

Adrenocorticotropic hormone   Secretion of the anterior pituitary gland which stimulates the adrenal cortex.

Adrenolutin   Breakdown product of noradrenalin; hallucinogenic substance.

Adrenolytic   Having the ability to offset the action of substances which stimulate the sympathetic nervous system.

Adrenosterone   Secretion of the adrenal cortex; related to sexual development.

ADS   Antidiuretic chemical secreted by the posterior pituitary gland.

Affect   Feeling or emotional tone.

Affective disorder   Personality disturbance marked by extremes in mood.

Affective incontinence   Lack of emotional restraint.

Afferent nerves   Peripheral nerves which carry impulses from receptors to the central nervous system; sensory nerves.

Aftercare movement   Program of assistance for mental patients following their release from the hospital.

Age regression   Technique in hypnosis by means of which a patient is taken back to an earlier period in life.

Agnosia   Inability to recognize persons or objects.

Agoraphobia   Fear of open places.

Aichmophobia   Fear of pointed objects.

Alarm reaction   First stage of the general adaptation syndrome.

Alcoholic hallucinosis   Brain syndrome due to alcoholism and characterized by delusions and hallucinations, often of a persecutory nature.

Alkalosis   Abnormally alkaline condition of the blood.

Alpha-2-globulin   Chemical suspected of influencing cell membranes and causing other chemicals to act abnormally both inside and outside the cell.

Alpha waves   Ten-per-second brain waves.

Alzheimer's disease   Presenile brain disorder.

Ambivalent   Having contradictory feelings or attitudes.

Amebic dysentery   Form of inflammation of the intestines.

Amenorrhea   Decrease or complete cessation of menstruation.

Amentia   Mental retardation.

Amitriptyline   Antidepressive drug.

Amnesia   Loss of memory.

Amniocentesis   Test of amniotic fluid to determine chromosome defects prior to birth.

Amok   Personality disturbance characterized by sudden outbursts of aggression; reported among the Malays.

Amotivational syndrome   Lack of motivation and initiative associated with excessive use of marihuana.

Amphetamine sulphate   Antidepressant drug; Benzedrine.

Anal stage   Level of psychosexual development.

Analeptic drug   Restorative drug, facilitating respiration and wakefulness.

Analytical psychology   Theory of personality advanced by Carl G. Jung.

Androgen   Male sex hormone.

Anemia   Decrease in red blood cells leading to a deficiency in the oxygen-carrying capacity of the blood.

Anencephaly   Complete absence of the cerebrum, cerebellum, and flat bones of the skull.

Anesthesia   Loss of sensitivity to stimuli.

Angina syndrome   Pain in the region of the heart.

Animism   Belief that the world is controlled by supernatural beings.

Anomaly   Obvious deviation from type.

Anorexia nervosa   Psychogenic loss of appetite.

Anoxemia   Deficiency of oxygen in the blood and tissues.

Anoxic shock therapy   Physical treatment based on shock induced by gas of various kinds.

Anticholinergic drug   Drug which inhibits action of parasympathetic branch of autonomic nervous system.

Antidepressant drug   Chemical used to treat depression.

Anti-insulin hormone   Secretion of the anterior pituitary gland influencing the insulin-producing tissue of the pancreas.

Antimetabolite   Chemical compound shaped to resemble a neurohormone but having minor structural differences.

Anxiety   Psychophysiologic reaction to threat.

Apathy   Absence of emotional response.

Aphasia   Inability to understand or use language meaningfully.

Aphonia   Inability to speak above a whisper.

Aplasia   Absence or impaired development of an organ or part of the body.

Apnoea   Breathing difficulty.

Apraxia   Loss of ability to perform purposeful movement in the absence of paralysis or sensory disturbance.

Archetype   Original model or type.

Arctic hysteria   Personality disturbance observed among the natives of Northern Siberia; marked by a high degree of suggestibility.

Argyll Robertson pupil   Neurological sign in which the pupil of the eye reacts to accommodation but not to light; sign of brain syphilis and other diseases.

Arteriosclerosis   Hardening of the arteries.

Ascorbic acid   Vitamin C.

Asphyxia   Condition caused by extreme lack of oxygen; may lead to brain damage.

Asthenic   Weak.

Asthenic type   Tall, thin body type described by Kretschmer.

Astrocytoma   Form of brain tumor.

Ataractic drug   Tranquilizing drug.

Ataraxia   State of detached serenity without loss of consciousness produced by tranquilizing drugs.

Ataxia   Impairment of muscular coordination.

Athetosis   Involuntary movements of the limbs due to inadequate control of the muscles.

Athletic type   Muscular body type described by Kretschmer.

Atrophy   Wasting or shrinking of body tissues.

Audiogenic seizure   Sound-induced convulsive seizure.

Aura   Characteristic warning experience preceding a convulsive seizure.

Autokinetic effect   Apparent movement of a fixed point of light in a darkened room.

Automatic behavior   Nonconscious behavior.

Automatic writing   Writing without conscious control.

Automatic   Self-governing; relatively independent.

Autonomic nervous system   Vegetative nervous system.

Avitaminosis   Vitamin deficiency.

Babkinski reflex   Neurological sign in certain organic disorders of the nervous system.

Barbital   Sedative drug.

Basal ganglion   Mass of gray matter in the subcortex.

Basal metabolic rate   Minimum rate at which heat is produced by a person at rest; a measure of vital functioning.

Benign   Relatively mild.

Benzedrine Synthetic stimulant to the central nervous system.

Berger rhythm Brain wave.

Beta rhythm Brain wave; shallower and faster than the alpha rhythm.

Bhang See *Marihuana*.

Bibliotherapy Use of reading for cure of psychological disorders.

Bimodal stimulant Drug having a direct stimulating action on the central nervous system and a slower-acting effect as a result of the inhibition of monoamine oxidase.

Binet test Comprehensive scale of intelligence.

Biofeedback Providing a person with information on the state of heart rate, blood pressure, brain waves, body temperature, or other biological functions.

Biorhythm Biological function that follows a regular pattern or cycle. Heartbeat, brain wave, menstrual cycle.

Biotelemetry Recording biological functions of animals or humans by means of radio signals and similar means.

Biotin Vitamin H.

Biotype Body type.

Biovular twins Fraternal twins; dizygotic twins.

Bipolar depression Mental disorder marked by periods of depression and elation. Assumed to have a genetic basis.

Birth trauma Shock of birth.

Birth-injury palsy See *Cerebral palsy*.

Bisexual Having the characteristics of both sexes.

BMR See *Basal metabolic rate*.

Body image Mental image one has of his own body.

Bromide Sedative and anticonvulsant drug.

Bufotenine Naturally occurring structural analog of serotonin; hallucinogenic substance.

Bulbocapnine Plant alkaloid used to induce experimental catatonia.

Bulimia Excessive appetite.

Cannabis indica Indian hemp.

Carbonic anhydrase Enzyme.

Cardiazol Metrazol.

Cardiovascular Pertaining to the heart and blood vessels.

Carotene Vitamin A.

Castration anxiety Fear of genital injury.

Catalepsy Characterized by muscular rigidity.

Catatonia Type of schizophrenia marked by decreased motor activity, mutism, and periods of waxy flexibility.

Catecholamines Chemical substances suspected of playing a role in certain types of depressions.

Catharsis Psychoanalytic term to denote emotional release during treatment.

Cathexis Channeling and fixation of libido.

Cerea flexibilitas Waxy flexibility sometimes seen in catatonic schizophrenia.

Cerebellum Brain structure related to the control of movement and body coordination.

Cerebral diplegia See *Cerebral palsy*.

Cerebral dysrhythmia Abnormal rhythm of the brain waves.

Cerebral injection Form of psychosurgery in which the frontal lobes are injected with alcohol, procaine, or other solutions.

Cerebral palsy Motor disability associated with organic brain damage or malformation.

Cerebral topectomy Form of psychosurgery in which a thin slice of cortical tissue is cut from each of the frontal lobes.

Cerebrotonia Personality type inclined toward intellectual pursuits; associated with the ectomorph body type described by Sheldon.

Cerebrum Largest and most recently developed part of the human brain; the two-lobed structure growing as an extension of the brainstem.

Ceruloplasmin Copper protein in the serum of the body.

CFF Critical flicker frequency.

Chloral hydrate Sedative drug.

Chlorodiazepoxide Minor tranquilizer.

Chlorpromazine Tranquilizer of the phenothiazine group.

Choleric Angry and irritable.

Cholesterol Unsaturated alcohol of the class of sterols; constituent of all animal fats and oils.

Cholinergic drug Drug which stimulates the parasympathetic nervous system.

Cholinesterase Enzyme.

Chorea Neurological condition marked by incoordinate movements of the head and extremities.

Choroid plexus Pertaining to a system of delicate blood vessels in the brain.

Circumstantial Irrelevant.

Classical conditioning Learning as a result of repeated pairing of an unconditioned stimulus with a conditioned stimulus; the Pavlovian model of learning.

Claustrophobia Fear of closed places.

Climacteric Change of life; the menopause.

Clonic phase Second phase of the *grand mal* convulsion; involuntary contractions and relaxations of the musculature.

Cocaine Drug obtained from the leaves of the coca plant.

Coconscious Not conscious but capable of becoming conscious.

Colitis Inflammation of the colon.

Collective unconscious That part of the unconscious which is inherited; racial unconscious.

Colloidal gold curve Biochemical index used in the detection of syphilis and other infectious disorders.

Coma Stupor.

Compensation Defense mechanism; attempt to overcome inferiority.

Complex Group of emotionally toned ideas that have been repressed.

Compulsion Unwelcome repetitive action.

Conceptual quotient Index of intellectual efficiency and mental deterioration.

Concordance Similarity of characteristics in twins.

Concussion Neurological disturbance produced by a severe blow to the head or spinal column; associated with such symptoms as shock, unconsciousness, and paralysis.

Condensation Telescoping images in a dream.

Confabulation Filling in memory gaps.

Congenital Existing from birth.

Conjunctival hyperemia Condition in which the eyes have a bloodshot appearance.

Constitution Total biological makeup of an individual.

Content analysis Analysis of projective test responses in terms of their symbolic meaning.

Contingencies Environmental conditions influencing the learning process.

Conversion reaction Neurotic condition in which anxiety is converted into physical symptoms.

Convolution Irregular fold of the outer surface of the brain.

Convulsion Pathological muscular contraction.

Coprophilia Sexual attraction to excretory processes and products.

Cortex Outer or surface layer of the brain or other organ.

Cortical frequency spectrum Range of electrical waves produced by the brain.

Cortical undercutting Form of psychosurgery in which brain tissue is cut at the junction of the gray and white matter in the prefrontal cortex.

Corticosterone Hormone of the adrenal cortex.

Corticotropin Anterior pituitary hormone which regulates the activity of the adrenal cortex.

Cortin Substance containing several hormones and extracted from the adrenal cortex.

Cortisone Hormone produced by the adrenal cortex.

Co-twin control Method of studying the hereditary factor in mental illness of twins.

Countertransference Emotional attachment of the therapist to the patient.

Covert Concealed or disguised.

CQ Conceptual quotient.

Cranial anomaly Abnormal structure of the bones of the head.

Craniostenosis Premature closing of the cranial sutures.

Cretinism Mental and physical retardation resulting from thyroid insufficiency during fetal life or early infancy.

Cryptogenic Of unknown origin.

Curare   Drug which paralyzes motor nerves.

CVA   Cerebrovascular accident; a "stroke."

Cyanocobalamin   Vitamin B_{12}.

Cyanosis   Bluish discoloration of the skin due to lack of oxygen.

Cyclazocine   Drug used in treatment of heroin addiction.

Cycloid   Pertaining to relatively marked fluctuations of mood.

Cyclothymia   Personality pattern marked by alternating periods of elation and depression.

Cyclothymic   Showing marked mood swings.

Cytomegalic inclusion body disease   Infectious condition in which a maternal virus infects the fetus; may be associated with mental retardation.

Cytosine   Basic chemical unit of the DNA molecule.

Death instinct   Tendency of the id to strive toward death and destruction; thanatos.

Decarboxylation   Metabolic breakdown process.

Decerebration   Removal of the cerebrum.

Decortication   Removal of the cortex, or parts of it.

Defense mechanism   Technique used by an individual to avoid what is unpleasant or anxiety-provoking.

Dehydrated   Lacking in water.

Delahara   Personality disturbance similar to Amok; observed in the Philippines.

Delirium tremens   Acute delirium precipitated by alcohol and associated with anxiety, tremors, hallucinations, and delusions.

Delta wave   Slow EEG wave seen during sleep and brain pathology.

Delusion   Belief contrary to reality and held in spite of evidence and common sense.

Dementia   Impairment of mental functioning.

Dementia paralytica   See *Paresis*.

Demerol   Narcotic derived from morphine.

Demography   Analysis of population variables.

Demonology   View that mental illness is caused by possession by the Devil.

Depersonalization   Loss of sense of reality or identity.

Depth therapy   Reconstructive psychotherapy

Dermatotropic   Influencing or involving the skin.

Desoxycorticosterone   Hormone produced by the adrenal cortex which acts on mineral metabolism.

Deterioration   Progressive impairment of function.

Deterioration index   Measure of intellectual deterioration.

Deuterium oxide   Heavy water.

Diabetes mellitus   Physical disorder characterized by an excess of sugar in the blood and other organs; associated with a disturbed insulin production.

Diagnosis   Identification of a disease or disorder.

Diazepam   Minor tranquilizer; Valium.

Diencephalon   Thalamus and hypothalamus; part of the forebrain.

Diplegia   Paralysis of legs and arms, with the legs more seriously affected.

Direct analytic therapy   Form of depth psychotherapy used with psychotic patients.

Directive psychotherapy   Psychological treatment in which the therapist actively manipulates the life of the patient; an authoritarian approach.

Disengagement   Defense mechanism based on noninvolvement.

Disorientation   Confusion about time, place, and person.

Displacement   Shifting of emotional emphasis.

Dissociation   Splitting of consciousness into two or more semi-independent parts.

Diurnal   Daily.

Dizygotic twins   Fraternal twins; biovular twins.

DNA (deoxyribonucleic acid)   Protein molecule which carries genetic information.

Dopamine   Chemical involved in the transmission of the nerve impulse.

Down's syndrome   A type of mental retardation; mongolism.

Dramatization   Changing abstract ideas into concrete images in dreams.

Dream work   Process by which the instinctual urges of the id are transformed into a dream.

Duodenum   First part of the small intestine.

Dysfunction   Abnormal functioning.

Dyskinesia   Disturbance of voluntary muscular reaction.

Dysmegalopsia   Hallucination in which the body is felt to be unsymmetrical.

Dysmenorrhea   Painful menstruation.

Dysplasia   Disharmony between different regions of the body.

Dysplastic type   Atypical body type associated with glandular disturbances.

Dysrhythmia   Disturbance of regular rhythm of brain waves.

Dystrophy   Impaired growth.

Echolalia   Repetition of the exact words spoken by someone else.

Echropraxia   Automatic imitation of another's movements.

Echul   Personality disturbance of a sexual nature seen among the Diegueno Indians.

Ecology   Study of the distribution of mental patients in the environment.

ECT   Electroconvulsive therapy.

Ectomorph   Fragile linear body type described by Sheldon.

Edema   Excessive accumulation of fluid in the tissue.

EEG   Electroencephalogram; brain waves.

EEG activation   Technique for enhancing the EEG response by drugs or other means.

Efficiency index   Measure of intellectual deterioration.

Effort syndrome   Neurotic heart disorder marked by fatigue, breathing difficulties, trembling, fainting, giddiness, and fear of effort.

Ego Self, person, or individual, as distinguished from others.

Egocentric Self-centered.

EKG Electrocardiogram.

Elaboration Altering a dream in retelling it.

Electra complex Repressed desire of a female for incestuous relations with her father.

Electrocardiogram Graphic record of the electric potential which accompanies the heartbeat.

Electroencephalography Recording the electrical waves of the brain.

Electromyography Measurement of muscle action potential.

Electronarcosis Electric sleep.

Electro-oculography Recording eye movements and pupillary reactions.

Electroshock therapy Treatment of a behavior disorder by electric shock to the brain.

Electrosome Instrument used to apply electric current to the brain to induce sleep for treatment purposes.

Embolism Stoppage of a blood vessel by a clot or obstruction.

Embryo Organism in the earliest phase of its prenatal development.

Emetic Drug which induces vomiting.

EMG Electromyogram.

Emotional catharsis Emotional release through the reliving of a traumatic experience.

Encephalitis Inflammation of the brain tissue.

Encephalitis lethargica Brain disorder associated with sleepiness.

Encephalopathy Brain disease.

Encounter group Therapeutic-like group interaction in which personal and interpersonal problems are worked out with the assistance of a group leader and other members of the group.

Endocrine gland Ductless gland.

Endogenous Arising from within the body.

Endomorph Round and fat body type described by Sheldon.

Enuresis Involuntary discharge of urine; bedwetting.

Enzootic ataxia Behavior disorder in sheep due to copper deficiency.

Enzyme Organic substance capable of producing other substances by catalytic action.

Eonism Transvestism.

Epidemiology Location and statistical study of psychiatric cases in a hospital or community.

Epilepsy Group of nervous diseases marked primarily by convulsions.

Epileptic furor Condition of excitement following a *grand mal* convulsion or substituting for it.

Epileptiform seizure Convulsion resembling those of epilepsy.

Epiloia Inherited neoplastic disease sometimes associated with mental retardation; tuberous sclerosis.

Epinephrine See *Adrenalin.*

Ergasias Reaction types of personality disturbance in the system of Adolf Meyer.

Ergotamine Naturally occurring structural analogue of serotonin; an hallucinogenic substance.

Erogenous Pertaining to sexual, libidinal, or erotic behavior or feeling.

Erotic Pertaining to sex sensations and their stimuli.

Erythrocyte Red blood cell.

Escape mechanism Defense mechanism.

Essential epilepsy See *Idiopathic epilepsy*.

Essential hypertension High blood pressure.

EST Electroshock therapy.

Estrogen Any female sex hormone.

Estrone Female sex hormone produced by the ovaries from the fetal period until menopause.

Ethnic Pertaining to groups of people believed to be biologically related.

Etiology Study of causes or origins of a disease.

Eukadol Narcotic derived from morphine.

Euphoria Exaggerated feeling of well-being.

Evoked memories Memories produced by stimulation of the cortex of the temporal lobe.

Exhibitionism Exhibiting one's sex organs to other people.

Existentialism Philosophical approach based on the importance of personal freedom, personal decision, and personal commitment.

Exogenous Originating outside the body or outside the nervous system.

Experimental neurosis Experimental behavior disorder induced in animals by means of conflict.

Extinction Decrease in behavior resulting from lack of reinforcement.

Extirpation Complete removal or surgical destruction of a part of the body.

Familial Pertaining to the family; hereditary.

Family-care system Treatment of the mentally ill through placement with private families.

Fantasy Daydream.

Fetishism Sexual deviation in which articles of clothing or parts of the body become a substitute for the love object.

Fetus Human embryo after the sixth to eighth week of pregnancy.

Field-dependent Dependent upon visual field cues in space orientation experiments.

Field-independent Dependent upon body cues in space orientation experiments.

Filtrable Capable of passing through a filter.

Fissure Furrow or groove on the surface of the brain.

Fistula Abnormal outlet from an internal organ to the outside of the body.

Fixation Arrest of psychosexual development.

Flaccid Limp; without normal tonus.

Flagellation Whipping.

Flooding Behavior modification involving direct exposure to stressful situations leading to a high level of anxiety.

Focal   Localized.

Focused ultrasound   Form of psychosurgery by means of high-frequency sound waves directed into the brain.

Folie à deux   Shared psychosis; usually of husbands and wives or close relatives.

Forebrain   Uppermost portion of the brain; cerebrum and diencephalon.

Formboard   Performance test of intelligence.

Freidreich's ataxia   Neurological disorder.

Frigidity   Absence of sexual feeling in women.

Frustration   Psychological state resulting from the blocking of goal-directed activity.

Frustration tolerance   Level of one's ability to accept frustration.

Fugue   Relatively long period of amnesia in which the patient usually leaves home.

Functional   Psychological; psychogenic.

Funkenstein test   Blood pressure reaction to an intramuscular injection of methacholine (Mecholyl).

GABA   Gamma amino butyric acid; chemical mediator in the transmission of the nerve impulse; neurohormone.

Galactosemia   Condition marked by an accumulation of galactos in the bloodstream; may be associated with mental retardation.

Galvanic skin response   Electrical skin resistance.

Ganglion   Nerve center.

Ganglion cells   Group of nerve cells usually located outside the brain and spinal cord.

Gargoylism   Disorder marked by a defect in the metabolism of connective tissue substance; may be associated with mental retardation.

GAS   General adaptation syndrome.

Gastritis   Stomach distress.

Genetic code   Chemical pattern in the DNA molecule which determines the physical structure of the organism.

Genital   Pertaining to the sex organs.

Glaucoma   Increased intraocular pressure; hardening of the eyeballs.

Glia cells   Supporting cells in the nervous system.

Glioma   Intrinsic tumor of the brain tissue.

Glutamic acid   Enzyme having anticonvulsive properties.

Gonadotrophic hormone   Secretion of the pituitary gland influencing the sex glands.

Gonads   Sex glands.

Grand mal   Major convulsive seizure.

Grantham lobotomy   Form of psychosurgery in which a needle electrode is inserted in the frontal area of the brain and tissue is destroyed through electrocoagulation.

Graphology   Analysis of handwriting characteristics.

Grieg's disease   See *Hypertelorism*.

GSR   Galvanic skin response.

Guamine   Basic chemical unit of the DNA molecule.

Gynandromorphy   Bisexuality of the physique.

Gyrus   Convolution of the brain.

Habitus   Body build.

Hallucination   Perception without an appropriate external stimulus.

Hallucinogen   Chemical substance capable of producing hallucinations.

Harmaline   Chemical substance capable of producing hallucinations.

Harmine   Naturally occurring structural analogue of serotonin; hallucinogenic substance.

Hasheesh   See *Marihuana*.

Hashish   Drug related to marihuana; derived from the hemp plant.

Hebephrenia   Type of schizophrenia marked by delusions, bizarre behavior, and inappropriate emotional responses.

Hemiplegia   Paralysis of one side of the body.

Hepatolenticular degeneration   See *Wilson's disease*.

Hermaphrodite   Individual with both male and female sex organs.

Heroin   Narcotic derived from morphine.

Heterosexual   Pertaining to erotic relations with members of the opposite sex.

Hindbrain   Lower brain structures including the pons, medulla, and cerebellum.

Hirsutism   Hairiness.

Histamine   Chemical mediator in the transmission of the nerve impulse; neurohormone.

Histidine   Amino acid source of histamine.

Homeostasis   Maintaining a balance or equilibrium in bodily processes.

Homosexual   Pertaining to erotic relationships between members of the same sex.

Hormone   Chemical substance secreted by the endocrine glands.

Humanism   Psychological approach in which human interests, values, and dignity predominate.

Hurler's disease   See *Gargoylism*.

Hutchinson's teeth   Notched or pegged teeth seen in congenital syphilis.

Hydrocephalus   Increased volume and pressure of cerebrospinal fluid in the ventricles of the brain.

Hydroxytryptamine   An intermediate product in certain metabolic processes.

Hyperemesis gravidarum   Nausea and vomiting of early pregnancy.

Hyperemia   Increased amount of blood in part of the body.

Hyperinsulinism   Overproduction of insulin.

Hyperkinesis   Excessive muscular action.

Hyperopia   Farsightedness.

Hypersomnic   Pertaining to excessive sleepiness.

Hypertelorism   Congenital cerebral defect characterized by an abnormal development of the skull; Grieg's disease.

Hypertension   High blood pressure.

Hyperthyroidism   Overactivity of the thyroid glands.

Hyperventilation syndrome   A combination of physical symptoms brought on by overbreathing.

Hypnoanalysis   Combination of the techniques of hypnosis with those of depth therapy.

Hypnosis   Sleep-like condition of heightened suggestibility.

Hypoadrenocorticism   Underproduction of adrenocortical hormones.

Hypochondria   Obsessive preoccupation with one's health.

Hypoglycemia   Lowered blood sugar.

Hypokinesis   Lethargy; underactivity.

Hypomania   Earliest stage in the development of the manic reaction.

Hypophrenia   Mental retardation.

Hypophysis   Endocrine gland located at the base of the brain; pituitary gland.

Hypoplasia   Underdevelopment of part of the body.

Hypotensive action   Ability to lower blood pressure.

Hypothalamus   Group of nuclei at the base of the brain involved in the regulation of various body processes.

Hypothyroidism   Thyroid underactivity.

Hysteria   Neurotic condition marked by an involuntary loss or disorder of function caused by psychological conflict.

Id   Deepest level of the unconscious; the source of instinctual impulses seeking immediate gratification of primitive needs.

Identification   Defense mechanism by means of which an individual affiliates himself with another person, group, or movement.

Ideomotor   Pertaining to a motor response elicited by an idea.

Idiopathic epilepsy   Convulsive disorder without known or specific organic cause; essential epilepsy.

Idiot savant   Form of mental retardation in which the patient exhibits a special ability or exceptional talent.

Imipramine   Antidepressive drug.

Impotence   Inability of the male to perform the sexual act.

Imu   Personality disturbance similar to Lata; observed among tha Ainu women of Japan.

Incest   Sex relations between close relatives of opposite sexes.

Incoherence   Disconnected and unrelated thoughts.

Individual psychology   Theory of personality advanced by Alfred Adler.

Indoleamine   Chemical substance involved in transmission of nerve impulse.

Infantile amaurotic family idiocy   See *Tay-Sach's disease*.

Infantile autism   Childhood psychosis.

Infantile cerebral lipoidosis   See *Tay-Sach's disease*.

Infantilism   Extreme immaturity and dependency.

Inkblot test   See *Rorschach test.*

Insight   Understanding; seeing meaningful relationships.

Instrumental conditioning   See *Operant conditioning.*

Insulin   Hormone produced by tissue imbedded within the pancreatic mass; related to sugar metabolism.

Insulin shock therapy   Physical treatment based on the induction of hypoglycemia or lowered blood sugar.

Intentional tremor   Tremor which appears when some specific movement is about to be performed.

Interaction chronograph   Instrument that gives a continuous recording of a number of interview interaction variables.

Interpersonal theory   View that personality disturbance is determined by social behavior and interpersonal situations rather than by constitutional factors.

Intrapsychic   Taking place within the mind or self.

Intrapsychic censor   Process by means of which unconscious strivings are kept out of consciousness.

Introjection   Absorption of the personality of another person into oneself; defense mechanism.

Involutional depression   Depression of late middle age.

Iproniazid   MAO-inhibitor type of antidepressant; Marsilid.

IQ   Intelligence quotient.

Isocarboxazid   MAO-inhibitor type of antidepressant.

Izoniazid   Energizing drug; antidepressant

Jacksonian seizure   Convulsive disorder in which the muscular contraction is limited to the arm, leg, or face.

Juramentado   Personality disturbance of an aggressive nature observed among the Mohammedan Moros.

Juvenile paresis   Syphilis of the brain and associated psychological symptoms in children and adolescents.

Kent-Rosanoff test   Standardized work-association test.

Kernicterus   Brain disorder resulting from a toxic condition during the first few days following birth; may be associated with mental retardation.

Ketogenic diet   Diet rich in fats; used to control convulsive disorders.

Kimilue   Personality disturbance of a sexual nature observed among the Diegueno Indians.

Kleptomania   Compulsive urge to steal.

Korsakoff's syndrome   Brain disorder associated with alcoholism.

KZ syndrome   Stress reaction observed in concentration camp survivors.

Lapsus linguae   Slip of the tongue.

Lata   Personality disturbance marked by extreme passivity and suggestibility; observed among the Malays.

Latency period   Stage in psychosexual development.

Latent   Inactive, dormant, hidden.

Latent dream   Deeper symbolic level of a dream.

Leptosomic type   Tall, thin body type described by Kretschmer; asthenic type.

Lesbianism   Homosexuality in women.

Lesion   Injury or wound.

Lethargy   Morbid drowsiness; inaction and apathy.

Leucotomy   Form of psychosurgery.

Libido   Constructive or destructive psychic energy.

Life instinct   Tendency of the id to strive toward integration of living substance into larger wholes; Eros.

Life stress units   A measure of stress in terms of specific life events.

Life style   Behavior pattern adopted early in life as a means of overcoming feelings of inferiority.

Lilliputian hallucination   Hallucination involving tiny figures of people or animals.

Limbic lobe   Ringlike convolution around the base of the cerebral hemisphere; visceral brain.

Lithium carbonate   Drug used to treat psychological depression.

Little's disease   See *Cerebral palsy*.

Lobectomy   Removal of a lobe.

LSD-25   Lysergic acid diethylamid; hallucinogenic drug derived from ergot.

Lues   Syphilis.

Lysergic acid   Naturally occurring structural analogue of serotonin; hallucinogenic substance.

MA   See *Mental age*.

Macrocephaly   Large-headedness.

Macrogyria   Condition in which the gyri and convolutions of the brain are few and broad while the sulci and fissures are short, shallow, and wide.

Macropsia   Hallucination in which the patient perceives his body or parts of his body as being unnaturally large.

Malnutrition   Deficiency in calories, proteins, and vitamins.

Mania   Overactivity, excitement, and violence.

Manifest dream   Dream as the dreamer remembers it.

MAO   Monoamine oxidase; enzyme.

Marihuana   Drug obtained from the hemp plant.

Masochism   Sexual pleasure derived from physical or psychological pain and suffering.

Medulla   Bulblike structure at the top of the spinal cord forming the lowest part of the brain.

Medulloblastoma   Form of brain tumor.

Melancholia   Depression.

Menarche   Age of onset of menstruation.

Meninges   Membranes of the brain and spinal cord.

Meningioma   Tumor arising from the membranes covering the brain.

Meningoencephalitis   Inflammation of the brain and its membranes.

Meningovascular   Involving the membranes of the brain and the cerebral blood vessels.

Menopause   Natural end of the menstrual cycle; "change of life"; climacteric.

Mental age   Level of intellectual development in terms of the average of a particular age group; MA.

Meprobamate   Tranquilizing drug derived from propanediol carbamate; *Miltown, Equanil.*

Mescaline   Hallucinogenic drug obtained from the cactus plant.

Mesmerism   Animal magnetism; hypnotism.

Mesomorph   Square muscular body type described by Sheldon.

Metabolism   Building up and breaking down of body cells.

Metastatic   Pertaining to the transfer of a disease from a primary source to a distant one.

Metastatic tumor   Tumor arising at a location in the body other than the primary source.

Methadone   Substitute drug used in treatment of heroin addiction.

Methamphetamine   Stimulating drug; antidepressant.

Methyl hydantoin   Anticonvulsant drug; Mesantoin.

Metrazol   Drug used in convulsive therapy.

Microcephaly   Small-headedness.

Microgyria   Condition in which the normal convolutions of the brain are replaced by a large number of small close-set convolutions separated by shallow grooves.

Micropsia   Hallucination in which the patient feels his body or parts of his body to be unusually small.

Midbrain   Part of the brain which developed from the middle of the primitive brain; mesencephalon.

Migraine   Severe form of familial headache.

Milieu therapy   Supportive type of psychological treatment based on the removal or modification of environmental stress.

Misala   Personality disturbance similar to Amok; observed among African tribes.

Modeling   Behavior learned through imitation.

Mongolism   Form of mental retardation in which the patient has the facial characteristics of a member of the Mongolian race; associated with a disturbance of the chromosomes.

Monoamine oxidase   Enzyme; MAO.

Monomania   Nineteenth-century term for mental illness marked by highly organized delusions.

Monoplegia   Paralysis involving a single limb of the body.

Monozygotic twins   Uniovular twins; Identical twins.

Moral insanity   Nineteenth-century term for character disorder.

Morphine   Narcotic drug derived from opium.

Mosaicism Chromosome disorder related to some cases of mental retardation.

Mutism Inability to speak.

Myopia Nearsightedness.

Myxedema Adult hypothyroidism.

Naloxone Drug which counteracts effects of opiates.

Narcissism Self-love.

Narcoanalysis See *Narcotherapy*.

Narcolepsy Neurotic attacks of sleep.

Narcosynthesis See *Narcotherapy*.

Narcotherapy Use of drugs to facilitate the release of unconscious material.

Natural areas Areas which develop during the growth of a city.

Naturalism View that illness is the result of natural causes.

Necrophilia Sexual attraction to death and dead bodies.

Negative transference Hostile and antagonistic feelings which the patient develops toward the psychotherapist.

Negativism Resistance; contrary behavior.

Neologism Made-up word having a private meaning for the mental patient.

Neoplasm Tumor.

Neurasthenia Neurotic reaction characterized by weakness, fatigue, and lack of physical vitality.

Neuritis Inflammation of a nerve.

Neurocirculatory asthenia See *Effort syndrome*.

Neurodermatosis Skin disorders occurring in cases of emotional instability.

Neurofibromatosis Neoplastic disorder associated in some cases with mental retardation.

Neurohormone Chemical mediator in the transmission of the nerve impulse.

Neurohumor Chemical substance involved in transmission of nerve impulse.

Neurosis Psychological disorder marked by anxiety or symptoms designed to control anxiety.

Neurosyphilis Syphilis of the nervous system.

Neurotropic Influencing or involving the nervous tissue.

Niacin See *Nicotinic acid*.

Nicotinamide See *Nicotinic acid*.

Nicotinic acid Vitamin of the vitamin B complex; niacin, nicotinamide.

Nondirective psychotherapy Psychological treatment in which the patient is largely responsible for the solution to his problems; a client-centered approach.

Nonspecific stress Stress resulting from cumulative effects of minor stressors.

Noradrenalin   Chemical mediator in the transmission of the nerve impulse; neurohormone; norepinephrine.
Norepinephrine   See *Noradrenalin*.
Nosology   Pertaining to classification.
Nucleotides   Chemical subunits of the DNA molecule.

Object love   Love directed toward other persons and things.
Obsession   Unwelcome recurring idea.
Occlusion   Closing of an artery.
Oculogyric   Referring to movements of the eyes.
Oedipal relationship   Erotic attachment of the young child to the parent of the opposite sex.
Olfactory brain   Limbic lobe; visceral brain.
Oligophrenia   Mental retardation.
Open-door policy   Program of unlocked hospital wards.
Operant conditioning   Learning in which the reinforcement of a response leads to the repetition of that response.
Ophthalmoplegic   Pertaining to a paralysis of the ocular muscles.
Overt   Open to objective observation.
Oxycephaly   Distortion of the skull giving the head a steeple-shaped appearance; acrocephaly.

Paleocortex   Limbic lobe; visceral brain.
Paleological thinking   Nonlogical nature of the thinking process of the schizophrenic patient.
Palsy   Paralysis.
Pantothenic acid   Calcium pantothenate; vitamin involved in the metabolism of fat, protein, and carbohydrate.
Papilledema   Edema or swelling of the optic nerve.
Paralogical thinking   See *Paleological thinking*.
Paralysis agitans   Shaking palsy; Parkinsons's disease.
Paranasal   Located near the nasal cavities.
Paranoid   Characterized by suspiciousness.
Paraplegia   Paralysis involving only the legs.
Paraprofessional   Nonprofessional person trained to assist professionals in their work.
Parasympathetic system   Segment of the autonomic nervous system.
Parataxic distortions   Disturbances of social perception.
Paresis   Brain disorder due to syphilis.
Parkinsonism   Neurological disorder characterized by rigidity, tremors, and impaired motor function.
Passive-aggressive   Characterized by rebellion through inaction and stubbornness.
Passive-dependent   Characterized by passivity and dependency.
Pathogenic   Causing disease or disorder.
Pathological   Abnormal, diseased, or disordered.

Pathological intoxication   Acute brain disorder characterized by a violent reaction to relatively small quantities of alcohol.

Pedophilia   Sexual inclinations directed toward children.

Pellagra   Physical disorder due to lack of nicotinic acid.

Pepsin   Protein-splitting enzyme.

Peptic ulcer   Lesion of the mucous lining of the stomach or duodenum.

Perceptual defense   Selective blocking of the input of anxiety-producing stimuli.

Performance test   Nonverbal psychological test.

Periodontal   Pertaining to the area of the teeth and gums.

Peristalsis   Rhythmic contraction of smooth muscles of gastro-intestinal tract.

Pernicious anemia   Physical symptom complex related to vitamin B_{12} deficiency.

Personal unconscious   That part of the unconscious which develops as a result of individual experience.

Petit mal   Convulsive disorder characterized by brief losses of consciousness.

PGR   Psychogalvanic response.

Phallic period   Stage in psychosexual development.

Phallus   Male sex organ.

Pharmacotherapy   Drug treatment.

Phenethylamine   Stimulating drug used in narcotherapy; Pervitin.

Phenothiazine   Chemical base of certain tranquilizing drugs.

Phenyl acetyl urea   Anticonvulsant drug; Phenurone.

Phenylethyl barbituric acid   Anticonvulsant drug; phenobarbital.

Phenylketonuria   Disturbance of protein metabolism frequently associated with mental retardation.

Phlebitis   Inflammation of a vein.

Phlegmatic   Cold and self-possessed.

Phobia   Pathological fear.

Photic activation   Technique for exaggerating the EEG by light stimulation.

Photophobia   Sensitivity to light.

Phrenology   Theory that character traits are localized in specific regions of the brain.

Pibloktoq   Personality disturbance marked by sudden episodes of excitement; observed among the Eskimos.

Pick's disease   Presenile brain disorder.

Pituitary   Endocrine gland located at the base of the brain; hypophysis.

Pleasure principle   Pertaining to the need for instinctual urges to be gratified immediately either directly or through fantasy.

Polygenic   Involving a combination of hereditary influences.

Polymorphous perversion   Pertaining to the theory that the sex drive in the child has no predetermined outlet and leads to behavior that would be deviant or perverse in an adult.

Polynucleotide   Enzyme.

Porencephaly   Congenital disorder in which there are funnel-shaped cavities in the brain communicating with the ventricles.

Porphyria   Metabolic disorder involving the excretion of porphyrins in the urine; transmitted as a dominant trait; may be associated with mental retardation.

Postpartum psychosis   Mental disorder following the birth of a child.

Preconscious   Not conscious but capable of becoming conscious.

Prefrontal lobotomy   Form of psychosurgery.

Prelogical thinking   Nonlogical nature of the thinking process of the schizophrenic patient.

Premenstrual tension   Emotional reaction in women prior to the onset of the menstrual cycle.

Presenile   Pertaining to premature aging.

Primal scene   Childhood memory of an early sexual experience, often related to parental sexual relations.

Prodromal   Early or warning signs of disease.

Progesterone   Female sex hormone produced by the ovaries during the active reproduction years.

Prognosis   Predicted outcome of a disorder.

Projection   Placing blame elsewhere; defense mechanism.

Projective test   Personality test based on responses to relatively unstructured materials and situations.

Prolonged narcosis   Sleep therapy.

Prostigmine   Chemical related to acetylcholine; stimulates the parasympathetic system.

Pseudocyesis   False pregnancy.

Pseudoneurotic schizophrenia   Marginal type of schizophrenia having strong neurotic components.

Pseudoretardation   Clinical condition which gives the appearance of mental retardation but in which the patient is not retarded.

Psychasthenia   Neurotic reaction characterized by obsessions, compulsions, and phobias.

Psyche   Human mind.

Psychedelic drug   Chemical that induces hallucinations. LSD, mescaline.

Psychiatry   Medical specialty dealing with the diagnosis and treatment of mental illness.

Psychoactive drugs   Drugs which affect the psychological functions of the individual.

Psychoanalysis   Freudian theory of personality and technique for treating personality disturbances.

Psychobiology   Psychiatric approach advanced by Adolf Meyer.

Psychodrama   Psychological treatment based upon the deliberate acting out of conflict situations.

Psychogalvanic response   Electrical skin resistance.

Psychogenic   Having a psychological origin.

Psychomotor   Motor behavior associated with psychological processes.

Psychomotor seizure   Convulsive disorder characterized by a wide range of behavior disturbances of a dissociative nature.

Psychopath   Antisocial personality.

Psychosis   Severe mental illness.

Psychosomatic   Referring to the relationship between psychological processes and body functions.

Psychosurgery   Brain surgery used to treat mental illness.

Psychotherapy   Treatment of emotional and behavior disturbances by psychological methods.

Psychotomimetic   Resembling a psychosis.

Psychotropic   Capable of influencing the mind.

Puerile   Childish.

Pupillometry   Measurement of pupillary changes as an indication of emotional reactions.

Purposive accident   Unconsciously motivated accident.

Pyknic type   Stout and compact body type described by Kretschmer.

Pyromania   Compulsive urge to set fires.

Quadriplegia   Paralysis of all four limbs of the body.

Quaternary stage   Stage in the development of syphilis.

Racial unconscious   That part of the unconscious which is inherited; collective unconscious.

Radio surgery   Form of psychosurgery in which proton rays are beamed into the brain tissue.

Rapport   Emotional acceptance of the therapist by the patient, and of the patient by the therapist.

Rationalization   Giving reasons and making excuses; defense mechanism.

Reaction formation   Denying a conflict; defense mechanism.

Reactive depression   Neurotic depressive reaction.

Reality principle   Pertaining to the necessity for instinctual urges to be adjusted to the demands of the environment.

Recall reaction   Third phase of the disaster syndrome.

Reciprocal inhibition   Principle of behavior therapy that assumes that incompatible states, namely anxiety and relaxation, cannot be experienced at the same time.

Recoil reaction   Second phase of the disaster syndrome.

Reconstructive psychotherapy   Psychological treatment directed toward a fundamental reorganization of the basic personality structure and dynamics of the patient.

Regression   Return to behavior used at an earlier period in life; defense mechanism.

Reinforcement   Rewarding a desired response in operant conditioning; following the conditioned stimulus with the unconditioned stimulus in classical conditioning.

Remission   Period of improvement in the course of mental illness.

Repetition compulsion   Need to repeat a behavior pattern over and over in an effort to reduce anxiety.

Repression   Unconscious tendency to exclude painful material from consciousness; defense mechanism.

Reserpine   Tranquilizing drug derived from the plant *rauwolfia serpentina*.

Resistance   Reluctance on the part of the patient in psychotherapy to produce significant material because of its anxiety-provoking nature.

Reticular activating system   See *Reticular formation*.

Reticular formation   Lower brain structure related to arousal, alertness, and consciousness.

Rhinencephalon   Visceral brain; limbic lobe.

Riboflavin   Vitamin B_2.

Ribonuclease   First enzyme to be artificially synthesized.

RNA (ribonucleic acid)   Chemical molecule involved in the transmission of genetic information.

Rorschach test   Projective personality test in which the subject is required to respond to a series of inkblots.

Rubella   Measles.

Sadism   Sexual satisfaction from giving pain to others.

Sanguine   Hopeful and confident.

Scaphocephaly   Distortion of the skull giving the head a long and narrow appearance.

Scatter   Irregularity of test performance on intelligence scales.

Schizoid   Seclusive, withdrawn, and unsociable; schizophrenic-like.

Schizophrenogenic   Contributing to the development of schizophrenia.

Scotophilia   Erotic satisfaction obtained from observing others; voyeurism.

Secondary gains   Secondary advantages derived from a neurotic symptom.

Secondary ventilation   Discharge of deeper levels of emotion-laden material during psychotherapy.

Self-confrontation   Treatment technique in which the individual observes his own deviant behavior by videotape or other means.

Self-stimulation   Technique by means of which animals are able to stimulate their brains electrically.

Senile   Pertaining to old age.

Senile plaque   Type of cell structure characteristic of the aging brain.

Sensory isolation   Experimental reduction of sensory cues.

Sequelae   Aftereffects of an injury or disorder.

Serotonin   Chemical mediator in the transmission of the nerve impulse; neurohormone.

Shock reaction   First phase of the disaster syndrome.

Sibling   Brother or sister born of the same parents.

Sibling rivalry   Rivalry between brothers and sisters.

Sociopath   Antisocial personality.

Sodium diphenyl hydantoinate   Anticonvulsant drug, Dilantin sodium.

Soldier's heart   See *Effort syndrome.*

Somatic   Pertaining to the body.

Somatotonia   Temperament expressed through exertion, exercise, and physical self-expression; associated with the mesomorph body type of Sheldon.

Somnambulism   Sleepwalking.

Somniloquy   Sleeptalking.

Spastic diplegia   See *Cerebral palsy.*

Spastic paralysis   See *Cerebral palsy.*

Spirochete   Organism of syphilis.

Stage of exhaustion   Third stage of the general adaptation syndrome.

Stage of resistance   Second stage of the general adaptation syndrome.

Status epilepticus   Succession of convulsive seizures without intervening recovery of consciousness.

Stigmatization   Psychogenic skin eruptions having religious significance.

Still reaction   Protective device used by certain animals when in danger; "playing dead."

Stimulus generalization   The spread of a response to a specific stimulus to a group of related stimuli.

Stress   Force applied to a system; physical and psychological pressures exerted on the body and personality.

Stressors   Events or conditions causing stress.

Structural analogue   See *Antimetabolite.*

Stupor   State of deep apathy and diminished sensibility.

Sturge-Weber syndrome   Condition in which an excessive growth of blood vessels in the skin causes a large birthmark on the face and neck.

Subcortical   Below the cerebral cortex.

Subcutaneous   Under the skin.

Sublimation   Gratification of primitive impulses in a socially approved manner; defense mechanism.

Substitution   Defense mechanism; adopting realistic goals in place of unrealistic ones.

Substrate   Underlayer.

Sulci   Shallow grooves on the surface of the brain.

Superego   That part of the personality structure which incorporates parental standards; conscience.

Supportive psychotherapy   Psychological treatment designed to remove symptoms by reinforcing existing personality defenses.

Surrogate mother   Substitute mother.

Sympathetic system   Segment of the autonomic nervous system.

Symptomatic   Pertaining to a specific symptom.

Syndrome   Group of symptoms which combine to form a particular disease or condition.

Systemic   Pertaining to a system of the body.

T-group   Training group; a form of encounter group.

Tabo-paresis   Form of syphilis of the nervous system involving the brain and spinal cord.

Tachycardia   Rapid heart rate.

Tarantism   Dancing mania.

Taraxein   Protein fraction related to ceruloplasmin; reported in schizophrenics.

TAT   Thematic Apperception Test; projective test of personality using a series of pictures.

Tay-Sach's disease   Hereditary disorder of fat metabolism; may be associated with mental retardation.

Telestimulation   Stimulation of the nervous system of a subject by means of radio or similar means.

Temporal lobe seizure   See *Psychomotor seizure*.

Tertiary stage   Stage in the development of syphilis.

Testosterone   Principal male sex hormone.

Thalamotomy   Form of psychosurgery in which electrodes are introduced into the thalamic region of the brain.

Thalamus   Lower brain structure serving as a sensory relay center.

THC (tetrahydrocannabinol)   Active chemical ingredient in marihuana.

Therapy   Treatment.

Thermocoagulation   Form of psychosurgery in which brain centers are destroyed by electricity.

Thiamine   Vitamin B_1.

Thiocyanate   Drug used to control high blood pressure.

Thrombosis   Blood clotting.

Thymine   Basic chemical unit of the DNA molecule.

Thyroid glands   Pair of endocrine glands on each side of the neck below the larynx.

Thyrotrophic hormone   Secretion of the anterior pituitary gland influencing the thyroid glands.

Thyroxine   Thyroid gland hormone.

Tic   Involuntary jerking of a small muscle group.

Tigretier   Form of dancing mania observed in Africa.

Token economy   Behavior modification method in which people are rewarded for appropriate behavior with tokens that can be exchanged for desired items or privileges.

Tonic phase   First phase of the *grand mal* convulsion; characterized by a contraction of the musculature.

Toxemia   Condition in which the blood contains toxic or poisonous substances.

Toxin   Poisonous substance.

Toxoplasmosis   Infection due to a protozoan-like organism; may be associated with mental retardation.

Transference   Process in psychotherapy in which the therapist assumes the role of a substitute parent; an emotional bond between the patient and therapist which is a reliving of childhood experiences.

Transference neurosis   Intense transference relationship which develops during depth therapy.

Translocation   Inappropriate shift in chromosome material.

Transorbital lobotomy   Form of psychosurgery in which the brain is entered through the thin bony structure behind the eye.

Transplacental   Transmitted by way of the placenta.

Transsexualism   Change from one sex to the other by means of surgery.

Transvestism   Wearing the clothing of members of the opposite sex.

Trauma   Shock or injury.

Tremor   Rhythmic and involuntary muscle movements.

Trephination   Cutting a small opening in the skull.

Trimester   Three-month period, usually with reference to pregnancy.

Trimethadione   Drug used to treat *petit mal* convulsions; Tridione.

Triplegia   Paralysis of three limbs of the body.

Trisomy   Having three chromosomes instead of the normal pair. Seen in Down's syndrome.

Tropenkohler   Personality disturbance similar to Amok; observed among African natives.

Tryptamine   Intermediate product in certain metabolic processes.

TTD   Tetraethylthiuram-disulphide; drug used in the conditioned aversion treatment of alcoholism; Antabuse.

Tuberous sclerosis   Inherited neoplastic disease sometimes associated with mental retardation; epiloia.

Tunnel vision   Progressive restriction of the visual field.

Type-token ration   Relation of the number of different words used in a speech sample to the total number of words used.

Tyrosine   Amino acid found in protein substances.

Ultrasonic   Pertaining to sound waves of higher frequency than can be heard by the human ear.

Unconscious   Below the threshold of consciousness; nonconscious.

Uniovular twins   Identical twins; monozygotic twins.

Unipolar depression   Depresssion related to specific life events.

Urethra   Duct that discharges urine from the bladder.

Urticaria   Hives; itching eruptions on the skin.

Uterus   Structure in which the embryo of mammals develops within the mother's body.

Vagus nerve   Tenth cranial nerve; pneumogastric nerve.

Vandalism   Malicious destruction of property.

Vasomotor   Pertaining to the expansion and contraction of the blood vessels.

Vasomotor rhinitis   Congestion of the nasal mucous membrane and the conjunctivae of the eyes.

Venesection   Bloodletting.

Ventricle   Small cavity within the heart or the brain.

Verbigeration Meaningless and stereotyped repetition of phrases or words.

Vertigo Dizziness.

Vesania Eighteenth-century term for all mental disorders.

Vicarious Pertaining to a substitute.

Virilism Development by a female of the secondary sex characteristics of a male.

Visceral Pertaining to the internal organs.

Visceral brain Ringlike convolution around the base of the cerebral hemisphere; limbic lobe.

Viscerotonia Relaxed, sociable, and convivial temperament, associated with the endomorph body type described by Sheldon.

Vital dye Substance used for staining living tissues.

Vitamin A Carotene.

Vitamin B_1 Thiamine.

Vitamin B_2 Riboflavin.

Vitamin B_6 Group of vitamins including pyridoxine, pyridoxol, and pyridoxamine.

Vitamin B_{12} Cyanocobalamin.

Vitamin C Ascorbic acid.

Vitamin H Biotin.

Von Recklinghausen's disease Neoplastic disorder associated in some cases with mental retardation; neurofibromatosis.

Voyeurism Erotic satisfaction obtained from observing others; scotophilia.

WAIS Wechsler Adult Intelligence Scale.

Wassermann test Test of the blood or cerebrospinal fluid for the detection of syphilis.

Wechsler tests Series of comprehensive tests of intelligence.

Wilson's disease Inherited disorder of protein metabolism which may be associated with mental retardation.

WISC Wechsler Intelligence Scale for Children.

Withdrawal symptoms Physical and psychological symptoms associated with the attempt to stop the use of certain drugs.

Witigo Personality disturbance in which the victim believes he is turning into a cannibal; observed among Canadian Indian tribes.

XYY variant Genetic deviation in which there are two Y (male) chromosomes rather than one, which is more common.

Zoophilia Sexual inclinations directed toward animals; bestiality.

Zygote Fertilized egg.

References

Ackerman, N. W. *The psychodynamics of family life.* New York: Basic Books, 1958.

Adler, N. E. Emotional responses of women following therapeutic abortion. *American Journal of Orthopsychiatry*, 1975, **45**(3), 446.

Aguilera, D. C., & Messick, J. M. *Crisis intervention: Theory and methodology* (2nd ed.). St. Louis: Mosby, 1974.

Aitken, R. C., et al. Treatment of flying phobia in aircrew. *American Journal of Psychotherapy*, 1971, **25**(4), 530.

Alper, T. An electric shock patients tells his story. *Journal of Abnormal and Social Psychology*, 1948, **43**, 201.

Ames, F. A clinical and metabolic study of acute intoxication with *cannabis sativa* and its role in the model psychoses. *Journal of Mental Science*, 1958, **104**, 991.

Andermann, E. Cited in the hearings before a subcommittee of the Committee on Appropriations, House of Representatives, 91st Congress, First Session, Pt. 3, 1969, p. 136.

Anthony, E. J. The influence of maternal psychosis in children—Folie à deux. In E. J. Anthony & T. Benedek (Eds.), *Parenthood.* Boston: Little, Brown, 1970.

Anthony, E. J. Children at risk from divorce: *A review*. In E. J. Anthony & C. Koupernik (Eds.), *The child in his family: Children at psychiatric risk.* New York: Wiley, 1974.

Anthony, E. J., & Koupernik, C. (Eds.) *The child in his family: Children at psychiatric risk.* New York: Wiley, 1974.

Antonovsky, A., & Maoz, B. Twenty-five years later: A limited study of sequelae of the concentration camp experience. *Social Psychology*, 1971, **6**(4), 186.

Arthur, R. J. Extreme stress in adult life and its psychic and psychophysiological consequences. In E. K. Gunderson & R. H. Rahe (Eds.), *Life stress and illness.* Springfield, Ill.: Charles C Thomas, 1974.

Ascough, J. C., & Sipprelle, C. N. Operant Verbal Conditioning of Autonomic Responses. *Behaviour Research and Therapy*, 1968, **6**, 363.

Atcheson, J. D. Problems of mental health in the Canadian Arctic. *Canada's Mental Health* (Ottawa), 1972, **20**(1), 10.

Ayllon, T., & Azrin, N. H. *The token economy: A motivational system for therapy and rehabilitation.* New York: Appleton-Century-Crofts, 1968.

Bacon, S. D. The process of addiction to alcohol. *Quarterly Journal of Studies on Alcohol*, 1973, **34**, 1.

Bagley, C. Social prejudice and the adjustment of people with epilepsy. *Epilepsia,* 1972, **13**, 33.

Baker, R., Hall, J. N., & Hutchinson, K. A token economy project with chronic schizophrenic patients. *British Journal of Psychiatry*, 1974, **124**, 367.

Ban, T. A. *Depression and the tricyclic antidepressants.* Montreal: Ronalds Federated Graphics, 1974.

440

Ban, T. A. Pharmacotherapy of depression: A critical review. *Psychosomatics*, 1975, **16**, 17.

Bandura, A. *Principles of behavior modification.* New York: Holt, 1969.

Bandura, A. (Ed.) *Theories of modeling.* New York: Atherton, 1970.

Bandura, A., Grusec, J. E., & Menlove, F. L. Vicarious extinction of avoidance behavior. *Journal of Personality and Social Psychology*, 1967, **5**, 16.

Bandura, A., & Walters, R. H. *Social learning and personality development.* New York: Holt, 1963.

Beaumont, W. *Experiments and observations of the gastric juice and the physiology of digestion.* New York: Dover, 1902.

Beck, A. T. *Depression: Clinical, experimental, and theoretical aspects.* New York: Harper & Row, 1967.

Beck, A. T. *Diagnosis and management of depression.* Philadelphia: University of Pennsylvania Press, 1973.

Beck, A. T., et al. Ideational components of anxiety. *Archives of General Psychiatry*, 1974, **31**(3), 319.

Beebe, G. W. Follow-up studies of World War II and Korean war prisoners. *American Journal of Epidemiology*, 1975, **101**(5), 400.

Beiser, M., et al. Illness of the spirit among the Serer of Senegal. *American Journal of Psychiatry*, 1973, **130**(8), 881.

Belmaker, R., Pollin, W., Wyatt, R. J., et al. A follow-up of monozygotic twins discordant for schizophrenia. *Archives of General Psychiatry*, 1974, **30**, 219.

Bennet, G. Psychological breakdown at sea: Hazards of single-handed ocean sailing. *British Journal of Medical Psychology.* 1974, **47**, 189.

Berger, H. Ueber das Elektrenkephalogram des Menschen. *Archiv Fuer Psychiatrie und Nervenkrankheiten*, 1929, **87**, 527.

Berlin, I. N. (Ed.) *Advocacy for child mental health.* New York: Brunner/Mazel, 1975.

Berne, E. *Principles of group treatment.* New York: Oxford University Press, 1966.

Berne, E. *Transactional analysis in psychotherapy.* New York: Ballantine, 1973.

Bernhardson, G., & Gunne, L. Forty-six cases of psychosis in cannabis abusers. *International Journal of Addiction*, 1972, **7**, 9.

Bhanji, S., & Thompson, J. Operant conditioning in the treatment of anorexia nervosa: A review and retrospective study of 11 cases. *British Journal of Psychiatry*, 1974, **124**, 166.

Birk, L., et al. Avoidance conditioning for homosexuality. *Archives of General Psychiatry*, 1971, **25**, 314.

Blatt, B. *Exodus from pandemonium.* Boston: Allyn and Bacon, 1970.

Bleuler, E. *Dementia praecox or the group of schizophrenias.* New York: International Universities Press, 1950.

Bleuler, M. The long-term course of the schizophrenic psychoses. *Psychological Medicine*, 1974, **4**, 244.

Block, J. Parents of schizophrenic, neurotic, asthmatic, and congenitally ill children. *Archives of General Psychiatry*, 1969, **20**, 659.

Bogoras, W. *The chukchee*, Jessup Expedition Report, 1904-1909. New York: 1910. American Museum of Natural History.

Bourne, P. G. The Viet Nam veteran: Psychosocial casualties. *Psychiatry in Medicine*, 1972, **3**(1), 23.

Bowlby, J. Psychopathology of anxiety: The role of affectional bonds. In M. H. Lader (Ed.), *Studies of anxiety*. London: Royal Medico-Psychological Association, 1969.

Braceland, F. J. Emotional accompaniments of cardiac surgery. *Postgraduate Medicine*, 1974, **55**(3), 130.

Breggin, P. R. Lobotomies: An alert. *American Journal of Psychiatry*, 1972, **129**, 97.

Brenner, M. H. *Mental illness and the economy*. Cambridge: Harvard, 1973.

Brill, A. A. Pibloktoq or hysteria among Peary's Eskimos. *Journal of Nervous and Mental Disease*, 1913, **40**, 514.

Brown, B. B. Heart beat and blood pressure: Acts of will. *Psychology Today*, 1974, **8**(3), 90.

Brozik, J., & Gentzkow, H. Psychologic effects of thiamine restriction and deprivation in normal young men. In N. L. Corak & E. N. Gale (Eds.), *The origins of abnormal behavior*. New York: Addison-Wesley, 1971.

Budzynsky, T. H., et al. EMG biofeedback and tension headeache: A controlled outcome study. *Psychosomatic Medicine*, 1973, **35**, 484.

Buss, A. *Psychopathology*. New York: Wiley, 1966.

Busse, E. W., & Wang, H. S. The multiple factors contributing to dementia in old age. In R. de la Fuente & M. N. Weisman (Eds.), *Psychiatry: Proceedings of the 5th world congress of psychiatry* (Pt.II). New York: American Elsevier, 1973.

Cade, J. F. Lithium salts in the treatment of psychotic excitement. *Medical Journal of Australia*, 1951, **2**, 349.

Cadoret, R. J., & Winokur, G. Genetic principles in the classification of affective illnesses. *International Journal of Mental Health*, 1972, **1** (1-2), 159.

Cadoret, R. J., & Winokur, G. Depression in alcoholism. *Annals of the New York Academy of Sciences*, 1974, **233**, 34.

Cadoret, R. J., & Winokur, G. X-linkage in manic-depressive illness. *Annual Review of Medicine*, 1975, **26**, 21.

Cahalan, D., et al. *Drinking practices and problems in the U.S. Army*. Washington, D. C.: Department of the Army, 1972.

Cahalan, D., & Cisin, I. H. *Report of a pilot study of the attitudes and* *behavior of naval personnel concerning alcohol and problem drinking.* Washington, D. C.: Bureau of Social Science Research, Inc., 1973.

Caine, D. B., & Lader, M. H. Electromyographic studies of tremor using an averaging computer. *Electroencephalography and Clinical Neurophysiology*, 1969, **26**, 86.

Caraven Surveys Opinion Research Corporation. *Executives' knowledge, attitudes, and behavior regarding alcoholism and alcohol abuse* (Study No. 2). Princeton, N.J.: Authors, 1974.

Carlson, G. A., et al. Follow-up of 53 bipolar manic-depressive patients. *British Journal of Psychiatry*, 1974, **124**, 134.

Carnahan, J. E. *The effects of self-monitoring of patients on the control of hypertension.* Ann Arbor: University Microfilms, 1973.

Carter, D., & Strickland, S. *A first hand look at the Surgeon General's report on television and violence.* Palo Alto: Aspen Program on Communications and Society, 1972.

Centerwall, W. R., & Centerwall, S. A. *Phenylketonuria: An inherited metabolic disorder associated with mental retardation.* Washington, D. C.: Maternal and Child Health Service, U. S. Department of Health, Education, and Welfare, 1972.

Chesler, P. *Women and madness.* New York: Doubleday, 1972.

Chess, S., & Thomas, A. (Eds.) *Annual progress in child psychiatry and child development.* New York: Brunner/Mazel, 1968.

Chicago Center for Policy Study *The social impact of urban design.* Chicago: University of Chicago Press, 1971.

Clausen, J. A., & Yarrow, M. R. The impact of mental illness on the family. *Journal of Social Issues*, 1955, **11**. (Entire issue)

Clayton, P. J., Desmarais, L., & Winokur, G. A study of normal bereavement. *American Journal of Psychiatry*, 1968, **125**, 168.

Cliffe, M. J. Reinstatement of speech in mute schizophrenics by operant conditioning. *Acta Psychiatrica Scandinavica*, 1974, **50**, 577.

Coate, M. *Beyond all reason.* London: Constable, 1964.

Cobb, S. Physiologic changes in men whose jobs were abolished. *Journal of Psychosomatic Research*, 1974, **18**, 245.

Cohler, B. J. et al. Social relations, stress, and psychiatric hospitalization among mothers of young children. *Social Psychiatry*, 1974, **9**(1), 7.

Comfort, A. *The biology of senescence.* New York: Rinehart, 1956.

Coombs, G. J., et al. Automated medical histories: Factors determining patient performance. *Computers and Biomedical Research*, 1970, **3**, 178.

Cooper, J. E., et al. *Psychiatric diagnosis in New York and London.* London: Oxford University Press, 1972.

Corsellis, J. A. N., et al. The aftermath of boxing. *Psychological Medicine*, 1973, **3**, 270.

Cuttler, B., & Reed, J. Multiple personality: A single case with a 15 year follow-up. *Psychological Medicine*, 1975, **5**, 18.

Deiker, T. E., & Pollock, D. H. Integration of hypnotic and systematic desensitization techniques in the treatment of phobias: A case report. *American Journal of Clinical Hypnosis*, 1975, **17**, 171.

Diagnostic and statistical manual of mental disorders (2nd ed.). Washington, D.C.: American Psychiatric Association, 1968.

Dohrenwend, B. S., & Dohrenwend, B. P. (Eds.) *Stressful life events: Their nature and effects*. New York: Wiley-Interscience, 1974.

Dorfman, W. The recognition and management of masked depression. In R. de la Fuente & M. N. Weisman (Eds.), *Psychiatry: Proceedings of the 5th world congress on psychiatry* (Pt. 1). New York: American Elsevier, 1973.

Eisinger, A. J., et al. Female Homosexuality. London: *Nature*, 1972, **238**, 106.

Eisler, R. M., et al. Effects of modeling on components of assertive behavior. *Journal of Behavior Therapy and Experimental Psychiatry*, 1973, **4**, 1.

Eitinger, L. *Concentration camp survivors in Norway and Israel*. Copenhagen: Universitetsforlaget, 1964.

Eitinger, L. Adjustment of survivors of Nazi concentration camps. In M. Lader & I. Marks (Eds.), *Clinical anxiety*. New York: Grune & Stratton, 1971.

Ekman, P., & Friesen, W. V. Nonverbal behavior and psychopathology. In R. J. Friedman & M. M. Katz (Eds.), *The psychology of depression*. New York: Winston, 1974.

Ellis, A. *Reason and emotion in psychotherapy.* New York: Lyle Stuart, 1962.

Ellis, A. *Humanistic psychotherapy: The rational-emotive approach* (Edward Sagarin, Ed.). New York: McGraw-Hill, 1974.

English, J. T. Sensitivity training: Promise and performance. *American Journal of Psychiatry*, 1969, **126**, 142.

Epstein, A. S. The fetish object: Phylogenetic considerations. *Archives of Sexual Behavior*, 1975, **4**(3), 303.

Epstein, A. W. Fetishism: A comprehensive view. In J. H. Masserman (Ed.) *Science and psychoanalysis*, New York: Grune & Stratton, 1969.

Esquirol, J. E. D. *Des maladies mentales considerée sous les rapports medical, hygienique et medico-legal.* Paris: J.-B. Bailliere et fils, 1838.

Evans, R. B. Physical and biochemical characteristics of homosexual men. *Journal of Consulting and Clinical Psychology*, 1972, **39**(1), 140.

Eysenck, H. J. The effects of psychotherapy: An evaluation. *Journal of Consulting and Clinical Psychology*, 1952, **16**, 319.

Faris, R. E. L., & Dunham, H. W. *Mental disorder in urban areas.* Chicago: University of Chicago Press, 1939.

Feighner, J. P., et al. Diagnostic criteria for use in psychiatric research. *Archives of General Psychiatry*, 1972, **26**, 57.

Fenton, G. Reappraisal: Special investigation in psychiatry. *Proceedings of the Royal Society of Medicine*, 1974, **67**, 912.

Ferster, C. B. Positive reinforcement and behavioral deficits of autistic children. *Child Development*, 1961, **32**, 437.

Fish, B. Contributions of developmental research to a theory of schizophrenia. In J. Hellmuth (Ed.), *Exceptional infant.* New York: Brunner/Mazel, 1971.

Fisher, G. Psychological needs of heterosexual pedophiliacs. *Diseases of the Nervous System*, 1969, **30**, 419.

Folling, A. Uber Ausscheidung von Phenylbrenz-traubensaure in den Harn als Stoffwechselanomalie in Verbindung mit Imbezilitat. *Zeitschrift fuer Physiologische Chemie*, 1934, **227**, 169.

Frankl, V. E. *The doctor and the soul: An introduction to logotherapy.* New York: Knopf, 1955.

Frankl, V. E. *Man's search for meaning.* Boston: Beacon, 1962.

Friedhoff, A. J., & Van Winkle, E. Isolation and characterization of a compound from the urine of schizophrenics. *Nature*, 1962, **194**, 897.

Friedman, M., & Rosenman, R. H. *Type A behavior and your heart.* New York: Knopf, 1974.

Frohman, C. E., Caldwell, D. F., & Gottlieb, J. S. Abnormalities in tryptophan metabolites in schizophrenia. *Psychopharmacology Bulletin*, 1974, **10**, 56.

Fuente, R. de la, & Weisman, M. N. (Eds.) *Psychiatry: Proceedings of the 5th world congress of psychiatry* (Pts. 1,2). New York: American Elsevier, 1973.

Fuller, John G. *The day of St. Anthony's fire.* New York: Macmillan, 1968.

Fulton, J. F., & Jacobsen, C. E. The functions of the frontal lobes: A comparative study in monkeys, chimpanzees, and man. *Abstracts of the second International Neurological Conference.* London: 1935.

Galton, F. *Inquiries into human faculty and its development.* London: Macmillan, 1883.

GAP: *The VIP with psychiatric impairment.* New York: Scribner, 1973.

Garmezy, N., & Nuechterlein, K. Invulnerable children: The fact and fiction of competence and disadvantage. *American Journal of Orthopsychiatry*, 1972, **42**(2), 328.

Geerlings, P. J., & Schalken, R. M. Acute adverse reactions to drug-taking. *Acta Psychiatrica Scandinavica*, 1972, **48**, 22.

Glass, A. J. Psychotherapy in combat zone. *American Journal of Psychiatry*, 1954, **110**, 725.

Glass, S. J. Homosexuality and testosterone. *New England Journal of Medicine*, 1972, **286**(7), 381.

Glasser, W. *Reality therapy.* New York: Harper & Row, 1965.

Glasser, W. *Reality therapy: A new approach to psychiatry.* New York: Harper & Row, 1975.

Goodhart, C. B. Female homosexuality. *London: Nature*, 1972, **239**, 174.

Goodwin, D. W., et al. Alcohol problems in adoptees raised apart from biological parents. *Archives of General Psychiatry*, 1973, **28**, 238. (a)

Goodwin, D. W., et al. The question of a genetic basis for alcoholism. *Quarterly Journal of Studies on Alcohol*, 1973, **34**, 1341. (b)

Greden, J. F., & Morgan, D. W. Patterns of drug use and attitudes toward treatment in a military population. *Archives of General Psychiatry*, 1972, **26**, 113.

Greist, J. H., et al. A computer interview for psychiatric patient target symptoms. *Archives of General Psychiatry*, 1973, **29**, 247.

Groh, C., & Rosenmayer, F. W. Epilepsy still kept a secret? *Epilepsia*, 1972, **13**, 480.

Grossman, J., et al. Computer acquired patient histories. *Journal of the American Medical Association*, 1971, **215**, 1286.

Grossman, H. J., et al. (Eds.) *Manual on terminology and classification in mental retardation.* New York: American Association oh Mental Deficiency, 1973.

Groth, A. N. *A differential classification of pedophiles determined by the nature of their object relations.* Ann Arbor: University Microfilms, 1972.

Grunebaum, H., et al. *Mentally ill mothers and their children.* Chicago: University of Chicago Press, 1975.

Gunderson, E. K., & Rahe, R. H. *Life stress and illness.* Springfield, Ill.: Charles C Thomas, 1974.

Haley, J. An interactional description of schizophrenia. *Psychiatry*, 1959, **22**, 321.

Hamburg, D. A., Moos, R. H., & Yalom, I. D. Studies of distress in the menstrual cycle and the postpartum period. In R. Michael (Ed.), *Endocrinology and human behavior.* London: Oxford University Press, 1968.

Hampton, P. T., & Tarnasky, W. G. Hysterectomy and tubal ligation: A comparison of the psychological aftermath. *American Journal of Obstetrics and Gynecology*, 1974, **119**, 949.

Hargrove, R. *EST: Making life work.* New York: Delacorte Press, 1976.

Harris, R. The relationship between organic brain disease and physical status. In G. Gaitz (Ed.), *Aging and the brain.* New York: Plenum, 1972.

Hathaway, S. R., & McKinley, J. C. *The Minnesota Multiphasic Personality Inventory.* New York: The Psychological Corporation, 1943.

Hausman, W., & Rioch, D. M. Military psychiatry. *Archives of General Psychiatry*, 1967, **16**, 727.

Heber, R., et al. *Rehabilitation of families at risk for mental retardation*, Progress Report. Washington, D. C.: Department of Health, Education, and Welfare, 1972.

Henry, G. W. *All the sexes: A study of masculinity and femininity.* New York: Holt, 1955.

Herridge, C. F. Aircraft noise and mental hospital admissions. *Sound*, 1972, **6**, 32.

Hersen, M. Effects of practice, instructions, and modelling on components of assertive behaviour. *Behaviour Research and Therapy*, 1973, **11**, 441.

Heston, L. L. Psychiatric disorders in foster home reared children of schizophrenic mothers. *British Journal of Psychiatry*, 1966, **112**, 819.

Hingten, J. N., Coulter, S. K., & Churchill, D. W. Intensive reinforcement of imitative behavior in mute autistic children. *Archives of General Psychiatry*, 1967, **17**, 36.

Hinton, J. *Dying*. London: Pelican Books, 1967.

Hoenig, J., & Kenna, J. C. The nosological position of transsexualism. *Archives of Sexual Behavior*, 1974, **3**(3), 273.

Hollingshead, A. B., et al. Social mobility and mental illness. *American Sociological Review*, 1954, **19**, 577.

Hollingshead, A. B., & Redlich, F. C. *Social class and mental illness*. New York: Wiley, 1958.

Holmes, T. H., & Rahe, R. H. The social readjustment rating scale. *Journal of Psychomatic Research*, 1967, **11**, 213.

Howel, L. M. Clinical and research impressions regarding murder and sexually perverse crimes. *Psychotherapy and Psychosomatics*, 1972, **21**(1-6), 156.

Hunter, R., et al. Alzheimer's disease in one monozygotic twin. *Journal of neurology, neurosurgery, and psychiatry*, 1972, **35**, 707.

Huttman, E. D. Public housing: Negative psychological effects on family living. *American Journal of Orthopsychiatry*, 1971, **41**(2), 244.

Itard, J. M. G. *Rapports et memoires sur le sauvage de l'Aveyron*. Paris: Bibliotheque d'Education Speciale, 1824.

Itil, T. M., Saletu, B., & Davis, S. EEG findings in chronic schizophrenics based on digital computer period analysis and analog power spectra. *Biological Psychiatry*, 1972, **5**, 1.

Jacobson, S., Fasman, J., & DiMascio, A. Deprivation in the childhood of depressed women. *Journal of Nervous and Mental Disease*, 1975, **160**(1), 5.

Janis, I. L. *Psychological stress: Psychoanalytic and behavioral studies of surgical patients*. New York: Wiley, 1958.

Janov, A. *The primal scream*. New York: Dell, 1970.

Jenkins, C. D., Rosenman, R. H., & Zyzanski, S. J. Prediction of clinical coronary heart disease by a test for the coronary-prone behavior pattern. *New England Journal of Medicine*, 1974, **290**, 1271.

Jessor, R., & Jessor, S. L. *Problem drinking in youth: Personality, social, and behavioral antecedents and correlates*. Boulder, Colo.: University of Colorado, Institute of Behavioral Science, 1973.

Jones, M. C. Elimination of children's fears. *Journal of Experimental Psychology*, 1924, **7**, 382.

Jowett, B. (Trans.) *The dialogues of Plato.* New York: Random House, 1953.

Kallmann, F. J. *Heredity in health and mental disorder.* New York: Norton, 1953.

Kalman, G., et al. Symptom clusters in various forms of depression. *Israel Annals of Psychiatry and Related Disciplines*, 1971, **9**(3), 219.

Kammeier, M. L. Adolescents from families with and without alcohol problems. *Quarterly Journal of Studies on Alcohol*, 1971, **32**, 364.

Kantor, R. E., & Herron, W. G. *Reactive and process schizophrenia.* Palo Alto: Science and Behavior Books, 1966.

Kantor, R. E., Wallner, J. M., & Winder, C. L. Process and reactive schizophrenia. *Journal of Consulting and Clinical Psychology*, 1953, **17**, 157.

Karlsson, J. L. An Icelandic family study of schizophrenia. *British Journal of Psychiatry*, 1973, **123**, 549.

Katchadourian, H. A., & Churchill, C. W. Social class and mental illness in urban Lebanon. *Social Psychiatry*, 1969, **4**(2), 49.

Kazdin, A. E. Covert modeling and the reduction of avoidance behavior. *Journal of Abnormal Psychology*, 1973, **81**, 87.

Keilholz, P. (Ed.) *Masked depression: An international symposium.* Baltimore: Williams & Wilkins, 1974.

Keller, M., et al. (Eds.) *Alcohol and health.* Rockville, Md.: National Institute on Alcohol and Alcoholism, 1974.

Keller, S. L. *Uprooting and social change.* New Delhi: Manohar Book Service, 1975.

Kesey, K. *One flew over the cuckoo's nest.* New York: New American Library, 1962.

Kety, S. S. Problems in biological research in Psychiatry. In J. Mendels (Ed.), *Biological Psychiatry.* New York: Wiley, 1973.

Kiev, Ari. *A strategy for handling executive stress.* Chicago: Nelson-Hall, 1974.

Kleinman, R. A. *The development of voluntary cardiovascular control.* Ann Arbor: University Microfilms, 1971.

Kogelschatz, J. L., Adams, P. L., & Tucker, D. M. Family styles of fatherless households. *Journal of the American Academy of Child Psychiatry*, 1972, **11**(2), 365.

Kolansky, H., & Moore, W. T. Toxic effects of chronic marihuana use. *Journal of American Medical Association*, 1972, **222**, 35.

Kondas, M. J. *Effects of biofeedback training of alpha rhythm on arousal and therapeutic gain as an adjunct to the rehabilitation of substance dependent population.* Ann Arbor: University Microfilms, 1973.

Kral, V. A. Stress and senile psychosis. In R. de la Fuente & M. N. Weisman

(Eds.), *Psychiatry: Proceedings of the 5th world congress of psychiatry (Pt. 1)*. New York: American Elsevier, 1973.

Kramer, B. M. Racism and mental health as a field of thought and action. In C. V. Willie et al. (Eds.), *Racism and mental health*. Pittsburgh: University of Pittsburgh Press, 1973.

Kretschmer, E. *Physique and character*. London: Kegan Paul, Trench, Trubner & Co., Ltd., 1925.

Krystal, H. The physiological basis of the treatment of delirium tremens. *American Journal of Psychiatry*, 1959, **115**, 137.

Laffal, J., & Ameen, L. Hypotheses of opposite speech. *Journal of Abnormal Social Psychology*, 1959, **58**, 267.

Laing, R. D. *The politics of experience*. New York: Pantheon, 1967.

Laing, R. D., & Esterson, A. *Sanity, madness, and the family: Families of schizophrenics* (2nd ed.). New York: Basic Books, 1971.

Lantz, H. R. Population density and psychiatric diagnosis. *Sociology and Social Research*, 1953, **37**, 322.

Laughlin, H. T. *The neuroses in clinical practice*. Philadelphia: Saunders, 1956, pp. 39–40.

Lazarus, A. A. *Behavior therapy and beyond*. New York: McGraw-Hill, 1971.

Lazarus, A. A. *Multimodel behavior therapy*. New York: Springer, 1976.

Le Dain, G., et al. *The non-medical use of drugs: Interim report of the Canadian government's commission of inquiry*. Ottawa, Canada: Information Center, 1970.

Leiderman, P. H. Mothers at risk: A potential consequence of the hospital care of the premature infant. In E. J. Anthony & C. Koupernik (Eds.), *The child in his family: Children at psychiatric risk*. New York: Wiley, 1974.

Leighton, A. H. *My name is legion. Volume 1. The Stirling County studies in psychiatric disorder and sociocultural environment*. New York: Basic Books, 1961.

Leighton, A. H., et al. *Psychiatric disorder among the Yoruba*. Ithaca: Cornell University Press, 1963.

Lejeune, J., et al. Etude des chromosomes somatiques de neuf enfants mongoliens. *Comptes Rendus Hebdomadaires des Seances de l'Academie des Sciences*, 1959, **248**, 1721.

Lesse, S. Depression masked by hypochondriasis and psychosomatic disorders. In R. de la Fuente & M. N. Weisman (Eds.), *Psychiatry: Proceedings of the 5th world congress of psychiatry* (Pt. 1). New York: American Elsevier, 1973.

Lesse, S. (Ed.) *Masked depression*. New York: Jason Aronson, 1974.

Levy, L., & Rowitz, L. *The ecology of mental disorder*. New York: Behavioural Publications, 1973.

Lidz, T. Schizophrenia and the family. *Psychiatry*, 1958, **21**, 21.

Lieb, J., et al. *The crisis team*. New York: Harper & Row, 1973.

Lieberman, M. A. Psychological effects of institutionalization. *Journal of Gerontology*, 1968, **23**, 343.

Lieberman, M. A., Yalom, I. D., & Miles, M. B. *Encounter groups*: *First facts*. New York: Basic Books, 1973.

Liss, J. L., Alpers, D., & Woodruff, R. A., Jr. The irritable colon syndrome and psychiatric illness. *Diseases of the Nervous System*, 1973, **34**(4), 151.

Loewi, O. Uber Humorale Ubertragbarkeit der Herznervenwirkung. *Pfluegers Archiv fuer die Gesamte Physiologie des Menschen und der Tiere*, 1921, **189**, 239.

Loney, J. Family dynamics in homosexual women. *Archives of Sexual Behavior*, 1973, **2**(4), 313.

Loquet, C. A. C. Sociocultural deprivation or difference? *Australian Journal of Mental Retardation*, 1973, **2**(8), 228.

Lovaas, O. I., et al. The establishment of imitation and its use for the development of complex behaviour in schizophrenic children. *Behaviour Research and Therapy*, 1967, **5**, 171.

Lubar, J. F., & Bahler, W. W. Behavioral management of epileptic seizures following EEG biofeedback training of the sensorimotor rhythm. *Biofeedback and Self-regulation*, 1976, **1**, 77.

Lubin, A. J. *Stranger on the earth . . . A psychological study of Vincent van Gogh*. New York: Holt, 1972.

Luccioni, H., & Scotto, J. C. Geographical mobility and maladjustment of children and youth. *Revue de Neuropsychiatrie Infantile*, 1974, **22**(6), 371.

Luce, G. G. *Body time*. New York: Pantheon, 1971.

Lumry, G. K., et al. Psychiatric disabilities of the Viet Nam veteran: Review and implication for treatment. *Minnesota Medicine,* 1972, **65**(11), 1055.

Lunde, D. T. Report to the meeting of the American Psychiatric Association, Miami Beach, Fla., 1969. Unpublished.

Lynch, J. J., & Paskewitz, D. A. On the mechanisms of the feedback control of human brain wave activity. *Journal of Nervous and Mental Disease*, 1971, **153**(3), 205.

Lynch, J. J., Paskewitz, D. A., & Orne, M. T. Some factors in the feedback control of human alpha rhythm. *Psychosomatic Medicine*, 1974, **36**(5), 399.

McCabe, M. S., et al. Psychiatric illness among paternal and maternal relatives of poor prognosis schizophrenics. *British Journal of Psychiatry*, 1972, **120** , 91.

Manual on terminology and classification in mental retardation (Rev. ed.). Washington, D.C.: American Association on Mental Deficiency, 1973.

Marihuana: A signal of misunderstanding. Washington, D. C.: U.S. Government Printing Office, 1972.

Marihuana and health. Third annual report to the U.S. Congress from the Secretary of Health, Education, and Welfare. Rockville, Md: National Institute on Drug Abuse, 1974.

Marks, M. W., & Vestre, N. D. Self-perception and interpersonal behavior changes in marathon and time-extended encounter groups. *Journal of Consulting and Clinical Psychology*, 1974, **42**(5), 729.

Marmer, S. S., Pasnau, R. O., & Cushner, I. M. Is psychiatric consultation in abortion obsolete? *International Journal of Psychiatry in Medicine*, 1974, **5**(3), 201.

Maslach, C., et al. Hypnotic control of peripheral skin temperature: A case report. *Psychophysiology*, 1972, **9**, 600.

Mandsley, H. *The Pathology of Mind* (3rd ed.). London: Macmillan, 1879.

Mayer-Gross, W. Model psychoses, their history, relevancy, and limitations. *American Journal of Psychiatry*, 1959, **115**, 673.

Mendels, J., & Frazer, A. Brain biogenic amine depletion and mood. *Archives of General Psychiatry*, 1974, **30**, 447.

Menninger, K., et al. The new role of psychological testing in psychiatry. *American Journal of Psychiatry*, 1947, **103**, 473.

Menninger, W. *Psychiatry in a troubled world*. New York: Macmillan, 1948.

Miller, E. Psychomotor performance in presenile dementia. *Psychological Medicine*, 1974, **4**(1), 65.

Miller, N. E., & DiCara, L. V. Instrumental learning of vasomotor responses by rats. *Science*, 1968, **159**, 1485.

Mills, E. Family counseling in an industrial job-support program. *Social Casework*, 1972, **53**, 587.

Miner, G. D. The evidence for genetic components in the neuroses: A review. *Archives of General Psychiatry*, 1973, **29**(1), 111.

Monckeberg, F. Malnutrition and mental development. *American Journal of Clinical Nutrition*, 1972, **25**, 766.

Moreno, J. L. *Psychodrama* (Vol. 1). Beacon, New York: Beacon House, 1946.

National Institute of Mental Health. *Statistical note 117*. Survey and Reports Branch, Division of Biometry. Rockville, Md.: 1975.

Nielsen, J. M. The neurology of alcoholism. In G. N. Thompson (Ed.), *Alcoholism*. Springfield, Ill.: Charles C Thomas, 1956, chap. 6.

Noyes, R., Jr., et al. Lithium treatment of depression. *Comprehensive Psychiatry*, 1974, **15**(3), 187.

Ochberg, F. M., & Brown, B. S. Key issues in developing a national minority mental health program. In C. V. Willie et al. (Eds.), *Racism and mental health*. Pittsburgh: University of Pittsburgh Press, 1973.

Older, J. Psychosurgery: Ethical issues and a proposal for control. *American Journal of Orthopsychiatry*, 1974, **44**(5), 661.

Orne, M. T., & Wilson, S. K. Paper presented at the meetings of the American Association for the Advancement of Science, Boston, 1976.

Osmond, H., & Smythies, J. Schizophrenia: A new approach. *Journal of Mental Science*, 1952, **98**, 309.

Pavlov, I. P. *Lectures on conditional reflexes*, Vol. 2: *Conditional reflexes and psychiatry*. London: Lawrence and Wishart, Ltd., 1941.

Paykel, E. S. Recent life events and clinical depression. In E. K. Gunderson & R. H. Rahe, *Life stress and illness*. Springfield, Ill.: Charles C Thomas, 1974.

Paykel, E. S., Prusoff, B. A., & Uhlenhuth, E. H. Scaling of life events. *Archives of General Psychiatry*, 1971, **25**, 340.

Pearson, M. Continuing education and the physician's emotional well-being. In R. Feldman (Ed.), *Eleventh annual training institute for psychiatrists-teachers*. Boulder, Colo: Western Commission for Higher Education, 1971.

Persky, H., et al. Relation of psychologic measures of aggression and hostility to testosterone production in man. *Psychosomatic Medicine*, 1971, **33**, 265.

Pfeiffer, E. Survival in old age: Physical, psychological and social correlates of longevity. *Journal of the American Geriatrics Society*, 1970, **18**(4), 273.

Pinsker, H. *The irrelevancy of psychiatric diagnosis*. Paper read at the American Psychiatric Association meeting, Detroit, May 1967.

Poinsard, P. J. Geriatric psychiatry. *Pennsylvania Medicine*, 1972, **75**(8), 33.

Potter, H. W. Mental retardation in historical perspective. In S. Harrison & J. McDermott (Eds.), *Childhood psychopathology*. New York: International Universities Press, 1972.

Psychopharmacology Bulletin (Appendix VII), 1972, **8**(3), 42.

Quackenbos, J. D. *Hypnotic therapeutics*. New York: Harper, 1908, p. 41.

Raimy, V. C. (Ed.) *Training in clinical psychology*. Englewood Cliffs, N.J.: Prentice-Hall, 1950.

Reed, J. L. The diagnosis of "hysteria." *Psychological Medicine*, 1975, **5**, 13.

Rickels, K., et al. Bromazepam and phenobarbital in anxiety: A controlled study. *Current Therapeutic Research,* **15**(10), 679.

Riederer, P., et al. The daily rhythm of HVA, VMA, (VA), and 5-HIAA in depression syndrome. *Journal of Neural Transmission*, 1974, **35**, 23.

Roberts, A. H., et al. *Individual differences and autonomic control: Absorption, hypnotic susceptibility, and the unilateral control of skin temperature*. Paper read at Biofeedback Research Society annual meeting, February 1974.

Roesler, T., & Deisher, R. W. Youthful male homosexuality: Homosexual experience and the process of developing homosexual identity in males aged 16–22 years. *Journal of the American Medical Association*, 1972, **219**(8), 1018.

Ross, M. Death at an early age. *Canada's Mental Health*, 1970, **18**, 7.

Rutter, M. *Children of sick parents: An environmental and psychiatric study.* London: Oxford University Press, 1966.

Rutter, M. Why are London children so disturbed? *Proceedings of the Royal Society of Medicine*, 1973, **66**, 1221.

Rutter, M., & Graham, P. Epidemiology of psychiatric disorder. In M. Rutter (Ed.), *Education, health behaviour.* New York: Wiley, 1970.

Sabbach, K. Biofeedback: Tuning in to the autonomic nervous system. London: *World Medicine*, 1972, **7**(24), 17.

Sachar, E. J., et al. Disrupted 24-hour patterns of cortisol secretion in psychotic depression. *Archives of General Psychiatry*, 1973, **28**, 19.

Sack, R., & Goodwin, F. K. The "pharmacological bridge," a view from the clinical shores. *Psychopharmacology Bulletin*, 1974, **10**, 52.

Satir, V. M. *Conjoint family therapy* (Rev. ed.). Palo Alto: Science and Behavior Books, 1967.

Schildkraut, J. J. The catecholamine hypothesis of affective disorders: A review of supporting evidence. *American Journal of Psychiatry*, 1965, **122**, 509.

Schless, A. P., et al. How depressives view the significance of life events. *British Journal of Psychiatry*, 1974, **125**, 406.

Schmale, A. H. *The role of depression in health and disease.* Presented at the American Association for the Advancement of Science meeting, Chicago, December 1970.

Schmidt, K. Beyond the study of prevalence of mental illness: Prevention. In R. de la Fuente & M. N. Weisman (Eds.), *Psychiatry: Proceedings of the 5th world congress of psychiatry* (Pt. 2). New York: American Elsevier, 1973.

Schuyler, D. *The depressive spectrum.* New York: Jason Aronson, 1975.

Schwartz, G. E. Biofeedback, self regulation, and the patterning of physiological processes. *American Scientist*, 1975, **63**, 314.

Scott, J. P., & Senay, E. C. (Eds.) *Separation and depression: Clinical and research aspects.* Washington, D. C.: American Association for the Advancement of Science, 1973.

Segal, J. (Ed.) *The mental health of rural America: The rural programs of the National Institute of Mental Health.* Rockville, Md: National Institute of Mental Health, 1973.

Selye, H. *The story of the adaptation syndrome.* Montreal: Acta, 1952.

Selye, H. *Stress without distress.* Philadelphia: Lippincott, 1974.

Serber, M., & Wolpe, J. Behavior therapy techniques. *International Psychiatry Clinics*, 1972, **8**, 53.

Seymour, F. Intestinal biofeedback in functional diarrhea: A preliminary report. *Journal of Behavior Therapy and Experimental Psychiatry*, 1973, **4**, 317.

Shagass, C. Psychopharmacology of evoked potentials in man. In *Psychopharmacology: A review of progress.* Washington, D.C.: U.S. Government Printing Office, 1973.

Sharma, R. G. The effects of malnutrition on mental growth and mental health of the children. *Indian Journal of Psychiatry*, 1973, **15**(3), 272.

Schepank, H., et al. *Hereditary and environmental factors in neurosis: Depth-psychological studies of 50 pairs of twins.* New York: Springer, 1974.

Sheldon, W. H. *Varieties of human physique.* New York: Harper, 1940.

Shields, J., & Gottesman, I. I. The genetic basis for schizophrenia. *Journal of Orthomolecular Psychiatry*, 1973, **2**(1-2), 1.

Shields, J., & Slater, E. Heredity and psychological abnormality. In H. J. Eysenck (Ed.), *Handbook of abnormal psychology.* London: Pitman, 1960.

Shopsin, B., et al. Psychoactive drugs in mania. *Archives of General Psychiatry*, 1975, **32**, 34.

Siegler, M., & Osmond, H. *Models of madness, models of medicine.* New York: Macmillan, 1974.

Sigal, J. J., & Rakoff, V. Concentration camp survival. A pilot study on effects on the second generation. *Canadian Psychiatric Association Journal*, 1971, **16**, 393.

Silver, L. B., Dublin, C. C., & Lourie, R. S. Does violence breed violence? Contributions from a study of the child abuse syndrome. *American Journal of Psychiatry*, 1969, **126**(3), 404.

Skinner, B. F. *The behavior of organisms*: *An experimental analysis.* New York: Appleton-Century-Crofts, 1938.

Skinner, B. F. *Science and human behavior.* New York: Macmillan, 1953.

Skinner, B. F., & Lindsley, O. R. *Studies in behavior therapy.* Status Report 1. Naval research contract N5, Ori-7662, 1953.

Slater, E. Hysteria 311. *Journal of Mental Science*, 1961, **107**, 359.

Slater, E. A. A review of earlier evidence on genetic factors in schizophrenia. In D. Rosenthal and S. S. Kety (Eds.), *The transmission of schizophrenia.* New York: Pergamon, 1968.

Smith, W. E. & Smith, A. M. *Minamata.* New York: Holt, 1975.

Snyder, R. B., & Kahne, M. J. Stress in higher education and student use of university psychiatrists. In E. Bower (Ed.), *Orthopsychiatry and education.* Detroit: Wayne State University Press, 1971.

Sobey, F. *The nonprofessional revolution in mental health.* New York: Columbia University Press, 1970.

Spitzer, R. L., & Fleiss, J. L. A re-analysis of the reliability of psychiatric diagnosis. *British Journal of Psychiatry*, 1974, **125**, 341.

Stampfl, T. G., & Levis, D. J. Essentials of implosive therapy: A learning-theory-based psychodynamic behavioral therapy. *Journal of Abnormal Psychology*, 1967, **72**, 496.

Stead, W. W., et al. Computer-assisted interview of patients with functional headache. *Archives of Internal Medicine*, 1972, **129**, 950.

Stein, A., et al. Changes in hydrochloric acid secretion in a patient with a gastric fistula during intensive psychotherapy. *Psychosomatic Medicine*, 1962, **24**, 427.

Stein, Z., et al. *Famine and human development: The Dutch hunger winter of 1944/45.* New York: Oxford University Press, 1975.

Stern, S. Schizophrenia and socioeconomic status. *Science News*, February 19, 1972, p. 123.

Stoller, R. J. Male transsexualism: Uneasiness. *American Journal of Psychiatry*, 1973, **130**(5), 536.

Suh, K. Y., et al. Seventeen cases of postpartum disorders of Korean women. *Neuropsychiatry*, Seoul, 1969, **8**(1), 39.

Surwit, R. S. Biofeedback: A possible treatment for Raynaud's disease. *Seminars in Psychiatry*, 1973, **5**(4), 483.

Sutton, T. *Tracts on delirium tremens.* London, 1813.

Swanson, D. W., et al. Clinical features of the female homosexual patient: A comparison with the heterosexual patient. *Journal of Nervous and Mental Disease*, 1972, **155**(2), 119.

Swingmann, C. A., & Pfister-Ammende, M. *Uprooting and after.* New York: Springer, 1973.

Syme, S. L., et al. Epidemiologic studies of coronary heart disease and stroke in Japanese men living in Japan, Hawaii and California: Introduction. *American Journal of Epidemiology*, 1975, **102**, 477.

Szasz, T. S. *The myth of mental illness.* New York: Dell, 1961.

Szasz, T. S. *Law, liberty, and psychiatry.* New York: Macmillan, 1963.

Szasz, T. S. *The manufacture of madness.* New York: Dell, 1971.

Talbott, J. A. Stopping the revolving door — A study of readmission to a state hospital. *Psychiatric Quarterly*, 1974, **48**, 159.

Tarter, R. E., Templer, D. I., & Hardy, C. Reliability of the psychiatric diagnosis. *Diseases of the Nervous System*, 1975, **36**(1), 30.

Taylor, D., & Bower, B. Prevention in epileptic disorders. *Lancet*, 1971, **2**, 1136.

Television and growing up: The impact of televised violence. Washington, D. C.: U.S. Government Printing Office, 1971.

Temerlin, M. K. Suggestion effects in psychiatric diagnosis. *Journal of Nervous and Mental Disease*, 1968, **147**, 349.

Templer, D. I. The obsessive-compulsive neurosis: Review of research findings. *Comprehensive Psychiatry*, 1972, **13**(4), 375.

Tennant, F. S., Jr., & Groesbeck, D. J. Psychiatric effects of hashish. *Archives of General Psychiatry*, 1972, **27**, 133.

Thomson, K. C., & Hendrie, H. C. Environmental stress in primary depressive illness. *Archives of General Psychiatry*, 1972, **26**, 130.

Thoresen, C. E., & Mahoney, M. J. *Behavioral self-control.* New York: Holt, 1974.

Thurrell, R. J., & Marshall, J. R. Difficulties in implementation of behavior therapies in a mixed or eclectic situation. *Journal of Nervous and Mental Disease*, 1974, **159**, 158.

Toffler, A. *Future shock.* New York: Bantam, 1970.

Tompkins, H. J. Psycho-physiological aspects of anxiety in the aged — An overview. In R. de la Fuente & M. N. Weisman (Eds.), *Psychiatry: Proceedings of the 5th world congress of psychiatry* (Pt. 1). New York: American Elsevier, 1973.

Tuke, D. H. *A dictionary of psychological medicine.* New York: McGraw-Hill, 1892.

Uhlenhuth, E. H., & Paykel, E. S. Symptom configuration of life events. *Archives of General Psychiatry*, 1973, **28**, 743.

Vaillant, G. E. Natural history of male psychological health, II. Some antecedents of healthy adult adjustment. *Archives of General Psychiatry*, 1974, **31**(1), 15.

Van Loon, F. G. H. Amok and Lattah. *Journal of Abnormal and Social Psychology*, 1927, **4**, 434.

Volynkina, G. Y., et al. Electromyographic investigation of emotional states. *Voprosy Psikhologii*, 1971, **4**, 49.

Wade, M. G., Ellis, M. J., & Bohrer, R. E. Biorhythms in the activity of children during free play. *Journal of the Experimental Analysis of Behavior,* 1973, **20**, 155.

Wald, E. D., & Mackinnon J. R. Endocrinological correlates of stress-induced ulcers, *Psychonomic Science*, 1972, **29**(5), 331.

Wallace, A. F. C. *Tornado in Worcester* (Publication No. 362). Washington, D. C.: National Academy of Sciences, National Research Council, 1956.

Watson, J. B., & Rayner, R. Conditional emotional reactions. *Journal of Experimental Psychology*, 1920, **3**, 1.

Weiner, H. J., Akabas, S. H., & Sommer, J. J. *Mental health care in the world of work.* New York: Association Press, 1973.

Weiss, R. & Parkes, C. M. *Mental health implications of conjugal bereavement*, Final Report. NIMH Grant MH-12042, 1971.

Weiss, T., & Engel, B. T. Operant conditioning of heart rate in patients with premature ventricular contractions. *Seminars in Psychiatry*, 1973, **5**(4), 439.

Welch, B. L. & Welch, A. S. Aggression and the biogenic amine neurohumors. In S. Garattini and E. G. Siggs (Eds.), *Aggressive behavior.* New York: Wiley, 1969.

Welgan, P. R. Learned control of gastric acid secretions in ulcer patients. *Psychosomatic Medicine*, 1974, **36**(5), 411.

Wender, P. H., Rosenthal, D., & Kety, S. S. Crossfostering: A research strategy for clarifying the role of genetic and experiential factors in the etiology of schizophrenia. *Archives of General Psychiatry*, 1974, **30**, 121.

West, A. Concurrent schizophrenic-like psychosis in monozygous twins suffering from CNS disorder. *British Journal of Psychiatry*, 1973, **122**(571), 675.

Westman, J. C., Ferguson, B. B., & Wolman, R. N. School career adjustment patterns of children. In E. Bower (Ed.) *Orthopsychiatry and education*. Detroit: Wayne State University Press, 1971.

Whanger, A. D., & Wang, H. S. Vitamin B-12 deficiency in aging psychiatric patients. *Gerontologist*, 1970, **10**(3), 31.

White, R. W. Strategies of adaptation: An attempt at systematic description. In G. V. Coelho, D. A. Hamburg, & J. E. Adams (Eds.), *Coping and adaptation*. New York: Basic Books, 1974.

Wickler, W. Socio-sexual signals and their intraspecific imitation among primates. In D. Morris (Ed.), *Primate ethology*. Chicago: Aldine, 1967.

Williams, T. A., Katz, M. M., & Schield, G. A., Jr. (Eds.) *Psychobiology of depressive illness*. Washington, D. C.: Department of Health, Education, and Welfare, 1973.

Wing, J. K., et al. *The measurement and classification of psychiatric symptoms*. London: Cambridge University Press, 1974.

Winick, M. Fetal malnutrition. In L. I. Mann (Ed.), *Fetal physiology*. New York: Harper, 1970.

Winokur, G. Genetic and clinical factors associated with course in depression. *Pharmakopsychiatrie/Neuro-Psychopharmakologie*, 1974, **7**(2), 122.

Winokur, G., & Reich, T. Two genetic factors in manic-depressive disease. *Comprehensive Psychiatry*, 1970, **11**, 93.

Winokur, G. W., Clayton, P. J., & Reich, T. *Manic-depressive illness*. St. Louis: Mosby, 1969.

Wolf, S. R. Emotional reactions to hysterectomy. *Postgraduate Medicine,* 1970, **47**, 165.

Woolley, D. W., & Shaw, E. Some neurophysiological aspects of serotonin. *British Medical Journal*, 1954, **2**, 122.

World Health Organization: *The international pilot study of schizophrenia* (Vol. 1). Geneva: Author, 1973.

Yap, P. M. The latah reaction: Its pathodynamics and nosological position. *Journal of Mental Science*, 1952, **98**, 515.

Young, J. P. R., et al. The inheritance of neurotic traits: A twin study of the Middlesex Hospital questionnaire. *British Journal of Psychiatry*, 1971, **119**, 393.

Yuwiler, A., et al. Increased blood serotonin and platelets in early infantile autism. *Archives of General Psychiatry*, 1970, **23**, 566.

Zigas, V., et al. New Guinea: Studies relating the medical and behavioral sciences (Pt. 1). *Urbanization, Culture, and Medicine*, 1972, **6** (6), 681.

Ziskind, E., et al. Psychophysiological, chemical, and therapeutic research on sociopaths: A search for a homogenous population. In R. de la Fuente & M. N. Weisman (Eds.), *Psychiatry: Proceedings of the 5th world congress of psychiatry* (Part 2). New York: American Elsevier, 1973.

Zung, W. W. K. The differentiation of anxiety and depressive disorders: A psychopharmacological approach. *Psychosomatics*, 1973, **14**, 362.

Figure Credits

Pringhorn, *Artistry of the Mentally Ill*, Springer Verlag, Heidelberg, Germany, 1972

Figure 11-3 "Hallucinations," René Magritte

Figure 11-4 Courtesy of Ciba Pharmaceuticals

Figure 11-5 Bill Bridges

Page 254 *Insania Pingens*, Ciba Pharmaceuticals, Basel, Switzerland

Figure 12-1 "Ecce Homo," from Pringhorn, *Artistry of the Mentally Ill*, Springer Verlag, Heidelberg, Germany, 1972

Figure 12-2 "Air Apparition," from Pringhorn, *Artistry of the Mentally Ill*, Springer Verlag, Heidelberg, Germany, 1972

Figure 12-3 Gianni Berengo-Gardin, *Internationales Jahrbuch des Fotografie*, 1970, #186

Figure 12-4 Costa Manos/Magnum

Figure 12-5 George W. Kisker

Figure 12-6 "Holy Sweat Miracle on the Insole," from Pringhorn, *Artistry of the Mentally Ill*, Springer Verlag, Heidelberg, Germany, 1972

Page 280 Museum of Modern Art, New York

Figure 13-1 New York Public Library

Figure 13-2 Shelton/Monkmeyer

Figure 13-3 Bettmann Archive

Page 294 Collection, Museum of Modern Art, New York; gift of Mr. and Mrs. E. Powis Jones

Figure 14-1 George W. Kisker

Figure 14-2 Suzanne Opton/Black Star

Figure 14-3 Virginia Hamilton

Figure 14-4 Courtesy of Dr. J. A. N. Corsellis, London

Figure 14-5 David Krasnor/Photo Researchers, Inc.

Figure 14-6 Shelly Rusten

Figure 14-7 George Silk/Time-Life Picture Agency © Time Inc.

Figure 14-8 American Psychiatric Museum Association

Page 322 Alan E. Cober, *New York Times*, May 6, 1972

Figure 15-1 Alan E. Cober, *New York Times*, May 6, 1972

Figure 15-2 George W. Kisker

Figure 15-3 Courtesy of Dr. Clemens E. Benda

Figure 15-4 Courtesy of the Columbus State Institute

Figure 15-5 Courtesy of the Columbus State Institute

Figure 15-6a,b Courtesy of the Columbus State Institute

Figure 15-7a,b Courtesy of the Columbus State Institute

Page 342 "Image of a Private World," *Art Psychotherapy*, 1973, **1**, 131.

Figure 16-1 Courtesy of W. W. K. Zung, M.D.

Figure 16-2 From E. M. Bridge, *Epilepsy and Convulsive Disorders in Children*, McGraw-Hill, New York, 1949, p. 534

Figure 16-3 EEG Laboratory, Longview State Hospital

Figure 16-4 "Lamb of God," from *Artistry of the Mentally Ill*, Springer Verlag, Heidelberg, Germany 1972

Figure 16-5 Courtesy of Hans Huber Verlag, Bern, Switzerland

Figure 16-6 Courtesy of Dr. Henry A. Murray and Harvard University Press

Figure 16-7 George W. Kisker

Figure 16-8 Psychiatric Clinic, Hamilton County Juvenile Court

Figure 16-9 George W. Kisker

Page 368 Colleen Browning, "Encounters, 1975." Courtesy of Kennedy Galleries, Inc., New York

Figure 17-1 John Briggs

Figure 17-2a,b,c,d *Insania Pingens*, Ciba Pharmaceuticals, Basel, Switzerland

Figure 17-3a Courtesy of Thomas Y. Crowell Company

Figure 17-3b Blackstone-Shelbourne, New York

Figure 17-3c Michael Fenster

Figure 17-3d United Press International

Figure 17-4 Baris of Boston

Figure 17-5 BAM Project, Oxnard, CA

Figure 17-6 Bernie Cleff

Figure 17-7 Ken Heyman

Figure 17-8 Ken Regan/Camera 5

Figure 17-9 J. M. Vincent/Camera 5

Page 394 Bettmann Archive

Figure 18-1 Culver Pictures

Figure 18-2 Courtesy of Dr. Jean Delay

Figure 18-3a,b Longview State Hospital

Figure 18-4 Courtesy of Dr. Almeida Lima and the Centro de Estudos Egas Moniz, Lisbon, Portugal

Figure 18-5 Courtesy of *Scientific American*

Figure 18-6 Courtesy of Charles C Thomas, Publishers

Name Index

Subject Index